GOD'S EMISSARIES

ADAM TO JESUS

Shaykh Rizwan Arastu

I.M.A.M.

ISBN: 978-0-9997877-2-4

Published by:
Imam Mahdi Association of Marjaeya (I.M.A.M.)
22000 Garrison Street
Dearborn, MI 48124
Tel: 313-562-IMAM (4626)
www.imam-us.org

Contents

Publisher's Foreword

In the name of God, the All-Beneficent, the Ever-Merciful. Praise is for God, Lord of all realms. May God shower all his prophets and messengers with mercy, particularly him who is foremost among them and their seal, Muḥammad, son of ʿAbd Allāh. And may God shower with mercy the progeny of Muhammad, his twelve pure and infallible successors.

People far and wide have expended great effort to record and relate the stories of great personalities, especially the stories of those who have sacrificed all that they have, whether property, family, or life itself, for the sake of their ideals in order to better humankind at large. The creations of those who convey the stories span the fields of painting and literature, carving and sculpture, and even graphic and digital design.

The stories of many of these great personalities are beneficial on some level. However, the stories of the prophets and their successors stand out as an inimitable exemplar of commitment to the ideals against which all ethical values should be compared. As God says in the Qurʾān, "We recount to you the best of narratives" (12:3).

Stories about prophets are exceptional in their flavor and lessons. They are true stories of real men who were of the highest caliber in human virtue. Their struggle, their commitment to the truth, and their triumph in the sight of God touches the human soul and our spiritual heart in profound ways. God's emissaries are true role models for inspiring the remembrance of God in us. The Qurʾān says, "There is certainly a moral in their accounts for those who possess intellect" (12:111).

Dear reader, this book that is now in your possession is not a simple book of stories. This is a product of intellectual and religious struggle to clarify truth. There are few original works in this era of materialism that seek to provide fuel and food for our souls. This is not a simple list of stories and narrative. Shaykh Rizwan Arastu (may Allah protect him) spent long hours of detailed research to deliver an authentic book that is based on original sources of narration and consistent with Islamic ideology. He worked hard to make sure that it is a useful product capable of having an impact on the life of the reader; otherwise, it would simply become one more title among the millions of other titles that offer no spiritual benefit in our lives.

Imam Mahdi Association of Marjaeya is proud that it has a share in providing this small service to the community of the prophets. We hope that these stories provide benefit not just for our brothers and sisters in faith but for humanity. Our hope is to deliver the message that these prophets do not just belong to one people, but rather they are a gift of mercy from God to all humankind. We hope that this book becomes a source of inspiration and a solid reference for works of art, movies, and children's writings, and we hope it delivers a long-term cultural impact.

Last but not least, again we thank the author for his efforts; and we hope that this effort will be followed up with a volume on the life of the last prophet, Muḥammad, to make the series complete. We would also like to express our gratitude to all those who helped to make publishing this book possible, especially Morteza Azarmnia. We ask God to guide us all to the service of humanity.

Sayyid M. B. Al-Kashmiri
Vice Chairman, I.M.A.M.
May 20, 2014

Transliteration

Arabic has been transliterated according to the following key:

ء	a, u, or i (initial form)	ط	ṭ
ء	ʾ (medial or final form)	ظ	ẓ
ب	b	ع	ʿ
ت	t	غ	gh
ث	th	ف	f
ج	j	ق	q
ح	ḥ	ك	k
خ	kh	ل	l
د	d	م	m
ذ	dh	ن	n
ر	r	ه	h
ز	z	و	w (as a consonant)
س	s	ي	y (as a consonant)
ش	sh	ة	ah (without iḍāfah)
ص	ṣ	ة	at (with iḍāfah)
ض	ḍ	ال	al-

آ = ءا	ā (initial form)	آ = ءا	ʾā (medial form)
ـَا	ā	ـَوْ	aw
ـُو	ū	ـَوّ	aww
ـِي	ī	ـُوّ	uww
ـَ	a	ـَيْ	ay
ـُ	u	ـَيّ	ayy
ـِ	i	ـِيّ	iyy (medial form)
		ـِيّ	ī (final form)

Introduction

The Emissaries

Traditions tell us that there were 124,000 prophets appointed by God to guide humanity.[1] Of these, the Qur'ān mentions twenty-six by name.[2] It briefly mentions another three without stating their

---

1. *Man lā yaḥḍuruhu al-faqīh* vol. 4 p. 180 tr. 5407

2. The following is a list of the 26 prophets mentioned by name in the Qur'ān:
    1. *Ādam* (Adam)
    2. *Idrīs* (Enoch)
    3. *Nūḥ* (Noah)
    4. *Hūd* (no English equivalent)
    5. *Ṣāliḥ* (no English equivalent)
    6. *Ibrāhīm* (Abraham)
    7. *Lūṭ* (Lot)
    8. *Ismā'īl* (Ishmael)
    9. *Isḥāq* (Isaac)
    10. *Ya'qūb* (Jacob)
    11. *Yūsuf* (Joseph)
    12. *Ayyūb* (Job)
    13. *Shu'ayb* (Jethro)
    14. *Mūsā* (Moses)
    15. *Hārūn* (Aaron)
    16. *Ismā'īl* (Ishmael son of Ezekiel)
    17. *Ilyās* or *Ilyā* (Elijah)
    18. *Al-Yasa'* (Elisha)
    19. *'Uwaydiyā* or *Dhū al-Kifl* (no English equivalent)
    20. *Dāwūd* (David)
    21. *Sulaymān* (Solomon)
    22. *Yūnus* (Jonah)
    23. *Zakariyyah* (Zechariah)
    24. *Yahyā* (John the Baptist)
    25. *'Īsā* (Jesus)
    26. *Muḥammad* (Muhammad)

names.[3] We know of a few dozen more from their mention in the traditions and in the Old Testament.

Affirmation of all God's prophets, along with the scriptures they brought, is a tenet of Islam. Muslims must affirm the following:

> *We believe in God and in what has been revealed to us and in what was revealed to Abraham, Ishmael, Isaac, Jacob, and the prophets from the Tribes of Israel and, in particular, in what was given to Moses, Jesus, and all the other prophets. We do not distinguish one of them from another insofar as they are prophets* (Qurʾān 3:84).

Problems With the Sources

There are formidable challenges facing anyone who wishes to know the details of these prophets' lives and legacies, whether through the Qurʾān or the traditions of Prophet Muḥammad and his family.

A large number of Qurʾānic verses do mention the prophets. Nonetheless, their stories are almost never told as a sequential narrative. Snippets are mentioned as they pertain to some larger theme, sometimes out of chronological order. At times, a mere allusion is all we are given. There is, in short, a scarcity of the kind of colorful details we expect in a good story.

The traditions (*aḥādīth*) give us many of these details and sometimes help to clarify the meaning of otherwise ambiguous verses. However, there are many problems with traditions, particularly those that convey the stories of the prophets.

Many are what are known as *Isrāʿīliyyāt*, Biblical quotations or otherwise distorted or fabricated stories that were cloaked early on in the guise of Prophetic traditions. Sometimes these *Isrāʿīliyyāt* may have been introduced innocently by early Jewish converts who believed their Biblical knowledge could add to the Islamic body of knowledge. But more often, they were introduced less innocently by people called *Qaṣṣāsūn* or *Quṣṣāṣ*, storytellers, who

---

3. i.e., al-Khiḍr, Ezekiel, and Samuel

falsely attributed Biblical passages to Prophet Muḥammad, thereby continuing their age-old tradition of maligning God's emissaries.

Some of the traditions were spoken by the imams in a state of dissimulation (*taqiyyah*). The larger Muslim community, because they had abandoned the guidance offered by the imams from the Prophet's family, were highly prone to accepting adulterated versions of the prophets' stories such as the *Isrāʾīliyyāt*. Sometimes, the imams felt the need to give lip-service to these adulterated stories, by accepting them as true or even promoting them, only because they had determined that there was some greater good to be had by turning a blind eye to relatively lesser evils.

Stories of the Prophets

The genre of *qiṣaṣ al-anbiyāʾ* or "stories of the prophets" developed as scholars began to compile and organize the verses and traditions concerning each prophet. Numerous such works have been written. Table 1 contains some of the most prominent of these works.

With all due respect to these authors for their efforts, as a western reader in the 21st century, I find their works problematic, or at least unsatisfying, for the following reasons:

- They seem to give priority to including all traditions they have found rather than selecting only those that are authenticated or plausible.
- They do not make much effort at reconciling discrepancies among the traditions.
- They do not make much effort at reconciling the traditions with Islamic beliefs in general.
- They do not lay out a solid, plausible chronology of events. Generally, they lay out tradition after tradition, and verse after verse, without stringing them together as a believable narrative.
- They do not synthesize the Qurʾānic verses with the traditions to show where they are mutually compatible, mutually corroborating, or mutually incompatible.
- They do not delve into a comparative analysis of the Islamic sources and the Judeo-Christian tradition.

Table 1

Title	Author	Sect	Title of Translation	Translator
Qiṣaṣ al-anbiyāʾ	Quṭb al-Dīn al-Rāwandī d.573	Shīʿī	-	-
al-Nūr al-mubīn fī qiṣaṣ al-anbiyāʾ wa al-mursalīn	Niʿmat Allāh al-Jazāʾirī d.1112	Shīʿī	-	-
Ḥayāt al-qulūb	Muḥammad Bāqir al-Majlisī d.1110	Shīʿī	*Ḥayāt al-qulūb* vol.1-3	Sayyid Athar Husayn S. H. Rizvi
Qiṣaṣ al-anbiyāʾ	Muḥammad ibn ʿAbd Allāh al-Kisāʾī	Sunnī	*Tales of the Prophets*	Wheeler M. Thackston
Arāʾis al-majālis fī qiṣaṣ al-anbiyāʾ	Aḥmad ibn Muḥammad al-Thaʿlabī d.1035	Sunnī	*Lives of the Prophets*	William M. Brinner
Qiṣaṣ al-anbiyāʾ	Ismāʿīl ibn Kathīr d.774	Sunnī	*Stories of the Prophets*	Rashad Ahmad Azami

- They understandably are not informed by modern research in archeology, history, or the natural sciences.
- They do not make for a good read, like a good solid novel.

About This Work

Over the course of the last three years, I have tried, with God's help, to fill some of these voids and compensate for some of these shortcomings. I have tried to make *God's Emissaries: Adam to Jesus* a comprehensive, theologically sound, captivating, and believable set of stories. I have tried to portray God's prophets as the heroes they were, possessed of the most stellar of human traits, exemplary in every aspect of their being.

I began my research by extracting all the verses related to a particular prophet. I then delved into a rigorous study of the commentaries on those verses. In a few instances, my thematic approach opened doors of understanding that seem to have remained closed to others who used only a sequential approach. Once I felt I had understood the verses, I translated them, one by one. Then I placed the verses in sequential order.

Next, I made a comprehensive study of the appropriate chapters from volumes 11 to 14 of ʿAllāmah Muḥammad Bāqir al-Majlisī's *Biḥār al-anwār*, which is indeed an "ocean of light." His tireless effort to compile Qurʾānic verses, commentary on those verses, and all extant traditions on a given topic from both Shīʿī and Sunnī sources, interspersed with the occasional expository notes, relieved me of the need to search any further, in most cases, for relevant traditions. I studied each tradition, weighing its contents against the verses of the Qurʾān and against theological principles. I reconciled discrepancies as far as possible, and where no reconciliation was possible, I built a case against the tradition so that I would be able to justify why I chose not to include it. I extracted every bit of information that I thought could add detail and interest to the bare bones of the Qurʾānic narrative.

In some cases, I found it necessary to take strategic digressions to research issues that were tangentially related to the stories. For instance, to understand the Islamic perspective on the astrological predictions of Āzar and the Pharaoh's magicians, I studied Shaykh Murtaḍā al-Anṣārī's discussions on the topic in *al-Makāsib*. I read several books on Egyptology to understand the process of mummification and to evaluate the various claims concerning the identity of the Pharaoh from Moses' story. From these books, I also got a sense of the geographical layout of a typical Egyptian city so that I could portray the setting of Moses' story realistically. I read articles on archeological excavations in Madā'in Ṣāliḥ to see if it could be identified with the city of Ḥijr in which the Thamūd used to live. A podcast of the radio show "On Being" gave me a lead on a book by David Montgomery called *The Rocks Don't Lie*. This book helped me to understand the interplay between the Christian and scientific communities over the question of Noah's flood. I read a few books and visited many websites on Wicca to better understand black magic. I studied maps to retrace routes and to evaluate the plausibility of certain events. I researched the history of the Temple Mount in Jerusalem and used scholarly reconstructions and diagrams of Herod's Temple to better understand some aspects of the story of Zechariah and Mary.

Next I turned to the Bible. I made a point of reading and studying the Old Testament stories, paying close attention to points of convergence, and more often, points of sharp divergence.

With research completed, I began the process of meticulously assembling the pieces of the puzzle. I wove together the verses and traditions, interspersing helpful commentary in the voice of the narrator. In a handful of places, I used my imagination to fill in missing details that I felt were necessary to make sense of the storyline. All the while, I made sure to document every detail with a citation or an admission of the exercise of creative license. I consigned research notes and supplemental commentary to footnotes so that they would not hinder the flow of the narrative while providing the curious with extra fodder for their minds.

I sincerely hope that this book is some of what I tried to make it.

Disclaimer

The study of history is far from a precise science. The study of prehistory is further still. For the most part, we have no information on the prophets that we can consider empirical. All our information is from revelation, which in and of itself is a far more reliable source of truth than our limited senses. That said, we must distinguish the pure revelation that is the Qur'ān and the teachings of Prophet Muḥammad and the twelve imams who succeeded him from the traditions (*aḥādīth*), which are merely historical archives of those teachings. Many factors make these traditions much less reliable, and we must treat them, accordingly, with more circumspection.

Without delving too much into the issue of authenticity of the traditions, I simply want to call your attention to an underlying assumption upon which much of this book is based. I have included traditions in my narrative and treated them as though they are correct as long as they passed the following litmus tests:

- that they did not contradict the Qur'ānic narrative
- that they did not contradict fundamental tenets of Islam such as the infallibility of the prophets
- that they did not contradict reason
- that they seemed plausible

Accordingly, it is prudent to refer to those parts of this narrative that are based on traditions or on my own interpretations with prudence by couching the sentence with appropriate uncertainty. By this I mean that we should not say, "Mary gave birth to Jesus in Karbalā'." Rather, we should say, "According to traditions, Mary gave birth to Jesus in Karbalā'" or "It seems or is likely that Mary gave birth to Jesus in Karbalā'." This language is more prudent, more truthful, and belies a higher level of wisdom and humility in us.

Acknowledgements

I thank God Almighty for the opportunity, motivation, and resources to complete this endeavor.

I also thank the Imam Mahdi Association of Marjaeya, and especially its vice chairman Sayyid Muhammad Baqir al-Kashmiri, and it's former executive Sayyid Haydar Bahrululoom, for believing in this project and providing me with the resources and encouragement to pursue it.

I also thank Philip "Hamza" Voerding who read the manuscript and offered comments informed by his deep knowledge of the Bible and Christian theology.

I also thank Dara Becker who efficiently edited the manuscript and offered much encouragement along the way.

I also thank my daughter, Asiyah, and my son, Yahya, who carefully and passionately read through much of the manuscript, and despite their youth, or perhaps because of it, caught many errors that eluded the rest of us.

I also thank Mohammed Alhadad for creating a unique and meaningful cover.

Finally, I also thank Taqwa Media for their tireless efforts in managing the layout and printing of this book.

Shaykh Rizwan Arastu
June 10, 2014
Dearborn, MI

Adam

Earth's Early Inhabitants

Eons had passed since God created the earth. He had filled it with life-giving water and air and all the resources his creatures would need until the end of time. For ages, myriad life forms—plant and animal—had inhabited the planet, each fulfilling its appointed role.[1] He had created winged angels and winged *jinn* who exalted him and extolled his praises tirelessly night and day. Then he created a race of humanoid creatures, called *nasnās*, with bodies and souls. They could not fly and needed food and drink to survive. They lived in communion with the *jinn*, and together they praised God.[2]

As time passed, the *nasnās* along with a group of *jinn* rebelled against God. They began spreading corruption on earth and spilling

---

1. Imam al-Bāqir is reported to have said, "It seems you think that God only created this world and that he did not create other than you. Rather, by God! He created millions of worlds and millions of Adams, and you are simply in the last of those worlds, descended from the last of those Adams" (*Nūr al-thaqalayn* vol. 1 p. 16). From his assertion that we are in the "last" of these worlds, we can infer that he is not referring to contemporaneous, parallel realms or planes of existence as some may be tempted to conjecture. Rather, he is clearly referring to worlds and races in sequence. From the word "last," we can also infer that we are now in the final world and that all the previous worlds and races are extinct. We are safe in construing his mention of "Adams" to be a figurative reference to other creatures, perhaps the *nasnās* (prehistoric humanoid creatures) or others. But it is not likely that the past creatures or races were similar in intellect and potential to Adam.

2. *Biḥār al-anwār* vol. 11 p. 322–3 tr. 5. We know very little about these *nasnās*. Shaykh Jawādī Āmulī believes it is possible that they are the same prehistoric humanoid creatures that modern paleontologists have uncovered (*Tasnīm* vol. 3 p. 60).

innocent blood. Their rebellion reached such a height that they began to reject God as their Lord.[3]

God allowed the *jinn* and *nasnās* to live like this for millennia. When, in his wisdom, he decided that it was time for them to be destroyed, he first assembled his angels to bear witness to the evil these creatures had wrought. When the angels saw them sinning unabashedly, spilling innocent blood, and causing corruption on earth, they were appalled. They became enraged for God's sake and said:

> Lord! You are the Invincible, the Omnipotent, the Compeller, the Dominant, the Great! And these feeble, meek creatures of yours live by your grace, upon your sustenance, and enjoy the well-being you have given them. Then they sin against you in such a horrible manner, yet you do not become angry at them, and you do not avenge yourself against them. This is too much for us to bear. We are outraged for your sake.[4]

God announced his plan to them saying, "I shall instate a vicegerent on earth."[5] He wished for this vicegerent to be a witness over his creatures and a proof against those among them who acted as the *nasnās* and *jinn* were acting.[6]

The angels, for millennia, had watched these earthly creatures destroy the earth and rebel against their creator. All the while, they themselves had tirelessly and happily carried out his every command, worshiping him along the way. The prospect of another race who would repeat the crimes of the former was abhorrent to them. From their past experience, they thought that anything created for the earth was inherently inferior to them.[7] They could not understand why God had decided to create such a species

---

3. *Biḥār al-anwār* vol. 11 p. 322–3 tr. 5

4. *Biḥār al-anwār* vol. 11 p. 103 tr. 10

5. Qur'ān 2:30

6. *Biḥār al-anwār* vol. 11 p. 104 tr. 10

7. *Biḥār al-anwār* vol. 11 p. 137 tr. 1 and p. 117 tr. 47

and, that too, to make him his vicegerent. Teeming with curiosity and bewilderment, they asked, "Will you instate therein one who will cause corruption therein and shed blood while we exalt you by praising you and proclaim your sanctity?"[8] Theirs was not an objection. They were, after all, angels, perfect servants of God. They would not venture to speak ahead of him, and they were wont to act only at his command.[9] However, they longed to understand God's wisdom, for they knew without a doubt that he was all-knowing and wise.[10]

God told them:

> I know what you do not.[11] I intend to create this creature and make of his progeny prophets and messengers, righteous servants, and guided imams. I shall make them my vicegerents to rule over all my earthly creatures. They will forbid them to sin against me, warn them of my punishment, guide them to obey me, and help them to traverse the arduous path that leads to me. I shall make them my proofs, *for* my creatures and *against* them.
>
> And I shall rid this world of the *nasnās* and purify the earth of their presence. And I shall move the sinful among the *jinn* and make them live in the air and in far off corners of the earth. They shall no longer live alongside the progeny of this new creature of mine. And I shall create a veil between this new creature and the *jinn* so that they do not see the *jinn* or befriend them or mix with them anymore.

---

8. Qur'ān 2:30

9. Qur'ān 21:27

10. Qur'ān 2:32

11. Qur'ān 2:30

> Thereafter, if any of these new creatures of mine sin against me, I shall cast them into the abode of past sinners without a second thought.[12]

The angels replied in meek comprehension, "Lord, let your will be done! We have absolutely no knowledge except what you have taught us."[13] Their question had been sincere. They had wished to understand God's reasons for actions of which they could not make sense. But perhaps it was the way they asked. Perhaps it was that they asked a question before unconditionally accepting God's will. There was something in their question that fell short of the lofty standards to which God holds his greatest servants. For this reason, he cast them away from his throne, distanced them from his mercy, and blocked his light from reaching them[14] to reprimand them.

When the angels realized they had earned God's displeasure, they were overcome. They began circulating around God's throne, begging his forgiveness.[15] After seven thousand years, God accepted their repentance and absolved them.[16] He ordered a house of worship to be built in the skies so that the angels could continue circulating indefinitely in worship.[17] This house of worship was built with four sides corresponding to the four symbolic legs of God's throne which are the four statements: "Exalted is God," "Praise is for God," "There is no god but God," and "God is greater than all."[18] Since then, each day, seventy thousand angels circumambulate that structure, and

---

12. *Biḥār al-anwār* vol. 11 p. 104 tr. 10

13. Qur'ān 2:32

14. *Biḥār al-anwār* vol. 11 p. 110 tr. 25

15. *Nūr al-thaqalayn* vol. 1 p. 49 tr. 74

16. *Biḥār al-anwār* vol. 11 p. 104 tr. 10

17. *Nūr al-thaqalayn* vol. 1 p. 49 tr. 77. In various traditions this "house" of worship is called *al-ḍarāḥ* or *al-bayt al-maʿmūr*. Some traditions even speak of these as two separate "houses," one in the fourth or sixth level of the sky and one in the first.

18. *Biḥār al-anwār* vol. 96 p. 57 tr. 9

having circled it once, never do so again.[19] They will continue in this way until the first horn blows announcing the end of the temporal world.[20] This structure in the skies was the prototype for the Kaʿbah, a four-sided edifice[21] God would later have built on earth. The angels' 7000 years of circumambulation around God's throne became the model for the seven symbolic circuits Adam would later fulfill as part of what came to be called Hajj.[22]

Dust to Make the Vicegerent

God decided that his vicegerent *over* the material world should be made *of* the material world. In particular, he wished to make him out of dust.[23] When he informed the earth that he would make a race of creatures from her dust and that these creatures would have the freedom to choose their actions—that some would choose to obey their creator and some would choose to sin, the earth shuddered.[24] She begged God not to make of her dust a creature that could potentially sin and then burn in hellfire. God assured her that his will would be done notwithstanding her reservations.[25]

He sent Archangel Gabriel with the task of gathering the dust. However, when he descended to collect it, the earth pleaded with him to give her respite so that she could beg God once again not to use her earth for this creature. God heard her cries and told Gabriel to return to the skies without taking her dust. In turn, God sent Archangels Michael and Seraphiel, and they met with a similar obstinacy. Then, when Archangel Azrael descended, the earth

---

19. *Nūr al-thaqalayn* vol. 1 p. 49 tr. 81

20. *Biḥār al-anwār* vol. 11 p. 108 tr. 17

21. *Biḥār al-anwār* vol. 96 p. 57 tr. 9

22. *Nūr al-thaqalayn* vol. 1 p. 49 tr. 77

23. Qurʾān 3:59

24. It is possible that this conversation between God and the earth is symbolic. However, it is perfectly plausible that a thing we consider inanimate actually has a level of consciousness that we cannot comprehend. Qurʾān 17:44 speaks of such a consciousness.

25. *Biḥār al-anwār* vol. 11 p. 121 tr. 55

protested again, but Azrael said, "My Lord has commanded me to do something. I shall fulfill this duty whether you like it or not."[26]

The earth renewed her protests saying, "God forbid that you take my dust."

Azrael retorted, "God forbid that I return to him not having fulfilled my duty."[27] With that, he proceeded to gather earth of different colors: white, red, brown, and black; of different temperaments: rocky, soft, sweet, and salty.[28] Then he gathered different kinds of water: fresh, salty, bitter, and putrid. From these varieties of earth and water, God would eventually create a diversity of colors and temperaments in his new creature.[29]

When Azrael had collected the dust and water as God had prescribed, God told him, "Just as you successfully seized this dust from the earth despite her resistance, from this day forward, you shall have the honor of seizing the souls of all my creatures at the time when I ordain their death."[30] From then on, Azrael became the Angel of Death.

The Creation of Adam's Form

God ordered one of his angels to mix the various portions of dry dust and water that Azrael had collected.[31] The angel poured the clay into the water forming dark foul-smelling clay.[32] He strained it to remove the stones and other foreign substances and to make the clay a homogeneous extract of clay.[33] Then he kneaded the clay for forty years[34] until it turned sticky and cohesive.[35] He let this sticky clay cure

26. *Biḥār al-anwār* vol. 11 p. 121 tr. 55

27. *Biḥār al-anwār* vol. 11 p. 113 tr. 34

28. *Biḥār al-anwār* vol. 11 p. 122 tr. 56

29. *Biḥār al-anwār* vol. 11 p. 101 tr. 6 and 7

30. *Biḥār al-anwār* vol. 11 p. 121 tr. 55

31. *Biḥār al-anwār* vol. 11 p. 121 tr. 55

32. Qur'ān 15:26-29

33. *Biḥār al-anwār* vol. 11 p. 122 tr. 56 and Qur'ān 23:12

34. *Biḥār al-anwār* vol. 11 p. 121 tr. 55

35. *Biḥār al-anwār* vol. 11 p. 122 tr. 56 and Qur'ān 37:11

for another forty years.[36] From this sticky clay, God fashioned[37] the hollow figure of a human being, standing upright, in perfect form,[38]

---

36. *Biḥār al-anwār* vol. 11 p. 121 tr. 55

37. The Arabic word *masnūn* has inspired great debate among linguists and scholars throughout Islamic history. Part of the debate centers around the meaning of the word. The other part centers around its role in verses 15:26–28 of the Qur᾿ān. There are four meanings for the word *masnūn* that are appropriate to the context of these verses:

- something that is poured
- something that is polished
- something that is fashioned
- clay that is made into pottery

All the commentaries to which I referred assumed *masnūn* to be an adjective of *ḥama᾿*, a dark foul-smelling clay. The only meaning that fits in this context is for *masnūn* to refer to "something that is poured." It seems that Imam ʿAlī used the word in this meaning when he described the stages by which God created Adam. He said, "Then God gathered dust from rocky terrain and from soft terrain, from sweet earth and salty earth, which he poured into water until it became homogeneous" (*Nahj al-balāghah* sermon 1). Most likely, he means that God poured the dust into water and then *strained* it to remove larger pieces and make it homogeneous (see *Minhāj al-bara᾿ah* of al-Rāwandī). This meaning for *masnūn* fits well in the context of this sermon, however, it does not fit well at all in the context of the verses 15:26–28 of the Qur᾿ān, for we would have to stretch its meaning and assume that many things were left unstated. If we turn a blind eye to these difficulties, the meaning of the verse would be that God created Adam "from hollow, resonant clay that is made from dark foul-smelling clay that has been poured, strained, and purified."

Because the previous interpretation is such a stretch, I believe that *masnūn* is an adjective, not for *ḥama᾿*, but for *ṣalṣāl*. Al-Samīn al-Ḥalabī mentions the possibility that *masnūn* is an adjective for *ṣalṣāl* but rejects it saying that it is not permitted for an adjective that is a *ẓarf* to come before a true adjective. This is not a sound rule since we have the exact same sentence structure in 43:31 where the word *ʿaẓīm* is undeniably an adjective for *rajul*. Similarly, we have this structure at the end of 15:41. Thus, not only is this interpretation within the bounds of good Arabic grammar, it also makes good sense to say that the dry resonant clay is "something that is fashioned" as opposed to being an amorphous lump. Thus, the meaning of the verse 15:26 is, "We created the first human from dry resonant clay fashioned from dark foul-smelling clay."

38. *Biḥār al-anwār* vol. 11 p. 122 tr. 56. In the Qur᾿ān, God mentions the stages of Adam's creation in detail. He tells us in the broadest of terms that he created him out of *al-arḍ* or "earth" (11:61). More specifically, he tells us that he made

and fully circumcised.[39] He made him precisely in the form he had ordained for him in the Protected Tablet since time immemorial.[40]

---

him from *turāb* or "dust" (3:59) and *mā'* or "water" (25:54). "Water" could be a reference to the semen from which all of Adam's progeny are born, but it could also be a reference to the water God mixed with the dust to create Adam. The combination of dust and water first made *ḥama'*, a "dark foul-smelling clay" (15:26), presumably mixed with other debris as is normal in naturally occurring clay. As Imam ʿAlī tells us in the first sermon of *Nahj al-balāghah*, God strained this foul-smelling mixture until it became *sulālah min ṭīn* or "a homogeneous extract of clay" (23:12). This refined *ṭīn* or "clay" (32:7) was then processed through kneading and drying until it became *ṭīn lāzib* or "sticky clay" (37:11). Then it was ready to be *masnūn* or "fashioned" (15:26) into the human form. It was allowed to dry until it hardened into *ṣalṣāl* or "hollow, resonant clay" (15:26). Despite its mean origin, it dried into *ṣālṣāl ka al-fakhkhār* or "hollow, resonant clay similar to fired pottery" (55:14). At this point God "blew" the spirit of life into the lifeless form and thereby created the first living human (15:29 and 38:72).

39. *Biḥār al-anwār* vol. 12 p. 3 tr. 4

40. *Biḥār al-anwār* vol. 11 p. 121 tr. 55. In the Book of Genesis we read, "Then God said, 'Let us make man in our image, in our likeness, and let them rule over the fish of the sea and the birds of the air, over the livestock, over all the earth, and over all the creatures that move along the ground.' So God created man in his own image, in the image of God he created him; male and female he created them" (1:26–27). The phrase "So God created man in his own image" is highly problematic since God is immaterial and is similar to nothing from his creation (see Qur'ān 42:11). The Qur'ān and the infallible guides have waged an age-old battle against the *Mushabbihah,* those who claim God has a form. Interestingly, this same phrase from the Bible has been transmitted in several traditions; however, the context of the traditions makes it clear that they are not telling us that "God created Adam in his *own* image."

- In one tradition it is related that Prophet Muḥammad passed by a Medinan man who was hitting one of his slaves in the face and saying, "May God make your face, and the face of anyone whom you resemble, ugly." The Prophet chided this man and told him, "This is an awful thing you have said, for God created Adam in his (i.e., your slave's) image" (*Tanzīh al-anbiyā'* p. 127). Adam, as the father of all human beings, resembles all human beings in some way. By asking God to deform the face of anyone whom his slave resembles, he is praying for damnation to befall the slave's forefather, Adam, whom God created in his (i.e., the slave's) image.
- In another tradition we read, "God created Adam in the image that he had ordained for him in the Protected Tablet" (*Biḥār al-anwār* vol.

For forty additional years[41] he let the figure dry and cure so that it would hold its shape.[42] Eventually it hardened into hollow, resonant clay[43] so fine it seemed like fired pottery.[44] In this state, God's new creature stood as a lifeless statue.

Reactions to Adam's Lifeless Form

During this time, the angels would pass by the figure and wonder to themselves, "For what have you been created?"[45] They did not yet know that this lifeless statue was to become the vicegerent God had vowed to create. One individual in particular by the name of Iblīs was a *jinn*[46] who had earned a place among the angels for his unwavering devotion to God and for his exceptional perseverance in worshiping God.[47] But now, gazing upon this meek figure, made of vile earth, it crossed his mind that God may have intended to make this his vicegerent. For the first time in his long life, he felt the distinct flame of jealousy kindle in his heart. He passed by the figure and said, "If this is what God wants to make into his vicegerent, I shall rebel."[48] He swiftly drove the thought from his mind and cast off the possibility as ludicrous, for he knew God was wise and would never do something that to him seemed so foolish.[49]

---

11 p. 121 tr. 55). Sayyid ibn Ṭāwūs has commented on this tradition saying, "Some Muslims have omitted part of this sentence and have narrated, 'God created Adam in his *own* image,' and have thus fallen prey to a belief that God has a form" (*Biḥār al-anwār* vol. 11 p. 121). It is not far-fetched to suppose the statement in the Bible suffered a similar fate at the hands of those Jews and Christians who, like these Muslims, abandoned God's guidance.

41. *Biḥār al-anwār* vol. 11 p. 121 tr. 55

42. *Biḥār al-anwār* vol. 11 p. 122 tr. 56

43. Qur'ān 15:26–29 and 55:14

44. Qur'ān 55:14

45. *Biḥār al-anwār* vol. 11 p. 109 tr. 22

46. Qur'ān 18:50

47. *Biḥār al-anwār* vol. 11 p. 119 tr. 51 and *Nahj al-balāghah* sermon 192

48. *Biḥār al-anwār* vol. 11 p. 119 tr. 53

49. *Biḥār al-anwār* vol. 11 p. 106 tr. 11

God assembled all of his angels along with Iblīs and announced to them, "I am creating a human being from dry, resonant clay fashioned from dark foul-smelling clay. So when I have fashioned him and blown into him of the human spirit, which is solely mine to give, fall prostrate before him."[50] It was a Friday,[51] and they prepared themselves to obey the divine command when God said to the figure, "Be!" and he was.[52] By one simple act, the divine will to create, the figure imbibed the spirit of life and changed from a mere clay statue to the first human being. God created him thus, without parents, as a testament for all the world to his omnipotence.[53] God named him Adam because he created him from *adīm al-arḍ*, dust from the surface of the earth.[54]

Adam Is Brought to Life

Adam felt life soaking into his body. As it reached his nose, he sneezed. God taught him to say, "Praise is for God, Lord of all realms."

He repeated, "Praise is for God, Lord of all realms."

Then God addressed him for the very first time and said, "May God have mercy on you. This is why I have created you—to know that I am one God, to worship me, to praise me, to believe in me and so that you do not reject me or associate partners with me."[55]

Adam Is Taught the Names

God turned his attention toward the assembly of angels. They were still ignorant of the great potential with which God had invested this new creature. Nonetheless, they were prepared to obey God's command and prostrate before him, only because of their conviction that God would only command what is good. However, before God ordered them to prostrate, he wished to demonstrate to them what

---

50. Qur'ān 15:28 and 38:72

51. *Biḥār al-anwār* vol. 11 p. 109 tr. 21

52. Qur'ān 3:59

53. *Biḥār al-anwār* vol. 11 p. 108 tr. 16

54. *Biḥār al-anwār* vol. 11 p. 100 tr. 3 and 4 and p. 101 tr. 6

55. *Biḥār al-anwār* vol. 11 p. 106 tr. 11 and p. 121 tr. 55

they had accepted on faith—that Adam was the most worthy of all creatures to hold the vicegerency of God, far superior to any angel.

Before the assembly of angels, in the span of an instant, God taught Adam all of the names of his creatures.[56] These names were not mere words.[57] They represented deep, complete knowledge of all of God's creatures, seen and unseen, those that had been created and those yet to be created, sentient and inanimate. Chief among these creatures were the divine guides, the myriad prophets, and other infallible beings God would eventually create.

God presented a representation of these creatures to his angels. Among them were the prophets and messengers from Adam's progeny, the best of whom were Prophet Muḥammad, his family, and their righteous companions and followers.[58] He said to the angels, "Inform me of their names if you were truthful in your prior implied claim that you are more worthy as vicegerents than he."[59]

They exclaimed, "Exalted are you! We have absolutely no knowledge except what you have taught us. You alone are the All-Knowing, the Wise."[60]

God addressed Adam and said, "O Adam! Inform them of the names of these creatures." When he had informed them of their names, God

---

56. Qur'an 2:31

57. Some have suggested that God simply taught Adam the words that refer to each of his creatures. Words were certainly not the subject of this first lesson for the following reasons:

- Words are simply conventions for ease of communication that change with time while what Adam was taught was something real and meaningful.
- If it were words that Adam learned, the angels would have become as knowledgeable as he as soon as he informed them of the words for everything. Rather, even after he told them what he knew, they remained ignorant of his knowledge.
- If God simply taught Adam words, the angels could have objected saying, "God, if you had taught us these words instead of Adam, then we could have become qualified to be your vicegerents instead of him."

58. *Biḥār al-anwār* vol. 11 p. 137 tr. 1

59. Qur'ān 2:31

60. Qur'ān 2:32

said to the angels, "Did I not tell you that I know whatever is unseen in the skies and the earth and that I know what you reveal and what you used to hide."[61] When they had asked God about the wisdom behind creating such a vicegerent, they had revealed part of their intent. But they had concealed within their hearts the sentiment that no earthly creature could become as close to God as they had. Now they began to see that they had sorely underestimated this creature.[62]

The Angels Bow Down

God addressed the assembly of angels saying:

> Adam and the righteous from his progeny are far superior to you because they will bear whatever burdens they are made to bear, and they will persevere against the predicaments in which they find themselves: against attacks by Satan's allies;[63] against their carnal souls; against the burdens of supporting a family; against the struggle to earn a lawful living; against the annoying fear of an attack by enemies like frightful bandits and tyrannical kings; against hardships in traveling on roads and through impasses and frightening places, through valleys and over mountains and hills to

---

61. Qur'ān 2:33

62. *Biḥār al-anwār* vol. 11 p. 137 tr. 1

63. Presumably, God refers here to a figure named Satan to foreshadow Iblīs' impending rebellion and mischief for which he is later banished and given the title *ṣhayṭān* or satan. It is interesting and appropriate that the Qur'ān always refers to Satan before he is outcast from the skies by his name, "Iblīs," and after he is outcast, by the derogatory "*al-Shayṭān*." I have conformed to this usage in my writing as well. It is also important to note that in several traditions we are told that Iblīs' name is derived from the word *iblās* which means hopelessness because "he lost all hope in receiving God's mercy" (*Biḥār al-anwār* vol. 46 p. 351 tr. 5). These traditions are problematic since, as I have just noted, Iblīs is the proper name he carried when he was a righteous servant of God. He only had reason to lose hope in God's mercy after his act of defiance at which point the Qur'ān refers to him, not by his given name, Iblīs, but by the epithet, *al-Shayṭān*.

> gather what lawful and good sustenance they can find to sustain themselves and their families...the best of the believers will bear all these hardships, fulfill their obligations, combat satanic forces and rout them, struggle against their carnal souls and bar them from attaining what they desire and overpower them despite the forces that have been combined within them: sexual desire, desire for fine clothes, food, honor, power, and an inclination to boastfulness and conceit...And you, my angels, are free from all of that. Neither does sexual desire arouse you, nor does the desire for food drive you, nor does fear for your worldly or spiritual well-being enter your hearts, nor will Satan be engaged in misguiding you, for you shall be protected from him. O my angels! Any of these humans who obeys me and guards his religion against these pitfalls and challenges has thereby borne for the sake of his love for me what you have not borne and has earned in proximity to me what you have not earned. For this reason, I hereby order you all to prostrate before Adam.[64]

Adam turned toward the vast assembly of angels. In unison, they all fell prostrate before him.[65] It was an act done in obeisance to God and in honor of his vicegerent[66] who was to be invested with authority over all God's creation. Through their prostration, they also honored the prophets and imams who would be born of Adam's progeny.[67] They placed their foreheads upon the earth to further ennoble this creature made of earth.[68] Since God himself had ordered them to prostrate to Adam, they knew they were

---

64. *Biḥār al-anwār* vol. 11 p. 137 tr. 1

65. Qurʾān 2:34 and 7:11 and 15:30 and 38:73

66. *Biḥār al-anwār* vol. 11 p. 139 tr. 4

67. *Biḥār al-anwār* vol. 11 p. 140 tr. 6

68. *Biḥār al-anwār* vol. 11 p. 139 tr. 3

worshiping, not him to whom they prostrated, but him who had commanded them to prostrate.[69]

Iblīs Rebels

There was only one individual from the ranks of the angels who failed to prostrate to Adam. It was Iblīs, the *jinn.*[70] God had created him, as he had created all the *jinn,* out of fire[71] so that he would have the opportunity to worship his creator in his oneness.[72] And Iblīs had fulfilled the true purpose of his creation with exceptional diligence for thousands of years.[73] However, the pangs of jealousy that had gnawed at his soul before, when he gazed on this human's lifeless form, now flared up within him.[74] He was certain he was superior to Adam, and he was certain God had made a terrible mistake. He flatly refused to prostrate and acted arrogantly and, thus, showed that, deep in his heart, he had always been among the unbelievers.[75] Thus, arrogance became the first sin ever committed.[76]

God addressed Iblīs demanding, "O Iblīs! What is the matter with you that you are not among those who prostrated?[77] What prevented you from prostrating when I commanded you to do so[78] before this creature whom I have created with my own two hands? Were you acting arrogantly just this once, or were you always from among the arrogant?"[79]

Iblīs replied, "It is not fitting for me to prostrate before a human being whom you have created from dry, resonant clay fashioned

69. *Biḥār al-anwār* vol. 11 p. 138 tr. 2

70. Qur'ān 2:34 and 7:11 and 15:30 and 38:73

71. Qur'ān 15:27

72. Qur'ān 51:56; *Biḥār al-anwār* vol. 11 p. 138 tr. 2

73. *Nahj al-balāghah* sermon 192

74. *Biḥār al-anwār* vol. 11 p. 141 tr. 7

75. Qur'ān 2:34 and 38:74

76. *Biḥār al-anwār* vol. 11 p. 141 tr. 7

77. Qur'ān 15:32

78. Qur'ān 7:12

79. Qur'ān 38:75

from dark foul-smelling clay.[80] I am better than he. You created me from fire, and you created him from clay."[81] He believed that God had issued an irrational command. He knew God had created him out of fire and Adam out of clay, and it was obvious that fire was more luminous than clay. Since he was created from something more luminous than Adam was, he concluded that he was better than Adam. Furthermore, he decided that it was senseless, even wrong, for God to order him to prostrate before Adam since one who is superior must never prostrate before an inferior.

Iblīs made several key mistakes in his reasoning. He knew that Adam was made of clay, but he did not know the full potential of clay. He did not know that clay was as precious as a gem because it had the potential to hold divine knowledge and wisdom when combined with the human soul. Iblīs could see only the material dullness of the clay, so he was oblivious that, from a spiritual perspective, it was more brilliant than fire.[82] Neither did he know what else Adam was made of. He did not know that God had combined in Adam four other major elements: light, fire, air, and water. Light gave him intellect and understanding. Fire allowed his body to digest food and drink. Air fed the flames of the fire and sustained his life functions. Water kept the fire in check and prevented it from drying his body and overheating it.[83]

If it had been only ignorance, God might have overlooked it. The angels had also been ignorant of these aspects of Adam. But they had not been arrogant. They had asked God, but Iblīs had defied him.

Iblīs attempted to assuage God by saying, "By your glory, if you excuse me from prostrating before Adam, I shall worship you with devotion unmatched by any of your creatures."[84]

God replied flatly, "I have no need for your worship. I wish but to be worshiped as *I* want, not as *you* want."[85] Then God ordered

80. Qur'ān 15:33

81. Qur'ān 7:12

82. See Islamic Texts Institute's commentary on *al-Kāfī* 2.19.18

83. *Biḥār al-anwār* vol. 11 p. 102 tr. 8

84. *Biḥār al-anwār* vol. 11 p. 119 tr. 52

85. *Biḥār al-anwār* vol. 11 p. 141 tr. 7

him, "Get down from here, for it is not appropriate that you act arrogantly herein. So get out! You are hereby among the abased.[86] Get out of this place, for you are hereby outcast, and you are hereby damned until the Day of Judgment."[87]

Iblīs' Concessions

Iblīs objected, "My Lord, how is this possible when you are just. Is the reward for all my deeds naught?" He knew very well that he had exceeded all bounds and transgressed against God, but he now appealed to God's ultimate justice. He knew God would not let a single deed pass without recompense.

God replied, "I shall not ignore the deeds you have done. Ask me for whatever reward you want in this temporal world for the deeds you have performed, and I shall give it to you."[88] He continued, "I have decided to compensate those who desire the life of this world and its glitter fully for their deeds therein, and they shall not be shortchanged. They are the ones for whom there shall be nothing in the hereafter but fire. Whatever they will have accomplished in the world will be obliterated, and their works will have come to naught."[89]

He said, "My Lord! First of all, since you have decided to cast me out and damn me, then at least give me respite until the day when these humans will be resurrected."[90]

God replied, "Since you have asked me for this, you shall be among those given respite until the day of the appointed hour." It was God's decree that every creature of his taste death.[91] He was not about to exempt his most despised creature from this law. So he gave him respite until the hour when Seraphiel would sound his trumpet

86. Qur'ān 7:13

87. Qur'ān 15:34-35

88. *Biḥār al-anwār* vol. 11 p. 141 tr. 7

89. Qur'ān 11:15–16

90. Qur'ān 15:36, 7:15, and 38:79

91. Qur'ān 29:57

announcing the end of the temporal world and everything in it.[92] It is an hour known only to God.[93]

Satisfied with God's answer to his first request, he pressed on, "Second, give me power over Adam's progeny."

God replied, "You shall have no power over my elect servants[94] who believe and trust in me.[95] You shall only have power over those who take you as their intimate friend and those who make you a partner of mine[96] and those who follow you from among those prone to misguidance."[97]

Iblīs was pleased again at receiving such a concession though it gave him more restricted power than he had hoped for. He began superfluously to explain to God his reason for making such a request saying, "Since you have misguided me, I swear to misguide them all, except your elect servants among them.[98] I shall adorn falsehood for them, and I shall misguide them all, except your elect servants among them.[99] I shall claim a set portion of them, and I shall misguide them, give them false hopes, and command them to worship false gods. As a result, they will slit the ears of their cattle to mark them for their gods. And I shall command them, and they will mutilate your creation."[100]

Pressing forward, Iblīs added, "Third, let me move freely among them as blood flows through their veins." When God conceded this too, Iblīs pledged, "I shall lie in wait for them upon this straight path you have ordained. Then I shall attack them from the front, from the

---

92. *Biḥār al-anwār* vol. 11 p. 108 tr. 17

93. Qur᾽ān 31:34, 41:47, and 20:15

94. Qur᾽ān 15:42

95. Qur᾽ān 16:99

96. Qur᾽ān 16:99

97. Qur᾽ān 15:42

98. Qur᾽ān 38:82–83

99. Qur᾽ān 15:39–40

100. Qur᾽ān 4:118–119. Perhaps the mutilation of God's creation is a reference to the practice of castration, the mutilation of enemies, and any other forms of mutilation, all of which are strictly prohibited in God's law.

rear, from their right flank, and from their left flank. And you shall not find most of them to be grateful.[101] I shall ruin Adam's progeny, except for a few."[102]

To this he added, "Fourth, for every one of them that is born, let two be born to me." God granted him this request too.

Iblīs pushed, "Fifth, let me see them, but let them not see me." Again, God conceded.[103]

Iblīs said once again, "Sixth, let me manifest myself before them in any form I wish."

God replied, "You shall not manifest yourself in the form of any of my prophets, their successors, or the righteous believers.[104] But you will be able to manifest yourself in any other form you wish."[105]

Finally, Iblīs thought to appeal to God's generosity and simply asked him to give him more, as though he had not been given enough. God told him, "I will make a place for you and your progeny in their hearts so that you can whisper to humankind."[106]

Iblīs Is Banished

Then with finality and disgust, God said, "Get out of this place, abased and outcast.[107] Lure whomever you can from among them with your voice; and rally your cavalry and your infantry against them; and share with them their wealth and children; and make them false promises![108] I swear if any among them follows you, I shall

---

101. Qur'ān 7:16–17

102. Qur'ān 17:62

103. Qur'ān 7:27

104. *Man lā yaḥḍuruhu al-faqīh* vol. 2 p. 584; *Kamāl al-dīn* vol. 1, p. 70

105. In his second letter to the Corinthians, Paul says, "Even Satan disguises himself as an angel of light" (2 Corinthians 11:14). He was correct in his assertion that Satan can disguise himself, although he was incorrect in claiming that he could disguise himself as an "angel of light."

106. Qur'ān 114:5; *Biḥār al-anwār* vol. 11 p. 141 tr. 7

107. Qur'ān 7:18

108. Qur'ān 17:64

fill hellfire with them and you altogether.[109] But, as I said, you shall have no power over my elect servants."[110] With that, Iblīs was cast out of the skies and sent to earth where he would live out his days in disgrace until the end of time. From then on, God would refer to him, not by his name, Iblīs, but by the derogatory epithet, Satan, or "distant one," for he was doomed to be banished from God's mercy for eternity.

Adam's Defenses Against Satan

As Adam witnessed this exchange between his creator and his newfound archenemy, he felt despondent. He felt God had empowered his enemy over him and his progeny, and he wondered how they would be able to serve God against such odds. When he asked God why he had done this, God answered, "Because of an act of his that I feel obliged to reward."[111]

Adam asked, "What act was it?"

God replied, "He prayed a single prayer that lasted 4000 years."[112]

---

109. Qur'ān 7:18

110. Qur'ān 17:65

111. God is omnipotent. He is not bound by anything or obliged by anyone. If he felt obliged to reward Iblīs, it was not because he owed Iblīs something. Rather, he felt obliged only to hold himself to his own policy of rewarding every good deed. He refers to this policy in the Qur'ān saying, "If anyone does a particle's weight of good, he shall see it" (Qur'ān 99:7).

112. *Biḥār al-anwār* vol. 11 p. 142 tr. 8. In the Qur'ān, God tells us that people can do something so heinous that they cause all their past deeds to be washed away. He refers to this phenomenon as *ḥabṭ*, the "obliteration" of deeds and mentions in particular apostasy, polytheism, and rejection of faith as causes for it. For instance, he says, "If any of you turns away from his religion (i.e., Islam) and dies as a non-believer, then they shall be the ones whose works are obliterated in this world and the hereafter. They shall be the inmates of the fire, and they shall remain in it forever" (2:117). Undoubtedly, Satan qualified to have all his acts of worship obliterated by this one ultimate act of defiance which was no less evil than apostasy, polytheism, and rejection of faith. The question is: Why did God not obliterate his deeds? Why did he agree to reward him, if only in this temporal world? Perhaps the answer is that God is not obligated to obliterate a person's deeds, even if he qualifies for this distinction. Especially if, as in Satan's case, rewarding him serves God's greater purpose. God had

Adam said to God, "You have given Satan all these advantages over me and my children. What advantages will you give us to counter him?"

God replied, "For you and your progeny I have ordained that each sin shall be punished in kind, while each good deed shall be rewarded tenfold."[113]

Adam said, "Lord, please give us more."

God said, "For every child born to you, I will assign two angels to guard him against sin."[114]

Adam said, "Lord, please give us more."

God said, "The gates of repentance shall remain open to you until your soul passes your throat at the time of death."

Adam said, "Lord, please give us more."

God said, "I shall absolve you of your sins without consideration for exacting justice."

Adam said, "That will suffice us."[115] He felt a renewed sense of hope since he realized that none of the concessions Satan had won would amount to anything as long as God had promised to graciously absolve the sins of humans. Sure, humans would sometimes be overwhelmed by Satan's machinations, but all except the most wretched would, in a moment of clarity, repent to God, and he would forgive them and render Satan's efforts null and void.

God told Adam to salute the angels who were still assembled using the sentence, "Peace be with you, and and may God's mercy and blessings be with you."

The angels replied in unison, "And peace be with you too, and may God's mercy and blessings be with you too."

---

ordained that human beings be tempted and tested. Satan, of his own free will, chose to fill this role. In one stroke, God absolved himself of even an imagined sense of obligation toward Satan for the deeds he had performed and found a candidate to fill the important role of tempter-in-chief.

113. *Biḥār al-anwār* vol. 11 p. 142 tr. 8; Qurʾān 6:160

114. *Biḥār al-anwār* vol. 11 p. 212 tr. 20; Qurʾān 6:61

115. *Biḥār al-anwār* vol. 11 p. 142 tr. 8

God told him, "This is the greeting you and your progeny are to use until the end of time."[116]

Adam's Wife

God had decided that Adam would have a spouse who would at once be a source of tranquility for him and a means for him to procreate.[117] He decided that he would create this spouse from Adam, not just from Adam's *kind*, but from the very clay he had used to create Adam.[118] Without telling Adam his plan, he made him sleep. As he

---

116. *Biḥār al-anwār* vol. 11 p. 143 tr. 11

117. Qur'ān 30:21

118. There is a difference of opinion with regard to the creation of Eve. One verse of the Qur'ān mentions her creation in ambiguous terms while the traditions convey at least two separate opinions that are mutually contradictory. I will first explain the verse of the Qur'ān and then turn toward the traditions.

The Qur'ān says, "O People! Fear your Lord who created you as a species from one being and created, from that being, a mate for him and spread forth, from those two beings, many men and women" (4:1). Clearly the verse is referring to the creation of Adam and his mate, Eve, and from them, the birth of the human race. The ambiguity lies in the Arabic phrase "*wa khalaqa minhā zawjahā*," which I have translated as "He created, from that being, a mate for him." There are those who claim that God created Adam's mate from the body of Adam, in particular from one of his left ribs, a view corroborated by numerous traditions and Genesis 2:21–23. There are those who claim that she was created, not from his body, but from the same clay from which he was made. Finally, there are those who believe that the phrase is better translated as "He created, from his *kind*, a mate for him." This last view is the one espoused by 'Allāmah al-Ṭabāṭabā'ī in *al-Mīzān*. He argues that the particle *min* in such a context indicates that one thing is of the same kind as another, not that one was created of another. He cites several other verses in the Qur'ān that use this same particle in similar contexts and argues that in all cases, the meaning is conclusively the former and not the latter. For instance, the Qur'ān says, "Among his signs is that he has created mates for you *from your own kind*, so that you may find tranquility in them" (30:21). It also says, "God made mates for you *from your own kind*" (16:72 and 42:11). It also says, "*From every kind of thing*, we made a pair" (51:49).

Nonetheless, I believe that verse 4:1 does in fact indicate that Eve was created *from* Adam, not just *from his kind*. There are several reasons why I favor this opinion:

- The first is based on an internal clue in the verse itself. Verse 4:1 says God "created you as a species from *one being*." This means that all

slept, he showed him a dream, the first dream ever dreamt.[119] In that dream, Adam saw God ordering an angel to take a portion of the clay he had used to create him, and from it, he created the form of a female. When her form was ready, God said to the figure, "Be!" In an instant, the clay figure was infused with the spirit of life and became the second human being, a perfect mate for Adam, made of his own flesh and blood.[120] In his dream, Adam gazed at her exquisite beauty

---

human beings were made from *one* being, not from *two* beings. If Eve were not made *from* Adam but as a separate being *from his kind*, then we could not say that we are all made from one being, rather we would have to say we were made from two beings. Thus, accepting that Eve was not created *from* Adam contradicts 4:1.

- The second reason is also based on an internal clue in the verse 4:1. God says he "created *you* as a species from one being." By "you" he means the entire human race. Eve was also part of the human race, so when the verse says that he created human beings from one being, it should also include Eve. If, on the other hand, we say that Eve was created separately and was not *from* Adam, we would have to concede that she was not human.
- Third, I believe that the particle *min* in 4:1 is different from the one in the verses ʿAllāmah al-Ṭabāṭabāʾī has cited. It is futile to argue about Arabic meaning through English medium, so I will simply refer you to a prominent commentator who has argued similarly—al-Ālūsī in *Rūḥ al-maʿānī*.

In conclusion, verse 4:1 tells us that Eve was created *from* Adam, but it does not give any more details of her creation. The traditions step in and offer some of these details. The problem though is that many of the traditions are what are known as *Isrāʾīliyyāt*, traditions fabricated and inserted into Islamic literature from Biblical origins. In particular, these traditions retell the story of Genesis—that Eve was created from Adam's rib. Some of these traditions are even attributed to the imams. However, one tradition in particular claims that all the others are lies and asserts that Eve was, in fact, created from clay remaining after the creation of Adam (*Biḥār al-anwār* vol. 11 p. 116 tr. 46). ʿAllāmah al-Majlisī believes that this tradition is reliable and that the rest were spoken in *taqiyyah*, or dissimulation (*Biḥār al-anwār* vol. 11 p. 117), though it is not far-fetched to conclude that they may be fabrications falsely attributed to the imams and Prophet Muḥammad.

119. *Biḥār al-anwār* vol. 11 p. 115 tr. 42

120. I have speculated on the details of her creation and carried over the descriptions of Adam's creation. It seems reasonable to assume that the process

and fell deeply in love with her. She told him, "I am a servant of God, and you are a servant of God, so ask God for my hand."[121]

When he awoke, he saw the woman from his dream sitting near his head. He modestly averted his gaze[122] and asked God who she was. God told him, "She is my servant. I have named her Eve."[123]

Adam asked, "For whom have you created her?"

God replied, "For anyone who will take her as a trust and show gratitude to me." Adam said, "I shall accept these stipulations. Please marry me to her." So God did, and they became husband and wife.[124]

Into the Garden

When they were married, God sent them forth to a lofty garden that had been prepared for them.[125] He told Adam, "Dwell with your wife

---

would have been the same.

121. *Mustadrak al-wasā'il* vol. 14 p. 324 tr. 17

122. The traditions do not mention that he averted his gaze, but I have assumed that he did because of what we know of the character of the prophets.

123. Eve's name in Arabic is *Ḥawwā'*. Several traditions mention that she was named *Ḥawwā'* because she was created from something *ḥayy*, or living, as opposed to Adam, who was created from *adīm al-arḍ*, dust from the surface of the earth (see *Biḥār al-anwār* vol. 11 p. 100 tr. 5).

124. *Mustadrak al-wasā'il* vol. 14 p. 324 tr. 17

125. It is impossible to say for sure where this "garden" was located. However, a careful analysis of the sources does help us to rule out certain false opinions and narrow the possibilities. Traditionally there have been three main opinions:

- The Old Testament calls it the Garden of Eden (Genesis 2:15). "Eden" (*'adn* in Arabic) means "permanence" and implies that this garden was the same as the gardens of paradise in which righteous people will live for eternity. 'Allāmah al-Majlisī claims that this has been the opinion of most Sunnī and Mu'tazilī scholars. There are also two traditions transmitted in *Biḥār al-anwār* that seem to indicate that their garden was one of the gardens of paradise (*Biḥār al-anwār* vol. 8 p. 146 tr. 68 and vol. 1 p. 326 tr. 120). However, we can rule this opinion out for the following reasons:
  - The gardens of paradise are reserved as a reward for those who earn them whereas Adam and Eve had not yet earned their place in them.
  - Those who enter the gardens of paradise are never made to leave,

for the Qur'ān tells us, "...and they shall not be expelled from it" (15:48), whereas Adam and Eve were eventually made to leave their garden.

- The blessings of paradise never end, for the Qur'ān tells us, "For them there is everlasting blessing therein" (9:21), whereas the blessings Adam and Eve enjoyed for a time ended when they were made to leave.
- Satan, who had been cast out of God's presence and stripped of God's mercy, would never have been allowed to enter the gardens of paradise, whereas he was able to enter their garden.
- Imam al-Ṣādiq also refutes this opinion in the following exchange, "Someone asked Imam al-Ṣādiq about the garden of Adam, 'Was it a garden of this world or a garden of the hereafter?' He replied, 'It was a garden of this world; the sun and the moon would shine upon it. If it had been a garden of the hereafter, Adam would never have been expelled from it, and Satan would never have entered it" (*Tafisīr al-qummī* under the aforementioned verses).

- As Imam al-Ṣādiq's aforementioned tradition states, the garden was a "garden of this world." Some have asserted that the garden was indeed "of this world" but not literally on earth. Their primary evidence for this claim is God's command, *ihbiṭū minhā* or "go down from the garden," which he said to Adam and Eve after they ate from the tree. They believe that it only makes sense to say "go down" to the earth if their garden was "up" above the earth (see *Manshūr-e jāwīd* vol. 11 p. 79). Among these scholars, there are some who believe the garden was in the sky, albeit within the temporal world (al-Majlisī attributes this opinion to Abū Hāshim; see *Biḥār al-anwār* vol. 11 p. 143). Shaykh Jawādī Āmulī believes the garden was in a sort of *barzakh* or "netherworld" (see *Tafsīr-e muwzū'ī* vol. 3 p. 245). Shaykh Ja'far Subḥānī does not specify where he thinks the garden was. He says only that it was not on earth and was the same place where Adam was originally created. He cites God's command, "*uskun*" meaning "dwell," to support his claim. He says that if Adam were not already in the garden, God would have told him to "enter" the garden. The fact that he says "dwell" and not "enter" shows that he was already in the garden (see *Manshūr-e jāwīd* vol. 11 p.78-79). These arguments have the following weak points:
  - It is true that God's command, *ihbiṭū minhā* or "go down from the garden," indicates that they were at some higher elevation and were commanded to go down to a lower elevation. However, this in itself does not mean that the garden they were in was in the sky or in some higher realm. It would have been appropriate for God to use this word even if their garden were at some elevated location

on earth, say on a hill or a mountain. After all, when God commands the Israelites to go into Jerusalem, he also says, "*ihbiṭū*" or "go down" (Qur'ān 2:61). They were presumably at an elevated earthly location, perhaps on a hill overlooking Jerusalem at the time. Similarly, God told Noah, "*ihbiṭ*" or "go down," when he wanted him to step out of his ark after the flood had subsided (Qur'ān 11:48). Accordingly, the phrase "*ihbiṭū minhā*" is not, by itself, conclusive evidence for this group's claim.

    - Similarly, Shaykh Subḥānī's argument based on the word "*uskun*" meaning "dwell" is weak. There is nothing far-fetched about God telling Adam to "dwell" in the garden even if he is not yet in the garden, so the use of this word does not form a conclusive argument.
    - The Qur'ān tells us that Satan was expelled from whatever place Adam, he, and the angels had been in after Adam had been created (Qur'ān 7:13, 7:18, and 15:34-35). If we accept, as Shaykh Subḥānī suggests, that Adam's garden was the same as the place where he was created, we would have to accept that Satan could have returned to that place to trick Adam after God himself had kicked him out. Since this is far-fetched, we can conclude that the garden was not in the same place where they were created but some other place where Satan had access to them.

- According to a third opinion, the garden was located on earth. Many traditions, mostly from Sunnī sources, but also in Shī'ī sources, identify its location as a place called *Sarandīb*, from which we get the word "serendipity." Many have understood this to mean Sri Lanka. Some traditions also mention *al-hind* or India. 'Allāmah al-Majlisī believes that the Shī'ī traditions among these, assuming they were actually spoken by the imams, were uttered in dissimulation (*taqiyyah*) since they agree with the opinion of Sunnīs and contradict the majority of traditions of the imams, to which I will refer shortly.

So far, I have summarized the three traditional viewpoints on this issue and offered some criticism of each. Based on these criticisms, I believe that the first and third opinions are unacceptable. Neither was their garden in paradise nor was it on earth. With regard to the second opinion, however, my criticisms were waged not at the opinion itself but, at the particular evidence its proponents have used to back it. In my opinion, there is, in the Qur'ān, no conclusive evidence to either support or refute the second and third opinions. Among the traditions, on the other hand, there is strong evidence that indirectly, albeit conclusively, supports the second opinion. These traditions tell us that Adam and Eve, after eating from the forbidden tree, were sent down from their garden to earth and placed respectively upon al-Ṣafā and al-Marwah, the two famous mountains next to the Ka'bah (*al-Kāfī* 4.3.4.1-2). The fact that they were "sent

in the garden and eat from it freely wherever you desire.[126] You are not to feel hungry herein or naked; and you shall not thirst herein or feel hot."[127] In the garden, they were to have all that their hearts desired. Food and drink were available freely. They neither had to sow nor cultivate nor harvest nor cook. Clothing was available as and when they wanted it. They neither had to spin nor weave nor sew nor wash. Shade was provided whenever they wished so that they should not suffer the least discomfort when the sun shone upon them.

It was midday and the sun was approaching its zenith. Adam and Eve exalted God for the blessings he had offered them. God decreed from then on that this time of each day would be reserved for prayer. This was the first prayer humans ever offered.[128]

After encouraging Adam and Eve to avail themselves freely of all the blessings of the garden, he advised them sternly saying, "But do not even approach this tree or you will be among the wrongdoers."[129] He was referring to one particular tree that was unlike any other in the garden. All the other trees bore but one type of fruit. This one, on the other hand, bore every kind of fruit and grain—wheat, grapes,

---

down" to earth from their garden indicates that the garden itself was not on earth. These traditions do not allow for the possibility that they were first sent to some garden on earth, say in Sri Lanka or India, and then "sent down" to al-Ṣafā and al-Marwah. Rather, they were sent down directly from their garden in some lofty place to these mountains. To my understanding, we cannot conclusively say more than this. Whether that garden was in the sky, in some higher realm, in a netherworld, or some other place, we cannot say with certainty. We can only say that it was part of the temporal world and somewhere physically above the earth.

126. Qur'ān 2:35 and 7:19

127. Qur'an 20:118-9

128. *Biḥār al-anwār* vol. 11 p. 197 tr. 52. In several instances in the story of Adam and Eve, we witness them performing acts that were not formally introduced as legal obligations until the advent of Islam. For example, they prayed the five daily prayers and they performed the Hajj. These parts of the story are not anachronisms. It is possible that Adam and Eve performed these rituals even though they did not become law until much later. These may have been duties specific to them, or they may have performed them voluntarily. Quite likely, God wished to honor them by codifying some of their practices within Islamic law.

129. Qur'ān 2:35 and 7:19

figs, and others.[130] There was nothing inherently harmful in this tree. For this reason, God did not forbid them outright from eating from it. He only advised them to avoid it and warned them vaguely of its consequences. He told them that if they ate from it they would no longer be able to remain in the garden and would need to toil to make their way in life.[131] Finally, he reminded them to beware of the guiles of Satan who had so recently pledged to misguide whomever he could. He said, "O Adam! This Satan is an enemy for you and your wife, so do not let him expel you from this garden, or you will need to toil to make your way in life."[132]

In this way, God accomplished two very important purposes. First, he set up a perfect training ground for Adam and Eve. He had decreed from the beginning that they would live their lives on earth, not in the garden, for Adam was God's "vicegerent *on earth*."[133] However, before they descended to earth, and were forced to bear the countless, hefty responsibilities of earthly life, he wanted to give them an opportunity to learn the meaning of responsibility. The garden, which was at the same time part of the temporal world and set apart from it, was the ideal training ground. God had not yet ordained a law to set limits for what was lawful and unlawful. There was nothing truly harmful in the garden. They could freely explore and learn without fear of harming their bodies or souls. Their state was much like that of a child who is raised in a nurturing household. He is not yet responsible for his actions, yet his parents teach, encourage, and discipline him in a safe environment, all in hopes of cultivating a responsible adult when the child comes of age. In this training ground, Adam and Eve needed to learn that there are consequences for acting against God's instructions. They also had to learn the true mettle of their archenemy Satan.[134]

The second purpose that God fulfilled by placing them in the garden was to give them a taste of what they could hope for in paradise.

---

130. *Biḥār al-anwār* vol. 11 p. 190 tr. 47

131. Qur'ān 20:117

132. Qur'ān 20:117-8

133. Qur'ān 2:30

134. *Manshūr-e javīd* vol. 11 p. 80

When they eventually ended up on earth, having to toil just to survive, he wanted them to remember the paradise they had lost so that they would strive to one day regain it.[135]

Adam Learns Intellect's Worth

Gabriel descended upon Adam and told him, "Adam, I have been commanded to offer you the choice of one of three traits, so choose one and leave two."

Adam asked him, "Gabriel, and what are these three traits?"

He answered, "They are intellect, decency, and devotion."

Adam said, "I most certainly choose intellect."

Gabriel told decency and devotion, "Go away and leave intellect with Adam."

Thereupon they said, "Gabriel, we have been ordered to remain with intellect wherever he may be."[136]

---

135. *Manshūr-e javīd* vol. 11 p. 80

136. This tradition's detailed account of the interaction and conversation between Gabriel and Adam prevents us from consigning it to allegory. However, the three personified human attributes mentioned here are problematic: How can human attributes that cannot exist independently of their possessor stand before Adam and speak? In traditions about purgatory and the hereafter, it is not uncommon for good and bad traits to appear in the form of beautiful and ugly figures. In fact, even in this temporal life, realities appear to some people in the form of visions. In the story of Joseph, for example, God depicts the ultimate reunion of Joseph and his family and his noble standing among them as eleven stars, the sun, and the moon prostrating before Joseph in a dream (Qur'ān 12:4). The king and Joseph's two cellmates also see similar visions that represent future events (Qur'ān 12:36 and 12:43). Thus, in the tradition at hand, there is nothing far-fetched about Gabriel's teaching Adam the nature of three human traits in tangible form. If it seems unusual, it is because we are used to dealing with mental concepts and words, not symbolic representations. However, because it is extremely important that a prophet of God know reality intimately, God chose to leave weaker, conventional methods of teaching with words and concepts and personified the three traits as figures to give Adam an unforgettable lesson about intellect's role in guiding decency and devotion.

Obviously, Adam possessed these three traits, especially intellect, before Gabriel's offer. Accordingly, perhaps Gabriel was asking him which of the three he would like to keep or which of the three he would like perfected in him.

Understanding this tradition requires an understanding of these three

Gabriel said, "As you wish." Then he ascended.[137]

The Boxthorn Staff

As they explored the garden, Adam came upon a boxthorn[138] tree with its long straight branches covered with thorns. He broke a branch and removed the thorns to make a sturdy staff for himself.[139]

Deceived by Satan

Just as God had warned them, Satan came to them, disguised so they could not recognize him.[140] He whispered to Adam saying, "O

---

human traits and their interactions with one another. Intellect, in the first sense of the word, is the human capacity to understand reality. Decency (*al-ḥayā'*) is a trait that makes a person recoil from anything he deems bad—whether it be bad in reality or not. Devotion (*al-dīn* in the sense of *al-diyānah*) is a trait that compels a person to do anything he deems good—whether it be good in reality or not. A person's intellect, inasmuch as it understands reality, realizes that decency and devotion are good in and of themselves and that he should acquire them. Once he acquires them, his intellect guides his decency so that it makes him recoil only from what is *truly* bad. Similarly, his intellect guides his devotion so that it compels him to do only what is *truly* good. It follows that if Adam had chosen decency or devotion instead of intellect, he would have been like a fledgling child whose misguided decency causes him to shy away from asking a question or conversing with an adult or like the pagans of Mecca or the Khawārij who devoted themselves to a religion founded on fantasies and misconceptions. However, by choosing intellect, he acquired a torch by which to guide his other two faculties. This footnote is taken from the Islamic Texts Institute's commentary on *al-Kāfī* 1.1.2.

137. *Al-Kāfī* 1.1.2

138. In Arabic boxthorn is called *'awsaj.*

139. *Biḥār al-anwār* vol. 13 p. 46 tr. 11

140. I have not found any evidence that explicitly states that Satan was disguised. However, it is reasonable to infer this detail for three reasons:

- First, God had given Satan the concession of manifesting himself in nearly any form he wished, and it is likely that he would have taken advantage of this concession at the first opportunity possible.
- Second, it seems unlikely that Adam would have forgotten Satan's face and his ruthless pledges to ruin him so soon after their previous encounter unless he was unaware that the person speaking to him was in fact Satan.

Adam! Shall I lead you to a tree that will give you immortality and a dominion that shall never perish?" God had told him they could eat from the garden freely wherever they desired,[141] so he was interested in finding out about the special tree this man spoke of. However, when he realized that the man was referring to the very tree God had advised against, he declined the offer and refrained from partaking of its fruit. With feigned sincerity, Satan leaned in close to them and whispered, "Your Lord only advised against eating from this tree lest you become angels or become one of the immortals." To drive the point home, he added, "I swear that I am one of your well-wishers."[142] Thus, he led them to eat from it through deception.[143]

Adam and Eve took his words to heart. He had spoken sincerely and sworn that he was well-wishing, so they naively abandoned God's advice[144] and accepted Satan's.[145] In this way, Adam disobeyed his Lord and went astray.[146] When they tasted the fruit of the tree,

---

- Third, the verse says, "Thus, he led them to it through deception" (Qur'ān 7:22). Disguise would have been the most appropriate form of deception for this particular mission.

141. Qur'ān 2:35 and 7:19

142. Qur'ān 7:20-1

143. Qur'ān 7:22

144. Qur'ān 20:116

145. Qur'ān 20:115 and *Biḥār al-anwār* vol. 11 p. 188 tr. 44

146. Qur'ān 20:121. It is crucial that we understand this verse in context of what was said before. God's statement, "Do not even approach this tree," was advisory (*irshādī*) not legislative (*mawlawī*). Thus, for Adam to eat from the tree did not constitute a sin against God's law; rather, he was simply acting against God's advice, following which was not binding upon him in the first place. The evidence for this claim lies in another verse where God warns Adam and Eve, "Do not let Satan expel you from the garden, or you will need to toil to make your way in life" (Qur'ān 20:117). God does not threaten them with his wrath or with hellfire. He only advises them of the consequences of their choice. Thus, when 2:35 warns them that they will be among the "wrongdoers" if they approach and eat from the tree, it in fact warns them of burdening themselves with the drudgery of worldly life, not of sinning against God, for Adam was a prophet of God and, thus, infallible and immaculate (Islamic Texts Institute. *Al-Nudbah: A Devotional Elegy for the Prophet Muḥammad and His Family*. 2009. p. 28).

the clothes God had provided them as a blessing were stripped from their bodies and their nakedness became apparent for themselves.[147] A sudden sense of shame overcame them both, and they began heaping leaves from the garden upon themselves. Their Lord called out to them, "Did I not advise you against eating from this tree and tell you that Satan is an open enemy of yours?"[148]

As the gravity of their actions became apparent to them, they felt as desperate as a child who has acted rashly, albeit innocently, and earned the displeasure of his parents and, in his naiveté, feels as though he has committed the most heinous crime in the world.

Out of the Garden

God addressed Adam, Eve, and Satan altogether and said, "Go down in mutual enmity. On earth is a temporary abode for you and a temporary means of sustenance.[149] On earth shall you live, on earth shall you die, and from earth shall you be brought forth."[150]

Thus, a mere seven hours after Adam and Eve were told to dwell in the garden, they were told to leave.[151] God's purpose for them had been served therein, and they were now prepared to enter the real world. It was the 25th of Dhū al-Qaʿdah.[152]

Before leaving the garden, Adam asked God humbly, "My Lord, tell me: Did you decree for me this act of disobedience, along with everything that I have done and ever shall do, before you even created me? Or did I do it myself before you decreed it for me, through my own baseness, such that it was my own act and from me and not your act?"

God replied, "O Adam! I created you and informed you that I would make you and your wife dwell in the garden. And it was through my blessing and through the power that I invested in you that you

---

147. Qurʾān 7:22 and 20:121

148. Qurʾān 7:22

149. Qurʾān 2:36 and 7:24

150. Qurʾān 7:25

151. *Biḥār al-anwār* vol. 11 p. 181 tr. 35

152. *Biḥār al-anwār* vol. 11 p. 217 tr. 29

gained the ability to disobey me with your own limbs. All the while, you never left my sight, and I never ceased to know of every act that you did or intended to do."

Adam said, "O Lord! All good is from you, and all evil is from me."

God said, "Adam, did I not advise you against eating from this tree? Did I not tell you that Satan is an enemy to you and your wife? Did I not warn you before you entered the garden? Did I not tell you that if you ate from the tree you would be wronging yourself and disobeying me? Adam, no one shall be with me in paradise who does wrong and disobeys me."

Adam replied, "Of course you told us all that, my Lord. You are absolutely right and there is no justification for what we did."[153] Then Adam and Eve exclaimed in unison, "Our Lord! We have wronged ourselves. If you do not absolve us and have mercy on us we shall be among the losers!"[154] They continued, "O God! There is no god but you. We exalt you with praise befitting you. We have acted wrongly and wronged ourselves, so forgive us, for you and you alone are the Clement, the Ever-Merciful. There is no god but you. We exalt you with praise befitting you. We have acted wrongly and wronged ourselves, so forgive us, for you and you alone are the best of forgivers."[155]

Their plea for forgiveness brought even the angels to tears. They beseeched God saying, "Lord, he is one of your creatures. You infused him with the spirit of life. You made all your angels prostrate before him. Yet, because of a single act of disobedience, you have reduced him to desperation!"[156]

Adam acquired certain words from his Lord.[157] In particular, God reminded him that among the names he had taught him there had been five creatures who were greater than all the rest, closer to God than all his other creatures. God ordered Adam and Eve to seek the intercession of those five creatures. They said, "O God! We beg you

---

153. *Biḥār al-anwār* vol. 11 p. 182 tr. 36

154. Qur'ān 7:23

155. *Biḥār al-anwār* vol. 11 p. 181 tr. 35

156. *Biḥār al-anwār* vol. 11 p. 171 tr. 18

157. Qur'ān 2:37

to absolve us through Muḥammad, ʿAlī, Fāṭimah, al-Ḥasan, and al-Ḥusayn."[158] Because they were sincere in their repentance and they earnestly sought the intercession of God's greatest creatures, he accepted their repentance, for he alone is the Clement, the Ever-Merciful.[159]

In this way, God selected and groomed Adam to be his first vicegerent on earth.[160] He was now ready to bear the trials that awaited him. He knew his goal. He knew his enemy. He knew how to battle his enemy. He knew how to attain his goal. God commanded them saying, "Go down from here altogether. Hereafter, if any guidance should come to you from me, then whoever follows that guidance from me shall not fear nor shall they feel remorse.[161] Whoever follows that guidance from me shall not stray in this world nor shall they find disgrace in the hereafter."[162] God gave them the following parting advice, "If you endeavor to better yourselves, I shall better you. If you act for me, I shall strengthen you. If you strive to do what pleases me, I shall rush to be pleased with you. If you fear me, I shall protect you from my wrath."

Adam and Eve broke into tears. They begged God saying, "Lord, help us to better ourselves and to do what pleases you."

God replied, "I shall, and if you do perpetrate evil, repent to me, and I shall accept your repentance, for I am the Clement, the Ever-Merciful."[163] Finally he said, "Adam, speak little, and you shall soon return to my company."[164]

Beseechingly, they said, "If you must send us down, at least send us to the place on earth that is most beloved to you."

---

158. *Biḥār al-anwār* vol. 11 p. 175 tr. 20 and p. 177 tr. 23

159. Qurʾān 2:37

160. Qurʾān 20:122 and 2:132

161. Qurʾān 2:38-39

162. Qurʾān 20:123

163. *Biḥār al-anwār* vol. 11 p. 183 tr. 36

164. *Biḥār al-anwār* vol. 11 p. 180 tr. 31

God sent the message to Gabriel, "Take them down to the blessed land of Bakkah."[165] Gabriel obeyed his orders. When he came to take Adam to Bakkah, he asked him why he had eaten from the tree. Adam replied, "Satan swore on God's name that he was my well-wisher, and I did not think any of God's creatures would falsely swear on God's name."[166]

He handed Adam a ring as a gift from God. Its inscription read, "There is no god worthy of worship except God, and Muḥammad is the Messenger of God."[167]

Adam toted the staff he had fashioned from boxthorn and prepared himself to be taken down.[168]

To Bakkah

Gabriel placed Adam atop one of Bakkah's mountains and Eve atop a neighboring mountain.[169] Adam's mountain would later come to be known as Mount Ṣafā because he, God's *ṣafwah* or "chosen servant," was the first to set foot upon it. Eve's mountain came to be known as Mount Marwah because she, the first *mar'ah* or "woman," was the first to set foot upon it.[170]

From a distance of 400 meters,[171] Adam could see where Eve had descended. But he thought to himself, "God must have separated her from me because it is no longer permissible for me to have conjugal relations with her. Otherwise, he would have sent her down with me on Ṣafā." So he would visit her during the daytime and speak with her but return at nightfall for fear that his desire for her would get the better of him.[172] They continued in this way for days.

---

165. Bakkah was the ancient name for Mecca.

166. *Biḥār al-anwār* vol. 11 p. 162 tr. 5

167. *Biḥār al-anwār* vol. 11 p. 107 tr. 13 and vol. 11 p. 62 tr. 1

168. *Biḥār al-anwār* vol. 13 p. 46 tr. 11

169. *Biḥār al-anwār* vol. 11 p. 183 tr. 36

170. *Biḥār al-anwār* vol. 11 p. 162 tr. 5 and p. 194 tr. 48

171. Ja'fariyyān, Rasūl. *Āthār-e islāmī makkeh wa madīneh*. p. 107

172. *Biḥār al-anwār* vol. 11 p. 194 tr. 48

One day when they were together on Marwah, they gazed around at the barren desert and jagged escarpments that surrounded them. In contrast to the idyllic garden from which they had descended, these stark surroundings appeared brutal and only added to their feeling of wretchedness. They stood where they were, gazing into the sky, and wailed with all their might, hoping God would hear them. Then they dropped their heads sobbing. God heard their sobs and asked, "What makes you cry so when you know that I am pleased with you both?"

They replied, "Lord, the lingering memory of our mistake makes us cry. Because of it, we had to leave your proximity. We can no longer hear the perpetual exaltation of the angels as we could in the garden. Our naked bodies are exposed, and we are compelled to till the earth and seek out our food and drink. And atop it all, we feel terribly lonely since you have split us apart." For his impassioned lamentations during these days, Adam would later be immortalized in history as one of the Five Lamenters.[173]

God spoke to Gabriel, "I am God, the All-Beneficent, the Ever-Merciful. And I wish to show mercy to Adam and Eve, for they have beseeched me. Take down to them a pavilion from paradise and bring them together inside of it." Gabriel erected the pavilion directly beneath the angels' house of worship in the skies, in the place where the Kaʿbah would eventually be built and of similar proportions. The tent poles were hewn from solid ruby that glowed red. The light from the ruby poles lit the surrounding mountains and beyond. God made all the areas illuminated by this light into his *ḥaram*, the sacred sanctuary that surrounds Bakkah. The ropes that supported the pavilion were anchored to the ground using large pegs. This ring of pegs eventually became the boundary of the Sacred Mosque of Mecca. Gabriel guided Adam down from Ṣafā and Eve from Marwah and allowed them to meet each other inside the pavilion. Then, on God's command, Gabriel ordered 70,000 angels to descend and surround the pavilion. They were instructed to circuit

---

173. *Biḥār al-anwār* vol. 12 p. 264 tr. 27. The others are Jacob, Joseph, Fāṭimah al-Zahrāʾ, and Imam Zayn al-ʿĀbidīn.

it as they used to circuit the house of worship in the skies, day and night, and, if necessary, to defend it against any mischievous *jinn*.

God reminded Adam that he would no longer provide for all his needs as he had done in the garden. Rather, he would have to till the land with his own hands and eat of his own labor. When he realized what a great blessing the garden had been, Adam fell prostrate for three consecutive days without lifting his head.[174] Gabriel taught him the following prayer through which he could ask for God's provision: "O God! Suffice me of all my needs in the temporal world, and spare me of every danger I may encounter until I reach paradise, and clothe me in well-being so that life be sweet."[175]

In answer to his supplication, God sent saplings of fruit trees from the garden for Adam to plant. There were date palms, grape vines, and olive and pomegranate trees. He also sent down a boxthorn like the one from which Adam had hewn his staff. Adam immediately set out to plant all of these so that he and his progeny would have food to eat.[176] He planted the boxthorn first.[177] The date palm was a species called *ʿajwah*. Adam had eaten from it in the garden and longed to enjoy its fruit in this world too, so he had asked God with yearning to send it down for him.[178] *ʿAjwah* was the original date palm from which all others are descended.[179]

When Adam ate the food he was able to collect, he felt an unusual heaviness in his belly that he had not felt in the garden. He complained about this discomfort to Gabriel who explained to him how he would now have to relieve himself regularly of the waste his body could not use.[180]

Adam and Eve did not have conjugal relations in their pavilion. Adam felt such an act would defile the sanctity of the sacred place.

---

174. *Biḥār al-anwār* vol. 11 p. 211 tr. 15

175. *al-Kāfī* vol. 5 p. 260

176. *Biḥār al-anwār* vol. 11 p. 215 tr. 26 and *Tahdhīb al-aḥkām* vol. 1 p. 326 tr. 120

177. *Biḥār al-anwār* vol. 13 p. 126 tr. 24

178. *Tahdhīb al-aḥkām* vol. 1 p. 326 tr. 120

179. *Biḥār al-anwār* vol. 11 p. 217 tr. 27

180. *Biḥār al-anwār* vol. 11 p. 114 tr. 37

Instead, he would take Eve with himself outside the confines of the sanctuary. When they were done, they would bathe and purify themselves before returning to Bakkah.[181]

The Kaʿbah Is Built

Some days later, Gabriel informed Adam and Eve that they must return to Mount Ṣafā and Marwah, respectively, and that their pavilion was to be removed from its place. Adam questioned Gabriel, "Has God ordered us to leave this place because he is displeased with us, or is this simply part of his plan for us?"

Gabriel replied, "He is not displeased with you; however, God may not be questioned about what he does. I will tell you though that the 70,000 angels whom God had sent to keep you company and protect your pavilion asked God to build a house of worship for them in place of the pavilion, similar to the house of worship they used to have in the skies. For this, God has ordered me to move you away and take your pavilion back to paradise."

Adam told him, "We are content with whatever God has planned."[182]

Before sending him back to Mount Ṣafā, Gabriel took Adam by the hand and led him to the place where the pavilion had stood. At that instant, God sent a cloud that cast a heavy shadow near where he stood. God said, "Adam, mark with your feet the outline of the shadow that this cloud now casts upon the ground. There I shall erect for you a house of worship that will be the focal point toward which you and your progeny will offer your prayers."[183]

God sent a host of angels with the mission of laying the foundations for the Kaʿbah along the perimeter Adam had outlined. In the meantime, Adam and Eve were escorted back to their vantage points atop their two mountains. From there they could watch the angels do their work.

Alone on Ṣafā, Adam felt a longing to be with Eve again. He walked briskly from Ṣafā to Marwah. He greeted her, and together they gazed down at the emerging structure and prayed to God that

181. *Biḥār al-anwār* vol. 11 p. 225 tr. 4

182. *Biḥār al-anwār* vol. 11 p. 185 tr. 36

183. *Biḥār al-anwār* vol. 11 p. 195 tr. 48 and p. 167 tr. 15

he would allow them to return to their home soon. When they were done praying, he returned to Ṣafā. He made this short excursion two more times to visit her. During each visit, their prayers were more intense and their tears more desperate. After the sixth leg of his journey, Adam stood atop Ṣafā, facing the Kaʿbah's foundations, praying, when Gabriel came to him. He told him to make a seventh trip to Marwah and join Eve. He told him that their prayers had been answered and that the Kaʿbah had been built. One cornerstone had been hewn from Ṣafā, another from Marwah, a third from Mount Sinai, and a fourth from the Mount of Peace in Kūfah. The rest of the stones had been hewn from Mount Abū Qubays which loomed high, less than a hundred meters due east of Ṣafā. The Kaʿbah had two doors: one facing northeast and the other facing southwest.[184] Within the eastern corner of the Kaʿbah, they installed a stone from the skies. This stone was whiter than milk.[185] It had been one of God's greatest angels, the first to answer God's call to obedience. To honor it, God entrusted it with the covenant he made with humankind.[186] Over the ages, people would renew their covenant with God through the stone, and in response to their sins, it would turn pitch black and become known as *al-ḥajar al-aswad,* the Black Stone.[187]

The First Hajj

No more than two weeks had passed since Adam and Eve had descended from the garden. It was approaching the 9th of Dhū al-Ḥijjah, and Gabriel was given the honor of teaching them how to perform the Hajj. He first took them from Bakkah to the plain of ʿArafāt. There, he told them to admit all their faults before God and told them that this would become a tradition among their progeny until the end of time. When the sun set, Gabriel took them to Muzdalifah and told them to combine their evening and night prayers there. The next morning, they went to Minā. Gabriel showed Adam the place where the Mosque of Khayf would eventually stand

184. *Biḥār al-anwār* vol. 11 p. 185 tr. 36

185. *Wasāʾil al-shīʿah* vol. 13 p. 318 tr. 17, 836

186. *Wasāʾil al-shīʿah* vol. 13 p. 318 tr. 17, 835

187. *Wasāʾil al-shīʿah* vol. 13 p. 318 tr. 17, 836

and asked him to mark its circumference with his feet as he had done for the Kaʿbah. When they had prayed, he told them to offer a sacrifice. Adam sacrificed an animal for God, and God sent down lightning from the sky to burn the offering, indicating that he had accepted it.

Gabriel told Adam, "God has blessed you by showing you these rites through which he will forgive your sins, and he has accepted your sacrifice, so shave your head as a sign of humility to him."[188] Gabriel wielded a blade fashioned of ruby from paradise, and with it, he shaved Adam's head.[189]

They began walking in the direction of Bakkah when Satan appeared before them. Gabriel ordered Adam to cast seven stones at him and say, "God is greater," with each throw. When he did this, Satan vanished. Then they proceeded to Bakkah to circuit the newly erected Kaʿbah.[190] Adam and Eve watched the angels circuit the Kaʿbah. They followed their lead and circuited it seven times and performed the first *ṭawāf* of the Kaʿbah.[191] Then Gabriel took Adam to a spot between the Kaʿbah's eastern door and the Black Stone called the *multazam*. He told him, "This is where you and your progeny must confess your sins before God."

Adam turned his attention to God and said, "Lord, he who worships is rewarded, and I have worshiped."

God said, "Ask what you would have."

Adam said, "O God! Forgive me my sin."

God said, "Adam, you have been forgiven."

Adam said, "And forgive my children after me."

God said, "O Adam! If any among them bring his sins here as you have brought them, then I shall forgive him."[192]

When they finished their pilgrimage, God told them to fast during the 13th, 14th, and 15th days of the month. He promised them that anyone from their progeny who fasted these three days of every

---

188. *Biḥār al-anwār* vol. 11 p. 168 tr. 15

189. *Biḥār al-anwār* vol. 11 p. 196 tr. 51

190. *Biḥār al-anwār* vol. 11 p. 169 tr. 15

191. *Biḥār al-anwār* vol. 11 p. 185 tr. 36

192. *Biḥār al-anwār* vol. 11 p. 179 tr. 29

month would be rewarded as though they had fasted perpetually.[193] He told them these fasts would whiten the spiritual blackness of sin and would thereafter be called the "white days."[194]

Having learned the rites of Hajj, Adam would continue to perform them year after year until, by the end of his life, he had performed the Hajj 700 times and the *'Umrah* 300 times.[195]

Adam's Beard

Once, Adam prayed to God saying, "Lord, make me handsome." God gave him a beard black as coal. Adam stroked his new beard and wondered what it was.

God told him, "It is a beard. I have given it to you and your male progeny to make you handsome."[196]

All Knowledge in Four Teachings

God told Adam, "I shall summarize all knowledge for you in four teachings: One relates to me, one relates to you, one relates to you and me, and one relates to you and others. The first is to worship me and not associate partners with me. The second is that I shall reward you for your deeds when you are most in need of it. Third is that it is upon you to pray, and it is upon me to answer. Fourth is that you must desire for others what you desire for yourself."[197]

---

193. The term for this perpetual fast is *ṣawm al-dahr*. In other traditions, we are told that *ṣawm al-dahr* comprises fasting the first Thursday, the middle Wednesday, and the last Thursday of every month (see *al-Kāfī* vol. 4 p. 90 tr. 3; see also *Wasā'il al-shī'ah* vol. 10 p. 436). There is no contradiction between the two since it is possible for God to promise a similar reward for two different deeds.

194. The 13th, 14th, and 15th of every lunar month are known as *al-ayyām al-bīḍ*. The tradition I have paraphrased in the text gives one explanation for this name. Another explanation is that the moon, on the eves of these three days, shines brightly for all or most of the night. Accordingly, the "white days" are actually the days after the "white nights" (see *Majma' al-baḥrayn*).

195. *Biḥār al-anwār* vol. 11 p. 114 tr. 38. The *'umrah* is similar to Hajj, but it is performed off season.

196. *Biḥār al-anwār* vol. 11 p. 172 tr. 18

197. *Biḥār al-anwār* vol. 11 p. 115 tr. 42

Adam Is Shown a Vision

Once, in the valley of Rawḥā', outside of Bakkah, God showed Adam a vision of all of his progeny until the end of time.[198] Adam was intrigued, in particular, by David and noticed that God had decided that he would only live fifty years. He asked God if he could give fifty years from his own life to make David's life 100 years. God said he would allow it. On his behest, Gabriel and Michael descended along with Azrael. Azrael recorded in his ledgers that fifty years were being transferred from Adam to David.[199]

Adam's and Eve's Children

Before long, Eve gave birth to a daughter whom they named ʿAnāq.[200] As she grew up, she proved to be an indecent and corrupt woman,

---

198. This tradition is clearly similar to the following verses of the Qur'ān: "Remember when your Lord extracted from the loins of the Children of Adam their descendants and he made them witness themselves, he said to them, 'Am I not your Lord?' They replied, 'Of course you are, we hereby witness.' He did this so that you can neither say on the Day of Resurrection, 'We were unaware of this,' nor can you say, 'It was only our forebears who ascribed partners to God before us, and we were only descendants after them following their lead. Will you then destroy us for what those misguided people did?'" (7:172–3).

There are two prevailing theories concerning these verses. One claims that these were real events that took place in history. The other claims that the story is an allegory. Sayyid al-Murtaḍā, who espouses the theory that these verses are an allegory, claims that traditions like the one I have paraphrased in the story, while clearly similar to the events narrated in the verse, are not speaking about the same event because of some major discrepancies between the stories. For one, the story in the tradition claims the progeny of Adam were extracted from his own loins while the verses speak of progeny being extracted from the loins of the progeny of Adam which seems to fit more with the phenomenon of birth, generation after generation, than it does with a miraculous display. In any case, I have included this story, but I have attempted to keep it separate from the allegory of the covenant.

199. *Biḥār al-anwār* vol. 14 p. 9 tr. 17. Another tradition says it was 60 years that he transferred (*al-Kāfī* vol. 7 p. 378 tr. 1). Another tradition gives much more detail; however, I have ignored much of it because it challenges the idea that Qur'ān 7:172–3 is allegorical (*Biḥār al-anwār* vol. 14 p. 9 tr. 18).

200. *Biḥār al-anwār* vol. 11 p. 226 tr. 6

and so God sent a wolf to kill her and a vulture to finish her off. Eve's second child was Cain.[201] When Cain grew to adulthood, God sent a female *jinn* in the form of a woman as a mate for Cain. Her name was Juhānah. On the command of God, Adam married Cain and Juhānah.[202]

Eve's third child was Abel.[203] When he grew to adulthood, God sent a female *ḥawrā'*, a creature from paradise, in the form of a woman. Her name was Turk. Adam married Abel and Turk upon God's command.

Some time later, God spoke to Adam and said:

> I had decided from time immemorial never to leave the earth without one endowed with knowledge through whom my religion could be known. I have decided to bring forth these guides from your progeny. Think now of your legacy of prophetic knowledge and of all the names that I have taught you and of all the guidance I have given you, which

---

201. In Arabic he is known as *Qābīl.*

202. There has always been debate surrounding the issue of marriage and procreation in the first generation after Adam. In particular, if all human beings, including Eve, are created from Adam as indicated by 4:1, then whom did Adam's and Eve's children marry? The Bible does not address this issue at all. However, Christian theologians commonly offer the explanation that Adam's and Eve's children must have had incestuous relationships with each other since no other humans existed. They justify this practice since incest was only outlawed in Moses' time. We can glean from Islamic traditions that this debate continued until the time of the imams. In several traditions, people have asked Imam al-Ṣādiq and other imams about this issue. When the imam asks the questioner what people say on the issue, he tells him that people say that they had incestuous relationships. In all these traditions, the imam rejects this opinion and states that God created a *jinn* and a *ḥawrā'*, each in the form of a human woman, and allowed the sons to marry them and procreate through them (see *Biḥār al-anwār* vol. 11 p. 226–8 tr. 6 for example). It is true that some traditions support the opinion of incest (see *Biḥār al-anwār* vol. 11 p. 225 tr. 4). However, in light of the explicit condemnation of this view in other traditions, we can comfortably consign these traditions to dissimulation (*taqiyyah*).

203. In Arabic he is known as *Hābīl.*

is vital to the prosperity of humankind. Turn all this over to your son Abel.

Cain's Conflict With Abel

Adam did as God commanded. He appointed Abel as his successor and shared with him his vast knowledge. When Cain learned of all this, he became enraged. He said, "Father, am I not older than my brother and more deserving of this appointment?"

Adam replied, "This matter is solely with God. He appoints whomever he wishes. Though you may be older, God has selected him because of his qualifications. However, if you believe I am mistaken and you do not believe me, then make God an offering."[204] He told them God would confirm his choice by accepting the sacrifice only from his chosen successor.[205]

Abel was a shepherd. He chose the finest, fattest ram of his flock[206] and offered it in hopes of pleasing God and his father. Cain was a farmer. He collected a mere handful of the hardest grains of wheat, grains that could not be ground in his stone mill, grains that even his animals could not eat. He made this meager offering, neither seeking the pleasure of God nor his father.[207] When Abel's sheep was offered to the ceremonial fire, it was consumed, but Cain's wheat was not.[208]

---

204. *Biḥār al-anwār* vol. 11 p. 227 tr. 6

205. *Biḥār al-anwār* vol. 11 p. 246 tr. 44

206. *Biḥār al-anwār* vol. 11 p. 230 tr. 8

207. *Biḥār al-anwār* vol. 11 p. 240 tr. 28

208. Qur'ān 5:27. There is no clear indication how they knew whether an offering had been accepted and the other rejected. But they did come to know this with certainty as indicated by Cain's strong reaction. It is likely that they knew this, as I have supposed in the story, because an offering that was accepted was consumed by a fire. The Qur'ān mentions that the Jews would recognize a prophet as legitimate if he brought them "an offering that the fire would consume" (Qur'ān 3:183). Whether this fire was a ceremonial fire or a flash of lightning from the sky, I do not know. See also *Oxford Companion to the Bible* p. 666–777. Also see Qur'ān 3:183 for further confirmation of this theory.

Cain felt a heightened sense of indignation and jealousy. In this moment of weakness, Satan whispered to him, "This affair will not end here with you and your brother. If you and he have children and your progeny increase, his descendants will gloat over you and your descendants until the end of time because your father favored him over you, and the fire accepted his offering and not yours. Kill him to stamp out his gloating progeny. If you do, your father will have no choice but to give you whatever he has given him."[209] Satan's insinuation was like fuel on Cain's fiery rage. He followed his brother discretely, seeking a moment when he was out of Adam's sight.[210]

When he found this moment, he seethed at Abel, "I swear that I shall kill you."[211]

Abel replied, "God only accepts offerings from the God-fearing."[212] Abel wanted Cain to know that it was no fault of his that Cain's sacrifice was not accepted. Cain had made his offering with a corrupt intention and, hence, had no one to blame but himself. Instead of threatening him, he should have endeavored to reform himself. Abel added, "Even if you extend your hand to me to murder me, I shall not extend my hand to you to murder you, for I fear God, Lord of all realms."[213] He would defend himself, but he was not about to strike preemptively at his brother for fear of earning the wrath of God. Their father had taught them that the murderer would be made to bear the sins of his victim along with his own sins,[214] and he cared to bear no such burden. He said, "I prefer that *you* return to God with my sins and your sins and that *you* be among the denizens of hellfire rather than I, for that is the recompense of the wrongdoers."[215]

---

209. *Biḥār al-anwār* vol. 11 p. 240 tr. 28 and p. 227 tr. 6

210. *Biḥār al-anwār* vol. 11 p. 241 tr. 30

211. Qur'ān 5:27

212. Qur'ān 5:27

213. Qur'ān 5:28

214. *Wasā'il al-shī'ah* vol. 29 p. 15 tr. 35036. This tradition is not attributed to Adam. However, the fact that Abel says, "I prefer that you return to God with my sins and your sins," shows that he has been taught this principle by his father, thus I have attributed it to him.

215. Qur'ān 5:29

Cain could hear nothing of his brother's reasoned admonishment for the cacophony of jealous thoughts and satanic voices in his head. He raised a rock he had concealed behind his back and swung a lethal blow at Abel's head. Abel moved to evade the strike, but too late. The rock smashed into his skull, and in an instant he lay dead on the ground.[216]

The momentary satisfaction of revenge swiftly gave way to the bitter aftertaste of guilt and shame. He worried that his father and mother would realize it was he who had killed Abel. In his rage, he had not given thought to how he would dispose of the body. Now he desperately sought a solution. He had not seen death before. There had been only the four of them. Now there would be only three.[217] There was no precedent for death and burial rites. After some time had passed and he was not able to think of anything, God sent a crow that dug in the earth and concealed something to show him how to conceal the corpse of his brother by burying it. He said, "Woe to me! Am I unable to be like this crow and conceal the corpse of my brother?" With this realization, he became among the regretful.[218] It was bad enough that he had killed his brother in a passion. What made him feel worse was that a mere bird had had more sense than he. Begrudgingly, Cain dug a grave and buried his brother as the

---

216. *Biḥār al-anwār* vol. 11 p. 230 tr. 8

217. It is narrated that Ṭāwūs al-Yamānī asked Imam al-Bāqir the following riddle, "When was a third of all people killed?" Imam al-Bāqir replied, "A third of all people was never killed. You meant to ask, 'When was a fourth of all people killed.' That was the day when Cain killed Abel. There had been four of them—Adam, Eve, Cain, and Abel. So one out of four was killed" (*Biḥār al-anwār* vol. 10 p. 156 tr. 6). According to the story as I have narrated it here, at the time of Abel's murder, there were six people including Cain's and Abel's wives. According to some other traditions, both Cain and Abel had twin sisters which brings the total to either six or eight depending on whether they were married at the time. In any case, according to the story as I have narrated it here, it seems the Imam should have told Ṭāwūs that a sixth of people died, not a fourth. Perhaps the Imam did not include Cain's and Abel's wives because they were not technically *human*, but a *jinn* and a *ḥawrāʾ*. ʿAllāmah al-Majlisī offers several other explanations for the Imam's answer (see *Biḥār al-anwār* vol. 11 p. 230 under tr. 7).

218. Qurʾān 5:31

crow had taught him.[219] Then he fled into the mountains, determined never to face his father as long as he lived.[220]

A Gift From God

God told Adam of Abel's murder.[221] Adam was heartbroken.[222] He mourned him for forty days.[223] Not only had he lost his son but his best student and successor too. He begged God to grant him another righteous son through Eve to inherit his prophetic knowledge. God answered his prayers saying, "I shall give you, in place of Abel, a son who shall be your successor, inherit your knowledge, and be a source of knowledge after you."[224]

Soon thereafter, Eve gave birth to a son, and on the seventh day from his birth, his foreskin and umbilicus were shed,[225] and Adam named him Seth.[226] God reminded Adam that Seth was a divine gift and asked him to give him the honorific title of *Hibat Allāh*, the "Gift of God."[227] Seth grew up to be righteous and God-fearing like his dead brother and his father.

Abel's wife, Turk, had been pregnant when he died. She soon gave birth to a son whom Adam named Abel, in memory of the child's late father.[228]

When Seth grew to be a man, God sent down another *ḥawrāʾ* named Nāʿimah. Adam married Seth to Nāʿimah. Soon thereafter, Nāʿimah gave birth to a girl whom Adam named Ḥūriyyah. When

---

219. *Biḥār al-anwār* vol. 11 p. 230 tr. 8

220. *Biḥār al-anwār* vol. 11 p. 263 tr. 11

221. *Biḥār al-anwār* vol. 11 p. 264 tr. 13

222. *Biḥār al-anwār* vol. 11 p. 265 tr. 14

223. *Biḥār al-anwār* vol. 11 p. 240 tr. 28 and p. 227 tr. 6

224. *Biḥār al-anwār* vol. 11 p. 265 tr. 13

225. *Biḥār al-anwār* vol. 12 p. 3 tr. 4. Another tradition mentions that he was born circumcised (*Biḥār al-anwār* vol. 14 p. 2 tr. 3).

226. In Arabic he is known as *Shayth.*

227. *Biḥār al-anwār* vol. 11 p. 265 tr. 13

228. *Biḥār al-anwār* vol. 11 p. 228 tr. 6

Ḥūriyyah and Abel, son of Abel, grew up, Adam married them at God's command.[229]

The First Prophet Prophesies the Last

Once, many years later, some of Adam's sons had gathered together. One of them asked, "Who is the best of God's creation?"

Each person offered an opinion. One said, "Our father, Adam, of course." Another said, "The archangels." A third said, "The bearers of the throne." When the discussion had become heated and they could come to no consensus, Seth entered. They felt relieved that their brother would be able to solve their dilemma. However, when they posed the question to him, he told them he would have to ask their father. When he went to Adam and asked him their question, Adam told him, "I have seen the following sentence written on the

---

229. *Biḥār al-anwār* vol. 11 p. 228 tr. 6. In several traditions, Imam al-Bāqir states that all the people alive at his time are the descendants of Abel and Ḥūriyyah (*Biḥār al-anwār* vol. 11 p. 228 tr. 6). In the story of Noah, we will see that there are many descendants of Cain. 'Allāmah al-Majlisī suggests that both Cain's line and Seth's line continued until Noah's flood. However, since Cain's descendants rejected Noah's call, they were all destroyed (see *Biḥār al-anwār* vol. 11 p. 242 under tr. 32). What follows is Adam's family tree:

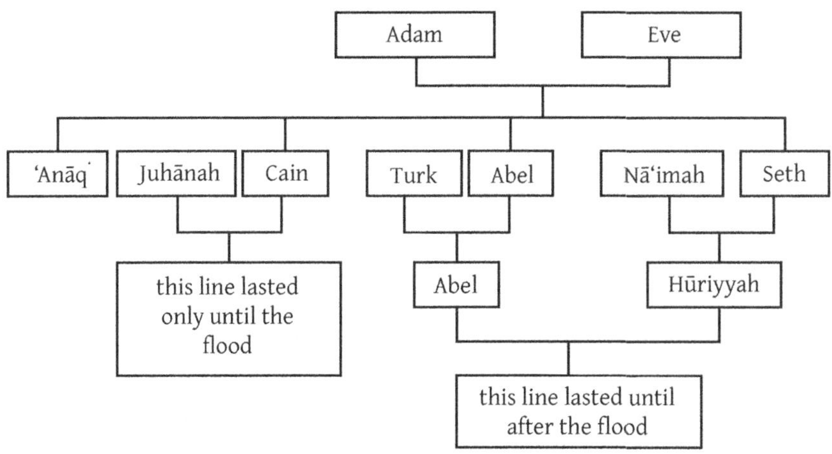

throne[230] of God Almighty: 'In the name of God the All-Beneficent, the Ever-Merciful. Muḥammad and the family of Muḥammad are the best of those whom God has created.'"[231] Then he remembered fondly something God had told him soon after he had created him. He narrated for Seth, "God told me, 'Adam, if it were not for two special servants whom I intend to create at the end of time, I would not have created you.' I asked, 'What are their names?' He told me to look at his throne, and I saw the following words written there: 'There is no god worthy of worship but God. Muḥammad is the Prophet of Mercy. And ʿAlī is the key to paradise. I have sworn to myself that I shall show mercy to whoever allies with them and to punish whoever shows them enmity.'"[232]

Adam's Successor

Years later, God told Adam:

> Your life and, hence, your term of prophethood is nearing an end. Think now of your legacy of prophetic knowledge and of all the names that I have taught you and of all the guidance I have given you that is vital to the prosperity of humankind. Turn all this over to the best of your children, the gift I gave you, Seth. And tell him to accept this appointment discreetly lest his brother, Cain, kill him as he killed Abel before. I had decided from time immemorial never to leave the earth without one endowed with knowledge through whom my religion could be known, who would judge according to my law, in whom those

230. The throne of God is not a physical throne but rather a symbol of God's sovereignty over his creation. As a king rules from his throne, so too the King of kings rules from his metaphorical throne. Perhaps the throne upon which Adam saw these inscriptions was a physical representation of God's sovereignty, shown to him to teach him an important lesson about Prophet Muḥammad and his family.

231. *Biḥār al-anwār* vol. 11 p. 114 tr. 40

232. *Biḥār al-anwār* vol. 11 p. 114 tr. 39

> who accepted his authority could find salvation, and who would be my proof against all who rejected me. I shall bring these guides forth from the progeny of Seth.[233]

Adam gathered all of his family except for Cain who had disappeared after murdering Abel. He told them:

> My children! God has told me that he will soon take my life. He has ordered me to appoint the best of my children as my successor. I hereby appoint God's gift, Seth. God himself has chosen him as my successor and your leader after me. So listen to him, and obey his command, for he is my heir and my successor over you.[234]

They replied in one voice, "We shall listen to him and obey him, and we shall not oppose him."[235]

Adam asked for a wooden chest to be constructed. He placed in the chest all relics of his knowledge, the names God had taught him, and his last testament to Seth. Then he addressed Seth saying:

> When I die, wash my body, shroud me, pray over my body, and place me in my grave. And when death comes to you, call upon the best of your children, who was your best disciple, and bequeath to him what I now bequeath to you. Never allow the earth to be without one endowed with knowledge from our household. My son! God Almighty sent me down to earth and made me his vicegerent upon it and his proof against all his creatures. I hereby make you God's proof on earth after me. Therefore, do not leave the world unless you have appointed a proof and successor after yourself. Bequeath to him this chest and its contents as I now bequeath it to you. Tell him that there will come a prophet

233. *Biḥār al-anwār* vol. 11 p. 265 tr. 14 and p. 227 tr. 6

234. *Biḥār al-anwār* vol. 11 p. 265 tr. 14

235. *Biḥār al-anwār* vol. 11 p. 265 tr. 14

> from my progeny named Noah. In his time, there will be a great flood and many will drown. Tell your successor to preserve this chest and its contents, and tell him that when death comes to him, that he must appoint his best son. Every subsequent successor must place his testament in this chest. Whoever among your descendants lives till the age of Noah must board his ark along with him. Noah must carry this chest with himself into the ark. Finally, I warn you, Seth, and all my children, of your accursed brother, Cain.[236]

Perhaps through a spy or perhaps through the help of Satan himself, Cain came to know what was happening. He secretly came to Seth and berated him saying:

> I know very well that Father has bequeathed to you his prophetic knowledge even though I am older than you and more deserving of it than you. However, just because I killed his other son, he is angry with me and has shown you preference over me. I swear by God, if you ever make any mention of this knowledge that he has given you, to assert your superiority over me or to vaunt it before me, I shall kill you just as I killed your brother.[237]

Seth wisely refrained from provoking Cain as long as Cain lived.

Adam's Death

Azrael came to end Adam's life. In the beginning, God had told Adam how long he was due to live, and, accordingly, Adam thought he still had fifty years to go. He told Azrael as much. Azrael reminded him that he had transferred fifty years to his descendant David. He showed him his ledger entry to this effect and had Gabriel and

236. *Biḥār al-anwār* vol. 11 p. 265 tr. 14

237. *Biḥār al-anwār* vol. 11 p. 241 tr. 31

Michael testify to the transfer that had taken place so many years before.[238]

As death overtook Adam, he lay on his deathbed and called on Seth. He told him:

> My son, my time is nearing its end, and I am sick. God ordered me to make you my successor and the keeper of the knowledge with which he had entrusted me, and I have done so. Under my head, you will find the scripture God sent down with me when I left the garden. When I die, take this scripture and be careful that no one else sees it. You yourself must not open it until next year, on the anniversary of my death. In it you will find everything you need for your religious and worldly affairs.[239]

> My son, I have always been fond of dates. I first tasted them in the garden. I liked them so much that I begged God to send me a date sapling on earth. Now that I am on the verge of death, I wish not to break this bond I have with the date tree. Please, when you shroud my body, take a green frond of the date palm, split it in half, and wrap these two halves close to my body.[240]

> My son, I am yearning for the fruit of paradise. Go up to this neighboring mountain. Convey my salutation of *salām* to whichever angels you meet there.[241] Inform them of my dying pains and ask them to give me a taste of the fruits of paradise before I die.[242]

---

238. *Biḥār al-anwār* vol. 14 p. 9 tr. 17

239. *Biḥār al-anwār* vol. 11 p. 262 tr. 11

240. *Tahdhīb al-aḥkām* vol. 1 p. 326 tr. 120

241. *Biḥār al-anwār* vol. 11 p. 262 tr. 11

242. *Biḥār al-anwār* vol. 11 p. 228 tr. 6

But he was destined not to eat from the fruits until he finally entered paradise. As soon as Seth left, Azrael, the Angel of Death, came to Adam. Adam made his last declaration of faith:

> I testify that there is no god but God who is one and has no partners. And I testify that I am the servant of God and his vicegerent on earth. He has shown me undeserved kindness since the beginning. He made the angels prostrate before me, he taught me all the names, and then he let me dwell in his garden. But he did not make it a permanent abode and a place to call my home. Rather, he created me to live on earth and to fulfill his purpose for me upon it.[243]

As he uttered these last words of praise for God, Azrael claimed his soul.

In the meanwhile, Seth ascended the mountain and was greeted by a host of angels, so he conveyed his father's message. Gabriel stepped forward and said, "Seth, your father has just died and we have come to attend his funeral. May God reward you greatly for enduring this hardship, give you patience to face your grief, and comfort you in your ensuing loneliness! Now let us return to your father's house."[244]

Adam's Burial

The first thing Seth did when he gazed upon his father's dead body was to take possession of the scripture that lay under his head as his father had bid him. Then he and the angels began washing Adam's body and shrouding it, all the while Gabriel coached Seth so he would know what to do. Seth made sure to include the pieces of the date frond as his father had requested him to do. When it was time to offer the funeral prayers, Gabriel urged Seth near Adam's body to lead the prayers, and he told all the angels to form lines behind

243. *Biḥār al-anwār* vol. 11 p. 265 tr. 14

244. *Biḥār al-anwār* vol. 11 p. 263 tr. 11

him. He told Seth to proclaim the *takbīr* saying, "God is greater than everything!" 75 times.[245]

Seth looked curiously at Gabriel and said, "Is it right for me to lead this prayer when you possess such a great status before God, and the greatest of God's angels are with you?"

Gabriel bowed his head submissively and replied, "Do you not know that when God created your father he made him stand before us and made all of us prostrate before him? On that day, he became our leader, and that leadership continues in his progeny. Today he has died and you are his successor, the heir to his knowledge, and you now stand in his place. How can we possibly step before you when you are our leader?"[246]

So Seth stepped forward and led the prayers as he had been taught, repeating the *takbīr* 75 times as he offered prayers for his father's soul. They carried Adam's body up to Mount Abū Qubays and buried him in one of its caves.[247] His remains would stay there until Noah would relocate them to their current resting place in modern day Najaf.[248]

After the burial, when the angels were set to return, Seth was overwhelmed with emotion and began to weep. Gabriel consoled him saying, "Seth, you shall never be alone, for God is with you. We too shall descend upon you with God's commands. So do not fret, and expect the best from God, for he is kind to you and compassionate."[249]

---

245. *Biḥār al-anwār* vol. 11 p. 263 tr. 11. A different number of *takbīrs* is mentioned in different traditions. Generally, traditions from Sunnī sources say it was thirty times. Some Shīʿī traditions say five times, some say seventy, and some say seventy-five. One tradition explains that five of the *takbīrs* were obligatory parts of the funeral prayer, similar to the way Shīʿī Muslims offer the funeral prayer today. The seventy *takbīrs* were extra, in honor of Adam (*Biḥār al-anwār* vol. 11 p. 267 tr. 15). Accordingly, we can comfortably say that some traditions mention only the obligatory *takbīrs*, some mention only the extra ones, and others mention both.

246. *Biḥār al-anwār* vol. 11 p. 263 tr. 11

247. *Biḥār al-anwār* vol. 11 p. 269 tr. 19

248. *Tahdhīb al-aḥkām* 6.34.10.12 and *Biḥār al-anwār* vol. 11 p. 260 tr. 3

249. *Biḥār al-anwār* vol. 11 p. 263 tr. 11

Cain's Last Stand

Sometime later, Cain emerged from hiding and angrily approached Seth. He demanded, "Where are the things our father gave you?" Seth denied having been given anything.[250] He could see in Cain's eyes that he would kill him if he so much as hinted that he had been given something. He said, "I killed Abel because his offering was accepted and mine was not. I feared that he would attain the very station that you have now attained. You have now become exactly what I hate. If you ever speak about anything that our father has given you, I shall kill you just as I killed Abel."[251]

Eve's Death and Burial

Eve survived Adam for an additional year. At the end of that year, she fell sick for fifteen days and finally passed on. Seth buried his mother next to his father in the cave on Mount Abū Qubays.[252]

After Cain's death, Seth was finally able to freely preach to the people. He was not only Adam's successor but a prophet in his own right. In the years to follow, God would reveal some fifty scriptures to him.[253] Seth would often speak to people about the coming of a prophet named Noah and encourage them to prepare the way for his advent.

---

250. Seth lied out of *taqiyyah*, lawful dissimulation, where a person lies to protect his life or the religion. Many traditions praise Seth for having practiced *taqiyyah* in his dealings with Cain.

251. *Biḥār al-anwār* vol. 11 p. 263 tr. 11

252. *Biḥār al-anwār* vol. 11 p. 269 tr. 19

253. *Biḥār al-anwār* vol. 11 p. 262 tr. 10

Enoch

From the progeny of Adam, there came a man named Enoch[1] who lived in the city now known as Kūfah.[2] God chose Enoch as a prophet to confirm the teachings of his forefather, Adam.[3] He was patient and righteous.[4] Each day more good deeds were written for him than for all other people of his age combined.[5]

A Message For a Tyrant

There was, during Enoch's time, a tyrannical king. During an excursion, this king came upon a verdant tract of land that he was told belonged to a man who had left the pagan religion to which the king subscribed and believed instead in the religion of Enoch. The king was taken with the beauty of the land. He ordered the man to be brought to him. He told the man how much he liked his land and asked him to give it to him. The man simply responded, "My family needs it more than you do."

The king said, "Very well, then, sell it to me for a handsome price."

The man insisted, "I shall not give it to you or sell it to you. You must forget about it completely."

The king became enraged but turned away and returned to his castle to deliberate over the affair. His wife was intelligent and cunning, and he often turned to her for advice. She told him, "My

---

1. This name is pronounced EE-nuk. In the Qur'ān, Enoch is referred to as *Idrīs*. We are told in traditions that Enoch was called *Idrīs* "because he studied (*darasa*) God's creation much" (*Biḥār al-anwār* vol. 11 p. 270 tr. 1) and "because he studied (*darasa*) books much" (*Biḥār al-anwār* vol. 11 p. 277 tr. 3).

2. We can infer that he lived in Kūfah because his house stood where Masjid al-Sahlah now stands (*Biḥār al-anwār* vol. 11 p. 280 tr. 10).

3. Qur'ān 19:56

4. Qur'ān 21:85–86

5. *Biḥār al-anwār* vol. 11 p. 279 tr. 9

king! Only one who is powerless to cause change worries and frets so. If you do not want to kill him without due cause, I can take care of him for you and deliver his land into your hands in a way that will justify your actions before your people. I shall send a host of my people to bring him to you and testify that he has abandoned your religion. After that, you will be justified in killing him and taking his property from him."

The king accepted her ploy and told her to execute it.

When the man was killed and his property was usurped, God became enraged. He sent a message to Enoch telling him, "Go to this tyrant and tell him, 'Was it not enough that you killed God's servant without just cause? Did you have to usurp his property and leave his family hungry and homeless too? God swears he will avenge these crimes on you in the hereafter, strip you of your dominion in this life, ruin your city, abase your very arrogance, and feed your wife's flesh to dogs, for she has beguiled you, and you in turn have overrun God's patience.'"

Enoch delivered God's message fearlessly. In response, the king threatened him and drove him out of his company for his audacity, but spared his life because of his reputation as a righteous man.

Once again, the king called on his wife and sought her counsel. She allayed his fears of the threats of Enoch's god and said, "I shall send my people to kill Enoch so that his god's threats are rendered meaningless."

She sent forty men to seek out Enoch. Enoch's companions learned of the king's plot and sent word to Enoch that his life was in danger. He turned to God and prayed, "O Lord! You sent me to this tyrant, and I conveyed to him your message. He now threatens to kill me. Rather, he *will* kill me if he captures me."

God communicated to him, "Flee from him. Abandon your city. Leave him to me, for I swear I shall do to him as I have threatened, and I shall bring to pass all that you conveyed to him from me."

A Prayer For Drought

Enoch said to God, "Lord, I must ask you something."

God said, "Ask and you shall be given."

He said, "Lord, I ask that you not let the sky rain on this city and its outlying areas until I ask you to."

God said, "Enoch, if I do this, then you understand that the city will be ruined, its people will be subjected to great hardship, and they will starve?"

Enoch replied, "Even so." God granted Enoch his wish and withheld rain from this city indefinitely.

Enoch gathered his companions, who numbered twenty, and told them of his prayer to God. He advised them to abandon their city along with him and make their home elsewhere. They did, and so did Enoch. He hid himself in a cave at the top of a distant mountain and remained there in solitude for the next twenty years. He would fast during the days, and God installed an angel to bring Enoch food every evening so that he could break his fast.

Just as he had promised, God stripped the tyrannical king of his dominion and killed him. He ruined his city and he fed his wife's flesh to dogs to avenge the death of his faithful servant.

Sadly, one tyrant was replaced by another. The successor ruled for twenty years in which time it never rained a drop. His people suffered and were forced to buy all that they could from distant lands. News spread during these years that it was Enoch's prayer that had brought this city to its knees. The people realized the error of their ways and understood that they would only find relief by begging God to show them mercy. They gathered together in humble clothing, covered their heads with dirt as a sign of humility, and began praying altogether with tears of repentance.

Enoch Is Tested

God told Enoch in his cave, "Your people have turned to me to seek my forgiveness with sincere tears. I am the All-Beneficent, the Ever-Merciful. I have accepted their repentance and wish to shower them with my mercy. The only thing preventing me from letting it rain is the promise I made to you not to let it rain until you asked me. Enoch, ask me now, so I may shower them with a merciful rain."

Enoch replied, "God, I shall not ask you this." He was not acting in rebellion to God. He was worried that his people's repentance was not sincere and that they would betray God once again. Their crimes were too great, and he felt they had not been punished enough. Of course, if God had ordered Enoch to ask, he would have complied. But God did not order him, perhaps because he was testing him to see if his love for his people would overcome his devotion to his divine mission. Instead, he sought to cajole him into compliance. He said, "Did I not answer you when you asked me your favor? But now when I ask you, you do not answer?"

When Enoch held his ground and showed fortitude, God increased the stakes to allow Enoch to grow in patience. God recalled the angel who brought Enoch food every evening. That evening, Enoch awaited his food and when it did not come, he was puzzled, but he was patient. On the second day, his hunger became harder to bear. On the third, he was unable to bear it any longer. He called out in prayer, "O Lord! You withhold your provision from me before taking my life from me."

God replied, "Enoch, you fret so much when I have withheld your provision for but three days, yet you do not fret for the people of your city though they have hungered for twenty years. When I told you that I wished to show them mercy and I asked you to ask me to let it rain and you refused, I made you taste hunger, but you have shown too little patience. Now go down from this cave and seek your own sustenance, for I hereby turn you over to your own designs."[6]

Half a Loaf

Hunger drove Enoch out of his cave and into the city in search of food. He saw smoke issuing from a chimney, so he hurried to that house. The woman who lived there had made two small loaves of bread from her ration of wheat—one for herself and another for

---

6. Since Enoch was a prophet of God, we know that what he did was neither a sin nor a mistake. His task to eke out a living was not punishment for a wrong action but an opportunity for him to practice patient perseverance so he could strengthen himself where he had been found to be lacking.

her child.[7] Enoch asked her to share some of her bread to save his life. She replied without recognizing him, "Prophet Enoch's prayer against us has left us with nothing extra to feed anyone. You must seek your provisions from the people of another city."

Enoch said, "At least provide me with enough to give my legs the strength to carry me to another city."

She replied, "I have only these two loaves—one for me and the other for my son. If I give you mine, I shall die, and if I give you his, he will die."

Enoch said, "Your son is small. Half a loaf will suffice him, and half will carry me to my destination." She complied, but when she gave half of her son's loaf to Enoch, her son became so upset that, in his weakened state, he died. She became overwhelmed with grief, but Enoch told her, "Do not fret. I shall revive him by God's leave." He grabbed the boy by his shoulders and called out, "O soul that has just departed from the body of this child! Return, by God's leave, to his body, for I am Prophet Enoch!"

The woman stared incredulously as her son came back to life. She looked at Enoch and could only manage to say, "*You* are Enoch?" When the full force of reality hit her, she ran out of her house calling, "O people! Glad tidings! Prophet Enoch has returned. Relief is near!"

The Path to Reconciliation

News spread rapidly and soon everyone had gathered in the city center. Enoch sat before the people of his city and they said, "Enoch, have you no mercy on us? These twenty years, we have suffered and starved. We beg you to ask God to send down rain upon us."

Enoch resolutely said, "No. Not until your king and every person in this city comes to me walking and barefoot, so I may know the sincerity of your repentance."

---

7. This story is very similar to one in the Old Testament in which Elijah asks the widow at Zaraphath for bread (1 Kings 17:7–24). Perhaps this is why some reports claim that Elijah and Enoch were the same person. (See *Biḥār al-anwār* vol. 13 p. 397 for a list of people's opinions.)

When the king heard of Enoch's return and his demands, he sent a force of forty men to capture him and bring him to him. Enoch prayed to God and cursed these men and they all died before they reached him. Again the king sent a force of 500. Enoch threatened them with a fate similar to that of their forty comrades. They exclaimed, "You nearly killed us by starvation for twenty years. Do you now want to curse us with death? Have you no mercy?"

He replied, "I shall not come with you, and I shall not pray for rain until your king comes to me walking and barefoot."

The soldiers returned to their king to convey Enoch's resolve in demanding the king's submission. Finally, under unbearable pressure from his people, the king submitted. Along with all the citizens of his city, he came in humility, walking and barefoot, to beg Enoch to ask God for rain.

Enoch raised his hands to beg God for rain, the clouds gathered, lightning flashed, and thunder boomed. It rained so much and with such force that they worried that their drought would be ushered out by a flood.[8]

God Ordains Worship

During those years in the cave, Enoch had spent much time contemplating God's greatness. He had often thought to himself, "This sky and this earth, all these creatures, the sun, the moon, and the stars, the clouds and the rain all indeed have a Lord who administers them and keeps them in order by his infinite power. What is my relationship to this Lord? How can I worship him as he deserves to be worshiped?"

He now addressed his people with these thoughts. He admonished them, reminded them, warned them, and called them to worship their creator. Gradually, they answered his call, one by one, until their numbers reached seven, then seventy, then seven hundred, and then one thousand. When they had reached one thousand, he proposed to them, "Let us choose the one hundred most righteous among us. Then let them choose the seventy most righteous. Then let them choose the ten most righteous. Then let

---

8. *Biḥār al-anwār* vol. 11 p. 272–276 tr. 2

them choose the seven most righteous. And let these seven pray to our creator while the rest of us follow them and say 'Amen.' Perhaps our creator will show us how we should worship him." When they did this, God inspired Enoch and showed him how they were to worship him. From then, for many years, people worshiped God without associating partners with him.[9]

Writing and Scripture

Enoch was the first human being to write.[10] God taught him, and he passed on this skill to others so that the written word could become a medium for the spread of divine knowledge. As people learned the written word, and the grounds were prepared for them to be further educated, God gave Enoch thirty scriptures replete with wisdom and guidance.[11]

Sewing and Weaving

God also taught Enoch how to weave and sew. Until that time, people dressed in the unstitched skins of animals. Enoch would sit in his house and sew clothes so that he and other believers could dress with dignity and preserve their chastity.[12] As he stitched he would repeat, "God is exalted. There is no god but God. God is greater than all."[13]

---

9. *Biḥār al-anwār* vol. 11 p. 271 tr. 1

10. *Biḥār al-anwār* vol. 11 p. 279 tr. 9

11. *Biḥār al-anwār* vol. 11 p. 277 tr. 5. We do not, and perhaps cannot, know the contents of these scriptures. In his book, *Sa'd al-Sa'ūd*, Sayyid ibn Ṭāwūs has quoted from a manuscript that he attributes to Enoch. However, there is no way to confirm the authenticity of this manuscript. It is interesting to note that the Falasha Jews of Ethiopia recognize *The Book of Enoch* as scripture. Reference is also made in the New Testament to a prophecy made by Enoch in the *Letter of Jude* 14–15.

12. It is transmitted that his house was where Masjid al-Sahlah now stands; that he used to sew and pray there. It is said that if one prays there, his prayers will be answered, and he will be raised to Enoch's lofty station on the Day of Judgment, and he will be given refuge from the hardships of temporal life and the machinations of his enemies (*Biḥār al-anwār* vol. 11 p. 280 tr. 10).

13. *Biḥār al-anwār* vol. 11 p. 279 tr. 9

Enoch and the Fallen Angel

During Enoch's time, there was an angel of lofty status who was expelled by God from the skies and sent to earth.[14] The angel

14. It is the opinion of the overwhelming majority of Muslim scholars that angels are infallible beings. Some have even claimed a consensus on this point (I have taken considerable help in writing this footnote from *Tafsīr ṣirāṭ al-mustaqīm* by al-Burujardī, vol. 5 p. 104–119). It may seem that the story I have narrated here, and the tradition on which it is based, pose a challenge to that opinion and that we must either accept the story or the consensus. I shall first present the case for the infallibility of the angels and then attempt to justify this tradition in light of their infallibility.

There are several verses of the Qur'ān that praise the angels graciously. Most of these speak of particular groups of angels and, thus, at most indicate the infallibility only of those groups. For instance the Qur'ān says, "O you who believe! Protect yourselves and your families from a fire whose fuel is people and stones, guarding over which are angels, hefty and severe, who do not disobey God in what he has commanded them to do, and they do what they are commanded" (66:6). This verse clearly speaks of these angels' infallibility; however, we cannot generalize from the verse to all angels. Another verse says, "Those who are in his proximity are not too arrogant to worship him, nor do they become weary" (21:19). This verse negates two common barriers to obedience, arrogance and fatigue, from God's closest angels, but again, we cannot generalize from this verse to all angels. A few verses later, we read, "These angels are not deities; rather, honored servants. They do not venture to speak ahead of him, and they act only at his command" (21:26–27). Here also we cannot generalize to all angels.

One verse does speak in general terms. "To God prostrates what creatures are in the skies and what creatures are on earth, and the angels, and they are not arrogant. They fear their Lord on high, and they do what they are commanded" (16:49–50). This verse seems to contain the strongest indication in the Qur'ān of the angels' infallibility.

Traditions, on the other hand, contain explicit pronouncements of the infallibility of all angels. I will quote here two examples. In one sermon, Imam ʿAlī says about the angels, "Not a one of them veers from the path to God's pleasure" (*Nahj al-balāghah* sermon 91). In another tradition, in response to a person who narrated the popular lies about the angels Hārūt and Mārūt, Imam al-Riḍā said, "The angels of God are infallible, protected against non-belief and everything reprehensible, by the grace of God" (*ʿUyūn akhbār al-Riḍā* vol. 1 p. 269).

Those who argue that angels are fallible usually cite three stories from the Qur'ān: The apparent objection of the angels to God's choice of vicegerent

(2:30); Satan's demotion from his status among the angels (2:34); and Hārūt and Mārūt who allegedly disobeyed God (2:102). In answer, these verses are at best ambiguous (*mutashābihāt*) and must be understood in light of the unequivocal verse (*muḥkamāt*) cited above (16:49–50). More specifically, the commentators have clearly and conclusively explained all of these stories and shown that they do not contradict the angels' infallibility. Very briefly, with regard to the first story, the angels' question to God was not an objection to his decision but a plea for an explanation of what they recognized to be beyond their reach. With regard to the second, we are told unequivocally that Satan was a *jinn* (18:50) and not an angel at all; thus, his disobedience does not reflect negatively on the angels at all. Finally, with regard to Hārūt and Mārūt, the verse clearly states that the magic they taught was according to God's will and was a test for people.

Aside from these three stories, this camp also refers to a handful of traditions like the one we are currently trying to understand that explicitly or implicitly indicate that angels are fallible. Quite simply, we have before us a verse that unequivocally says all angels are infallible (16:49–50) and traditions that explicitly support this assertion. On the other hand, we have three ambiguous verses that may seem at first to put some angels in a negative light, but for which sound and reasonable explanations are available. Clearly, considering the evidence, we must conclude that all angels are indeed infallible. As for the handful of traditions that seem to indicate otherwise, we must see if there is a reasonable explanation that jives with the angels' infallibility, and if we cannot find any such explanation then, by order of the Prophet himself, we must "throw it against a wall," (Islamic Texts Institute, *Al-Nudbah: A Devotional Elegy for the Prophet Muhammad and his Family* p. x–xi) for it is a fabrication falsely attributed to him.

The question remains: How do we understand this story from the time of Enoch? Can an infallible angel do something for which he is "expelled by God from the skies and sent to earth"? To answer this, we must understand the nature of their infallibility. As with the prophets and imams, the angels are not forced to be infallible such that they cannot choose otherwise. Rather, they are free to choose; however, they always choose obedience to God over disobedience. The prophets and imams choose obedience because their intellect shows them its merit, and they have the will to overpower their carnal desires. The angels also possess an intellect that guides them to obedience; however, they lack carnal desires altogether, and so their choice is relatively easier, but it is their choice nonetheless (see *Mishkāh al-anwār* p. 251). That angels choose to be infallible is the traditional view of Muslim theologians.

Several verses corroborate the view that angels are infallible by choice. One verse says, "If anyone among the angels says, 'I am a god alongside God,' we shall compensate him with hellfire" (21:29). This verse indicates that the angels have it within themselves to make such a claim, but they do not. Generally speaking,

appeared before Enoch and asked him to intercede for him before God. Enoch proceeded to fast and pray for three days. Then he prayed to God on behalf of the angel. God accepted his prayer and readmitted the angel into the skies.

The angel told Enoch, "I wish to repay you for your favor. Ask me anything."

Enoch told him, "I wish to meet the Angel of Death and become acquainted with him, for I am not able to enjoy anything as long as I think of him."

The angel spread his wings and allowed Enoch to mount his back. They searched for the Angel of Death in the lowest level of the sky,[15] but they were told that he had ascended, on a mission,

---

all the praise that is doled out to the angels in the Qur'ān and traditions indicates that they are what they are by choice, for it does not make sense to praise someone for doing something unless they had the choice to do otherwise.

Until this point, we have drawn the following conclusions: 1) Angels are infallible and never sin against God; 2) Angels have the power to choose their actions.

The question remains: Can one who is infallible by choice be "expelled by God from the skies and sent to earth"? The answer is that he can if what he did to be expelled was not a sin. An infallible, of course, does not perpetrate anything God has made unlawful (*ḥarām*) or fail to do anything that he has made obligatory (*wājib*). Beyond this, he is not obligated in any way. Nevertheless, God holds him to an extremely high standard. He expects him to refrain even from what is *makrūh* (disliked by God) even though perpetrating it is not a sin. Similarly, he expects him to do even what is *mustaḥabb* (loved by God) even though failing to do so is not a sin. Among the infallibles, there are some who fulfill all these expectations and some who do so to a lesser extent. In Islamic theology, a failure to live up to any one of these high standards is called *tark al-awlā*, "forsaking the better." Because God's standard for these individuals is so high, he treats their seemingly slight shortcomings like major transgressions and even refers to them as *dhanb, ma'ṣiyah, ithm, and ẓulm*, all of which are usually reserved for true sins. Thus, whenever we see mention of an infallible individual being reprimanded by God, it is because he has forsaken the better, not because he has sinned.

In conclusion, we can accept this story and tradition and still hold fast to our well-founded belief in the infallibility of the angels. We do not have any evidence to tell us what this angel did to be expelled, but we can say with certainty that it was not a sin.

15. I am using "sky" to refer to the space above the earth including outer space and what lies beyond what we know to be the universe. These "seven levels of

to a higher level. They caught up with him between the fourth and fifth levels of the sky. When the Angel of Death saw them approach, he looked quizzically at them. Enoch asked him why he looked surprised and he said, "I was standing in the shade of God's throne when I received the command to take your soul between the fourth and fifth levels of the sky. At the time, I was unsure how I was to fulfill this task. But now I see."

When Enoch heard this, he knew his time had come. He slid off the angel's back and stepped forward so the Angel of Death could take his soul.[16]

After Enoch's death, under the guidance of his successors,[17] people continued to follow his teachings and worship God as he had commanded them. Eventually, however, his followers began to grow old and die until only a few were left. People began to fabricate lies about God and introduce false beliefs and practices into the religion until hardly a semblance remained between people's religion and what Enoch had taught them.[18]

---

the sky" or "seven heavens" as the Qur'ān calls them, are definitely part of the temporal world, though not necessarily part of the material world. They are not to be confused with the "heaven" that is paradise, which is beyond this temporal realm in the hereafter.

16. *Biḥār al-anwār* vol. 11 p. 278 tr. 7

17. No mention is made of his successors in the sources; however, I have inferred their presence because of the general principle that all prophets had successors and that there is always a divine guide on earth.

18. *Biḥār al-anwār* vol. 11 p. 271 tr. 1

Noah

The Beginning of Polytheism

In the generations that followed Adam and Enoch,[1] their message of monotheism and basic human morality devolved into polytheism and moral depravity. The seeds of polytheism were planted by Satan himself. There was a group of righteous men bearing the names *Wadd, Suwāʿ, Yagūth, Yaʿūq,* and *Nasr*. At their passing, their deaths weighed heavily on their survivors, and they mourned them intensely. Satan sensed a golden opportunity and crafted images of these men. He disguised himself and introduced these images to the people as mementos. During the winter months, the people brought these revered images into their homes to shelter them from the elements. Benign veneration of these images continued for a generation. Then Satan returned to their descendants and insinuated that these images were in fact deities worshiped by their forebears. Many were deceived and the seeds of idolatry took root.[2]

As devotion to the one God waned, so did morality. The human population grew, and increased numbers gave rise to conflict. The wealthy asserted their superiority over the poor, the powerful over the weak. The simple ethical system that had prevailed since the time of Adam was no longer adequate. God knew the time had come to renew the message of Adam and Enoch and to introduce into human civilization, for the first time, a system of law.

God Chooses Noah

For this task God chose Noah.[3] As with all his prophets, God knew before creating Noah that he possessed exceptional virtue and

---

1. This name is pronounced EE-nuk. In the Qurʾān he is referred to as *Idrīs*.
2. *Biḥār al-anwār* vol. 11 p. 315 tr. 8
3. Qurʾān 3:33 and 29:14

that he would obey his every decree.[4] So he provided him with the means for spiritual development and nurtured him to be absolutely righteous and infallible. He was one of the few in history who was born circumcised.[5]

Noah's name was al-Sakan,[6] although he was also known as ʿAbd al-Ghaffār,[7] ʿAbd al-Malik,[8] ʿAbd al-Jabbār,[9] and ʿAbd al-Aʿlā.[10] He was called Noah (*Nūḥ* in Arabic) because of his profuse lamentations (*nawḥ*) during his worship of God. In particular, he lamented over the state of humankind for its recalcitrance throughout the 950 years during which he tirelessly preached to them.[11] He lamented over his own state,[12] perhaps because he felt alone, rejected by his people, and mocked openly for 950 years. And he lamented throughout the 500 years he lived after the flood during which he must have felt great remorse for the failure of humanity to accept his call and the need for them to be destroyed.[13]

---

4. Islamic Texts Institute, *Al-Nudbah: A Devotional Elegy for the Prophet Muḥammad and his Family*. p. 25–26

5. *Biḥār al-anwār* vol. 14 p. 2 tr. 3

6. *Biḥār al-anwār* vol. 11 p. 286 tr. 3

7. *Biḥār al-anwār* vol. 11 p. 286 tr. 4

8. *Biḥār al-anwār* vol. 11 p. 286 tr. 5

9. *Biḥār al-anwār* vol. 11 p. 226 tr. 44

10. *ibid.* tr. 6. I have reconciled these five traditions by postulating that his name was al-Sakan while the other four names, ʿAbd al-Ghaffār, ʿAbd al-Malik, ʿAbd al-Jabbār, and ʿAbd al-Aʿlā were epithets praising him for his servitude to God (*ʿIlal al-sharāʾiʿ* 1.20.3).

11. *Biḥār al-anwār* vol. 11 p. 286 tr. 3

12. *Biḥār al-anwār* vol. 11 p. 286 tr. 4

13. It is also possible that the 500 years mentioned in traditions 5 and 6 coincided with a portion of the 950 years mentioned in tradition 3. In this case, I would have to retract the assertion that he lamented after the flood.

Noah lived to the ripe old age of 2,500 years[14] in a time when others lived an average of 300 years.[15] During his first 850 years, Noah lived a relatively normal life. He lived in modern-day Kūfah, and his home was within the confines of the great Mosque of Kūfah.[16] He was a carpenter by trade. He was brown-skinned with a small face and wide eyes. His arms were small and his legs were heavy. His belly was robust and his beard was long. Being an artisan, he was tall and hefty.[17]

During this time, he witnessed the moral and spiritual degeneration of humanity around him; yet he held fast to the religion of his forefathers Enoch and Adam and continued to worship the one God and act with impeccable virtue in all aspects of life. In particular, he was an exemplar of unflagging gratitude to God.[18] Whenever he wore a garment or ate food or drank water, he would say, "In the name of God," when he began and, "Praise is for God," when he finished.[19] Morning and evening he would say, "O God! I call on you to witness my admission that all blessings and

---

14. Most of our traditions confirm his age at 2,500 years (*Biḥār al-anwār* vol. 11 p. 285 tr. 2). The Qur'ān in 29:14 tells us that he remained among his people for 950 years during his mission as a prophet. This timeframe does not account for the 850 years he lived before becoming a prophet or the 200 years during which he built the ark or the 500 years he spent after the flood. We know about the rest of his life only because of traditions from Prophet Muhammad and his family (*Biḥār al-anwār* vol. 11 p. 285–6 tr. 2). Some believe that Noah's life was extended to 2,500 years miraculously or that they used to count each month as a year. However, there is nothing in Noah's story to suggest that his longevity was miraculous. His people never mention it as an oddity, nor does he mention it as a miracle to bolster his credibility. Furthermore, considering that others in his time lived to 300 years, which is itself hard for us to imagine, it seems we cannot consign his long age to a miracle. ʿAllāmah al-Ṭabāṭabāʾī explains that there is no cap on the age a human can live. Especially if a person lives a simple and healthy life, there is no reason he cannot live long if God wills.

15. *Biḥār al-anwār* vol. 11 p. 289 tr. 12

16. The Mosque of Kūfah has now been shifted from its original location where it had been erected by Adam and where it still stood in Noah's time (*Biḥār al-anwār* vol. 11 p. 331 tr. 54).

17. *Biḥār al-anwār* vol. 11 p. 287 tr. 9

18. Qur'ān 17:3

19. *Majmaʿ al-bayān* under 17:3

well-being in this world and the hereafter are from you alone who has no partner. For all that, praise and thanks are for you, such that you are pleased and even after you are pleased."[20]

It was after 850 years that Noah was appointed by God as his prophet and messenger. God made a covenant with him just as he had done with Adam and Enoch before him and just as he would do with every one of the nearly 124,000 prophets who would follow him.[21] According to this covenant, they were to believe in and worship the one God, to support one another, and to work sincerely for the guidance of all people.[22] However, the covenant with Noah was special, for he was to be the first of an elite group of five, immortalized in history as "The Messengers of Great Resolve."[23] These five were chosen for their exceptional resolve to carry out the ultimate divine command. They were bearers of law to all of humanity whose legal systems set the precedent for all legal systems and who were instrumental in nurturing humanity from the lawlessness of primitive society into refined and advanced civilizations.

We know very little of the law of Noah.[24] We know it consisted of exhortations to worship only one God and to abandon all idols. It

20. *Biḥār al-anwār* vol. 11 p. 291 tr. 2

21. Qur'ān 33:7. In this verse, God mentions his covenants with all the prophets and then singles out the five Messengers of Great Resolve. Four of them are mentioned in chronological order. Prophet Muḥammad is mentioned first, though he was chronologically last, because of his station above them all.

22. Qur'ān 3:81

23. This epithet is mentioned for them by the Qur'ān in 46:35. Imam al-Ṣādiq has said, "The leaders of the prophets and messengers are five, and they are the Messengers of Great Resolve. Around them does the world revolve. They are Noah, Abraham, Moses, Jesus, son of Mary, and Muḥammad—may God shower his mercy on him and his family and on all the prophets" (*al-Kāfī* 1.4.2.3). The prevailing view based on traditions from Prophet Muḥammad and his family is that they were sent to all humankind and *jinn*. For instance, in one tradition, Abū Ḥamzah al-Thumālī asks Imam al-Sajjād the meaning of the phrase "the Messengers of Great Resolve" to which he replies, "They were sent to the East and the West, to *jinn* and humankind" (*Biḥār al-anwār* vol. 11 p. 33).

24. Biblical scholars refer to the seven Noahide laws:

1. Idolatry is forbidden.

obligated people to pray toward the east[25] and to enjoin good and forbid evil. And it designated things as permissible or prohibited. There was, on the other hand, no penal code and no laws of inheritance.[26]

The Mission Begins

With this basic but no less revolutionary message, which at once confirmed the teachings of his predecessors and catered to the most pressing needs of his time, Noah began to call his people. His first task was to establish his credibility. He did this, as all prophets must, by performing a miracle—a supernatural act that no human

2. Incestuous and adulterous relations are forbidden.
3. Murder is forbidden.
4. Cursing the name of God is forbidden.
5. Theft is forbidden.
6. Eating the flesh of a living animal is forbidden.
7. Mankind is commanded to establish courts of justice.

They claim, based on an esoteric interpretation of Genesis 2:16, that these laws were first given to Adam. The third, sixth, and seventh laws are mentioned explicitly as follows:

> But you must not eat meat that has its lifeblood still in it. And for your lifeblood I will surely demand an accounting. I will demand an accounting from every animal. And from each human being, too, I will demand an accounting for the life of another human being. Whoever sheds human blood, by humans shall their blood be shed (Genesis 9:4–6).

The Pseudepigraphic Book of Jubilees (7:20–28) mentions some additional Noahide laws:

> Noah began to enjoin upon his sons' sons the ordinances and commandments, and all the judgments that he knew, and he exhorted his sons to observe righteousness, and to cover the shame of their flesh, and to bless their Creator, and honour father and mother, and love their neighbour, and guard their souls from fornication and uncleanness and all iniquity. For owing to these three things came the flood upon the earth ... For whoso sheddeth man's blood, and whoso eateth the blood of any flesh, shall all be destroyed from the earth (Charles, R.H. *The Apocrypha and Pseudepigrapha of the Old Testament*. Oxford: Clarendon Press, 1913).

25. *Jesus Through Shi'ite Narrations* p.288

26. *Biḥār al-anwār* vol. 11 p. 331 tr. 53

could possibly do without divine intervention.[27] He reminded his people that he had been impeccably trustworthy throughout his life and would continue to maintain their trust as a messenger of God.[28] Accordingly, he promised to convey God's guidance to them without altering so much as a letter. He also dispelled their doubts by renouncing any ulterior motives.[29] He did not want them to think he was trying to fool them into obeying him so that he could take undue advantage of them for his own political or financial benefit.

When he had sufficiently established his credentials, he called them saying, "O people! Worship God other than whom you have no deity worthy of worship. I fear for you the punishment of a momentous day."[30] He told them, "I am for you a clear warner, sent with the message, 'Do not worship any but God.' I fear for you the punishment of a painful day."[31] He told them, "O people! Worship God other than whom you have no deity worthy of worship. Do you not fear God?"[32] And he told them, "O people! I am for you a clear warner, sent with the message, 'Worship God, fear him, and obey me.'"[33] The fundamental message that he repeated over and over

---

27. On a purely rational basis, we can say that every prophet must have a miracle to prove his divine mandate. The Qur'ān confirms that many of the prophets brought miracles in the following verse. After recounting the stories of several prophets beginning with Noah, it says, "These are cities some of whose stories we recount to you. Their messengers brought them proofs (*bayyināt*)..." (7:101). *Bayyināt* is a reference to the miracles brought by these prophets, among whom was Noah. Unfortunately, we do not have any evidence in the Qur'ān or traditions to describe Noah's particular miracle. He only refers off-handedly to his miracle when he says, "My people! Tell me: If I have a miracle from my Lord and he has given me a book and divine knowledge as mercy from him, but you have been blinded to this, should we force this upon you against your will?" (11:28).

28. Qur'ān 26:106–108

29. Qur'ān 26:109–110

30. Qur'ān 7:59

31. Qur'ān 11:25–26

32. Qur'ān 23:23

33. Qur'ān 71:2–3

was for people to worship the one God and to live life knowing that they would one day stand before him in judgment.

If they heeded his call, he promised them that God would absolve them of their past sins and they could begin afresh. He also warned them that if they persisted in their evil ways, their lives would be cut short by a disastrous punishment. If on the other hand, they reformed themselves, God would allow them to live to their full life expectancy.[34] Thus, their fate in this world and the next was squarely in their own hands.

The Line of Seth

People's response to Noah was generally poor. There were certain segments of the population who accepted his teachings. In particular, the descendants of Seth, Adam's son and successor, saw that Noah's teachings corroborated everything they had inherited from their forefathers, so they readily accepted him and supported him.[35] Unfortunately, they were generally the destitute and disenfranchised of society.[36] They had nothing to lose and everything to gain. By accepting complete servitude to God, they freed themselves from bondage to the aristocracy that had come to dominate society and realized the real purpose of their existence.

One of the first to heed his call was a woman named ʿAmūrah, a granddaughter of Enoch. When her father found out about her newfound faith, he chastised her saying, "Have Noah's words affected you so swiftly?" She admonished him, and he threatened her. Finally, when he saw her resolve, on the advice of his clan, he imprisoned her in a room and tried to starve her to her senses. Her resolve never faltered, and God sustained her miraculously until her family gave in and released her. Noah married her, and she bore him children and remained faithful until the end.[37]

---

34. Qurʾān 71:4

35. *Biḥār al-anwār* vol. 11 p. 323 tr. 34

36. Qurʾān 26:111 and 11:27

37. *Biḥār al-anwār* vol. 11 p. 342. This tradition also mentions Noah's other wife, Rābiʿā, who was faithless and was destroyed by the flood. She will make her appearance in the story a little later.

The Line of Cain

This was not everyone's reaction. The descendants of Cain, in particular,[38] who were the leaders of society, summarily dismissed Noah. They realized immediately that his message was a direct attack on them. Without thought for what he was saying, they assaulted him viciously, hoping to thwart the revolution he was about to foment. They told him without reserve, "We deem you to be in clear error."

He replied, "O people! I am not in error; rather I am a messenger from the Lord of all realms."[39] The concept of a single Lord who ruled over the various realms of existence was one they had long since forgotten and replaced with multiple gods, each with a limited dominion. He continued, "I convey to you the messages of my Lord," reemphasizing that he did not speak on his own behalf but as a trusted messenger of God. He said, "I wish you well, and I know of God what you do not know."[40] He constantly needed to reaffirm his credibility by confirming his good intentions for them and his qualifications as one who was superior to them in knowledge.

The leaders parried telling the masses, "He is but a man like you who wants to rule over you." They assumed Noah, like them, was driven by ulterior motives—to use government as a means to amass personal wealth and power. They also promoted a fallacy that God would only communicate to humankind through angels when they said, "If God had wished to guide you he would have sent down angels. We have not heard of such as this in the history of our forefathers." In saying this, they forgot that prophets were not only messengers but the ultimate role models, subject to all human frailties and temptations, who had overcome the challenges of their carnal nature to surpass the greatest of angels.

Noah addressed this objection of theirs when he said, "Are you surprised that a reminder from your Lord has come to you through

38. *Biḥār al-anwār* vol. 11 p. 323 tr. 34

39. Qur'ān 7:60–62

40. Qur'ān 7:60–62

a man from among you who has been sent so he can warn you and so you can fear God and in hopes that you will be shown mercy"?[41]

When their other arguments seemed not to have their desired effect, they attacked him ad hominem saying, "He is nothing but a man afflicted with insanity, so give him respite for a while."[42] By asking for respite, they sought to reduce people's sense of urgency and get them to wait until he either came to his senses and stopped preaching or died. Unfortunately for them, he never "came to his senses," and he outlived three generations of them.

One of the reasons the leaders refused to accept him was outright jealousy. They could not understand what advantage Noah had that God would choose him over them. They said, "We deem you to be but a man like us, no better."[43]

Without arrogance, he explained to them what advantages he had saying, "My people! Tell me: If I have a miracle from my Lord and he has given me a book and divine knowledge as mercy from him, but you have been blinded to this, should we force this upon you against your will?"[44] In other words, "You say I am just a man like you; however, I am a man who has brought a miracle to prove to you that I am from God. Additionally, I have brought divine knowledge, a book of guidance, and a law. In short, I am a man, but not *like you*. And I have sufficiently proven this to you. It is you who have blinded yourselves to the truth. The only other thing I could possibly do is to force you to believe. However, this is absurd because there is no room for compulsion in belief."

In addition to their personal attacks on Noah, the leaders criticized him for the kind of followers he attracted. In their mind, if he were a prophet, he would attract the wealthiest and most refined segments of the population. The fact that it was the dregs of society who were with him set up another barrier against them believing since they could not stand to be associated with such people. They told Noah, "Should we believe in you when the meek

---

41. Qur'ān 7:63

42. Qur'ān 23:24–25

43. Qur'ān 11:27

44. Qur'ān 11:28

have followed you?"[45] And they said, "We see no one following you but those who are the meekest of us and have followed you at the drop of a hat."[46] Not only was their social standing too low for them, but they could not believe that the uneducated masses could have based their decision to follow him on anything but impulse, certainly not intelligence.

Noah responded brilliantly to this red herring. He said, "What do I know about what they used to do? Their reckoning for their past is only up to my Lord. If only you would think."[47] He distanced himself from the past deeds and low character of his followers and let it be known that their past was irrelevant to his own legitimacy. If in the past, they acted badly, God, and not him or they, would judge them. But now, they had reformed themselves and chosen to obey God's messenger, and this put them into a whole new class of people. This is why he continued and said, "And I am not one to drive away the believers, for I am but a clear warner."[48] He would not push away those who had answered his call simply because of their past history for the sake of people who were wealthy and powerful, yet refused to submit to the truth. He added, "And I shall not drive away those who have believed, for they shall meet their Lord. However, I see that you are a people who are ignorant about the Judgment. O people! Who will defend me against God's wrath if I were to drive them away? Do you not realize?"[49] Not only would disparaging the lower classes be immoral, but he feared the consequences of such actions on the Day of Judgment. Noah went beyond declaring that his followers' social class was irrelevant; he used their very lowliness to show once again that he had no ulterior motives. He said, "My people! I do not ask you for any money for this guidance—my compensation is solely with God."[50] He had told them this before; however, in the context of their new objections,

---

45. Qurʾān 26:111

46. Qurʾān 11:27

47. Qurʾān 26:112–113

48. Qurʾān 26:114–115

49. Qurʾān 11:29–30

50. Qurʾān 11:29

this declaration took on new meaning. It is as though he were saying, "Is it not obvious that I want nothing from you? Just look at my current followers. They are the poor and disenfranchised. They have nothing for themselves, much less for me."

When they saw the solidarity between Noah and his followers, the leaders attacked them both saying, "We deem you all to have no advantage above ours; rather we believe you to be liars."[51] In this statement it is evident they were preparing for war. They were sizing up their enemy, and they liked what they saw. They had all the advantages of power, wealth, and alliances.

Noah and his followers, on the other hand, had no power, wealth, or support to match theirs. To this, Noah replied that he had never claimed to have the kinds of powers they imagined a prophet should have. "I do not tell you that I possess the treasuries of God" to make my poor followers rich. "Nor do I know the unseen." At least independently of what God bestows on me, I do not have knowledge of the unseen to be able to avoid all harm and procure all good. "And I do not say that I am an angel." None of these things is relevant to my mission. What is relevant is that I have divine knowledge, that I am trustworthy, that I want what is best for you, and that I have brought miracles to prove it to you. He continued saying, "And I do not say to those whom you look upon with disdain that God will not give them goodness, for God knows better what is in their souls. If I were to say such a thing, I would be among the wrongdoers."[52] In other words, he did not believe as they did—that the lower classes were beasts of burden who existed only to serve the rich and who were bereft not only of the right to worldly pleasure but of access to God's mercy. God alone judges people and decides who receives goodness.

As time passed, tensions increased between Noah and the leaders of society. Their attacks became more bellicose and irrational. They would announce to all that "he is insane," and they would do everything in their power to ostracize him from society.[53] Aging

---

51. Qur'ān 11:27

52. Qur'ān 11:31

53. Qur'ān 54:9

fathers began exhorting their heirs from their deathbeds saying, "My Son! If you survive me, you must not follow this madman!"[54]

Women's Reaction

It was not only men who opposed Noah. There were women who began dressing and acting indecently, dousing themselves in perfume, and mingling with men in illicit pleasure. They would adorn themselves with jewelry and don silken garments and sit with men in public celebration. Until that time, all women menstruated only once annually. To impede these women's lust, God made them menstruate every month to diminish their desire, to occupy them with their bleeding, and so the men would distance themselves from them. This retribution initially affected only these corrupt women who numbered some 700. However, in coming generations, the progeny of the women with monthly cycles interbred with the progeny of the righteous women with annual cycles. Since the women with monthly cycles were more successful at conceiving and bearing children, this trait came to dominate and eventually drove the other trait to extinction.[55]

300 Years

Three hundred years had passed since Noah began his mission. He was now 1,150 years old, and he felt increasingly each day that his efforts were futile. So few had believed, and so many stood against him. He began to entertain thoughts of giving up, not because he lacked resolve, but because he felt people were too far gone to come back to God. Once, they beat him so severely that he lay unconscious for three days with blood oozing from his ears. When he recovered, he resolved to pray to God for their destruction.[56] At sunrise after the morning prayers, when he was about to ask God to send down his wrath upon them, he was approached by an army of 12,000 tribes of angels from the lowest level of the sky. They had come to beg him not to lose hope in his people just yet. Witnessing

54. *Biḥār al-anwār* vol. 11 p. 287 tr. 9

55. *Biḥār al-anwār* vol. 11 p. 326 tr. 47

56. *Biḥār al-anwār* vol. 11 p. 327 tr. 48

this massive display of God's mercy, Noah found a renewed sense of purpose and announced to the angels that he would continue to preach for another generation, 300 years, before giving up on them, if God allowed him to live that long.[57]

With characteristic zeal and patience, Noah resumed his mission, calling his people night and day, in public and in private. He conveyed to them God's promises of mercy and forgiveness and of worldly blessing. He later recounted his effort in a conversation with God:

> My Lord! I have summoned my people night and day. However, my summons has only increased them in flight. Whenever I have summoned them, so that you might absolve them, they have stuck their fingers in their ears, drawn their cloaks over their heads, and persisted in their refusal to hear me, and they have been incredibly arrogant. I summoned them openly. And I spoke to them publicly and in private and told them, "Seek your Lord's forgiveness, for he is All-Forgiving. If you do, he will send down upon you abundant rains from the sky and aid you with wealth and sons and provide you with gardens and provide you with streams. What is the matter with you that you do not look upon God with veneration, though he has created you through various stages? Have you not seen how God has created the sky in seven layers and how he has made therein the moon for light and the sun for a lamp? It is God who made you grow from the earth. Then he will return you to it and then bring you forth from it. And it is God who has made the earth expansive for you so that you can travel upon its wide roads."[58]

---

57. *Biḥār al-anwār* vol. 11 p. 310 tr. 5

58. Qur'ān 71:5–20

600 Years

The response he received from this generation was no better than their parents'. They were as stubborn and as arrogant as their parents had been. And so, Noah considered, at the end of their generation, to call down God's wrath upon them. Once again, a massive envoy of 12,000 tribes of angels, this time from the second level of the sky, came to him to beg him to reconsider. Once again, he agreed to persevere for another generation, resolving to have patience with his people as long as God did.[59]

900 Years

It was during the year 900 of his mission, as he approached his own 1,750th year, that it became clear to him that his people had already sealed their own fate. Nothing he could say or do could affect them. The believers numbered in the mere hundreds,[60] and many of these were weak in their faith.

As a last resort, he issued one final threat to his people of severe divine retribution. Defiantly, they responded, "Noah, you have argued with us, and you have argued a lot. Bring down that with which you threaten us if you are truthful."

He said, "Only God can bring it down if he wishes. And when he does you will not be able to thwart it. If God wants to lead you astray,[61] even my good wishes could not benefit you—if I were to wish you well. He is your Lord and to him shall you be returned...If I have fabricated this, then my sin shall be upon me. But if you are wrong, then I am absolved of your sins."[62]

---

59. *Biḥār al-anwār* vol. 11 p. 310 tr. 5

60. Traditions tell us that the number who boarded the ark were between 8 and 80. They also tell us that a series of God's tests decimated the ranks of the believers during the last 250 years before the flood. Based on this, I have estimated their numbers at this time in the hundreds.

61. God does not lead people astray until they themselves decide that they want to go astray and abandon his guidance. Once they seal their hearts, he fastens the seal; once they shut their ears and eyes to the truth, he reinforces their deafness and blindness.

62. Qur'ān 11:32–35

As always, Noah turned to God to seek his help. He said beseechingly, "Lord! Aid me through that which they deny."[63] He wanted God to follow through on his threats and prove him right by crushing them with the very same divine retribution that they had so vehemently denied.

With renewed determination, Noah told his people, "O people! If it is hard on you that I have stayed so long among you and constantly reminded you of God's signs, then do what you will and know that in God have I put my trust. So conspire together, along with the idols you believe to be God's partners. And let nothing of your plan cause you the least remorse. Then carry it out against me without giving me any respite. If you turn your backs on me, you shall not harm me in the least, for I have not asked you for any compensation. My compensation is solely with God, and I have been commanded to be among those who submit to him."[64]

Noah's followers also begged him importunately to ask God for relief from the torment they constantly faced for his sake.[65] So he turned to God and said, "O Lord! My people have rejected me. So judge between them and me, and save me and the believers who are with me."[66] And he prayed, "I am vanquished, so come to my aid."[67]

Their Fate Is Sealed

For those who live their lives in devotion to God, their prayers' answer comes swiftly. God confirmed Noah's conclusion and justified his feelings of hopelessness when he told him, "No one from your people shall believe except those who have already believed, so do not grieve for what they used to do."[68]

---

63. Qur'ān 23:26

64. Qur'ān 10:71–72

65. *Biḥār al-anwār* vol. 11 p. 327 tr. 48

66. Qur'ān 26:117–118

67. Qur'ān 54:10

68. Qur'ān 11:36

It was then, when he heard God's judgment and confirmation of what he had perceived to be true, that he called down God's wrath with abandon. He said:

> My Lord! They have disobeyed me and followed those whose wealth and children only add to their loss; who have plotted to deceive outrageously; who tell them, "Do not abandon your gods. Do not abandon Wadd, nor Suwāʿ, nor Yaghūth or Yaʿūq or Nasr." And these leaders have already led many astray. O God! Add only to the wrongdoers' error...O Lord! Do not leave a single being from the non-believers on Earth. If you do leave them, they will misguide your servants, and they will only bear sinful and faithless progeny. O Lord! Forgive me and my parents and those believers who have entered my house from my followers and all believing men and women. And add only to the wrongdoers' destruction.[69]

Seven Date Pits

He had hardly finished praying when Gabriel came to him and informed him that God had heard his prayers and answered them. He brought with him seven date pits and ordered Noah to command his followers to plant them. He communicated to them God's promise that they would find their salvation from their tribulations when these date pits grew into mature trees and gave fruit.[70] They were elated and could hardly wait for the day when they would witness God's promise fulfilled.

Wisdom in Delay

God had two reasons for postponing his promised salvation of the believers and destruction of the non-believers. On the one hand, he chose not to destroy the non-believers immediately because of

---

69. Qur'ān 71:21–24 and 26–28

70. *Biḥār al-anwār* vol. 11 p. 327 tr. 48 and p. 329 tr. 51

his forbearance and his unshakable sense of justice. He was loath to leave room for anyone to even conjecture that he had wronged someone. In particular, the ranks of the non-believers comprised newborn infants and children, and he wanted no one to look back and think, "Maybe those children would have grown up and answered Noah's call." So he made the women sterile for the next 40 or so years.[71] In this way, any child born up to the 900th year of Noah's mission was be able to grow up, mature to the age of 50, and make his own choice before his fate was sealed. In the meantime, God commanded Noah to continue to preach to them, despite his knowledge that none who had not yet believed would believe.[72] He told him, "Noah! They are my creatures and my servants. I shall only destroy them after you have redoubled your efforts and sealed my case against them. So redouble your efforts to call the people, for I shall reward you for it."[73] Thus, God sealed his case against every human being—whether adult or child—while maintaining his immaculate record of justice. On the other hand, he chose not to grant Noah's followers swift salvation to test them and separate the sincere in faith from the weak.

When the seven date trees matured and bore fruit, Noah's followers eagerly collected the harvest and brought it to him. God had told them that they would find their salvation from their tribulations when these date pits grew into mature trees and gave fruit, and they looked to Noah to make good on this promise. He turned to God and prayed on their behalf. Against their expectations, God once again commanded them to eat these dates and plant their pits, repeating his promise that they would find their salvation from their tribulations when these date pits grew into mature trees and gave fruit. A large contingent of the believers, perhaps a third, felt they had been abandoned by God and betrayed by Noah. They left the fold of faith and joined with

---

71. *Biḥār al-anwār* vol. 11 p. 311 tr. 6 and p. 320 tr. 25

72. Qurʾān 11:36

73. *Biḥār al-anwār* vol. 11 p. 329 tr. 51

his enemies. Others remained steadfast and did as they were commanded by God.[74]

When the new crop of date palms matured and ripened, the same series of events repeated itself, and once again a large contingent of the believers, perhaps a third, turned coat. Only seventy-odd loyalists remained steadfast and did as they were commanded by God. When the dates ripened for the third time, the remaining believers pleaded with Noah saying, "Only a few of us are left. If you delay our salvation any further, we fear we may not be able to remain strong in faith."[75] One man expressed such loyalty that he said, "O Prophet of God! Whether you do for us what you promised or not, I testify that you are a truthful prophet sent by God, we shall not doubt in you no matter what you do."[76] Noah conveyed their desperate cries and their sincere loyalty to God whereupon he replied:

> At last, morning has broken through the black of night, and truth has been filtered of all impurities...If I had destroyed the non-believers and left in your ranks those who have now turned their backs on you, I would have failed to fulfill my promise to those who have sincerely worshiped me and held fast to you as their prophet. I had promised them that I would make them my vicegerents in the land and give them freedom to practice religion; that I would replace their fear with sanctuary by removing any vestiges of doubt

74. *Biḥār al-anwār* vol. 11 p. 327 tr. 48 and p. 329 tr. 51. It may seem cruel and unfair for God to renege on his promise. However, this is not the case. As God himself will explain to Noah shortly, he delayed their relief two, and in some traditions, six or even nine times to weed out the weak in faith. He was justified in apparently "breaking his promise" based on *badā'*, the apparent changes in some of God's decrees contingent upon human action. His promise to give them relief was contingent upon the absence of any whose faith was weak. As long as such people remained in their ranks, he continued to delay the fulfillment of his promise so that they would be weeded out.

75. *Biḥār al-anwār* vol. 11 p. 327 tr. 48

76. *Biḥār al-anwār* vol. 11 p. 340 tr. 76

> from their hearts so that they could worship me alone. How could I have fulfilled this for them when I knew the weakness of those who have now left? For whenever they would have gained power over the land, their hypocrisy would have shown its countenance, and they would have shown their brethren enmity and vied with them for power.[77]

Building the Ark

After 950 years as a prophet, when Noah was in his 1,800th year, God sealed the fate of those who had chosen not to believe. He ordered Noah to take an ax to the date palms, and after felling the trees, to use the timber to build an ark.[78] He told him, "Build an ark under our gaze and with our guidance."[79] Noah had been a carpenter all his life,[80] but no human had ever built a vessel to float on water before.[81] He desperately needed God's help to design and build it to the specifications and purpose only God knew. God sent Gabriel to show him the way.[82] Its dimensions were to be on the order of 1200 cubits in length by 800 cubits in width by 80 cubits in height.[83] He was to build ninety compartments within it to

---

77. *Biḥār al-anwār* vol. 11 p. 327 tr. 48 and p. 329 tr. 51

78. *Biḥār al-anwār* vol. 11 p. 311 tr. 5 and p. 323 tr. 35. Another tradition (*Biḥār al-anwār* vol. 11 p. 328 tr. 49) mentions that he was commanded to split planks of teak (*sāj*) although it seems this tradition may be lacking in authenticity for several reasons, and it leaves the cut date palms, which are mentioned in several traditions, with no purpose.

79. Qur'ān 11:37

80. *Biḥār al-anwār* vol. 11 p. 287 tr. 9

81. *Biḥār al-anwār* vol. 11 p. 332 tr. 54

82. *Biḥār al-anwār* vol. 11 p. 328 tr. 49

83. *Biḥār al-anwār* vol. 11 p. 311 tr. 5. Its dimensions in another tradition are 800 cubits in length, 500 cubits in width, and 80 cubits in height (*Biḥār al-anwār* vol. 11 p. 320 tr. 23). A cubit is something on the order of half a meter making the ark between 400m by 250m by 40m to 600m by 400m by 40m.

house all the animals.[84] On God's orders, he solicited help from his followers promising anyone who helped him with gold and silver in paradise.[85]

Ridicule and Mockery

He began construction on the grounds of the Mosque of Kūfah. It was next to his own house[86] and near the temple where the pagans housed their idols.[87] The pagans ridiculed him to no end. This was nothing new. They had been mocking him all along. When he had planted the date palms, they called him a farmer and ridiculed him for having planted trees in old age, for conventional wisdom said old men never live to see the fruits of their labor. When he had chopped the trees down, they called him a lumberjack and ridiculed him and called him mad for destroying the trees he had taken so much effort to plant just when they were entering their prime. And now when he began construction on the ark, they called him a carpenter and a sailor and ridiculed him for building a ship in the middle of Kūfah, far from any sea.[88] Whenever the leaders from his people would pass by him, they would mock him.

He told them, "If you mock us now, it is no matter, for we shall soon mock you as you now mock us.[89] And you shall soon know upon whom among us a degrading punishment will come down and upon whom among us a lasting punishment will descend."[90]

---

84. *Biḥār al-anwār* vol. 11 p. 319 tr. 22

85. *Biḥār al-anwār* vol. 11 p. 311 tr. 5

86. *Biḥār al-anwār* vol. 11 p. 312 tr. 6

87. *Biḥār al-anwār* vol. 11 p. 332 tr. 54

88. *Biḥār al-anwār* vol. 11 p. 311 tr. 5 and p. 323 tr. 35

89. To initiate mockery and ridicule is morally reprehensible. However, as just retaliation in kind, it is completely justified. God attributes such ridicule to himself when he says that he will ridicule those who ridicule believers who give charity freely and others who simply have nothing to give (Qur'ān 9:79). He also says that the believers who are laughed at in this world will laugh at those who laughed at them on the Day of Judgment (Qur'ān 83:34).

90. Qur'ān 11:38–39

Oven Gushing With Water

It took all of 200 years for Noah and his few followers to complete the ark's construction.[91] Back when God had issued orders to build the ark, he had told Noah, "When our command comes and your oven gushes with water, then lead into the ark a pair from each kind of animal along with your family—except for those among them who have already been condemned. And do not speak to me about the wrongdoers. They shall be drowned."[92] The oven God referred to was one in Noah's house in which his faithful wife, ʿAmūrah, used to bake bread.[93] He warned her to watch for the day when water would gush out of this oven for that would be God's sign that the great punishment was imminent. So they waited.

When one day she hollered in alarm, Noah rushed to her aid to find water gushing out of her oven, and he knew it was time. He did as God had commanded him—to "lead into the ark a pair from each kind of animal along with your family—except for those among

---

91. *Biḥār al-anwār* vol. 11 p. 285 tr. 2. There are discrepancies in the time it took to build the ark. Our traditions are in agreement on Noah's total age (2,500 years) and the timeline of the other segments of his life (850 years before becoming a prophet, 950 as a prophet, and 500 years after the flood). Two hundred years are left to account for. The tradition cited above explicitly says that he spent 200 years building the ark. Another tradition says it took him only eighty years, no more, because God facilitated things for him (*Biḥār al-anwār* vol. 11 p. 232 tr. 54). We can possibly reconcile these differences if we assume that the entire 200 years was not spent actually *building* the ark. Perhaps the 200 years included the time it took to plant the three or more generations of date palms to produce the timber for the ark.

92. Qurʾān 23:27

93. One tradition mentions that the oven was "in the house of an old, faithful woman just behind the current *qiblah* on the right side of the mosque where a cornerstone of *Bāb al-Fīl* currently lies" (*Al-Kāfī* vol. 8, tradition 421). Another tradition says that "Noah's wife used to bake" there (*Biḥār al-anwār* vol. 11 p. 312 tr. 6). Considering that Noah had two wives as I mentioned earlier, and that the woman who witnessed this miracle and informed Noah of it was almost certainly one of his followers, I have concluded that these two traditions are mutually compatible and are referring to the same woman—ʿAmūrah, Noah's righteous wife.

them who have already been condemned. And do not speak to me about the wrongdoers. They shall be drowned."[94]

A Pair of Each Animal

Noah called out, "Every beast and living thing, come!" And they came from all around. When they approached, he led a pair of each onto the ark and into its special holding pen so that he would be able to restore the world's animal population after everything was destroyed. He also loaded whatever provisions they would need for the duration of their trip.[95] He sent word to all the believers, who after all these years, numbered on the order of 80 people.[96] As the first drops of rain fell on the first of *Rajab*,[97] Noah told them, "Board the ark. May its launching and docking be with God's name. He is the All-Absolving, the Ever-Merciful."[98]

They boarded as they had been planning for so long, grateful to God and to Noah for saving them and fulfilling their promise to them. When they were situated, they extolled God saying, "Praise is for God who saved us from the wrongdoers."

Then Noah added, "Lord! Disembark me in a blessed place. You are the Best to Disembark."[99]

Noah's Flood

Then the rains began in full force. God flung open his celestial floodgates to let torrential rains pour down. And he made the earth burst forth with geysers, at which the two waters met according to a plan that was ordained. As chaotic as the ensuing destruction

---

94. Qur᾿ān 23:27

95. *Biḥār al-anwār* vol. 11 p. 312 tr. 6

96. Various numbers have been mentioned in the traditions between six and eighty. We cannot say with any certainty which is right (see *al-Mīzān* vol. 12, p. 234). I have chosen eighty only because it is the most famous account. Otherwise, all we can say for sure is what the Qur᾿ān tells us, "Only a few had believed with him" (23:27).

97. *Biḥār al-anwār* vol. 11 p. 318 tr. 18

98. Qur᾿ān 11:41

99. Qur᾿ān 23:28–29

must have seemed, not a drop rose or fell except according to God's precise plan. And he planned to carry Noah and his followers on an ark of planks and nails that sailed under his gaze. All this, as recompense for one who had been rejected.[100]

Noah's Evil Wife, Rābiʿā

God had foreshadowed for Noah that all of his family would not join him on the ark when he said, "Lead into the ark...your family—except for those among them who have already been condemned."[101] One of these who had been condemned and chose not to board the ark was one of Noah's wives, Rābiʿā.[102] Despite being so close to one of God's greatest prophets, she refused to believe. On the Day of Judgment she will be told, "Enter the fire along with the others."[103]

Noah's Son, Canaan

More surprising, even to Noah himself, was the refusal of his son, Canaan,[104] to board. He had been a believer, like his brothers, Shem, Ham, and Japheth, or so Noah had thought, and he had expected him to join the others. But the water was rising fast and there was no sign of him. It was almost time to seal the hatch when he finally spotted him in the distance. Noah called out to him saying, "O my son! Board the ark with us, and do not remain with the non-believers." He did not know that his son was himself *among* the non-believers.

He replied, "I shall seek refuge on a mountain which will protect me from the water."

Noah said, "There is nothing on this day that can protect anyone from God's command except him upon whom God has mercy." But

---

100. Qurʾān 54:11–14

101. Qurʾān 23:27

102. *Biḥār al-anwār* vol. 11 p. 342

103. Qurʾān 66:10

104. Canaan is named as the son of Ham in the Bible (Genesis 9:22). However, this name is mentioned in some traditions as the name of Noah's son who was destroyed (*Biḥār al-anwār* vol. 11 p. 317 tr. 15). Whatever his name, the Qurʾān explicitly describes him as Noah's son.

the prerequisite for God's mercy is belief and obedience. With that, a wave surged between them, and he became one of those who were drowned.[105]

Noah called out to his Lord and said, "My son is from my family and your promise is true and you are the Best of Judges."[106] Noah had no qualms about the necessary destruction of the non-believers. After all his merciful efforts to teach them and convince them of the truth, only the most wretched of people had refused. Once God told him, "No one from your people shall believe except those who have already believed,"[107] he had called down God's wrath upon every last one of them saying, "O Lord! Do not leave a single being from the non-believers on Earth."[108] Noah, the first of the Messengers of Great Resolve, was not one to compromise on principles and duty for the sake of familial ties. Even if his son were to reject his call, he would have no compunction about seeing him destroyed by God's wrath and cast into hellfire. So it was not weakness that called Noah to plead with God. It was concern over his own duty. He had been ordered to "Lead into the ark... your family,"[109] and his son was certainly from his family. He had also been promised that all the believers would be saved,[110] and to the best of his knowledge, this son of his had been a believer. He wanted to know whether it was his duty to bring his son on board, or whether he had truly joined the ranks of the accursed. However, he knew that whatever God's judgment, it would be just, for he is the Best of Judges.

God replied, "Noah, he is not from among those family members whom I promised to save,[111] for he is the embodiment of an

105. Qur'ān 11:42–43

106. Qur'ān 11:45

107. Qur'ān 11:36

108. Qur'ān 71:26

109. Qur'ān 23:27

110. *Biḥār al-anwār* vol. 11 p. 327 tr. 48 and p. 329 tr. 51

111. Some are of the opinion that this son, Canaan, was not truly Noah's son, but an illegitimate child Noah's wife had fooled Noah into thinking his own. However, the verses of the Qur'ān clearly state that he was *his* son. Imam al-Riḍā

unrighteous act. So do not ask me for that about which you have no knowledge. I warn you about this lest you be among the foolish." Noah, of course, had not asked for his son to be spared; he had only skirted gingerly around the question so that he could know the truth about his son's state. Nonetheless, God is strict with his closest servants, and so he warned him to ensure that he remained within the bounds of propriety.

In turn, Noah, in complete subservience to God said, "O Lord! I seek refuge in you from asking that about which I have no knowledge. If you do not absolve me and have mercy on me, I shall be among the losers."[112]

All People Are Drowned

The waters rose so high that all the earth was submerged.[113] God drowned those who rejected his signs, for they were a people

---

refutes these defamatory claims saying, "He was indeed his son. But when he sinned against God, God disowned him on Noah's behalf" (*ʿUyūn akhbār al-Riḍā* vol. 2, p. 75 and *Biḥār al-anwār* vol. 11 p. 320 tr. 24 and tr. 26 and p. 321 tr. 28).

112. Qurʾān 11:46–47

113. The predominant opinion of our scholars is that the flood covered the entire earth, and so I have deferred to their opinion. However, there is no textual evidence in the Qurʾān that explicitly states that this was so. We do have substantial and, in some cases, explicit evidence for the following:

- Noah was a prophet to *all* human beings alive at his time. We know this because the Qurʾān tells us he was the first of the Messengers of Great Resolve, and the traditions tell us that the Messengers of Great Resolve had a mandate to guide all human beings.
- Every last human being alive at the time of the flood was destroyed by the flood except those few people who boarded the ark with Noah.

Based on these two facts, if it so happened that there were people all over the earth, then necessarily the flood must have covered the entire earth. However, if people only lived in a limited part of the world, then the flood need only have covered that portion. In a situation like this, we need not commit too strongly to either possibility.

In any case, we need not heed the many irreverent attempts by modern scientists to falsify the flood as described in the Old Testament. Unlike the Bible, the Qurʾān places no timeline on Noah's flood, neither does it indicate that the flood covered the entire earth, so we need not limit our search for geological evidence of the flood to the last 5–7 millennia, and we need not search for a

blinded by their foolishness.[114] They had been sufficiently warned.[115] They were an evil people, so he drowned them all.[116] He made them a sign of warning for all people, and he has prepared a painful punishment for those wrongdoers.[117] Therein they shall not find anyone to aid them against God.[118]

God had told Noah before he had boarded the ark, "Whenever you fear that your ark may fail, hail my oneness a thousand times and beg me for salvation, and I shall grant it." At one point, a gale pressed on the ark with such force Noah felt a pang of desperation and fear. He remembered God's admonishment but felt he had no time to repeat his prayer one thousand times. At the last moment, he said, "There is no god but God, one thousand times! Lord, through my children, Muḥammad and his family,[119] save us!" The gale abated, and the ark sailed smoothly once again. Later, after the flood, Noah would recall these words through which God had saved him and etch them into the facet of his ring.[120]

Thus did God save Noah and his family from their tremendous grief. And he saved him from a people who had rejected God's signs.[121] He made him and those who were with him in the ark succeed their predecessors.[122] In all that is a sign;[123] a sign that God's threats of punishment are not empty; a sign that God has invincible power; a sign that God unfailingly fulfills his promises to the believers; and a sign that he is ever-merciful in his dealings

---

global flood.

114. Qur'ān 7:64

115. Qur'ān 10:73

116. Qur'ān 21:26

117. Qur'ān 25:37

118. Qur'ān 71:25

119. *Biḥār al-anwār* vol. 12 p. 40 tr. 28

120. *Biḥār al-anwār* vol. 11 p. 285 tr. 1

121. Qur'ān 21:26–27

122. Qur'ān 10:73

123. Qur'ān 26:121

with his friends. As for the ark, he made it a sign for all people.[124] He left the ark as a sign. Is there any who will heed his sign? How terrible was his punishment and how complete his warning![125] It will remain preserved for people to discover, so they will know that this story is real, that God is real, that his promise is real, and that his threat is real.

Noah Passes Through Bakkah

Only the Kaʿbah was protected miraculously from being submersed. Because it was saved from the flood, it came to be known as *al-Bayt alʿAtīq*, "The House that was Spared."[126]

The waters carried the ark to Bakkah. There God commanded Noah to descend from the ark onto Mount Abū Qubays so that he could collect the remains of Adam. He stowed these remains in a wooden chest in the ark, and they continued their journey.[127]

The *jinn* survived the flood by changing into spirits and floating on the wind above the water.[128] Presumably creatures of the sea survived without any special effort on Noah's part.

The Flood Ends

Noah and his companions remained in the ark for some time[129] until God decreed, "O Earth! Swallow up your water. O Sky! Cease your

---

124. Qurʾān 29:15

125. Qurʾān 54:15–16. These verses and the previous verse explicitly state that God has preserved the ark as a sign for all people, not just the story of the ark, but the ark itself. The fact that we have not yet conclusively found the ark does not contradict these verses since it is possible that it will act as a "sign" at some later time when it is finally discovered. Perhaps it will be discovered in a time when human confidence in the Qurʾān's validity ebbs to an all-time low in order to bolster people's waning faith.

126. *Biḥār al-anwār* vol. 11 p. 313 tr. 6 and vol. 11 p. 325 tr. 43. In Arabic, *iʿtāq* means "to free something" or "to save something." Based on this, one meaning of *al-Bayt alʿAtīq* is "The House that was Spared."

127. *Biḥār al-anwār* vol. 11 p. 268 tr. 18

128. *Biḥār al-anwār* vol. 11 p. 319 tr. 21

129. Different traditions mention different durations for the flood. Some say

downpour."[130] The sky withheld its moisture. The earth absorbed its water according to God's decree and abstained from absorbing the water of the sky which remained on the earth's surface. Gabriel was commissioned to guide this water to the earth's oceans and lakes.[131] And the ark came to rest upon a great mountain.[132] At this, God declared, "Gone are the wrongdoers!"[133]

Then he said, "O Noah! Go forth with our peace and blessings with you and with those communities who will issue from those who are with you.[134] And there will be communities among them whom we shall make prosper, and afterward, they will be afflicted by our painful punishment."[135]

He continued, "I hereby make the rainbow a sign of sanctuary and a covenant with my servants from now until the Day of Judgment

---

seven days (*Biḥār al-anwār* vol. 11 p. 333 tr. 56), others say 150 days, 5 months, and 6 months (*Biḥār al-anwār* vol. 11 p. 334–335).

130. Qur'ān 11:44

131. *Biḥār al-anwār* vol. 11 p. 313 tr. 6

132. Some say that *al-Jūdī* is the proper name of the mountain. Others say that *al-jūdī* is a common noun for a large mountain. The latter opinion is supported by a tradition (*Biḥār al-anwār* vol. 11 p. 339 tr. 74).

133. Qur'ān 11:44

134. This verse indicates that there will be "communities" issuing from those who were on the ark with Noah. Coupled with the fact that all human beings not on the ark were killed, we can conclude that all subsequent generations can trace their lineage back to those on the ark. However, another verse, "We made his progeny alone those who lasted" (Qur'ān 37:77), indicates that only Noah's line has continued, not the others. This could either indicate that the lineage of the others on the ark eventually died out or that through intermarriage, the lineage of the others converged with Noah's such that all modern generations can trace their lineage back to Noah, at least through one parent. One tradition attributed to Imam al-Bāqir contradicts this interpretation and claims that verse 37:77 does not mean that all people can trace their lineage back to Noah but that God placed "the truth, prophethood, the book, and faith in his progeny" (*Biḥār al-anwār* vol. 11 p. 310 tr. 3). 'Allāmah al-Ṭabāṭabā'ī does not accept that this tradition is strong enough to make us abandon the clear and apparent meaning of the above-mentioned verses.

135. Qur'ān 11:48

that I shall not drown them again. And who is more faithful to his covenant than I?"[136]

After the Flood

Noah lived for 500 years after the flood. During this time, he was responsible for repopulating the earth, rebuilding its cities, and establishing the first civil society based on the law of God.[137] With eighty or so people and an ark full of animals, he did this and became the second father of humankind.[138]

One of the first things Noah did upon alighting from the ark was to take the chest with Adam's bones and bury it outside of Kūfah in modern day Najaf.[139]

Satan's Admonishment

Once, Satan came to Noah and told him, "I owe you for a favor you have done me."

Noah responded disdainfully, "It is repugnant to me that I should have done you a favor."

But God spoke to Noah and told him, "Speak with him and ask him what he has to say, for I shall cause him to speak to his own detriment."

Noah ordered Satan to speak, so he said, "When we find that a son of Adam is miserly, greedy, jealous, arrogant, or impatient, we pounce upon him to misguide him. And when all these traits join together in a person, we call him a devil."[140]

Noah asked him, "What is this favor I have allegedly done you?"

Satan replied,

> That you prayed for your people's destruction, and, in response, God destroyed them. Now my work has been made much easier, at least

---

136. *al-Jawāhir al-saniyyah* p.17

137. *Biḥār al-anwār* vol. 11 p. 285 tr. 2

138. *Biḥār al-anwār* vol. 11 p. 313 tr. 6

139. *Tahdhīb al-aḥkām* 6.22.7.8

140. *Biḥār al-anwār* vol. 11 p. 288 tr. 10

> until another generation comes along for me to misguide. I shall repay this favor by teaching you some things: Think of me during three instances, for it is then that I have the most influence over one of God's servants. Think of me when you are angry. Think of me when you arbitrate between two parties. And think of me when you are illicitly alone with a woman.[141]

Noah's Legacy

As Noah neared the end of his life, he was approached by Gabriel who told him on God's behalf,

> Your prophethood is nearing its end, and you have lived out your days. Think now of your legacy of knowledge and the relics of past prophets and turn these over to your son Shem, for I never leave the earth without one endowed with knowledge through whom people can be guided and know how to obey me between the death of one prophet and the commencement of the mission of another. And I would never leave people without one who knows me to witness their deeds and call them to me and guide them to my path. I have decided to set up 'for every people a guide' through whom I can guide those who choose to be felicitous and who will be my witness against those who choose to be wretched.

Noah turned over his legacy of knowledge and the relics of past prophets to his son Shem. Then he turned to his closest followers and said:

> After I am gone, there will be a time when no prophet will be among you. During this time, evil people will rise to power. God Almighty

141. *Biḥār al-anwār* vol. 11 p. 293 tr. 7, p. 317 tr. 14, and p. 318 tr. 20

> will relieve you through one from my progeny who will rise up. His name will be Hūd. He will be demure and dignified. He will look and act like me. During his time, God will destroy your enemies with a wind.[142]

He then exhorted Shem to open the written mandate he had given him every year and read it so that the anniversary would become a festival for all people.[143] And he exhorted people to fast on the first of *Rajab*, on the anniversary of their salvation from God's enemies by means of the flood.[144]

When the Angel of Death finally came to him to claim his soul, Noah was standing in the sun. He asked permission to move from the sun to the shade. Then he reflected momentarily on his long life and said to the Angel of Death, "All that happened to me in this temporal world seems as short-lived as my movement from the sun into this shade." With that, the Angel of Death claimed his soul.[145]

Shem buried his father on the outskirts of Kūfah in modern day Najaf next to the new resting place of Adam's bones.[146]

---

142. *Biḥār al-anwār* vol. 11 p. 363 tr. 27

143. *al-Kāfī* vol. 8 p. 285 tr. 430

144. *Biḥār al-anwār* vol. 11 p. 318 tr. 18

145. *Biḥār al-anwār* vol. 11 p. 286 tr. 2

146. *Tahdhīb al-aḥkām* 6.34.10.12

Hūd

ʿĀd and Their Wonders

Generations had passed since the death of Noah. The descendants of ʿĀd, a great-great grandson of Noah,[1] had settled in the southern parts of the Arabian Peninsula.[2] They were organized into thirteen different clans who were collectively known as ʿĀd after their common ancestor.[3] They were the heirs of the antediluvian civilization that Noah's flood had obliterated.[4] God had showered them with innumerable blessings. He endowed them with enormous physical size and strength.[5] He endowed them with land unparalleled in Arabia in its fertility and verdure.[6] There were countless springs to water their farms and gardens and no dearth of pasture for their herds of cattle.[7]

---

1. *Biḥār al-anwār* vol. 11 p. 346
2. *Majmaʿ al-Bayān* under Qurʾān 46:21
3. *Biḥār al-anwār* vol. 11 p. 357–8 tr. 15
4. Qurʾān 7:69
5. Qurʾān 7:69. Many Muslims, including commentators of the Qurʾān, have concluded from this verse and several traditions that these people, including Hūd, were literally giants of fairytale proportions. When Hūd tells his people, "Remember when God...enhanced you vastly in your physique," he could be referring to them as giants, but he could simply be referring to their above-average physiques. Samuel describes Saul (*Ṭālūt*) using a similar phrase when he tells those who feel he is unfit to rule over them, "...and God has enhanced him vastly in his physique and knowledge" (Qurʾān 2:247). In other words, verse 7:69 is ambiguous with regard to their giantism. Unless there is valid archeological evidence to prove that such massive humans once existed or physiological evidence to show that it is possible for a human to grow to such proportions, we should not commit ourselves to the more unlikely of two interpretations.
6. *Biḥār al-anwār* vol. 11 p. 357 tr. 15
7. Qurʾān 26:133–134

Among the winding, sandstone mountains of Yemen,[8] the ʿĀd had crafted a magnificent city they called Iram, the City of Pillars.[9] It was a city destined to become a legend in human history, never to be paralleled.[10] They had used their immense physical strength and their advanced technological skills to hew massive monolithic pillars as long as the mountains, from which they hewed them, were tall. They would ingeniously haul these pillars of stone into Iram, affix them in the earth, and then build their palatial residences atop them.[11] Upon every hill and mountain, they erected monuments to display their wealth and power to the world.[12] Their buildings were such solid edifices that it seemed to all who saw them that they would last for eternity.[13] Their military might made them invincible. When they struck at their enemies, they struck with such brutality that they left no one and nothing standing.[14]

ʿĀd's Decline

Counter to their great technological, artistic, agricultural, and military advancements, the ʿĀd found themselves in a steep, downward spiral of religious and moral decay. In the centuries following Noah's death, one by one, each of the prophecies he had delivered to his followers from his deathbed had been fulfilled. All the evil that had drowned with the flood had gradually resurfaced and shown its face. More and more people had devoted themselves to idol worship; those unfit to rule had assumed power; and injustice and immorality were rampant.[15]

---

8. This is a translation of the term *aḥqāf* which the Qurʾān uses to describe the area where Iram was built (see 46:21).

9. Qurʾān 89:7

10. Qurʾān 89:8

11. *Biḥār al-anwār* vol. 11 p. 355 tr. 12 and p. 357–8 tr. 15

12. Qurʾān 26:128

13. Qurʾān 26:129

14. Qurʾān 26:130

15. *Biḥār al-anwār* vol. 11 p. 363 tr. 27

For the few surviving believers, the only glimmer of hope that remained was the savior who Noah had promised would rise up from among his progeny and purge the world of evil once again. The dwindling ranks of the righteous held on to this thread of hope. They knew what his name would be. They knew what sort of character he would have. They even knew what he would look like. But with the passing of each year, this unfulfilled prophecy emaciated their hope. Many abandoned their vigil and renounced their faith because they felt God had abandoned them.[16]

Hūd Is Chosen

When only a fraction of the believers remained and their oppression at the hands of the pagans had reached an apex, God determined that it was time to appoint his new prophet to warn and guide the citizens of Iram.[17] For this role, he chose Hūd.

Hūd was born into a prominent and honorable family of Iram, and so, commanded great respect among his people.[18] He was a merchant by profession.[19] He had been successful in the markets and had added a sizable fortune to his distinguished lineage.[20] Most importantly, for his impeccable honesty and integrity in all his dealings, he had gained the unfailing trust of his people.[21] Like his people, he spoke Arabic.[22] He was demure and dignified and looked and acted like his forefather, Noah.[23] He also resembled his forefather, the patriarch of all people, Adam. He was dark-skinned,

---

16. *Biḥār al-anwār* vol. 11 p. 363 tr. 27

17. *Biḥār al-anwār* vol. 11 p. 363 tr. 27

18. *Biḥār al-anwār* vol. 11 p. 357 tr. 15

19. *Biḥār al-anwār* vol. 11 p. 359 tr. 15

20. *Biḥār al-anwār* vol. 11 p. 357 tr. 15

21. *Biḥār al-anwār* vol. 11 p. 361 tr. 21

22. *Biḥār al-anwār* vol. 11 p. 346. Hūd was the first Arabic-speaking prophet we know of. The others were Ṣāliḥ, Shuʿayb, Ishmael, and Muḥammad, may God's peace be with them all. The fact that Hūd, Ṣāliḥ, and Shuʿayb are considered "Arab" debunks the conventional wisdom that Ishmael is the "Father of the Arabs" since Hūd and Ṣāliḥ predated him and Shuʾayb was not from his line.

23. *Biḥār al-anwār* vol. 11 p. 363 tr. 27

had a full head of hair and was, by all standards, good looking.[24] His name derived from the Arabic word for guidance because he was destined to guide his people out of the darkness and toward God.[25]

He Calls and They Refuse

Hūd began his prophetic mission at the age of forty[26] by boldly telling his people, "O people! Worship God other than whom you have no deity worthy of worship. Do you not fear him?"[27] It was the same message Adam, Enoch, and Noah had brought before him, and he hoped it would strike a chord with their descendants. He told them, "I am for you a trustworthy messenger," and they knew in their hearts that it was so. Until this day, they had trusted him implicitly. He continued, "So fear God and obey me. I do not ask you for any recompense for this work. My recompense is solely with the Lord of all realms."[28] He wanted no reward from them, and they knew he needed none. His mission was not one of self-interest. He wanted what was best for them. To his message of monotheism he added the same warning the prophets before him had repeatedly issued, "Worship none other than God, for I fear for you the punishment of a momentous day."[29]

The leaders of society replied, "If our Lord had wished to send a messenger, he would have sent down angels. Since he has not, we reject that with which you have been sent."[30] It was the same fallacy their ancestors had used against Noah—that God would only

---

24. *Biḥār al-anwār* vol. 11 p. 357 tr. 15

25. *Biḥār al-anwār* vol. 11 p. 357 tr. 14. The name *Hūd* is not from the same root as *hudā* (guidance) since the second and third root letters have been transposed. Nonetheless, it is common to see such associations in the traditions between names and their linguistic roots. Some have conjectured that these associations are based on what is known as *al-ishtiqāq al-kabīr,* where two words share a common meaning and a common root, but the letters are transposed.

26. *Biḥār al-anwār* vol. 11 p. 361 tr. 21

27. Qur'ān 7:65

28. Qur'ān 26:125–127

29. Qur'ān 46:21

30. Qur'ān 41:14

communicate to humankind through angels. They did not realize that prophets, aside from being messengers, are also the ultimate role models and that angels, who are not subject to human frailties and temptations, could never fulfill this role.

Hūd replied, "Are you surprised that a reminder from your Lord has come to you through a man from among you who has been sent so he can warn you? Remember when God made you inheritors of the earth after the people of Noah were destroyed and enhanced you vastly in your physique. So remember all of God's blessings. Hopefully you will attain success."[31] By reminding them of the countless blessings that surrounded them, he hoped to stir their conscience to remember God who had provided them these blessings and who had saved their ancestors from the flood. Once they recalled the flood, they would have to remember Noah who, as great as he was, had been but a man like himself.

The leaders from among his people refused to let their conscience be cajoled and said, "We deem you to be steeped in foolishness, and we believe you to be among the liars."[32] They could see only two explanations for Hūd's denunciation of their gods: either he had lost his mind and actually believed what he was saying, or he was sane and spoke with malicious intent using lies to misguide them. If the latter was true they were prepared to label him a liar, as they had done to all the other prophets who had come before him.

With characteristic dignity and forbearance, Hūd replied, "O people! I am not afflicted with foolishness. Rather, I am a messenger from the Lord of all realms. I convey to you the messages of my Lord and I am your well-wisher and I am trustworthy.[33] He felt no need to emphasize his rebuttal. He was saying only what they already knew to be true. First, they knew very well that he was no fool. To believe in only one God when all of creation is clearly the coherent product of a single will is perfectly rational. Second, if he were lying to them, it would either be out of malice, whereby he would intentionally adulterate the message he had been given, or

31. Qurʾān 7:69

32. Qurʾān 7:66

33. Qurʾān 7:67–68

out of careless inattention, whereby he would botch the message and fail to communicate it to them faithfully. Hūd, on the other hand, as they knew very well, was their well-wisher and bore them no ill-will and was exceptionally trustworthy and would therefore convey his charge with absolute integrity.

Having failed in their first two attacks, the leaders charged, "Have you come to us so that we worship God alone and abandon what our forefathers used to worship? If so then bring on that with which you threaten us if you are among the truthful."[34] It did not matter to them that what he said was true or that it made sense to them, they honored the tradition of their forebears above all, no matter how nonsensical they knew that tradition to be.

He told them, "The punishment and wrath of your Lord shall undoubtedly befall you. Do you argue with me concerning empty names that you and your forefathers have chosen, for whose existence God has sent down no proof? If you insist, then wait for the impending punishment. I, along with you, am among those who will wait."[35]

It was too much for the leaders of ʿĀd to tolerate such blatant insubordination. They were a people infamous for their use of excessive force. Without compunction, they lashed out at Hūd and beat him savagely to the verge of death. As he hovered on the boundaries of consciousness, they warned him, "If you ever speak of these ideas again, we will beat you so severely that you will think back to today's beating fondly."

He remained unconscious for an entire day. When he came to, he immediately turned to God in prayer and said, "My Lord! I did as you commanded, and you see what they have done."

Gabriel told Hūd, "Your Lord orders you to persevere in your mission. He gives you his word that he will cast terror into their hearts so that they never dare to raise a hand to you again.[36]

---

34. Qurʾān 7:70

35. Qurʾān 7:71

36. *Biḥār al-anwār* vol. 11 p. 361 tr. 21

Hūd Perseveres

As soon as he had recuperated from his battering, he was on the streets calling people again. The leaders reminded him of their threat, but he spoke with such courage and determination that they were forced into silence. He proclaimed, "My people! You have sunken into paganism as the people of Noah did before you. I would now be justified in calling down God's wrath upon you as Noah did upon his people."

They replied defiantly, "Hūd! The gods of Noah's people were weak, but our gods are strong. You see how powerful they have made us."[37]

Afflicted by Drought

When the leaders of ʿĀd so recalcitrantly rebuffed Hūd, God gave them a taste of his chastisement as a foreshadowing of what was in store for them if they continued on their course. For as long as anyone could remember, the rains had soaked the fields of Iram, and the springs had gushed forth with abundant fresh water. For their senseless rejection of the truth, God withheld his rain, and, for the first time, the people of Iram felt the bite of drought.[38]

Hūd hoped that the drought would humble his people enough to remind them how much they depended on God for their sustenance. He may have failed to convince the leaders of Iram, but he now turned successively to other segments of its citizenry. He was determined to convey his teachings to every person who would hear him. On one occasion he told his people, "O people!

---

37. *Biḥār al-anwār* vol. 11 p. 361 tr. 21

38. There is no explicit mention of this drought in the Qurʾān. However, two verses hint at it. In one verse, Hūd tries to entice his people to believe by promising that, in exchange, God "will send down rain upon you in torrents," (11:52) which would only be enticing if they were experiencing a shortage of rain. In another verse, when the people of Iram spotted the clouds on the horizon that eventually would destroy them, they exclaimed in a misguided moment of jubilance, "This is a cloud bringing us rain!" (46:24). Several traditions explicitly mention this drought and corroborate my inference (see *Biḥār al-anwār* vol. 11 p. 351 tr. 2).

Worship God other than whom you have no deity worthy of worship. You all are but fabricators of lies against God. O people! I do not ask you for any recompense for this work. My recompense is solely with the one who created me. Will you not then use your reason to understand this? O people! Seek forgiveness from your Lord, then turn to him and he will send down rain upon you in torrents and he will add strength to your strength. And do not turn away from him like criminals."[39]

Penitent Farmers and Hūd's Wife

Seven years into the drought, a group of penitent farmers from a neighboring city heard his call. When the brunt of the drought hit them, they realized that Hūd's God was real. They came in search of Hūd to seek forgiveness and to ask him to pray to deliver them from the drought. He was not at his home, so they spoke to his wife. She told them mockingly, "If the god who caused this drought really listened to my husband's prayers, do you think his own crops would be scorched by the heat as they are?"

Dejected, they began to second guess their decision to come to Hūd. They thought to themselves, "If his own wife feels this way about him, then maybe he is a false prophet." As they prepared to return to their city, Hūd approached. He heard them out, reassured them that they had made the right decision and prayed to God to give them rain. When they asked him about his wife who so obviously rejected his claims, he simply shook his head and said, "May God give her a long life." They were confused by this prayer, so he explained with great wisdom, "God has made a nemesis for every believer, and she is my nemesis. To have my nemesis under my custodianship is better than to be under the custodianship of my nemesis."[40]

Hūd Severs Ties

Sadly, most of the denizens of Iram did not use their reason as these farmers had. They said, "O Hūd! You have not brought us any proof

---

39. Qur'ān 11:50–52

40. *Biḥār al-anwār* vol. 11 p. 351 tr. 2

for your claims, and we are not going to abandon our gods based solely on what you say, nor shall we believe in you without proof."[41] This was a false indictment since he had shown them numerous miracles[42] as all prophets must. It was they who had been blinded by their stubbornness and failed to accept his miracles for what they were. They continued, "With regard to the reason for your ranting, we believe only that some of our gods have afflicted you with insanity."[43]

Hūd replied to them, "I call on God as a witness, and you also witness, that I hereby sever ties with what you worship other than him. I do not fear your reprisal, so plot altogether against me and give me no respite."[44] If Hūd's previous miracles had had no effect on their hardened hearts, he hoped that his standing alone against them, despite their numbers, wealth, power, and gods, would make them realize that he drew his strength from his faith in, and reliance upon, the one with infinite power.[45] He continued, "I have no fear because I rely upon God, my Lord and your Lord. There is no creature, including all of you, whom he does not hold in absolute control as if by the forelock. My Lord is on a straight and constant path, for he is constant in his aid and just in his retribution. If you persist in turning away, it will not be for any shortcoming on my part, for I have conveyed that with which I was sent to you. My Lord will replace you with another people, and you shall not harm him in any way. He knows what punishment you deserve because my Lord is mindful of everything."[46]

---

41. Qurʾān 11:53–54

42. There is no mention in the Qurʾān of any specific miracles presented by Hūd. However, verse 7:72 explicitly mentions that ʿĀd "denied our miracles" which confirms that Hūd had brought them miracles. More generally speaking, we know that all God's prophets presented miracles to establish their credibility whether or not we know what their specific miracles were (see Qurʾān 7:101).

43. Qurʾān 11:53–54

44. Qurʾān 11:54–55

45. See *Tafsir Muwzu'i* of Shaykh Jawādī Āmulī vol. 6 p. 405.

46. Qurʾān 11:56–57

Moral Decay

Not only were the ʿĀd corrupt in their beliefs, their lifestyle and moral behavior were reprehensible. Their technological advancement had deceived them into thinking themselves invincible. Hūd brought this to their attention and said, "Do you pointlessly build monuments upon every peak? And do you erect buildings in hopes that you will live therein eternally? And when you strike, do you strike excessively? If you are guilty of these crimes, then fear God and obey me. Fear him who has provided you with all these blessings that you know of—provided you with cattle, sons, gardens, and springs. I admonish you thus because I fear for you the punishment of a momentous day."[47]

His admonishments fell on deaf ears. God had endowed them with ears, eyes, and hearts so they could perceive truth. However, their ears, eyes, and hearts did not avail them at all.[48] They callously responded, "It is the same to us whether you admonish or are not among those who admonish. These rantings about a "momentous day" are just like the myths of the ancients.[49] We are not going to be punished."[50]

---

47. Qur'ān 26:128–135

48. Qur'ān 46:26

49. It has been suggested that their sentence "These rantings about a 'momentous day' are just like the myths of the ancients" could alternatively be translated as "These practices of ours are but the traditions of our forefathers." However, upon closer examination, this would have been an unlikely way for them to express this idea. First, they respected the traditions of their forefathers and would not refer to them as "nothing but the traditions of our forefathers" since this expression slights the importance of those traditions. Second, their next statement, "We are not going to be punished," follows naturally after a denial of Hūd's message, not after an assertion that their practices come from their forefathers. In other words, it makes sense for them to say, "Since Hūd's warnings about a day of judgment are false, thus, we shall not be punished." It does not make sense for them to say, "Since our practices originated with our forefathers, thus, we will not be punished," since it is possible that both they and their forefathers be punished.

50. Qur'ān 26:136–138

In one last attempt to fulfill his mission or to conclusively seal his case against the ʿĀd, Hūd told them, "Worship none other than God, for I fear for you the punishment of a momentous day."[51]

They replied, "Have you really come to us to turn us away from our gods? If you really want to do this, then you must bring down upon us that with which you have threatened us, assuming you were truthful in your threats." With this they announced that their commitment to their gods was so complete that only death would make them cease worshiping them.[52]

He told them, "Knowledge of that punishment is only with God. I simply convey to you that with which I have been sent. However, it is no wonder that you understand none of this and challenge me to do what is solely for God, for I find you to be a people wont to be foolish."[53]

Their Fates Are Sealed

In this way, the vast majority of the ʿĀd sealed their own fates. They behaved arrogantly on earth and abandoned what they knew to be right. They boastfully challenged, "Who is more powerful than we?" seemingly oblivious to the fact that God who had created them and given them their power was more powerful than they.[54] They rejected the miracles sent by their Lord, disobeyed his messengers, and followed the orders of every obstinate tyrant.[55]

When every citizen of Iram had heard the call and made his choice to obey or reject, God decreed that all who had rejected must be destroyed. When the command came to destroy them, he sent word to Hūd and those who believed with him letting them know of the fate of their people and ordering them to flee from Iram before the destruction began. God would never unleash his wrath on people who were innocent. He promised to deliver them

---

51. Qurʾān 46:21

52. Qurʾān 46:22

53. Qurʾān 46:23

54. Qurʾān 41:15

55. Qurʾān 11:59

from his wrath in this world and to grant them salvation from his wrath in the hereafter.[56]

Escape From Iram

As Hūd and the believers prepared to leave Iram, they saw ominous clouds on the horizon as a storm brewed. The people of Iram, still intoxicated by their delusions of invincibility, rejoiced at the sight of what appeared to them as clouds approaching their valley. After suffering the effects of a long drought, they were elated and exclaimed, "This is a cloud bringing us rain!"

Hūd ruefully informed them, "Rather, it is what you hastened upon yourselves—a gale in which there is a painful punishment. It will destroy everything by its Lord's leave."[57]

God delivered Hūd and the believers with him out of his mercy, and as they fled, the wind began to pick up. It was a Wednesday, the last Wednesday of the month, a day of the month that would be known evermore as "a day of perpetual misfortune."[58]

Iram Is Utterly Destroyed

For the next seven ill-fated nights and eight ill-fated days, without a moment's respite, God released upon Iram a tempestuous, howling gale to purge them.[59] God had decided to make them taste a degrading punishment in this temporal life, as a foreshadowing of their even more degrading punishment in the hereafter.[60] It was a gale that issued from the very belly of the earth, from below its seventh layer. Never before had such a wind been released upon a people;[61] and never again would it be released until the end of time, for this was the very wind God would use at the end of time

56. Qur'ān 11:58

57. Qur'ān 46:24

58. *Biḥār al-anwār* vol. 11 p. 362 tr. 22 and p. 363 tr. 23–25

59. Qur'ān 69:6–7

60. Qur'ān 41:16

61. *Biḥār al-anwār* vol. 11 p. 352 tr. 3

to destroy the earth completely.[62] He ordered the angel in charge of this wind to release but a modicum of it.[63] On the Day of Judgment, it will be released in full force.[64]

As Hūd had threatened, it "destroyed everything by its Lord's leave."[65] It was a gale like no other, bereft of all benefit. It sought out every person and pursued them mercilessly like fugitives no matter how thoroughly they had barricaded themselves in their homes, and it left their corpses as though they were uprooted palm trunks strewn around.[66] At the end of the eighth day, not a single living thing remained in Iram.[67] In fact, it had turned everything it touched into rubble.[68] Only their empty residences were left standing in ruins.[69]

In all this, God left us a sign—a sign to the believers that God unfailingly fulfills his promises to them; a sign to those who choose to reject God's guidance that his threats of punishment are not empty; and a sign to all people that God has unfathomable power. He is invincible in his dealings with his enemies, the ever-merciful in his dealings with his friends.[70]

A New Beginning

Hūd and the few people who believed along with him fled from Iram and traveled north to the city of Bakkah[71] which was ruled by a man whose mother was a descendant of ʿĀd and who was, thus,

62. *Biḥār al-anwār* vol. 11 p. 354 tr. 5 and p. 355 tr. 12

63. *Biḥār al-anwār* vol. 11 p. 354 tr. 6 and *al-Kāfī* vol. 8 tr. 63–64

64. *Biḥār al-anwār* vol. 11 p. 354 tr. 5 and p. 355 tr. 12

65. Qur'ān 46:24

66. Qur'ān 54:20 and 11:60

67. Qur'ān 69:8 and 7:72

68. Qur'ān 51:41–42

69. Qur'ān 46:25

70. Qur'ān 26:139–140

71. Bakkah was the ancient name for Mecca.

their cousin.[72] In Bakkah, they lived out their days, free to worship God as they had never been free in Iram.[73]

Years later, when Hūd lay on his deathbed, he appointed his successor and prophesied the coming of Ṣāliḥ.[74] When he died, they buried him near the Kaʿbah, the house of worship built by the angels during the time of Adam.[75]

---

72. *Biḥār al-anwār* vol. 11 p. 364

73. *Biḥār al-anwār* vol. 11 p. 359 tr. 15

74. *Biḥār al-anwār* vol. 11 p. 359 tr. 16

75. There are four opinions on the place of Hūd's burial.

- According to one tradition, his grave is in a cave near Ḥaḍramawt in Yemen with a Hebrew inscription over it saying, "I am Prophet Hūd. I believed in God. I showed compassion for the people of ʿĀd despite their non-belief. Nothing could turn back what God commanded" (*Biḥār al-anwār* vol. 11 p. 360 tr. 19). While this is possible, two aspects of the tradition seem out of sorts.
  - First, it is strange that the inscription would be in Hebrew since Hūd was an Arab prophet sent to an Arab people and is not even recognized by the Jewish tradition as a prophet.
  - Second, it is strange that the Yemeni man who reportedly described the grave to Imam ʿAlī was able to read the Hebrew inscription since he was Arab.
- According to a second tradition, his grave is on a mountaintop near Maharah in Yemen in a church where people say a magician is buried. In this same tradition, Imam ʿAlī is reported to have said that the grave in al-Nukhaylah near Kūfah, which people attributed to Hūd, actually belonged to Yahūdā, son of Jacob (*Biḥār al-anwār* vol. 11 p. 360 tr. 18).
- According to a third set of traditions, the same grave in al-Nukhaylah is mentioned as the grave of Hūd, which is named as an important station for the army of Imam al-Mahdī (*Biḥār al-anwār* vol. 52 p. 272 tr. 167). This opinion is further corroborated by a report from Imam ʿAlī's deathbed. He reportedly told Imam al-Ḥasan, "When I die, bury me on the outskirts of this city in the grave of my two brothers, Hūd and Ṣāliḥ" (*Biḥār al-anwār* vol. 5 p. 379 tr. 4)
- ʿAllāmah al-Majlisī mentions that a fourth opinion is that he is buried in the semicircular enclosure next to the Kaʿbah now known as Ḥijr Ismāʿīl, however I could not find this tradition.

There is no apparent way to decide among these opinions. Al-Majlisī entertains the possibility that he was buried in one of these sites and then moved supernaturally to the other sites (*Biḥār al-anwār* vol. 11 p. 360). I simply chose

---

the opinion that made the most sense in the context of the story. Since he reportedly left Yemen and settled in Mecca, it seems reasonable that he would have been buried in Mecca. But God alone knows the truth.

Ṣāliḥ

Thamūd and Their Wonders

After the annihilation of Iram and most of the ʿĀd people in southern Arabia, God's favor shifted to another branch of Noah's Semitic descendants,[1] the tribe of Thamūd. The Thamūd settled in northwestern Arabia near modern-day Tabūk. There they founded a splendid city called Ḥijr in an area known until the early Islamic era as Wādī al-Qurā, the "Valley of a Thousand Cities."[2] They derived their name from their patriarch,

---

1. Qur'ān 23:31 and 7:74. Verse 23:31 says, "Then after their (i.e., the people of Noah's) destruction, we brought about another people," but does not explicitly mention the name of the people. Some commentators have assumed from the phrase "after their (i.e., Noah's people's) destruction" that it is referring to the ʿĀd. However, at the end of this section of the Qur'ān, we are told that these people were destroyed when "a blast (*ṣayḥah*) seized them as they deserved" (23:41). Two other verses, 11:67 and 15:83, tell us explicitly that the Thamūd were destroyed by a *ṣayḥah* or a "blast," but no verse tells us that the ʿĀd were destroyed in such a way. Thus, in my opinion, it is better to attribute the story to Thamūd, who did technically come *after* Noah's people—even if the ʿĀd lived in the intervening years.

2. Qur'ān 15:80. It is commonly believed that Ḥijr was located at the site currently referred to as Madā'in Ṣāliḥ, halfway between Medina and Tabūk, in the Kingdom of Saudi Arabia. Some traditions recount that Prophet Muḥammad stopped there, along with his army, on his way to the Battle of Tabūk in 9 A.H. He ordered his troops not to drink the water of this God-forsaken city and not to perform their ablutions with their water. Then he led them to a well that had belonged to Ṣāliḥ, and they quenched themselves from it. He told them, "Do not demand a sign from your prophet. The Thamūd, to whom Ṣāliḥ was sent, demanded a sign from their prophet. The camel used to come to them out of this canyon and provide them with milk on the days when it was her turn to drink their water. Yet, they slaughtered her and were given an ultimatum of three days. God's promise was not proven false. A squall seized them, and not a single person under the sky was spared." The next day, Prophet Muḥammad allowed his soldiers to explore the ruins of Madā'in Ṣāliḥ and encouraged them to ponder their fate and to instill fear in themselves lest they earn a similar fate (*Mawsūʿah al-ta'rīkh* vol. 2 p. 450-452). The ruins at Madā'in Ṣāliḥ still stand.

Thamūd, son of ʿĀthir, son of Iram, son of Shem, son of Noah.[3]

The Thamūd were especially resourceful in the construction of Ḥijr. They carved intricate complexes with hundreds of interconnected cells deep into the sandstone mountains thereby transforming the mountains of Wādī al-Qurā into secure homes.[4] Yet they did not stop at carving homes into the mountains. They made use of the excavated stone to build grand palaces in the valleys[5] thereby alleviating the problem of disposing of enormous quantities of stone debris while saving the unnecessary effort of hewing new rock for their palaces.[6]

The city of Ḥijr was surrounded by exquisite natural beauty. There was abundant water flowing in springs, and these allowed the Thamūd to cultivate their crops, lush gardens, and date orchards, which yielded especially supple fruits.[7]

Sadly, God's innumerable blessings were not enough to hold the attention of the Thamūd, and, like so many before them, they fell prey to their own whims and desires. They eventually came to worship a pantheon of no less than seventy idols.[8]

There are magnificent stone tombs hewn into the mountains (Savingac, Peter and Pere Jaussen. "The Monuments-II." *Saudi Aramco World* Sept-Oct. 1965: 18-19) which are reminiscent of the description we are offered in the Qurʾān (15:82 and 89:9).

However, archeological studies date these structures to the 1st century C.E., to the Nabataean people (Harrigan, Peter. "New Pieces of Mada'in Salih's Puzzle." *Saudi Aramco World* July-Aug. 2007: 14-23), not to the prehistoric Thamūd who likely lived thousands, if not tens of thousands, of years before the Common Era. Apparently, the Nabataeans built their city on the ruins of the Thamūd's Ḥijr. It is even possible that the stone tombs belonged, not to the Nabataeans, but to the Thamūd. This would explain why Prophet Muḥammad encouraged his troops to walk through these ruins to remind them of the fate of Ṣāliḥ's people.

3. *Biḥār al-anwār* vol. 11 p. 377 tr. 1

4. Qurʾān 15:82, 89:9, and 26:149

5. Qurʾān 7:74

6. Harrigan, Peter. "New Pieces of Mada'in Salih's Puzzle." *Saudi Aramco World* July-Aug. 2007: 14-23

7. Qurʾān 26:147-8

8. *Biḥār al-anwār* vol. 11 p. 377 tr. 2

Ṣāliḥ is Chosen

Among the Thamūd people, there was a boy named Ṣāliḥ.[9] From an early age, he demonstrated keen aptitude and moral excellence. His tribesmen came to rest their hopes upon him, believing that he would one day become their leader.[10] They were correct in presaging his future as their leader but not at all in the manner in which they expected.

When Ṣāliḥ reached the age of sixteen, God appointed him as a prophet to the Thamūd.[11] Ṣāliḥ diligently set out to call his people to God saying, "My people! Worship God other than whom you have no deity worthy of worship, for he created you from the earth and made you dwell upon it. Since he is your only creator and Lord, seek absolution from him for your polytheism and sin and turn toward him from now on. My Lord is near and answers my prayers."[12] They believed in God and knew he was their creator. But they insisted that he was too great and too distant for them to worship and that they must worship lesser gods who were nearer at hand and could, thus, hear their prayers better. Ṣāliḥ wanted them to know that no lesser gods existed. Their creator was the only god, and despite his greatness, he was always near to his servants, ready to hear their every prayer.

As with all God's prophets, Ṣāliḥ confirmed his legitimacy not only through his strength of character and well-reasoned message but by means of multiple miracles.[13]

---

9. *A'lām al-qur'ān* has collected several different possible lineages for Ṣāliḥ (p. 501).

10. Qur'ān 11:62

11. *Biḥār al-anwār* vol. 11 p. 378 tr. 3 and p. 383 tr. 8

12. Qur'ān 11:61

13. The Qur'ān does not tell us what Ṣāliḥ's initial miracles were. It only tells us that there were multiple miracles, all of which the majority of Thamūd rejected (15:81).

Thamūd's Response

Nonetheless, when he told his people, "Worship God," they immediately fell into two quarreling factions.[14] There were a few who, like Ṣāliḥ, were attuned to their natural disposition to worship the one God[15] and had never bowed to any pantheon of idols. They heard Ṣāliḥ's simple call with eagerness and responded with their hearts and minds. The vast majority of Thamūd, on the other hand, were arrogant and blind to anything but worldly gain, and they saw their purpose better served by maintaining the status quo. They rejected God's prophet and defied God himself because of their propensity for excess.[16]

They were surprised by what they perceived to be Ṣāliḥ's sudden betrayal of their heritage. They said, "Ṣāliḥ, You were one in whom we placed our hopes before all this. Do you now forbid us to worship that which our forefathers have worshiped even though we are in doubt about that to which you call us?"[17]

He replied, "My people, tell me: If I have a miracle from my Lord, and he has given me divine knowledge as a mercy from him, then who will defend me against God if I disobey him and abandon my mission? In asking me to do so, you add only to the loss in which you seek to place me."[18]

The Thamūd thought perhaps Ṣāliḥ had devised some ploy to exploit his position among them or that he had fallen prey to some sorcery. They said, "You are but from among those bewitched."[19]

But he declared to them, "Do you not fear God? I am for you a trustworthy messenger. So fear God and obey me. I do not ask you

14. Qur'ān 27:45

15. Qur'ān 30:30

16. Qur'ān 91:11

17. Qur'ān 11:62

18. Qur'ān 11:63

19. Qur'ān 26:153

for any recompense for this work. My recompense is solely with the Lord of all realms."[20]

Ṣāliḥ's Wife

Even Ṣāliḥ's wife worked against him. Her name was Ṣadūf. She was renowned to be beautiful and came from a wealthy family. Her wealth was from cattle: camels, cows, and sheep. She was one of Ṣāliḥ's worst enemies who encouraged the people of Ḥijr to defy her husband and to hold fast to their old ways.[21]

Ṣāliḥ Calls and Thamūd Rejects

Ṣāliḥ tried to remind them of God's great blessings to them, past and present. He told them, "Remember when God made you inheritors of the earth after the people of ʿĀd and established you in this land so that you now erect palaces on its plains and carve homes into the mountains. Thus, remember these gifts of God and do not cause corruption in this land."[22] He asked them, "Do you really think you will be left, safe from God's inquisition, immersed in what vast blessings that are here in the land of Ḥijr, immersed in gardens and springs and crops and date palms whose fruits are supple while you expertly carve dwellings from mountains? So fear God and obey me. And do not obey the commands of the excessive who cause corruption on earth, not reform."[23]

Seeing that Ṣāliḥ's logic and goodwill were having their effect on their people, the leaders from among Thamūd, who were arrogant, said to those who were helpless, to those who believed from among them, "Do you really think that Ṣāliḥ is a messenger from his Lord?!"

They replied, "We truly believe in that with which he has been sent."[24]

---

20. Qurʾān 26:142-145

21. *Majmaʿ al-bayān* vol. 4 p. 682

22. Qurʾān 7:74

23. Qurʾān 26:146-152

24. Qurʾān 7:75

Those who were arrogant said, "We deny that in which you believe."[25] These leaders from among his people, who had refused to believe and had denied that they would meet their maker in the hereafter and whom God had made affluent in the temporal world, said to those who had declared their faith, "This man is but a human being like you. He eats of what you eat, and he drinks of what you drink. We swear, if you obey a man who is like you, then you shall be losers."[26] They clothed their objection in the cloak of a genuine theological problem. However, that their prophet was a mere mortal and not an angel was not their primary difficulty. They were actually jealous that God should choose Ṣāliḥ over them. They said, "Shall we follow one single man who is from among us? We shall then be in error and insanity. Has this reminder been sent to him to the exclusion of all of us? No, rather he is an arrogant liar."[27]

They also rejected Ṣāliḥ's claim that there would be an afterlife and a Day of Judgment. They said, "Does he promise you that when you die and become dust and bones that you shall be brought forth from the grave? Absurd! Absurd is what you are being promised! There is but our temporal life. Some of us die and others live in their place, but we shall not be raised. He is but a man who has falsely attributed lies to God, and we do not believe in him."[28] They not only denied the Day of Reckoning but also the great catastrophe of Armageddon that would end this world order and mark the beginning of the hereafter.[29]

Ṣāliḥ did all he could to guide the Thamūd, but they preferred remaining blind to heeding his guidance.[30] After debating with them to no avail, he turned to God and prayed, "Lord! Aid me through that which they deny." He felt that the only cure for their adamant denial was for them to witness the life after death themselves.

25. Qur'ān 7:76

26. Qur'ān 23:33-34

27. Qur'ān 54:24-25

28. Qur'ān 23:35-38

29. Qur'ān 69:4

30. Qur'ān 41:17

God replied forebodingly, "After a short while, they shall become remorseful.[31] They shall know tomorrow at Judgment Day who is truly the arrogant liar. We shall send them a she-camel to test them, so give them respite and persevere in calling them. And inform them that the water is to be divided between them and the camel. Each one's turn at the water will be monitored."[32]

A Contest of the Gods

When Ṣāliḥ had spent a lifetime preaching to his people, trying to convince them to leave their idols and worship God alone, all to no avail, he addressed them with great fervor saying, "I was sent to you when I was but 16 years old. I have now reached 120 years. I present to you two choices: If you wish, ask something of me that I can in turn ask of my God to see if he answers. And if you wish, I shall ask something of your gods. If they answer my request, I shall leave your midst, for you are tired of me, and I am tired of you."

His people said with uncharacteristic sincerity, "This is very fair of you." And they agreed on a day and a place to have the contest. For three days prior to the contest, they gathered at the foot of their sacred mountain where they were wont to gather annually to worship their idols and offer blood sacrifices and food and drink to them.[33] They brought their idols to this mountain and told Ṣāliḥ to begin by asking their gods what he wished.

Ṣāliḥ approached the greatest of all their idols and asked them his name. When they told him, he called on the idol by his name, but it did not respond. Ṣāliḥ turned to his people and asked, "What is wrong? Why does he not answer?" His people were puzzled and told him to ask another. He asked another and another, taking each one's name, but none of them answered. He told his people, "You have seen me call each of your gods, and not one of them has

---

31. Qur'ān 23:39-40

32. Qur'ān 54:26-28. God knew ahead of time that the Thamūd would challenge him to produce a camel from the mountain. He devised his plan accordingly, long before they even thought to challenge him.

33. *Biḥār al-anwār* vol. 11 p. 385 tr. 11

answered me. Now, ask anything of me, and I shall ask my Lord to answer you immediately."

The people of Thamūd turned in desperation to their idols and asked, "What is the matter? Why do you not answer Ṣāliḥ?" When they still did not answer, they asked Ṣāliḥ to give them some room to speak in private with their gods. They smeared themselves in dirt to humble themselves before their gods and told them, "If you do not answer Ṣāliḥ, we shall be disgraced."

When they called Ṣāliḥ to address them again, he said, "The entire day has passed, and I do not believe your gods are going to answer me. Ask anything of me, and I shall ask my Lord to answer you immediately."

Seventy of the most esteemed men from the city were elected. They said, "Ṣāliḥ, we shall ask you something."

Ṣāliḥ asked them, "Do the rest of the people accept you to speak on their behalf?"

The people replied unanimously, "Yes. If these seventy accept your claim, we shall also accept."

The seventy men said, "Ṣāliḥ, we shall ask you for something. If your lord answers us, we shall follow you, and everyone in our city will follow you."

Ṣāliḥ said, "Ask whatever you wish."

They said, "Let us go to that mountain, for we shall ask you over there." So they walked together toward the mountain. When they were at its base, they said, "Ṣāliḥ, you are but a human like us, so it is hard for us to accept that you are God's messenger to us. Bring us a miracle if you are truthful.[34] Ask your lord to bring forth for us from this mountain this very instant a she-camel with a thick, deep-red coat that is heavy with calf. It must bear its calf immediately and its udders should be ladened with milk."

The She-Camel

Ṣāliḥ replied, "You have asked for something that is impossible for me but easy for my Lord." Ṣāliḥ turned his focus to God and begged him to answer them. In an instant, there was a deafening,

34. Qur'ān 26:154

maddening explosion as the mountain split apart. The mountain trembled like a mother at the climax of labor. Then they could see the camel's head poking out of the crack. And then it pulled itself completely out of the mountain and stood upright.

The Thamūd exclaimed, "How fast has your Lord answered us! Ask him to also bring forth her calf. So he did, and she bore her calf, and, after some moments, it ran tremulously in circles around her.

Ṣāliḥ asked them, "Is there anything else?"

They said, "No. Let us go back to our people so we can tell them what we have seen. They will undoubtedly believe in you."[35]

The Thamūd were anxiously awaiting the return of Ṣāliḥ and their seventy tribesmen. Those who believed in Ṣāliḥ were eager to hear of Ṣāliḥ's victory. The leaders of Thamūd were nervous that their entire social order was on the brink of revolution.

With a beaming expression, Ṣāliḥ approached his people drawing behind him a magnificent camel and her newborn calf. He stood before the gathered crowd and announced in a tone that all could hear, "My people! Worship God other than whom you have no deity worthy of worship. A clear sign has come to you from your Lord. This is God's camel which has come as a sign for you. So let it graze on God's earth, and do not let the slightest harm come to her lest a painful punishment befall you."[36]

Then Ṣāliḥ announced, "This camel is a test for you. The water of Ḥijr is to be divided between you and her.[37] She gets a turn at the water on an appointed day, and you all get a turn at the water on an appointed day.[38] Each one's turn at the water will be monitored."[39]

On the camel's day, she would miraculously drink all of their water, first thing in the morning, until the wells ran dry. Then she would stand in the middle of the city and allow the Thamūd to milk her, and, miraculously, her milk would suffice them all. The

---

35. *Biḥār al-anwār* vol. 11 p. 378 tr. 3 and p. 383 tr. 8 and p. 389-90 tr. 14

36. Qur'ān 7:73, 11:64, and 26:156

37. Qur'ān 54:27-28

38. Qur'ān 26:155

39. Qur'ān 54:28

following day, the camel would not even approach the water, but would allow the Thamūd to draw water at will for themselves and their livestock.[40] In short, it was a test of discipline more than anything material. God wanted to see if the Thamūd were willing to modify their lives to accommodate the camel he had created for them. In return, he gave them the blessing of unlimited milk. Nevertheless, the intrusion was too much for a people who loathed bowing to any will but their own. Repeatedly, Ṣāliḥ reminded them, "Mind God's camel and its drinking rights."[41]

The Plot to Kill Her

In the city of Ḥijr, there were nine men from among the leaders who spread corruption in that land and did not work for its betterment.[42] They had watched their power dwindle as their people began to honor Ṣāliḥ's camel and heed his message of monotheism and social justice. Now, they decided, was their final chance to conspire together to rout Ṣāliḥ once and for all.[43] They believed their people would revert to their old ways in an instant if only they could rid themselves of the dreaded camel. They elected from their midst a man named Qudār whom they made their henchman and to whom they entrusted the task of destroying the camel.[44] Qudār was a fair-skinned and ruddy man with blue eyes. He had been an illegitimate child,[45] yet he commanded respect among his people.[46] Nonetheless, for his unparalleled heartlessness and stalwart defiance of truth, he would go down in history as the most wretched person[47] from

40. *Biḥār al-anwār* vol. 11 p. 386 tr. 11 and p. 388 tr. 14

41. Qur'ān 91:13

42. Qur'ān 27:48

43. *Biḥār al-anwār* vol. 11 p. 384 tr. 8

44. Qur'ān 54:29

45. *Biḥār al-anwār* vol. 11 p. 386 tr. 11

46. *Majma' al-bayān* vol. 4 p. 682

47. Qur'ān 91:14

all past generations, from the time of Adam until the advent of Islam, thousands of years later.[48]

The next day, it was the camel's day to drink. Qudār lay in wait for her near the well. As she began to drink, he drew his blade and struck at her throat and, in so doing, rebelled against his Lord's commandment.[49] She staggered, and he struck her again, and she fell. Her calf, who had been cowering next to her, ran off in alarm and scampered up a nearby mountain to safety.[50]

The commotion of the bloody slaughter attracted the attention of the citizens of Ḥijr. The first people to arrive at the scene looked on, aghast at what Qudār had done. They reminded him of Ṣāliḥ's warning—"Do not let the slightest harm come to her lest a painful punishment befall you."[51]

However, Qudār and his eight co-conspirators allayed their fears with cool bravado. They cried out in defiance to no one in particular but for all to hear, "O Ṣāliḥ! Bring down upon us that with which you threaten us if you are truly among the messengers."[52] With their actions and their words, they sought to prove that Ṣāliḥ, notwithstanding his fancy words and his flashy trick, was bluffing and touting empty threats. After all, if the camel had truly belonged to Ṣāliḥ's god, would that god not have protected it?

Their actions and words had the desired effect. The Thamūd's prior gasps of astonishment faded into silent consent and finally into zealous nods of support. Qudār finished butchering the camel while the others kindled a fire. In no time at all, the camel's meat was roasted and everyone, adults and children alike, had partaken

---

48. *Biḥār al-anwār* vol. 11 p. 393. It might seem puzzling that Qudār earned such a superlative as *ashqā al-awwalīn,* "the most wretched person from all past generations," even though his crime was only killing a camel which hardly seems like the worst of crimes, even if that camel was a miraculous gift from God. Perhaps the answer lies in realizing that his superlative wretchedness refers, not to the nature of this particular crime, but to him as a person and the supreme wretchedness of rebelling against God.

49. Qur'ān 7:77

50. *Biḥār al-anwār* vol. 11 p. 386 tr. 11

51. Qur'ān 7:73, 11:64, and 26:156

52. Qur'ān 7:77

of an extemporaneous feast on its forbidden flesh.[53] Only a handful of Ṣāliḥ's devotees abstained and launched a silent protest by leaving the gathering and reporting to Ṣāliḥ who had not yet learned of the day's events.

A Second Chance

When Ṣāliḥ arrived on the scene, he witnessed the carnage in sheer horror. His hope for his people's salvation was rapidly waning. The Thamūd's defiance had earned them God's wrath, but the All-Beneficent was willing to give them one final chance to redeem themselves. Ṣāliḥ said, "Live at ease in your homes for three final days. This is an ultimatum not to be defied." He told them that during these three days they would see signs of God's power. On the first day, their faces would turn yellowish; on the second day, they would become reddish; and on the third and final day, they would turn blackish.[54] "During these three days," he told them, "if you are able to seek out the camel's calf and treat it as you were supposed to treat its mother, God may still forgive you."[55]

Qudār and his co-conspirators repeated their defiant challenge, "O Ṣāliḥ! Bring down upon us that with which you threaten us if you are truly among the messengers."[56]

Ṣāliḥ felt sorely disappointed. He said, "My people! Why do you hasten the onslaught of evil rather than goodness? If only you would seek God's forgiveness, perhaps you would be shown mercy."[57] Granted, they had committed a terrible sin; but he wondered why, instead of seeking forgiveness for what they had done, they were daring God to punish them.

---

53. *Biḥār al-anwār* vol. 11 p. 386 tr. 11

54. *Biḥār al-anwār* vol. 11 p. 386 tr. 11

55. *Biḥār al-anwār* vol. 11 p. 392

56. Qur'ān 7:77

57. Qur'ān 27:46

Yellow in the Face

The Thamūd heeded neither his warnings nor his pleading. They celebrated heartily that evening giving no thought to either. In the morning, when they found that their faces appeared unusually sallow, even yellowish, their nine leaders convinced them that Ṣāliḥ was playing tricks on them. They found Ṣāliḥ and berated him and his followers saying, "We trace all our misfortune to you and to those who are with you."[58] They felt their status quo had been upset only because Ṣālīh had blasphemed their gods and cast doubt upon their powers.

Ṣāliḥ retorted, "Your misfortune is written with God and is only a result of your own evil deeds." To blame Ṣāliḥ for their "misfortune" was like blaming a doctor for the disease he diagnoses. The blame lay squarely with them for clinging to false ideas and defying truth, not with him whose aim was but to guide them back to God. He continued, "However, do not think this is the full extent of your misfortune, for you are a people who shall be punished."[59] He wished to let them know that the "misfortune" they had seen until then was nothing compared to the punishment God had in store for them for their crimes.

The Plot to Kill Him

The confederation of nine men swore to God and then said to one another, "We shall kill him and his family by night, then we shall tell his avenger that we were not present at the death of that avenger's relatives and that we are truthful."[60] With the notable exception of his wife,[61] Ṣāliḥ's relatives comprised a large contingent of his meager ranks of followers, so they knew that killing these would guarantee the eradication of Ṣāliḥ's movement, and they thought this would render Ṣāliḥ's god impotent to be able to destroy them as he had threatened. They accounted for the unfortunate

---

58. Qur'ān 27:47

59. Qur'ān 27:47

60. Qur'ān 27:49

61. *Majmaʿ al-bayān* vol. 4 p. 682

consequences: Ṣāliḥ's other relatives, though not with him, would nonetheless be up in arms over his murder insofar as he was their relative. With this compact, they wished to prevent any such retribution by them, for if they could not find anyone willing to implicate the guilty parties, they would have no one upon whom to take their revenge.

They plotted in this way, and God plotted too though these men did not perceive it.[62] On the next day, God made the whole city's faces reddish, and, on the third day, blackish, all in preparation for their final destruction.[63]

Deliverance of the Innocent

On the eve of the appointed day, God sent word to Ṣāliḥ and those who believed with him and were God-fearing.[64] He wished to deliver them from the land of Ḥijr to reward them for their selfless devotion to his cause. He delivered them from the destruction and disgrace of that fateful day through a special mercy of his which he reserves for believers.[65] They set out together under the cover of darkness. As Ṣāliḥ led them out, his final words to his people were, "My people! I conveyed to you the message of my Lord, and I was your well-wisher, but you clearly do not love well-wishers."[66]

Thamūd's Destruction

As dawn drew near, a fierce quake struck Ḥijr[67] accompanied by a terrible blast.[68] It was a single blast, but when it struck, the denizens of the city became like fodder mulched by a shepherd for his sheep to eat.[69] The blast struck them like a thunderbolt as they but gazed

---

62. Qur'ān 27:50

63. *Biḥār al-anwār* vol. 11 p. 386 tr. 11

64. Qur'ān 27:53 and 41:18

65. Qur'ān 11:66

66. Qur'ān 7:79

67. Qur'ān 7:78

68. Qur'ān 15:83

69. Qur'ān 54:31

on, helpless to defend themselves.[70] The earth let up a sound, as it swallowed them, like that of an iron pickaxe striking, but once, at rocky soil.[71] In an instant, all of them were left as corpses in their homes.[72] They were not able to so much as stand to evade the punishment themselves nor were they aided by anyone else.[73] When it happened, what they had been amassing—their vast wealth and their dwellings, which they had carved into the mountains—did not avail them in the least.[74] It was, by all estimations, an overwhelming punishment,[75] a demeaning punishment,[76] but a well-deserved punishment[77] that enveloped them and leveled their city.[78] Their entire civilization and everything and everyone in it was reduced to debris.[79]

Their dwellings were completely razed to the ground[80] such that it was impossible to imagine that they had been inhabited only a few instants before.[81] It made no difference to God that only one man had actually killed the camel, for people are bound together by their approval and dissatisfaction of deeds, their loyalty to and disavowal of ideals. God punished them all because they all approved of his deed and, in so doing, adopted it as their own.[82]

---

70. Qur'ān 51:44

71. *Nahj al-balāghah* sermon 201

72. Qur'ān 7:78 and 11:67

73. Qur'ān 51:45

74. Qur'ān 15:84

75. Qur'ān 69:5

76. Qur'ān 41:17

77. Qur'ān 23:41

78. Qur'ān 91:14

79. Qur'ān 23:41

80. Qur'ān 27:52

81. Qur'ān 11:68

82. *Nahj al-balāghah* sermon 201

Whereas they had schemed to prevent Ṣāliḥ's heirs from avenging his death, God did not have the slightest fear of retribution for destroying them,[83] for God is the Powerful, the Invincible.[84]

The Lessons in Their Destruction

In the story of the Thamūd and their ultimate destruction, there is a sign for those willing to consider.[85] God blessed them profusely, guided them with a prophet and miracles, forgave their repeated transgressions, and gave them multiple chances to reform. But they persisted in their evil ways, rebuked and reviled God's prophet, defied God's warnings, denied the final judgment, and slaughtered God's gift to them. Let it be known! The Thamūd rejected their Lord. Let it be known! The Thamūd are forever outcast from God's mercy.[86]

A Fresh Start

With his small band of faithful followers, Ṣāliḥ proceeded eastward to the city of Kūfah where his forefather Noah had lived generations before.[87] There, they began the work of building a community of

---

83. Qur'ān 91:15

84. Qur'ān 11:66

85. Qur'ān 51:43

86. Qur'ān 11:68 and 23:41

87. We do not have any reliable indication of Ṣāliḥ's life with his followers after they left Ḥijr. All we do know is that he was buried in Najaf since Imam ʿAlī told Imam al-Ḥasan, "When I die, bury me on the outskirts of this city in the grave of my two brothers, Hūd and Ṣāliḥ" (*Biḥār al-anwār* vol. 5 p. 379 tr. 4). (Incidentally, this tradition is the main evidence for the third opinion on Hūd's burial place as I mentioned at the end of his story.)

There are two traditions that speak of Ṣāliḥ's life after the destruction of Ḥijr.

- The first says that he left his people for many years and returned as an old man. His people were first divided as to whether he was truly Ṣāliḥ. Finally, he was able to convince them (*Kamāl al-dīn* vol. 1 p. 168). This tradition is problematic for several reasons.
    - It tells us that Ṣāliḥ looked significantly different from what he had looked like when they knew him. It seems, from the tradition, that he actually looked like a totally different person, not just that he

faith, free from the obstinacy and arrogance of Thamūd. Ṣāliḥ lived out his years in this city, and when he died, was buried next to his ancestors, Noah and Adam, on the outskirts of Kūfah in modern-day Najaf.[88]

---

had grown old and decrepit. While this is possible, it is unusual.

- His people asked him to tell them something that would convince them that he was Ṣāliḥ. He told them he was the one who brought forth the she-camel and that it was supposed to drink one day and the people were allowed to drink on the alternate days. When he told them this, they declared their renewed faith and accepted him as Ṣāliḥ. It seems very unlikely that these two pieces of information would have served to convince these people of Ṣāliḥ's identity. Anyone could have known this, so it hardly seems like proof.
- This tradition refers to verses 7:75-76. However, it attributes the quotations in these verses in a strange way. In particular, the phrase "Do you really think that Ṣāliḥ is a messenger from his Lord?!" was originally a rhetorical question asked of the believers by the arrogant leadership of Thamūd. However, in this tradition, it is trimmed to "Ṣāliḥ is a messenger from his Lord" which is a declarative statement and is attributed to God as though God is affirming for the people that Ṣāliḥ is indeed his prophet. Not only is such an allusion strange, what makes it stranger is that the statement "Ṣāliḥ is a messenger from his Lord" is totally irrelevant to the immediate problem facing Ṣāliḥ's followers at that moment. None of those people doubt that Ṣāliḥ was a messenger of God. Their only question is, "Is this man before us really Ṣāliḥ?"

Because I have not been able to answer these questions about this tradition, I have not incorporated it into my narrative.

- The second tradition tells us that Ṣāliḥ is later sent to a people called *Aṣḥāb al-Rass* who are different from the *Aṣḥāb al-Rass* mentioned in the Qur'ān (25:38 and 50:12). According to this tradition, these people killed him. Then God sent two more people to guide them. When the people continued to reject, they were cast into the ocean by a wind (*Biḥār al-anwār* vol. 11 p. 388 tr. 13). While this story is plausible, I did not incorporate it into my narrative, mainly because I have no way of linking it with the story told in the Qur'ān. We know nothing about these *Aṣḥāb al-Rass* or the other guides who were sent to them or their destruction by a wind. In the end, God knows best, and I refer this tradition back to him without rejecting it outright.

88. *Biḥār al-anwār* vol. 11 p. 379 tr. 4

Abraham, Ishmael, & Isaac

An Ill-Omen in the Sky

Nimrod[1] was the first king to rule all of Mesopotamia as a unified entity.[2] He ruled from his capital at Kūthā Rubā which was located in the vicinity of modern-day Kūfah.[3] He was the first king to ever mint gold and silver coins.[4] However, he became so intoxicated with power that he deluded himself into thinking he was a god.[5]

---

1. He is known in Arabic as *Numrūd ibn Kan'ān.* He is mentioned in the Old Testament as the ruler of Babel (Genesis 10:8–12). However, there has not been any archeological finding that would help us place this king in a particular time in history ("Nimrod." *Encyclopædia Britannica. Encyclopedia Britannica Online Library Edition.* Encyclopædia Britannica, 2011. Web. 19 May 2011).

2. The tradition tells us that four kings "ruled all the earth;" two of these were good: Solomon and Dhū al-Qarnayn, and two were evil: Nimrod and Nebuchadnezzar (*Biḥār al-anwār* vol. 12 p. 36 tr. 13). I believe it is more plausible to translate the phrase *malaka al-arḍ kullahā* as "ruled all the Holy Land" or "ruled all *the Land*," rather than saying they "ruled all the earth." None of these kings, nor any king yet, has ruled all the earth. No one even ruled all of the inhabited world at the time. At most, they were unique for ruling over the Middle East, or Mesopotamia, or the Holy Land as a unified entity.

3. The city of Abraham's birth is referred to in traditions as Kūthā. Al-Ḥamawī says, "Kūthā is the name given to three places: one is a place near Kūfah in Iraq in the land of Babel; the second is a place in Mecca. The Kūthā in Iraq is itself two places (thus, making the three that he promised)—one is called Kūthā al-Ṭarīq, and the other is Kūthā Rubā which is the city in which Abraham was born in which he was cast into the fire and in which his grave is located (I will quote a tradition from Imam al-Ṣādiq that places his death in the Holy Land, though it is remotely possible that his grave be in Kūfah as mentioned here). These are two distinct places in the land of Babel" (*Mu'jam al-buldān* vol. 4 p. 487). Al-Mas'ūdī says that Ur is a city from the area of Kūthā which is located near modern day Kūfah (see *Encyclopaedia of Islam.* Leiden: E.J. Brill, 1913–1936. p. 1169). Since there is no clear record of these places, it seems we have to suffice ourselves with these conjectures. What is clear is that Kūthā or Ur or both were located near Kūfah.

4. *Biḥār al-anwār* vol. 10 p. 80. tr. 1

5. Qur'ān 2:258

Nimrod's closest advisor and confidante was an astrologer and idol-maker named Āzar.[6] Once, Āzar spent the entire night studying the stars and planets and contemplating their unusual movements.[7] Near dawn, he burst into Nimrod's palace frantically

---

6. *Biḥār al-anwār* vol. 12 p. 29 tr. 6

7. Shaykh al-Anṣārī (d.1281/1864) has discussed the legality of astrological calculations and predictions at great length in his opus, *al-Makāsib* (vol. 1 of 6 p. 201–232). However, what concerns us here is not the legality but the legitimacy of such predictions. The predominant view of Shīʿī scholars is that there is no causal link between the movements of the stars and planets and natural phenomena. They do however believe that their movements and formations are *indicators* of natural phenomena. However, for two main reasons, astrological predictions are usually incorrect and should never be relied upon.

- First, there is such a tremendous amount of data to be considered that human beings, with their limited capacities, cannot consistently make accurate predictions.
- Second, the destiny of the world and its components is contingent upon human actions (this contingency of destiny is known as *badāʾ*). Just because the stars tell us one thing today does not mean that what they predict will actually occur since it is possible for something to happen that changes the course of destiny.

I will share several traditions that show, on the one hand, that the movements of the stars and planets do provide information and, on the other, that we must not pay this information any heed.

- ʿAbd al-Raḥmān ibn Sayābah told Imam al-Ṣādiq, "People say that it is not permissible to study the stars. However, they (i.e., the stars) amaze me. If they are harmful to me from a religious perspective, then I shall never study them since I have no need for what harms me from a religious perspective. But if they are not harmful to me from a religious perspective, then, by God, I yearn for them and I yearn to study them."

  Imam al-Ṣādiq told him, "It is not as they have said. Studying them (i.e., the stars) does not harm you from a religious perspective. However, you (i.e., people in general) study an aspect of them, much of which cannot be known, and little of which has no benefit" (*Wasāʾil al-shīʿah* vol. 17.2.24.1 tr. 22195).
- A village chief from the Persians approached Imam ʿAlī as he set out for battle against the Khawārij. After saluting him, he said, "O Commander of the Faithful! The rising stars bring an ill omen...On a day like this, any sensible person would hide. This day is to be a difficult day for you. Two planets have changed places, the fire has faded from your zodiac, and war is not in your best interest." Imam ʿAlī proceeded to inform

searching for his king. Upon entering the king's chambers, he exclaimed, "I have seen something strange in the stars this night! According to my calculations, a child is to be born soon in Kūthā who will bring an end to our religion and our civilization. He will destroy us and call people to a new religion. It is not long before he is born. We must act fast."[8]

Nimrod asked him, "Has this boy been conceived yet?"

Āzar replied, "He has not. And that is why you must act immediately to separate all the men and women of Kūthā so this monster cannot be conceived."

---

him of so many events that had occurred throughout the world, about which the chief, despite his calculations, knew nothing. Then he said, "My master, Prophet Muḥammad, and I are neither of the east nor of the west. We are the pole around which the stars turn and the beacons to which the heavens look for guidance. As for this that you say, 'The fire has faded from your zodiac,' it was more fitting that you deem it a good omen for me than an ill omen. Its brilliance is still with me, and its burning has left me. This is a very complex issue. Make your calculations only if you think you are qualified" (*al-Iḥtijāj* vol. 1 p. 239).

- In another tradition, someone tells him not to ride to Nahrawān because the stars are not good. He replies, "Do you really think you can guide me to the moment in which I shall be saved from harm if I travel and that you can warn me of the moment in which I shall be harmed if I travel? If anyone believes you, he has thereby rejected the Qur'ān and deemed himself needless of God's help in attaining what he likes and avoiding want he dislikes..." Then he turned to the people and said, "O people! Beware of studying the stars except for the purpose of navigating on land or on sea, for it leads one to fortune-telling. The fortune-teller is like a magician, and the magician is like an unbeliever, and the unbeliever is doomed to hellfire." Then he ordered his troops, "In the name of God, forward march!" (*Nahj al-balāghah* sermon 79).

8. I have relied on several traditions to write the story of Abraham's birth and childhood. They can be found in *Biḥār al-anwār* vol. 12 p. 29 tr. 6 and p. 41 tr. 30 and p. 42 tr. 31. Notably, these traditions are not completely consistent with each other. I have had to use some discretion in choosing which facts to use. I have tried to choose those facts that fit most naturally in the story.

Against All Odds

Immediately, the royal edict was issued and executed. For several days, no men were permitted to have any contact with their women. Only in the palace and in Āzar's household was the edict not enforced since they knew that the king and his closest advisor's family could not conceivably give birth to the child in the prophecy. This is why Āzar's brother, Terah,[9] was not barred

---

9. There is a lot of confusion over the identity of Abraham's father and the relationship of Āzar to Abraham. The Qur'ān and many traditions refer to Āzar as the *ab* (literally "father") of Abraham. Nonetheless, for several reasons, we cannot take this usage literally and must construe *ab* to mean "uncle" or "maternal grandfather," not "father." I will first present evidence from the Qur'ān and traditions that prevent us from accepting that Āzar was his father. I will then present evidence from the Qur'ān that shows that *ab* can indeed be used for an uncle or grandfather.

Evidence from the Qur'ān:

- During Abraham's childhood, after exhausting all possible ways to guide Āzar, Abraham finally realized that Āzar was an enemy of God with no hope of ever reforming. Because of this, he severed ties with him and disowned him (Qur'ān 9:114). On the other hand, when Abraham grows old, he offers a prayer for the forgiveness of both his parents (Qur'ān 14:39–41). Definitely, Āzar with whom he severed ties as a child was not one of the two parents for whom he prayed as an adult. This claim is bolstered by the fact that Āzar is always referred to as *ab* while he refers to his parents as *wālidāy*.

Evidence from the traditions:

- It is reported that Prophet Muḥammad said, "I was born of legitimate marriage, not fornication, right back to the time of Adam" (*Biḥār al-anwār* vol. 15 p. 117 tr. 63). He is also reported to have said, "God perpetually transferred me through my ancestors from the loins of pure men to the wombs of pure women until he brought me out into this realm of yours. He never defiled me with the filth of the Age of Ignorance" (*Biḥār al-anwār* vol. 15 p. 117 tr. 63). These traditions, especially the latter one, indicate that all of Prophet Muḥammad's ancestors, back to Adam, were "pure" of the "filth of the Age of Ignorance," chief among which was polytheism. Accordingly, Āzar, who was clearly a polytheist, could not have been Abraham's father and, hence, Prophet Muḥammad's ancestor.
- Some traditions explicitly call Abraham's father *Tārukh* (*Biḥār al-anwār* vol. 15 p. 42 tr. 31) or *Tāraḥ* (*al-Burhān fī tafsīr al-Qur'ān* vol. 2 p. 443). In the Old Testament, he is referred to as *Terah* or *Terach* (Genesis 11:26–

from his wife, Sarah, who was a righteous lady and the daughter of Prophet Lāḥij.[10] That night, unbeknownst to all, Terah and Sarah conceived a child, the only one to be conceived in all of Kūthā during those nights.

When Āzar learned that his brother and sister-in-law had been together, he grew suspicious and called in the midwives. He ordered them to examine her and inform him if they found any signs of pregnancy. God hid the signs from them, and they reported truthfully that they could see no signs that she was pregnant.

Abraham Is Born

Sarah finally gave birth to a boy on the first of Dhū al-Ḥijjah.[11] She and Terah named him Abraham.[12] Āzar discovered their secret and decided to take the infant to Nimrod and report him. His loyalty to his king had numbed his humanity. Terah and his wife convinced him not to take his nephew to the king, lest he bear the full responsibility for the child's death. Rather, Sarah volunteered

---

28). Thus, Āzar was not his father.

The question remains: Why do the verses of the Qur'ān and many traditions refer to Āzar as Abraham's *ab* (literally "father") if he was not really his father. One tradition from Imam ʿAlī explains, "Āzar was Abraham's father in that he raised him" (*al-Burhān fī tafsīr al-Qur'ān* vol. 2 p. 443). From this, we can surmise that Abraham's biological father must have died before he escaped from his cave. It is not without precedent to refer to a person's uncle or grandfather with the word *ab*. The Qur'ān refers to Abraham, Isaac, and Ishmael as Jacob's *ābā'* (plural of *ab*; Qur'ān 2:133), when only Isaac was his true father. Abraham, on the other hand, was his grandfather, and Ishmael was his paternal uncle (the ideas for this footnote were taken from *al-Mīzān* vol. 7 p. 162–5 under Qur'ān 6:74 and *al-Bayān fī al-muwāfaqah bayn al-ḥadīth wa al-qur'ān* vol. 4 p. 86).

10. *Biḥār al-anwār* vol. 12 p. 44 tr. 38

11. *Biḥār al-anwār* vol. 12 p. 31 tr. 7

12. Two explanations are given for his name:

- It is derived from *hamma* and *barra*. In other words, "he was concerned" (*hamma*) with the hereafter, so "he was righteous" (*barra*) (*Bihar al-anwar* vol. 12 p. 4 tr. 7).
- It is derived from *hamma* and *bari'a*. In other words, "he was concerned" (*hamma*) with the hereafter, so "he cut himself off" (*bari'a*) from the temporal world (*Bihar al-anwar* vol. 12 p. 4 tr. 7).

to take Abraham to a cave and leave him there to meet his fate on his own terms. Āzar conceded.[13]

Into the Cave

She secretly smuggled her son out of the city to a cave she knew. There she cuddled the child and nursed him one last time. She begged God to protect him by some miracle and sought his

---

13. The Qur'ān makes no explicit mention of Abraham's childhood in the cave. However, there are elements in several verses that only make sense if he had lived in complete isolation from his people and the world at large.

- He asks his uncle and people, "What are you worshiping?" (26:70). For someone to ask this question who has grown up in the capital of idolatry (Babylon), in the same city with a king who claims to be a god, in a household of that king's chief priest and idol-maker seems odd unless he has not witnessed them worshiping until that moment. This is why he asks his question with the word *what*. "*What* are you worshiping?" is the question of one who is seeing people worship for the first time and does not know how to categorize the object of their worship. Once the priests answer saying, "We are worshiping idols," Abraham assumes that the idols must be sentient beings since it only makes sense to worship a sentient being, so he asks, "Do they hear you when you call them? Or do they benefit you or cause you harm?" (26:72–73) referring to the idols with a pronoun used in Arabic only for sentient beings.
- When Abraham sees the sun he exclaims, "This is my Lord!" referring to the sun with the masculine demonstrative pronoun *hādhā* even though the sun is feminine in Arabic. His use of the masculine pronoun for the sun shows that he is referring to the sun, not as the sun per se, but as a luminous body of which he knows only that it is brighter and more magnificent than anything else he has seen. Had he recognized the sun, he would have referred to it with the appropriate feminine pronoun as he did later on when challenging Nimrod to make the sun rise from the west (Qur'ān 2:258).
- When he sees a star, the moon, and the sun, he postulates that each could be his Lord. He does not refute his hypothesis until he actually sees each one set. This shows that he did not know that they would set until they did so. If, on the other hand, he had seen these three heavenly bodies rise and set many times before, he would have refuted his hypothesis even as he uttered it saying, "This could be my lord except that it sets." (In writing these three points, I have relied heavily on *al-Mīzān* in his discussion on 6:74–79.)

forgiveness for not being able to fulfill her motherly duties any more than this. She swaddled him, left him on the floor of the cave, and with eyes full of tears, left him. At the mouth of the cave she stacked rocks until she had sealed the entrance completely. Trusting in God, yet with a heavy heart, she returned home.

The prayers of the desperate and faithful never go unanswered. God made milk flow from Abraham's thumb. He nursed himself on this miraculous nourishment and proceeded to grow at an exceptional rate. He grew in a day as another infant might grow in a week. On the seventh day of his birth, his umbilical cord and foreskin were shed.[14] All of his needs were fulfilled by angels sent by God for this express purpose.[15]

After some days, Abraham's mother took Terah's permission and escaped to the cave. Her dread of so many days melted when her gaze fell on her son who seemed to be thriving despite his predicament. She hugged him and nursed him. Soon she had to return, and so once again she bade him farewell and sealed the cave's entrance with stones.

She visited him as frequently as she could without attracting the suspicious eye of her brother-in-law, Āzar. Months and years passed. Abraham grew healthy and strong, nurtured only by his mother's infrequent visits and the host of angels but sheltered otherwise from any contact with the world beyond the entrance to his cave.

In the intervening years, Terah passed away. Left with little choice, his widow married his brother, Āzar.[16]

---

14. *Biḥār al-anwār* vol. 12 p .3 tr. 4

15. There is no mention of angels taking care of him, but it is only natural that there would have been some such provision for bathing him and cleaning him.

16. There is no concrete evidence that Terah died or that his wife married Āzar. However, it seems the only natural way for Āzar to have played a fatherly role to Abraham. We can only conjecture that he married Abraham's mother or that she too passed away, leaving him as Abraham's only guardian.

Escape From the Cave

In Abraham's thirteenth year, despite his mother's warnings against the danger of being discovered, Abraham felt he could remain in the cave no longer. He now had the strength to move the rocks that imprisoned him. Rock by rock, he cleared the way for his escape.

He took his first step out of the cave with a rising sense of excitement coupled with trepidation.[17] It was dusk, yet even the fading light on the western horizon was more than he was used to in his cave. He did not know which way to go, but he caught a faint glimpse of a single trail leading away from the cave's mouth. He decided this was his best chance for finding his mother and his home. Even as darkness set in, he followed the faint hint of the trail through the dense forest, musing all the time at the fresh new scents that reached his nose for the first time.

After some time, he reached a clearing, and, across the clearing, he saw the walls of a city. He had reached Kūthā. He could hardly contain his excitement as he rushed toward the city gates. He informed the guards that he wished to go to the house of Āzar, who, as he had learned from his mother, had become his step-father.

Reunited With His Family

When Āzar first realized who Abraham was, he was appalled to see that he was still alive. Forebodings of the prophecy he had deciphered thirteen years before still loomed in his mind. However, his wife instinctively allayed his worries by telling him that the gods of Kūthā must have preserved their son precisely because he was *not* the boy in the prophecy. Against his own better judgment, Āzar softened to the boy as he saw his dead brother's semblance in him. He embraced him and resolved to treat him as one of his own sons.

Abraham bathed and donned fresh clothes borrowed from one of his cousins. They ate and became acquainted after their long

---

17. This segment of the story is pure speculation. I have simply tried to imagine how he might have gone from the cave to Āzar's house in the most natural way.

hiatus. The next morning before sunrise, Āzar decided to take Abraham to the temple to offer thanks to the gods for his safe return. All these years, Abraham had been instinctively drawn toward God. He had had many silent conversations with him and had worshiped him in his own way. He grew excited to think that he would finally learn how to worship him correctly.

First Visit to the Temple

When they entered the magnificent temple, Abraham was amazed by the sights, sounds, and aromas. Priests like his uncle were engaged in all sorts of rituals before statues of stone and wood. This puzzled Abraham. He knew his creator was sublime, greater than any of his creatures. He thought perhaps these were some lesser gods the Almighty had appointed to manage the affairs of the people of Kūthā and this is why they worshiped them.

Āzar joined the ranks of the priests and engaged in their extraordinary rituals. Hours passed, and Abraham simply watched their every move and listened to their every word intently.

His consternation increased as he realized that the statues remained stoically silent and still no matter how ecstatically the priests called out to them or what gifts they offered them. Towards evening, when the day's rituals came to an end, Abraham asked some of the priests with the confidence that comes of innocence and prodigious intelligence, "What are you worshiping?"

They looked curiously at the unfamiliar boy then replied, "We are worshiping idols. We spend our days in devotion to them."

Abraham looked again at the statues, trying to catch a glint of consciousness in their glassy eyes. Seeing nothing to belie life or intelligence in them, he turned back to the priests and probed, "Do they hear you when you call them? Or do they benefit you or cause you harm?"

The priests cast nervous glances at each other and at Āzar. Then one of them broke the silence, "We do not know whether they hear us or not. But we worship them nonetheless because we found our forebears worshiping like this."[18]

---

18. Qur'ān 26:69–74

Abraham had seen and heard enough. These idols were no gods. A god must be powerful and wise. A god must hear its devotees' supplications and be able to answer. A god must be actively engaged in providing for all the needs of its subjects. Only such a god deserved to be worshiped, and these idols were nothing but lifeless forms.

Āzar quickly intervened. He grabbed the boy by the arm and led him out of the temple. It was evening now, and he wanted to speak to Abraham in the privacy of the ensuing darkness. Before Āzar could speak, Abraham asked him, "Do *you* take idols for gods? I believe you and your people are in clear error."[19] Āzar could hardly believe the blasphemy he was hearing. Yet he silenced his inner rage when he remembered that the boy was seeing these things for the first time. He was sure he would come around in time.

He explained to Abraham that the idols in the temple were indeed not truly gods. They were but representations of the true gods of Kūthā.[20] The priests carried out these rituals all day long to appease the true gods who lived in the heavens. He promised Abraham to introduce him to these gods shortly.

Meeting the Real Gods

Again Abraham grew excited. He walked with Āzar back to the temple. This time they climbed to the top of the temple to an open-air arena. Again, he noticed priests earnestly engaged in worship, all staring fixedly at a single brilliant star above the western horizon.[21] Since, Abraham had escaped from his cave the

---

19. Qur'ān 6:74

20. See *al-Mīzān* vol. 7, p. 175 under his discussion on verse 6:76 and *al-Taḥrīr wa al-tanwīr* vol. 6, p. 176.

21. The traditions identify this "star" as the planet Venus (*Biḥār al-anwār* vol. 12 p. 30 tr. 6). Indeed the word *kawkab* refers to the most brilliant objects in the sky, many of which we now identify as planets. Nonetheless, I have translated it as "star" to avoid an anachronistic usage of the term "planet." Even in English, Venus is often poetically referred to as the "Morning Star."

'Allāmah al-Ṭabāṭabā'ī has used certain clues in these verses to determine that this incident must have taken place in the fall or winter during the second half of a lunar cycle. He has determined that it took place in the fall or winter

night before, he had not had an opportunity to look into the sky. In the black firmament, this single star looked pristine. Abraham joined the ranks of the priests and exclaimed, "This is my Lord!" For an hour or more, he stood with the priests and thanked God for guiding him to the lord of Kūthā.

Then the star dipped below the horizon and set. Abraham looked puzzled again and said to himself, "I do not like those who set."[22] A lord must be constantly engaged in his subjects' affairs. Abraham knew that a god whose contact could be severed was no god.

Soon after, the priests turned in unison toward the eastern horizon. There was a glowing halo rising into view. Within minutes, a waning gibbous moon began to show itself, and again the priests began their incantations. Again, Abraham, seeing the moon for the first time, exclaimed, "This is my Lord!" With renewed hope, he joined the priests in their prayers and spent the better part of the night worshiping with them.

Then the moon too, set. Utterly distraught, Abraham said, "If my Lord does not guide me, I shall surely be among the misguided."[23] Not much time passed before the eastern horizon began to glow. The priests turned to face the incipient light from the east and carried on their rituals with renewed fervor. Abraham focused quizzically at the light and color that seemed to be exploding out of the horizon. He stood transfixed as he witnessed his first sunrise. He exclaimed, "This is my Lord! This is bigger." He felt this source of light, which was blindingly bright, must be the Lord for which he had been searching. Again, he joined the priests in their prayers for the remainder of the day. However, at the end of the day, once again, the sun set just as the star and moon had set before it.

---

because Venus sets soon after the sun only during these seasons. He determined that it took place during the second half of a lunar cycle because the story indicates that there was a time lag between the setting of the sun and Venus and the rising of the moon. During the first half of the lunar cycle, the moon is already in the sky when the sun sets. Only after the full moon does the moon rise after the sun sets.

22. Qur'ān 6:76

23. Qur'ān 6:77

The Epiphany

As if by epiphany, Abraham declared, "O my people! I hereby sever ties with what you take as God's partners.[24] I hereby disavow what you worship, except for the one who created me, for he will guide me.[25] I hereby turn my focus exclusively toward him who created the skies and the earth, and I shall not be among the polytheists."[26] He had attained certainty that the singular and unique creator whom he had been worshiping all these years was in fact the Lord of all creatures. The idols and other gods that his people had taken to worshiping were merely creatures like him, subjects of the true Lord, with no power to hurt or help themselves except by God's leave.

Abraham Is Chosen

It was through these encounters with his people that God showed Abraham his dominion over the skies and the earth so that, among other things, he would be among those with certitude.[27] It was

---

24. Qur'ān 6:78

25. Qur'ān 43:26–27

26. Qur'ān 6:79

27. Qur'ān 6:75 and *Biḥār al-anwār* vol. 12 p. 28 tr. 1 and *al-Iḥtijāj* vol. 1 p. 213. Traditionally there have been many attempts to understand and justify Abraham's statement, "This is my Lord!" Some have said that he must have been too young to be responsible for what he was saying. Others have said he was pretending to worship with his people to attack their beliefs from within. Yet others have said that he said it, not as a statement, but as a rhetorical question: "This is my Lord?" My narrative is most closely in line with *al-Mīzān*'s interpretation of these verses though I have departed from his understanding on some points. I believe I am justified in construing Abraham's statement as a sincere attempt to find the truth because of the clues within the verses, which I have pointed out in previous footnotes, and because of two traditions that corroborate my opinion. It is narrated that Imam al-Ṣādiq was asked about this verse and whether it meant that Abraham was a polytheist at the time. He replied, "It was not polytheism that drove Abraham; rather, he was in pursuit of his Lord" (*Biḥār al-anwār* vol. 12 p. 31 tr. 6). In another tradition, Imam al-Ṣādiq said, "In his youth, Abraham remained upon his innate, godly disposition until God guided him" (*Biḥār al-anwār* vol. 12 p. 45 tr. 38).

when Abraham advanced from his innate God-consciousness to well-reasoned certitude that God made a covenant with him and appointed him as his prophet and began to actively guide him.[28] He was yet a child,[29] but he was already an ardent follower of Noah,[30] and his mission had begun in full force. Before it would end, Abraham would become the great Patriarch of Monotheism, the second of the Messengers of Great Resolve.[31]

Debating With the Priests

The priests of Kūthā surrounded Abraham, enraged by his blasphemy. They threatened him with their gods' wrath which would not spare anyone who defied them as he had done. They insisted that their gods, and not the creator, were his lords.[32]

Abraham retorted, "Do you argue with me about God's lordship over me when he has guided me?" It made no sense for them to insist on worshiping their gods when their gods could not even speak, much less call anyone to themselves or guide them. Yet they denied God as their Lord when he was eloquent and eager to guide all who were willing to listen and heed his call.

Abraham answered their empty threats saying, "I do not fear the partners you ascribe to my Lord unless my Lord wishes for something to happen to me through them." Their idols, the sun, the moon, and the planets were powerless if left to their own devices. However, as creatures of God, they were each subject to God's will. If he wished for a stone idol, for instance, to fall upon

---

28. Qur'ān 21:51

29. According to the information I quoted earlier, he was 13 years old (*Biḥār al-anwār* vol. 12 p. 29 tr. 6). But another tradition says he was 15 years old when he became enlightened (*al-Iḥtijāj* vol. 1 p. 213).

30. Qur'ān 37:83

31. Qur'ān 33:7. In this verse, God mentions his covenants with all the prophets and then singles out the five Messengers of Great Resolve. Four of them are mentioned in chronological order. Prophet Muḥammad is mentioned first, though he was chronologically last, because of his station above them all.

32. Qur'ān 6:80. The verse does not mention what their argument was, but we can infer their meaning from Abraham's response in the following verses.

him, it would cause him harm, not of its own volition or power, but because of the properties and forces that God had put into play.

He continued, "My Lord's knowledge spans all things so whatever harm befalls me through your gods is known to my Lord and under his control. Do you not then heed?[33] How can you expect me to fear the partners you have ascribed to him, yet you do not fear the consequences of ascribing partners to God for which he has sent down no proof?" They knew God, and they knew they had no justification for ascribing partners to him, yet they did so without compunction. He concluded, "Thus, tell me which of our two sides is more justified in feeling safe, if you know.[34] If you are tongue-tied, I shall answer for you—it is those who believe and do not corrupt their belief with falsehood; they alone have amnesty and are guided."[35]

Admonishing His Uncle

The priests and worshipers were dumbfounded. Again Āzar thought it best to extricate Abraham from the situation and speak to him privately. He summarily goaded Abraham out of the temple and led him briskly home. No sooner had they entered their home than Abraham turned to his uncle with compassion in his eyes and asked, "Uncle, why do you worship that which neither hears nor sees and is of no avail to you in any way?"[36] To warrant people's devotion, a god must be able to comprehend their prayers and fulfill the needs of which their prayers are but an expression. Āzar's gods, on the other hand, could not hear their incantations or see their acts of worship and sacrifice, much less fulfill even the slightest of their myriad needs.

Not giving Āzar time to parry, Abraham pressed forward saying, "Uncle, knowledge has come to me that has not come to you, so follow me, and I will guide you to a straight and level path."[37]

---

33. Qur'ān 6:80

34. Qur'ān 6:81

35. Qur'ān 6:82

36. Qur'ān 19:42

37. Qur'ān 19:43

Abraham wanted Āzar to know that he was amply qualified to serve as his guide. Yet even as he asserted his divine knowledge, he adroitly avoided the snare of vanity by making it clear that his knowledge had *come to him*, not that he had *gained it* though his own devices. He also wanted Āzar to know that he had his best interests at heart and was not after any personal gain. This is why he wished to guide him to a way of life that, while filled with challenges of its own, was far simpler and satisfying than the path of idolatry and sin.

Abraham added, "Uncle, do not obey Satan, for Satan has always been disobedient to the All-Beneficent. Uncle, I fear that some punishment from the All-Beneficent may touch you and that you will then be dependent on Satan who is himself powerless to help you."[38] He wanted his uncle to understand that worshiping false gods was not only a futile act that led to no good; it was a veritable act of treachery that would bring down great punishment upon its perpetrators from which they would be helpless to escape.

Despite Abraham's efforts to disarm his uncle and maintain due decorum, Āzar's response was far from cordial. He bellowed, "Abraham! Are you renouncing my gods? If you do not desist, I shall stone you. Get away from me forever."[39] He had observed Abraham all day, and he was now convinced that there was no hope of guiding him. He wished to disown him, and if he refused to go, he would subject him to the most degrading punishment he knew: death by stoning.

They Part Ways

Seeing that Āzar was no longer prepared to listen to him, Abraham said softly, "Peace be to you. I shall plead with my Lord to forgive you. Indeed he has always been solicitous of me."[40] His was a great act of magnanimity and forbearance. He countered Āzar's threats with a pronouncement of peace and goodwill. And he promised to

---

38. Qur'ān 19:44–5

39. Qur'ān 19:46

40. Qur'ān 19:47

seek forgiveness for Āzar if he ever came around to the truth,[41] for he saw in his uncle the potential to reform. But in the meantime, he agreed to keep his distance saying, "I shall distance myself from you and whatever you invoke besides God. And I will pray to my Lord. Hopefully, I will not be disappointed in my prayers to my Lord."[42] With that, Abraham left his uncle's house disappointed yet hopeful that he might one day come around.

Calling the People of Kūthā

In the following months and years, Abraham tried tirelessly to talk sense into his people.[43] Only a small number came to believe.[44]

---

41. *Biḥār al-anwār* vol. 12 p. 28 tr. 3

42. Qur'ān 19:48

43. There is no indication of exactly how long this period of his life lasted. There are a few pieces of evidence that suggest that Abraham remained in Kūthā until he was old enough to marry and gather a following.

- One verse in the Qur'ān tells us, "When he distanced himself from them and from what they worshiped besides God, we granted him Isaac and Jacob" (19:49). The phrase "when he distanced himself from them" refers to his eventual flight from Kūthā to the Holy Land. For God to ordain that a son and a grandson be born to him—even if it was years before God's promise was fulfilled—it seems only natural that he would have been married and desirous of children at the time.
- Another verse refers to "Abraham and those who were with him" (60:4), indicating that he had a following before he left Kūthā.
- One tradition says that Abraham married Sarah and lived in Kūthā for years and built a considerable fortune before he was sentenced to the fire and finally expelled from the city (*al-Kāfī* vol. 8 p. 370 tr. 560).
- When Abraham is eventually brought to trial for destroying the idols, the people mention that he is a *fatā*, an Arabic word that applies to a boy or to a young man (*Lisān al-ʿarab*).

All said, it seems Abraham spent many years in Kūthā and presumably engaged his people on many different occasions. Accordingly, I have fashioned the narrative to take place over the course of years before he is finally expelled.

44. There is no indication how many followers he had. They are only mentioned in passing in Qur'ān 60:4. Prophet Lot (Lūṭ) is mentioned as one who believed in him in Qur'ān 29:26. And of course his wife Sarah believed in him and was a great source of support to him, as indicated in the traditions. I have accordingly made mention of his followers only vaguely.

Among the first believers were his cousins, Lot[45] and Sarah.[46] They were brother and sister,[47] and their mother, Waraqah,[48] and Abraham's mother, Sarah, were sisters and the daughters of the Prophet Lāḥij.[49] Both were righteous in the superlative and accepted Abraham's prophethood as soon as he first laid claim to it.

A Lesson in Mercy

When God showed Abraham the dominion of the heavens and the earth, in addition to seeing God's grandeur, he also saw, with his newfound perception, the deeds of God's creatures, good and evil. Among the first deeds he witnessed were several instances of adultery. He was so angered by the impudence of the perpetrators that he called down God's punishment and had them destroyed. After several such incidents, God intervened and told Abraham:

> Cease calling down my punishment upon my servants, for I am the Absolver, the Merciful, the Compassionate, and the Forbearing. My servants' sin does not harm me just as their obedience does not benefit me. I do not train them, as you have been of late, by taking revenge upon them. So cease calling down my punishment upon my servants, for you are but a warner, not a partner in my dominion or an overseer for me and my servants. My servants who sin against me fall into one of three categories, and I treat them accordingly. If they repent, I accept their repentance and conceal their faults. If they do not

---

45. Qur'ān 29:26. In Arabic his name is *Lūṭ*. Many commentators have inferred from the verse, "So Lot believed in him," that Lot was the *first* to believe in him. While it is highly likely that Lot would have been the first to believe in him, there is no indication of this in the verse.

46. In Arabic her name is *Sārah.*

47. *Biḥār al-anwār* vol. 12 p. 148 tr. 1

48. *Ruqayyah* is given as an alternative possibility for her name (*Biḥār al-anwār* vol. 12 p. 45 tr. 38).

49. *Biḥār al-anwār* vol. 12 p. 45 tr. 38

> repent, but I know that they will have righteous progeny, I withhold my punishment from them for a while so that their progeny can be born. Once they are born, I mete out my punishment upon the sinful parents. And if they neither repent nor will they have righteous progeny, I punish them. And the punishment I have prepared for them is far more severe than anything you could imagine, for I punish them according to my might and grandeur. So, Abraham, leave my servants' judgment to me, for I am more merciful than you are and I am the Compeller, the Forbearing, the Omniscient, and the Wise. I manage their affairs through my knowledge and enforce upon them my decrees.[50]

Abraham and Sarah Are Married

As the years passed, Abraham and Sarah came of age and decided to be married. At the time of their marriage, Sarah stipulated that Abraham must never reject any of her lawful requests or disobey her.[51] Abraham deemed this a minor concession for marrying such a virtuous woman. In addition, Sarah had inherited a sizable fortune from her father. Her estate included an enormous tract of land and a large herd of livestock. She believed unwaveringly in her new husband's message and supported him with all of her heart. She voluntarily gifted to Abraham her entire estate so that he could use it to further his cause. Abraham took charge of this estate and managed it adeptly, increasing his land holding and herd size until he was the wealthiest man in all of Kūthā.[52]

---

50. *Biḥār al-anwār* vol. 12 p. 60 tr. 5 and 6

51. *Biḥār al-anwār* vol. 12 p. 112 tr. 38

52. *Biḥār al-anwār* vol. 12 p. 45 tr. 38

Admonishing the Priests

One day Abraham returned to the temple to address the priests who served Kūthā's idols. He told them, "You know these things you have been worshiping, you and your ancestors? They are my enemies except the Lord of all realms[53] who created me and is thus the one who guides me; who provides me with food and drink; and when I get sick, he is the one who cures me; who will make me die and then bring me to life; and who, I hope, will forgive me my

---

53. Qur'ān 26:75–77. These verses from 26:75 to 26:102 are apparently a continuation of the preceding verses from 26:70 to 26:74. However, after much deliberation, I have come to the conclusion that these verses are not telling one contiguous story but rather narrate two separate conversations between Abraham and his people. These verses cannot be a contiguous story for the following reasons:

- As we saw, verses 26:70–74 took place immediately after Abraham came out of his cave and witnessed idol worship for the first time. In that conversation, he asked them if their idols could hear and see or bring them benefit or harm. It only makes sense for Abraham's conversation with his uncle, which is narrated in verse 19:42, to have taken place *after* the exchange of 26:70–74. Otherwise, if he already knew that the idols could not hear or see or bring him benefit or harm, he would not have needed to ask the priests these questions. Thus, 19:42 definitely took place chronologically after 26:70–74. On the other hand, verse 26:87 narrates Abraham's prayer to God to forgive his uncle. This verse is clearly the fulfillment of his promise to Āzar to ask God to forgive him which is narrated in 19:47. Thus, 26:87 definitely took place chronologically after 26:87. This line of reasoning confirms that the verses of chapter 26 are not contiguous.
- In verse 26:75, Abraham refers to the gods of the people of Kūthā with the phrase "These things you have been worshiping...they are my enemies." If he had said this as part of the same contiguous conversation, he would have simply said, "*they* are my enemies" without clarifying the antecedent of his pronoun.
- At the beginning of 26:70, Abraham is speaking to his people and his uncle. However, in the end of this section in 26:86, he prays for his uncle's forgiveness in the third person, indicating that he is probably not present. This further corroborates my conclusion that this story is not contiguous.

iniquities on the Day of Retribution."[54] His message to them was that there was no room for their gods in the cosmology of the world. God, the Creator, fulfilled every role they had falsely attributed to their gods in addition to roles they had never imagined a god could play.

As he remembered God as the Lord and Sustainer, Abraham became so overcome with passion for God that he virtually forgot about the priests gathered before him and turned his undivided attention toward God and said, "My Lord! Grant me sound judgment and unite me with the righteous. Let me be remembered well in coming generations and make me one of the heirs to a paradise filled with blessings. And forgive my uncle, for he is one of those who are astray."[55] He had promised Āzar that he would seek forgiveness for him, and he wished to fulfill his promise,[56] hoping that his faithfulness to his word would impress Āzar and soften his heart to the truth. He continued:

> Do not disgrace me on the day when people will be resurrected; the day when neither wealth nor children shall avail anyone—but he who comes to God with a sound heart shall benefit from the

---

54. Qur'ān 26:75-82

Many verses in the Qur'ān seem to attribute sin to the prophets. Our intellect dictates that God should only choose infallible people to guide us, for if they were fallible, we could never be certain that the guidance they preach is correct. There would always be room to doubt in them, and God's system of guidance and judgment would fall apart. Since our intellect is our only way of knowing truth, we must cling to the rational proof and favor the possibility that all these verses are speaking of shortcomings and imperfections, not sin, for it is not uncommon to use the same words to describe both. For instance, in English I might say, "I am sorry I am late," or, "Please forgive me for being late," even if my being late was no fault of my own.

One reason the prophets attribute such things to themselves is that they, being the closest of all creatures to God, feel sincerely that nothing short of total and undivided worship of God is worthy of him. They know his perfection, and they feel utterly impoverished before him and that they are utter failures before him.

55. Qur'ān 26:83–86

56. Qur'ān 9:114

> soundness of his heart—the day when paradise will be brought near for the God-fearing and hell will be brought into view for the errant and they will be asked, "Where are those whom you used to worship besides God? Do they now come to your aid or find aid for themselves?" Then they will be cast into hell on their faces: the gods, the errant who worshiped them, and all the hosts of Satan. They will say, as they quarrel with their gods therein, "By God, we were in clear error when we equated you with the Lord of all realms. However, it was these criminals, these hosts of Satan, who led us astray. Thus, we now have no intercessors; nor do we have even a single sympathetic friend. Would that we had another chance so that we could be among the faithful."[57]

As his soliloquy came to a close, he and his audience were so caught up in the fervor of what he had said that there came no response from them. Leaving a wake of deafening silence, Abraham solemnly strode out of the temple.[58]

And so things continued for years. Abraham tirelessly called his people to abandon their false gods and worship the one God. Perhaps because he was from a prominent family, or perhaps because he held sway over only a paltry number of followers, Āzar and the other priests let him be, engaging him only when he forced them to do so but otherwise ignoring him.

Excursion to Bāniqyā

Once, Abraham traveled with Lot to a neighboring town where they hoped to spread their teachings and sell some of their sheep. When they wished to stay the night, the people of that town warned them of the small earthquakes that plagued them each night, but they slept there nonetheless. That evening, to everyone's surprise,

57. Qur'ān 26:87–102

58. There is no indication in the Qur'ān that the idol worshipers responded to Abraham.

there was no earthquake. The people wondered if their guests had something to do with it, so they asked them to stay another night, and, again, they were spared of their nightly tremors. They begged them to remain in their town and promised to give them anything they wished in return. Abraham declined but told them he wished to buy a barren tract of land he had seen on the outskirts of their city and that if they sold it to him, the earthquakes would stop permanently. They told him, "The land is yours."

Abraham insisted, "I will only take it if I can pay you for it. I will give you one hundred sheep for the land." They happily took his sheep and Abraham occupied his barren land.

Lot asked his cousin, "Abraham, what do you intend to do with this land that is bereft of animal and fodder?"

Abraham told him, "God will raise 70,000 people from this land whom he will admit to paradise without reckoning." This land came to be known as Bāniqyā[59] because, in the Nabatean tongue, *bā* means "100" and *niqyā* means "sheep," thus immortalizing the price Abraham paid for it.[60]

One day, back in Kūthā, Abraham asked his uncle and his people, with an air of derision in his voice, "What are these statues to which you are so devoted?"[61]

They evaded his question and simply replied, "We found our forebears worshiping them."[62] They were tired of hearing Abraham's attacks on their gods—that they were blind, deaf, and dumb, that they were impotent, that they could not even help themselves. For them, the mere fact that their ancestors had worshiped these same idols was sufficient justification for ignoring the voice of their own conscience.

Abraham told them frankly, "Truly, you and your forebears have been in clear error."[63]

---

59. Bāniqyā is now known as Najaf.

60. *Mustadrak al-wasāʾil* vol. 2 p. 308, *Biḥār al-anwār* vol. 12 p. 77 tr. 2, and *Muʿjam al-buldān* vol.1 p. 331 under "Bāniqyā"

61. Qurʾān 21:52

62. Qurʾān 21:53

63. Qurʾān 21:54

They asked, "Have you come to us seriously, or are you just playing?"[64]

He said, "I am not playing; rather, your Lord is the Lord of the heavens and the earth, who originated them; and to this do I attest."[65]

Then he thought to himself, "I swear by God, I shall carry out a stratagem against your idols after you have left me behind and gone to your retreat."[66] It was customary for all the people of Kūthā to retreat from the city once a year to celebrate and worship. That day was approaching, and Abraham had devised a plan he hoped would make them realize the truth.

Festival Day

On the day of the festival, there was a great fanfare in the city as they all prepared to leave for the celebration. As the preparations came to a head, Abraham approached his uncle and his people and asked them once again, "What do you worship? Is it out of deviance that you seek gods besides God? If you think these lesser gods of yours deserve your worship, then what do you think about the Lord of all realms who rules your gods? Is he not more deserving of your worship?"[67]

Āzar tried to quiet Abraham and discourage him from his arguments on this of all days. He told him to get ready to come with the rest of the people hoping that the festivities would curb his zeal for his one God.

Abraham glanced from Āzar up at the stars and then turned to Āzar and said, "I am going to be ill. I do not feel I can come today."[68]

---

64. Qur'ān 21:55

65. Qur'ān 21:56

66. Qur'ān 21:57

67. Qur'ān 37:83–87

68. Literally Abraham says, "I am ill." There is much debate among commentators of the Qur'ān over the meaning of his glance into the stars and the meaning of his statement, "I am ill." With regard to his statement, some have said he was really ill. Some have said he was ill of spirit over his people's continued defiance—a tradition attributed to Imam al-Ṣādiq tells us, "By God,

Iconoclast's Ruse

So they left him behind. When all the inhabitants of the city had left, he slipped into the temple and stole over to their idols with a club in hand. Arranged before them were elaborate dishes of food and other offerings. He pointed insistently at the offerings laid before them and asked sarcastically, "Will you not eat?" When they did not reply, he asked them, "What is wrong with you that you do not speak?" When they still did not respond, he took the club he had brought with him and attacked them, striking with his right hand.[69] He smashed them into pieces, all except the biggest of them so that his people might come back to it.[70] Around this idol's neck, he suspended the strap of his club.[71]

When Kūthā's people returned in the evening, the priests led them into the temple so they could pay their respects to their gods. They were hardly prepared for the utter melee that awaited them. In a state of shock mixed with outrage, the leaders asked, "Who did this to our gods? He is indeed a wrongdoer!"[72]

Several people in the crowd called out, "We heard a young man speaking ill of them. He is called Abraham."[73]

---

he was not sick, nor did he lie. Rather, he just meant that he was sick for the sake of his religion" (*Biḥār al-anwār* vol. 12 p. 29 tr. 5). Some have said he knew he was going to be ill. And others have said he was telling a white lie (*tawriyah*) to set the stage for his ruse. With regard to his glance into the stars, some have said that he looked into the stars as part of his ruse to make his uncle believe his claim since it was through the stars that his people believed they could tell the future. Some have said he glanced at the stars to mark the time of some recurring illness he was alleged to have. And others have said he glanced at the stars to foresee the future.

Out of these possibilities, it is not easy to determine exactly what he wanted to say. The only thing that is clear is that he effectively communicated his excuse to his people, and this allowed him to carry out his plan.

69. Qur'ān 37:88–93

70. Qur'ān 21:58

71. *Biḥār al-anwār* vol. 12 p. 44 tr. 37

72. Qur'ān 21:59

73. Qur'ān 21:60

The priests issued the order, "Bring him before these people so that they may bear witness that he is indeed the one guilty of speaking ill of the gods."[74]

A zealous mob streamed out of the temple and went running towards Abraham's house.[75] They dragged him into the temple. Silence fell over the crowd as the priests prepared to adjudicate. Āzar scowled at his nephew and asked in a bellowing voice, "Was it you who did this to our gods, Abraham?"[76]

He replied with smug provocation, "No, rather it was this one, the biggest of them, who did it! Ask your gods, if they can speak."[77]

A Moment of Clarity

The absurdity of his proposal struck them dumb. It was as if they had suddenly awoken from a long stupor of self-deception. The same thought crossed every person's mind: "Actually it is *we* and not Abraham who are the wrongdoers!"[78] In utter bewilderment, without realizing what he was saying, Āzar uttered, "You know very well that they cannot speak."

Finally, Abraham had succeeded in getting his uncle to admit to something to which he never thought he would admit and that, too, in front of all of Kūthā. Triumphantly, he seized on the moment and said,

> Do you then worship, besides God, that which cannot cause you any benefit or harm?[79] Do you worship what you carve with your own hands when it is God who created you and what you make?[80] I am exasperated with you all and with what you worship besides God. Will you not then

74. Qur'ān 21:61

75. Qur'ān 37:94

76. Qur'ān 21:62

77. Qur'ān 21:63

78. Qur'ān 21:64

79. Qur'ān 21:65

80. Qur'ān 37:95–96

> use your minds?[81] Worship God and fear him. That is better for you if only you knew. You worship in place of God nothing but idols, and, in so doing, you invent a lie. Those whom you worship in place of God have no power over your sustenance, so seek your sustenance with God, worship him, and thank him, for to him shall you be returned. If you reject my message, I shall not be surprised, for nations before you rejected their prophets likewise. The messenger is responsible only for clearly conveying his charge.[82]

Āzar was unable to answer any one of Abraham's challenges, much less the entire maelstrom that had just been let loose upon him. He felt a surge of desperation as he saw his grip over the people's hearts so rapidly dissolving. Spontaneously, from behind him, erupted the furious shouts of the priests, "Kill him! Burn him."[83]

Abraham's Sentence

Taking their lead, the crowd joined in. Some roared, "Kill him!" Others, thinking a quick death too kind an end for such heresy, insisted, "Burn him!"[84]

Regaining his will as he felt the people rallying behind him, Āzar, as vizier of Nimrod and high priest of Kūthā, ruled that his nephew's crimes warranted no less than that he should be burned to death.[85] With cold finality, he proclaimed, "Burn him and aid your gods if you truly wish to aid them.[86] Construct a massive structure for him and cast him into the inferno therein."[87] They

81. Qurʾān 21:67

82. Qurʾān 29:16–18

83. Qurʾān 29:24

84. *Biḥār al-anwār* vol. 12 p. 38 tr. 23

85. *Biḥār al-anwār* vol. 12 p. 44 tr. 37

86. Qurʾān 21:68

87. Qurʾān 37:97. Some commentators have construed this *bunyān* or "structure" to be a catapult they used to cast Abraham into the fire. However, it had burned criminals before; but never had one threatened the very foundation of their civilization as Abraham had. Over the years, he had slowly but steadily attracted a following. With this latest act, though, he had exposed their gods' impotence like no argument of words could ever have done. They needed to make an example of him, and, by destroying him, they wished to destroy any seeds of his ideas that might still lay dormant in the people's hearts. This had to be a fire that would not only incinerate his body but his very memory; that would instill a level of terror in people's hearts that would block them from ever recalling Abraham or his ideas again. For this reason, they called on every citizen of Kūthā to collect what wood he or she could find and to deposit it at the execution grounds so that it could be used in the construction of the giant fire pit.[88] It was an ingenious way to regain people's commitment, for when people contribute to a cause, they feel a sense of ownership toward that cause. With each contribution, they were affirming their culpability in Abraham's destruction and, with it, the destruction of any vestiges of Abraham's ideas they harbored within themselves.

When the judgment was passed and the plans were made, Abraham berated them saying, "You have taken to worshiping idols besides God only because of your regard for one another in this temporal world." He had made it amply clear to them that their gods deserved no veneration in their own right. The only reason they persisted in worshiping them was because of their regard for their forebears and for each other. The idols were the backbone of their civilization, and their loyalty to that civilization, no matter how irrational, was greater than their collective conscience. He issued one final warning saying, "On the Day of Judgment, you will

---

seems more appropriate that they first speak of building the structure to contain the fire and only afterward of the means to cast him into the fire. Furthermore, if the fire was to be a normal-sized fire, there would have been no need to speak of a catapult since they could easily have placed him in the fire without it. This is not to deny that they used a catapult to cast him into the fire, for this is mentioned repeatedly in the traditions. Here I am only claiming that this verse is referring to one and not the other.

88. *Majmaʿ al-bayān* under Qurʾān 21:68

repudiate one another and curse one another. Your refuge will be the fire, and you shall not have therein anyone to aid you."[89]

Gabriel's Outrage

Gabriel witnessed Abraham's heroic defiance of falsehood against all odds. But he saw that the people were blind to the truth, and he feared they would kill him and this infuriated him. God asked Gabriel, "What angers you so?"

He said, "Lord, he is your servant, your friend.[90] There is no one else on earth who worships you as he does. Yet you have released upon him your enemy and his!" He felt time was slipping away, and, without God's intervention, Abraham would certainly be killed.

God replied, "Be silent! For only he makes haste who fears, as you do, that an opportunity will escape him. As for me, I know he is my servant and in my care; I shall deliver him whenever I wish to." God's words comforted Gabriel.[91]

Even the earth itself exclaimed, "Lord, there is no one upon me who worships you as he does. He will be burned in the fire!"

God told the earth, "If he calls on me, I shall suffice him."[92]

The First Catapult

Over the next few days, the people of Kūthā built a towering structure more akin to a small fortress enclosed by four thick walls than to a fire pit. It dawned on them that the blaze created by this much timber would be so hot as to make it impossible to throw

89. Qur'ān 29:25

90. I have translated Abraham's title *al-khalīl* as "friend." All the traditions that describe the circumstances under which God gave him this title seem to indicate that it was conferred on him later in his life, after he was exiled from Kūthā. This is the only tradition that refers to him as God's "friend" from the period before he is exiled. It could be that this is an anachronism inserted unwittingly into the tradition by transmitters intending only to mention Abraham's name with more honors not realizing that he did not have this title at this time. In any case, I did not feel this inconsistency was important enough to disqualify this tradition altogether.

91. *Biḥār al-anwār* vol. 12 p. 35 tr. 11 and p. 39 tr. 24

92. *Biḥār al-anwār* vol. 12 p. 44 tr. 37

Abraham into its center. Satan, who is always near at hand when mischief is in short supply, manifested himself in human form and offered to build a contraption that would propel Abraham into the fire pit from a safe distance. Thus, he constructed for them the first, rudimentary catapult.[93]

The Execution

All the preparations were made by Wednesday of that week,[94] and, once again, the people of Kūthā were summoned. Even Nimrod, the god-king, was present along with Āzar. They watched from a special viewing tower that had been constructed especially for this occasion.[95] On Nimrod's orders, the structure was ceremoniously lit at all four corners, and Abraham was made to sit in the catapult.

Gabriel descended upon Abraham full of concern. He asked, "Do you need anything?"

With complete serenity and composure, he replied, "Not from you."[96] It was not insolence or stubbornness that made him reply in this way, nor did he intend to show ingratitude for Gabriel's solicitousness. Rather, it was his absolute trust in God's providence that made him look to no one's help besides God's, not even his greatest angel's.

Deliverance From Death

Poised in the catapult, staring death in its fiery face, Abraham turned with a sincere heart toward his creator and exclaimed, "O God! O Singular! O Referent in times of need! O you who neither bear children, nor were you born, nor is there anyone to match

---

93. *Biḥār al-anwār* vol. 12 p. 36 tr. 14. Another tradition indicates that he taught them how to build it, not that he built it himself (*Biḥār al-anwār* vol. 12 p. 38 tr. 23).

94. *Biḥār al-anwār* vol. 12 p. 37 tr. 19

95. *Biḥār al-anwār* vol. 12 p. 39 tr. 25 and tr. 26

96. *Biḥār al-anwār* vol. 12 p. 35 tr. 11, p. 38 tr. 21, and p. 5 tr. 12

you. Deliver me from this fire through your mercy[97] by the right of Muḥammad and his family."[98]

In answer to his prayers, God sent Abraham a silver vial that hung from a chain and a silver ring. When Abraham opened the vial he was amazed to see a fine tunic woven with fabric from paradise unfurl before him.[99] The ring bore in minuscule letters the following six inscriptions: "There is no god worthy of worship but God," "Muḥammad is the Messenger of God," "There is no power except through God," "I surrender my affairs to God," "I derive my support from God," and "God suffices me." God told him, "Don this tunic and ring, for through them I shall make the fire cool and peaceful."[100] Abraham obeyed and donned both the tunic and ring. He studied the inscriptions on the latter and read each one to himself. When he read the second one, he mused over the name of Muḥammad, who God had told him would be from his progeny and would, along with his illustrious descendants, be the fulfillment of Abraham's deepest prayers. This knowledge dispelled any vestiges of fear from his heart and filled him with joy.[101]

Meanwhile, Nimrod nodded to his executioner, the catapult was fired, and Abraham was hurtled through the air into the heart of the inferno. The crowd cheered and hailed their god-king, Nimrod, and his chief priest, Āzar, for their swift dispensation of justice in defense of their gods.

Cool and Peaceful

As Abraham fell into the fire, God ordered the blaze, "O Fire! Be cool and peaceful for Abraham."[102] In an instant, guaranteed death turned to a cool sanctuary and a restful haven for Abraham. Concealed from the gazes of Kūthā by the light, heat, and the high

---

97. *Biḥār al-anwār* vol. 12 p. 39 tr. 24

98. *Biḥār al-anwār* vol. 12 p. 40 tr. 27

99. *Biḥār al-anwār* vol. 12 p. 249 tr. 14 and p. 279 tr. 55 and tr. 56

100. *Biḥār al-anwār* vol. 12 p. 35 tr. 11

101. *Biḥār al-anwār* vol. 12 p. 35 tr. 2

102. Qur'ān 21:69 and 28:24

walls of timber around him, Abraham's landing was cushioned, to his surprise, by soft verdure. Neither did he feel the slightest discomfort from the fire, nor was he so much as scratched as he made his landing. Gabriel greeted him and showed him to his place at the center of the fire upon a pedestal draped in a lush carpet the likes of which even Nimrod had never seen. God had made pristine, lush, verdant plants grow around him in the fire and filled his surroundings with blossoms, the likes of which exist only in the combination of the four seasons of the year. All this, God did for the sake of Muḥammad and his family whose light lay dormant in the loins of Abraham.[103] Gabriel brought him another tunic, this one forged of silver from paradise, which he donned.[104] The two of them sat together worshiping and enjoying the blessings of God that surrounded them.

Poverty Would Be Worse

While Abraham sat with Gabriel, God said to him, "I created you and tried you with Nimrod's fire. If I had instead tried you with poverty and stripped you of your patience, what would you have done?"

Abraham replied, "My Lord, poverty is worse than Nimrod's fire."

God said, "Indeed, by my might, I have not created anything in the sky or on earth worse than poverty."

Abraham asked, "O Lord! If a person feeds one who is hungry, what is his reward?"

God said, "His reward shall be forgiveness, even if his sins fill the sky and the earth."[105]

After the Inferno

Three days passed, and it was Saturday when the fire began to abate. Nimrod and Āzar, surrounded by an entourage of guards, climbed the viewing tower that had been built for this very occasion. As

---

103. *Biḥār al-anwār* vol. 12 p. 40 tr. 28

104. *Biḥār al-anwār* vol. 12 p. 43 tr. 33

105. *Biḥār al-anwār* vol. 69 p. 47 tr. 58

they gazed down, they were dumbstruck as they gazed upon the magnificent garden that lay nestled in the wide circumference of smoldering ashes. They saw Abraham sitting with his angelic companion surrounded by a veritable heaven on earth. Nimrod's first reaction was to say, "How dear must Abraham be to his God! Whoever wants a god should take a god like Abraham's."[106]

One of his priests overheard him and offered obsequiously, "I am the one who ordered the fire not to burn him." He hoped his assertion, false though it was, might earn him a closer place to the king. But no sooner had he spoken than God sent a sudden blast of fire up from the ashes to burn him dead and silence his insolent claim.[107]

Debate With Nimrod

Despite his desperation at the way things had unfolded, Nimrod regained his composure and ordered his guards to retrieve Abraham from the fire and bring him to his court immediately. When he arrived, Nimrod asked him, "Who is your lord?"[108]

Abraham replied, "My Lord is he who gives life and brings death."[109]

Nimrod quickly retorted, "*I* am he who gives life and brings death."[110] He finally saw an opportunity to outmaneuver Abraham and win back the confidence of his people. He ordered his guards to bring him two prisoners from the dungeons whom he had sentenced to death. When they were brought, he had the death sentence carried out upon one of them, and then he gave the other one reprieve and let him live.[111] Nimrod had adeptly twisted Abraham's words. Abraham had meant that God creates the living and takes their life, leaving them dead. Nimrod demonstrated only

---

106. *Biḥār al-anwār* vol. 12 p. 39 tr. 25 and p. 39 tr. 26

107. *Biḥār al-anwār* vol. 12 p. 39 tr. 26

108. *Biḥār al-anwār* vol. 12 p. 34 tr. 9

109. Qur'ān 2:258

110. ibid.

111. *Biḥār al-anwār* vol. 12 p. 34 tr. 9

that he could let someone live or cause his death. The difference between the two was substantial; however, his courtiers overlooked the fallacy and gestured obsequiously in approval of their king. With smug triumph, Nimrod turned to Abraham.

Abraham felt equally triumphant, for Nimrod had unwittingly taken his bait. By asserting that he, and not God, was the lord of life and death, he was claiming to be Lord of lords, more powerful than God himself. Abraham said casually, "If that is the case, then since God brings the sun from the east, you bring it from the west." Nimrod's smugness transformed in an instant to consternation.[112] If he were to say, "You are wrong. God does not make the sun rise from the east, I do," Abraham would have told him, "So if you can make it rise from the east, then humor me and make it rise once from the west." And if he were to say, "I cannot make it rise from the west," he would be admitting that he was not, as he had just claimed to be, Lord of lords.

Banished From Kūthā

Nimrod was furious, but helpless. He could not defeat Abraham with ideas; he could not kill him. All that was left to do was to exile him and his followers and hope that their dangerous ideas would leave with them. He issued the edict to expel them.[113] Abraham insisted that he would take all of his livestock and possessions. After much back and forth, Nimrod deemed it wiser to concede than to risk further strife. Ironically, he and his people had wished to harm Abraham, but God had turned the tables and made them the greatest losers[114] and the lowliest.[115]

Abraham's followers were fortified that day with a surge of new converts who had witnessed the blaze and the subsequent debate and become convinced of the truth of Abraham's claims. One clan

---

112. Qur'ān 2:258

113. *Biḥār al-anwār* vol. 12 p. 154 tr. 8

114. Qur'ān 21:70

115. Qur'ān 37:98

in particular joined their ranks from whose descendants God would later raise Prophet Job, Prophet Jethro, and Balaam, son of Beor.[116]

Final Disavowal

Abraham's followers rallied around him and together declared before all of Kūthā with triumphant finality, "We hereby disavow you and what you worship besides God. We hereby repudiate you. Enmity and hatred has now sprung up between us and you and will continue unless you come to believe in God alone." Then they offered in prayer, "Our Lord, upon you do we rely, to you do we turn, and to you is our return. Our Lord, do not make us the means by which you test those who do not believe, and forgive us, our Lord. You alone are the Invincible, the Wise."[117]

Emigration

Within a few days, they packed all their belonging, gathered their herds, and prepared for their exile. They asked Abraham where he planned to go. He told them, "I am emigrating to a place where I can be free to worship God. He shall guide me. And may he grant me righteous children."[118] In response, God ordained that severance from all false gods would be a lasting legacy in Abraham's progeny so that those among them who would deviate from strict monotheism would return to God.[119]

Lot pledged to join him saying, "I too shall emigrate with you to a place where I can be free to worship God, for God alone is the Invincible, the Wise."[120] Because of his unfailing devotion to truth, God appointed Lot as a prophet. God began speaking to him through dreams and through his angels, though he was not yet able to see angels.[121]

---

116. *Biḥār al-anwār* vol. 12 p. 384 tr. 9

117. Qur'ān 60:4–6

118. Qur'ān 37:99–100

119. Qur'ān 43:28

120. Qur'ān 29:26

121. *al-Kāfī* 4.2.1

For their eagerness to emigrate for God's sake, God saved Abraham and Lot along with their families and conveyed them to a land that he had blessed for all mankind, the Levant.[122] In this way, Abraham fulfilled his promise to Āzar which he had made so many years before: "I shall distance myself from you and whatever you invoke besides God. And I will pray to my Lord. Hopefully, I will not be disappointed in my prayers to my Lord."[123] Most of Abraham's other followers took their own paths, each hoping to find a place where he could begin anew. Only the one clan who had come to believe in him after seeing him delivered from the fire chose to emigrate with him.[124]

Nimrod's Last Stand

When they had left, Nimrod made a last feeble attempt to regain his power. With great fanfare, he climbed atop the viewing tower he had had constructed, armed to the teeth, ready to fight in single combat with Abraham's God. From the top of the tower, he shot a single arrow, which he had slyly coated with blood, high into the sky. When the arrow fell back to the crowd below, they saw it coated in blood. Nimrod descended from the tower victoriously and proclaimed, "I have dominated all who are on earth and killed him who is in the sky."[125] The people of Kūthā cheered and felt relieved that their king had killed Abraham's God and that life could return to normalcy.

To completely disgrace this tyrant who had rebelled against God and denied his lordship, God released upon him one of the weakest of his creatures, the gnat, to show him the Almighty's power and

---

122. Qur'ān 21:71

123. Qur'ān 19:48

124. *Biḥār al-anwār* vol. 12 p. 384 tr. 9

125. *Biḥār al-anwār* vol. 25 p. 372 tr. 24. I did not find any explicit mention of Nimrod climbing the tower to "shoot" God. However, it was the best way I could put his statement, "I have dominated all who are on earth and killed him who is in the sky," into perspective.

greatness. It entered one of his nostrils, burrowed into his brain, and killed him.[126]

God's wrath did not end with the effortless destruction of Nimrod, for he ruled only with the support of a people foolish enough to call him god. With Abraham and all the believers gone, there was no reason left for God to withhold his punishment. God razed their buildings from the very foundations, so their roofs caved in on them from above, and punishment came at them whence they did not perceive it.[127]

Encounter With ʿArārah

When God informed Abraham that he had destroyed Kūthā, he and Lot were well on their way to the Holy Land with Sarah and the newly converted clan. Abraham had constructed a litter atop one of his camels to house Sarah. Once she was comfortably inside, he secured the door with a lock, for they both felt that she would be safer that way, not only from the gazes of men but from any other harm anyone may wish to inflict upon a woman of her beauty.

When they crossed from the territory over which Nimrod had ruled into the territory of the Egyptian king, ʿArārah, they were stopped by a tax collector whose duty it was to collect a one-tenth tax in the name of his king on all wealth that crossed the border. The tax collector assessed all of Abraham's and Lot's possessions. When his gaze fell upon the litter atop Abraham's camel, he demanded, "You must open this litter so that I can assess its contents."

---

126. *Biḥār al-anwār* vol. 12 p. 37 tr. 18 and tr. 19

127. Qurʾān 16:26. There is no indication in this verse that it refers to the destruction of Kūthā. However, Shaykh al-Ṭūsī quotes a tradition from Ibn ʿAbbās and Zayd ibn Aslam that claims that this verse refers to Nimrod's people. In another tradition Imam ʿAlī says, "...and on a Wednesday 'their roofs caved in on them from above,'" which is a verbatim quote from this verse (*Biḥār al-anwār* vol. 12 p. 37 tr. 19). In a third tradition, Imam al-Ṣādiq says that God told Abraham to order Lot to "remind his people of what befell Nimrod and his people" (*al-Burhān fī tafsīr al-qurʾān* under Qurʾān 66:10). Based on these clues, I have incorporated this verse into this story.

Abraham told him, "Assess whatever gold or silver you think such a litter might contain, and I will pay a tenth of that amount; however, I shall not open it."

The tax collector insisted that he would accept nothing short of seeing its contents. Against his will, Abraham stood down, and the man opened it. When he saw Sarah, wrapped completely in her cloak, he was startled and asked Abraham, "What relation has this woman to you?"

Abraham replied indignantly, "She is my wife and my cousin."

He asked, "What brought you to imprison her like this in this litter?"

Abraham replied, "We felt this was better for her safety so that no one's gaze should fall upon her."

The tax collector said, "I cannot let you go until I notify my king of your situation." So he sent a messenger who soon returned with instructions to bring Abraham to court.

Abraham told him, "I shall not leave my wife's litter until my soul departs my body!" They agreed to take them altogether to avoid further trouble.

When they arrived at King ʿArārah's court, the king ordered Abraham to open the litter. He objected saying, "My king, my wife is in it. If you accept, I would like to offer you all of my possessions if only you forgo opening the litter." Nevertheless, ʿArārah insisted.

When the door was drawn open, he saw Sarah wrapped in her cloak. His curiosity got the better of him, and he extended his hand to touch her. Abraham looked away as he felt his honor about to be violated. Under his breath, he whispered in prayer, "O God! Prevent his hand from touching my wife and cousin."

ʿArārah's hand froze just short of Sarah's face, and he could neither extend it further or retract it. In utter astonishment, he craned his neck toward Abraham and asked, "Did your Lord do this to me?"

Abraham, having regained his composure, said, "Yes. My Lord has honor and hates sin. It is he who prevented you from committing the sin that you intended."

ʿArārah begged him for forgiveness. He said, "Please, ask your Lord to give me my hand back. If he does, I give my word: I shall not touch her."

Abraham, sensing his sincerity said in prayer, "O God! If this man is truthful, then let him retract his hand."

The king's hand came free and he retracted it, staring with awe at Abraham. He was amazed at Abraham's sense of honor and at the power he wielded through his God. He honored him and told him, "Rest assured, neither I nor anyone else in my kingdom will harm your wife or touch any of your possessions. Go freely wherever you wish. But I do have one wish. I would like your permission to offer your wife an Egyptian handmaid, one who is both beautiful and wise." When Abraham granted him permission, ʿArārah gifted to her his slave named Hagar.[128]

Abraham thanked ʿArārah and offered him parting words of wisdom and advice. Then he, Sarah, Hagar, and Lot set out with all their belongings to continue their journey. ʿArārah walked a few steps behind Abraham, feeling dwarfed by his tremendous presence. God told Abraham, "Stop. Do not walk in front of this king. Walk behind him and show him respect, for he rules over this land. And every land needs a ruler, whether he be good or evil."[129]

---

128. Her name in Arabic is *Hājar.*

129. The statement, "And every land needs a ruler, whether he be good or evil," is attributed in this story to God. Imam ʿAlī echoes this truth when he says, "People must have a ruler, whether he be good or evil" (*Nahj al-balāghah* sermon 40). The need for a ruler who is good should be clear enough. The need for a ruler even if he is evil may come as a surprise. Even an evil ruler maintains order and enforces the rule of law. Despotic rule is better than no rule at all. Under despotic rule, only one person has the power to exercise his whims. In an anarchy, as many whims are exercised as there are people.

In the case of King ʿArārah, it seems God wants two things to happen:

- First, he does not want Abraham to undermine his authority, for after Abraham leaves, it is he who has to rule over his people and maintain order there. If Abraham allows him to lose his status in the eyes of his own people without replacing him with someone more qualified, he will leave a power vacuum in which the potential for civil strife will be too great.
- Second, he sees that this king has potential to be a great ruler since he

Abraham obeyed and told ʿArārah, "Please go ahead, for God has commanded me to honor you and let you walk ahead of me to show deference to you."

ʿArārah asked incredulously, "God told you that? I testify that your Lord is kind, forbearing, and generous. You have convinced me to follow your religion." Abraham embraced him and welcomed him into his faith and taught him its most essential tenets. Then they bade farewell, and Abraham and his companions continued on their way to the Holy Land.[130]

Innovative Garments

In those days, it was not customary for men to wear undergarments beneath their outer robes. As Abraham walked with his family and animals, the earth felt ashamed of what it could see of him from its perspective. It begged God to ask Abraham to cover himself from below. That night, as his family slept, Abraham sewed the first undergarment, akin to shortened pants, which he wore beneath his robes to increase his decency and chastity.[131]

As they continued their journey, Abraham felt that his feet could not bear the rough terrain any longer, for in those days there were no shoes. God taught Abraham how to tie a piece of tough leather with thongs to his foot and ankle. Thus, he also became the first person to ever wear shoes.[132]

---

responded with such humility when he experienced the power of God firsthand. He hopes that by honoring him, he will be able to completely win his heart so that he becomes a truly God-fearing king.

130. *Biḥār al-anwār* vol. 12 p. 45–47 tr. 38. The Holy Land is referred to in the traditions and commentaries as *al-Shām* or *al-Shāmāt* which roughly corresponds to the Levant which comprises modern day Syria, Lebanon, Israel, Palestine, and Jordan.

131. *Biḥār al-anwār* vol. 12 p. 77 tr. 3

132. *Biḥār al-anwār* vol. 12 p. 13 tr. 38

Homestead at the Crossroads

Abraham settled with Lot, Sarah, Hagar, and his few followers in Hebron.[133] He strategically chose this location which lay at the crossroads of the trade routes between Yemen and Syria and Babylon.[134] There he built a house and established his estate with all the livestock and possessions he had hauled from Kūthā.

When they were settled, Abraham and Lot turned to preaching and calling people to God. They fared much better here than they ever had in Kūthā. Travelers and caravans constantly passed by. Abraham became famous far and wide as "the one who did not burn when Nimrod threw him into the fire." He hosted them all generously and called them to faith and obedience to God.[135] Many accepted his teachings and turned toward God.

Lot Sent to Sodom

One day, news reached Abraham of trouble to the north in the city of Sodom[136] located near the Sea of Galilee. People began to complain to him of the Sodomites' extreme immorality and decadence. He decided to send Lot as his deputy to Sodom to warn its people and guide them back to the truth.[137]

---

133. *Biḥār al-anwār* vol. 12 p. 45–47 tr. 38. This tradition mentions that Abraham and Sarah settled in *Aʿlā al-Shāmāt* and he sent Lot to *Adnā al-Shāmāt*. While it is tempting to construe these terms to mean northern and southern Syria or Palestine, there is no good reason to do so. The two qualifiers might be an indication of elevation. Since the Sea of Galilee is located in the Jordan Valley, it is at a lower altitude than Hebron. Hebron is known as *al-Khalīl* in Arabic and is reputed to be the site of Abraham's and Sarah's graves.

134. *Biḥār al-anwār* vol. 12 p. 155 tr. 8

135. ibid.

136. In one tradition, Gabriel tells Prophet Muḥammad that Sodom was located near *Buḥayrat Ṭabariyyah* (Tiberias) which corresponds to the Sea of Galilee (*Biḥār al-anwār* vol. 12 p. 153 tr. 7).

137. *Biḥār al-anwār* vol. 12 p. 155 tr. 8

Friend of God

Abraham spent numerous years in God's service. He sought out the poor and hungry and fed them generously out of what God had given him.[138] He would pass long hours of the night prostrating upon the earth[139] worshiping the Almighty while others slumbered.[140] His perpetual invocation was to ask God to shower his mercy upon his descendants—Muḥammad and his family.[141] And throughout his life, no matter what tribulations he faced, he never sought the help of anyone besides God.[142] Every morning and evening, as part of his daily routine, he would say, "I awaken in the morning, praising my Lord. I awaken in the morning without ascribing partners to God or calling any other alongside God or taking any other as a helper."[143] For all this, God wished to bestow on him a unique rank.

One day, according to his habit, Abraham went out to search for a poor person to bring home as a guest. As always, he locked the door so that Sarah and Hagar would be safe inside and he took the key with himself. After some hours, he returned, unsuccessful in his search for a guest. But when he unlocked and opened the door, there was a handsome man standing before him. Puzzled, he asked, "By whose permission did you enter this house?"

The man answered, "I entered by the permission of its *owner*."

Abraham understood the man's innuendo and heartily greeted him as the Archangel Gabriel. He asked him what had brought him here to which Gabriel answered, "God Almighty has sent me to one of his servants. He wants me to award him with the rank of *al-Khalīl*, the Friend of God."

Abraham eagerly asked, "I beg you to tell me who he is so that I may serve him for the rest of my life."

---

138. *Biḥār al-anwār* vol. 12 p. 4 tr. 10

139. *Biḥār al-anwār* vol. 12 p. 4 tr. 8

140. *Biḥār al-anwār* vol. 12 p. 4 tr. 10

141. *Biḥār al-anwār* vol. 12 p. 4 tr. 9

142. *Biḥār al-anwār* vol. 12 p. 4 tr. 5

143. *Biḥār al-anwār* vol. 12 p. 70 tr. 13

Gabriel gave him a knowing smile, impressed by Abraham's utter humility and unassuming nature. He said, "Abraham, you are he."[144] Abraham was taken aback. Gabriel told him, "It is because you never asked anybody besides God for anything. And he never asked you for anything but that you said, 'Yes.'"[145]

Sand into Flour

One year, their crops did badly due to drought, so Abraham traveled to borrow some flour from a friend of his in Egypt where the crops had not been affected by the shortage of rain. When he arrived, his friend was not there and so he could not ask him for a favor. He was ashamed to return empty-handed to Sarah, so he filled his donkey's saddlebags with sand to give her hope until he could make a plan for another journey. When he got home, he slept right away.

In the morning, Sarah opened the saddlebags and found them filled with the best flour she had seen. She baked bread with it for breakfast. Abraham was surprised and asked where she got the flour. She told him, "It is the flour that you brought back from your Egyptian friend."

---

144. Qur'ān 4:125

145. *Biḥār al-anwār* vol. 12 p. 13 tr. 40. The story is told in a slightly different way in another tradition: "The Angel of Death was given the task of giving him the tidings of this appointment. Abraham's habit was to lock his door when he left for the protection of his wife. Once, he left to do an errand locking the door behind him. When he returned, a handsome young man dressed in white opened the door from the inside and greeted him at the door. Abraham felt his honor violated. He asked, "Who let you into my house?" The man replied, "Its lord did." Abraham understood his innuendo and said, "Indeed, its lord has more right over it than I. But who are you?" He replied, "I am the Angel of Death." Abraham felt a sense of panic and asked, "Then you have come to take my soul?" He said, "No, rather God has chosen one of his servants as his friend, and I have come to give him tidings." Abraham asked, "Who is this servant? Perhaps I can spend my life in his service until I die." The angel said, "It is you." Abraham entered his house and told Sarah, "God has taken me as his friend" (*Biḥār al-anwār* vol. 12 p. 5 tr. 11).

Abraham, now understanding what God had done, said, "He is my friend, but he is not Egyptian."[146]

Scriptures of Abraham

God revealed twenty different scriptures to Abraham, all consisting of wisdom, moral lessons, and a canon of law that would supersede the law of Noah. These books came to be known simply as *Ṣuhuf Ibrāhīm*, the Scriptures of Abraham.[147] They were revealed to him on the eve of the first of Ramaḍān.[148] The following are some of the teachings they contained:

> O king who is afflicted and deceived! I did not make you a king so that you should amass the material world. Rather, I made you a king so that you should answer the call of the oppressed on my behalf, for I do not refuse the call of the oppressed even if it comes from one who does not believe in me.
>
> One with intellect, as long as his intellect is not compromised, should schedule the following times into his daily routine, a time in which he speaks intimately with his Lord; a time when he takes account of himself; a time when he contemplates what God has done to him; and a time when he avails himself privately of his lawful share of God's blessings. This last time is important because it fortifies him to make the best of the other three times and relaxes his mind.
>
> One with intellect should be insightful with regard to the issues of his times, proactive in his

---

146. *Biḥār al-anwār* vol. 12 p. 6 tr. 13 and p. 11 tr. 30

147. *Biḥār al-anwār* vol. 12 p. 71 tr. 14

148. *Biḥār al-anwār* vol. 12 p. 75 tr. 29. It is not clear from this tradition whether all twenty were revealed on the same evening in the same year or over the course of many years.

own interests, and mindful of his tongue, for if one considers his words to be part of his deeds, he shall say little more than what concerns him.

One with intellect ought to seek the following three things: advancement of his livelihood; provisions for the final return to God; and enjoyment through lawful means.

It is strange how one who is certain of death can exult; and how one who is certain of the fire can laugh; and how one who sees the temporal world and how it undulates with its denizens can find comfort in it; and how one who believes that God is the provider in due portion would exhaust himself in reckless pursuit of more; and how one who is certain of the reckoning does not work for it.[149]

He has succeeded who has given charity and remembered his Lord's name and prayed. Instead, you give priority to this temporal life when the hereafter is better and longer lasting.[150]

No soul shall bear the burden of another. A person only receives the results of his own efforts. And his efforts shall be examined. Then he will be given full recompense for them. To God is the final return. He makes some laugh and others cry. He doles out death and gives life. He created the sexes, male and female, from sperm, which was secreted. And it is up to him to bring them to life once again. He is the one who gave riches and bounty. He is the Lord of Sirius. And he is the one who destroyed the ʿĀd of old and the

149. *Biḥār al-anwār* vol. 12 p. 71 tr. 14

150. Qur'ān 87:14–17 and *Biḥār al-anwār* vol. 12 p. 71 tr. 14

> Thamūd of whom he spared none and the people of Noah before that. They were more unjust and rebellious. And he buried the overturned cities of Lot's people. And before that he had enshrouded them in unspeakable terror. Thus, about which of your Lord's bounties do you wish to dispute?[151]

Abraham's Code of Law

Abraham's new law also ordained ten practices for personal hygiene. Five of these related to the head:

- The men would trim their hair regularly.[152]
- They would trim their mustaches.
- They would let their beards grow long.
- They would brush their teeth.
- And they would pick their teeth clean after meals.

The five other practices relate to the rest of the body:

- They would bathe after sexual activity.
- They would clean themselves with water after relieving themselves.
- They would trim their nails regularly.
- They would remove their body hair.
- They would circumcise their male children on the seventh day.[153]

---

151. Qur'an 53:37–55

152. *Ṭamm al-sha'r* could alternatively be translated as "shaving of the head."

153. *Biḥār al-anwār* vol. 12 p. 7 tr. 16. One tradition says that Abraham circumcised himself at the age of eighty (*Biḥār al-anwār* vol. 12 p. 10 tr. 25). It seems this is a view held by Sunnīs and is possibly rooted in the Biblical story (see Genesis 17:10–11). When a man presented this story to Imam al-Ṣādiq, he refuted it vehemently saying, "It is not as they have said. They have spoken falsely!" Then he added that Abraham's and the other prophets' foreskins fell off on the seventh day along with their umbilical cords (*Biḥār al-anwār* vol. 12 p. 9 tr. 22). In another tradition, Imam al-Kāẓim says, "Adam was created circumcised. Seth, Enoch, Noah, Shem, Abraham, David, Solomon, Lot, Ishmael, Moses, Jesus, and Muḥammad were all born circumcised" (*Biḥār al-anwār* vol. 12 p. 3 tr. 4). Perhaps by saying they were "born circumcised," he means they were born in such a way that their foreskins fell off naturally on the seventh day, so this tradition does

A Lesson on Death

Once, Azrael, the Angel of Death, visited Abraham to teach him about death. Abraham asked him, "Can you show me the countenance you carry when you extract the soul of a believer?"

Azrael told him to turn away for a moment and when he turned back, he saw before him an exquisitely handsome young man with fine clothes, fine features, and a fine scent. Abraham said, "If seeing you were all the reward given to a believer, it would be enough. Now, show me the countenance you carry when you extract the soul of an unbeliever."

Azrael said simply, "You do not have the stomach for it." When Abraham insisted, Azrael told him to turn away for a moment and when he turned back, he saw before him a hideous man with hair bristling, emitting a putrid odor, wearing blackened clothes. From his mouth and nostrils issued fire and smoke. Abraham passed out at the sight. When he came to, Azrael had returned to his normal state.

Abraham said, "If seeing you in that state were all the punishment given to an unbeliever, it would be enough."[154]

Yearning For a Child

Since Abraham and Sarah had married, they had remained without child. Ironically, even though Sarah was the first daughter of a prophet to menstruate,[155] she remained unable to conceive. They were exceptionally patient people and completely submitted to God's decree, yet they never stopped praying for a child, even as their ages crept ever higher.

---

not necessarily contradict the previous one. The tradition continues to say that Abraham was the first prophet to be commanded to circumcise (*ibid.*). However, he did not circumcise himself as some have alleged, but rather Isaac. According to another tradition, because Sarah insulted Hagar, God did not allow Isaac's foreskin to fall off automatically. He commanded Abraham to remove it with a blade (*Biḥār al-anwār* vol. 12 p. 101 tr. 7).

154. *Biḥār al-anwār* vol. 12 p. 75 tr. 25

155. *Biḥār al-anwār* vol. 12 p. 12 tr. 107

Abraham suggested to Sarah that she sell him her slave, Hagar. He said, "Perhaps, through her, God will grant us a child and an heir." Sarah agreed that this was a wise idea,[156] but, according to custom, before she could free her slave or sell her, she had to have her circumcised, which she did.[157]

Despite their redoubled efforts and earnest prayers, many more years passed without any sign of a child from either woman, yet they nurtured hope within themselves, for they knew God often postpones answering his most patient servants' prayers precisely because he knows they will pray ever more earnestly, and he loves to hear his servants pray.[158]

---

156. *Biḥār al-anwār* vol. 12 p. 47 tr. 38

157. *Wasā'il al-shī'ah* 21.6.58.27536. Female circumcision (*khafḍ*) is condoned in Islamic sources. However, the kind of circumcision that is condoned is not the genital mutilation that is often perpetrated in Islamic and non-Islamic societies today. In modern terms, what Islam condones seems to be clitoridotomy, not clitoridectomy or infibulation. The following tradition demonstrates this:

- Imam al-Ṣādiq said, "When women immigrated to the Messenger of God in Medina, a woman called Umm Ḥabīb immigrated. She was a circumciser. She used to circumcise girls. When the Messenger of God saw her, he asked her, 'O Umm Ḥabīb! Do you still do the work you used to do?'

  She answered, 'Yes, O Messenger of God, unless it is now unlawful, in which case you may prohibit me from doing it.'

  He said, 'No, it is lawful, but come near so that I may teach you something.' She drew near to him and he told her, 'O Umm Ḥabīb! When you do it, do not overdo it, and do not remove it completely, and remove only a little, for this will make her face more radiant and bring her more pleasure with her husband...'" (*Wasā'il al-shī'ah* 17.2.18.22170).

In any case, it is clear that what Sarah did to Hagar was according to custom and was an acceptable thing to do. It was not an act of aggression akin to rape. Accordingly, her repentance for this act many years later must be construed as remorse for having sold Hagar to Abraham since this eventually made her jealous and angry toward Hagar. She is not repenting for the act of circumcision itself.

158. *Nahj al-balāghah* letter 31

Prayers Are Answered

One day, Sarah gazed at Abraham and said, "You have grown old. Why not beg God again to provide you with a child who will make us happy. God has made you his Friend, and he will answer your prayer if he wills."

Abraham prayed with renewed fervor for a child who would be righteous[159] and forbearing.[160] God replied, "I shall give you a forbearing child,[161] and, thereafter, I shall test your obedience to me through him."

Ishmael Is Born

It would be another three years before his prayer was actually realized.[162] To Sarah's deep chagrin, the answer to Abraham's prayers came, not through her womb but through Hagar's. She bore him a son whom they named Ishmael.[163] On the seventh day, his foreskin was shed with his umbilicus, an early sign that he was chosen for the prophethood.[164]

Sarah's Struggle

As virtuous as Sarah was, she could not help but feel deeply disappointed and envious of Hagar. Her state of mind was only worsened when she found that she was no longer experiencing her

---

159. Qur'ān 37:100

160. *Biḥār al-anwār* vol. 12 p. 131 tr. 16. Al-Majlisī has most likely recorded *ʿalīm* mistakenly instead of *ḥalīm* as it has been transmitted in the original source.

161. This is an allusion to 37:101. This forbearing child is Ishmael (*Ismāʿīl*) who was born to Abraham through Hagar. We can say this with confidence because the story of this child's birth is narrated in 37:101–111. Then verse 37:112 says, "And we gave him glad tidings of Isaac, a prophet among the righteous," indicating that the son about whom the previous verses spoke was not Isaac, and thus, Ishmael (see *Biḥār al-anwār* vol. 12 p. 130 tr. 11).

162. *Biḥār al-anwār* vol. 12 p. 131 tr. 16

163. In Arabic his name is *Ismāʿīl.*

164. *Biḥār al-anwār* vol. 12 p. 3 tr. 4

monthly cycle.[165] She began complaining intolerably to Abraham about this sour turn of fate.[166] When Abraham in turn complained to God about her, God told him to be patient with her "for women are like a bent rib. With a rib, if you try to straighten it, you will break it, but if you leave it bent, you will benefit from it; so too are women."[167]

It was natural for Sarah to feel as she did. God did not wish to aggravate her further in this difficult situation, so he commanded Abraham to take Hagar and his newborn son to another place,[168]

---

165. There is no explicit mention of this detail in the traditions. However, the fact that she suddenly menstruated five years later, just before the angels prophesied the birth of Isaac (as per Qur'ān 11:71) indicates that she must have ceased menstruating at some point.

166. *Biḥār al-anwār* vol. 12 p. 97 tr. 6

167. *Biḥār al-anwār* vol. 12 p. 116 tr. 50. Apparently this means that there are aspects of a woman's nature that cannot be altered without ruining what it means to be a woman. In this instance, he may be referring to a woman's innate desire to be a mother. If a woman loses her maternal instinct by choice or by force, she loses part of her womanly nature. In this way, God is helping Abraham cope with Sarah's emotional response to what she feels is a tremendous failure on her part to be what she most wanted to be: a mother. In particular, rather than stopping her from being emotional, he should be patient with her until she is able to cope herself.

I do not see anything in this tradition that disparages the nature of women as inherently faulty.

168. With regard to the character of Sarah and Hagar, there are some conflicting messages among the traditions and between the traditions and the Old Testament. The latter portrays both in a bad way. It tells us, "So after Abram (Abraham) had been living in Canaan ten years, Sarai (Sarah) his wife took her Egyptian maidservant Hagar and gave her to her husband to be his wife. He slept with Hagar, and she conceived. When she knew she was pregnant, she began to despise her mistress. Then Sarai said to Abram, 'You are responsible for the wrong I am suffering. I put my servant in your arms, and now that she knows she is pregnant, she despises me. May the Lord judge between you and me.' 'Your servant is in your hands,' Abram said. 'Do with her whatever you think best.' Then Sarai mistreated Hagar; so she fled from her" (Genesis 16:3–6).

Within the traditions, Sarah is generally portrayed as an exceptional woman. Two traditions are revealing since they indicate that she has a high status in the hereafter:

- One tells us that she and Abraham are given temporary custody not because they had done anything wrong, but to relieve Sarah, on one hand, and to carry out his divine plan for Ishmael and his progeny on the other.

Abraham asked, "Lord, where shall I take them?"

God replied, "To my sanctuary, to the first place I created on earth—to Bakkah."[169] God sent Gabriel with the creature called Burāq[170] to carry Abraham, Hagar, and Ishmael to Bakkah.

Before they left, Sarah made him promise that he would not dismount where he left them but return to her immediately. Because of the promise he had made to her when they married, he conceded.

---

of children in paradise until the children can be given back to their parents (*Biḥār al-anwār* vol. 5 p. 293 tr. 18 and vol. 12 p. 14 tr. 43) which indicates that she is in paradise and that she has a special role to play in caring for people who die in infancy.

- Another tells us that she came to Prophet Muḥammad's wife, Khadījah, along with Āsiyah, Mary, and Kulthum (Miriam), Moses' sister, to help her with her delivery (*Biḥār al-anwār* vol. 6 p. 246 tr. 79) which also indicates that she had a status akin to these women, three of whom are the best women this world has ever seen.

In light of the high praise afforded to her in these two traditions in sharp contrast to her disparagement in the Bible, I have decided it wisest to look skeptically upon those traditions that agree with the biblical attitude of disparagement. It is possible that these traditions are correct, but if I must err, I would rather err on the side of assuming the best of Sarah than of mistakenly treating her with contempt.

169. Some traditions tell us that Sarah spitefully ordered Abraham to take Hagar and Ishmael "to a land without pasture or livestock" (*Biḥār al-anwār* vol. 12 p. 114 tr. 45). Other traditions tell us that it was God who chose the place and the attributes of the place. If Sarah had acted so spitefully, she would not be praised as highly as she is. Additionally, Abraham would not have had reason to listen to her. For these reasons, I have decided to disregard the former traditions and accept the latter, if only because I would rather err on the side of portraying Sarah in the best possible light.

170. This is apparently the same creature, or the same kind of creature, that would carry Prophet Muḥammad from Mecca to Jerusalem and then into heaven on the Ascension (*miʿrāj*) many generations and perhaps millennia later. Another tradition says they traveled on a donkey (*Biḥār al-anwār* vol. 12 p. 115 tr. 48).

Journey to Bakkah

Every time they passed over a verdant tract of land with trees and pasture, Abraham would ask Gabriel, "Is this it?"

Each time, Gabriel would reply, "No, we must go further." Then they arrived at Bakkah, and Burāq set them down in a barren desert amidst some ruins that appeared as a mound of red clay.[171] Abraham, bound by the promise he made Sarah, remained upon Burāq without dismounting. He raised his hands and prayed, "Lord, I leave my family in this valley which is bereft of pasture, near your sacred house, not for worldly gain, but according to your command so that they may establish the prayer; so make people's hearts incline toward them and provide them with sustenance so that they may be thankful."[172]

Hagar looked to him imploringly and said, "Abraham, why do you leave us in a place where we have neither friend nor water nor pasture?" All he left with them were some meager provisions and a small amount of water in a skin.[173]

With tears in his eyes, he replied, "The one who ordered me to leave you in this place will take care of you."

Gabriel concurred, "Abraham has left you in the care of one who will suffice you."[174] And with that, they left.

Struggle For Water

There was a single decrepit tree near the ruins. Hagar improvised a lean-to with her cloak and laid her child in its shade. As the day advanced, the sun rose higher and Ishmael grew thirsty. They needed water, so Hagar rose, ran to the nearest mountain, which she later discovered was called Ṣafā, and called loudly, "Is there any friend in this valley?" From this vantage point she could not see Ishmael, so she returned to him. Then she saw a mirage on a neighboring mountain, Marwah, and ran toward it. As she reached

171. *Biḥār al-anwār* vol. 12 p. 115 tr. 48

172. Qur'an 14:37

173. *al-Kāfī* vol. 4 p. 201 tr. 1

174. *al-Kāfī* 15.7.2

it, she realized it was nothing, and she could not see Ishmael again, so she returned to him. Like this, she ran back and forth between Ṣafā and Marwah seven times. Exhausted and nearly abject as she returned to Ishmael, she saw that water had miraculously begun to gurgle and collect at Ishmael's feet. She quickly packed sand around the area to allow the water to collect. This water came to be known as Zamzam.[175]

Alliance With Jurhum

On the nearby plain of ʿArafāt, the nomadic tribe of Jurhum had set up camp. In the distant horizon they saw birds, indicating that there was water. They sent scouts to explore the area. The scouts found Hagar and Ishmael, huddled beneath their lean-to next to an oasis like they had never seen. They asked her who she was. She replied, "I am a handmaid of Abraham, the Friend of God, and this is his son. God commanded him to leave us here."

They asked, "Would you give us permission to set up camp near you?"

She said, "I give you permission until Abraham returns."

Three days later, when Abraham returned to visit them, she asked for his permission which he gladly gave. He prayed, "Lord, make this a safe city, and provide its denizens—those among them who believe in God and the Last Day—with sustenance."[176]

---

175. *Biḥār al-anwār* vol. 12 p. 97–99 tr. 6

176. Qur'an 2:125. I have placed this verse at this point in the story for two reasons.

- He prays saying, "Make this *a safe city*," as opposed to his prayer in 14:35, "make this *city safe*." The wording of the former indicates that no city existed but that he had reason to hope that a city would one day exist. The wording of the latter presupposes the existence of a city.
- He prays in general for "its denizens" as opposed to praying specifically for his family as he does in 14:37. When he first left his family, it made sense for him to pray for them and his progeny through them. However, as the Jurhum people began to settle around them, it made sense for him to pray for the city's denizens as a whole.

God replied, "I shall provide for them. However, I shall give those who do not believe only a little respite; then I shall force them to enter the torment of hell. What a terrible place to end up!"[177]

The tribe of Jurhum settled down in Bakkah and became a source of comfort and help for Hagar. Each Jurhumī family gave Ishmael a sheep as a gift. This sizable flock of sheep supported Hagar and Ishmael until he grew up and could fend for himself.[178]

Caravans, which used to avoid Bakkah because of its lack of water, now saw the birds and other signs of an oasis. Hagar and Ishmael provided them with water for which the caravans bartered with food and other supplies.[179] It gladdened Abraham and Hagar that God had upheld his promise to suffice them of all their needs from the very day they set foot in Bakkah.

Rescuing Lot

In the intervening years, there was a war in Sodom and Gomorrah, and Lot was taken captive. Abraham assembled an army in the Holy Land and freed Lot. With this action, he became the first person ever to wage war in the way of God,[180] and he became the first of four prophets who would fight with the sword.[181]

A Lesson on Resurrection

Abraham once visited the sea and found the corpse of an animal that lay strewn on the beach. Part of the body was submerged

---

177. Qur'an 2:125

178. *Biḥār al-anwār* vol. 12 p. 97–99 tr. 6

179. *al-Kāfī* vol. 4 p. 201 tr. 2

180. *Biḥār al-anwār* vol. 12 p. 10 tr. 25. This tradition attributed to Imam al-Kāẓim contains some questionable details which I have left out. For instance, it says the Romans were responsible for capturing Lot. Even if Romans refers to the Byzantines, any reference to these civilizations is highly anachronistic. This tradition also speaks of Abraham circumcising himself, the falsehood of which I discussed earlier. Nonetheless, I have included those aspects of the tradition that are not problematic. This story is also narrated in great detail in Genesis 14.

181. *Biḥār al-anwār* vol. 14 p. 2 tr. 2. The others would be Moses, David, and Muḥammad.

under water and part of it extended onto the sand. All sorts of scavenging sea creatures tore at the body and consumed it. These were, in turn, devoured by larger fish. The part on land was also consumed by scavenging birds and animals, some of whom were in turn attacked and eaten by larger predators. Abraham observed this carnage for some time. Then it crossed his mind that resurrection of the dead must be a complicated affair since a single body fed so many, and their bodies in turn fed so many, leaving the dead body strewn far and wide, incorporated into the bodies of many. He knew God Almighty could do anything, and he knew that he would indeed resurrect all creatures on Judgment Day;[182] but he wanted to see how this happened with his very own eyes, so he said, "Lord, show me how you resurrect the dead."

God asked, "Do you not believe?"

He replied, "Of course I do, however, I ask you to show me so that my heart may be at ease."

God said, "Then take four birds." Abraham found a peacock, a rooster, a pigeon, and a crow.[183]

God told him, "Cut them up after training them to come to you." He trained the four birds, slaughtered them, chopped them into pieces and mixed the pieces,—bones, flesh, and feathers—altogether.

God told him, "Place a portion of their bodies on every surrounding mountain." He placed a portion of the mixture upon each of the ten mountain tops surrounding his city. He carried only the four beaks with himself.

God told him, "Now call to them, and they will flock to you."

Abraham set out some seed and water before the beaks of the birds and then called out, "Answer my call, by God's leave!" No sooner had he finished his command then the flesh and bones of each bird whirled toward him, and they self-assembled in front of his eyes. When each bird was assembled perfectly, every feather in

---

182. *Biḥār al-anwār* vol. 12 p. 63 tr. 8, p. 73 tr. 21

183. In another tradition we are told there was a hoopoe and a shrike in place of the rooster and pigeon.

its correct place, the birds stirred to life, rose to their feet, cooing and calling, pecking at the seed as if nothing had happened.

God gave the birds the ability to speak, and they addressed Abraham in unison saying, "O Prophet of God! You gave us life. May God give you life."

Abraham bowed his head and said solemnly, "Rather, God is the one who gives life and takes it."[184]

God told him, "Thus know that God is invincible and wise."

Abraham fell prostrate before God and declared, "God is indeed invincible and wise,"[185] for even a seemingly impossible task poses no challenge to him, and he accomplishes it in the best possible way.[186]

Abraham's Dream

When Ishmael came of age,[187] Abraham came to visit him.[188] Abraham loved Ishmael very much, and he saw in him his only legacy. One night, Abraham saw in a dream that he must do what, for any other man, would have been impossible. He awoke and roused his son and said, "My son, I have seen in a dream that I am slaughtering

184. *Biḥār al-anwār* vol. 12 p. 63 tr. 9 and tr. 10 and p. 74 tr. 22

185. Qurʾān 2:260 and *Biḥār al-anwār* vol. 12 p. 65 tr. 11

186. *al-Mīzān* under the verse 2:260

187. The only clear indication of his age is in verse 37:102 which says, "When he came of age." There is a tradition that claims that he was five when Isaac was born (*Biḥār al-anwār* vol. 12 p. 130 tr. 11), however, we can confidently reject this number in light of the aforementioned verse. Some commentators have claimed he was thirteen without citing any tradition to back themselves. I have simply used the term "coming of age." If we assume that "coming of age" meant the same to them as it does to Muslims, we can guess that he was fifteen; however, it is safer not to guess.

188. Several traditions place the story of the sacrifice within the context of Abraham's first Hajj (*Biḥār al-anwār* vol. 12 p. 126 tr. 2). However, these traditions are problematic for the following reasons:

- They mention that the boy's mother was Sarah instead of Hagar.
- The timeline is odd. These traditions act as though Hajj is already a ritual that people engage in at the time, when it is not until later, when Ishmael grows up, that he and Abraham rebuild the Kaʿbah and resurrect the rituals of Hajj.

you. Tell me, what is your opinion?"[189] As a prophet, Abraham saw only clairvoyant dreams, and it was clear to him that this message was a command from God. Nonetheless, as God was testing him, he wished also to test his son.[190]

Ishmael replied, "O Father! Do as you have been commanded. You shall find me, if God wills, among the patient."[191] He did not so much as hesitate. Even at a young age, he fully understood who his father was and who God was, and he knew that God could see great wisdom where man could see none. He continued, "I only ask you to bind my limbs so that I do not move; and tie your clothes back so they are not sprayed with my blood, lest my mother see; and sharpen your blade; and move it swiftly across my throat to make it easier on me, for indeed death is difficult."

---

189. Qur'ān 37:102

190. There is an age-old debate between followers of the Judeo-Christian tradition and Muslims as to whether the son Abraham offered as a sacrifice was Ishmael or Isaac. The Bible states explicitly that it was Isaac (Genesis 22:1–19) but also refers to Isaac as Abraham's "only son" despite having conceded that Ishmael was born before Isaac (Genesis 16:15–16) raising the question: How could Isaac be his *only* son if he was born after Ishmael?

Regardless, within the traditions attributed to Prophet Muḥammad and the imams, there are also some traditions that say it was Isaac, not Ishmael (*Biḥār al-anwār* vol. 12 p. 126 tr. 2, p. 131 tr. 14 and 15). However, the majority of traditions name Ishmael.

While the traditions are somewhat equivocal, the Qur'ān is not. True, it does not name Ishmael when it narrates the story of the sacrifice (37:101–111). Nonetheless, after narrating the story, it says, "And we gave him (i.e., Abraham) glad tidings of Isaac, a prophet among the righteous" (37:112), indicating that the son about whom the previous verses spoke was not Isaac, and thus, Ishmael. The imams explicitly referred to this verse as proof that it was Ishmael (see *Biḥār al-anwār* vol. 12 p. 130 tr. 11). Another solid argument revolves around the verses that narrate the tidings given by the angels to Abraham and Sarah. They were told before Isaac was born that he would live long enough to have a son named Jacob (11:71). Thus, if Isaac was the one Abraham was to sacrifice, he would have known that the child would survive the ordeal and that it was just a test. The fact that he did not know it was a test shows that the sacrificial boy could not have been Isaac.

191. Qur'ān 37:102

Abraham gazed at him with tears in his eyes and said, "You are such a great support to me in fulfilling God's command."[192]

Satan Speaks to Abraham

Abraham and Ishmael set out under the pretense of collecting firewood[193] from Minā, for it was there that God had ordered the sacrifice to be carried out. Along the way, Satan presented himself to Abraham as an old man.[194] He asked, "Abraham, what do you plan to do to this boy?"

Abraham replied, "I must slaughter him."

The old man exclaimed, "Exalted be God! You will slaughter a boy who has never sinned against God in the least!"

Abraham said with resolve, "God has commanded me to do it."

The old man objected, "Rather, God has forbidden you to do it. It is *Satan* who has commanded you to do this."

Abraham retorted, "No, the one who has raised me to my current station is the one who commanded me to do it. I shall not speak to you any further." By this time, Abraham had reached Minā, and he began making preparations for the slaughter.

The old man interjected, "Abraham, you are a leader. People will follow your lead. If you kill your son, others will kill their children." But Abraham had resolved to ignore this man and follow only the command of God, so the man slipped away unnoticed.

Satan Speaks to Hagar

Meanwhile, Hagar was going about her duties when the same old man appeared before her shaking his head saying, "What do you know about this old man whom I saw?"

Hagar said, "That is my husband."

---

192. *Majmaʿ al-bayān* under 37:102

193. *Majmaʿ al-bayān* under 37:102

194. The story of Satan presenting himself to Abraham and Hagar is narrated in the same tradition which I previously dubbed problematic (*Biḥār al-anwār* vol. 12 p. 126 tr. 2). Nonetheless, I have transmitted this portion of the tradition because it falls within the realm of possibility and adds to our understanding of Abraham's and Hagar's resolve to obey God despite Satan's machinations.

He continued, "And the boy who was with him?"

She said, "That it my son."

He said in disgust, "I saw the old man lay your son on the ground and take a blade to his throat to slaughter him!"

She protested, "You are a liar. Abraham is the most compassionate of people. How could he slaughter his son?"

He swore, "By the Lord of the sky and the earth and the Lord of this place, I saw him lay him on the ground and put a blade to his throat."

She asked, "And why would he do such a thing?"

He replied, "He thinks his Lord commanded him to do it."

With a sense of relief she said, "Then he is right to obey his Lord."[195]

The Sacrifice of Ishmael

In Minā, Abraham bound Ishmael's limbs and tied his own clothes back as Ishmael had advised. He sharpened his blade and laid Ishmael's temple upon the ground so that his face looked in the direction of the ruins of the Kaʿbah. With tears in his eyes and resolve in his heart, Abraham drew the blade swiftly across his son's throat. He expected to feel the tremors of death surge through Ishmael but was surprised to see that his blade had failed to cut and the boy remained unusually tranquil.

As Abraham and Ishmael struggled to make sense of this anticlimax, God's voice rang out, "O Abraham! You have fulfilled my command from the dream. This is how we reward the righteous. We have tested you rigorously to prepare you to receive the greatest rewards in paradise. This was the manifest test I had promised you[196] some years ago when I said, 'I shall give you a forbearing child, and, thereafter, I shall test your obedience to me through him.'"

---

195. *Biḥār al-anwār* vol. 12 p. 126 tr. 2

196. Qurʾān 37:103–106

The Substitutionary Ram

Gabriel brought a majestic ram from the neighboring mountain of Thabīr[197] and presented it to Abraham.[198] The ram had long, spiraling horns and a roan coat. God had created it miraculously and sent it directly from the skies. Wherever it trod, ate, gazed, or defecated, the ground burst forth in verdure.[199] Gabriel told Abraham that this ram, the noblest of animals,[200] would replace Ishmael as his sacrificial offering to God.[201]

Abraham, immensely relieved, eyes streaming with tears of joy, untied his son and embraced him, and together they slaughtered the ram and praised God.

When they had finished butchering the ram and had prepared its meat to be distributed among the poor, Satan appeared, this time in his own form. He demanded, "Abraham, give me my share of this ram."

Abraham, perplexed, asked, "What share do you get of this ram, for it was a sacrificial offering for my Lord and a replacement for my son?" At that moment, God spoke to Abraham telling him that Satan was to receive a share—the spleen and the testicles. Abraham gave these parts to Satan, and it has since become unlawful for people to eat these parts of an animal.[202]

The Highest Rank

Almost from birth, Abraham had faced some of the most rigorous trials a human being can bear. He was consigned to live in a cave from his birth until he was old enough to escape. He was catapulted into a blazing fire. He was banished from family and home. He was deprived of the joy of parenthood until old age, and when he was

197. Mount Thabīr forms the northern boundary of Minā. If you stand atop the Mountain of Light, facing the Ka'bah, Mount Thabīr is on your left side.

198. *al-Kāfī* 15.7.9

199. *Biḥār al-anwār* vol. 12 p. 131 tr. 17

200. *Biḥār al-anwār* vol. 12 p. 131 tr. 12 and 13

201. Qur'ān 37:107

202. *Biḥār al-anwār* vol. 12 p. 130 tr. 10

finally granted a son, he was ordered to slaughter him. Throughout all of these trials, Abraham had remained unwaveringly steadfast in his devotion to God. And God had rewarded him accordingly. He had made him a prophet and then a messenger. He chose him as his friend. After having fulfilled the herculean task of surrendering his son,[203] God told him, "Submit!" at which he replied, "I hereby submit to the Lord of all realms."[204] So God told him, "I hereby appoint you an imam, a leader, of all people."[205]

Abraham urged, "And will you appoint anyone from my progeny?"

God replied, "This covenant shall not include the wrongdoers among them," thus, promising him at once that there would be imams in his progeny and that some would be wrongdoers and hence disqualify themselves from this lofty position.

The Visitors

Sarah and Abraham continued to beg God for a son in earnest through their old age, although the cessation of her monthly cycle had acutely curbed their will to hope.

Then one day, Abraham gazed out over his land when he spotted four men, dressed in white, approaching. They wore turbans and had drawn the ends of their turbans over their faces to protect themselves from the elements.[206] They hailed, "Peace," and he replied, "Peace,[207] O strangers to our land!"[208] In those few moments, from their movements and their speech, Abraham realized that these were special guests, and he wished to honor them. He stole

---

203. *Biḥār al-anwār* vol. 12 p. 12 tr. 36 and 37 mention the order in which these ranks were conferred upon him. *Biḥār al-anwār* vol. 12 p. 59 tr. 1–2 and 4 indicate that it was the sacrifice of Ishmael that was the final test.

204. Qur'ān 2:131

205. Qur'ān 2:124

206. *al-Kāfī* 18.171.6

207. Qur'ān 11:69

208. Qur'ān 51:25

over to his wife, Sarah,[209] and they decided they would serve the best they could offer.

Abraham ordered his servants[210] to slaughter the choicest, fattest calf from his ample herd. Then, he had them roast the entire calf until its meat was exquisitely tender and its juices ready to burst forth.[211] He offered the roasted meat to them.[212] They thanked him courteously, but they did not touch the meat. He asked them, "Will you not eat?"[213] When he saw that they did not extend their hands to partake in it, he looked disapprovingly at them and felt fearful of them.[214]

He cast a nervous glance at Sarah whom he had instructed to stand by in case their guests should need anything.[215] Then he looked back at his guests and said quite frankly, "We are frightened of you."[216]

A Second Son Prophesied

At last, the men pulled aside the coverings from their faces, and Abraham immediately recognized the angels: Gabriel, their leader,[217] and Michael, Raphael, and Carobiel.[218] They said, "Do not

---

209. Qur'ān 51:26

210. There is no mention of servants at this point in the story, but it seems only natural that Abraham, with all his wealth and in his old age, would have some servants in his employ. In a tradition in *al-Durr al-manthūr* (under verse 11:70), Sarah reassures Abraham saying, that he, his wife, and his servants outnumber their four guests, in case they wish him harm, thereby indicating that he did have servants.

211. *al-Kāfī* 18.171.6 and Qur'ān 51:26 and 11:69

212. Qur'ān 51:27

213. Qur'ān 51:27

214. Qur'ān 11:70

215. Qur'ān 11:71 and in *al-Durr al-manẓūm* under the same verse

216. Qur'ān 15:52

217. *Biḥār al-anwār* vol. 12 p. 5 tr. 12

218. *al-Kāfī* 18.171.6

be frightened. We have been sent to the people of Lot."[219] He was both relieved and elated to see his old friends, not yet registering the foreboding in their primary mission.

Little did Abraham realize that Sarah, at that moment, had, after decades of infertility, suddenly begun to menstruate.[220]

The angels continued, "We have come to give you tidings of a boy endowed with knowledge who is to be born to you."[221]

He asked, "Do you give me such tidings despite my old age? I could not have heard correctly, so what is it again of which you give me tidings?"

They said, "We have given you these tidings in all seriousness, so do not be among the despondent."

He said, "Of course not, for who except the errant despair of the Lord's mercy?"[222]

Sarah, who had overheard the entire conversation, came forward with a gasp and slapped herself in incredulity and said, "Shall an old, barren woman like me bear a child?"

They said, "This is what your Lord has said. He is the Wise, the Omniscient."[223] Then they turned to Abraham and said:

> We give you tidings of a son who shall be called Isaac,[224] a prophet from among the righteous. God

---

219. Qur'ān 11:70

220. Qur'ān 11:71. The word *ḍaḥikat* has two possible meanings. It could mean that she laughed (from *ḍiḥk* meaning "to laugh"). It could also mean that she menstruated (from *ḍaḥk* meaning "to menstruate"). Many commentators, like al-Zamakhsharī and al-Fakhr al-Rāzī, have favored the former and say that she laughed in relief when she learned that these men did not wish them ill. Traditions from Prophet Muḥammad and his family, on the other hand, say that the latter is intended (see *al-Burhān fī tafsīr al-qur'ān* vol. 3 p. 124 and vol. 4 p. 316). Apparently, allowing her to menstruate after so many years of being barren was a way to prepare her for the news they were about to deliver. She had, after all, been disappointed once before when another promise was made, but not about her.

221. Qur'ān 15:53

222. Qur'ān 15:54–56

223. Qur'ān 51:29–30

224. Qur'ān 11:71. His name in Arabic is *Isḥāq*.

> shall bless you and Isaac. From his progeny there shall be some who are righteous and some who will clearly wrong themselves.[225] We also give you tidings of a grandson who will come after Isaac who shall be called Jacob.[226] We shall make each of them righteous. And we shall make them leaders to guide by our mandate, and we shall reveal to them admonishment to do good deeds, establish prayer, and give charity. And they shall be our worshipers.[227]

She said, "O my! Am I to bear a child when I am old and my husband here is also old? This is something surprising."

They said, "Are you surprised by an act of God? God's mercy and his blessings have been upon you, O household of Abraham! He is praiseworthy and magnanimous."[228]

When Abraham's fear was dispelled and the tidings of Isaac and Jacob had sunk in,[229] he said, "Enough about my son—what is your mission, O messengers?"

The Angels' Mission

They replied, "We have been sent to punish a criminal people.[230] We shall destroy the denizens of this city where Lot has been sent, for its denizens have been wrongdoers."[231]

---

225. Qur'ān 37:112–3

226. Qur'ān 11:71. ʿAllāmah al-Ṭabāṭabā'ī believes that the phrase "who will come after Isaac" is a backhanded attack on the Torah which says Jacob was named *Yaʿqūb* because he was born holding the heel (*ʿaqib*) of his twin brother (see Genesis 25:26). Rather, he was called Jacob (*Yaʿqūb*) because his birth was prophesied after (*ʿaqiba*) his father's.

227. Qur'ān 21:72–73

228. Qur'ān 11:72–73

229. Qur'ān 11:74–75

230. Qur'ān 15:57–58

231. Qur'ān 29:31

Abraham began arguing with the angels about God's impending punishment for the people of Sodom and Gomorra, for Abraham was forbearing, solicitous, and always turned to us in his affairs.[232] He asked Gabriel, "If there were one hundred believers among them, would you destroy them?"

Gabriel said, "No."

Abraham asked, "And if there were fifty?"

Gabriel said, "No."

Abraham asked, "And if there were thirty?"

Gabriel said, "No."

Abraham asked, "And if there were twenty?"

Gabriel said, "No."

Abraham asked, "And if there were ten?"

Gabriel said, "No."

Abraham asked, "And if there were five?"

Gabriel said, "No."

Abraham asked, "And if there were one?"

Gabriel said, "No."[233]

Abraham said, "Well Lot is among them."[234] He believed that God's decree for them was still pending and could be altered by his intercession.[235]

They said, "O Abraham! Cease this effort.[236] We know better who is among them.[237] Your Lord's decree has been issued. A punishment shall befall them which cannot be repealed.[238] We have been sent... to cast upon them a barrage of sandstone pebbles, earmarked by God for those who are excessive.[239] As for Lot and his family, we

---

232. Qur'ān 11:74–75

233. *al-Kāfī* 18.171.6

234. Qur'ān 29:32

235. See *Sharḥ uṣūl al-kāfī* by al-Māzandarānī vol. 12 p. 437.

236. Qur'ān 11:76

237. Qur'ān 29:32

238. Qur'ān 11:76

239. Qur'ān 51:33–34

shall deliver them all from the punishment except for his wife who is among those who must remain and be punished."[240]

The Birth of Isaac

Nine months later, Sarah gave birth to a boy whom, in accordance with God's instructions, they named Isaac.[241] On the seventh day, Sarah noticed that the boy's umbilicus was shed; however, she became worried when she saw that his foreskin was intact. It was known that the foreskins of the prophets were shed on the seventh day of their birth, and she feared that God's plan for her son had somehow changed. She asked Abraham about this, and he, in turn, asked God. God reassured them that Isaac would be a prophet but that his foreskin would not be shed on its own because of the bad feelings Sarah harbored toward Hagar all those years before. He ordered Abraham to remove his foreskin with a blade.[242] Sarah felt so remorseful for her ill feelings toward Hagar that she begged God saying, "O God, do not take me to task for what I did to Hagar."[243]

Admiration For His Brother

Years later, when Isaac was a young man, Abraham told him the story of his brother's sacrifice and of his high station before God. Isaac wished that he could have been the one and that he could

---

240. Qur'ān 15:59–60 and 29:32

241. In Arabic his name is *Isḥāq*. One tradition claims that Sarah was 90 years old and Abraham was 120 years old at the time of Isaac's birth (*Biḥār al-anwār* vol. 12 p. 111 tr. 36). While we can comfortably say that they were both old, and past the normal age of parenthood, the thirty-year age difference that this tradition implies is improbable. As we mentioned in previous footnotes, Abraham and Sarah married in Kūthā long before Abraham was thrown into the fire. When he was thrown into the fire, the people referred to him as a *fatā* (Qur'ān 21:60) which, in this context, refers to a young man, probably not exceeding 25 or 30 years old. Accordingly, there is no way Sarah could be 30 years his junior.

242. *Biḥār al-anwār* vol. 12 p. 101 tr. 7

243. *Biḥār al-anwār* vol. 12 p. 108 tr. 29. It is true that the end of this tradition says that she was speaking about the time when she had Hagar circumcised. However, it is possible that this explanation is not part of the tradition, but an explanation from the transmitter based on misinformation from the Bible.

also have attained a similarly high station. Because of his sincere and righteous intention, God promised to reward him like his brother.[244]

Māriyā ibn Aws

There was an old, pious man named Māriyā ibn Aws who lived in a swamp that was surrounded by deep waters. Every three years, he would emerge from his home to gather supplies and to worship upon one of the mountains around Jerusalem. On one such occasion, he came upon Isaac who was tending to Abraham's flock of sheep. Māriyā was impressed by the beauty of the animals and by the radiance in Isaac's countenance. He inquired, "To whom does this flock belong?"

Isaac replied, "To Abraham, the Friend of God, and I am his son, Isaac." They spoke at length, and when Māriyā had gone, Isaac returned to his father and told him about his encounter. Abraham wished to meet Māriyā and so he went in his pursuit. It was not until three years later, as Abraham walked in the mountains around Jerusalem, that he came upon a man deep in prayer with his arms outstretched to the sky and his eyes closed, flowing with tears. Abraham waited patiently for him to finish. Then he addressed him saying, "What is your name and to whom do you pray?"

Māriyā replied, not knowing to whom he spoke, "My name is Māriyā, and I pray to the God of Abraham."

Abraham asked, "And who is the God of Abraham?"

Māriyā replied, "The one who created me and you."

Abraham said, "I am pleased to meet you, and I wish to befriend you for God's sake. Tell me where your home is, if I ever wish to visit you."

Māriyā told him, "My home is in a swamp surrounded by waters that you will not be able to cross. But you may find me here in my place of worship."

---

244. *Biḥār al-anwār* vol. 12 p. 123 tr. 1. Isaac's attitude toward his brother is known in Arabic as *ghibṭah* or "admiration," and must not be confused with *ḥasad* or "envy" or "jealousy." One who is jealous wishes to have what another has instead of that person. One who admires also wishes to have what the other has but at no cost to that person.

Abraham asked him, "How do *you* cross the water?"

Māriyā said, "I walk on it."

Abraham said, "Let us go together. Perhaps the one who placed the water at your service will do the same for me."

Māriyā gathered his things, and they set off together for his home. When they reached the water's edge, Māriyā said, "In the name of God," as he stepped upon the water and his foot rested upon it without sinking in. Abraham also said, "In the name of God," and stepped onto the water's surface, and, to Māriyā's surprise, he too was able to walk without sinking.

When they reached his home, Abraham marveled at the beauty and simplicity of his home in the swamp. He told Māriyā, "Let us raise our hands in prayer. I shall pray and you say 'amen', and you should pray and I will say 'amen'."

Māriyā asked, "For what do you propose we pray?"

Abraham said, "We should pray for the guidance and forgiveness of those believers who have sinned, and we should beg God to spare us the hardships of the Day of Judgment."

Māriyā suddenly looked dejected and said, "What good is my prayer? I have been praying to God for three years for one thing and he has not answered me. I feel ashamed to ask him anything else until I know that he has heard me."

Abraham told him, "Māriyā, certainly God has heard your prayer, for he is the All-Hearing. Nonetheless, he delays his answer to those whose prayers he loves so that they pray more and plead more fervently. Tell me: For what have you been praying?"

Māriyā told him the story of the young shepherd he had met and said, "I have been begging God to allow me to meet his Friend, Abraham."

Abraham exclaimed, "Good tidings, for God has answered your prayers. I am Abraham." They embraced in joy and tears, and it is said that the tradition of embracing other believers began with their embrace.[245]

---

245. *Biḥār al-anwār* vol. 12 p. 9 tr. 23 and p. 76 tr. 1 and p. 81 tr. 10. I have done my best to combine these three narratives into one.

Restoration of the Kaʿbah

In Bakkah, the Kaʿbah had remained much as Abraham had found it when he first left Hagar and Ishmael there—little more than a mound of red clay. Although God had saved the Kaʿbah from the deluge in Noah's time,[246] weather and neglect had worn it down. Ishmael and Hagar had built their small home adjacent to the northwestern side of these ruins, precisely where Abraham had first left them.[247] Now that Abraham and Ishmael had successfully passed one of God's most difficult tests, God deemed it the right time for them to begin the restoration of the Kaʿbah. Their task was to rebuild the Kaʿbah upon the foundations left from Adam's time.

They used the water of Zamzam and the plentiful clay from the area to make mud bricks. These they layered, each day adding an entire layer of bricks. When they had built the wall to about waist high, Abraham heard a voice from the neighboring mountain, Abū Qubays, saying, "I have something for you which has been entrusted to me these many years."[248]

Abraham climbed the mountain and retrieved the Black Stone which had been stashed away in one of its caves. They placed the Black Stone in the eastern corner of the building so that it could be seen and touched from the outside.[249] Then they continued to build row after row. God sent a cool breeze from paradise called *Sakīnah* upon them to give them strength and comfort through their toil.[250] They made two doors, one facing northeast from which to enter and the other facing southwest from which to exit.[251] Just outside the entrance door was the place Ishmael had built a corral for his sheep. He used to feed them *ḥaṭīm* or "hay" there, and so this area

---

246. *Biḥār al-anwār* vol. 11 p. 313 tr. 6 and vol. 11 p. 325 tr. 43

247. The site of their home is now known as Ḥijr Ismāʿīl.

248. *al-Kāfī* 15.7.4

249. *al-Kāfī* 15.7.4

250. *al-Kāfī* 15.7.5

251. *al-Kāfī* 15.7.7

came to be called *Ḥaṭīm* and became one of the best places in the world to pray.[252]

Abraham and Ishmael found the work exhilarating, and they said as they toiled, "Lord, accept this from us, for you alone are the All-Hearing, the All-Knowing. Lord, make us subservient to you and, of our progeny, make a nation subservient to you, show us our rites of worship, and accept our penance, for you alone are the Clement, the Ever-Merciful. Lord, raise in their midst a messenger from among them who will recite your verses to them and teach them the law and wisdom and purify them, for you are the Invincible, the Wise."[253]

To build the lower half of the Kaʿbah, they were able to stand on the ground. As the walls grew taller though, they found they needed a raised platform upon which to stand. Abraham stood on a nearly cubical stone, tall enough for him to stand on to extend his reach but small enough to facilitate moving it. In no time, they had completed the four walls. The Kaʿbah stood 9 cubits tall and had no roof.[254]

God commanded Abraham to stand in the center of the stone before coming down. For a moment, he made the stone soften under his feet leaving a distinct impression. Then he made the stone hard again.[255] For all time, this stone would be known to the world as *Maqām Ibrāhīm*, the Station of Abraham.[256] Abraham placed this stone adjacent to the wall, just to the north of the door. There it would remain for centuries to come.[257]

---

252. *Biḥār al-anwār* vol. 65 p. 86 tr. 11

253. Qurʾān 2:128–9

254. *al-Kāfī* 15.7.7–8

255. *al-Kāfī* vol. 4 p. 223. tr. 1

256. Jaʿfariyān, Rasul. *Āthār-e islāmī-e makkeh wa madineh* Qum: Nashr-e Maʿshar, 2002. p. 99.

257. *al-Kāfī* vol. 4 p. 223. tr. 2 and *Biḥār al-anwār* vol. 31 p. 33 tr. 1. These traditions tell us that the Station of Abraham was originally adjacent to the Kaʿbah. Prior to Prophet Muḥammad's time, it was moved to where it now stands. The Prophet moved it back to where Abraham had placed it, and ʿUmar ibn al-Khaṭṭāb, during his caliphate, ordered that it be moved back where it had been

God told Abraham, "Do not associate any partners with me, and purify my house for those who circulate around it, who stand before it in worship, who frequent it, and who bow and prostrate toward it.[258] We hereby designate this house as a place of pilgrimage and as a sanctuary. Make of the Station of Abraham a place of prayer.[259] And proclaim the Hajj among people, and they will come to you if even on foot or on any scrawny camel that will bring them from every far-flung canyon."[260]

Proclamation of Hajj

Abraham climbed upon one of the corners of the building[261] and proclaimed to the people who had settled in Bakkah and, through them, to all the world, "God commands you all to make a pilgrimage to his house, so come![262] This is the first house of God built for all people here in Bakkah. It is blessed, and it is a guide for humankind. In and around this house are clear signs such as the Station of Abraham. Whoever enters it is hereby granted amnesty. All people owe God a Hajj if they are able to go. If anyone refuses, it is to their own detriment, for God is free from need for people."[263]

God amplified his voice and made it resonate in the hearts of everyone on earth in the east and west and in the heart of every unborn child and unfertilized seed in the loins of man until the end of time.[264]

---

in the Age of Ignorance. And there it stands till the present day. In one tradition, Imam ʿAlī wishes he could move it back to where Abraham and the Prophet had placed it, but he regrets that the "*sunnah* of ʿUmar" had so thoroughly eclipsed the *sunnah* of the Prophet that if he were to try, his troops would mutiny against him (*al-Kāfī* vol. 8 p. 59 tr. 21).

258. Qurʾān 22:26 and 2:24

259. Qurʾān 2:124

260. Qurʾān 22:27

261. *al-Kāfī* 15.7.6. Another tradition says he climbed atop Mount Abū Qubays (*Biḥār al-anwār* vol. 12 p. 115 tr. 47).

262. *al-Kāfī* 15.7.4

263. Qurʾān 3:96–7

264. *Biḥār al-anwār* vol. 12 p. 115 tr. 47, p. 106 tr. 18, and p. 107 tr. 20

Then he turned his attention to God once again and said:

> Lord, make this city safe, and keep me and my progeny from worshiping idols. Lord, idols have led many people astray. Those who follow me are with me, and those who disobey me will, I hope, be guided by you in some other way, for you are absolving and merciful. Lord, I had settled some of my progeny in a valley bereft of pasture near your sacred house and prayed, "O Lord, I settled them here so that they would establish the prayer, so make people's hearts incline toward them, and provide them with sustenance so that they may be thankful." O Lord! Of course, I need not tell you all this, for you know what we conceal and what we reveal. In fact, nothing on earth or in the sky is concealed from God. Praise is for God who has granted me Ishmael and Isaac despite my old age. My Lord is the Hearer of Prayers. Lord, make me and my progeny steadfast in prayer. And Lord, accept my prayers. Lord, forgive me and my parents and all the believers on the day when the reckoning will be taken.[265]

Abraham's First Hajj

The people of Bakkah and surrounding areas began pouring in for the pilgrimage in answer to Abraham's call. God charged Gabriel to teach Abraham and Ishmael the rites of Hajj just as he had taught Adam and Eve before. On the 9th of Dhū al-Ḥijjah, he led them to the Plain of ʿArafāt and told them *to confess their sins* before their Lord.[266]

---

265. Qur'ān 14:35–41

266. *Biḥār al-anwār* vol. 12 p. 108 tr. 27. The Arabic word *iʿtirāf,* which means "to admit or confess," is derived from the same root as the name ʿArafāt, hence the connection.

That night, as the sun set, he took them to Muzdalifah and told them *to proceed* onto the sacred ground.[267] There, Abraham and his followers collected pebbles for the coming rituals. The next morning, they proceeded to Minā where Gabriel told them to pray for whatever *they could wish for*.[268] As they approached the place known as al-Jimār, where years before Satan had tried his utmost to thwart Abraham from sacrificing Ishmael, once again Satan was made to appear. Gabriel told them to stone him as Adam used to, and they did, with seven stones each. Satan slunk back into the ground at the place where the obelisk, *Jamarat al-ʿAqabah*, would later be erected.[269]

They then sacrificed animals to commemorate Abraham's sacrifice of the ram in place of Ishmael so many years before. They shaved their heads and then returned to Bakkah and completed the *ṭawāf* around the Kaʿbah. When they began to walk between Ṣafā and Marwah, Satan was made to appear again, and at Gabriel's command, Abraham and his followers began running from him in what came to be called the *harwalah*.[270] They then returned to Minā, and each day Satan was made to appear at the sites where the three obelisks, *al-Jamarat al-Ūlā*, *al-Jamarat al-Wusṭā*, and *Jamarat al-ʿAqabah* would later be erected. Every time he appeared, Abraham and his followers would stone him with seven pebbles each, and he would slink into the ground.[271] In this way, every year, Abraham invited people to complete the pilgrimage called *Hajj*.

---

267. *Biḥār al-anwār* vol. 12 p. 108 tr. 28. The Arabic word *izdilāf* means "to proceed or move forward." It is true that this meaning of *izdilāf* would imply that the correct pronunciation is *muzdalafah* (*ism mafʿūl* or *ism al-makān*) instead of *muzdalifah* (*ism al-fāʿil*); however, these rules are rarely observed in proper names.

268. *Biḥār al-anwār* vol. 12 p. 108 tr. 25. The Arabic word *tamannī* means "to wish" and *munyah* pl. *munā* means "wish(es)," hence the connection.

269. *Biḥār al-anwār* vol. 12 p. 110 tr. 33

270. *Biḥār al-anwār* vol. 12 p. 108 tr .23–4

271. *Biḥār al-anwār* vol. 12 p. 102 tr. 8 and p. 110 tr. 32

Taming of the Horses

When the first Hajj was complete, Abraham stood near the Kaʿbah and made an unusual call unlike any the people had heard. Before they knew what was happening, all the horses of the world, which were wild as of yet, gathered and submitted themselves before Abraham and Ishmael.[272] Ishmael was the first person to ever tame and ride horses.[273]

Hagar's Death

When Hagar passed away, Ishmael was distraught. She had raised him and loved him, and he was very fond of her too. He buried her in the *Ḥijr* right next to the Kaʿbah and built a wall around it so no one would trample her grave unwittingly.[274]

Ishmael Marries

In time, Ishmael was ready to marry. He first married a woman from the local tribe of Jurhum named Zaʿlah or ʿImādah, but he divorced her because she had borne him no children. Then he married al-Sayyidah bint al-Ḥārith who bore him children.[275] He also married a woman from the ʿAmāliqah people named Sāmah.[276]

Abraham longed to see his son, but he could not visit often because of the agreement he had made with Sarah. Finally, he decided to visit him, but Sarah made him promise not to alight from his camel until he returned to Hebron and that he not spend a night away from her. God folded the earth[277] for him and miraculously let

---

272. *Biḥār al-anwār* vol. 12 p. 104 tr. 16 and p. 114 tr. 46

273. *Biḥār al-anwār* vol. 12 p. 107 tr. 21

274. *Biḥār al-anwār* vol. 12 p. 104 tr. 13

275. *Biḥār al-anwār* vol. 12 p. 113 tr. 40

276. *Biḥār al-anwār* vol. 12 p. 111 tr. 38. We do not know much about the ʿAmāliqah. Fayrūzābādī simply tells us they are the descendants of ʿImlīq ibn Lāwidh and that they have since vanished (see *al-Qāmūs*).

277. This supernatural process is referred to as *ṭayy al-arḍ* in this and other traditions.

him travel the long distance in a few moments.[278] Nonetheless, he arrived after Hagar had died. He met Ishmael's wife, Sāmah, and spoke to her without letting on who he was. He was disappointed to learn that Ishmael was away from home hunting. He asked her about their life there and she replied, "Our situation is tough, and our life is tough." Before leaving her, he told her to give the following message to her husband, "Tell your husband that an old man visited and told him to change the threshold of his door."

When Ishmael returned, he sensed someone had visited and asked his wife excitedly. She conveyed her guest's message. He understood the message but did not tell his wife anything. He simply replaced the threshold of his door as her guest had ordered.

Sometime later, Abraham visited again under similar circumstances, and, once again, Ishmael was out hunting. This time, when he asked about their life, Sāmah replied, "Our life is well, and we are well. Please come in and be our guest." He saw the tidy cages Ishmael had built to house his pigeons.[279] Despite her insistence, he declined to accept and returned home. Later, when Ishmael returned, she told him of their guest, and Ishmael informed her that it was his father, Abraham, who had visited her.[280]

Grey Hair

When Isaac reached adulthood, he looked so similar to his father that people had trouble distinguishing them. In those days, people's hair did not turn grey, so the vast difference in their ages did not help set one apart from the other.[281] Then one day, when Abraham was grooming himself, he noticed a grey hair in his beard. He had never seen a grey hair, and so he asked God concerning this, and God told him, "It is a sign of dignity."

---

278. *Biḥār al-anwār* vol. 12 p. 112 tr. 39

279. One traditions says that the pigeons that now live around the Sacred Mosque are the descendants of Ishmael's pigeons (*Biḥār al-anwār* vol. 12 p. 118 tr. 56).

280. *Biḥār al-anwār* vol. 12 p. 112 tr. 38

281. *Biḥār al-anwār* vol. 12 p. 111 tr. 36

Hearing this Abraham prayed, "God, increase my dignity.[282] Praise is for God who has brought me to this ripe old age without my having sinned for a moment."[283]

A Lesson on Death

Once Sarah told Abraham, "You have become old and your end may be near. Why do you not ask God to delay your death and extend your life so you can live with us and continue to bring us joy?"

Abraham prayed as she asked him to. God told him he could ask him to extend his life for as long as he wished. When he told Sarah, she advised him to ask God to extend his life indefinitely until he himself asked for death. His prayer was answered, and Sarah encouraged him to show gratitude to God by serving a great feast for the destitute. One of his many guests that night was a blind, decrepit man who came with the help of a guide. He sat down and began to eat. When he tried to take his first morsel of food, his hand began to tremble from his weakness. He missed his mouth, and his hand went to his forehead. Only with the help of his guide did he manage to put the food in his mouth. The next morsel hit his eye before finding its mark.

All the while, Abraham stared incredulously at this blind man and how he was eating. He thought to himself, "If I grow old, I too may become like him." Abraham turned his focus to God and said, "Lord, take my life whenever *you* deem it best, for I have no need for an extended life after what I have seen today."[284]

Mercy in Illness

Over the years, Abraham witnessed the deaths of many people around him. He was always saddened to see their lives come to an abrupt end, for until that time, people died for no apparent reason other than old age or some accident. One of the hardest

---

282. *Biḥār al-anwār* vol. 12 p. 8 tr. 19 and p. 13 tr. 39

283. *Biḥār al-anwār* vol. 12 p. 8 tr. 20

284. *Biḥār al-anwār* vol. 12 p. 79–80 tr. 9

of these deaths for him to bear was the death of Ishmael.[285] When he died, Abraham buried him next to his mother, Hagar,[286] and his daughters[287] in the Ḥijr. After him, his descendants ruled Bakkah generation after generation. They managed the Hajj for people and guided them in their religion until the time of ʿAdnān ibn Udad.[288] Abraham asked God to make some cause for death so that people would have the opportunity to earn reward by persevering through the sickness and so that their survivors would feel some closure by knowing the reason for their loved-ones' deaths.[289] Thus, God created fatal sicknesses which he would dole out in due measure when he intended to take a person's life.

Abraham's Death

As he reached the age of 175, Abraham's life was drawing to a close.[290] He was in Hebron at the time[291] with Sarah, Isaac, and some of his other sons and daughters[292] by his side. He told them, "My

---

285. Several traditions mention that Ishmael died before Abraham (*Kāmil al-ziyārāt* p. 65 tr. 3). No traditions contradict this claim by saying that Ishmael was Abraham's successor. However, the traditions that mention Ishmael's age at the time of his death say he was either 120 years old (*Biḥār al-anwār* vol. 12 p. 113 tr. 42), 130 (*Biḥār al-anwār* vol. 12 p. 113 tr. 41), or 137 (*Biḥār al-anwār* vol. 12 p. 113 tr. 40). If Abraham died at 175 and Ishmael died at 120, that would make Abraham's age less than 55 when he had Ishmael. While there is nothing far-fetched about this, it seems that he would have been much older considering the details surrounding Ishmael's birth. In any case, I have given precedence to the tradition that says Ishmael died before Abraham because it is transmitted by Ibn Qūlawahy who is renowned for his reliability and because it is hard to put much stock in the ages mentioned in traditions.

286. *Biḥār al-anwār* vol. 12 p. 117 tr. 54

287. *Biḥār al-anwār* vol. 12 p. 118 tr. 56

288. *Biḥār al-anwār* vol. 12 p. 113 tr. 41

289. *Biḥār al-anwār* vol. 12 p. 13 tr. 41

290. *Biḥār al-anwār* vol. 12 p. 11 tr. 27

291. *Biḥār al-anwār* vol. 12 p. 79 tr. 8

292. There is no specific mention of Abraham's other sons besides Ishmael and Isaac. There is also no evidence that places Ishmael at his side on his deathbed. Yet, the verse of the Qurʾān tells us, "Abraham exhorted *his sons* to follow it (i.e.,

children, God has chosen this religion for you, so make certain you die in submission to him."[293] Then he made his special testament to Isaac. He hung the vial containing the tunic from paradise on Isaac's neck and commanded him to pass it on to his son when death came to him.[294]

When the Angel of Death came to take his soul, Abraham was pleased to see him, for he was more handsome than anyone Abraham had ever seen. He asked, "Who could possibly dread your visit when you come looking like this?[295] Are you here to invite me or to take me by force?"

Azrael told him that he was there to invite him. Abraham asked him, half in jest, "Have you ever seen a friend who takes the life of a friend?"

God sent back the message, "Have you ever seen a lover who dislikes meeting with his beloved?"[296] Abraham smiled deeply and prepared for death. He was buried near his home in Hebron.

After the death of Abraham, Ishmael's descendants continued to rule in Bakkah. Isaac became his successor in the Holy Land. When Isaac died at the age of 180, he was buried near his father and succeeded by his son, Jacob.[297]

God's religion), as did Jacob, saying, "My sons, God has chosen this religion for you, so make certain you die in submission to him" (Qur'ān 2:132). Considering all this, we can infer that Abraham must have had at least two other sons besides Isaac who were by his side on his deathbed. We can also safely say that he had at least one daughter because he once prayed for a daughter who would mourn for him after his death (*Biḥār al-anwār* vol. 12 p. 117 tr. 53), and his prayers were always answered.

293. Qur'ān 2:132

294. *Biḥār al-anwār* vol. 12 p. 249 tr. 14

295. *Biḥār al-anwār* vol. 12 p. 79 tr. 8

296. *Biḥār al-anwār* vol. 12 p. 79 tr. 7

297. *Biḥār al-anwār* vol. 12 p. 113 tr. 42

Lot

Childhood in Kūthā

Lot[1] was born in Kūthā Rubā into a family with a prophetic legacy. His mother, Waraqah,[2] was the daughter of Prophet Lāḥij.[3] She had married Harān[4] and gave birth to a girl named Sarah and then to her son, Lot.[5]

During his childhood, Lot had witnessed the evils of paganism and the deterioration of his grandfather's legacy as he watched his fellow citizens prostrate before their king and before idols of their own fashioning.

One day, a cousin of his, who no one seemed to know had ever existed, appeared after having been tucked away in a cave outside of Kūthā all his life. His name was Abraham. Few were as happy to get to know him as Lot was. Especially when Abraham began challenging the priests and their idols, Lot felt that what his cousin said resonated with his own conscience. When Abraham declared that he was a prophet, Lot and his sister, Sarah, immediately believed in him and became his most ardent followers.[6]

---

1. In Arabic his name is *Lūṭ*.

2. Ruqayyah is given as an alternative possibility for her name (*Biḥār al-anwār* vol. 12 p. 45 tr. 38).

3. *Biḥār al-anwār* vol. 12 p. 45 tr. 38

4. This is the name given for Lot's father in the Old Testament (Genesis 11:27). There, Harān is described as the brother of Abraham, and, accordingly, Abraham would have been Lot's paternal uncle. On the other hand, a tradition from Imam al-Bāqir tells us that Sarah and Lot were siblings and that Abraham was their maternal cousin (*Biḥār al-anwār* vol. 12 p. 148 tr. 1), not their uncle. Naturally, I have given precedence to the tradition from Imam al-Bāqir over the Bible. Nonetheless, I have kept the name Harān for lack of any other information about Lot's and Sarah's father's name.

5. *Biḥār al-anwār* vol. 12 p. 148 tr. 1

6. Qur᾿ān 29:26

Over the years, Lot remained Abraham's greatest supporter and helper. He traveled with him to surrounding lands to spread the message of God's unity. He was with Abraham when he bought Bāniqyā.[7] He offered his blessings when his sister, Sarah, was married to Abraham. He helped him plan the destruction of the idols on the festival day. And when Abraham was finally banished from Kūthā, Lot was the first to declare his own willingness to emigrate with him. He said, "I shall emigrate with you to a place where I can be free to worship God, for God alone is the Invincible, the Wise."[8] Because of his unfailing devotion to truth, God appointed Lot as a prophet. He began speaking to him through dreams and through his angels, though Lot was not yet able to see the angels as his cousin could.[9] And God saved Abraham and Lot along with their families and conveyed them to a land that he had blessed for all mankind, the Levant.[10]

A New Life in Hebron

Abraham settled with Lot, Sarah, Hagar, and some of their followers in Hebron. He strategically chose this location which lay at the crossroads of the trade routes between Yemen and Syria and Babylon.[11] There he built a house and established his estate with all the livestock and possessions he had hauled from Kūthā. When they were settled, Abraham and Lot turned to preaching and calling people to God. They fared much better here than they ever had in Kūthā. Travelers and caravans constantly passed by. Abraham became famous far and wide as "the one who did not burn when Nimrod threw him into the fire." He hosted them all generously and called them to faith and obedience to God.[12] Many accepted his teachings and turned toward God.

7. *Mustadrak al-wasāʾil* vol. 2 p. 308, *Biḥār al-anwār* vol. 12 p. 77 tr. 2, and *Muʿjam al-buldān* vol. 1 p. 331 under "Bāniqyā"

8. Qurʾān 29:26

9. *al-Kāfī* 4.2.1

10. Qurʾān 21:71

11. *Biḥār al-anwār* vol. 12 p. 155 tr. 8

12. *ibid.*

Sent to Sodom

One day, news reached Abraham of trouble to the north in the city of Sodom located near the Sea of Galilee.[13] People began to complain to him of the Sodomites' extreme immorality and decadence. He decided to send Lot as his deputy to Sodom to warn its people and guide them back to the truth.[14] Abraham's parting words to Lot were, "Go to Sodom and its sister cities. Call its people to worship God, warn them of God's punishment, and remind them of what befell the people of Kūthā who followed Nimrod."[15] For this

---

13. In one tradition, Gabriel tells Prophet Muḥammad that Sodom was located near *Buḥayrat Ṭabariyyah* (Tiberias) which corresponds to the Sea of Galilee (*Biḥār al-anwār* vol. 12 p. 153 tr. 7). Admittedly, we no longer know for sure where Sodom was located. There are claims that archeological remains found in and around the Dead Sea belong to Sodom. However, there is no way to confirm this as of yet. One tradition mentions that the distance between Abraham's home (presumably Hebron) and Sodom was seven farsakh, about 24 miles (*Biḥār al-anwār* vol. 12 p. 155 tr. 8). This does not fit with the modern locations of Hebron and Tiberias and also does not make much sense considering the violence with which Sodom was destroyed. What is certain is that the site was known to the Quraysh at the time of the Qur'ān's revelation as indicated by the following verses:

- "And we left clear evidence of them for people who think" (29:35).
- "You Quraysh pass by their ruins in the morning and by night. Do you not then think that a similar fate may await you?" (37:137–8).
- "We left therein a sign for those who fear a painful punishment" (51:37).

14. *Biḥār al-anwār* vol. 12 p. 45–47 tr. 38. This tradition mentions that Abraham and Sarah settled in *a'lā al-shāmāt,* and he sent Lot to *adnā al-shāmāt*. While it is tempting to construe these terms to mean northern and southern Syria or Palestine, there is no good reason to do so. The two qualifiers might be an indication of elevation. Since the Sea of Galilee is located in the Jordan Valley, it is at a lower altitude than Hebron. Hebron is known as *al-Khalīl* in Arabic and is reputed to be the site of Abraham's and Sarah's graves.

The Old Testament tells us that Abraham and Lot parted company because they each owned so many possessions that they could not both live in the same place together without quarreling (Genesis 13:5–9). In typical fashion, the Old Testament authors have attempted to degrade the prophets by making them out to be worse than ordinary people. Certainly, Abraham sent Lot to Sodom for the purpose of guiding those people not because they could not get along.

15. *al-Burhān fī tafsīr al-qur'ān* under Qur'ān 66:10

purpose, God gave Lot wisdom and knowledge[16] and raised him to the rank of a messenger and a warner.[17]

The History of Sodom

Sodom was actually a confederation of four cities known separately by the names *Sadūm* (Sodom), *Ṣadīm* (Siddim), *Ladmā'* (Admah), and *'Umayrā'* (Gomorrah).[18] The Sodomites had been a noble and righteous people. They were communal farmers. All the men would go out to the fields during the day and leave their women and children at home. They worked hard and were rewarded with bountiful crops and a peaceful and wholesome life. They were generous with their wealth and prided themselves as excellent hosts to the multitude of traders whose caravans continuously passed through their city.

Then God tried them with a drought. As their crops dried, their coffers emptied, and they began to second-guess their culture of hospitality. They became less willing to extend a helping hand to those who passed through. The Sodomites became inordinately stingy with their resources.[19] Where travelers once found open arms, they now found only closed doors. When travelers could not replenish their supplies within the city through fair commerce, they began pilfering supplies from the meager, but still-yielding, crops that surrounded it.[20]

Satan Plants the Seed

In each divine trial, Satan sees an opportunity. He came to the Sodomites, posing as a wise, old man and said, "I have devised a plan by which you will be able to prevent these vagrants from raiding your crops and absconding with your meager and hard-

16. Qur'ān 21:74

17. *Biḥār al-anwār* vol. 12 p. 148 tr. 1

18. *al-Kāfī* vol. 5 p. 549 tr. 2. In some traditions *Ṣarīm* is mentioned instead of *Ṣadīm*. In others, *Ladnā* is mentioned instead of *Ladmā'* (*Biḥār al-anwār* vol. 12 p. 162 tr. 14).

19. *Biḥār al-anwār* vol. 12 p. 147 tr. 1

20. *al-Burhān fī tafsīr al-qur'ān* under Qur'ān 66:10

earned harvest." The Sodomites were all ears. He continued, "Whenever you catch someone taking from your fields, you must make an example of him. Strip him of his clothes and rape him."[21]

The Sodomites cringed in disgust and horror at the thought. But having planted the seed in their minds, Satan left.

During the next few nights, Satan manifested himself as a young, handsome boy. He began stealing into their fields by night and trampled through their crops and carried off loads of produce. When they noticed and grew irate at the repeated trespasses, the men of Sodom decided they would lie in wait to catch the culprit. When they had captured him, they found he was a handsome boy. Satan's proposal crossed their collective mind for a fleeting instant, but they silenced the horrid thought and agreed among themselves that the boy must simply be executed, lest he continue to unscrupulously destroy all their crops. One of the men volunteered to imprison the boy for the night so that they could carry out the execution in the morning.

In the middle of the night, the man who had imprisoned the boy woke to the boy's heart-wrenching sobs. He asked him what was the matter. The boy said, "My father always used to lull me to sleep on his chest."

The man's heart went out to the seemingly innocent boy, and he said, "Come and sleep on my chest." The boy grew calm and began snuggling with the unsuspecting man. Seamlessly, the boy's innocent movements grew sinister, and he began fondling himself while the man observed in a rapture. When the man became fully aroused, the boy coaxed him to copulate with him. They passed the remainder of the night like that, and, by morning, the man was so exhausted that he fell into a deep slumber, and Satan managed to escape and flee from the city altogether.[22]

When the other Sodomites came to the man's house and saw that the boy was nowhere to be found, they were understandably upset. But the man began describing to them what he had done with the boy during the night, and his graphic description piqued

---

21. *Biḥār al-anwār* vol. 12 p. 155 tr. 8

22. *Biḥār al-anwār* vol. 12 p. 164 tr. 17 and *al-Kāfī* vol. 5 p. 544

their interest. He showed them the way the boy had shown him. They were still disgusted, but they began thinking that the wise man's proposal may be a workable solution after all.

Satan's Seed Takes Root

As time passed, they caught more and more people rummaging through their fields or stealing uninvited into their city. They stripped these people on the spot and disgraced them publicly. With time and repetition, disgust turned to pleasure. When no outsiders were to be found, the men began to look to one another, taking turns. They shunned their wives in favor of other men. With time, their appetites increased, and they began to copulate with younger and younger boys as well.

The Women Too

Satan was elated to see how well his plan had worked. He decided to try his hand with the women of Sodom. He manifested himself in the form of a woman visiting their city. This woman began speaking to the women, noting that the men seemed to be involved only with other men leaving the women unfulfilled. With a bit of insinuation and a tone of indignation, she was able to coerce the women to satisfy their needs among themselves, partly out of desperation, and partly to seek revenge against their neglectful husbands.[23]

Depravity Becomes the Norm

With time, the last vestiges of nobility and virtue left the people of Sodom. They became gluttonous, not only in their appetites for carnal pleasures, but for food and drink as well.[24] They were blinded by their drunken lust.[25] Even as the drought ended and their crops demanded their attention, they found little time to work their fields, and so they had fewer resources and could no

---

23. *Biḥār al-anwār* vol. 12 p. 164 tr. 17, p. 162 tr. 13, p. 147 tr. 1, vol. 12 p. 155 tr. 8, and *al-Kāfī* vol. 5 p. 544

24. *Biḥār al-anwār* vol. 12 p. 152 tr. 7

25. Qur'ān 15:72

longer afford to be generous. Thus, miserliness, which had once been only an expedient, became second nature to them.[26] Their sensibilities toward basic hygiene atrophied, so they stopped cleaning themselves after defecating[27] and after sexual activity.[28] They became extravagant and indecent in their ways of dressing. They began wearing transparent fabrics that revealed their skin and the contours of their bodies.[29] They would leave their garments unfastened in the front to expose their chests.[30] Some would wear their togas draped over their left shoulders and leave their right ones uncovered.[31] They would wear their pants long so that they trailed luxuriantly.[32] In short, they became a people wont to acts of filth, and they became an evil and corrupt people.[33]

Lot Enters Sodom

Battling such depravity would have been a formidable challenge for any prophet, but for Lot it proved especially so. Most prophets were sent to their own people who knew them and with whom they had a history. Lot was a foreigner. He knew no one and had no supporters among them.[34] Despite these odds, he was unshakable in his determination to fulfill his duty to God. As he approached the outskirts of Sodom, he drew his garments about himself and

---

26. *Biḥār al-anwār* vol. 12 p. 147 tr. 1, p. 152 tr. 7

27. *Biḥār al-anwār* vol. 12 p. 148 tr. 1, p. 152 tr. 7

28. *Biḥār al-anwār* vol. 12 p. 148 tr. 1, p. 152 tr. 7

29. *Man lā yaḥḍuruhu al-faqīh* vol. 1 p. 260 tr. 799 and *Tahdhīb al-aḥkām* vol. 2 p. 371 tr. 74

30. *Biḥār al-anwār* vol. 12 p. 151 tr. 3

31. *Man lā yaḥḍuruhu al-faqīh* vol. 1 p. 260 tr. 799 and *Tahdhīb al-aḥkām* vol. 2 p. 371 tr. 74

32. *Biḥār al-anwār* vol. 12 p. 151 tr. 3. This tradition also mentions that they used to hunt with sling shots, play marbles, and chew a resin called *'ilk* or "mastic," however, I refrained from including these in the text because I do not know that modern jurists would even consider these activities *makrūh*, much less *ḥarām*, based on a singular transmission such as this.

33. Qur'ān 21:74

34. *Biḥār al-anwār* vol. 12 p. 148. tr. 1 and p. 152 tr. 7

covered his head leaving only a narrow portion of his face exposed, hoping not to draw undue attention to himself.

He was immediately shocked when he entered the city. There was an air of unabashed lewdness. The way people dressed, the way they carried themselves, the way they interacted with one another, the way they leered, all suggested that they were a people without an iota of shame or decency left in them. He meandered through the main thoroughfare and market and sized up the enormous task at hand. Then, unexpectedly, a group of men turned their attention to him. They saw from his dress and his manner that he was a foreigner, and they were immediately interested. Lot turned to remove himself, but the excitement had drawn a large mob and there was no way out. Lot knew he was in God's care, and he collected his thoughts and realized that, despite appearances, he had been presented with an ideal opportunity to introduce himself to these people.[35]

He turned to face his would-be assailants and drew back his head-covering to reveal his face. In an authoritative voice he announced, "I am Lot, son of Harān. I am the cousin of the prophet, Abraham, who did not burn when Nimrod threw him into the fire; for whom God made the fire cool and peaceful. He has now settled near to you, so fear God, and do not perpetrate these acts for which you are notorious, and cease the worship of idols,[36] otherwise God will destroy you.[37] God has sent me to you as a prophet and a messenger. Do you not fear him? I am for you a trustworthy messenger. So fear God and obey me. I do not ask you for any recompense for this work. My recompense is solely with the Lord of all realms."[38]

The Sodomites were defiant, but they could not deny that Abraham wielded fearsome power. His reputation had preceded him, and when he settled in Hebron, the Sodomites had taken notice. Though they wanted to laugh Lot out of their city, for fear of Abraham, they vowed not to touch him.

---

35. I have described his arrival at Sodom as I imagine it to have happened.

36. *al-Burhān fī tafsīr al-qur'ān* under Qur'ān 66:10

37. *Biḥār al-anwār* vol. 12 p. 155–6 tr. 8

38. Qur'ān 26:161–166

Lot Is Married

Lot settled in Sodom and established his home there. He found a wife[39] named Qiwāb who was one of the first people in Sodom to believe in him.[40] Over the next 30 years,[41] she would bear him three outstanding daughters.[42] For all intents and purposes, Lot became one of them.[43]

---

39. *Biḥār al-anwār* vol. 12 p. 156 tr. 8

40. I found only one tradition that named his wife (*al-Burhān fī tafsīr al-qurʾān* under Qurʾān 66:10). This tradition asserts that she was his second wife, taken after his first one had died. It also asserts that Qiwāb (assuming this is the correct pronunciation of her name) was a believer but does not mention that she ever turned against faith. I am hesitant to accept that he was married before he arrived at Sodom for the following reasons:

- There is no mention of a wife in the other stories about Abraham's and Lot's emigration from Kūthā.
- It seems highly unlikely that Lot would have brought his wife into such a depraved society as Sodom.

With all that said, for the purpose of this narrative, I am going to use Qiwāb as the name of Lot's first and only wife, who was eventually destroyed along with her people. This is based on many assumptions and is not to be taken as fact.

41. *Biḥār al-anwār* vol. 12 p. 148 tr. 1 and p. 152 tr. 7. This is also the number of years he spent as a prophet to Sodom before they were destroyed.

42. *Biḥār al-anwār* vol. 12 p. 156 tr. 8. We do not know exactly how many daughters Lot had. The Bible claims there were only two (Genesis 19:30–38) and shamefully maligns them by inventing a terrible story about them. However, the Qurʿān and traditions always refer to them as *banāt*, which is the plural of *bint*, indicating that there were at least three. Furthermore, that they were delivered from Sodom along with their father indicates that they were righteous and deserving of praise.

43. The Qurʾān calls Hūd *akhū ʿĀd,* literally "the brother of the ʿĀd people." Similarly, it calls Ṣāliḥ *akhū Thamūd,* literally "the brother of the Thamūd people." This makes sense for them because they were from the ʿĀd and Thamūd people, respectively. However, Lot was not one of the Sodomites. He had emigrated from Kūthā to Hebron and was then sent to Sodom on this mission. Nonetheless, the Qurʾān, in one place calls him *akhū ahl Sadūm* (26:116), presumably to show that, when he emigrated there, he completely assimilated and became as one of them.

Lot's Mission to the Sodomites

Day and night, Lot strove to guide the Sodomites. He confronted them over their deviant sexual practices asking them, "Do you perpetrate an abomination which no one in the world before you ever perpetrated?[44] Do you go to men in lust instead of women? Do you, of all people, go to men in lust and abandon the wives God has made for you?[45] Do you go to men in lust and thereby sever the path to procreation, and, moreover, do you perpetrate this evil in public gatherings[46] while you watch one another?"[47] He hoped desperately to awaken their conscience with his repeated questioning. He wanted them to see that their forefathers, for whom they claimed to have so much respect, never sanctioned such behavior, thus they should abandon their innovation for fear of incurring their forefathers' displeasure. More to the point, having relations with the same sex, besides being inherently reprehensible to human sensibilities, is tantamount to ingratitude to God for the spouses with which he has provided us. It is to cast aside a gift and usurp, in its place, what is not ours to have. Furthermore, practically speaking, it is a genealogical dead end for, naturally, no offspring can be born of such relations. But arguably more heinous than their homosexuality itself was their willingness to hold their orgies in public gatherings where all were obliged to participate or at least watch.

They ignored his admonishments because they were a foolish people[48] and a people given to excess.[49] They told him, "If you do not cease talking, Lot, you shall be among those who are banished."[50]

---

44. Qur'ān 7:80 and 29:28

45. Qur'ān 26:165–166

46. Qur'ān 29:29

47. Qur'ān 27:54

48. Qur'ān 27:55

49. Qur'ān 26:166

50. Qur'ān 26:167

They sarcastically added, "You and your family are a people too *pure* for us."[51]

He said, "I do not care if you banish me, for I hate your acts of indecency."[52]

When it became clear that their sense of propriety was too far gone to be repaired, he warned them of God's punishment as Abraham had advised.[53] However, his people's only response was to say, "Bring on God's punishment if you are truthful in your threats."

Lot prayed to God saying, "Lord, help me against these corrupt people.[54] Lord, deliver me and my family from the destruction they are doomed to face for what they are doing."[55]

Lot's Hospitality

Despite the great adversity Lot faced in Sodom, or perhaps because of it, he felt his character and nobility blossom. He became renowned for his generosity, especially as a host. Like his cousin, Abraham, he loved to entertain guests, seizing upon every opportunity to show them kindness and to open their hearts to the guidance he offered. However, Lot saw hospitality not only as a means of calling people to truth but as a way to save them from the clutches of the Sodomites who, were it not for his protection, would gladly have attacked anyone unfortunate enough to enter their city.[56] Nonetheless, his wife secretly betrayed his activities to her people. Whenever Lot would smuggle guests into their house, Qiwāb would secretly signal her people by lighting a fire atop her

---

51. Qur'ān 27:56

52. Qur'ān 26:168

53. *al-Burhān fī tafsīr al-qur'ān* under Qur'ān 66:10. Interestingly, the Qur'ān never quotes Lot warning them about God's punishment. However, his people's response clearly indicates that he did warn them as corroborated by the aforementioned tradition.

54. Qur'ān 29:30. Also see *Biḥār al-anwār* vol. 12 p. 156 tr. 8.

55. Qur'ān 26:169

56. *Biḥār al-anwār* vol. 12 p. 155–6 tr. 8

roof if they came by night or through smoke signals if they came by day.[57]

Repeatedly, the Sodomites warned Lot about trying to protect the visitors to their city under the pretense of hosting them. They told him, "We forbid you from interfering in our affairs with people. Do not host any guest who comes to you. If you do, we vow to attack them and disgrace you."[58]

After 30 Years

Thirty years had passed since Lot had first come to Sodom. Despite his tireless efforts to guide these people, no one but his own daughters had heeded his message.[59] The earth wept so much for their evil that news of her tears reached the sky; and the sky wept so much that news of its tears reached God's throne. Thus, God told the sky that it would soon stone them, and he told the earth that it would soon swallow them up.[60]

Four Guests

God sent four angels, Gabriel, Michael, Raphael, and Carobiel,[61] to give the Sodomites one final test, and if they failed, to destroy them. He told them to wait until Lot testified against his people three times.[62] They arrived on a Tuesday[63] when Lot was working

---

57. *Biḥār al-anwār* vol. 12 p. 157 tr. 8. Another tradition says that she used to signal them by whistling (*Biḥār al-anwār* vol. 12 p. 163 tr. 15). This is also possible, but I chose to include the tradition about fire and smoke because it seems more natural that she would use an inaudible signal so that she could keep her signals secret from Lot.

58. *Biḥār al-anwār* vol. 12 p. 148 tr. 1

59. Qur'ān 51:36. Shaykh al-Ṭabarsī mentions that the names of two of Lot's daughters were Za'ūrā' and Raythā' (see *Biḥār al-anwār* vol. 12 p. 161 tr. 12), though he does not mention his source. I shall write more about his daughters in a few pages.

60. *Biḥār al-anwār* vol. 12 p. 167 tr. 22

61. *al-Kāfī* 18.171.6 and *Biḥār al-anwār* vol. 12 p. 169 tr. 27

62. *Biḥār al-anwār* vol. 12 p. 169 tr. 27

63. *Biḥār al-anwār* vol. 12 p. 151 tr. 4

in his fields, irrigating his crops. He saw the four men, dressed handsomely in white, but since their faces were concealed, he did not recognize them. As they approached, he grew troubled on their account and feared he would be powerless to protect them, and he said to himself, "This promises to be a calamitous day."[64]

The four men asked if he would host them for the night. He replied, "My brothers, the people of this city are evil. May God damn them and destroy them. They will rape you and loot all your possessions."

At this, Gabriel thought to himself, "This is Lot's first testimony against his people."

They replied that they had no choice as it was getting late, and so they insisted. He reluctantly agreed, torn between his eagerness to help them and his dread of the Sodomites. He reluctantly led them toward the city gates. When they came near, he turned and whispered in earnest, trying desperately to make them reconsider their decision, "You have come to a city with the worst of God's creatures in it."

Gabriel thought to himself, "This is Lot's second testimony against his people."

Once they entered the city, Lot led them quietly through back alleys, far from anyone's gaze as was his wont. When they neared his house, Lot repeated once again, "These are the worst of God's creatures."

Gabriel thought to himself, "This is Lot's third testimony against his people."

They entered Lot's residence. While they washed and made themselves comfortable, Lot went to his wife and confided in her, "I have brought home some guests for the night. You must keep their presence secret. I know you have betrayed me countless times before, but if you honor my request this time, I shall forgive you for all the other times." She promised him, but no sooner had he left to see to his guests than she proceeded to the rooftop to light her signal fire.

---

64. Qur'ān 11:77

The Sodomites Arrive

Seeing her signal, the Sodomites came to their house as if driven by lust.[65] Shortly thereafter, they arrived at Lot's gate in good spirits.[66]

Lot had barely begun preparing a meal for his guests when he heard the frenzied pounding at his gate. Alarmed and distraught, Lot understood that his wife had again betrayed him. He cautiously opened the gate, hoping he would once again be able to deter his people from attacking. He told them, "These are my guests, so do not disgrace me by harming them. Fear God and do not embarrass me."[67]

They replied, "Did we not forbid you from interfering in our affairs with people?"[68]

Now he knew he would not be able to hold them off this time. As a last ditch effort, he offered, "These daughters of mine are purer for you, if only you will marry them."[69] Thus, fear God, and do not shame me by attacking my guests. Is there not among you a sensible man?"[70] If it was sexual gratification they sought, he offered his own daughters' hands in marriage to anyone who sought to reform himself and return to decency.[71]

---

65. Qur'ān 11:78

66. Qur'ān 15:67

67. Qur'ān 15:68

68. Qur'ān 15:69

69. Qur'ān 15:71

70. Qur'ān 11:78

71. Some have suggested that he was not literally offering his own daughters for two reasons:

- According to the Bible, he only had two daughters, while he refers here to "daughters" in the plural indicating that he intended three or more women.
- His two daughters would hardly have sufficed all the men of Sodom even if Lot was proposing adulterous relations, which he certainly was not. Rather he was telling them to go back to their own wives, who, as part of his spiritual flock, were his spiritual "daughters."

In response, we must reiterate, first, that the Bible is not proof, especially where it contradicts the Qur'ān. Just because the Bible asserts that he had two

They replied, "You know we have no right to your daughters according to our customs. You know what we really want."[72]

With great anguish in his voice, Lot exclaimed, half to himself, "If only I had the strength to stop you or could avail myself of some strong support."[73]

His Guests Defend Him

From behind him, he heard his guests address him in a heartening voice, "Do not fear, and do not fret. We shall deliver you and your family, except for your wife."[74]

Lot turned to them, construing their words as mere bravado in the face of an invincible enemy. He told them, "You are apparently strangers to this land!"[75] Certainly, the four of them could do nothing to help themselves, much less Lot and his daughters.

They replied, "No, rather we are the ones who brought you that revelation in which they have been in doubt. And we have brought you truth once again, and we are truthful."[76]

When he looked puzzled, they removed their face coverings and said, "Lot, we are your Lord's messengers. They shall not reach you."[77] These were God's angels in human form. These were Lot's

---

daughters does not make it so. Second, for Lot to have referred to the Sodomite women as his "daughters" he would have had to have a "fatherly" connection to them. This was clearly not the case since none of them believed in him. It is even more unlikely that the Sodomite men would have stood for him referring to their women as his daughters without retorting in some way. Thus, he was definitely referring to his biological daughters. Furthermore, he intended for them to take his daughters in marriage. As for the disproportionate number of men compared to his daughters, he presumably wished to make the offer for any man who was willing. He basically sealed his case against them by removing all excuses for their abomination and offering a way out to any who wished to do so.

72. Qur'ān 11:79

73. Qur'ān 11:80

74. Qur'ān 29:33

75. Qur'ān 15:62

76. Qur'ān 15:63–64

77. Qur'ān 11:81

friends and helpers. Just as they had brought him truth before by way of revelation, once again, they had brought him truth, though this time of a different nature. It was a guarantee of punishment for his people and of salvation for himself and his daughters. They continued:

> We have been sent to these criminal people to send upon them shards of sandstone, earmarked by God for those who are excessive. We sought to remove those in the city who were believers, but we found therein but one house of believers,[78] and that is yours. So flee with your family sometime this night, and bring up the rear, and let no one among you look back, and proceed wherever you are commanded to go. As for your people, their appointed time of destruction is this morning. Every last one of them shall be destroyed by morning. Is morning not so very near? As for your wife, what befalls them shall befall her,[79] for God has deemed her to be among those who must remain.[80]

Lot felt an immense sense of relief. For thirty years he had suffered at these people's hands. At last, he would be free of them. Gabriel told him, "Back away from the gate, and let them enter." Lot glanced into his eyes in a moment's hesitation, and again, Gabriel assured him, "We are your Lord's messengers. They shall not reach you."[81]

Lot let the gate swing open and the leering eyes of his people fell upon the four men standing there. As a group of them rushed to advance on them, Gabriel raised two fingers and with a sweeping movement, blinded them all.[82] Bewildered, they stumbled aimlessly

---

78. Qur'ān 51:32–36

79. Qur'ān 15:65–6 and 29:33

80. Qur'ān 27:57

81. Qur'ān 11:81

82. *Biḥār al-anwār* vol. 12 p. 164 tr. 15 and Qur'ān 54:37

and collided with one another. Their lust had been transformed into confused anger. They scrambled back out of the house and warned the others about the magic Lot had used against them. With menacing finality, they told Lot, "We shall return in the morning, and neither you nor your guests will escape us then."[83]

When the mob had cleared, he locked the gate and turned to his guests. They reminded him that he must flee from the city before morning so that they could carry out their divine mandate. He called his daughters and explained to them the task ahead, and all began earnestly packing what they wished to salvage from their life in Sodom.

Qiwāb, his wife, was nowhere to be found. She had slipped out of the house amidst the chaos and had returned to her own family. Gabriel reminded Lot that he need not concern himself with her, for God had deemed her to be among those who must remain.[84] He prophesied to him that God would immortalize her as an example for those who reject faith. He would tell them, "She was under the care of our righteous servant, Lot, yet she betrayed him, and so he could not benefit her or defend her against God at all. It would be said to her on the Day of Judgment, 'Enter the fire along with the others.'"[85]

Deliverance For the Righteous

Early Wednesday morning,[86] before the sun rose,[87] Lot and his daughters moved furtively through the streets of Sodom for the last time. All around, they heard the drunken revelry of orgiastic parties, thankful that they would soon have to hear them no more. When the sun rose, they were well on their way south to Hebron.[88] Then they felt the faint tremors beneath their feet, and Lot knew

---

83. *al-Burhān fī tafsīr al-qur'ān* under Qur'ān 54:37

84. Qur'ān 27:57

85. Qur'ān 66:10

86. *Biḥār al-anwār* vol. 12 p. 151 tr. 4

87. Qur'ān 54:34

88. *Biḥār al-anwār* vol. 12 p. 152 tr. 7

that it had started. He reminded his daughters not to look back, and so they marched on to freedom and deliverance.

The Destruction of Sodom

There was an explosion near Sodom at sunrise.[89] The earth began heaving and trembling as a gale[90] rained down sandstone shards upon them, each earmarked for its target in God's plan.[91] The

---

89. Qur'ān 15:73. 'Āllāmah Ṭabāṭabā'ī suggests that the punishment meted out to the Sodomites was a volcano accompanied by three distinct phenomena, all of which are used in the Qur'ān to describe their punishment:

- seismic activity that upturned their city as indicated by the name *al-Mu'tafikah*, "The Overturned City," that was "thrown down" and "buried" (Qur'ān 53:53-4)
- explosions that produced blasts and howls as described in Qur'ān 15:73
- raining down of lava and volcanic rock upon them, referred to in many verses as "sandstone shards"

His explanation makes the punishment of Sodom very believable. However, it does not take into account the seemingly mythical descriptions that are given in several traditions of the angels lifting the city into the sky and then smashing it down upon itself in the sea. To be fair, he does not deny that these traditions are true but only says that there is a lack of evidence to positively confirm what these traditions describe.

In this work, I will incorporate these traditions into the story for two reasons.

- First, what they say is possible and does not contradict anything in the Qur'ān.
- Second, I believe Qur'ān 53:53–4 confirms the meaning of the tradition since the verb *ahwā* literally means "he threw down" implying that they were first raised to a height.

90. Qur'ān 54:34

91. Qur'ān 11:82–3. The verses that describe the overturning of their city and the raining down of sandstone shards place them in this respective order (see Qur'ān 15:74–5 and 11:82). However, in Arabic simply mentioning that "A and B happened" does not necessarily mean that A happened before B. In this case, it seems to make more sense that the "rain of sandstone shards" would have occurred before the city was overturned. Otherwise, no one would have been left alive to receive the pelting, and it would have been a punishment in vain. For this reason, and because of a lack of any alternate explanation in the traditions, I have changed the order of these two events.

The shards are called both *ḥijārah min ṭīn* and *ḥijārah min sijjīl*. Lexicographers and commentators have mentioned that the word *sijjīl* comes from the Persian

calamitous explosion, the gale, and the rain of shards overwhelmed the people of Sodom. Those who were caught out in the open were gruesomely pelted, their bodies beaten and cut by the projectiles. Those who found sanctuary within their homes and buildings were, a moment later, subjected to an even more harrowing experience. The four angels, Gabriel, Michael, Raphael, and Carobiel, having doffed their human forms for their angelic ones, spread their massive wings. Each one sank his wings into the ground on one side of the city. Their wingtips reached the furthest depths of the earth. Then they lifted in unison and raised the entire city into the air so that the denizens of heaven could hear the barking of its dogs and the crowing of its roosters.[92] There they held it until God gave the word. Then they hurtled it down into the sea to the west, and they buried it decisively.[93] The "Overturned City"[94] formed a small island before it crumbled into the sea.[95] The giant hole that had been Sodom,[96] along with some ruins that the angels purposely left standing, would serve as a sign to all who passed along that trade route for generations to come.[97]

Gabriel would later recount the events of that fateful morning as follows:

---

sang-e gil meaning "stone of clay." Some have described it as petrified clay. I have translated both phrases as "sandstone shards." There is no need to construe these stone shards as heavenly objects that were rained down upon them. Rather, it is reasonable to assume that they were earthly material hurled into the air by a volcanic explosion or some other seismic activity, before raining back down fatally upon them.

92. *Biḥār al-anwār* vol. 12 p. 158 tr. 8

93. Qurʾān 53:53–4

94. This is a translation of *al-Muʿtafikah.*

95. *Biḥār al-anwār* vol. 12 p. 153 tr. 7

96. I am tempted to speculate that the Sea of Galilee may be the result of their destruction. The fact that Gabriel told the Prophet that their city was located at Lake Tiberias, which seems to refer to the Sea of Galilee, along with this description of their city being wrenched out from its roots and cast into the sea, seems to allow for us to speculate that the Sea of Galilee is on the spot where Sodom once stood.

97. Qurʾān 15:76–77, 37:137–8, and 51:37

> Before dawn broke, I received a message from the throne saying, "Gabriel, God's order for the punishment of Lot's people is hereby final and irrevocable. Therefore, go down to the city of Lot's people and the surrounding areas and uproot it down to the seventh layer of the earth, then lift it into the sky and hold it there until God the Compeller's command comes to overturn them upon themselves. But leave behind the house of Lot as a sign for passing caravans."
>
> I descended upon the city of those criminals. I buried my right wing into their eastern border and my left wing into their western border. Then I ripped out their city down to the seventh layer of the earth. I spared only Lot's house as a sign for caravans. Then I lifted them between my wings and held them suspended so that the angels in the skies could hear the crows of their roosters and the barks of their dogs. As the sun rose, I received a message from the throne saying, "Gabriel, now turn the city upon its denizens." I turned them upside down. All this after God had rained down shards of sandstone upon them.[98]

Return to Hebron

Lot and his daughters[99] returned to Hebron where they spent the rest of their days by Abraham's side helping him to preach God's message to all who happened their way. On Abraham's suggestion, Lot married his daughters to three of the clansmen who had emigrated with them to Hebron from Kūthā. From the descendants

98. *Biḥār al-anwār* vol. 12 p. 152 tr. 7

99. The Bible claims that Lot's daughters seduced him and bore children from their incestuous relation with their father (see Genesis 19:30–8). This licentious claim is preposterous and need not be dignified with a rebuttal.

of these three virtuous couples would arise Prophet Job, Prophet Shuʿayb, and Balaam, son of Beor.[100]

100. *Biḥār al-anwār* vol. 12 p. 384 tr. 9. This tradition actually adds that "all prophets after the time of Abraham until the Israelites were from their descendants." Since this part of the tradition disregards the presence of Ishmael, Isaac, and their descendants, I have rejected it.

Jacob & Joseph

Jacob Is Heir to Isaac

As Isaac[1] lay on his deathbed in Hebron, he delivered his last testament to his son Jacob.[2] He hung the small silver vial containing Abraham's tunic around his son's neck as Abraham had instructed him.[3] Then he bequeathed him a special belt of his[4] and appointed him as his successor. With his last duty fulfilled, he passed away.

Jacob's Family

Jacob continued to live in Hebron in the Land of Canaan, near the graves of his ancestors, Abraham, Sarah, Lot, and Isaac. He married his maternal cousin, Leah,[5] and over time, she bore him six sons: Reuben, Simeon, Levi, Judah, Issachar, and Zebulun. In the intervening years, he also had children through two of his slave-women. Bilhah bore Dan and Naphtali, and Zilpah bore Gad and Asher. When Leah died, Jacob married her younger sister Rachel,[6] and she bore him Joseph and Benjamin, the youngest of his sons.[7]

---

1. In Arabic his name is *Isḥāq*.
2. In Arabic his name is *Yaʿqūb*.
3. *Biḥār al-anwār* vol. 12 p. 249 tr. 14
4. *Biḥār al-anwār* vol. 12 p. 250 tr. 1
5. In Arabic her name is *Layā.*
6. In Arabic her name is *Rāḥīl.*
7. The Old Testament portrays the interactions among Jacob's wives and slave-women as one of intrigue and rivalry (Genesis 29:15 to 30:24). In contrast, a tradition from the imams says that he married the sisters in succession, not contemporaneously, and does not mention that the servants belonged to the two wives or that they bore their sons as surrogate mothers (*Biḥār al-anwār* vol. 12 p. 220 tr. 1).

Jacob was given the honorific *Isrā'īl*, meaning "Power of God" because he struggled in God's way.[8]

From an early age, Joseph and Benjamin proved to be precocious children with a deep sense of piety and virtue, especially so Joseph. Jacob saw in Joseph the burgeoning qualities of a prophet and lavished appropriate love and honor upon him. He was due to become a fourth generation prophet, a great honor for which God had chosen him.[9]

Aunt Sarah's Plot

Young Joseph was also especially dear to his Aunt Sarah, Jacob's sister. For extended periods, she would invite him to stay with her. One time, she even plotted to keep him with her indefinitely. Jacob had lent Sarah the belt their father had given him. It reminded her of her father, so she had asked to hold on to it for a time. When Jacob sent Joseph to her house to fetch the belt back, she secretly tied the belt under Joseph's clothing, unbeknownst to him. Then she sent him home with a message for Jacob, "Please leave the belt with me tonight so that I may reminisce about our father. I shall send it to you in the morning." The next day, she came to Jacob and told him that the belt had gone missing and that she suspected

---

8. *al-Mīzān* under Qur'ān 3:93. Genesis tells us that God, in the form of a man, tried to wrestle with Jacob but was unable to beat him. He did manage to hurt him on the hips. Thus, God named him *Isrā'īl* because "you have struggled with God and with man and have overcome." And thus, "the Israelites to this day do not eat the tendon that attaches to the socket of the hip because the socket of Jacob's hip was touched near this tendon" (Genesis 32:22–32). In stark contrast, Islamic sources tell us that he earned the honorific *Isrā'īl*, meaning either "Servant of God," "Power of God" (*Biḥār al-anwār* vol. 12 p. 265 tr. 30 and p. 284 tr. 65), or "Devotee of God" (*Biḥār al-anwār* vol. 12 p. 218 tr. 1), because he struggled *in God's way* not *with God*. The Qur'ān also rebuts the claim that Jacob made the hip tendon unlawful in 3:93. It tells us, "All food was lawful for the Israelites before the Torah was sent down except for what Isrā'īl (i.e., Jacob) made unlawful for himself." The traditions clarify that he gave up camel meat because it caused him some pain whenever he ate it. But when the Torah was sent down, camel meat was not prohibited on the Israelites in general (*Biḥār al-anwār* vol. 12 p. 299 tr. 87).

9. *Biḥār al-anwār* vol. 12 p. 284 tr. 64

Joseph had taken it from her. Jacob searched Joseph and found the belt on him. Sarah reminded her brother that the law demanded that Joseph become her servant as ransom for the stolen belt. Jacob reluctantly acquiesced, on principle, on condition that she not sell him or give him to any other. Sarah agreed and conceded that she would free Joseph voluntarily as long as Jacob never took him from her unless she agreed to let him go herself.[10]

Jacob and Dhimyāl

God blessed Jacob with copious wealth, a large family, and a high position in society. Jacob showed his gratitude, in part, by being generous. Every day, it was his wont to have one of his sheep slaughtered. He would send a crier out morning and evening proclaiming, "Whoever would like a meal, come to the house of Jacob!"[11] The city's poor would flock to his house, and they and his family would partake in the victuals with a spirit of communion.

For years, Jacob fed the poor and called them to God. One day, a man named Dhimyāl entered the city. He was a stranger to those parts. He was a believer and held a high station in God's eyes, but he was a poor vagrant. It was a Thursday evening, and it was the Night of Apportionment,[12] and Dhimyāl had been fasting. He arrived too late to partake in the daily communion at Jacob's house. Nonetheless, hoping to find some scraps to break his fast,

---

10. *Biḥār al-anwār* vol. 12 p. 250 tr. 15, p. 262 tr. 24, and p. 298 tr. 86. This story is problematic in that it portrays Sarah, who otherwise seems to be a virtuous person, as being guilty of lying and conspiring against Joseph. Nonetheless, it has been transmitted in various traditions and accepted by our scholars, thus, I have included it here in the spirit of being comprehensive. Verse 12:77 adds further credence to this story. In it, Joseph's brothers say, "If Benjamin has stolen today, it is no surprise, for a brother of his (i.e., Joseph) stole something before." This is a clear allusion to some past incident in which Joseph was accused of stealing. We are safe in assuming that the brothers knew Joseph was innocent and that they rehashed this old indictment only to exonerate themselves of Benjamin's alleged crime and take one more jab at the two brothers who were the object of their collective envy.

11. *Biḥār al-anwār* vol. 12 p. 284 tr. 66

12. In other words, *laylat al-qadr. Biḥār al-anwār* vol. 12 p. 218 tr. 1

he came to Jacob's door and called out, "Feed a vagrant beggar who is a stranger to this town. Give him your scraps!"

Jacob and his sons faintly heard a man's voice, but as the hour was late and they felt they had fulfilled their duty for the day, they did not attend to him. Seeing that there was no one to pity him, Dhimyāl turned away and began to weep. He complained to God that he was hungry and finally huddled into a lonely spot and slept hungry.[13]

The next morning, God severely rebuked Jacob for his unwitting negligence. He said:

> Jacob, you have disparaged one of my servants, and you have thereby invoked my anger. You have earned disciplinary action, and, thus, you and your sons shall be afflicted with tribulation. Jacob, the most beloved and honored of my prophets are those who are merciful to the destitute among my servants, who draw them near and feed them and are a shelter and refuge for them. Jacob, why did you not show mercy to my servant Dhimyāl? For he is persistent in worshiping me, and he is content with a meager portion from this temporal world. Yet last night, when he presented his need at your door at the time when you had broken your fast, you fed him nothing. He awoke this morning hungry but grateful, and you and your sons awoke with full bellies and extra food to spare. Jacob, do you know that my tribulations and reprimands befall my beloved friends more swiftly than they befall my enemies. This is so that I can nurture greatness in my friends and ensnare my enemies. Beware! For, by my might, I shall send down tribulations upon you, and I shall make you and your sons a target for my afflictions. Therefore, ready yourselves,

---

13. *Biḥār al-anwār* vol. 12 p. 271–2 tr. 48

> be content with my decree, and have patience with my trials.[14]

Joseph's Dream

Jacob sat lamenting his terrible mistake[15] when Joseph, who was yet a young boy of about nine,[16] came to him. He said, "O Father! I saw in a dream eleven stars, the sun, and the moon—I saw them prostrating to me."[17] He had seen this wondrous dream during the night and had understood its meaning with complete clarity and realized that it was a harbinger of great things to come. The sun was his mother, Rachel. The moon was his father. And the eleven stars were his brothers. Their prostration signified a position of honor to which he was destined to attain.[18] He wished to share his joyous dream with his father.

Yet his father, with the specter of God's reprimand still looming in his mind, perceived that the goodness of this prophecy would only be realized after much hardship had befallen them. And he now understood that the tribulation God had promised him would strike at him through Joseph.[19] It made perfect sense to him that it should be so, for God tests most severely those who have the greatest capacity to succeed. Among his sons, only Joseph had

---

14. *Biḥār al-anwār* vol. 12 p. 272 tr. 48

15. Clearly, I have used "mistake" in a loose sense. Jacob was a prophet and, thus, infallible. His charity was voluntary, and, thus, his lapse was not a true sin. However, as God says in the quote above, "My tribulations and reprimands befall my beloved friends more swiftly than they befall my enemies."

16. *Biḥār al-anwār* vol. 12 p. 275 tr. 48

17. Qur'ān 12:4. The Bible also narrates this dream but under very different circumstances (Genesis 37:9). It portrays Joseph gloating over the dream to his brothers, seemingly to exacerbate their jealousy. It portrays Jacob to be in shock and even to be angered at the prospect of bowing down to his son (Genesis 37:10).

18. *Biḥār al-anwār* vol. 12 p. 217 tr. 1. Other traditions identify Jacob as the sun and Joseph's aunt as the moon (*Biḥār al-anwār* vol. 12 p. 219 tr. 1).

19. *Biḥār al-anwār* vol. 12 p. 271–2 tr. 48

such mettle.[20] Through these trials, Joseph would attain the station for which he was destined. These thoughts brought a medley of bittersweet thoughts to Jacob's mind.

His Brothers' Jealousy

He told Joseph, "My dear child, do not recount your dream for your brothers, or they will certainly plot against you. Satan lies in wait for the jealous, for Satan is a clear enemy to man."[21] He knew God's will would be done, and he was prepared to submit to God's plan, but he deemed that he must do what was in his reach to mitigate the impending trial. He had always been good and fair to all his sons. But fairness did not necessitate equality, for the rest of his sons were certainly not equal to Joseph whom God had chosen for prophethood. Joseph's outstanding spiritual and moral qualities dictated that Jacob love and honor him more.[22] Nonetheless, Jacob was judicious in this regard and sensitive to his other sons' feelings. However, now that he saw that Joseph was doomed to suffer for what Jacob considered his own mistake, he naturally began doting

---

20. *Biḥār al-anwār* vol. 12 p. 270 tr. 44

21. Qur'ān 12:5

22. Al-Fayḍ al-Kāshānī has collected the following traditions clearly indicating that it is natural and permissible for a parent to have differential love for his or her children according to their different levels of virtue (*al-Wāfī* vol. 23 p. 1396):

- Muḥammad ibn Qays said, "I asked Abū Ja'far al-Bāqir whether a man may favor some of his children over others. He replied, 'Yes, and the same goes for his wives.'"
- A person asked Imam al-Ṣādiq about children whom he has had with different mothers and whether he may favor some of them over others. He replied, "This is not a problem." According to another transmitter, the Imam added, "'Alī did so to his son al-Ḥasan. Al-Ḥusayn did so to his son 'Alī. My father did so to me, and I have done so to my son."

The last of these traditions encourages a parent to try to treat his or her children fairly.

- The Messenger of God saw a man with two sons. He kissed one and did not kiss the other. The Prophet said, "Why did you not treat them equally?"

on him more than usual, and thereby, ironically, incited his other sons' jealousy all the more.[23]

Having taken due precaution, Jacob looked past the immediate future and prophesied for his son, "As he has shown you this dream, so will your Lord choose you and teach you the interpretation of dreams and complete his blessings upon you as he completed them upon your forefathers before you, Abraham and Isaac. Your Lord is knowing and wise."[24] Then he brought forth the silver vial that his father had given him and fastened it with a chain around Joseph's neck.[25]

Joseph's brothers misconstrued their father's newly increased concern for Joseph. Their latent jealousy for Joseph and Benjamin blazed within them. The ten oldest met in private to revile their youngest brothers and what they perceived to be their father's imprudence. They said, "Joseph and his full brother are more beloved to our father than we, even though we are able-bodied men who take care of all his needs. Certainly, our father is in clear error in this regard."[26] They were in their prime, and they helped their father by tending his flocks and maintaining his estate. Joseph and Benjamin were but children and hardly pulled their weight. Thus, in their shortsightedness, they thought themselves more worthy of favor than the other two.[27]

Plot to Eliminate Joseph

One of them proposed to his brothers, "Let us kill Joseph or banish him to some land, and our father's attention will be solely ours, and

23. *Biḥār al-anwār* vol. 12 p. 271–2 tr. 48

24. Qur'ān 12:6

25. *Biḥār al-anwār* vol. 12 p. 249 tr. 14

26. Qur'ān 12:8

27. The Bible and some traditions (*Biḥār al-anwār* vol. 12 p. 271–2 tr. 48) claim that Joseph revealed his dream to his brothers. This is certainly not the case. Jacob explicitly forbade him from doing so (Qur'ān 12:5), and there is nothing to indicate that he disobeyed him. Rather, the Qur'ān praises him for his strength of character and his devotion to God and to his father.

thereafter, we can repent, make amends, and be upright people."[28] His jealousy had so eroded his sense of morality that he thought it possible to erase the sin of premeditated murder by paying lip-service to repentance.

Among the ten brothers, Levi's[29] jealousy was somewhat less, and he said, "Do not kill Joseph; rather, if you must do something, then cast him onto the hidden recess of our cistern, and some passing caravan will find him.[30] In this way, he felt they could be rid of Joseph without needlessly sullying their hands with his blood. They all agreed that this was the best course of action.

Having reached a consensus, they came to their father and said, "O Father! Why is it that you do not trust us with Joseph when we are his well-wishers?"[31] They had decided the best way to coerce their father to comply was to place him on the defensive. They knew he would not openly admit that he did not trust them, so they hoped he would comply simply to avoid inciting their jealousy. When they saw that he was at a loss for words, they pressed, "Send him with us tomorrow so that he may frolic and play. We shall protect him."[32]

Jacob reassured them that it was not that he feared that they would hurt him or let something hurt him intentionally. Rather, he said, "It is I who am pained by your taking him."[33] He assumed full blame for having been protective and, thus, graciously shifted all

---

28. Qur'ān 12:9. Many Sunnī commentators follow the lead of the Biblical tradition and believe that Joseph's brothers were also prophets. This deviant belief was also commonplace during the time of the imams. In one tradition, Imam al-Bāqir has said, "They were not prophets but the children of a prophet. They departed this world in felicity because they repented and made amends" (*Biḥār al-anwār* vol. 12 p. 220 tr. 1).

29. *Biḥār al-anwār* vol. 12 p. 218 tr. 1

30. Qur'ān 12:10

31. Qur'ān 12:11

32. Qur'ān 12:12

33. Qur'ān 12:13

blame from them. As a last resort, he admitted, "I fear that a wolf may eat him while you are distracted from watching him."[34]

His sons had planned their strategy well. They said, "Your concern is completely unfounded, for we swear if a wolf were to eat him despite our being such able-bodied men, then we would indeed be losers."[35] They staked their reputation as managers of his estate upon their ability to take care of Joseph. There was nothing left for Jacob to say. They had truly been good shepherds, strong and trustworthy. They had never lost a sheep to a wolf. For him to prevent Joseph from going on this pretense would have been unreasonable. So he gave in.

The following day, they packed their supplies as they did every day and prepared for a day in the pasture minding their father's sheep. They packed extra supplies for Joseph and said their usual farewells to their father reassuring him that they would bring Joseph back to him safely.

Joseph Into the Cistern

The day progressed normally, and for the first time, ironically, Joseph felt loved by his older brothers. Their usual coldness was lacking and he felt disarmed by them. Then they reached the outskirts of their pastureland. There was a cistern that lay on the caravan route to Egypt. This cistern was not encased in stone like the others. The only way to get in was to be lowered from above by a rope or to be thrown. Once inside, the cistern opened up into a wide underground vault at the bottom of which was potable water. At the water's edge, the ground formed a flat recessed embankment upon which a person could stand.

They all gathered at the cistern's mouth, and then Joseph saw a glint of ill-will in his brothers' eyes. They all seemed to be in agreement about something, and suddenly he found himself surrounded by them on three sides with only the cavernous opening to the cistern behind him. Joseph was surprised to hear Levi say, "Cast him onto the hidden recess of this cistern, and some

---

34. Qur'ān 12:13

35. Qur'ān 12:14

passing caravan will find him."[36] They had chosen this well because Joseph would be able to swim to the embankment and not drown, but he would be unable to climb out unless he was thrown a rope from above.

Joseph was overcome with terror. He beseeched, "Fear God, brothers, and do not cast me into this cistern!"

Ignoring him, Levi perfunctorily ordered him, "Remove your tunic."[37]

Joseph looked at them in horror. He pleaded, "My brothers, fear God, and do not strip me."

One of them held a knife to his throat and threatened, "If you do not remove your tunic, I shall kill you."[38] With no choice but to comply, Joseph removed his tunic. They each lay a hand on him and unceremoniously shoved him backward into the abyss.

They callously walked away, indifferent to the muffled cries of their brother splashing in the depths. At a few paces, they could no longer hear his cries. They stood together with a sense of accomplishment and discussed how they should proceed. They agreed that they would tell their father that Joseph had been killed by a wolf. They slaughtered a small lamb from their herd and doused Joseph's tunic with its blood.[39] Armed with their story, their cool confidence, and his bloodied tunic, they set off for home.

At the Bottom of the Cistern

Meanwhile, Joseph had overcome his initial shock. He had swum to the water's edge and heaved himself gasping for air onto the slick embankment. There he lay, drenched, crying, and praying to God. He said, "O Lord of Abraham and Isaac and Jacob! Have mercy on me in my weakness and my inability to help myself and in my young age."[40] He remained trapped in the dark cistern for days.

---

36. *Biḥār al-anwār* vol. 12 p .221 tr. 2

37. *Biḥār al-anwār* vol. 12 p. 221 tr. 2

38. *Biḥār al-anwār* vol. 12 p. 252 tr. 17

39. Qur'ān 12:18

40. *Biḥār al-anwār* vol. 12 p. 222 tr. 2

At one point, Gabriel came to Joseph in the well. He taught him the following prayer.

> O God! I ask you because all praise is for you. There is no god but you. You are the Compassionate, the Benevolent, the Originator of the heavens and earth, the Possessor of might and honor. Shower your mercy upon Muḥammad and his family, and make for me an escape from my current predicament. Provide for me from whence I expect it and from whence I do not expect it.[41]

Lying to Jacob

His ten brothers reached home earlier than usual that evening. They came to their father, weeping.[42] Jacob greeted them solicitously asking, "My sons, why do you weep and lament? And why do I not see Joseph among you?"[43]

They said, "O Father! We went racing and left Joseph with our things, and a wolf ate him. But you would not believe us even if you thought we were truthful; and since you think we are liars, it is out of the question to expect you to believe us."[44] Once again, they thought the best way to manipulate their father was through self-deprecation.

To bolster their claim, Judah[45] showed him Joseph's tunic splattered with the fraudulent sheep's blood.[46]

When he saw the tunic doused in blood, he fainted. As he awoke, he still clung to the tunic. He raised it to his face to kiss it but stopped

---

41. *Biḥār al-anwār* vol. 12 p. 248 tr. 13

42. Qur'ān 12:16

43. *Biḥār al-anwār* vol. 12 p. 286 tr. 70

44. Qur'ān 12:17

45. In one tradition, we learn that, at the end of this story, Joseph sends Judah with his tunic and tells him to cast it over their father's face to bring back his sight, to atone for having been the bearer of Joseph's bloodstained tunic all those years before (*Majma' al-bayān* under 12:88).

46. Qur'ān 12:18

short. He smelled it and then examined it with an increasingly quizzical expression. He turned to his sons and asked, "Why do I not smell Joseph's scent on this tunic? Why is there not even a tear in it?"[47] Then he exclaimed sardonically, "O God! What a kind wolf it must have been that it did not tear his tunic!"[48] He stared his sons in the face with a stern expression and said knowingly, "It is not as you claim; rather, you have fooled yourselves into doing something awful."[49] Then, suddenly composing himself, he said calmly, "But graceful patience shall be my motto, and from God shall I seek help against what you allege."[50]

Joseph's Conversation With God

Three days had rendered Joseph physically and emotionally spent. With a sense of humility characteristic of God's prophets, he felt that God had not answered his prayers only because he himself was not worthy. He cried out, "O God! If my sins[51] have dishonored me in your eyes and prevented my voice from rising to you and prevented you from answering me, then I ask you through my father, Jacob. Have mercy on him in his weakness and bring us together, for you know how tender his heart is for me and how much I yearn for him."[52]

At last, God saw that he had tested Joseph's patience enough and he gave him tidings saying, "You shall disclose to them the reality of these deeds of theirs one day when they will not even recognize you because your state will be so much better than it is at this moment."[53] With this prophecy, Joseph understood that he would live to escape this watery prison and that his state would

---

47. *Biḥār al-anwār* vol. 12 p. 286 tr. 70

48. *Biḥār al-anwār* vol. 12 p. 300 tr. 89

49. Qur'ān 12:18

50. Qur'ān 12:18

51. As I have mentioned before, "sins" of the prophets are not true acts of disobedience. Rather, they view their own shortcomings before God as sins.

52. *Biḥār al-anwār* vol. 12 p. 255 tr. 19

53. Qur'ān 12:15

drastically improve before he would eventually be reunited with his brothers.

A Passing Caravan

Some days later, around midday on the third of Muharram,[54] Joseph heard the faint sounds of animals and human voices. A caravan was preparing to stop, and they had sent their water-drawer ahead of them to begin drawing water for the thirsty animals and riders. Joseph heard the man making a racket at the mouth of the cistern as he checked his knots and equipment. Before Joseph realized what was happening, the man released a large bucket into the middle of the cistern, and it came down with a splash sending a cascade of water onto Joseph. He cried out to the man above and pleaded with him to help him out of the cistern. Initially surprised, when the water-drawer realized that the voice had come from within, he exclaimed excitedly to the first caravan riders who were approaching, "What good fortune! There is a boy here!"[55]

They told Joseph to grab onto the bucket so they could heave him up. His eyes had become accustomed to the darkness, and the midday sun was blinding. He was famished and greatly emaciated from his ordeal. They fed him and gave him dry clothes. As he recuperated, the caravan leaders discussed in earnest what they should do with him. They knew he must belong to a family in the area, but the prospect of profiting from selling him as a slave was far too tempting to resist. They moved him while he still slept and stowed him in one of the slave cages lest he should escape or his family should come and claim him.[56]

---

54. *Biḥār al-anwār* vol. 12 p. 256 tr. 21 and p. 268 tr. 41

55. Qur'ān 12:19

56. Qur'ān 12:19. Some traditions allege that Joseph's brothers came back and sold him to the caravan for 20 silver pieces (*Biḥār al-anwār* vol. 12 p. 222 tr. 2, p. 274 tr. 48, and p. 282 tr. 61). This corresponds to the story narrated in the Old Testament (Genesis 37:28). However, it is highly unlikely that they would go to the trouble of throwing him into the well if they were going to sell him anyway. They could have sold him directly and saved themselves the trouble of throwing him in the well, risking him dying, convincing the caravan owners that he belonged to them, and negotiating a price. Furthermore, to say that the verse of

Jacob's Patience

Jacob held true to his promise. He was gracefully patient, never complaining about the trial that had befallen them.[57] Nonetheless, he lamented his separation from Joseph in private, with only God as his audience,[58] saying, "My beloved Joseph, whom I loved more than all of my children, has been stolen from me. My beloved Joseph, for whom, among all my children, I had such great hopes, has been stolen from me. My beloved Joseph, who used to keep me company in my loneliness, has been stolen from me. O my beloved Joseph! If only I could know upon which mountain they have cast you or in which sea. O my beloved Joseph! If only I could have been with you so that what has befallen you had instead befallen me."[59]

The Slave Market

When Joseph awoke, he was at once relieved to be safely out of the cistern and distraught that he was being held captive like a slave. He protested vehemently but to no avail.[60]

Eighteen days later,[61] at the slave market in Egypt, the caravan drivers were eager to sell Joseph as quickly as possible to avoid being exposed as the boy's kidnappers. The first person to show interest was a nobleman whom everyone referred to respectfully

---

the Qur'ān that speaks of Joseph being sold for a paltry price (12:20) is speaking of his brothers selling him is far-fetched. For one thing, all the pronouns in the previous verse refer to the caravan riders, and there is no evidence that the pronoun in the phrase "They sold him for a paltry price" suddenly refers back to the brothers. Second, the following verse (12:21) speaks of "the one who bought him." This juxtaposed to the phrase "They sold him for a paltry price" clearly indicates that the two verses are speak of two sides of the same transaction, not two separate transactions.

57. *Biḥār al-anwār* vol. 12 p. 267 tr. 38

58. Qur'ān 12:86

59. *Biḥār al-anwār* vol. 12 p. 286 tr. 70

60. *Biḥār al-anwār* vol. 12 p. 224 tr. 2

61. *Biḥār al-anwār* vol. 12 p. 275 tr. 48

as "'Azīz."[62] He asked to know the price, and they eagerly informed him that they would be willing to take twenty silver pieces for him.[63] He was astounded at the bargain and quickly paid them lest they change their mind. Twenty silver pieces was, according to Egyptian law, the restitution one would pay for accidentally killing another's hunting dog.[64] The 'Azīz thought to himself that the merchants had been blind to sell such a noble boy for the paltry price of a dog, but he knew their loss was his gain.[65]

His brief conversation with Joseph on the way home confirmed his initial hunch. The boy was refined and good-natured and seemed to be of noble stock. When they arrived at his residence, his wife, Zalīkhā,[66] came to greet her husband. She was beautiful and dressed in fine clothes, yet the 'Azīz did not seem to take note of her beauty. He introduced her to Joseph and said, "Give him a place of honor in our household. Perhaps he will profit us, or we can adopt him as a son."[67] They did not have any children, for the 'Azīz had forsworn relations with women.[68] He hoped now that Joseph could fill this void in Zalīkhā's life.

Childhood in Egypt

Thus began the next chapter in Joseph's life. God established Joseph in the land of Egypt to prepare the way for the fulfillment of his promise to him. Joseph's brothers and the caravan drivers had abused him and used him to reach their own short-sighted goals. All the while, God reigned supreme over his affairs, turning

---

62. "'Azīz" is an honorific used for nobles or government officials roughly equivalent to "Noble One." It probably does not refer to a particular position, such as the king's vizier, but to several different positions. For this reason, when Joseph assumes the position as head of food rationing, he is also called *'Azīz.*

63. *Biḥār al-anwār* vol. 12 p. 222 tr. 2 and p. 300 tr. 89

64. *Biḥār al-anwār* vol. 12 p. 300 tr. 94

65. Qur'ān 12:20

66. According to *Lisān al-'arab,* the correct pronunciation of her name is Zalīkhā, not Zulaykhā.

67. Qur'ān 12:21

68. *Biḥār al-anwār* vol. 12 p. 254 tr. 18

their efforts to push Joseph down into the very means for lifting him up.[69]

Joseph lived the next nine years of his life in their household. Until he reached puberty, Zalīkhā loved him and nurtured him with motherly devotion. But as he entered adulthood, he became more and more handsome. Her husband's indifference to her was weighing heavily on her, and she began to look at Joseph with different eyes. Her feelings for him escalated over the course of years. All the while, Joseph kept his eyes peeled to the ground in her presence for fear of God.[70]

Plot to Seduce Him

When Joseph reached the age of eighteen, he entered his prime.[71] God gave him sound judgment and knowledge to reward him for his virtue and goodness.[72] Physically too, he reached full maturity,[73] and Zalīkhā was no longer content with subtle overtures and innuendo. Thus, she plotted one day to seduce him. She chose a time when her husband was out. She sent all of her other servants away, and, with only Joseph with her in the house, she bolted all the doors from within.[74] She adorned herself in fine clothes and jewelry and said to him, "Come to me!"

He exclaimed, "In God do I seek refuge! I am from a family that does not partake in fornication."[75] And he said, "In God do I seek refuge! My Master gave me a place of honor in your household. Those who do wrong by their masters never succeed."[76] He spoke wisely and with double entendre, at once admonishing himself of his duty to God who had blessed him with so much and reminding

---

69. Qur'ān 12:21

70. *Biḥār al-anwār* vol. 12 p. 270 tr. 45

71. *Ashudd* is from the age of 18 to 40.

72. Qur'ān 12:22

73. *Biḥār al-anwār* vol. 12 p. 284 tr. 68

74. Qur'ān 12:23

75. *Biḥār al-anwār* vol.12 p.275 tr.48

76. Qur'ān 12:23

her of the need for chastity and loyalty to her husband. But his words fell on deaf ears.

"Lift your gaze and look at me," she ordered.

He said, "I fear I may go blind."

She said, "How beautiful are your eyes!"

He said, "In my grave, they will be the first part of my body to spill their fluid onto my cheeks."

She said, "How sweet is your scent!"

He said, "If only you could smell my decaying body three days after I have died, you would flee from me."

She said, "Why do you not come close to me?"

He replied, "By refraining thus, I hope to become close to my Lord."

She said, "My bed is lined with silk, so stand and fulfill my needs."

He said, "I fear that I will lose my place in paradise."

She threatened, "I shall turn you over to my husband's torturers."

He replied, "Then my Lord will protect me."[77]

But she was unyielding in her insistence. She began advancing upon him. As he retreated, his eyes fell on her household idol, which strangely had some cloth cast over its head. Joseph asked, "Why did you do that?" pointing to her idol.

She replied, "I would be ashamed if my idol saw us today."

He desperately admonished, "Is it right that you should feel ashamed before one who neither hears nor sees nor comprehends nor eats nor drinks, yet I should not feel ashamed before one who has created humankind and taught them?"[78] It was not that Joseph was not attracted to her, for she was beautiful and he was youthful. Just as she desired him, so he would have desired her had he not seen his Lord's proof. With the utmost clarity, he saw his Lord's magnificence, his own desperate indebtedness to him, and the reality of the sin she desired, and it was abhorrent to him.[79] In this

---

77. *Biḥār al-anwār* vol. 12 p. 270 tr. 45

78. *Biḥār al-anwār* vol. 12 p. 266 tr. 35

79. One tradition tells us that God will use him on the Day of Judgment to argue against those men who believe their inordinate handsomeness justifies their acts of sexual indecency. He will present Joseph to them and ask, "Are you

way, God staved off from him evil desire and sexual indecency, for he was among God's select servants.[80]

In a fit of desperation, Zalīkhā thrust herself at Joseph. He turned and bolted for the door, and she raced after him. When he reached the main gate, he fumbled with the lock, and she caught up with him. As he struggled to open the door, she caught hold of his tunic and tried dragging him back into the house. His tunic ripped and was wrenched completely off his body just as the door opened. There, at the house's threshold, was the ʿAzīz.[81]

The ʿAzīz Arbitrates

The ʿAzīz was shocked by the scene before him. Joseph was relieved that he was safe from Zalīkhā's advances. But Zalīkhā, without skipping a beat, seamlessly played the part of the victim and questioned accusatorially, "What punishment can there be for one who intended to violate your wife but that he be imprisoned or subjected to some painful punishment?"[82]

Joseph exclaimed indignantly, "*She* is the one who sought to seduce *me*!"[83]

With nowhere to turn and no one to defend him, Joseph turned to his constant protector in silent prayer. God inspired an infant from Zalīkhā's family,[84] who had been visiting her, to counsel with wisdom beyond his years, "If his tunic is ripped from the front, then she has told the truth and he is a liar. But if his tunic is ripped from the back, then she has lied, and he is truthful."[85]

The ʿAzīz calmed his nerves enough to examine Joseph's shirt. When he saw that his tunic was torn from the back, he said to his

---

more handsome or he? We made him handsome, yet he was not tempted" (*Biḥār al-anwār* vol. 12 p. 341 tr. 2).

80. Qurʾān 12:24

81. Qurʾān 12:25

82. Qurʾān 12:25

83. Qurʾān 12:26

84. *Biḥār al-anwār* vol. 12 p. 275 tr. 48

85. Qurʾān 12:26–27

wife, "This is the plot of a woman. Women's plots are heinous."[86] Having shifted the full brunt of his anger to his treacherous wife, the ʿAzīz said, "Joseph, turn a blind eye to this." He wished the shame of his wife's actions to be known no further than his household. Then he turned to her and said, "And you, woman, seek forgiveness for your sin, for you were in the wrong."[87]

News Spreads

In the days following this incident, tensions were high in the ʿAzīz's household. The ʿAzīz kept close tabs on his wife. He made Joseph work outside of the house for a while so he would be away from Zalīkhā. Despite Joseph's tact and sworn secrecy, news of the incident leaked through other members of the household.[88] Zalīkhā became the laughing stock of high society. Women throughout the city began to say, "The ʿAzīz's wife is seeking to seduce her man-servant. She is smitten with him. We believe she is clearly acting inappropriately."[89]

Zalīkhā's Party

Their gossip and ridicule was too much for Zalīkhā to bear. She knew she had acted wrongly, but she believed their ridicule was unfair since they would have fared no better had they been in her shoes. She devised a plan to silence them and perhaps win them over to her side, if only through blackmail. She sent word to all of them that she was throwing a party for all the society women. She prepared fine food and drink for them[90] and arranged a place for each of them to recline. When the meal was done, she served them fruits and gave each one of them a paring knife. As they busied

---

86. Qurʾān 12:28

87. Qurʾān 12:29

88. Some traditions do allege that Joseph himself spread the news (*Biḥār al-anwār* vol. 12 p. 276 tr. 48). However, this would have been beneath Joseph's character as a prophet, so I have rejected this notion.

89. Qurʾān 12:30

90. *Biḥār al-anwār* vol. 12 p. 276 tr. 48

themselves with their fruits, she gave Joseph a fool's errand and said, "Go out to them."

When they saw him, they were bewitched by his countenance, and they stared wide-eyed, and they cut their hands. They exclaimed, "Glory be to God! This is no mortal. This is nothing less than a venerable angel!"[91]

Zalīkhā's arrow had hit its mark. She looked contentedly at her peers and said, "It was for this precisely that you were blaming *me*."[92] She had successfully blackmailed the city's women and made them unwitting accomplices in her scheme. All of her guests had fallen head over heels when they saw Joseph. They had done so in plain sight of every other woman. With so many witnesses, no one could say she was immune to Joseph's spell. Zalīkhā was now free to make her advances on Joseph. None of the society women had any moral leverage to disparage her. If anyone dared to speak, Zalīkhā and all the other women could testify to what they had witnessed from her on this day. With complete impunity, she admitted, "Yes, I did try to seduce him, but he resisted." Then she delivered her coup-de-grâce, "If he does not now do what I order him to do, he shall be imprisoned and he shall be among the disgraced."[93]

Joseph immediately understood the gravity of the situation. He had escaped from Zalīkhā once by the tail of his shirt. But this time, she had maneuvered a strong position for herself and he felt even the ʿAzīz would be unable to avail him. He turned his focus to God and said in prayer, "Lord, to be thrown in prison is more to my liking than this to which they invite me. If you do not stave off their guiles, I may give in to them and be among the foolish."[94]

His Lord answered his prayer and staved off their guiles, for he is the Hearer of his servants' prayers, the Knower of their worthiness.[95]

---

91. Qur'ān 12:31

92. Qur'ān 12:32

93. Qur'ān 12:32

94. Qur'ān 12:33

95. Qur'ān 12:34

Scapegoat

True to her pledge, Zalīkhā and her friends lobbied their husbands and convinced them that Joseph, chaste and unwavering as he was, was a threat to the integrity of their families. True, the ʿAzīz had seen much evidence to exonerate him. He had seen an infant speak in his defense. He had seen that his tunic was torn from behind. Now they had seen that he was strong enough to resist the temptation of so many women willing to give themselves over to him. And they had witnessed Zalīkhā's public admission of her guilt and his innocence. Nonetheless, they decided to make him a scapegoat and imprison him for a time until the whole affair was utterly forgotten.[96]

Into Prison

Joseph was cast mercilessly into prison. Two other men entered the prison at the same time as Joseph.[97] One was the king's cupbearer, and the other was his baker.

As Joseph entered the prison, God rewarded him for having exercised his moral strength and for his patience by fulfilling his promise to him—a promise that Jacob had conveyed to him so many years before—he taught him the interpretation of dreams.[98] The prisoners, having nothing better to do, were wont to recount, each morning, the dreams they had seen the previous night for the prisoners in their own and adjacent cells. When Joseph heard his neighbors' dreams, he could see clearly, by God's leave, exactly what those dreams meant. By turn, each would tell his dreams, and Joseph would interpret them, revealing things about their past and uncovering secrets that only a true clairvoyant could know. Thus, they came to accept that Joseph was truly gifted.

---

96. Qurʾān 12:35

97. Qurʾān 12:36

98. *Biḥār al-anwār* vol. 12 p. 290 tr. 73

His Cellmates' Dreams

Joseph's two cellmates, who had initially been skeptical of Joseph's ability, witnessed his gift firsthand and so decided to present their own dreams to him. The king's former cupbearer said, "I see myself squeezing grapes to make wine."

The king's former baker said, "I see myself carrying, atop my head, bread from which birds are eating."

"Inform us of their interpretation," they requested, "for we see that you are knowledgeable[99] in the interpretation of dreams."[100]

Joseph told them, "No meal that sustains you shall come to you before I inform you of the interpretation of these dreams."[101] In prison, there was little more to punctuate their day than the meager meals they were served. Thus, he promised them that he would answer their request soon enough, but duty demanded that he first use this opportunity to guide his new friends to the one God. "This ability to interpret dreams is from what my Lord has taught me, for I have abandoned[102] the religion of a people who

---

99. I have translated *muḥsin* as "knowledgeable." This is a legitimate translation as it fits in the context, and this word, especially in its verbal form, *aḥsana,* is often used in traditions to mean "to know." Most commentators, on the other hand, have construed the word *muḥsin* as "doer of good." This meaning presupposes that Joseph's cellmates believed that righteous people could naturally interpret dreams which seems to be a baseless presupposition.

100. Qur'ān 12:36

101. Qur'ān 12:37. It is also possible to translate this sentence as follows, "Whenever a meal comes to you for your sustenance, I shall inform you what it is to be before it comes to you." The purpose of such a statement would have been to confirm their belief that he is able to interpret dreams and to ensure that they know his gift is from God, not a craft that a person can learn through his own endeavor. He only used such a strange medium to show his skills because they are prisoners, and prisoners do not have much else other than their meals to surprise them. The problem with this interpretation is that it is odd that he would use the word *ta'wīl* for foretelling what their meals will be when it has been used throughout this story for the interpretation of dreams. It is also far-fetched to suppose that prisoners in that time would have received a varied and unpredictable menu.

102. He says he "abandoned" false religion, not because he had followed it and

do not believe in God and who deny the hereafter.[103] And I have followed the religion of my forefathers Abraham, Isaac, and Jacob. It is not for us to associate any partners with God. This protection from polytheism is from the grace God has shown us and shown people through us; nonetheless, most people are not grateful for it."[104] He continued his soliloquy, "O cellmates! Are various gods better or God, the One, the All-Dominating?[105] You worship besides God nothing but empty names that you and your forefathers have concocted for which God has sent down no basis. Commands are only for God to give. He has ordered you to worship none but him. This is the upright religion, but most people do not know it.[106] Having delivered his charge and called them to the truth, he came to offer them what they wanted. He said, "O cellmates! One of you will serve his master wine once again. The other will be crucified, and birds will feed on his head. The matter about which you ask has been ordained."[107] He wanted them to know that his prophecy was based on divine decree that could not be changed, not on the mere interpretation of dreams like some others are capable of doing.

Only a few days passed before the prison guards came for the baker. They announced that he was to be executed by crucifixion, just as Joseph had prophesied. He pleaded with them to spare his life, but they ignored his cries and dragged him out. That same day, the guards came for the king's cupbearer. They announced that he had been pardoned and that he was to resume his previous position immediately.

---

then abandoned it, but because he made a conscious decision to reject it in favor of the true religion of his forefathers.

103. Qur'ān 12:37

104. Qur'ān 12:38

105. Qur'ān 12:39

106. Qur'ān 12:40

107. Qur'ān 12:41

Mention Me to Your Lord

As Joseph bid him farewell, he told him, "Mention me to your lord."[108] Joseph knew that none but God could help him, but he also knew that God worked through the means at his servants' disposal. Joseph hoped that this may be the means through which God would choose to deliver him his freedom. But in the excitement of the moment, the cupbearer paid little heed to Joseph's request, and Satan made him forget to mention Joseph to his lord, so he remained in prison for some years.[109]

Bread Into Stew

In the intervening years, life in prison became a drab monotony. The prisoners' only excitement was their dreams and the lessons Joseph taught them. They complained to him about their uneventful diet of bread and salt. He conveyed their complaint to God and asked him to provide him and his prison mates with

---

108. Qurʾān 12:42

109. Qurʾān 12:42. Many commentators have construed this verse as follows, "Satan thereby made him, i.e., Joseph, forget to remember his Lord." While the language of the verse supports both possibilities, I consider this latter interpretation to be weak for the following reasons:

- Verse 12:45 mentions "the one cellmate who had been saved and *now remembered after so long.*" When we juxtapose this verse with verse 12:42, it is clear that the one who forgot and then remembered after a long time was the cellmate and not Joseph.
- Joseph simply tried to avail himself of the means at his disposal. Doing so in no way contradicts having trust (*tawakkul*) in God. Even an ordinary Muslim would realize that natural means work only insofar as God allows them too and would not place them alongside God Almighty. Thus, it is a disparagement of Joseph to assume that he believed his cellmate to be an independent means of helping him alongside God.
- The Qurʾān tells us that Joseph was "among God's select (*mukhlaṣ*) servants" (12:24). It also tells us that Satan has no access to mislead the select (*mukhlaṣīn*) among God's servants (38:82). Thus, Satan could not have made Joseph forget his Lord for even an instant.

For these reasons, I have also disregarded the traditions that support this weaker interpretation (*Biḥār al-anwār* vol. 12 p. 231 tr. 5, p. 302 tr. 100, p. 246 tr. 12, and p. 303 tr. 103).

some soup or gravy so they could dip their bread in it and escape their tedium. God told Joseph to collect their dried bread and place it in a tub and pour water and sprinkle salt over it. Miraculously, God changed the concoction into a delicious hot stew, and they all rejoiced in the blessing.[110]

Prayers From Prison

Gabriel taught Joseph the following supplication and ordered him to recite it thrice after every prayer: "O God! Give me relief and escape from my current predicament, and sustain me from whence I expect it and from whence I do not expect it."[111]

As the years trailed on and he saw no sign of deliverance, Joseph recalled the prayer he had offered many years before in the cistern. He cried out, "O God! If my sins have dishonored me in your eyes and prevented my voice from rising to you and prevented you from answering me, then I ask you through my father, Jacob."[112]

In answer to his prayer, God sent Gabriel. He told Joseph, "God has tested you and your father. He now wishes to deliver you from this prison, so ask him through Muḥammad and his family to deliver you from your current predicament."

Joseph prayed, "O God! I ask you through Muḥammad and his family to hasten my deliverance and relieve me from my current predicament."

Gabriel told him, "Glad tidings! For God has sent word that he will deliver you from this prison within three days."[113]

The King's Dream

Outside the prison walls, Joseph's memory had been all but forgotten. On the same night Joseph offered this prayer, the king of Egypt saw a wondrous dream. Early the next morning, he assembled his advisors, who were reputed to be versed in dreams,

---

110. *Biḥār al-anwār* vol. 12 p. 268 tr. 40

111. *Biḥār al-anwār* vol. 12 p. 256 tr. 20 and p. 301 tr. 99

112. *Biḥār al-anwār* vol. 12 p. 268 tr. 39

113. *Biḥār al-anwār* vol. 12 p. 291–2 tr. 7

to seek their counsel, for he felt that his was a message and not an ordinary dream. He summoned his cupbearer to pour wine for them all. As they drank, he closed his eyes and recounted his dream which he could see as clearly as if it were unfolding at that moment: "I see seven lean cows eating seven fat cows and seven green ears of wheat and seven others that are dry. My advisors, give me your opinion concerning my dream, if you are truly able to interpret dreams."[114]

They deliberated at length with quizzical expressions on their faces. Each one hoped the others had an answer to offer. At last, with no clue as to the meaning of the dream, they said, "This is a patchwork of dreams, and we do not know how to interpret such dreams."[115]

His Dream Interpreted

The cupbearer had witnessed the entire event unfold. Hearing mention of a dream that could not be interpreted, he suddenly remembered his old cellmate whom he had forgotten for so long. He addressed his king excitedly, "I can inform you of its interpretation; rather, I know someone who can interpret it for you. He was my cellmate in prison. If you send me to him, I can ask him."[116]

The king dispatched his cupbearer immediately with a retinue of guards toward the prison. Joseph saw his old cellmate and felt as though he were meeting an old friend. Magnanimously, he did not think for a minute to question him about the favor he had failed to do for all these years. The cupbearer explained that the king had seen a dream. He said, "Joseph, you who are impeccably truthful, give us your opinion concerning seven lean cows eating seven fat cows and seven green ears of wheat and seven others that are dry. I hope to return to the people and convey to them what you say so that they can know its meaning."[117]

---

114. Qur'ān 12:43

115. Qur'ān 12:44

116. Qur'ān 12:45

117. Qur'ān 12:46

Joseph, acquiesced and said, "You shall farm for seven consecutive years. You must leave whatever you harvest in its ear besides a small portion from which you will eat. Then after that will come seven years of hardship which will veritably consume all that you had stored away for them besides a small fraction which you will preserve for seed. Then after that will come a year in which people will receive rain and be able to press oil and juice from their crops."[118]

The cupbearer excitedly returned to the king, pleased to have been of such great service to him. He conveyed Joseph's message, and the king peremptorily ordered, "Bring him to me."

Exoneration First

The cupbearer returned to Joseph to bring him to the king, but Joseph refused to come and said, "Return to your lord, and ask him about those women who cut their hands, for my Lord is well aware of their tricks."[119] Of course, Joseph meant his Lord, God, but he knew the king would think he meant him and would be pleased to have been shown such respect.

He delivered the message. The king, who was anxious to see Joseph as soon as possible, summoned the women who had accused Joseph of indecency and questioned them. He asked, "What do you women have to say about the time when you seduced Joseph? Was he guilty of any wrongdoing?"

They answered resoundingly, "Glory be to God! We know of no blame that we can lay on him."

Even the ʿAzīz's wife said, "Alas, the truth has surfaced! *I* am the one who seduced *him*, and he was indeed telling the truth."[120]

Thus, Joseph's name was cleared, and three days after Gabriel had promised Joseph, the messenger returned to have him freed. The messenger asked Joseph why he had insisted on proceeding as he did. He replied, "I did all this so the ʿAzīz would know that I did not betray him in his absence and that God does not guide

---

118. Qur'ān 12:47–49

119. Qur'ān 12:50

120. Qur'ān 12:51

the traitor's tricks.[121] However, in saying all this I do not mean to absolve my soul of its natural inclinations, for the soul prompts us all to evil except insofar as my Lord shows us mercy. Indeed, my Lord is all-absolving, merciful."[122]

A Place of Eminence

The cupbearer brought Joseph to court but before presenting him to the king, entered by himself and recounted for him Joseph's wise words. The king, ever eager to meet the sage who spoke thus urged, "Bring him to me, for I wish to appoint him to my personal service." When he was brought before him, he spoke with him at length asking about his dream and its practical implications, and he told him, "As of today, you hold, in our eyes, a place of eminence and our complete trust."[123]

Joseph said, "Appoint me to oversee the granaries of this land, for I am prudent with whatever is placed in my care and knowledgable of the administration of this program and of the languages spoken by your subjects."[124] Joseph was not a boastful person, but it was critical for the welfare of the Egyptian people that a qualified individual assume this momentous role, so he let his abilities be known to the extent that was necessary to secure the position.[125]

The king easily accepted his request and conferred on him the title of ʿAzīz, Minister of Agriculture and Food Distribution, and consigned to him his ring and his silver goblet which was the standard of measure in the kingdom.[126] Thus, God established Joseph in that land in which he had once been a slave. He could now move freely among them wherever he wished. God delivers

121. Qurʾān 12:52

122. Qurʾān 12:53

123. Qurʾān 12:54

124. Qurʾān 12:55 and *Biḥār al-anwār* vol. 12 p. 284 tr. 63

125. *Biḥār al-anwār* vol. 12 p. 305 tr. 112

126. *Biḥār al-anwār* vol. 12 p. 292 tr. 76

his mercy to whomever he wishes. And he does not forsake the reward of those who do good.[127]

Seven Years of Prudence

For the next seven years, Joseph issued a mandate requiring all wheat farmers to sell their surplus wheat to the king's treasuries at fair market value. In this way, Joseph gave the farmers an incentive to produce more and to honestly disclose their surplus crops. He had acres of massive granaries constructed in which they stored the whole ears of wheat, dried, but otherwise unprocessed, just as God had instructed them in the king's dream. As he acquired seven years worth of grain, he nearly completely depleted the king's treasuries, but with good cause, for at the end of seven years, when famine struck, Joseph, on behalf of the king, held a monopoly over the most crucial commodity needed by every Egyptian subject, and he proceeded to sell it back to them at a reasonable price and according to an equitable system of rations, thereby deflecting the brunt of the famine.[128]

Famine Mitigated

As families' personal food stores were depleted, they began thronging to Egypt to buy their rations. Expecting to have to fight tooth and nail through a corrupt system, the people were pleasantly surprised to find an efficient and equitable system in place that left no Egyptian without sufficient rations.

First Trip to Egypt

Jacob gathered his sons and told them, "It has reached me that good wheat is still sold in Egypt, and the man in charge of it is a righteous man who does not withhold from people what is due to them. So go to him, and buy wheat from him. He shall be good to

---

127. Qur'ān 12:56

128. The details of Joseph's plan are not stated in the Qur'ān or traditions, but I have inferred that his plan must have looked something like this.

you, God-willing."[129] The caravan from Canaan traveled for eighteen days[130] bringing Joseph's ten older brothers to Egypt.

First Encounter With Joseph

They appeared before Joseph, and he immediately recognized them. But they failed to recognize him[131] because God prevented them from doing so through supernatural means.[132] He attended to them before the others in the Canaanite caravan and asked them, "Who are you?"

They replied, "We are the children of Jacob, son of Isaac, son of Abraham, the All-Merciful's Friend whom Nimrod cast into the fire, but he did not burn, rather God made the fire cool and peaceful for him."[133]

Joseph said, "Then, according to you, three prophets bore you, yet none of you appears to be a wise man, nor are any of you dignified or humble. Perhaps you are actually spies sent by some other king to my country!"

They replied, "O ʿAzīz! We are not spies or warriors. If you knew our father, you would like us, for he is a prophet of God and a descendant of prophets, and he is very sad."

Joseph asked, "And why is he sad if he is a prophet of God and a descendant of prophets, and paradise is his final abode, and he has sons as numerous and strong as you? Perhaps he is sad because of your foolishness or ignorance or your lies or tricks or deception?"

They said, "O ʿAzīz! We are not fools or ignoramuses. His sadness is not because of us. Rather, he had a son named Joseph who was younger than we. He went hunting with us, and he was eaten by a wolf. Ever since, our father has been miserably sad and tearful."

Joseph said, "Are all of you from one father?"

They said, "Our father is one, but our mothers are several."

---

129. *Biḥār al-anwār* vol. 12 p. 257 tr. 23

130. *Biḥār al-anwār* vol. 12 p. 282 tr. 61

131. Qurʾān 12:58

132. *Biḥār al-anwār* vol. 12 p. 283 tr. 61

133. *Biḥār al-anwār* vol. 12 p. 236 tr. 8

He asked, "Then what drove your father to send you all on this trip without keeping even one of you behind to bring himself comfort and peace of mind?"

They said, "He did so. He kept one of us behind. He is the youngest of us."

He asked, "And why did he choose him out of you all?" They said, "Because he is the most beloved of us after Joseph."[134]

Satisfied that he had made enough of a pretense of suspicion to prevent them from discovering his identity, Joseph told them he was satisfied with their answers and believed their story. He told his servants to take care of their needs as quickly as possible and show them great hospitality while they waited.[135]

Rations were provided based on the number of people in a household, so the brothers explained to Joseph that they needed ten rations for themselves, two for their parents, and one for their half brother, in addition to their servants. Joseph told them that he would provide them with all their rations, including their absent brother's. They paid the price of the wheat in frankincense which they had brought with them,[136] and Joseph ordered his workers to begin filling their saddlebags with their rations. Then he added, "Bring me this half brother of yours next time. Do you not see that I give you your full portion and that I am a most gracious host?"[137] But he sensed that mere encouragement may not be enough to convince them to bring Benjamin, so he added, "If you do not bring him next time, then you shall not receive any portion from me or even be able to approach me."

They replied, "We shall persuade his father to let him come. We shall indeed do this."[138]

Still not convinced that they would do as he told them, he discretely ordered his servants, "Place their frankincense, with which they bartered for their rations, in their packs. Hopefully they

---

134. *Biḥār al-anwār* vol. 12 p. 257 tr. 23

135. *Biḥār al-anwār* vol. 12 p. 287 tr. 71

136. *Biḥār al-anwār* vol. 12 p. 236 tr. 8

137. Qur'ān 12:59

138. Qur'ān 12:61

will recognize it when they return to their families, and hopefully they will return to me once more, this time with Benjamin."[139]

Benjamin Must Come

When they returned to their father, they recounted for him the events of their journey and confirmed that they had been dealt with justly and graciously. However they said, "We shall be deprived of part of our rations next time if we do not take our brother with us, so send him with us when we go for our rations, and we shall protect him."[140]

Jacob replied, "Can I possibly entrust him to you any more than I entrusted to you his brother before him? No promise you make me will fully reassure me, but God is his best protector, and he is the Most Merciful."[141] Thus, he agreed reluctantly to let him go, not because they had earned his trust back, but because he trusted in God and saw there was no other option for them.

When they opened their packs to unload their contents, they found that their frankincense, with which they had bought their rations, had been returned to them. They exclaimed with redoubled motivation to return to Egypt, "O Father! What more could we want? Here is our capital. It has been returned to us. We shall provide for our family, protect our brother, and increase our provisions by one camel-load. That is an easily attained ration."[142]

Second Trip to Egypt

Six months later[143] when their stores had been nearly depleted, Jacob's sons prepared to join another caravan heading to Egypt, this time with their half brother, Benjamin, in their midst. But Jacob, still wary about his sons' lack of trustworthiness said, "I

---

139. Qur'ān 12:62

140. Qur'ān 12:63

141. Qur'ān 12:64

142. Qur'ān 12:65

143. Several traditions mention that they used to go to Egypt once every six months, in the summer and winter (*Biḥār al-anwār* vol. 12 p. 287 tr. 71).

shall not send him with you until you swear an oath to me before God that you will bring him back to me unless you are destroyed."[144] They agreed to this condition for, despite their continued ill will for Benjamin, they were eager for their father's trust.

When they had sworn the oath to him, Jacob solemnly said, "God is witness to what we have said."[145] He continued, "My sons, when you go to Egypt, do not enter together from a single gate; rather, enter from various gates so that you do not raise suspicions." He was concerned that the sight of eleven strong men entering the city together might draw unnecessary attention and needlessly give the authorities a scare. He continued, "Nonetheless, I cannot avail you of anything against God's wish, for such decisions are only for God to make. Thus, I trust in him, for it is in him that people must trust."[146]

They departed with the caravan but separated themselves when they approached the city. They entered the city from whence their father had advised them, in small groups entering from different gates. Nonetheless, his advice did not avail them of anything against God's wish. Though it did fulfill a need for prudence in Jacob's heart. Jacob possessed the knowledge that prudence, while necessary, cannot thwart God's will. He had this knowledge by virtue of what God had taught him, for most people do not have such knowledge.[147]

Joseph Speaks to Benjamin Privately

Once again, they came before Joseph, still not recognizing him except as the ʿAzīz. Joseph showed them special favor again and invited them to join him for a meal. He had several spreads of food laid out and he asked them to sit in groups with their full brothers. When they were all seated, he saw that one brother, Benjamin, was left standing. He asked him, "Why have you not sat at a spread?"

Benjamin said, "I do not have a full brother among them."

---

144. Qurʾān 12:66

145. Qurʾān 12:66

146. Qurʾān 12:67

147. Qurʾān 12:68

Joseph pressed, "Do you have a full brother at all?"

Benjamin replied, "Yes, I do. They claim he was eaten by a wolf, but I believe they caused some mischief to separate him from our mother and father."

Joseph asked, "Have you married? And do you have children?"

Benjamin answered, "Yes, God has given me three sons, and I have named each of them something to remind me of my lost brother."

Joseph said, half in jest, "I see that you have embraced a woman and had children despite your brother's loss," as though true grief for his brother should have prevented him from marrying.

Benjamin justified himself saying, "I have a good father. He told me to marry in hopes that God would bring forth from my loins children who would fill the world with his praise."[148]

"Then sit with me at my spread," Joseph told him.[149] Everyone was busy eating, and Joseph felt he could speak privately with Benjamin. He told him, "I wish to be your brother to replace the one you lost."

Benjamin told him, "Who could ask for a better brother than you; but alas, you are not the son of Jacob and Rachel!"[150]

Joseph's tears welled up as he drew close to Benjamin and told him secretly, "I am, in fact, your brother, and I will protect you, so do not fret over what they used to do to us."[151]

Benjamin took the news in stride so as not to raise his other brothers' suspicion, but he was elated within to have found his beloved brother and immensely relieved at the prospect of escaping the constant torments of his older brothers. He said, "I shall not ever leave your side."

Joseph Schemes to Keep Benjamin

Joseph said, "I can only keep you here if I accuse you of something awful."

---

148. *Biḥār al-anwār* vol. 12 p. 259 tr. 23

149. *Biḥār al-anwār* vol. 12 p. 238 tr. 9 and p. 287 tr. 71

150. *Biḥār al-anwār* vol. 12 p. 289 tr. 71

151. Qur'ān 12:69

Benjamin said, "I do not care. Do what you must."

Joseph told him, "I have ordered my servants to plant the king's goblet in your saddle bags. I will then accuse you of stealing to keep you here with me."[152]

The meal was complete, and Joseph's workers informed him that his guests' rations were packed and ready to be taken. They also furtively let him know that they had acted on his instructions and planted the king's goblet in his youngest brother's pack. Joseph bade them all farewell and sent his regards to their father.

The caravan had not traveled far when Joseph raised the alarm. Within minutes, he had sent out a retinue of soldiers to intercept the caravan promising, "Whoever brings the goblet to me shall receive a camel-load of rations. I guarantee it."[153] The soldiers' crier announced as they approached from behind, "O camel-riders! You are thieves!"[154]

The brothers asked as they turned toward the source of the accusation, "What is it that you are missing?"[155]

Joseph's soldiers replied, "We are missing the king's goblet."[156]

The brothers said, "For God's sake, you had determined that we did not come here to cause mischief in this land and that we are not thieves."[157] Nonetheless, the soldiers ordered the entire caravan to return to Egypt so that the ʿAzīz could decide how to proceed.

When they were brought before Joseph and they repeated their denial of their accusations, Joseph challenged, "Perhaps you are telling the truth; however, what shall be the consequence for stealing if you are lying?"[158]

They said, "Its consequence shall be that he in whose pack it is found shall remain with you. This is how we punish wrongdoers

---

152. *Biḥār al-anwār* vol. 12 p. 290 tr. 71

153. Qurʾān 12:72

154. Qurʾān 12:70

155. Qurʾān 12:71

156. Qurʾān 12:72

157. Qurʾān 12:73. They refer here to the conversation that I narrated from *Biḥār al-anwār* vol. 12 p. 257 tr. 23.

158. Qurʾān 12:74

in Canaan."[159] They were so confident of their innocence that they boldly made this offer even though they knew it could potentially contradict their oath to their father.

He accepted this proposal and had his workers begin searching the older brothers' packs before Benjamin's pack. Then they brought it out from Benjamin's pack.[160] Benjamin's brothers suddenly changed their tune. They said viciously, "If he has stolen today, it is no surprise, for a brother of his stole something before."[161] They sought to distance themselves from Benjamin and Joseph by rehashing their aunt's false accusation from so many years before and dismissing both brothers as morally degenerate.

Joseph bore their accusations and did not expose the truth to them. He simply said to them, "Your current predicament is worse than your two brothers', for you have just contradicted your own previous claim that you are not thieves. Now you are admitting that two of you were in fact thieves and that you had prior knowledge of this." He shook his head in disbelief and said, "God knows better whether what you allege about your brother is even true."[162] They lied to him despite his inordinate hospitality and kindness, thus placing their current accusation against their lost brother under question.

In this way, Joseph succeeded, with God's special aid, in keeping his brother, Benjamin, in Egypt under the pretext of him having stolen. If it had not been for God's special favor, he would not have been able to do so within the dictates of the king's customs, for it allowed for such severe punishment only if the criminal himself agreed to it, which in this case, he had.[163]

Their Oath to Their Father

Then they realized the full extent of their folly. They realized that they would have to face their father having broken their oath to

159. Qur'ān 12:75

160. Qur'ān 12:76

161. Qur'ān 12:77

162. Qur'ān 12:77

163. Qur'ān 12:76

him. They begged Joseph saying, "O ʿAzīz! He has an old father, so take one of us in his place, for we believe you to be among the righteous."[164]

Joseph replied, "God forbid that we take anyone but him with whom we found our property. If we were to do so we would be wrongdoers."[165]

When they lost hope in convincing him to take one of them in his place, they met privately on the side. The eldest of them, Reuben, said, "Do you not remember that our father made us swear an oath before God that we would bring our brother back to him unless we were destroyed, and before that, remember how we fell short of our promise with respect to Joseph? Therefore, I shall not leave this land until my father gives me leave or God himself ordains a way for me to return. He is the best to ordain."[166] Reuben continued, "Go back to your father and tell him, 'O Father! Your son stole, and we only proposed that the thief be taken as punishment for his crime based on our knowledge that we were all innocent. We could not have known the unseen.'"[167]

Facing Their Father

So nine of them left, leaving Benjamin and Reuben behind, dreading their impending encounter with their father. When they arrived home, they tried to explain to their father all that had transpired, the truth this time, but one too many lies had eroded the last vestiges of his trust in them. In desperation they said, "Ask the people who live in the city where we were and who traveled in the caravan with which we returned. We are telling the truth."[168]

Jacob told them, "It is not as you claim; rather, you have fooled yourselves into doing something awful."[169] It was not just that

164. Qurʾān 12:78

165. Qurʾān 12:79

166. Qurʾān 12:80

167. Qurʾān 12:81

168. Qurʾān 12:82

169. Qurʾān 12:83

he did not trust his sons' story. Rather, he scolded them because they had acted foolishly. First, they had not been clever enough to realize that the presence of the goblet in Benjamin's pack was circumstantial evidence and did not prove that he stole it. Second, they had foolishly proposed a punishment that, if enforced, would prevent them from fulfilling their oath to their father. Thirdly, when Benjamin was detained, aside from Reuben, they had all failed to fulfill their oath. Like their brother, they should not have returned without Benjamin.

Nonetheless, Jacob once again submitted to the circumstances that had been doled out to him and said, "But graceful patience shall be my motto. Perhaps God will bring them all back to me, for he is the All-Knowing, the Wise."[170]

Jacob's Grief

Jacob pulled away from his sons and resigned to mourn his loss in solitude. In prayer, he exclaimed, "O how I grieve for Joseph!" He wept for Joseph and the tribulations God had ordained for them until his eyes went blind from sadness because he could all but contain it.[171]

He said, "Lord, will you not have mercy on me? You took my sight, and you took my two sons."

God replied to him, "Even if they were to die, I would bring them back to life to bring you together. However, I have lengthened your separation to reprimand you. Do you not remember that you once slaughtered a sheep and roasted its meat and ate it? There was a wayfarer who had been fasting, yet you did not offer him any of the meat."[172] To be reminded that he was cause of Joseph's suffering only made his pain greater.

Weeks passed, and Jacob continued to spend his time in private mourning. His sons, still haunted by their age-old jealousy of their brother, told him spitefully, "By God, it seems you will never cease thinking of Joseph and praying for his return until you ruin

---

170. Qur'ān 12:83

171. Qur'ān 12:84

172. *Biḥār al-anwār* vol. 12 p. 264 tr. 28

your health or die."[173] They had disposed of Joseph hoping to gain their father's exclusive attention, yet even in Joseph's absence, his memory reigned supreme over their father's thoughts, and rather than giving them his exclusive attention, he turned away from them in remembrance of Joseph.

Jacob replied, "I only present my worries and grief to God who can answer my prayers, not to you who are the very source of my grief."

Reassured by the Angel of Death

Jacob needed to know whether Joseph was still alive. So he called down ʿAzrāʾīl, the Angel of Death. He appeared before him in a most beautiful form and asked, "Of what service can I be?"

Jacob asked, "Tell me, do you personally take all people's souls or are they taken separately by various angels of death?"[174]

He replied, "My helpers take them separately, but all people's souls are presented to me."

Jacob pressed eagerly, "If that is the case, then I ask you for the sake of the God of Abraham, Isaac, and Jacob, has the soul of Joseph been presented to you?"

ʿAzrāʾīl said, "No." It was then that Jacob felt certain that Joseph was still alive and hopeful that their reunion would be soon.[175]

Messenger From Egypt

Around the same time, in Egypt, a villager came to Joseph to buy rations for his household. When he had packed his rations, Joseph asked him where he lived. He mentioned his town's name and Joseph's eyes lit up. He said, "On your way, when you reach such and such a valley, stop and call out 'O Jacob! O Jacob!' An honorable

---

173. Qurʾān 12:85

174. ʿAllāmah al-Majlisī has construed this phrase to mean that he wanted to know whether ʿAzrāʾīl waited until all people were dead to take their souls all at once or whether he took each person's soul individually at the time of his or her death (*Biḥār al-anwār* vol. 12 p. 278 tr. 50). However, this explanation does not fit with ʿAzrāʾīl's answer. I believe my explanation is more suitable.

175. *Biḥār al-anwār* vol. 12 p. 244 tr. 11 and p. 278 tr. 50

and handsome man will answer your call. Tell him, 'In Egypt, I met a man who conveys to you his salutations and says that the trust that you had consigned to God's care has not been forsaken.'"

This villager did what Joseph requested of him and delivered the message to Jacob. No sooner had he heard the message than he fell unconscious. When he awoke and recovered his composure, he asked the villager if he had any needs that he could fulfill for him in repayment for bearing the message. The man said that he did. He said, "I am a man with much wealth, yet my wife has not borne me any children. So I wish for you to pray to God to provide me with a child."

Jacob performed his ablutions and prayed as the man requested. God answered his prayer, and the villager was eventually granted four blessed sons. In this way, Jacob was repeatedly reassured by God that his beloved son was alive and well.[176] Accordingly, he told his sons, "I know, by the grace of God, what you do not know."[177]

Third Trip to Egypt

Another six months had passed, and Jacob's family's rations were running low once again. Jacob sent some[178] of his sons again to Egypt and told them, "My sons, go and also seek out Joseph and his brother, and do not lose hope in the mercy of God. Only unbelievers lose hope in the mercy of God."[179]

He composed a letter to send with his sons to the ʿAzīz who had enslaved his son Benjamin, not realizing he was writing to his own Joseph. He sealed this letter and entrusted it to one of his sons.

They arrived in Egypt and appeared before Joseph saying, "O ʿAzīz! Hard times have come upon us and our family. We have come with few goods with which to buy our rations; nonetheless, we beg

---

176. *Biḥār al-anwār* vol. 12 p. 285 tr. 69

177. Qurʾān 12:86

178. The evidence that he only sent some of his sons on this trip lies in 12:94–5, for while some of his sons are returning from Egypt, Jacob tells some others that he smells Joseph's scent, and they in turn accuse him of reverting to his previous state of error.

179. Qurʾān 12:87

you to give us our full ration and be charitable with us by releasing our brother.[180] God rewards the charitable."[181]

Jacob's Letter

They presented to him their father's letter which read:

> In the name of God, the All-Beneficent, the Ever-Merciful. To the ʿAzīz of Egypt, justice incarnate, who gives in full measure, from Jacob, son of Isaac, son of Abraham, the All-Merciful's Friend...
>
> Peace be with you. I praise God other than whom there is no god.
>
> We are a family upon whom God has always sent tribulation to try us in thick and thin. My grandfather, Abraham, was thrown into the fire because of his obedience to the Lord, and, as a result, God made the fire cool and peaceful for him. God also commanded my grandfather to slaughter my uncle but then replaced him with a ram. For the last twenty years, tribulations have rained down upon me. The first was that I had a son whom I called Joseph. He was my joy and the light of eyes. His half brothers asked me to let him go with them to play and frolic. So I sent him with them in the morning, and they returned to me in the evening weeping. They brought me his tunic splattered with fraudulent sheep's blood and claimed that a wolf had eaten him. My grief for his loss was immense, and my weeping for his separation from me was intense, so much that it blotted out my vision. He had a

---

180. I have construed "charity" to specifically mean "releasing our brother" for two reasons. First, it would be beneath the dignity of a prophet's family to beg for charity. Second, a tradition transmitted in *Majmaʿ al-bayān* (under 12:88) explicitly explains charity as "releasing our brother."

181. Qurʾān 12:88

> brother with whom I was pleased. He was my comfort. Whenever I missed Joseph, I would hug this brother of his to my chest, and that would mitigate some of my grief. This son's brothers told me that you asked them about him and ordered them to bring him to you, and you threatened to deny them their rations if they failed to bring him. So I sent him to you with them so they could bring us our wheat rations. But alas, when they returned, he was not among them. They told me that he had stolen your king's goblet. However, I call you to witness that I am no thief, and I did not sire a thief. You have taken him prisoner and caused me much heartache. My grief over his separation from me is immense, so much that it has weighed down my feeble back. So I beg you to do me a favor and let him go free. Provide us with good wheat, and charge us a fair price. Give us our complete ration, and quickly release the family of Abraham.[182]

Joseph was noticeably affected by his father's letter. He took it from his brother and kissed it and touched it to his own eyes. And he weeped so profusely that his tears fell upon the robes he was wearing. Jacob's sons were visibly surprised to see him so affected. But Joseph momentarily ignored his brothers and composed a reply to his father. He wrote, "Be patient as your forefathers were patient, and you shall prevail as they prevailed."

When Jacob would later read this reply he would say, "These are not the words of kings and pharaohs but of prophets and sons of prophets."[183]

---

182. I have combined two separate transmissions of this letter, taking the best parts of each (*Biḥār al-anwār* vol. 12 p. 269 tr. 4 and *Majmaʿ al-bayān* under 12:88).

183. *Biḥār al-anwār* vol. 12 p. 269 tr. 43

Joseph Reveals Himself

Joseph then turned his attention back to his brothers and reprimanded them saying, "Do you remember what you did to Joseph and his brother in your foolishness?[184] You took Joseph from his father, you cast him into a well, and you conspired to kill him; then you separated Benjamin from his older brother, and you mistreated him and made him speak to you as a slave speaks to his master; and worse than all this, do you see what you have done to your own father?"[185] As he said this, he remembered God's voice comforting him in the cistern, "You shall disclose to them the reality of these deeds of theirs one day when they will not even recognize you."[186]

As the clues added up, God lifted the veil of obscurity from his brothers' eyes and they asked incredulously, "Are *you* Joseph?"

He replied, "I am Joseph, and this is my brother. God has shown us favor." But he wanted to ensure that they finally understood that God's favor is not arbitrary–that anyone who fulfills the prerequisites can attain it, so he continued, "If anyone is God-fearing and patient, God shall show him favor, for God does not neglect to reward the righteous."[187]

They admitted, "By God, he has indeed favored you over us, and we have indeed acted wrongly."[188]

Tidings For Jacob

Joseph said, "I shall not reproach you again from this day on. May God forgive you, for he is the Most Merciful."[189] He then tugged at the chain around his neck until a small silver vial appeared from beneath his robes. This was the same vial that his father had given

184. Qur'ān 12:89

185. *Majma' al-bayān* under 12:88

186. Qur'ān 12:15

187. Qur'ān 12:90

188. Qur'ān 12:91

189. Qur'ān 12:92

him so long before. Joseph pried it open and unfurled his great-grandfather's tunic which had been given to him by Gabriel to protect him from Nimrod's fire.[190] He handed this to his brother Judah and said, "Take this tunic of mine, and cast it over my father's face, and he will see once again. And bring me your entire family."[191] Judah had been the bearer of Joseph's bloodstained tunic all those years before because of which their father had gone blind, so Joseph wanted him to be the one to bear this tunic and cast it over their father's face to bring back his sight and atone for the past.[192] With that, he ordered their saddlebags to be filled with rations and sent them on their way.

When the caravan had only just departed from Egypt, their father who was yet in Canaan, said to his sons who had stayed behind, "I swear I smell a hint of Joseph." It was the scent of paradise that emanated from Abraham's tunic that he smelled.[193] He continued, "If you did not consider me senile, you would believe me."[194]

But alas, they had still not escaped from the clutches of jealousy and they said thoughtlessly, "By God, you are still in error in this regard as you have always been."[195]

Gabriel came to Jacob and asked, "Shall I teach you a supplication through which God will restore your sight and bring back your sons?" When Jacob answered in the affirmative, he continued, "Pray as Adam prayed when he wanted God to forgive him. And pray as Noah prayed when he wanted God to bring his ark to rest on the mountain and save him from the flood. And pray as your grandfather Abraham prayed when he was thrown in the fire. Say, 'O God! We ask you through Muḥammad, ʿAlī, Fāṭimah, al-Ḥasan,

---

190. *Biḥār al-anwār* vol. 12 p. 249 tr. 14

191. Qurʾān 12:93

192. *Majmaʿ al-bayān* under 12:88

193. *Biḥār al-anwār* vol. 12 p. 279 tr. 56

194. Qurʾān 12:94

195. Qurʾān 12:95

and al-Ḥusayn, to bring Joseph and Benjamin back to me and to restore my vision.'"[196]

Jacob did as Gabriel taught him, and eighteen days later, the caravan arrived from Egypt. Jacob's household stirred to life in anticipation of the news it brought. Jacob's sons, in stark contrast to their melancholy departure, returned elated, even celebratory. They greeted their father and their families with a confused cacophony of reports about the events that had transpired in Egypt. Then Judah, humble and yet joyous, approached his father with Joseph's tunic spread in his hands. As Joseph had instructed him, he cast the tunic upon his father's face, and his sight returned.[197]

Jacob beamed as he looked upon his sons and their families for the first time in decades. Then he told them knowingly, "Did I not tell you that I know, by the grace of God, what you do not know?"[198] Never again would they dare say that he was in error, for it was made plain to them that he drew his knowledge from a divine source.

The Sons of Jacob Are Redeemed

All of his sons gathered around their father, penitent and broken. They begged, "O Father! Seek forgiveness from God for our sins. We have acted wrongly."[199]

He promised, "I shall seek forgiveness for you from my Lord. He is the Absolver, the Merciful."[200] Joseph had prayed for their forgiveness as soon as they requested it and without hesitation,[201] for it was his own right they had trampled and, thus, his prerogative to forgive, and he was young and light-hearted.[202] Jacob's pain, though largely vicarious, had been greater, and he needed time to

---

196. *Biḥār al-anwār* vol. 12 p. 260 tr. 23

197. Qur'ān 12:96

198. Qur'ān 12:96

199. Qur'ān 12:97

200. Qur'ān 12:98

201. Qur'ān 12:92

202. *Biḥār al-anwār* vol. 12 p. 280 tr. 57

clear his heart, so he waited until early Friday morning,[203] before sunrise, for that is a time when hearts are ready to supplicate and God is ready to answer.[204]

At last, Jacob's and Joseph's patience paid off. These sons and brothers who had been ensnared by envy for so long had finally freed themselves by submitting before the objects of their former envy, and, in so doing, gained honor and dignity in God's eyes. Their penance was accepted and their past deeds effaced. Rather than making them symbols of jealousy and malice, God made them fathers of the twelve great tribes of Israel.[205]

Jacob's Family Arrives in Egypt

According to Joseph's instructions, his brothers packed all their belongings and brought their entire family to Egypt. Light-footed and light-hearted, they completed the journey from Canaan to Egypt in nine days, half the time it would normally have taken.[206] When they came before Joseph, he hugged his parents[207] to himself and said, "Enter Egypt in safety, if God wills."[208]

He brought his parents up to the king's throne to honor them,[209] and they and his eleven brothers all spontaneously fell prostrate

---

203. *Biḥār al-anwār* vol. 12 p. 251 tr. 16

204. *Biḥār al-anwār* vol. 12 p. 266 tr. 34

205. *Biḥār al-anwār* vol. 12 p. 291 tr. 75

206. *Biḥār al-anwār* vol. 12 p. 282 tr. 61

207. There are several opinions about the woman who was there with Jacob. Some say it was Rachel, so the reference to his parents is literal. Others say that Rachel had died in childbirth, so the woman who was with Jacob was Rachel's sister. Apparently, this was another sister besides Leah because she died before Rachel married Jacob (*Biḥār al-anwār* vol. 12 p. 290 tr. 71).

208. Qur'ān 12:99

209. According to several traditions, Joseph was guilty of remaining seated and not rising to honor his father. According to these traditions, as punishment, Gabriel extracted the light of prophethood from his hands so that no prophets would ever be born in his progeny and the light was instead given to his brother Levi (see *Biḥār al-anwār* vol. 12 p. 251 tr. 17 and p. 260 tr. 23 and p. 281 tr. 58 and tr. 59). This indictment of Joseph is problematic for the following reasons.

- First, it does not fit with the impeccable moral character for which

before him in gratitude to God.[210] Joseph said to Jacob, "O Father! This is the realization of my earlier dream. God has made it a reality. He was kind to me when he brought me out of prison, and he brought you from the desert even though Satan had caused a rift between me and my brothers. My Lord is kind to whomever he wishes. He is the All-Knowing, the Wise."[211] Then he turned to God in prayer and said, "Lord, you gave me power and taught me the interpretation of dreams. O Fashioner of the heavens and the earth! You are my master in this world and in the hereafter. Take my soul as I submit to you, and raise me among the righteous."[212]

Joseph is known. The Qur'ān praises him throughout this story and, even at this particular juncture, does not indicate that he has acted in an unfavorable way. On the contrary, it tells us that he "hugged his parents to himself;" that he greeted them respectfully saying, "Enter Egypt in safety, if God wills;" and that "he brought his parents up to the king's throne," presumably to honor them.

- Second, these traditions maintain that Levi earned the honor of having the light of prophethood pass through his progeny through two acts. First, he persuaded his brothers not to kill Joseph but to cast him into the cistern instead. Second, he was the one who held true to his oath to his father and remained in Egypt when Benjamin was detained. Both of Levi's alleged honors are problematic. That he persuaded his brothers not to kill Joseph is good, but this does not indicate that he had any great love for Joseph or that he was altogether free from the others' jealousy. He did, after all, follow through with their plot, and it was he who demanded that Joseph remove his tunic before they cast him into the cistern. Certainly, the goodness of this act of his cannot be compared to Joseph's goodness and cannot earn him a merit of which Joseph was unworthy. Furthermore, it is probably incorrect to claim that the brother who stayed back was Levi, for the Qur'ān explicitly says it was the eldest of them who stayed back (Qur'ān 12:80) while all accounts suggest that Levi was in the middle of the brothers and not the eldest (*Biḥār al-anwār* vol. 12 p. 220 tr. 1).

For these reason, I have rejected the aforementioned traditions and maintained that Joseph acted in an exemplary fashion as he was supposed to. It follows that the prophethood was placed in Levi's progeny, and not his, for some other reason that God alone knows.

210. *Biḥār al-anwār* vol. 12 p. 217 tr. 1

211. Qur'ān 12:100

212. Qur'ān 12:101

The Culmination of Joseph's Plan For Egypt

Even after his family and he were reunited, Joseph continued his program of selling rations on behalf of the king according to his original plan. During the first year, people had paid with their silver and gold coins until, by the end of the year, there was hardly a coin left in Egypt and the surrounding lands that was not in the king's treasuries.

During the second year, people paid with their jewelry and precious stones, until by the end of the year, there were hardly any jewelry or precious stones left in Egypt and the surrounding lands that were not in the king's treasuries.

During the third year, people paid with their livestock and pack animals until, by the end of the year, there were hardly any livestock or pack animals left in Egypt and the surrounding lands that were not in the king's possession.

During the fourth year, people paid with their slaves until, by the end of the year, there were hardly any slaves left in Egypt and the surrounding lands who were not in the king's possession.[213]

Jacob's Death

Jacob died during this fourth year, two years after coming to Egypt. He had been God's proof and guide, spreading the teachings of Abraham throughout Egypt, using Joseph's power and influence to do God's work.

As he lay on his deathbed, he gathered his children around and asked them, "What will you worship after me?"

They replied unanimously, "We shall worship your God and the God of your forefathers, Abraham, Ishmael, and Isaac as one God to whom we all submit."[214]

Pleased with their answer, he admonished them as Abraham had once admonished his children, "My children, God has chosen this religion for you, so make certain you die in submission to him."[215]

---

213. *Biḥār al-anwār* vol. 12 p. 292 tr. 76

214. Qur'ān 2:133

215. Qur'ān 2:132

He was 120 years old when he passed away.[216] Joseph carried his body to Jerusalem and buried him there.[217] With Jacob dead, God appointed Joseph as his messenger to the people of Egypt.[218]

During the fifth year of the famine, people paid with their homes and landholdings until, by the end of the year, there was hardly any property left in Egypt and the surrounding lands that was not in the king's lease.

During the sixth year, people paid with their wells and water rights until, by the end of the year, there was hardly any water left in Egypt and the surrounding lands that was not in the king's control.

During the seventh year, people, having nothing left, paid by indenturing themselves until, by the end of the year, there was hardly a free man or woman left in Egypt and the surrounding lands who was not in the king's indenture.

Eventually, as the seventh year of the famine drew to a close, Joseph addressed the king. He showed him how he had taken possession of all of Egypt by the grace of God. Then he said, "I hereby testify before you that I free the people of Egypt and return to them what was theirs. And I return to you your ring and goblet on condition that you rule justly and follow my counsel in all affairs, for God has saved you and the people of Egypt at my hand."

The king accepted his condition and he declared, "There is no god but God, who is singular and has no partner, and you, Joseph, are his messenger."[219]

Zalīkhā Is Redeemed

In the following years, the ʿAzīz who had bought Joseph as a child passed away. The king also passed away, and Joseph became king. Zalīkhā, old and haggard, found herself utterly destitute, begging on the street for her daily subsistence.[220] Some of her old

216. *Biḥār al-anwār* vol. 12 p. 298 tr. 85

217. *Biḥār al-anwār* vol. 12 p. 295 tr. 77

218. *Biḥār al-anwār* vol. 12 p. 295 tr. 77 and Qurʾān 44:34

219. *Biḥār al-anwār* vol. 12 p. 292 tr. 76

220. *Biḥār al-anwār* vol. 12 p. 253 tr. 17

acquaintances suggested that she should go before King Joseph and ask him for help. But others expressed their concern saying, "We fear what he might do to you in revenge for what you did to him."

Zalīkhā quieted their fears saying, "I do not fear him who fears God."[221]

So she stood upon a route that Joseph traveled daily. When she caught sight of him, she called out, "Exalted is he who makes slaves out of kings when they disobey him and makes kings out of slaves when they obey him. I have been stricken by poverty, so give me charity."[222]

Joseph immediately recognized his old mistress, and despite all she had put him through, his heart went out to her. Zalīkhā apologized profusely for what she had done to him but justified her transgression saying, "Do not blame me too much for what I did, for I was tempted by four things that made it impossible for me to avoid what I did: I was the most beautiful woman in Egypt; you were the most handsome man in all of Egypt; I was wealthy beyond imagination; and my husband, the ʿAzīz, was impotent and had forsworn women, thus leaving me a virgin."[223]

Joseph asked her, "If you considered me handsome, what would you have done if you had been tested through a prophet named Muḥammad whom God will send at the end of time? He will be more handsome, with better character, and more generous than I."

Joseph and Zalīkhā Are Married

She realized that her test had been just and that it was she who had been weak. Then she added that, as Joseph had described Muḥammad, she had felt a deep sense of love for him in her heart. Joseph turned his attention toward God and asserted that he had fallen in love with Zalīkhā because of her newfound love for

---

221. *Biḥār al-anwār* vol. 12 p. 269 tr. 42 and p. 296 tr. 79

222. *Biḥār al-anwār* vol. 12 p. 253 tr. 17

223. *Biḥār al-anwār* vol. 12 p. 269 tr. 42 and p. 296 tr. 79 and p. 253 tr. 17

Prophet Muḥammad. He asked God to restore her youth so that he may marry her. God answered his prayer, and they were married.[224]

Joseph and Zalīkhā lived out their long lives as king and queen of Egypt. Joseph spread the teachings of Abraham throughout his kingdom and ruled justly as God's proof and vicegerent on earth.

Joseph's Death

At the age of 120,[225] as Joseph lay on his deathbed, he assembled his followers and eighty members from the family of Jacob[226] to deliver to them his last testament. He began by praising God and then said, "Great hardship is set to befall you. These Egyptians will subjugate you and inflict a terrible torment on you. Your men will be murdered. The bellies of your pregnant women will be slit. Your newborn boys will be slaughtered. This will continue until God reveals the truth through one who will rise up from the descendants of Levi, son of Jacob. That man will be dark-skinned and tall." He was describing Moses, son of Amram. Then he said, "Hold fast to him."[227] And with that Joseph passed on.

224. *Biḥār al-anwār* vol. 12 p. 282 tr. 60

225. *Biḥār al-anwār* vol. 12 p. 298 tr. 85

226. *Biḥār al-anwār* vol. 13 p. 38 tr. 9

227. *Biḥār al-anwār* vol. 13 p. 36 tr. 7 and p. 38 tr. 9

Job

Joseph's Legacy Fades

Joseph's legacy had been strong. Admittedly, there were many in the ruling class of Egypt who had harbored doubts in his prophethood and decided for themselves that God would never send another prophet after him.[1] Nonetheless, he had caused a revolution that had brought Egypt and its surrounding lands under the fold of monotheism for a time.

God sent a series of successors to carry on the mission and propagate the message of Joseph and his forebears.[2] Two generations on, he chose Job,[3] a great-great grandson of Isaac,[4] as a prophet and guide.

---

1. Qur'ān 40:34

2. There is no concrete evidence of these successors, except for the Prophet Efram, whom I will introduce shortly. Nonetheless, countless traditions tell us that God sent successors after every prophet and that he would never leave the earth without an infallible guide.

3. In Arabic Job is known as *Ayyūb*. In English his name is pronounced *jobe,* which rhymes with "globe."

4. Three traditions describe different lineages for Job and place him at different points in history:

- One claims that Job's father had been a believer and follower of Abraham and that his mother was Lot's daughter. It further claims that he was married to Ilyā, Jacob's daughter, making him Jacob's son-in-law (*Biḥār al-anwār* vol. 12 p. 352 tr. 23). I have rejected this tradition for two reasons:
  - Its chain of transmission does not reach to an imam or to the Prophet but to Wahb ibn Munabbih who is known to have been a transmitter of *Isrā'īliyyāt*, stories taken from other religious traditions and inserted into the Islamic tradition in the guise of Prophetic traditions.
  - It seems far-fetched, if Job was a contemporary of Jacob and Joseph, that he would never be mentioned in their story, nor they in his.

Job Settles Down

Job was thirty years old when his father, Amos,[5] passed away.[6] Amos had been a wealthy man with sizable herds of camels, cattle, goats, donkeys, mules, and horses. There was virtually no one in the Levant as wealthy as he. Job, who was a wise and forbearing man despite his youth, inherited this fortune and immediately set out to find a wife and begin his life in earnest.

He had heard about a girl in Egypt named Raḥmah, the daughter of Prophet Efram,[7] son of Joseph. Efram loved his daughter very much, the more so because he had seen his father, Joseph, in a dream. In the dream, Joseph doffed his tunic and draped it over Raḥmah and told her, "Raḥmah, this is my beauty and resplendence. I hereby bequeath it to you." From that day forward, she grew to resemble Joseph more than any of his other descendants did. More importantly, she was devout and aloof of worldly pleasures.

- Another claims that Job was the son of Amos, son of *Rāzikh* (or *Tārikh*), son of *Rūm*, son of Esau, son of Isaac and that his mother was a descendant of Lot (*Biḥār al-anwār* vol. 12 p. 356). While there is nothing inherently problematic with this geneology, its transmitters are Wahb ibn Munabbih and Kaʿb al-Aḥbār and, thus, lacks independent credibility for this reason.
- A third tradition, attributed to Imam al-Ṣādiq, tells us that Job was the son of Amos, son of Rūʿīl, son of Esau, son of Isaac (*al-Burhān fī tafsīr al-qurʾān* vol. 4 p. 664). While it is admittedly not important to place Job in a specific historical context and know his genealogy, it is interesting, and so I have based my story on this third tradition only because it is attributed to an infallible imam by a respected scholar in an important book. It is interesting to note that Job was not an Israelite prophet since he was not from the descendants of Israel, i.e., Jacob, as confirmed by *Biḥār al-anwār* vol. 12 p. 350 tr. 16.

5. In Arabic Amos is known as *Amūṣ*.

6. I have adapted most of this story from *al-Burhān fī tafsīr al-qurʾān* vol. 4 p.664–72. Abridged versions of the same story can be found in *Biḥār al-anwār* vol. 12 p. 342 tr. 3 and p. 345 tr. 4.

7. In Arabic Efram is known as *Ifrāʾīm*. Many traditions claim that he was a prophet.

Job had his heart set on marrying Raḥmah. Efram, despite his attachment to his daughter, married her to him because of his righteousness and piety. Together the new couple traveled back to the Levant, to Job's hometown of Bathnah.[8] There they settled down, and God granted them many children.

Job Enjoys Countless Blessings

Some years later, God appointed Job as a prophet and messenger to the people of Bathnah and the neighboring town of Ḥawrān. Because of his outstanding character and gentle nature, and because of his and his father's status, he was not opposed or repudiated by his people. He promulgated the law of Abraham and built houses of worship. He served food to the destitute and to the wayfarers. He was like a father to the orphans, a husband to the widows, and a guardian to the weak. Whenever he ate, he would eat with orphans or some other guests at his spread.[9] He instructed his agents not to bar anyone from his orchards and fields. He even extended his hospitality to the birds and the beasts whom he allowed to graze freely in his fields. Whenever he was faced with a choice between two good deeds, he chose the harder of the two.[10] For Job's devotion and generosity, God rained down his blessings upon him more and more by the day and made his animals bear twins every year.

Despite God's myriad blessings upon him, Job never exulted or felt conceit. Rather he would say, "Lord, if this world is like this, then how wonderful must your paradise be, for you have created it specially for those whom you wish to honor." Decades passed until Job reached the age of seventy-three.[11]

---

8. The name of this city has been recorded as *al-Bathnah* and *al-Bathaniyyah.* It was apparently a city between Damascus and Adhruʿāt (modern day Daraa, Syria; see *Muʿjam al-buldān* vol. 1 p. 338).

9. *Biḥār al-anwār* vol. 12 p. 343 tr. 3

10. *Biḥār al-anwār* vol. 12 p. 343 tr. 3

11. *Biḥār al-anwār* vol. 12 p. 352 tr. 23

Satan's Jealousy of Job

Satan used to roam those parts seeking a way to undermine Job's devotion to God. With great vexation, he found that Job was extraordinarily grateful for all his wealth and diligent in paying charity. This made Satan feel bitterly jealous of Job. So he ascended to the highest levels of the sky and approached the throne of God.[12]

God, who knows what is hidden as well as what is apparent, knew the jealousy he harbored, yet he asked, "O you who are damned![13] From what activity have you come?"

Satan replied, "I circled the earth to misguide all who would obey me. Yet, I have not been able to misguide those servants of yours whom you have specially selected."

God pressed, "What do you feel about the blessings I have showered upon Job? Have you been able to shake him despite his lengthy devotions to me? Does he not counter every blessing I give with renewed thanks?"[14]

Satan spoke to the Almighty patronizingly, "Lord, Job has not shown you proper gratitude for these blessings of yours. I have examined him closely. He is a person upon whom you have bestowed well-being, and so he has welcomed your bestowal; for whom you have provided, and so he has accepted your provision. However, you have not yet tested him through tribulation. I swear, if you were to try him with tribulation, you would find him to be contrary to what he now appears. If you were to grant me, my Lord, dominion over his wealth, you would see how quickly he forgets you."

God Almighty conceded, "O you who are damned! I hereby grant you dominion over his wealth to show you that you are wrong in your assessment of him." It was a Wednesday, the last Wednesday

12. According to this and other traditions (*Biḥār al-anwār* vol. 12 p. 342 tr. 3 and p. 345 tr. 4), the *jinn* were still able to ascend into the skies in those days. In the time of Jesus, they were barred from anything above the fourth sky. And when Prophet Muḥammad was born, they were barred from the skies altogether. This also corresponds to Qur'ān 72:8–9.

13. This is my translation of *mal'ūn*.

14. *Biḥār al-anwār* vol. 12 p. 351 tr. 19

of the month, which had been, and would always remain, an inauspicious day.[15]

The Destruction of Job's Wealth

Satan descended from the heavens and summoned his army of devils from the east and west. He announced, "I have been given an opportunity unlike any since the time I removed Adam and Eve from the garden. I have been granted dominion over Job's wealth. I shall ransack his wealth and make him destitute."

One devil volunteered, "Give me charge of his trees and fields, for I shall become fire and burn them all to ashes." Satan granted him this charge.

Another volunteered, "Give me charge of his animals, for I shall become a fearsome squall to frighten them dead." Satan granted him this charge.

The people of Bathnah spotted thick smoke on the horizon and heard a fearsome squall. Satan manifested himself as one of Job's shepherds. Injured and coated in soot, he ran desperately to Job, who was praying, and panted, "Help me, master. I am your only shepherd to survive. A tremendous blaze came from the sky and scorched your trees and fields and killed all of your animals and shepherds except me. And I heard a herald from the heavens cry out, 'This is retribution for one who has been ostentatious in his worship, who worships to please people instead of God. This is the fire of God's rage!'"

Without batting an eye, Job turned away from this man and engaged in his prayer all the more fervently. Calmly, he completed his prayer and then turned back to the man and said, "It was not *my* wealth that was destroyed. It was God's. He does with it as he wishes." Then half to himself, he said, "Praise is for God for whatever he has decreed. To him belongs praise for what he has given and for what he has taken back."[16]

---

15. *Biḥār al-anwār* vol. 12 p. 351 tr. 20. This was also the day of the month when God reportedly sent his punishment upon the ʿĀd.

16. *Biḥār al-anwār* vol. 12 p. 351 tr. 19. A similar statement is attributed to Job in the Bible. In the *Book of Job* he says, "Naked came I out of my mother's womb,

Then Job turned to the man and asked, "Who are you again? You seem to be one whom God has damned and stripped of his blessing. If there had been any good in you, God would have informed me of it, and he would have taken your life as he took the lives of my other righteous servants. Rather, he removed you from their noble ranks the way chaff is removed from grain. Therefore, leave my presence in disgrace."

The man retorted indignantly, "A wise man once said, 'Do not dare to serve the arrogant.' Job, I now see that you are one of the arrogant and that you were purely ostentatious in your worship. I am but your lowly servant who wants nothing but the best for you. I have been protective of your wealth, I was injured in its defense, and I came now to report to you. Yet you reward me for all my service by maligning me."

Job, seeing the cunning in the man's words, refused to speak another word and turned back to his prayer.

Satan left Job and ascended to God's throne once again. God exulted, "O you who are damned! How did my servant, Job, fare? Did you see how patient he was despite losing all his wealth and how he praised me?"

Satan obsequiously said, "My God! My Master! You have availed him of healthy children and a beautiful home. If only you would grant me dominion over his children and his home, you would see that he is not truly grateful for your blessings." God granted him what he asked, and cast him away.

The Destruction of Job's Children and Home

Satan descended once again, this time upon Job's home where Job's children had gathered. He seized the edifice and made it quake from its foundation, crushing and mutilating Job's children until none survived.

Secretly, God communicated to the earth saying, "Protect the bodies of Job's children, for my plans for them are not yet complete."

---

and naked shall I return thither: the Lord gave, and the Lord hath taken away; blessed be the name of the Lord" (Job 1:21).

As Job stood gaping at the carnage, Satan approached and taunted, "Do you see what I have done to your children? I buried them with its walls, anointed them with its mortar, and shrouded them in their own clothes. If only you could have seen how their lovely faces were spoiled with blood and dirt. If only you could have heard their bones being crushed and their flesh being torn and their skin being shredded." He mercilessly recounted every horrid detail of their murder until Job began to sob. Satan, sensing that he had succeeded in breaking Job's patience, egged him on.

But Job felt a sudden sense of regret at having wept, not because it was wrong to weep for great loss, but because he had made himself vulnerable before his sworn enemy. He sought forgiveness from God for ceding even that much to Satan. When he had fully regained his composure, Job glared at Satan with bloodshot eyes and said with resolute patience, "Get away from me in disgrace. O you who are damned! For my children were but a trust from God from whom separation was inevitable. And, if God wills, I shall be reunited with them, if not in this life, then in the next."

Having failed once again, Satan ascended to God's throne. God exulted, "O you who are damned! How did my servant, Job, fare in his test? Did you not see him repent for having cried in front of you?"

Satan said, "My God! My Master! You have availed him of a healthy body, and this gives him resilience to endure the loss of wealth and children. If only you would grant me dominion over his body, you would see how swiftly he forgets you and ceases thanking you."

God acquiesced saying, "O you who are damned! Leave my presence. I hereby give you dominion over his body except for his eyes, his intellect by which he can know and worship me,[17] his tongue which never ceases remembering me, and his ears."

The Destruction of Job's Health

Satan found Job at his alter. He was singing God's praises, beseeching him, thanking him for his immense blessings, and praising him for

---

17. *Biḥār al-anwār* vol. 12 p. 341 tr. 1

the tribulations he had chosen for him. He said in prayer, "By your might and majesty! Your tribulations only cause me to thank you more. And if you perpetually enshroud me in tribulations, I shall only advance in my patience to endure them."

Seeing him in such serene devotion enraged Satan all the more. As Job bowed his head in prostration, Satan entered the earth and blew searing flames onto Job's body starting from his nostrils, thereby scorching his face and body. Job writhed in pain. His body was charred. Then his skin began to blister from head to foot. He shed his hair, his body began to swell, and his wounds became infected. By the sixth day, parasitic worms had taken up residence in his flesh and his wounds began exuding pus.[18]

---

18. All but one tradition say that Job's affliction extended to his physical body in the way I have described here. Only one tradition, attributed to Imam al-Ṣādiq, says, "Job's body never smelled, his face never became hideous, pus and blood never oozed from his skin, nobody who saw him saw anything repugnant about him, no one was irked by what they saw in him, and his body was not afflicted with parasitic worms...people only abandoned him because he became poor and apparently weak..." (*Biḥār al-anwār* vol. 12 p. 348 tr. 13). We could make a strong case for what this tradition says and write off the other traditions as having bent to Sunnī or Biblical influence (i.e., *taqiyyah*) if we were to base our judgment purely on theological grounds since we have a general rational principle that dictates that God's infallible guides must be free from any defects or deformities that would make people fear or even hesitate to approach them for guidance. However, the traditions that speak of his physical ailments and decrepitude are too many and too strong in their chains of transmission to be cast aside so easily (*Biḥār al-anwār* vol. 12 p. 349 in his *bayān* of the aforementioned tradition). Accordingly, I have favored the majority of traditions over this single one in writing my story while conceding that the truth may lie in that single one.

We must, however, still address the theological problem that such physical tribulations raise. Considering Job's story, it is plausible to say that he had already established himself as a prophet and fulfilled his role of guiding the people of Bathnah before he was afflicted. In this way, his affliction did not interfere with his mission as a prophet. At most, it only created an additional test for his people, to see whether they would remain loyal to him or fall prey to Satan's insinuations. Thus, there is no theological ground for rejecting the prevailing view embodied in the majority of traditions about him (*Biḥār al-anwār* vol. 12 p. 349 in his *bayān* of the aforementioned tradition; also see *Tanzīh al-anbiyā'* p. 62).

When his lesions began to itch, he scratched relentlessly until his fingernails fell off. Then he scratched with jagged stones. Despite his agony, when a worm would fall off his body, he would pick it up and return it to its place saying, "Eat of my flesh and blood until God sends relief."

Raḥmah's Faithfulness

Job's loving wife, Raḥmah, looked at him abjectly and said, "Your wealth and our children are gone. Now your body has also been stricken!"

Job comforted her saying, "God tried the prophets before me, and they were steadfast and patient, and God has promised great things to those who are patient." Then he fell prostrate before God and said, "My God! My Lord! Even if you were to enshroud me in tribulations perpetually, I would advance only in my gratitude to you. But God, please do not give my accursed enemy, Satan, occasion to gloat over me."

Raḥmah wept and wailed for Job's tribulations. He comforted her and told her to restrain herself saying, "Are you not a daughter of prophets? Do you not know that I too am a prophet? I must follow the example of the past prophets and messengers, especially your forebears, Abraham, Ishmael, Isaac, Jacob, Joseph, and Efram." Then he prayed that God would give her patience to endure whatever befell him.

Turned Out by His People

He asked her to find another place for him to rest as he feared desecrating his altar with his bodily secretions. Raḥmah did not know where else to take him, and she was unable to move him by herself, so she went into town to solicit help from people whom Job had always helped in their times of need. To her astonishment, when she presented her need to them, they refused and said, "God is angry with Job because his devotion to God has been ostentatious. We wish he would go as far from us as the east is from the west, for if there had been any virtue in him, God would not have afflicted him thus."

With a broken heart, Raḥmah returned to Job and sobbed, "Our trials have become even greater. Our hopes for the help of those whom you have taught and served have been dashed."

Job said knowingly, "This is the fate of those who are tested. Never mind all that. Come to me and say, 'There is no power except God's.' Then, place your right hand under my head and your left hand under my legs, and you will be able to lift me by the power of God." And she did. She carried him singlehandedly from his altar to the courtyard where Job had always set out spreads of food for the indigent and needy.

Raḥmah Must Work

When he had made himself as comfortable as he could, he said, "Raḥmah, we are prohibited from taking charity. Now that my wealth is gone and my health has failed, you will have to work to support us." As he said this, he began weeping. When she asked him why, he said, "Raḥmah, you are from a line of prophets. And you are immeasurably beautiful. Nobody has ever had your beauty except your grandfather, Joseph. But there are lecherous men in this city, and you will be laboring in their houses, and I fear Satan's machinations."

Hurt by the insinuation, Raḥmah said, "I deserve better than for you to suspect me of such impropriety, for I am from the line of the pure and righteous prophets. I swear by my forebears, my eyes shall never gaze at any man except you."

Having elicited this oath from her and evoked her sense of honor as he had hoped, he allowed her to go out and find work.

She began working in the homes of the denizens of Bathnah. She drew water for them, swept their floors, cleared their garbage, and washed their clothes. They paid her her wages which she dutifully spent on Job's upkeep.

Satan Turns Them Against Her

Satan transformed himself into an old man and addressed the townspeople saying, "People of Bathnah! How is it that you allow a woman to serve you who nurses her husband's festering sores and pus-covered body, for she then enters your homes and puts her contaminated hands on your dishes and in your food and your drink?"

His ruse worked. From that day forward, they refused to let Raḥmah into their homes. She was distraught, but she refused to tell Job, lest she add to his sadness. Fortunately, some families, while refusing to employ her, gave her food, and out of desperation, despite Job's admonishment against taking charity, she accepted the offering and fed it to Job.

Meanwhile, Satan strengthened his grip on Job's deteriorating health. The stench that emanated from his wounds became unbearable for the people of Bathnah. They threatened to force him to leave their city. He told them there was no need for threats, for he understood their plight. He asked them to carry him to the dumping grounds at the outskirts of the city so that they could be relieved of his stench, and he could rest without worrying about bothering others. The people's answer was, "We are disgusted by you when we are far from you. How can we possibly come near you to carry you there?"

When he lost hope in their help, he turned to his devoted wife once again and said, "O faithful and good wife! You have witnessed how these people have turned against me and how they have come to detest me. I want you to go out to the crossroads and wait for any travelers who may be passing that way. Tell them my story and ask them to help you to move me to the dumping grounds."[19]

Two Passersby

Raḥmah went first to the dumping grounds and built a shelter for Job and herself, then she went to the crossroads to carry out his command. When she had been waiting a while, two handsome men, whose faces shone like the moon, approached. A beautiful scent wafted from their direction. She felt that they were very good, so she became embarrassed to present her need to them. Fortunately

19. It seems odd that he did not have her carry him miraculously with the power of God again as he did the time before. Perhaps he wanted to give travelers a chance to pass the divine test of serving their fellow man, in this case a prophet of God, after the people of Bathnah failed a similar test.

for her, they spoke first and asked, "How is our friend Job? How is he coping with his affliction?" She told them how severe his condition had become and how his people had abandoned him and how she had built a shelter for him at the dumping grounds. She requested them to pray for his speedy recovery."

They told her, "When you return to him, convey our greetings to him." No sooner had she mustered the courage to ask them her favor than they made to leave. So she returned to Job and told him about the two men she had met.

On hearing her account, Job exclaimed, "O how I long to see Gabriel and Michael! Raḥmah, how blessed you are to have been spoken to by God's angels."

Hurriedly, Raḥmah made to go back to the crossroads in hopes of finding the two angels. When she approached, she saw four men, the same two from before with two others. This time, they asked her immediately if they could be of service to her.

Their reunion with Job was bittersweet. They admonished him to continue to be patient in the face of his tribulations, and they prayed for his health. Then they carried him altogether to the shelter Raḥmah had made for him and took their leave.

Humble Shelter

Raḥmah led Job to the bed she had made of soft dirt. Ashamed of what little she could do for her husband, she said sarcastically, "Welcome, Job, to your bed of dirt which is a far cry from the plush rugs we once slept on. Now your pillow is a rock which is a far cry from the luxuriant pillow upon which you once rested your head."

Job gently scolded her saying, "Did I not tell you to refrain from thinking of our past blessings lest we fail to show gratitude for those we now have?"

Job threw himself upon the earth, praising God saying, "Glory be to God who is mighty and near! Glory be to God who is lofty and high. He is glorious and almighty!"

Raḥmah draped him in their only blanket. She covered the door with branches and leaves and busied herself with tending to Job's wounds and finding food for them both. Without his knowledge, she went door to door to procure what she could. She asked one woman who barked, "Get away from here, for Job's God is angry with him." She met with similar rejection everywhere she went.

She returned to Job sobbing. She told him, "Everyone has shunned us. They have shut their doors on us."

Job comforted her saying, "It is no matter if they shut their doors on us, for God's door is never shut, and his mercy descends without fail." But he knew the burden on her was great, and he wished to offer her a way out. He asked, "Raḥmah, do you wish to leave me?"

Raḥmah, surprised by the question, answered, "God forbid me from even thinking that. What excuse would I have before God for having abandoned his prophet?" Having allayed his worries, she said, "Perhaps I can take you to another city where the people are kinder than they are here."

To Another City

With great difficulty and with great pain to Job, she managed to take him to the neighboring city of Ḥawrān. She left him outside the city gates and asked God to protect him from wild animals. In the city, she entered the marketplace and announced, "If anyone needs clothes washed, floors swept, trash carried out, or water drawn, I will do it in exchange for food."

Not recognizing her, a woman said some unkind words to her. Raḥmah asked her, "Why do say such things about me? Do you not realize that I am Raḥmah, daughter of Efram, son of Joseph, son of Jacob, son of Isaac, son of Abraham, and I am the wife of Job, God's prophet?"

The woman grew ashamed and asked eagerly to see Job. Raḥmah took her to see him, but when she saw him, she wept at the state he was in. She asked incredulously, "Is this Job who once owned so much land and animals and servants?"

Job replied, "Indeed, I am Job, God's slave and messenger, whose hunger is not sated except by God's remembrance and whose thirst is not quenched except by God's praise."

Raḥmah said to the woman, "Please bring me an axe with which I may cut some trees and build a shelter to protect Job from the heat and cold and in which I may prepare food for him." She brought her an axe, and Raḥmah set to work.

She began working in five different houses. In exchange for her labor, she was able to earn enough wheat to bake ten loaves of bread. Bursting with excitement, she told Job, "I procured much food today. I promise not to leave your side until this food runs out." She baked the bread and soaked it in water before feeding it to Job, for his teeth had fallen out and he could no longer chew.

Job told her, "May God reward you handsomely, Raḥmah. You are indeed from the line of prophets." Then he turned his attention to God and said, "Praise is to him who does not forget those who remember him and does not abandon those who thank him and does not disgrace those who place their trust in him. Dominion is his. To him do all things return, and he has power over all things."

Satan As a Doctor

One day, Raḥmah was on her way back from work when Satan, disguised as a doctor, met her. He said, "I am a doctor from the west. I heard about your husband's illness, and I have come to treat him. I plan to pay him a visit tomorrow. In the meantime, tell him he must do the following if he wishes to be cured. He must slaughter a sparrow without mentioning God's name and eat from its flesh. He must drink a full glass of wine. And he must smear blood over his body. He must do these things if he wants relief."

Raḥmah, thinking only of the hope this doctor had given her, rushed back to Job to tell him what he must do to be cured. She finished her jubilant recounting, and, in place of the joy she expected, she saw only rage in Job's face—rage like she had never thought possible. He asked her coldly, "When have you ever seen me eat anything upon which God's name has not been taken? When have you known me to even touch wine? When have you known me to pollute my body with filth? Raḥmah, you were once the messenger of Gabriel and Michael. But today you have become the messenger of Satan himself!"

She realized her folly. Unawares, she had fallen victim to one of Satan's ruses. She profusely apologized and begged Job to forgive her, and he did. Then he warned her never to let her guard down like that again.

Satan's Final Ruse

On another day, as she returned from work, Satan appeared before her again, this time with pomp and majesty. As he approached, he noted, "I believe I know you. Are you not Raḥmah, daughter of the prophet Efram and wife of the afflicted prophet, Job?"

She replied, "Yes."

He continued, "I knew you to be a family of wealth and sufficiency. What brought you to this state?"

Raḥmah told him, "We have been tried by having all our wealth destroyed, all our children killed, and, worst of all, by this current blight that has afflicted my husband, Job."

The man asked, "Why do you think all of these tribulations have afflicted you?"

She replied resolutely, "Because God Almighty wanted to test our patience in the face of his trials."

He rebutted, assuming a sudden tone of derision, "You could not be more wrong. Rather, there is a god of the heavens, Allāh, and there is a god of the earth, who is I. I wished for you to exclusively be my servants, but you worshiped the god of the heavens instead. So I punished you like this. All of your wealth and your children and servants are with me. Follow me, and I shall show them to you, for I have kept them in a valley just over that hill."

At hearing all this, Raḥmah was dumbfounded. She thought she could easily verify whether or not he was telling the truth by following him to this valley he mentioned. So she did. As they approached the overlook, Satan bewitched her eyes so that she saw all of her possessions and her children and her servants gathered below. He asked her, "Do you believe me now? Or do you still think I am lying?"

But Raḥmah remembered Job's warning, and she told him, "I do not know what else to say to you. I must first talk to my husband, Job."

So she escaped from that place and returned home. When she recounted her adventure, Job exclaimed, "To God do we belong and to him shall we return! Please, Raḥmah! Do you not know that there is no other god but the one God? If God takes a person's life, then no one can revive him except God."

With great chagrin, she managed to say, "I know this."

Job continued to berate her, "If only you had employed your intellect, you would not have lent Satan your ear, and you would not have allowed him to bewitch your eyes."

She sobbed, "O Prophet of God! Forgive me for this grave mistake. I shall never do it again."

Raḥmah's Penance

Job said, "I forbade you once to listen to this damned creature. And now you have perpetrated the same thing twice. I hereby swear an oath to God that if he restores my health, I shall give you 100 lashes for talking with Satan."[20]

---

20. It is clear from Qur'ān 38:44 that Job swore to beat someone and that God commanded him to fulfill his oath in a less severe manner than that to which he had originally sworn. The traditions are unanimous on the point that the person he swore to beat was his wife, Raḥmah However, there is a discrepancy as to the reason for this severe punishment.

- One tradition alleges that he swore to beat her because she cut her two braids of hair and traded them for two loaves of bread so that she and Job would have something to eat (*Biḥār al-anwār* vol. 12 p. 344 tr. 3). There are two compelling reasons to reject this story.
  - First, Job is rightfully characterized as the very embodiment of patience and gratitude, yet according to this story he is supposed to have jumped to the conclusion that she had done something wrong and so he swore to beat her without even investigating her reason for cutting her hair.
  - Second, assuming he had sworn such an oath on a false pretext, why would God make him hold true to his oath and not release him from it? God himself has said, "God does not hold you to your empty oaths" (Qur'ān 2:225).
- The other version of the story is the one I have incorporated into my story. According to this version, Raḥmah actually did something deserving of discipline, especially since she was a daughter of prophets and the wife of a prophet.

Raḥmah admitted her mistake and repented for it, and she herself wished to be expiated. To this end she used to say, "I wish Job would recover quickly and give me the one hundred lashes he swore to mete out along with another hundred!"[21]

All the tribulations God let Satan inflict upon Job were tolerable, and Job maintained unswerving patience throughout. Once, Raḥmah suggested to Job that he pray to God to cure him. Job replied, "We lived in comfort for 70 years, so let us be patient in hardship for something on that order."[22]

The Last Straw

At last, when Satan saw no other way to break Job, he went to some monks who lived in the surrounding mountains and had been Job's companions and made them suspect Job and convinced them to ask him about the tribulations he had faced.[23]

They traveled to him on their mules, but when they approached his shelter, the mules refused to go closer for the stench that emanated from Job's body. So they bound the animals to each other to prevent them from running far and then proceeded on foot to see their old friend.

When they saw his decrepit body and the bare squalor of his shack, the suspicions Satan had planted in their heads were confirmed. They told him quite frankly, "Job, until now we have had no better opinion about anyone than we have had of you. However, we believe God has punished you in this way because of some sins you have secretly perpetrated or because your good deeds and acts of worship were done ostentatiously, not for the sake of God. We beg you to tell us what secret sins you have perpetrated to anger God so."

---

21. I have adapted most of the aforementioned story from *al-Burhān fī tafsīr al-qur'ān* vol. 4 p. 664–72.

22. *Biḥār al-anwār* vol. 12 p. 348 tr. 12. A similar statement is attributed to Job in the Bible. He said, "Shall we receive good at the hand of God, and shall we not receive evil?" (Job 2:10).

23. *Biḥār al-anwār* vol. 12 p. 351 tr. 21

Job was deeply hurt by their accusation. He protested, "I swear by the Lord's majesty, God knows that I never used to eat a meal without an orphan or a guest at my side to share in my food. And never have I been presented with two options, both good, except that I have chosen the more arduous of the two." He wanted them to know that, if they thought him exemplary before, he was exemplary still by God's grace, and tribulation had not befallen him because he had committed any sin or fallen from God's favor.[24]

A young man from among the monks saw the sincerity in Job's eyes and reprimanded his cohorts saying, "Shame on you all. You have attacked a prophet of God and accused him and thereby forced him to reveal good deeds he had managed to conceal from all except God Almighty all these years."[25]

Job had been sorely hurt by his friends' suspicions. He could take Satan's worst attacks, but he could not stand to be humiliated and accused of improprieties. He would later tell that the worst trial he ever faced was the false allegations people leveled at him and the gloating of his enemies.[26]

He turned in his hour of desperation to God. He needed affirmation from God himself that he had not displeased him or been insincere in the least. He said, "My Lord, you know that I never used to eat a meal without an orphan or a guest at my side to share in my food. And never have I been presented with two options, both good, except that I have chosen the more arduous of the two. I have done all this to please you."[27]

God asked him rhetorically, "Job, who was it that inspired you to such service?"

Job burst out in tears. He had only wanted God to edify him; he had not meant to imply that he had done God any favor, but his words had been wanting. He grabbed a handful of dirt from

24. *Biḥār al-anwār* vol. 12 p. 347 tr.8–9 and p. 348 tr. 13

25. *Biḥār al-anwār* vol. 12 p. 343 tr. 2 and p. 345 tr. 5

26. *Biḥār al-anwār* vol. 12 p. 352 tr. 21

27. *Biḥār al-anwār* vol. 12 p. 346 tr. 5

beneath himself, and thrust it into his own mouth to reprimand himself for misspeaking in God's presence.[28]

Begging For Relief

He realized he had reached his limit. Seven years had passed since his trials began,[29] and Job was now 80 years old.[30] Never once during this time had Job asked God to lighten his burden or relieve him of his hardship.[31] But he turned to God now in utter devotion and said, "Hardship has befallen me, and you are the Most Merciful."[32] And he said, "Satan has afflicted me with exhaustion and torment."[33] And he said:

> O God! On this day, I seek refuge in you, so grant me refuge.
>
> On this day, I seek sanctuary in you from the strain of your trials, so grant me sanctuary.
>
> On this day, I seek your succor, so grant me succor.
>
> On this day, I cry out for your aid against your enemy and mine, so come to my aid.
>
> On this day, I seek your reinforcement, so reinforce me.
>
> On this day, I seek your help to fulfill my task, so help me.
>
> On this day, I place my trust in you, so suffice me.

---

28. *Biḥār al-anwār* vol. 12 p. 346 tr. 5

29. *Biḥār al-anwār* vol. 12 p. 347 tr. 9

30. *Biḥār al-anwār* vol. 12 p. 352 tr. 23

31. *Biḥār al-anwār* vol. 12 p. 350 tr. 18

32. Qur'ān 21:83

33. Qur'ān 38:41

On this day, I hold fast to you, so hold fast to me.

On this day, I seek your protection, so protect me.

On this day, I beg you, so give me.

On this day, I seek your sustenance, so sustain me.

On this day, I beg your forgiveness, so forgive me.

On this day, I remember you, so remember me.

And on this day, I seek your mercy, so show me mercy![34]

Immediate Relief

Immediately, God sent Gabriel with the message, "Strike the earth with your leg," for he could move little else of his body. He feebly did as he was instructed, and a spring gushed forth, and Gabriel told him, "This is a cool spring to bathe in and a cool drink."[35] As Job managed to douse his body with the cool water, his skin and flesh and limbs were restored completely. He cupped his hands and took a deep draft. The stench that once emanated from him dissipated, and his entire body was as healthy as it had been seven years before.

Job was instructed to take Raḥmah and return to his property in Bathnah. When they arrived, they found their home completely restored, their animals fattened and grazing happily on the land. As they drew nearer to their house, a door swung open, and their entire family filed out to greet them. God promised Job he would let him live another seventy-three years to match the years he had lived before his trial began,[36] and he promised he would redouble the number of children he already had. He did all this out of mercy

34. *Muhaj al-daʿawāt* p. 309

35. Qurʾān 38:42

36. *Biḥār al-anwār* vol. 12 p. 352 tr. 23

and as a reminder to those with intellect[37] who are devoted to the worship of God.[38]

Job was overwhelmed with gratitude to God. He fell prostrate with tears streaming down his cheeks.

The reunion complete, Job set off with his sons to inspect their land. It was now the middle of the growing season, and, as Job looked into the distance, he saw that the neighboring farms were teeming with verdure. In stark contrast, his own land lay fallow since, naturally, he had not yet been able to replant it since Satan had destroyed it seven years prior. He looked toward the heavens and said, "My Lord! My Master! You restored this lowly servant to health, but his fields lie fallow while the Israelites' fields teem with verdure."[39]

God replied to him, "Job, take a clump of clay and cast it into your fields, for I shall make your fields grow." When he did as he was commanded, his fallow land sprouted before his eyes, and he was blessed with a healthy crop of chickpeas.[40]

God told him, "Job, you have now realized the true meaning of your name, for you have "returned" to health, blessing, family, property, and children after your lengthy affliction.[41]

He Fulfills His Oath

One matter remained. Job had taken an oath to punish his wife with one hundred lashes for having given Satan an audience one too many times. Now that his strength was restored, he would have to make good on his oath. Raḥmah was compliant. She wanted only to be purged of her weakness and freed from the burden of her sin. But Job's heart now faltered, and he wished their was a way to circumvent his oath. He turned to God and begged him to forgo

37. Qur'ān 38:43

38. Qur'ān 28:84

39. This is the tradition to which I referred earlier which seems to confirm that Job was not from the descendants of Jacob.

40. *Biḥār al-anwār* vol. 12 p. 350 tr. 16

41. According to this tradition, Job, or Ayyūb, is derived from *āba ya'ūbu* meaning "to return" (*Biḥār al-anwār* vol. 12 p. 350 tr. 17).

his oath. God replied, "Take in your hand a cluster of one hundred small branches and hit her lightly with it, but do not go back on your oath. This is my concession to you because you have been patient[42] and an outstanding servant and because you have turned to me for clemency."[43]

---

42. One tradition tells us that God will use Job on the Day of Judgment to argue against those people who believe their inordinate hardships justify their acts of moral corruption. He will present Job to them and ask them, "Was your affliction greater or his? We afflicted him, yet he was not corrupted" (*Biḥār al-anwār* vol. 12 p. 341 tr. 2).

43. Qur'ān 38:44

Jethro

Corruption in Midian

Midian[1] was a city located in the northwestern region of the Arabian Peninsula, west of Tabūk and east of the Gulf of Aqaba.[2] It was a fertile land covered with dense woods, and so the people of Midian came to be known as *Aṣḥāb al-Aykah*, the People of the Woods.[3]

The Midianites were a prosperous people;[4] however, their prosperity had, instead of fortifying their devotion to the Bestower of prosperity, made them decadent and degenerate. They were ruled by a tyrannical king. In his vain effort to safeguard Midian's prosperity, he ordered his subjects to stockpile what they harvested so prices would spike and allow them to reap more profit. He encouraged fraud in the marketplace. Merchants rigged their weights and measures so they could give less merchandise than what was warranted by the exorbitant prices they charged. Yet when they bought from their suppliers, they insisted that everything be weighed and measured in full. And they ruthlessly undervalued their suppliers' merchandise,

---

1. Midian is known in Arabic as *Madyan*. The city is mentioned in Exodus 18:1–27 among other places in the Bible.

2. We do not know the exact location of Midian. I feel comfortable with the conjecture that it is located in northwest Arabia because of the following clues we can glean from Islamic sources:
    - The Qur'ān tells us that Sodom and Midian were both located "on a road evident to your caravans" (15:79). The major caravan routes for the Quraysh were to Yemen in the south and the Levant (Syria) in the north (106:2). Sodom was clearly located in the Levant, and this verse places both Sodom and Midian on the same "evident road." Thus, Midian should be located between Mecca and the Levant.
    - *Tafsīr al-qummī* tells us that Midian is a "city on the way to the Levant (*al-Shām*)" (*Biḥār al-anwār* vol. 12 p. 381 tr. 2). Admittedly, this statement is not explicitly marked as a tradition from an infallible. But, assuming it is true, it presumably means it is on the way from Mecca to the Levant.

3. Qur'ān 26:176 and 50:1 and *Biḥār al-*anwār vol. 12 p. 382 tr. 4

4. Qur'ān 11:84 and *Biḥār al-anwār* vol. 12 p. 384 tr. 9

finding fault where there was none to be found so they could buy their goods for less than they were worth. But more egregious than all, they had forgotten the teachings of Abraham and Lot and had begun worshiping, alongside God, a pantheon of idols.[5]

God Chooses Jethro

To the north, in the city of Hebron, lived Jethro.[6] He was a descendant of one of Lot's daughters whom Lot had married to one of Abraham's followers who had emigrated with them when they came from Kūthā to Hebron.[7] Jethro was an exceptional man. He was devoted to God and to the law of Abraham, and he spent longs hours in prayer,[8] his eyes filled with tears.[9]

God chose Jethro as a prophet and messenger and bequeathed to him the relics of past prophets including the staff Adam had fashioned from a boxthorn of the garden.[10] God sent him to guide the Midianites.[11] He moved there along with members of his clan[12]

---

5. *Biḥār al-anwār* vol. 12 p. 385 tr. 9

6. Jethro is known in Arabic as *Shuʿayb*. He is known as the fourth of the five "Arab prophets" (*Biḥār al-anwār* vol. 12 p. 385 tr. 11). Clearly, he was not Arab from the perspective of descent since his parents came from Kūthā in Iraq, and he was born in Hebron in the Levant. So it seems this adjective only applies to him loosely, as it did to Ishmael, because he was sent to Arab people and he lived among them and became like one of them.

Jethro is known to Jews and Christians alternatively as "the Priest of Midian," "Reuel," "Hobab," and "Jethro" (see Exodus 18, for example; in Arabic Jethro is *Yathrūn* (*Biḥār al-anwār* vol. 12 p. 387 tr. 14)). Unfortunately, as usual, his impeccable personality has been defiled by the current Bible.

7. *Biḥār al-anwār* vol. 12 p. 384 tr. 9

8. Qur'ān 11:87

9. He earned the epithet *al-Bakkāʿ* for his profuse tears of devotion (*Biḥār al-anwār* vol. 12 p. 385 tr. 11).

10. *Biḥār al-anwār* vol. 13 p. 45 tr. 11

11. Qur'ān 7:85

12. I have deduced this point from a statement made by the Midianites much later. They tell Jethro, "If it were not for our courtesy to your clan, we would stone you, for you are not at all dear to us" (Qur'ān 11:91). Their threat implies that Jethro's clan was also present in Midian and that they had gained some

and lived among them for many years, establishing his credibility as an upstanding person with moral integrity and compassion for his fellow man.[13] With time, they began to recognize that he was sensible and forbearing.[14]

When he felt that his influence in Midian was strong, and the Midianites had accepted him as one of their own, Jethro made his first strong efforts to reform them. He presented the miracles with which God had empowered him to prove beyond a shadow of a doubt that he was indeed a prophet of God.[15]

---

standing among the Midianites.

13. That he lived among them before he began preaching to them is mere speculation on my part. However, I feel justified in my speculation for the following reasons:

- God refers to him as *akhāhum* meaning "their brother" or "one of their own" (26:116). Considering that he was from Hebron and not Midian, the justification for this description should be similar to what we offered for Lot whom the Qur'ān describes in one place as *akhū ahl Sadūm* (26:116), presumably to show that when they emigrated to their respective cities, they completely assimilated and became as one of them.
- Jethro refers to his people with the evocative "*yā qawmi*" meaning "My people!" Doing so requires a connection and a mutual sense of belonging. Even Lot, after all his thirty years in Sodom, is never once quoted as saying "*yā qawmi*" to his people.
- The Midianites recognize that Jethro is "forbearing and sensible" (Qur'ān 11:87). It is unlikely that they would have conceded these two qualities to him after he began battling with them. Thus, it is most likely that he established these credentials from before the start of his outward mission.

Thus, it seems that all the conversations quoted in the Qur'ān between Jethro and the Midianites occurred after he had assimilated as one of them.

14. Qur'ān 11:87

15. We do not know exactly what his miracles were; however, we know as a general principle that all prophets were given miracles to prove their claim (see 7:101). The Qur'ān also quotes Jethro as saying, "Proof has now come to you from your Lord" (7:85) which seems to be a reference to miracles he had presented to them.

Jethro Calls His People

He addressed his people saying, "My people! Worship God. You have no god besides him.[16] Will you not fear him?[17] I am a trustworthy messenger sent to you.[18] So fear God, and obey me,[19] and await the Last Day.[20] I do not ask you for any money for this guidance—my compensation is solely with the Lord of all realms."[21]

Then, alluding to the miracles he had shown them, he said, "Proof has now come to you through me from your Lord, so you have no excuse but to heed my admonishment. Measure and weigh in full and do not undervalue people's goods and do not thus cause corruption on earth when God has perfected it[22]—for this is better for you—if you have believed after seeing my proof."[23] And he told them, "I see that you are well off, and I fear for you the punishment of an inescapable day."[24] The Midianites had no reason to cheat and act corruptly, for God had blessed them beyond measure, and he would increase their bounty if they would only turn to him and deal fairly with one another. And he told them, "What God has left for you by way of fair gain would be better for you if you were believers. But I am not your keeper, so you must choose your own path."[25]

---

16. Qur'ān 7:85 and 11:84–85

17. Qur'ān 26:177

18. Qur'ān 26:178

19. Qur'ān 26:179

20. Qur'ān 29:36

21. Qur'ān 26:180

22. To a great extent, a society's happiness is dependent upon a fair system of commerce. A system that deprives producers, service providers, middlemen, or retailers of their rightful pay is not sustainable. Consequences of such social injustice include poverty, crime, social unrest, political turmoil, and a general lack of security. While Jethro's two or three points of reform may seem minor and specific, he was in fact addressing the very core of his people's problems.

23. Qur'ān 7:85 and 11:84–85 and 26:181–183

24. Qur'ān 11:84

25. Qur'ān 11:86

Midian's Response

They said, "Jethro, do your prayers give you the right to order us to abandon what our forefathers have worshiped or to do with our money what we wish?" They believed he was forgetting himself and overstepping his bounds, considering himself to be better than they because he prayed differently than they. They continued, "Far be it from you to order us thus, for we know you to be forbearing and sensible."[26]

He replied, "O people! Tell me: Should I cease guiding and admonishing you if I am with clear proof from my Lord and he has provided me with the spiritual sustenance of divine revelation?" He was morally compelled by the knowledge God had given him to guide others. "Furthermore," he said, "rest assured that I am not trying to unduly limit your freedom because I do not intend to act differently from you by perpetrating what I forbid for you." All too often those who set out to reform others forget to begin with themselves. But Jethro, like all the prophets before and after him, was committed to implementing every reform in his own life before expecting anyone else to follow. He added, "I wish only to effect reform as much as I can. But my success in doing so is only from God. In him do I trust and to him do I turn."[27]

And he told them, "O people! Do not let your defiance of me cause such a punishment to afflict you as that which afflicted Noah's people, Hūd's people, or Ṣāliḥ's people. Even Lot's people were not long before you, so you should not have forgotten their fate and

---

26. Qurʾān 11:87. Many commentators have construed their statement "You are forbearing and sensible" to have been spoken with sarcasm and ridicule. However, *al-Mīzān* and *Rūḥ al-maʿānī* believe it was spoken with an air of incredulity. They knew him to be forbearing and sensible, so they felt it was not fitting that he should rush to condemn them without understanding their rationale or to claim a right that they believed him to be lacking.

27. Qurʾān 11:88

the actions that led them to it.[28] Seek your Lord's forgiveness; then turn to him. My Lord is merciful and loving."[29]

Jethro's Missionaries

In the intervening years, as he persisted in calling the Midianites to faith, he also began sending missionaries to surrounding lands. To one civilization in Africa, he sent Ḥassān ibn Sinān al-Awzāʿī. This missionary faithfully called those people to Jethro's religion, but they refused to believe, and in the end, they buried him alive and left him to die.[30] Likewise, Jethro sent others to outlying regions, but none were successful.[31]

Back in Midian, the leaders of the city told Jethro, "Jethro, we do not comprehend much of what you say," for they heard but were not listening and saw but were not looking, so God sealed their hearts to the truth. And they sought at once to insult him and threaten him by saying, "We consider you to be among our weak ones. If it were not for our courtesy to your clan, we would stone you, for you are not at all dear to us."[32]

He said, "My people, is my clan really more dear to you than God is, and do you disregard him as a thing consigned to oblivion?" Neither had they any regard for him nor for God but only for the formalities of tribal structure. He warned, "Beware, for my Lord

---

28. Qur'ān 11:89. Some commentators believe his statement "وَ مَا قَوْمُ لُوطٍ مِّنكُم بِبَعِيدٍ" to indicate that the people of Lot were not geographically far from Midian. While this is true in and of itself, their proximity alone does not justify being singled out in this verse since Thamūd was much closer to them than Sodom. Temporally, on the other hand, Sodom was closer (i.e., in the more recent past) than the rest, having been destroyed only a few generations before Midian, that too, at the hands of angels who served Jethro's forefather, Lot.

29. Qur'ān 11:90

30. *Biḥār al-anwār* vol. 12 p. 384 tr. 8

31. Al-Karājikī mentions another missionary by the name of al-Ḥārith ibn Shuʿayb al-Ghassānī, but he describes him as "Jethro's missionary to Midian" (*Biḥār al-anwār* vol. 12 p. 384 tr. 8). There seems to be some sort of mistake. In any case, these two traditions suggest that Jethro was actively proselytizing to the people of his time beyond the borders of Midian.

32. Qur'ān 11:91

comprehends fully what you do.[33] Fear the one who created you and the generations who have passed before you."[34]

Ad Hominem

Unable to find fault in anything he had said, they indicted, "You are but from among those bewitched.[35] And you are only a human being like us. We firmly believe you to be a liar.[36] So we challenge you to bring down a heavenly body upon us if you are truthful in your threats."[37]

He replied, "My Lord knows better what you do and whether you deserve such a punishment."[38]

When they saw that they could not dissuade Jethro from his mission, they sought to ensure that at least their own people would not follow him. They staked out the roads and alleys that led to his house and, by turn, waited there to intercept all who wished to visit him. They harassed them and did their best to convince them that it was Jethro, and not they, who was corrupt.

Jethro told them, "My people, do not lie in wait upon every road that leads to me, threatening those who believe in God and dissuading them from the path to God by portraying it as crooked. And remember when you were few and God made you many. And consider the end of those who cause corruption.[39] If it comes to pass that a group of you has believed in that with which I have been sent and another portion has not believed, then I call upon you all to be patient until God judges between us, for he is the Best Judge."[40]

---

33. Qur'ān 11:92

34. Qur'ān 26:184

35. Qur'ān 26:185

36. Qur'ān 26:186

37. Qur'ān 26:187

38. Qur'ān 26:188

39. Qur'ān 7:86

40. Qur'ān 7:87

The leaders among his people who were arrogant said, "We shall expel you, Jethro, from our city and, with you, those who believe, or you must revert to our religion."[41]

Jethro asked, "Must we revert even if we are unwilling?[42] If we were to revert to your religion after God has delivered us from it, then we would be fabricating lies about God." He meant that professing the Midianite's religion when they knew that only their own was true was tantamount to lying. They would be claiming that God had partners when they knew that he had none. He continued, "It is not for us to revert to your religion unless our Lord God were to wish it." Of course, Jethro knew God would never wish such a thing. However, he knew being steadfast is contingent upon God's help, without which one can neither find, nor remain on, the straight path. He explained this saying, "I defer thus to God because God's knowledge encompasses all things," and he could not claim to know the fate of his or his people's faith, so he proclaimed, "Upon God do we rely." Then in an aside to the Almighty, he said, "Lord, judge truthfully between us and our people, for you are the Best Judge."[43] At last, with finality and exasperation, he said to his people, "My people, do as you have been doing. I too shall do as I am doing. Soon you shall know who is to be struck by a degrading punishment and who is a liar. Wait! I too shall wait."[44]

Midian Is Destroyed

God sent word to Jethro that Midian's destruction was imminent. He instructed him to leave with his followers and head south to Bakkah,[45] so Jethro and his followers hurriedly packed what they could and prepared to evacuate the city.

---

41. Jethro was speaking on behalf of the believers in general, all of whom had previously subscribed to the Midianite's false religion. For this reason, they give them the option of being banished or "reverting," even though, for Jethro, he would not be reverting but accepting their false religion for the first time.

42. Qur'ān 7:88

43. Qur'ān 7:89

44. Qur'ān 11:93

45. *Biḥār al-anwār* vol. 12 p. 385 tr. 9. This tradition says that they remained in

The leaders among his people who refused to believe said to the believers as they prepared to leave Midian with Jethro, "If you follow Jethro, you shall be among the losers."[46]

The next morning, when God gave his command, he had mercifully delivered Jethro and, with him, those who believed to safety beyond the horizon. And then a massive earthquake[47] and a terrible squall befell the wrongdoers as the day of the overshadowing cloud overtook them. It was a punishment on a terrible day.[48] By day's end, they were left as corpses in their homes.[49] It was as though they had never lived there. Just like that, Midian was destroyed just as Thamūd had been destroyed before.[50] In all, God annihilated one hundred thousand Midianites. Of these, only fourty thousand were truly evil. Nevertheless, he destroyed the other sixty thousand with them because they had been complacent and accepting of evil and had failed to take a stand against it alongside Jethro.[51]

The People of the Woods were wrongdoers.[52] They had repudiated Jethro and thereby repudiated all God's messengers.[53] So God took revenge on them.[54] In the end, an earthquake befell them, and they were left as corpses in their homes.[55] It was as though those

---

Bakkah (Mecca) till the end of their lives. This does not seem likely since Moses meets Jethro and lives with him for ten years in Midian, and that is after Jethro has reached old age (Qur'ān 28:23). It seems more likely that Jethro left Midian for Bakkah temporarily while God destroyed its citizens. Then he must have returned to Midian and lived out his days there with his daughters and, for a short time, Moses.

46. Qur'ān 7:90

47. Qur'ān 29:37 and 7:91

48. Qur'ān 26:189

49. Qur'ān 11:94

50. Qur'ān 11:95

51. *Biḥār al-anwār* vol. 12 p. 386 tr. 12

52. Qur'ān 15:78

53. Qur'ān 26:176

54. Qur'ān 15:79

55. Qur'ān 7:91

who repudiated Jethro had never lived there. It was those who repudiated Jethro who were in fact the losers.[56] As Jethro turned to witness Midian's final destruction from a distant horizon, he said to them, "My people, I conveyed my Lord's messages to you and was your well-wisher. So I feel no compunction seeing you destroyed thus. How can I possibly fret over the fate of a people who refused to believe?"[57]

Life in Bakkah

When Jethro and his fellow believers arrived in Bakkah, they were greeted by the descendants of Ishmael and his followers. They performed the Hajj according to the teachings of Abraham and spent the coming years enjoying the camaraderie of living among fellow believers, free from the persecution to which they had become accustomed in Midian.[58]

Jethro married in Bakkah.[59] Years later, he returned to Midian with a handful of his followers to rebuild the destroyed city of Midian and repopulate it. His wife bore him two beautiful daughters who were devoted to their father, and after their mother died, lovingly cared for him into his old age.

Jethro's Tears

Jethro spent long hours in prayer. Out of love for God, he would weep intensely.[60] One day, he wept until he lost his sight. God showed him mercy and restored his vision. But again, in the passion of prayer, he cried and lost his sight. Again God restored his vision, and again, a third time, he lost his sight, and God restored it. When

---

56. Qur'ān 7:92

57. Qur'ān 7:93

58. *Biḥār al-anwār* vol. 12 p. 385 tr. 9

59. This is mere speculation, however, we know that he had two young daughters at the time when Moses stumbled into Midian, so I have conjectured that Jethro must have married a younger wife in Bakkah who gave birth to these two daughters.

60. He earned the epithet *al-Bakkāʿ* for his profuse tears of devotion (*Biḥār al-anwār* vol. 12 p. 385 tr. 11).

it happened a fourth time, God asked him solicitously, "Until when do you plan to continue in this way? If you weep out of fear of the fire, I tell you I shall not let it touch you. And if you weep out of a yearning for paradise, I tell you, you shall enter it freely."

Jethro replied, "Lord, you know very well that my tears are not of fear for your fire, nor of yearning for your paradise. Rather, my love for you has enraptured my heart, so I cannot wait to meet you."

God told Jethro, "Endure in your patience. To reward you for your devotion and service to me, I shall bring the greatest man alive, my prophet Moses, into your service."[61] And so he did, many years later.

For his years of patient discourse and eloquent appeals to his people, Jethro earned the honorific, *khaṭīb al-anbiyāʾ*, "The Orator of the Prophets."[62] He lived to the age of 242 years.[63]

---

61. *Biḥār al-anwār* vol. 12 p. 380 tr. 1

62. *Biḥār al-anwār* vol. 12 p. 385 tr. 9

63. *Biḥār al-anwār* vol. 12 p. 387 tr. 13

Moses & Aaron

Joseph's Prophecy Is Realized

It was just as Joseph had predicted four centuries before.[1] The religious awakening and economic prosperity he had ushered in as king of Egypt eventually degenerated along with his teachings. The Children of Jacob, the Israelites, had enjoyed a short burst of happiness when their numbers, wealth, and power had been on the rise. But as their worldly interests superseded their spiritual ones, and as their stewardship of, and commitment to, Joseph's teachings waned, God withdrew his blessing from them. They were cast into one of the darkest episodes in their history.

This darkness came in the form of a ruthless and cunning Egyptian who toppled the Israelite government and reclaimed the throne of Egypt and, with it, the title Pharaoh.[2] This new Pharaoh

1. *Biḥār al-anwār* vol. 13 p. 36 tr. 7. Another tradition mentions that this occurred 500 years after Abraham (*Biḥār al-anwār* vol. 13 p. 6 tr. 2). Both traditions corroborate one another.

2. The Qur'ān simply refers to him as *Fir'awn* (the Pharaoh). His name is given in one tradition from Imam al-Kāẓim and one Sunnī source as al-Walīd ibn Muṣ'ab (*Biḥār al-anwār* vol. 13 p. 134 tr. 40 and p. 50 quoting from al-Tha'labī's *'Arā'is al-majālis*). We cannot say for certain whether this was actually his name. This name is obviously Arabic and bears no resemblance to any of the known names from the 32 Egyptian dynasties that ruled from 3100 B.C.E.–395 C.E. With the discovery of the mummy of Ramesses II in 1881 C.E. and restoration efforts on his mummy in 1974 C.E., many Muslims overeagerly came to believe that he was the Pharaoh from Moses' story. Some have claimed it was his son Merneptah because of the salt that was found on his body, suggesting, perhaps, that he died in the sea (El Mahdy, Christine. *Mummies, Myth and Magic in Ancient Egypt*. 91. London: Thames and Hudson, 1989). Sadly, there is no conclusive scientific evidence to date that can help us identify which Pharaoh lived and died in Moses' time.

The dearth of evidence should come as no surprise considering the fate of the vast majority of the Egyptians' mummies. Grave robbers pillaged their graves almost as soon as they were buried. From the 12th century C.E., Europeans

and his closest confidante and advisor, Hāmān, were sorcerers of unmatched skill[3] able to conjure and control with prowess. It was largely through their mastery of the dark arts that they were able

---

discovered that mummies were a great source of bitumen or asphalt which the Egyptians had used as an adhesive to bind the mummies, but the Arabs, and later the Europeans, used to treat certain skin ailments. During the following centuries, literally tons of mummies were collected, traded, and destroyed for their bitumen and for other medicinal properties and even as fuel and a source of linen for paper (El Mahdy, Christine. *Mummies, Myth and Magic in Ancient Egypt.* 24–33. London: Thames and Hudson, 1989, and Zayn Bilkadi. *Saudi Aramco World.* 1984. vol. 35 number 6. p. 2–9). That any mummies survived into this century is nothing short of miraculous.

3. In the modern world, we tend to dismiss magic and consign it to the realm of fairy tales and fiction. Nonetheless, the Qur'ān treats magic as a real force. In particular, it confirms the power of magic in the story of Moses. Thus, we must understand, and come to terms with, magic to fully understand this story.

Magic (*siḥr*) is the production of supernatural effects by any of the following four methods:

- By drawing on the secrets and/or powers of nature. This type of magic is broadly called "natural magic." It relies on the qualities of herbs, stones, stars, planets, and animals, among other things, to make predictions, uncover information, or to cause supernatural effects.
- By using the spirits of angels, *jinn*, or deceased humans. This type of magic is broadly called "invocative magic." The practitioner invokes or summons a spirit and solicits information or compels it to cause supernatural effects.
- By combining the powers of the stars and planets with earthly powers. This type of magic is broadly called "talismanic magic" and entails the use of amulets for protection and/or talismans for actively producing supernatural effects.
- By controlling others' perceptions and emotions. This type of magic is broadly called "illusionary magic." A practitioner of this kind of magic may cause feelings of love or hatred in others. Or he may make them see hallucinations (al-Anṣārī, Murtaḍā. *al-Makāsib.* Beirut: Mu'assasat al-Nūr li al-Maṭbū'āt, 1990. vol. 3 p. 41–49 and http://www.tarotforum.net/library/5/2002-09/7-types-of-magic-20020911.shtml).

Of these four kinds of magic, it is the fourth that is attributed to the Pharaoh and his magicians. Their magic was not mere sleight of hand, for sleight of hand is only an illusion, not a real supernatural feat. As we will see as this story unfolds, they were able to control people's perceptions and emotions.

to seize power so quickly.[4] They dominated the land of Egypt and reduced its people into factions, abasing and enslaving their former Israelite lords and restoring their fellow Egyptians to their lost glory.[5] With great hubris, the new Pharaoh said, "If their god cares about his people, as they fancy he does, he would not let me subjugate them so."[6]

From the ranks of the conquered Israelites, Pharaoh chose his bride. Her name was Āsiyah, the daughter of Muzāḥim.[7] Her father had been noble and pious, and these qualities were manifest in her as well. When the Pharaoh laid eyes upon her, he was sure she would make an outstanding queen as soon as he won her loyalty. This she gave him but in outward expression only. The Pharaoh sought an heir from her, but to his great frustration, in vain, for she was barren.[8]

Joseph's prophecy had not only predicted the hardships to which the Israelites would be subjected but also promised them deliverance from those hardships at the hands of a savior from the tribe of Levi.[9] When times were good, the Israelites paid only lip service to their awaited savior, but when the Pharaoh brought his iron fist to bear upon them, they grew ever more anxious for his arrival.[10]

---

4. *Biḥār al-anwār* vol. 13 p. 120 tr. 21

5. Qur'ān 28:4

6. *Biḥār al-anwār* vol. 13 p. 106 tr. 1

7. *Biḥār al-anwār* vol. 13 p. 39 tr. 9

8. *Biḥār al-anwār* vol. 13 p. 39 tr. 9

9. *Biḥār al-anwār* vol. 13 p. 36 tr. 7

10. *ibid.* Some traditions mention that Joseph told them that his name would be Moses, son of Amram and that, as a result, Israelites eagerly named their sons Amram and their grandsons Moses hoping that theirs would be the one (see *Biḥār al-anwār* vol. 13 p. 38 tr. 9). However, it seems unlikely that the prophecy would mention his name for two reasons:

- First, if his name and his father's name were known, Pharaoh, who was well aware of the prophecy, would have targeted those Israelites with these names, and no one among the Israelites would have dared to keep these names.
- Second, another tradition tells us that it was the Pharaoh's wife, Āsiyah, who gave Moses his name since she found him in the water among the trees or reeds, and *mū* meant "water" and *sā* meant "tree"

The Awaited Savior

Murmurs of this awaited savior caught the attention of the Pharaoh's informants. During this time, he also saw a dream in which a ball of fire came to Egypt from Jerusalem and surrounded and burnt its houses in a great conflagration.[11] He realized that the rumored salvation of the Israelites meant his own demise, and he was determined not to undo all that he had striven to achieve. He called on his court of magicians and sought their counsel. They divined the lineage of the awaited savior and determined that he would be an Israelite and that he was due to be conceived soon. The Pharaoh gave the midwives of Egypt strict orders to report the gender of every Israelite child born. He appointed two soldiers to each midwife with orders to summarily kill every male child reported, and if the midwife resisted or was found to be lying, to execute her on the spot. Female infants were of no consequence and were to be left alone.[12] He also ordered his army to round up all of the Israelite men and to detain them indefinitely until he was sure the impending danger had been neutralized.[13]

Amram's Hope

News spread, and, day by day, more men were rounded up. The Israelites' hope was evaporating quickly, for they could see no way for their savior to be born in the face of such a sweeping infanticide. The Israelite men who had not yet been captured decided that, against such odds, it was senseless to even try to conceive a child when it would inevitably be slaughtered even as it gasped its first breath. There was only one man from the tribe of

---

in Egyptian (*Biḥār al-anwār* vol. 13 p. 4 and p. 7 tr. 7). Assuming that this tradition is true, then it was she and not Moses' mother who named him. Furthermore, it is impossible to expect that the Pharaoh would allow a child to be named Moses and then be admitted to his household if he knew that a person named Moses was destined to destroy him.

11. *Biḥār al-anwār* vol. 13 p. 52 tr. 21

12. Qur'ān 28:4

13. *Biḥār al-anwār* vol. 13 p. 25 tr. 2 and p. 47 tr. 15

Levi named Amram, son of Izhar, son of Kohath,[14] who still clung to his hope in God's promise. Amram and his wife, Jochebed,[15] already had two children, an older daughter named Miriam[16] and a two-year-old son named Aaron.[17] Amram told his fellow Israelites, "We must try to conceive, for God's will will be done though these pagans loathe it." When he saw that his cry fell upon deaf ears, he turned to God and said, "Even if others refuse, I shall not. Even if others have abandoned hope, I shall not." He lay with his wife, and they conceived a child.[18] At the crack of dawn, the Pharaoh's soldiers came and bore Amram away in chains, and he was never seen again.[19]

Moses Is Born

According to Pharaoh's policy, a midwife was charged to make daily visits to Jochebed. As the months progressed, the signs of motherhood became increasingly visible. When she finally bore a son, she was distraught at the thought of him being slaughtered like some 20,000 of his Israelite brothers before him.[20] But when the midwife laid eyes on him, her countenance filled with compassion.[21]

14. In Arabic his name is *ʿImrān*, son of *Yaṣhar*, son of *Qāhith* (*Biḥār al-anwār* vol. 13 p. 4). His lineage is also mentioned in the Old Testament (Exodus 6:16–25).

15. It is pronounced "JAW-kə-bed." This is the name mentioned for her in the Old Testament. No name is mentioned for her in the Qurʾān or Islamic traditions. She is simply referred to as *Umm Mūsā*, the "Mother of Moses." Sadly, the Bible identifies her as Amram's father's sister (Exodus 6:20), no doubt to bring undue shame on these noble people.

16. Their daughter is named *Kulthum* (with a short "u," not *Kulthūm*, which is a man's name) in some traditions (*Biḥār al-anwār* vol. 19 p. 19 tr. 11). But in the Old Testament she is called Miriam (Exodus 15:20).

17. His name is *Hārūn* in Arabic.

18. *Biḥār al-anwār* vol. 13 p. 38 tr. 9

19. We cannot say for certain that he was killed, but his conspicuous absence from the rest of Moses' story suggests that he must have been.

20. *Biḥār al-anwār* vol. 13 p. 47 tr. 15

21. In the Qurʾān, God tells Moses, "And I cast upon you love as a gift from me" (20:39). God made people love Moses, at least as a child, when they laid eyes on him.

She whispered to his mother, "Do not fear,[22] for I shall keep your secret."[23] She swaddled the infant and hid him safely in a storage chest. Then she went out to the guards stationed by the door and reported that it had been a miscarriage, and only some clotted blood had come out.[24]

After witnessing the power of God firsthand, Jochebed felt the hope she had always seen in her husband rekindled within her. The midwife left, and Jochebed lay quietly, surrounded by her two older children, with her newborn in her arms. Then she heard a voice. It was Archangel Gabriel, and he said, "Nurse him, and when you fear for him, cast him into the river and neither fear nor grieve, for we shall return him to you and make him one of the apostles."[25]

The voice startled her, but it inspired her with calm. She asked, "How shall I cast him in the river, for he is a helpless child? And what will become of him?"[26]

Gabriel presented a small wooden box to her[27] and said, "Place him in this wooden box, and throw him into the river. The river will cast him onto its bank, and he shall be picked up by an enemy of mine and an enemy of his."[28]

Cast Into the Nile

For the next few days, she took care of her children and nursed her newborn, wary that the Pharaoh's guards might sweep her neighborhood again and find her child. Then it happened. A rumor swept through that the guards were coming. She frantically swaddled the baby and placed him in the box as Gabriel

---

22. *Biḥār al-anwār* vol. 13 p. 25 tr. 2

23. *Biḥār al-anwār* vol. 13 p. 38 tr. 9

24. ibid.

25. Qur'ān 28:7

26. I have inferred this question. It is not in the Qur'ān or traditions.

27. One tradition mentions that the box was "sent down" to her (*Biḥār al-anwār* vol. 13 p. 25 tr. 2). Another says that she was told to make one (*Biḥār al-anwār* vol. 13 p. 39 tr. 9), and Sunnī sources say that she had an Egyptian carpenter make the box for her (*Biḥār al-anwār* vol. 13 p. 54).

28. Qur'ān 20:39

had instructed her. She furtively crept through the alleyways undetected and found her way to the edge of the Nile. The sheer breadth of the river made it seem like a vast ocean. She feared it would swallow her child in a second. But the memory of Gabriel's voice rang in her ears, and she took comfort in God's promise as she let the box slip away. The steady current carried the box, and she watched as it floated, as if guided by the hand of God, directly toward the palace grounds of the Pharaoh himself.

At Āsiyah's Pavilion

Earlier that day, the Pharaoh's queen, Āsiyah, had told her husband, "It is such a beautiful spring day. I would like to enjoy the weather on the shore of the Nile. Please have a pavilion erected for me." He had a pavilion erected, and Āsiyah went to it with her retinue of servants. They spent the day swimming and exploring the reed beds along the river. As Āsiyah gazed out over the water, she saw something dark floating toward the near shore. Out of curiosity she went to see what it was.[29] She called out to her ladies-in-waiting. Together they pulled the box from the water.[30] Her eyes fell upon the swaddled child, and, in a moment, her heart melted. For a barren woman like her, the sight of the child was like a sip of water to parched lips or a gasp of air to one drowning.

In the distance, Jochebed's pulse raced as she watched the queen hold her child. Anyone weaker than she would have considered rushing to the palace to divulge the whole affair in what would no doubt have been a futile attempt to retrieve her child. But God had fortified her heart so that she would have faith in his promise. Even as her helpless child entered the very jaws meant to crush him, her heart became free from all worry,[31] for he had been conceived against all odds; he had been born against all odds; he had escaped execution against all odds; and he had just been picked up by his and God's greatest enemy, just as Gabriel had promised her.

---

29. *Biḥār al-anwār* vol. 13 p. 39 tr. 9

30. Qur'ān 28:8

31. Qur'ān 28:10

Āsiyah spent the remainder of the day coddling the infant and holding him close. When the Pharaoh arrived to check on his queen and bring her back to the palace, he saw the baby. From its skin color and features, he immediately recognized it as an Israelite. He perfunctorily wrenched it from her arms, and, without a thought, ordered his guards to kill it. Āsiyah threw herself at his feet and begged him saying, "This infant will be a source of comfort for me and for you. Do not kill him. Maybe he will benefit us or we can adopt him as a son."[32] He heard the anguish in her voice, and for a moment, his glance fell upon the baby's face, and his heart also melted.[33]

He asked her, "What name shall we give him?"

She said, "Let us call him Moses, because I found him in the water among the reeds."[34]

The Search For Milk

Their newfound joy turned abruptly to deep consternation when Moses began to cry. He had been away from his mother for a few hours, and he was hungry. Arrangements were made for a wet nurse, but Moses refused to drink. Another was called, but he refused her too.

News quickly spread among the ruling elite that Pharaoh had adopted a son and desperately needed a wet nurse. Every husband with a nursing wife hoped that his wife might be appointed to the position so his family could earn favor with the Pharaoh. They flocked to the palace that evening, but Moses refused every one of them. The Pharaoh and Āsiyah grew ever more weary. As their options evaporated, the Pharaoh told Hāmān to look beyond the palace walls and past the elite families and to turn away nobody, poor and wretched though they may be.[35]

---

32. Qur'ān 28:9

33. Qur'ān 20:39

34. In Egyptian, *mū* meant "water" and *sā* meant "tree" or "reed" (*Biḥār al-anwār* vol. 13 p. 4 and p. 7 tr. 7). In Arabic his name is *Mūsā*.

35. *Biḥār al-anwār* vol. 13 p. 39 tr. 9

Meanwhile, Jochebed was beside herself in anticipation of the fulfillment of God's promise. She sent Miriam toward the palace gates with instructions to track down any information she could about her brother. She did as she was instructed and saw a line of anxious woman being admitted into the gates of the palace and another line of women shrouded in disappointment heading out. She staked out a vantage point from which she could peer through the gates without attracting notice. From there she could make out the unmistakable form of a swaddled baby, her brother.[36]

One after another, the women took a seat and tried to feed the wailing infant but to no avail.[37] Āsiyah and the others were justifiably frazzled. Miriam, seeing her opportunity, furtively approached one of the guards and asked, "Shall I show you a family that will take care of him for you and be his well-wishers?"[38]

The guard was reluctant to heed the word of a young girl, especially after so many women had tried and failed. However, the possibility that she might be right and that he could gain favor with the Pharaoh if he was the one who brought this woman she spoke of, was too great to pass up. He went with Miriam to bring her mother.

Jochebed could hardly contain her delight as she nursed her son with complete impunity in the palace of the very tyrant whose guards had sought to murder him just yesterday without anyone suspecting her relationship to him. She felt her grief melt away, replaced with comfort and tranquillity and a renewed conviction that God indeed fulfills his promises.[39]

---

36. Qur'ān 28:11

37. Qur'ān 28:12

38. Qur'ān 28:12 and 20:40

39. Qur'ān 28:13. Some traditions say that it took three days before mother and son were reunited. While this is possible, it is far-fetched to think of a newborn surviving for three days without any milk. For this reason, I have shortened the timeframe to what seems natural.

Jochebed Befriends Āsiyah

Jochebed came and went freely in the palace. She and Āsiyah spent considerable time together, and in private they confided in each other. Through Jochebed, Āsiyah was able to reconnect with her faith in a way she had longed for since she was forced into marriage, despite the Pharaoh's eagerness to purge her of it. When Jochebed saw her piety and devotion to God, she confided in her God's promise to make Moses into a prophet. Together they dreamed secret dreams of a day when he would rise up to destroy the Pharaoh.

Moses' Upbringing

Moses developed into an outstanding person.[40] His two mothers fostered in him complete subservience to God and an acute sense of social justice and compassion for the plight of his people. When he reached the age of eighteen, God fortified him with divine knowledge and wisdom.[41]

Beyond the Palace Gates

Moses saw the Pharaoh's injustices from a unique vantage point. As prince and heir-apparent, he was privy to the inner workings of the royal court. He also vicariously felt the pain and suffering

40. I have consciously left out a story that is transmitted in a few traditions. According to these traditions, Moses, as a child, once sneezed in Pharaoh's presence and said the phrase "*al-ḥamdu lillāh*." The Pharaoh became angry, Moses yanked his beard, the Pharaoh threatened to kill him, and finally Āsiyah intervened. To prove that Moses had no sense and didn't mean what he said or did, they decided to offer him a burning coal and a date to see if he had the sense to choose the date. Gabriel made him choose the coal, he burnt his tongue (but apparently not his fingers), and that is why he allegedly stuttered (*Biḥār al-anwār* vol. 13 p. 26 tr. 2). This story more closely resembles a myth conjured to explain his alleged speech impediment than history. It is not clear why Moses did not have the sense to hold his tongue when he sneezed and why Gabriel, who steered his actions later in the story did not steer him clear of aggravating the Pharaoh earlier on. In short, it is a problematic story, and so I chose to omit it.

41. Qur'ān 28:14 and *Biḥār al-anwār* vol. 13 p. 49 tr. 19

of the people of Egypt, especially of the Israelites, who were his people. Pharaoh had enslaved them and pressed them into labor. They cut stone, made bricks, hauled huge loads, and did everything too hard and too dangerous for Egyptian laborers to do.[42] If the hard labor did not kill them, the cruel punishments did. Pharaoh's favorite form of punishment was to make the unfortunate soul lie face down in the hot sand with legs and arms splayed. He would then have stakes driven through his hands and feet and leave him to die. For this he is remembered in infamy as *Dhū al-Awtād*, "The Stake-Driver."[43]

Moses would secretly slip out of the palace and visit the Israelites. He would bring aid and relief as he could. He would admonish them and give them hope that God was with them and would soon deliver them. He taught them about the great prophet, Muḥammad, who would come at the end of time ushering in an age when justice would rule supreme. He taught them to say the following prayer before they began work, "O God! Shower your mercy upon Muḥammad and his family," and he promised that, as a result, their work would become easy and they would be protected from harm.[44]

The Savior Is Sighted

A group of Israelites used to meet in secret with one of their priests who knew of the ancient prophecies from Joseph. He would speak to them and remind them of the attributes of their awaited savior. On one occasion, Moses stumbled across their meeting place. The priest immediately recognized him as the one described in the prophecies. He threw himself at Moses' feet and exclaimed, "Praise be to God for letting me live to see you."

---

42. *Biḥār al-anwār* vol. 13 p. 47 tr. 16

43. The Qur'ān refers to the Pharaoh as *Dhū al-Awtād*, "The Stake-Driver" (89:10). One tradition explains the reason for this epithet as I have described it above in the story (*Biḥār al-anwār* vol. 13 p. 136 tr. 44).

44. *Biḥār al-anwār* vol. 13 p. 47 tr. 16

Moses simply replied, "May God hasten the appearance of your savior."[45] News soon spread that the savior had been seen, and a sudden wave of hope rippled through the ranks of the Jews.

Satan's Work

Some ten years later, when Moses was just shy of thirty, he was on one of his excursions outside the palace into the main city.[46] It was after sunset,[47] at a time when people were resting. He found there two men fighting—one from among his followers[48] and the other, an Egyptian, from the Pharaoh's supporters.[49] The one who was from his followers caught a glimpse of him and called out to him in desperation to seek his help against the other. Moses rushed to them and tried his best to break up the fight, but the Egyptian

45. *Biḥār al-anwār* vol. 13 p. 36 tr. 7

46. Based on two clues in the Qur'ān, we can infer that the Pharaoh's palace was located just outside, or on an extremity of, the city. One verse tells us, "One day he entered the city..." (Qur'ān 28:15), implying that while in the palace he had been outside the city; then he entered it for his excursion. Another verse tells us, "There came a man from the outskirts (furthest outpost) of the city, running" (Qur'ān 28:20). According to traditions, this man was Ezekiel, the Pharaoh's treasurer, and he had just left the court to warn Moses of the plot against him. Thus, the palace must have been on the "outskirts" of the city, far from where Moses was entrenched. We also know from Egyptologists that most of the cities in ancient Egypt were built on the eastern shores of the Nile since they believed the west to be associated with death as evinced by the sun's setting in that direction. Thus, they built tombs to the west and cities to the east. We also know that the Nile used to flood annually, so the palaces and other enduring buildings were built farther from the Nile, beyond the floodplain.

47. *Biḥār al-anwār* vol. 13 p. 32 tr. 6

48. The reference to this man as "one of his *Shī'ah*," indicates that Moses had a following by this time. There is no mention of this in the traditions, and it seems hard to imagine that he could have been active in any public way without alerting the Pharaoh's spies. Nonetheless, he must have attracted some following, if only in a secret, underground manner.

49. The Qur'ān labels this man as Moses' enemy; however, I believe he is called an enemy only because he was, *in reality* an enemy, not because he and Moses had some history of enmity. In general, all evidence suggests that Moses lived in a state of dissimulation (*taqiyyah)* during his years in the palace so as not to raise the ire of the Pharaoh before he was prepared to face the consequences.

would not relent. With no option left but force, Moses punched him. In a stupor, the man stumbled backward, tripped and struck his head against a rock. Moses rushed to make sure he was not hurt too badly but found him dead.

Moses thought for a long minute about this situation. He had just aided an Israelite slave against an Egyptian. He had taken the life of an Egyptian to save an Israelite slave from a few bruises. It would not matter that he was Moses, heir to the throne. It would not matter that he had acted for justice to defend one who was in need. The Pharaoh would see his actions as evidence that his allegiance was with the Israelites and that he was a traitor to Egypt. Filled with frustration, he looked to the Israelite and pointing aimlessly at the corpse before them and to the ground where they had been fighting and to everything in their vicinity, he declared, "This predicament in which we now find ourselves[50] is the work of Satan. He is a clear enemy who misguides."[51] Just as Satan leads people into sin, so does he lead them into hardship and trouble. And Moses saw that he was now in severe hardship and impending trouble.

A Night in Hiding

He told the Israelite to go home and to hide until this incident was forgotten. But he himself had nowhere to go. He could not return to the palace, of course. He did not want to go to Jochebed's home, for he did not want to bring down any trouble upon his family. So he hurried into the alleyways, leaving the Egyptian's body where it lay.

He found a secluded place and hunkered down for the night. His thoughts careened through the events of the last hour, and he turned his attention to God and said, "My Lord, I have wronged myself. Forgive me." He had been ensnared by Satan's ruse which was meant to make him fall from favor with the Pharaoh. He knew he had done the right thing by defending the Israelite, but he still

---

50. *Biḥār al-anwār* vol. 13 p. 32 tr. 6

51. Qur'ān 28:15

regretted that the Egyptian had died and that his own cover had been breached.

Of course, God forgave him, for he is the All-Forgiving, the All-Merciful.[52]

Moses continued to say to God, "My Lord, because you have blessed me with countless blessings since my birth, I shall never be a supporter of wrongdoers."[53] Striking the Egyptian had been his first opportunity to actually stand up to injustice. While the practical ramifications of this particular incident promised to cause much trouble for him, he was hooked. Before this, he had been a champion of justice in principle only, but from now on, he would be its champion in practice too.

The rest of the night passed uneventfully. Moses rose at dawn in the city, fearful and vigilant. He concealed his face and walked casually through the streets, eavesdropping on peoples' conversations. He learned that the Egyptian's body had been found, that the Pharaoh's soldiers were aggressively searching for his murderer, and that they had no leads on his identity.

Another Fight

Relieved, he circled back to the scene of the previous night's events, when behold, he saw the same Israelite who had sought his help the night before, once again in a fray with another Egyptian. When he saw Moses, he shouted for his help once again. Moses ran to where they were fighting. Once again, he pulled them apart and tried to defuse the situation, but the Egyptian kept charging at the Israelite. Moses looked incredulously at the Israelite and said, "You are clearly twisted."[54] Moses had assumed yesterday's fight was an anomaly, and so he had intervened whole-heartedly. But two fights

52. Qur'ān 28:16. It is not clear whether Moses was able to perceive God's forgiveness or not. He was not yet a prophet, however, it is possible that God communicated this to him through a vision or through some other means. It is also possible that God is telling us after the fact but did not tell Moses at the time.

53. Qur'ān 28:17

54. Qur'ān 28:18

in as many days meant that the Israelite was also at least partly to blame. But he would have to deal with him later. The immediate priority was to stave off the Egyptian.

Moses reared to strike the Egyptian, but the Israelite, scared that *he* was the intended target of Moses' blow, thoughtlessly blurted out, "Moses, do you want to kill me just as you killed that person yesterday? You simply want to be a tyrant in the land. And you clearly do not want to be a reformer."[55]

Appalled but helpless, Moses darted into the alleyways and disappeared before the bedazzled Egyptian realized that he had just been handed the solution to the previous day's murder. He rushed to the Pharaoh's court and informed them that Moses was their man.

Arrest Warrant

The Pharaoh summoned his advisors and deposed his witness in their presence to make it clear to them that Moses was guilty, not only of killing an Egyptian, but worse, of sympathizing with an Israelite. His suspicions, he now felt, had been correct. He had been blinded by emotion, but he had always suspected that Moses harbored a loyalty to his own people. Pharaoh issued a summary warrant for Moses' arrest and execution.

There was among the Pharaoh's advisors one named Ezekiel.[56] He was the Pharaoh's treasurer and an elderly man and one of his distant relatives. He had always liked Moses and had admired his strength of character and goodness. He now feared for Moses' well-being and so decided to warn him of the plot against him.

He rushed from the palace, which lay on the outskirts of the city, eager to beat the Pharaoh's death squad. He roamed the streets around where Moses had last been seen. At last, he found him and

---

55. Qur'ān 28:19

56. His name in Arabic is mentioned alternatively as *Ḥizqīl*, *Ḥizbīl*, and *Ḥirbīl*. This Ezekiel should not be confused with Prophet Ezekiel who is the third successor to Moses or the Ezekiel whom David met in a cave.

informed him, "Moses, the court is conspiring to kill you. Flee from here. I am your well-wisher."[57]

Moses Flees Egypt

Without an opportunity to bid his family farewell or to gather any provisions, he left the city, fearful and vigilant, with only the shirt on his back. He said in prayer, "My Lord, deliver me from these unjust people."[58]

He moved north along the Nile. With the city behind him, he shifted course and headed northeast. He headed toward Midian where, he had heard, there was a prophet of God. He said to himself, "I hope my Lord will show me the best path to take."[59] He traveled by night, slept by day, always imagining the sound of hoofbeats in hot pursuit. He ate whatever he could gather along the way.

Moses Reaches Midian

On the eighth day, he awoke to the bleating of sheep and the sharp calls and whistles of shepherds. He was on a hill overlooking a watering hole. From a distance he saw a throng of shepherds vying with one another to water their flocks. He also saw, at a closer distance, two young women holding back their flock. He approached and asked the young women, "What is the matter? Why do you not water your sheep along with the rest?"

They replied, "We do not water our flock until the other shepherds have driven out theirs. Otherwise, it is not decent for us to vie with them for a place for our sheep. Our father would water them himself, but he is now an elderly man, and cannot."[60]

As exhausted and emaciated as he was, Moses watered their flock for them. When he was done and he had returned their flock to their care, he withdrew to the shade of a tree and collapsed. The last thought that flitted across his mind before he slept was a

---

57. Qur'ān 28:20

58. Qur'ān 28:21

59. Qur'ān 28:22

60. Qur'ān 28:23

prayer of utter desperation. He said, "My Lord, I am in dire need of any goodness you may send down to me."[61] He would have been content with but a morsel of bread because since he had left Egypt, he had only eaten leaves and herbs. He had grown so emaciated that you could virtually see the leaves through his stretched skin and atrophied muscle.[62]

Not long after, one of the two young women approached him,[63] walking bashfully. She made some noise to stir him, and when he started from his slumber, she said, "My father extends to you an invitation to pay you the wages for watering our flock for us."[64]

As she set off to lead the way home, Moses bid her stop. He said, "I would rather you walk behind me. You can guide me from there. I am from a people who do not look inappropriately at women."[65]

Moses Meets Jethro

They arrived at a simple house surrounded by pasture. Moses saw the sheep he had herded earlier. He was greeted at the door by an elderly man who introduced himself as Jethro. Moses immediately recognized him as Prophet Jethro, "The Orator of the Prophets,"[66] and threw himself at his feet. They embraced, and Jethro led him into a small sitting room.

Moses recounted his entire adventure for Jethro and his daughters. Jethro comforted him saying, "Do not fear. Your prayer has been answered. You have been delivered from those unjust people."[67]

---

61. Qur'ān 28:24

62. *Biḥār al-anwār* vol. 13 p. 50 tr. 20 from *Nahj al-balāghah* sermon 160

63. One tradition tells us that this was the older of the two sisters, Ṣafrā', to whom Moses would later be married (*Biḥār al-anwār* vol. 13 p. 45 tr. 10).

64. Qur'ān 28:25

65. *Biḥār al-anwār* vol. 13 p. 32 tr. 5

66. *Biḥār al-anwār* vol. 12 p. 385 tr. 9

67. Qur'ān 28:25

They enjoyed a meal together, and then Jethro showed Moses to a small room where he could recuperate from his strenuous journey.

When the hosts were alone, the elder of Jethro's daughters, Ṣafrāʾ,[68] said, "Father, hire him to help you with the farm. The best person you can hire is someone strong and trustworthy."[69]

Curious, Jethro asked his daughter, "I understand how you know he is strong since you witnessed him handle our flock of sheep with ease. But how have you perceived that he is trustworthy?"

Ṣafrāʾ told him how Moses had insisted that she walk behind him lest he see something inappropriate from her.[70] Jethro nodded with an approving smile.

Marriage to Ṣafrāʾ

Later, when Moses was rested, he came out of the guest room and sat again with Jethro. Jethro told him earnestly, "I would like to marry you to one of these two daughters of mine," as he pointed to his daughters who were preparing a meal near the fire, "on condition that you work for me for eight years. And if you complete ten, that will be up to you.[71] I do not want to be hard on you, so the work I shall give you will not be too taxing. God-willing you will find that I am one of the righteous."[72]

Moses had seen the strength and goodness in Ṣafrāʾ, so he chose her. He was grateful that Jethro had not only offered his daughter in marriage but offered Moses a respectable way to pay her his bridal

68. *Biḥār al-anwār* vol. 13 p. 365 tr. 8

69. Qurʾān 28:26

70. *Biḥār al-anwār* vol. 13 p. 45 tr. 10

71. The details of this marriage raise several questions: Why does Jethro not specify which of his daughter he wishes Moses to marry? Why does he not specify whether it is eight or ten years that Moses must serve him? Is the service to him a bridal gift (*mahr*) or a separate stipulation within the marriage contract? Qurʾānic commentators have discussed these issues at length. But in the final measure, it is important to keep in mind that Abrahamic law, as practiced by Jethro, was not necessarily the same as Islamic law; thus, we need not be able to reconcile the two completely.

72. Qurʾān 28:27

gift. He presently had nothing to give her save the shirt on his back, but he could work, and by working, could earn wages and then offer Ṣafrā᾽ a worthy gift. He said, "Let this hereby be an agreement between you and me. I shall marry Ṣafrā᾽, and in exchange, I shall work for you. Whichever of the two terms I complete, let there be no blame on me. I shall work for at least eight years. Then I shall see whether I can complete the extra two or not. Let God be witness to what we say."[73] When they had completed the marriage arrangements, Jethro confided in Moses how God had promised to bring him into his service."[74] They praised God for having fulfilled his promise.

Ten Years in Midian

These years were the best of Moses' life. He found in Jethro a willing and able teacher and a spiritual and practical role model. After living a dual life in Egypt, pretending to be the heir to the Pharaoh while trying desperately to help those oppressed by him, he was relieved to be in the company of believers. He was happy with his new wife and she with him. Through mutual agreement, they decided to consummate their marriage before he had completed the term they had stipulated.[75] Soon afterward, Ṣafrā᾽ gave birth to their first child and then another, a boy.[76]

---

73. Qur᾽ān 28:28

74. *Biḥār al-anwār* vol. 12 p. 380 tr. 1

75. *Biḥār al-anwār* vol. 13 p. 37 tr. 8. In this tradition, Imam al-Ṣādiq implies that they were only able to consummate the marriage before the stipulated time was over because Moses had knowledge from God that he would live long enough to fulfill his commitment. It seems there is a difference of opinion about the authenticity and meaning of this tradition. As such, I have offered the additional justification that whatever they did was through mutual agreement, for if a wife wishes, it is her prerogative to forgive the bridal gift or defer it.

76. There is no concrete evidence that they had children. However, later, when they traveled to Egypt, Moses told his wife and at least two other people to wait (Qur᾽ān 28:29). The plural form of the verb is used indicating that he was addressing at least three people, at least one of whom must have been male. Based on this reasoning, they must have had at least two children before leaving Midian, and at least one was a boy.

As their tenth anniversary approached,[77] Moses decided it was time to return to Egypt. As a parting gift, Jethro gave Moses the staff he had inherited from Adam which he had fashioned from a boxthorn from the garden.[78] With that, Moses, along with his wife and children, set off westward.[79]

Return to Egypt

As they passed through the mountains, they lost their sense of direction. Darkness and the chill of the desert night descended upon them. From the mountain pass where they stood, they could see the glow of fire ahead on the side of the mountain, to the right of the valley that lay before them. Moses told his wife and children, "Wait here for me. I see fire. I might be able to bring some information about our route or find a brand of fire so that you can be warm."[80]

He left his family where he felt they would be safe until he returned. Then he walked briskly into the valley so he could get as close to the fire as possible before ascending the right flank of the mountain. As he walked, he was miraculously transported hundreds of miles to the northeast, across the vast Arabian desert, to the land that, many centuries later would come to be known as Karbalāʾ.[81]

---

77. *Biḥār al-anwār* vol. 13 p. 37 tr. 8

78. *Biḥār al-anwār* vol. 13 p. 45 tr. 11, p. 45 tr. 10, p. 45 tr. 11 and p. 138 tr. 51

79. Qurʾān 28:29

80. Qurʾān 28:29 and 20:10

81. Among Biblical historians, there is much debate over the location of the mountain where God spoke to Moses. Because Moses climbed the mountain on his way from Midian (in northwestern Arabia) to Egypt, it makes sense that the mountain should be located on this route. For this reason, people have traditionally identified various mountains on what is now known as the Sinai Peninsula. Jabal Mūsā is the most famous. Some have also identified Jabal al-Lawz which is located west of Tabuk. Neither the Qurʾān nor the traditions give us enough information to confirm or refute these claims.

However, interestingly, many traditions from the Prophet's family identify the area around Karbalāʾ and Najaf as the location where God spoke to Moses. A quick look at the map of the area reveals two challenges to these traditions:

God Speaks to Moses

The surrounding mountains were barren, but this one was *saynā'*, covered with trees—olive trees to be precise.[82] As he neared the glow, a voice sounded, "Blessed is he who is in the fire and he who is near the fire, and exalted is God, Lord of all realms."[83] Moses started and peered through the darkness toward the flickering light,

---

- Karbalā' and Najaf are about 1000 km in the wrong direction for someone traveling from Midian to Egypt.
- There are no mountains to speak of in Karbalā' and Najaf or the surrounding areas.

If he were transported to Karbalā' miraculously, there would be no limit on the distance he might have traveled. His travel would then be similar to Mary's travel from Jerusalem to Karbalā where she reportedly gave birth to Jesus.

In response to the second challenge, I can offer the following defense. The mountain need not have been an immense mountain. The entire episode clearly takes place on the "side of a mountain," not on top. Even a hill would satisfy this description. If there is not even a hill left in modern day Najaf and Karbalā', that does not preclude the possibility that there may once have been one that has since eroded or been destroyed.

If we only had the Qur'ānic verses to examine, we could say with confidence that these events occurred somewhere between Midian and Egypt. However, with the additional guidance of the Prophet and his family we must allow that the apparent meaning of the verses may not be intended. If there were only one such tradition, we may have been justified in dismissing it. But when all the traditions from the imams assert the same thing, we cannot ignore them.

82. The Qur'ān does not name a specific mountain upon which these events took place. It refers to the place as *al-ṭūr* which simply means "the mountain" (see 19:52, 28:29, 28:46). In two verses, it does mention the words *ṭūr saynā'* (23:20) and *ṭūr sīnīn* (95:2). *Ṭūr saynā'* is not mentioned in the context of this story and is not a proper noun but a common noun apparently referring to a kind of mountain, not a specific one. According to one tradition from Ibn 'Abbās, both terms, *ṭūr saynā'* and *ṭūr sīnīn*, refer to any mountain upon which something beneficial grows like trees and herbs. Mountains on which there is nothing growing of benefit are simply called *ṭūr* or "mountain" (*Biḥār al-anwār* vol. 13 p. 65 tr. 3). The prevailing view among Qur'ānic commentators is that both terms are synonymous and refer to any mountain that is covered with trees or any blessed mountain. With time, we have come to refer to the specific mountain where this story took place as Mount Sinai, but this is not the Qur'ānic usage.

83. Qur'ān 27:8

and the voice suddenly boomed again, "Moses![84] I am your Lord, the Invincible, the Wise,[85] the Lord of all realms."[86] God spoke to Moses, and thereby showed him one of his greatest signs, without the use of any appendage or accessory or voice box or uvula.[87] "Remove your sandals," he continued, "for you are in the sacred valley of Ṭuwā.[88] And as you doff them, doff your love for anything besides me and your fear of losing anything besides me."[89] Moses unquestioningly doffed his sandals and moved furtively toward the fire which, he could now see, emanated from the base of an olive tree[90] about halfway up the mountainside.

The voice continued, "I have chosen you, so listen to this revelation:[91] I am God. There is no god but me. So worship me, and establish prayer in my remembrance.[92] The hour of judgment undoubtedly shall come so that every person may act and be recompensed for his effort, though I have almost completely hidden it from the eyes of humankind.[93] So do not let yourself be

84. Qur'ān 20:11

85. Qur'ān 27:9

86. Qur'ān 28:30

87. *Biḥār al-anwār* vol. 13 p. 50 tr. 21 from *Nahj al-balāghah*

88. Qur'ān 20:12

89. Commentators have proposed various symbolisms for the doffing of the shoes. 'Allāmah al-Majlisī has collected these into a list of six (*Biḥār al-anwār* vol. 13 p. 65). It seems the prevailing view among Sunnīs was that he had to remove his shoes because they were made of impure donkey hide (*Biḥār al-anwār* vol. 13 p. 64 tr. 1). In one tradition, Imam al-Mahdī refutes this opinion and says that Moses was very fond of his family, perhaps too fond. By commanding him to remove his shoes, he was commanding him to love only God and to love his family only through God (*Biḥār al-anwār* vol. 13 p. 65 tr. 4). Because this last view has been attributed to an imam, I have used it for my story.

90. *Biḥār al-anwār* vol. 13 p. 65 tr. 3

91. Qur'ān 20:13

92. Qur'ān 20:14

93. Qur'ān 20:15

distracted from it by those who do not believe in it and who have followed their desires, lest you perish."[94]

Moses' Staff

After a moment, God called attention to Moses' staff by asking, "Moses, what is that in your right hand?"[95]

The question caught Moses off guard. He had forgotten that he still clenched anything at all. As if waking from a stupor, he said, "It is my staff." Then he nervously rambled on, "I lean upon it, and with it I beat down leaves for my sheep, and I have other uses for it."[96]

God ordered, "Moses, throw it down."[97] So he threw down his staff, and, suddenly, it became a slithering snake.[98] When he saw it writhing as a serpent writhes, he wheeled around to flee, not daring to look back. God said, "Moses, come forward, and do not be afraid. You are safe, for you are my messenger, and my messengers fear nothing in my presence except me.[99] And likewise those people have no fear who do wrong and then replace that wrong with some good, for I am the All-Absolving, the Ever-Merciful.[100] Take hold of the snake, and do not fear. We shall restore it to its former state."[101] Emboldened, Moses grabbed the snake, and instead of scales and musculature, his fingers wrapped around the rigid coldness of his familiar wooden staff.

The White Hand

Then God told him, "Insert your hand under your lapel, and place it between your arm and chest. When you pull it out, it will emerge

---

94. Qur'ān 20:16

95. Qur'ān 20:17

96. Qur'ān 20:18

97. Qur'ān 20:19 and 28:31

98. Qur'ān 20:20

99. Qur'ān 28:31

100. Qur'ān 27:11

101. Qur'ān 20:21

white but unharmed by leprosy.[102] We have shown you this because we wanted to show you some of our great signs. Keep a stiff upper lip, and muster your strength against the fearsome task that lies ahead.[103] Go to Pharaoh. He has rebelled.[104] Your staff and your white hand shall be two proofs from your Lord to Pharaoh and his court. You will need such proofs, for they are a corrupt people."[105]

---

102. Mention of the phrase "white but unharmed by leprosy" seems to be an indirect rebuttal of the Biblical account of this story. There we read, "Then the Lord said, 'Put your hand inside your cloak.' So Moses put his hand into his cloak, and when he took it out, the skin was *leprous*—it had become as white as snow" (Exodus 4:6). One of the symptoms of leprosy is whitened skin. The Jewish authors of the Bible used this fact to twist one of God's great miracles into a blemish with which to mar their prophet.

103. This part of the story is narrated three times in the Qur'ān. The clearest of these is 27:12 which reads, "Insert your hand under your lapel, and it will emerge white but unharmed." The first part of 28:32 is also clear. Only the verb insert (*adkhil*) has been replaced with another synonym (*usluk*). However, the confusion starts when comparing this same phrase as it appears in 20:22, "وَ اضْمُمْ يَدَكَ إِلى جَناحِكَ تَخرُجْ بَيْضاءَ مِنْ غَيْرِ سُوءٍ" in which the verbs *adkhil* and *usluk* have been replaced with "*uḍmum,*" with a similar phrase from 28:32, "وَ اضْمُمْ إِلَيْكَ جَناحَكَ مِنَ الرَّهْبِ" for there is a striking resemblance between the two phrases. My first instinct was to assume that these two similar phrases convey the same meaning. Al-Zamakhsharī also favors this opinion. However, there are serious problems with this assumption:

- 28:32 would then contain a redundant phrase, for the meaning of the phrases "*usluk yadak*" and "*wa uḍmum ilayka janāḥak*" would be the same, and a redundancy like this is beneath the Qur'ān's eloquence.
- The phrase "*min al-rahb*" clearly sets "*wa uḍmum ilayka janāḥak*" in this verse apart from "*wa uḍmum yadak ilā janāḥika*" for it makes it clear that the purpose of pulling his arms in was to counter his fear and muster his strength, not to make his hand white. In conclusion, since this phrase is idiomatic, instead of translating it literally as "keep your arms drawn to your sides," I have translated it as "keep a stiff upper lip," which I believe conveys the same meaning.

104. Qur'ān 20:24

105. Qur'ān 20:22–23 and 27:12 and 28:32

Moses' Prayers

Moses said, "Lord, I accept whatever duty you charge me with,[106] but I have killed one of their men, so I fear they will kill me.[107] My Lord, I fear they will reject me[108] and that I will lack the capacity to bear this burden and that my tongue will fail me, so send for Aaron.[109] My brother, Aaron, is more eloquent than I, so send him with me as a helper to affirm me."[110]

Moses continued in fervent prayer, "My Lord, increase my capacity to bear this burden; make this mission easy for me; remove the hitch from my tongue so that they may understand my message.[111] Appoint for me a minister from my family—my brother, Aaron. Through him, strengthen me. And make him my partner in my mandate so that together we may glorify you much and remember you much. I ask and hope all this of you because you have always kept watch over us."[112]

---

106. He does not say this in any verse, but I inserted it to remind us that his list of potential problems is not a set of excuses he is offering to shirk duty. He certainly accepts the charge but also needs reassurance that these challenges will not prevent him from discharging his duty.

107. Qurʾān 28:33

108. Qurʾān 26:12

109. Qurʾān 26:13. See *al-Mīzān* for a justification of this meaning as it is based on the recension that reads "*yaḍīqa*" in the accusative case instead of "*yaḍīqu*" in the nominative case.

110. Qurʾān 28:34

111. One tradition explains that it was not a physiological impediment but a psychological one. He was ashamed to speak to others with the same tongue he used to speak to God (*Biḥār al-anwār* vol. 13 p. 64 tr. 2). It is also plausible to say that he had no "hitch" at all. As he prepares for the momentous task of combatting the Pharaoh, he prays for heightened strength, courage, and fortitude. He is simply asking God to make his tongue fluent at a time when tongues not fortified with the strength of God fall silent. This does not imply that he stuttered or was in any other way impaired.

112. Qurʾān 20:25–35

God's Answer

God replied, "Your requests have been granted, Moses. And rest assured that I shall support you always just as I showed you favor once before.[113] Let me remind you of the time when I spoke to your mother through inspiration[114] and told her, 'Place him in this wooden box and throw him into the river. The river will cast him onto its bank, and he shall be picked up by an enemy of mine and an enemy of his.' And bear in mind that I cast love upon you as a gift from me, for many reasons, one of which was that you be reared under my auspices.[115] Recall also when your sister walked to the Pharaoh's palace and asked, 'Shall I show you a family that will take care of him?' Thereby we returned you to your mother to brighten her eyes and so that she would not fret. And recall that you killed a person, but we saved you from hardship and thereafter tested you in so many ways. Then you resided for years among the people of Midian and you progressed just as I envisioned, O Moses![116] And thus I chose you for my service.[117]

What Is the Reward?

Moses asked, "Lord, what is the reward for one who accepts that I am your prophet and messenger with whom you have spoken?"

He replied, "My angels will visit him and give him tidings of paradise."

Moses asked, "Lord, what is the reward for one who stands before you in prayer?"

He replied, "I shall be proud of him before my angels whenever he bows, prostrates, stands, or sits. And when I am proud of someone before my angels, I never punish him."

Moses asked, "Lord, what is the reward for one who feeds a poor person to seek your pleasure?"

113. Qur'ān 20:36–37

114. Qur'ān 20:38

115. Qur'ān 20:39

116. Qur'ān 20:40

117. Qur'ān 20:41

He replied, "I shall have a crier announce on the Day of Judgment that so-and-so is among those freed by God from the fire."

Moses asked, "Lord, what is the reward for one who maintains ties with his family?"

He replied, "I shall delay his appointed death, and I shall lighten the throes of death, and the guardians of paradise will call out to him, 'Come! Enter from whichever of heaven's gates you please!'"

Moses asked, "Lord, what is the reward for one who refrains from harming others and does good to them?"

He replied, "The fire will call out to him on the Day of Resurrection, 'I cannot touch you!'"

Moses asked, "Lord, what is the reward for one who remembers you with his tongue and in his heart?"

He replied, "I shall shelter him on the Day of Resurrection with the shade of my throne, and I shall admit him into my proximity."

Moses asked, "Lord, what is the reward for one who follows your law in public and in private?"

He replied, "He shall cross the bridge (*ṣirāṭ*) that spans hellfire quick as lightning."

Moses asked, "Lord, what is the reward for one who perseveres in the face of people's persecution and disparagement?"

He replied, "I shall help him to face the terror that afflicts people on the Day of Resurrection."

Moses asked, "Lord, what is the reward for one whose eyes shed tears in fear of you?"

He replied, "I shall guard his face from the fire of hell and give him sanctuary on the Day of Great Distress."

Moses asked, "Lord, what is the reward for one who abandons treachery because he feels shame before you?"

He replied, "He shall be safe on the Day of Resurrection."

Moses asked, "Lord, what is the reward for one who loves those who obey you?"

He replied, "I shall forbid the fire to touch him."

Moses asked, "Lord, what is the punishment for one who murders a believer intentionally?"

He replied, "I shall not even look at him on the Day of Resurrection, and I shall not overlook his faults."

Moses asked, "Lord, what is the reward for one who invites an unbeliever to faith?"

He replied, "I shall give him leave to intercede on behalf of whomever he wishes on the Day of Resurrection."

Moses asked, "Lord, what is the reward for one who prays all his prayers on time?"

He replied, "I shall answer his prayers and give him free access to paradise."

Moses asked, "Lord, what is the reward for one who performs the ablutions perfectly because he fears you?"

He replied, "When I resurrect him, there will be a light sparkling between his eyes."

Moses asked, "Lord, what is the reward for one who fasts the month of Ramaḍān in hopes of your reward?"[118]

He replied, "I shall give him a station in which he will not fear."

Moses asked, "Lord, what is the reward for one who fasts the month of Ramaḍān for the sake of people?"

He replied, "His reward will be like one who did not fast."[119]

Moses asked, "Lord, what kind of a person will live in your closest proximity?"

God replied, "Those whose eyes never gazed upon what was unlawful; whose money was never tainted with usury; who never accepted bribes for their judgment. Moses, never denigrate the poor, and never envy the rich."[120]

God's Exhortations

God also told him, "Moses, he is a liar who says he loves me but sleeps away from me when night falls. Does a lover not love to be intimate with his beloved?"[121]

He also said the following:

---

118. According to this tradition, fasting during the month of Ramaḍān was prescribed, at least as a supererogatory act even in Moses' time.

119. *Biḥār al-anwār* vol. 13 p. 327 tr. 4

120. *Biḥār al-anwār* vol. 13 p. 329 tr. 6

121. *Biḥār al-anwār* vol. 13 p. 330 tr. 7

> Moses, I exhort you regarding the son of the Virgin, Jesus, son of Mary, who shall ride a donkey, dress in a burnoose, live in a place famed for olives, olive oil, and for the Holy of Holies.
>
> And I exhort you regarding the one who will come after him who will ride a red camel; who is good and pure. He is described in your book as one who is superior in his knowledge of all books. He will bow and prostrate. His companions will be the poor. His helpers will be from another people... his name is Aḥmad and Muḥammad, the Most Trustworthy of those who are past and those who are left. He will believe in all of my scriptures, and he will confirm all of my messengers. His nation will be full of mercy and blessing. They will have specific times designated in which they will pray. Accept him, for he is your brother. He is my trustee. He is a good servant. Whatever he touches is blessed...so tell the wrongdoers among the Israelites not to conceal his name and not to desert him, but, alas, they will do so anyway...[122]

God also told him, "Moses, I shall only accept the prayers of those who are humble before my greatness, whose hearts are ever-fearful of me, who pass their days in remembrance of me, who do not persist in a sin, and who recognize the station of my friends and those I love."

Moses asked, "Lord, by 'your friends and those you love' do you mean Abraham, Isaac, and Jacob?"

God replied, "They are indeed my friends, and I do indeed love them. However, I meant him because of whom I created Adam and Eve; him because of whom I created heaven and hell."

Moses asked, "Who is he, Lord?"

God replied, "Muḥammad or Aḥmad. I derived his name from mine, for I am *al-Maḥmūd*, the Praiseworthy."

---

122. *Biḥār al-anwār* vol. 13 p. 332 tr. 13

Moses begged, "Lord, include me in his nation."

God said, "Moses, you are from his nation as long as you recognize him and his station and the station of his family. He and his family are to the rest of my creation as paradise is to every other garden, for its leaves never wither, and its scent never fades. If a person recognizes them and their station, I shall replace his ignorance with knowledge and fill his darkness with light. I shall answer his prayers before they are uttered, and I shall give him before he asks."[123]

God also exhorted him, "Moses, thank me as I deserve to be thanked."

Moses said hopelessly, "Lord, how can I thank you as you deserve to be thanked when every thanks I offer requires yet another thanks?"

God said, "Moses, by recognizing this very fact, you have thanked me as I deserve to be thanked."[124]

Moses Is Chosen

Then God asked Moses, "Do you know why I have chosen you out of all my creatures and singled you out to speak to?"

Moses replied, "No, my Lord!"

God said, "I looked upon the earth, and I saw no one more humble before me than you." Upon hearing this, Moses threw himself prostrate and rubbed his cheeks in the dirt out of meekness before God. God told him, "Moses, lift your head, and pass your hand over the place on the ground where you just prostrated, and wipe that hand over your face and whatever you can reach of your body, for this will keep you safe from every sickness, affliction, and disability."[125]

Finally, God said, "Go now. We shall strengthen you through your brother and empower you both with such proofs that they

---

123. *Biḥār al-anwār* vol. 13 p. 338 tr. 14

124. *Biḥār al-anwār* vol. 13 p. 351 tr. 41

125. *Biḥār al-anwār* vol. 13 p. 7 tr. 6 and tr. 8

shall not touch you. Through our signs, you two and all who follow you shall overcome."[126]

Moses had come to this mountain searching for a flame. He would now return from it blazing with divine inspiration, for he would henceforth be one of God's prophets and messengers;[127] the third of God's "Messengers of Great Resolve"[128] and the first of 600 prophets God would eventually send to the Israelites, culminating in Jesus, son of Mary.[129] God gave him a ring with the inscription, "Be patient, and be rewarded. Speak the truth, and be saved."[130] He walked, dazed and pensive at first, and then with a quickened gait, down the mountain. Seamlessly, he was transported back from Karbalāʾ, and he soon returned to find his family where he had left them. At first dawn, they were on their way home.

First Encounter With His Followers

They neared Egypt, and on the outskirts of the city, they came upon the meeting place of the small band of Israelites who regularly met with their priest to discuss the prophecies of the savior and to do what they could to hasten his return. Moses had stumbled into their meeting many years before. This time he walked to the site intentionally.

Hours before, these Israelites' priest had informed them that he had received inspiration from God that their savior would return to them after forty years. These people had already waited in patience for eons, so they accepted God's decree and exclaimed, "Praise is for God."

At that moment, God told the priest, "I shall make it thirty years because they said, 'Praise is for God.'"

These people became elated at the prospect of only waiting thirty short years. They exclaimed, "Every blessing is from God."

Again, God told the priest, "I shall make it twenty years."

126. Qurʾān 28:35

127. *Biḥār al-anwār* vol. 13 p. 32 tr. 3

128. Qurʾān 46:35

129. *Biḥār al-anwār* vol. 13 p. 7 tr. 5

130. *Biḥār al-anwār* vol. 11 p. 63 tr. 1

They overflowed with ebullience and joy and said, "Only God brings goodness."

Again, God told the priest, "I shall make it ten years."

They celebrated, "Only God dispels falsehood."

Finally God told him, "Do not disperse from this gathering, for I have decreed that your savior return to you this evening." No sooner had he delivered this message than Moses rode into their gathering on the back of a donkey, followed by his wife and children.

The priest wished to introduce Moses to his followers. He asked, "What is your name?"

Moses replied, "I am Moses, son of Amram."

"What is your mission?" He asked.

Moses replied, "I have come with a message from God for you and for the Pharaoh." The priest laid hold of Moses' hand and kissed it deeply. Moses sat with them much of that night, teaching them, admonishing them to help him when he called on them, and preparing them for the long road ahead.[131]

Homecoming

When they finally reached Egypt, Moses disguised himself to forestall any chance that someone might recognize him. They entered the city uneventfully, and he took his wife and children directly to his family for what proved to be an emotional homecoming.

Moses, with plenipotentiary power from God, informed his older brother, Aaron,[132] that God had also chosen him as a prophet to aid him in his mission. They would work hand in hand to bring Pharaoh to his knees. Henceforth, God would speak to Moses, and he in turn would communicate the message to Aaron who would be his deputy and aid.[133]

---

131. *Biḥār al-anwār* vol. 13 p. 37 tr. 7

132. *Biḥār al-anwār* vol. 13 p. 11 tr. 15

133. *Biḥār al-anwār* vol. 13 p. 27 tr. 2

Preparing to Meet the Pharaoh

That night the message came, "Go forth with my signs, you and your brother, and do not flag in remembering me.[134] Both of you go to the Pharaoh, for he has rebelled.[135] Speak to him softly. Maybe he will take heed or fear me.[136] Ask him, 'Are you inclined to purify yourself? Shall I guide you to your Lord so that you fear him as he ought to be feared?'"[137]

The two brothers discussed their plan. Moses said, "Lord, we fear that he will forestall us or overstep the bounds."[138]

God said, "Do not be afraid, for I shall be with the two of you, hearing and seeing whatever happens.[139] Approach him and say, 'We are envoys of the Lord of all realms. Let the Israelites go free with us and cease torturing them. We have brought you proofs from the Lord. May God's peace be upon him who follows this guidance.'"[140]

Moses and Aaron prayed earnestly that God strengthen them and soften the Pharaoh's heart and open his ears.

In the Pharaoh's Court

The next morning, they proceeded to the palace dressed only in their coarse woolen cassocks with their shepherd's staffs in hand.[141] They requested permission to speak with the Pharaoh. Though he was in session with Hāmān and his other advisors, they were admitted. They entered an enormous hall lined with massive columns that ascended skyward. The walls and ceiling were ornate with gold leaf and brightly colored hieroglyphs extolling the

---

134. Qur'ān 20:42

135. Qur'ān 20:43

136. Qur'ān 20:44

137. Qur'ān 79:18–9

138. Qur'ān 20:45

139. Qur'ān 20:46

140. Qur'ān 20:47

141. *Nahj al-balāghah* sermon 192 and *Biḥār al-anwār* vol. 13 p. 110 tr. 14

Pharaoh they were about to meet. It was a hall meant to belittle all who dared enter.

But Moses and Aaron pressed unperturbed toward the far side of the hall where the Pharaoh sat majestically upon his golden dais, bejeweled from head to foot and donning the finest garments imaginable. Next to him stood Hāmān and behind them both, two columns of advisors.

God whispered to his prophets:

> Do not let his garments instill fear in you, for his forelock is in my grasp. And do not be amazed by the trappings and luxury of this world with which he has been provided, for if I had wanted, I could have adorned you with such trappings that, upon seeing them, the Pharaoh would have ceded that all his power pales before it. Instead, I steer you clear of all that and steer all that clear of you. This is how I treat all of my friends. I steer them clear of this world's trappings like a shepherd steers his flock clear of perilous terrain...and this is not to disparage you but rather so that you may fully and soundly be availed of my true blessings to you. My friends adorn themselves with humility, subservience, and fear which spring spontaneously from their hearts and become manifest upon their bodies. These attributes constitute their mettle and their mantle, the source of their salvation, their station, and their greatness, and the very mark by which they are known. Moses, if you meet one of them, be humble and gracious with him, and soften your heart and tongue to him. And keep in mind: If anyone terrorizes my friends, then he has thereby declared war on me, and I shall avenge my friends on the Day of Resurrection."[142]

---

142. *Biḥār al-anwār* vol. 13 p. 49 tr. 18

Moses offered a silent prayer saying, "O God! I shall defend you if even by striking at his throat. I seek your protection against his evil, and I seek your help." In response to this prayer, God would replace the Pharaoh's arrogance with fear.[143]

Assuming they were some lowly shepherds come to talk about some petty matter, the Pharaoh paid them little heed. He only humored them with some formalities as they approached.

Moses and Pharaoh Speak

When they were before him, Moses addressed him in the most respectful of terms as God had ordered him to.[144] He said, "Abū Muṣʿab,[145] we are envoys from your Lord,[146] the Lord of all realms.[147] It is not fitting for me to say anything about God except truth.[148] Let the Israelites go free with us, and cease torturing them. We have brought you proofs from the Lord. May God's peace be upon him who follows this guidance.[149] And it has been revealed to us that punishment awaits whoever repudiates this message and turns away.[150] Abū Muṣʿab, are you inclined to purify yourself? Shall I guide you to your Lord so that you fear him as he ought to be feared?"[151]

Stunned by both the content of these statements and the confidence and eloquence with which they were spoken, the Pharaoh peered closer at his guest. He asked, "Are you not Moses?"

Moses conceded that he was.

The Pharaoh shook his head incredulously and asked, "What gives you the gaul to enter my court and speak to me? Did my wife

---

143. *Biḥār al-anwār* vol. 13 p. 132 tr. 36

144. Qurʾān 20:44

145. *Biḥār al-anwār* vol. 13 p. 134 tr. 40

146. Qurʾān 20:47

147. Qurʾān 26:16 and 7:7

148. Qurʾān 7:8

149. Qurʾān 20:47

150. Qurʾān 20:48

151. Qurʾān 79:18–9

and I not raise you in our midst as our own child, and did you not live with us for years of your life?"[152] Moses conceded that this was true.

The Pharaoh continued with a tone of derision, "But then you perpetrated that heinous deed of yours, thereby joining the ranks of these Israelite ingrates!"[153]

Moses paused a moment and said thoughtfully, "I did that when I was lost."[154] In his heart he meant that he had killed the Egyptian before he had been graced with divine guidance, when he had had only his limited intelligence to go on. He had deemed intervention between the Egyptian and the Israelite the best path without knowing that the Egyptian would accidentally die or that the Israelite was unworthy of his help. But when he said, "I was lost," he knew the Pharaoh would hear what he wanted to hear—that Moses had perpetrated his crime and was now vindicating himself because he had been ignorant and foolish at the time. Moses hoped that such an admission might soften the Pharaoh's heart to listen to what he now had to say.

Moses continued, "So I fled from you because I feared you. Then my Lord gave me sound judgment and made me one of his apostles."[155] Having vindicated himself and laid claim to his credentials, he went on the offensive and took issue with the favor the Pharaoh apparently felt he had the right to hold over him and his people. He asked rhetorically, "And is this the favor you hold over my head—that you enslaved the Israelites?"[156] It was true that the Pharaoh and his wife had ostensibly raised him. However, he considered it no great favor since it was the Pharaoh's oppressive rule and genocidal policies that had left his mother no choice but to cast him into the river in the first place.

The Pharaoh deftly sidestepped Moses' attack and abruptly asked, "Who is this Lord of yours, Moses?"

---

152. Qur'ān 26:18

153. Qur'ān 26:19

154. Qur'ān 26:20

155. Qur'ān 26:21

156. Qur'ān 26:22

Moses replied, "Our Lord is he who gave everything its existence and then guided it."[157] This answer surprised the Pharaoh. Moses seemed to be speaking of the creator, but everyone knew that the creator was sublime, too sublime in fact to have anything to do with the day-to-day running of the world. This, the Egyptians believed, he had consigned to the gods. It was absurd in their mind for Moses to lay claim to being a messenger from the creator.

The Pharaoh pressed, "You mentioned something about a 'lord of all realms.' What is this 'lord of *all realms*' of which you speak?"[158] The Egyptians had created a mythology with a pantheon of gods, lords of the natural elements. There was a lord of the river, a lord of the rain, a lord of the wind, and of every other realm upon which human prosperity depended. The Pharaoh touted himself as the highest of these Egyptian lords.[159] But he and his underling lords only ruled over the land of Egypt. Neighboring civilizations presumably had their own lords. The concept of one singular lord who directly ruled all realms was a concept long forgotten, driven out of their collective memory with the demise of Joseph.

Moses replied, "He is the Lord of the sky and the earth and all that is between them, if you seek the path to certainty."[160]

Pharaoh mockingly said to his courtiers around him, "Do you not hear what he is babbling?"[161]

Moses, ignoring his derisive air, said, "He is your Lord and the Lord of your forefathers."[162]

At the mention of his forefathers, Pharaoh found a segue to question something else Moses had said earlier. He asked, "You mentioned something about punishment awaiting whoever repudiates this message of yours and turns away. Then what about

---

157. Qur'ān 20:50

158. Qur'ān 26:23

159. Qur'ān 79:24

160. Qur'ān 26:24

161. Qur'ān 26:25

162. Qur'ān 26:26

the generations who have passed?[163] How is this Lord of all Realms of yours going to bring people to justice who have long since turned to dust?"

Moses replied, "Knowledge of them and all they did is with my Lord, recorded in a book. My Lord neither botches their records nor forgets them.[164] He is the one who made the earth level and accessible for you, and made roads therein for you, and sent down water from the sky, and with it brought forth various kinds of vegetation,[165] and told you 'Eat from this, and graze your cattle.' In all of that are signs for those with intellects.[166] From earth has he created us, into the earth shall he inter us, and from the earth shall he bring us forth once again."[167] He hoped the Pharaoh would realize that a god who could create and nurture thus could easily resurrect and carry out judgment.

Ad Hominem

But Pharaoh, finding no rational rebuttal, doffed his cool demeanor and lashed out ad hominem decrying, "This messenger who has been sent to you is mad."[168]

---

163. Qur'ān 20:51

164. Qur'ān 20:52

165. Qur'ān 20:53. There is a difference of opinion among the commentators over verses 20:53–55. Some consider these lines to be an interjection by God, only tangentially related to Moses' conversation with the Pharaoh. Others consider it to be a continuation of Moses' conversation with the Pharaoh. The problem with the latter view is that the voice shifts to the first person plural which makes it seem God is speaking, not Moses. Nonetheless, because the ideas are so suited to Moses' response, I have favored this opinion and made minor adjustments to the pronouns in translation to accord with good English style. Incidentally, such a sudden shift in voice is not uncommon in the Qur'ān.

166. Qur'ān 20:54

167. Qur'ān 20:55

168. Qur'ān 26:27

Again Moses turned a deaf ear to the insult and continued, "He is the Lord of the east and the west and whatever is between them. If only you would use your reason."[169]

Beyond the limits of his patience, having cast aside his façade of reason, Pharaoh seethed, "If you dare take up a god other than me, I shall cast you into my dungeon."[170]

The Staff and White Hand

Moses realized that no amount of talk would convince this Pharaoh. Thus, he fell back to his arsenal of miraculous signs. He said, "What if I show you something clear and undeniable?"[171]

Pharaoh's interest was slightly piqued. He said, "Bring it forth, if you be truthful."[172]

Moses uttered a word and threw down his staff, and it suddenly became a serpent.[173] Pharaoh and his courtiers reared in terror. Their eyes were still affixed on the snake when Moses placed his hand under his lapel and drew it out, white to the onlookers.[174] The writhing serpent and the luminous hand each seemed to outdo the other in magnificence.[175] When Moses felt his miracles had done

---

169. Qur'ān 26:28

170. Qur'ān 26:29

171. Qur'ān 26:30

172. Qur'ān 26:31

173. Qur'ān 26:32 and 7:107

174. Qur'ān 26:33 and 7:108

175. Qur'ān 43:48. There are two possible meanings given for this verse. It could mean that every sign that Moses showed them was increasingly great, meaning number two was greater than number one; number three greater than number two, and so forth. One problem with this interpretation is that no qualifier exists in the verse to say that each sign was greater than *the one before it*. We would have to infer this qualifier which would not be so hard but that there is nothing apparently greater about the white hand than there is about the serpent. Both are great miracles, and to compare them is to compare apples and oranges.

Accordingly, I believe another interpretation is better. The verse is not saying that one miracle was greater than the other. Rather, it is saying that each one was so great that, if we were shown one, we would say that it is the greatest

their work, he let the whiteness fade from his hand and calmly lay hold of the snake which once again became his staff. Moses had made it eminently clear that he spoke the truth and that he drew his power from a higher source than the Pharaoh did. Nonetheless, seizing power was not his primary goal. He magnanimously promised the Pharaoh that he could keep his kingdom and his honor on condition that he submit to God.[176]

The Pharaoh's head was reeling. In a fleeting moment of clarity, he was prepared to submit to Moses' God, but Hāmān, sensing his weakness, deterred him saying, "How can you be a god to be worshiped if you answer to a slave?"[177] These words fortified the Pharaoh's recalcitrance.[178] He had his guards escort Moses and Aaron out of the court so that he could deliberate with his advisors in private.

Private Council

When they were gone, Pharaoh turned to his courtiers with renewed muster and scoffed,[179] "Are you not amused by these two? They dare place conditions on *my* keeping *my* kingdom and *my* honor when

---

miracle ever, and if we were shown the other, we would say it too is the greatest miracle ever. It is like an art gallery filled with masterpieces. A person would be hard-pressed to rank them by beauty. Instead, whichever one he looks at, he feels that it is the most beautiful until he looks at another and is forced to revise his judgment.

176. *Nahj al-balāghah* sermon 192

177. *Biḥār al-anwār* vol. 13 p. 110 tr. 14

178. Qur'ān 27:14

179. Qur'ān 43:47 says that they "laughed" when they saw his two miracles. It is unlikely that their first reaction to the snake was to laugh. Even Moses, as courageous as he was, reared when he first saw it on the mountain. If they were so unperturbed by the serpent as to simply laugh derisively at it, then we would have to admit that God chose a poor miracle to send to them. Rather, I believe that their first reaction, as I described in the story, was terror. The tradition that mentions that the Pharaoh was on the verge of submitting corroborates this notion. It was only after deliberation that Pharaoh was able to feign derision. It was at this time that they "laughed" in condescension at Moses and his miracles, more as a tactic than a reaction.

they are, as you see, in such a state of poverty and dishonor! Why have they not even been decorated with bracelets of gold?" He said this because he thought the world of his own hoards of gold and because he disparaged the woolen cassocks they wore. If God the Exalted had wanted to lay open for the prophets whom he sent his treasuries and mines of gold and his fruit-laden gardens; if he had wanted to surround them with the birds of the sky and beasts of the land, he would have done so. But if he had done so, there would be no test; there would be no reward for passing those tests; the tidings of reward and punishment would be meaningless; those who accepted the prophets would no longer deserve the reward of those who succeed against tribulation; the believers would no longer deserve the reward of the righteous...[180] Then he admitted to his courtiers who stood around him with an air of nonchalance, "He is indeed a skilled sorcerer."[181] Then, suggestively, he said, "He seeks to expel you from your land with his magic. So what do you advise?"[182]

They were silent at first. Then they said, "He is, as you say, a skilled sorcerer,[183] and he does, as you say, wish to expel us from our land with his magic.[184] Give him and his brother respite for a while, and send heralds to every city[185] to bring you every skilled sorcerer."[186] The Pharaoh had hoped his courtiers would advise to kill Moses, but they did not because they were all of legitimate birth,[187] and no one has the audacity to kill God's prophets except bastards.[188]

---

180. *Nahj al-balāghah* sermon 192

181. Qur'ān 26:34

182. Qur'ān 26:35

183. Qur'ān 7:109

184. Qur'ān 7:110

185. Qur'ān 26:36 and 7:111

186. Qur'ān 26:37 and 7:112

187. *Biḥār al-anwār* vol. 13 p. 137 tr. 50

188. *Kāmil al-ziyārāt* p. 79

Moses and Aaron Return

The Pharaoh readmitted Moses and Aaron into his court. He told them, "What you have shown us is clearly sorcery."[189]

Moses retorted incredulously, "*This* is what you say about truth when it stares you in the face? Do you really think this was sorcery? It most emphatically was not, for sorcerers never succeed."[190]

The Pharaoh persisted to ask rhetorically, "Have you two come to dissuade us from the religion of our forefathers and to establish supremacy for yourselves in this land? Because we believe this to be your motive, we shall never believe in you.[191] Rather, we shall counter your magic with similar magic. So let us set a day for a contest between us which neither you nor we shall fail to attend; a contest to be held in wide open grounds."[192]

Moses saw that further discussion was futile, thus, he proposed, "The day of the contest shall be the Day of Adornment with the people gathered together at high noon."[193]

Preparing for the Day of Adornment

Weeks passed, and the Pharaoh and his advisors made their preparations.[194] From throughout his kingdom, Pharaoh summoned one thousand magicians. He tested their prowess and narrowed their pool to one hundred who were more proficient than the others. Then he tested them again and narrowed their pool to the top eighty sorcerers.[195]

The Pharaoh explained to his sorcerers the task at hand. They told him, "You know that there is no one more skilled in magic

---

189. Qur'ān 10:76

190. Qur'ān 10:77

191. Qur'ān 10:78

192. Qur'ān 20:58

193. Qur'ān 20:59

194. Qur'ān 20:60 and 79:22

195. *Biḥār al-anwār* vol. 13 p. 120 tr. 21

than we. If we defeat Moses in this contest, then what will be our prize?[196] Is there a reward for us if we happen to be the victors?"[197]

He replied, "Of course. You shall, in that case, be my closest counselors,[198] and I shall share my power with you."[199]

They then asked, "And if Moses defeats us and overpowers our magic, then we shall know that what he has is not magic or any sort of illusion, and we shall have no choice but to believe in him and confirm his prophethood."

The Pharaoh patronizingly said, "If Moses defeats you, I too shall confirm his prophethood along with you. But that will not happen. Prepare yourselves well for the great festival!"[200]

The Day of Adornment

On the Day of Adornment, Egypt was abuzz with excitement. Thousands had gathered from far and near to enjoy the festivities and to witness the Pharaoh's contest with Moses. An enormous pavilion was erected for the Pharaoh, Hāmān, and his other courtiers. The Pharaoh's garments were completely covered with tiny plates of shimmering, polished metal. When he stepped into the sunlight, the glare from these garments blinded all who dared look.[201]

It was announced to the people, "If you please, gather together."[202] Then with great fanfare, the Pharaoh set the stage for the contest and explained the stakes. He introduced Moses and Aaron who wore their simple cassocks. He proclaimed to his people, "O my people! Do the kingdom of Egypt and these rivers that run at my feet not belong to me? Do you not perceive?[203] Am I not better than

---

196. *Biḥār al-anwār* vol. 13 p. 120 tr. 21

197. Qur'ān 7:113

198. Qur'ān 7:114

199. *Biḥār al-anwār* vol. 13 p. 121 tr. 21

200. *Biḥār al-anwār* vol. 13 p. 121 tr. 21

201. *Biḥār al-anwār* vol. 13 p. 121 tr. 21

202. Qur'ān 26:39

203. Qur'ān 43:51

this vile person who cannot even speak clearly?[204] Why have no bracelets of gold been cast upon him to match my bracelets, nor have angels come with him as escorts?"[205] Feeding off the energy of the crowd and his overwhelming sense of invincibility, he shook his fists in the air and declared, "I am your highest lord!"[206] In this way he made fools of his people, so they obeyed him. His people were a transgressing lot,[207] for they would never have obeyed him if they had listened to their conscience.

Moses interjected, "May God punish you. Do not fabricate a lie against God, or he will annihilate you with a great punishment. He who fabricates lies surely fails."[208]

Upon hearing this, the sorcerers secretly argued with one another about Moses, for many believed these were not the words of a mere sorcerer.[209]

Oblivious to the argument among the sorcerers, the Pharaoh proclaimed to the people, "These two men are sorcerers whose goal is to expel you from your land using their sorcery and to do away with your outstanding way of life.[210] Therefore, I call on the sorcerers of Egypt to summon their ingenuity and then come forward in ranks. Whoever has the upper hand on this day shall be prosperous."[211] Then to entice his sorcerers, he announced, "Perhaps we shall follow the sorcerers if they be victorious."[212]

---

204. Qur'ān 43:52. Most scholars construe his insult as a reference to the speech impediment Moses had as a child which was removed by God when he made him a prophet. In my view, since he had no impediment, his insult may have been aimed at something as petty as Moses' accent. Perhaps, after living away from Egypt for 10 years, he had acquired an accent, and the Pharaoh was capitalizing on his people's xenophobia.

205. Qur'ān 43:53

206. Qur'ān 79:24

207. Qur'ān 43:54

208. Qur'ān 20:61

209. Qur'ān 20:62

210. Qur'ān 20:63

211. Qur'ān 20:64

212. Qur'ān 26:40

The Sorcerers' Trick

The leader of the sorcerers stepped forward to address Moses. He offered, "Moses, either you cast your spell, or we shall be the first to cast ours."[213]

He replied, "You cast yours first."[214]

The sorcerers acted in unison according to their plan. They pulled ropes from beneath their robes and raised their staffs. As they threw these to the ground, they conjured a force to overpower the senses and emotions of all who looked on. The people saw writhing snakes and felt a shudder of terror surge through their hearts.[215] Even to Moses, their ropes and staffs appeared to wriggle swiftly because of their magic.[216] There were gasps of horror followed by pin-drop silence as people stood mesmerized.

Moses' voice cut through the silence as he exclaimed, "What you have done is nothing but magic. God will debunk your claim to power which is nested in your magic. God never supports the deeds of those who cause corruption.[217] Instead, he will establish the truth through a miracle that requires but a word from him, and he will do this in spite of you criminals."[218]

But as he spoke these words, Moses saw how thoroughly the sorcerers had mesmerized the people. He felt a pang of fear in his heart.[219] It was not fear of failure or of being forsaken by God or of the sorcerers' skill or of the Pharaoh's wrath. He feared that these foolish people would fall for the sorcerers' tricks, and, as a result, those who wished to misguide them would easily rule over them.[220]

---

213. Qur'ān 7:115

214. Qur'ān 7:116

215. Qur'ān 7:116

216. Qur'ān 20:66

217. Qur'ān 10:81

218. Qur'ān 10:82

219. Qur'ān 20:67

220. *Nahj al-balāghah* sermon 4

God fortified him saying, "Moses, do not be afraid. You have the upper hand.[221] Throw what is in your right hand, and it will swallow what they have conjured. What they have conjured is but a magician's trick. And the magician fails wherever he may go."[222]

Moses' Staff

Without a moment's hesitation, Moses threw his staff. It transformed into a giant serpent as it had twice before, on the mountain and in the Pharaoh's court. In an instant, it began swallowing what the sorcerers had conjured.[223] The fanfare of the sorcerers' tricks abruptly stopped. People's vision returned to normal, and their fear subsided.

The Sorcerers Believe

This time, it was the sorcerers who stood aghast. They fully understood what power and skill it had taken them to do their magic. And they knew the limits of the dark arts. As they watched Moses' serpent devour their ropes and staffs, they clearly saw the truth of his claim and the futility of what they had been doing.[224] They murmured, "This is not magic. If it had been magic, our ropes and staffs would have been left intact."[225] They instantly admitted defeat and felt the shame of failure.[226] Then, it occurred to them that their failure as magicians was actually their key to success, for they now knew with utmost certainty that Moses and the God of which he spoke were true. Spontaneously, as if on cue, the

---

221. Qur'ān 20:68

222. Qur'ān 20:69

223. Qur'ān 7:117 and 26:45

224. Qur'ān 7:118

225. *Biḥār al-anwār* vol. 13 p. 110 tr. 14

226. Qur'ān 7:119

sorcerers fell down prostrate.[227] They declared, "We believe in the Lord of all realms,[228] the Lord of Moses and Aaron."[229]

The Pharaoh was infuriated. He saw his kingdom crumbling before him. He intimated to the sorcerers, struggling to contain his fury, "You dare to profess your faith in Moses' Lord without my permission?" Then, in a voice loud enough for the crowds to hear, he roared, still addressing the sorcerers, "It seems Moses is your master who has taught you magic![230] This is clearly a plot you devised in conspiracy with him to expel the people of this city from it. You shall soon know the consequences of these fateful choices of yours."[231] It was a masterful move on the part of the Pharaoh. At once, he managed to disavow himself of the sorcerers, steal the limelight from Moses' victory, and save face before his subjects, all in one fell swoop.

Mass Execution

Without allowing them a chance to defend themselves, he summarily passed judgment upon them. He decreed with rancor, "I shall chop off your hands and your opposing feet, and I shall crucify you, one and all, upon the trunks of these date palms that surround this field. You will soon come to know whose punishment is more severe and more lasting."[232]

Unfazed by his threats, they said:

> Your judgment upon us is of no consequence, for we shall return to our Lord, and it is his judgment that matters.[233] Hereafter, we shall never give preference to you over the manifest proofs that have been presented to us nor to him who has

---

227. Qur'ān 7:120

228. Qur'ān 7:121

229. Qur'ān 7:122

230. Qur'ān 20:70

231. Qur'ān 7:123

232. Qur'ān 7:124 and 20:17

233. Qur'ān 26:50 and 7:125

> created us. Judge as you may; your jurisdiction is but this temporal world. We have decided to believe in our Lord in hopes that, because we are the first to believe,[234] he will forgive us our past iniquities and the magic you compelled us to perform. God is better than you and more lasting.[235] From what we have learned from Moses, we now know that whoever returns to his Lord laden with sin, for him there shall be hell where he will neither live nor die.[236] But whoever returns to him with faith, having done righteous deeds, for such shall be the highest ranks:[237] everlasting forests with streams flowing through them in which they will reside forever.[238] You begrudge us only because we have believed in our Lord's proofs when they were presented to us when you did not."[239]

They then turned their attention to their newfound God and prayed, "Lord, bestow on us the capacity to be patient and let us die in submission to you."240

The Pharaoh was in a quandary. He had lost the contest. His prized sorcerers, whom he had touted so much, had betrayed him. He could no longer convince or fool his people into submission. The only tactic left was to instill fear, for fear would keep his people's conscience in check. He decided to carry out the threat he had issued to the sorcerers.

On the spot, while the crowds still gazed on, he ordered his guards to surround the sorcerers and take them into custody. He

---

234. Qur'ān 26:51

235. Qur'ān 20:71

236. Qur'ān 20:74

237. Qur'ān 20:75

238. Qur'ān 20:76

239. Qur'ān 7:126

240. Qur'ān 7:126

pronounced his sentence against them for the crime of disavowing him as their god. One by one, he had them brought before his pavilion. His executioner severed their right arms at the elbow and then their left legs at the knee. Then two other guards dragged their writhing bodies, one by one, to the date palms that encircled the fair grounds. They strung each bleeding corpse upon a separate tree. Within the hour, the Day of Adornment was transformed into a bloodbath. Before the royal pavilion lay a pile of severed limbs, and all around the field hung 80 corpses dressed in fine robes, each missing an arm and a leg.[241]

Moses had been relieved, even elated for a few moments following his victory. He had found an army of devout believers in the most unlikely of people. But no sooner had they believed in the truth than they were snatched away, and Moses' brief moment of happiness was enshrouded in deep sorrow for the martyrdom of these noble souls.

After the Contest

Moses' success in the contest proved a great boon to his burgeoning movement. Even though Pharaoh had managed to distract people from comprehending the true meaning of the outcome and thereby mitigated the impact of the blow, he could no longer persecute the Israelites with the impunity he had come to enjoy. Instead he was forced to try to ignore them altogether.

Nonetheless, only small numbers of young Israelites joined Moses. Most of the others refrained in part because of a residual fear of the Pharaoh. Though his policy toward them had temporarily changed, they felt there was no guarantee that he would not as suddenly resume his former persecution of Israelites in general, and Moses' followers in particular, for he was a tyrant and he was an unrestrained despot. Additionally, they were afraid of the Israelite leaders who ironically were more interested in maintaining the

---

241. The description of this massacre is my own. Besides the threat that the Pharaoh issued to them, we have no indication that they were killed or any description of how they might have been killed. However, it seems far-fetched to think that the Pharaoh would have let their transgression slide.

status quo in which they enjoyed a place at the top of their society, even if it was only a society of slaves.[242]

Korah's Betrayal

In particular, they feared Korah.[243] He was an Israelite[244] from the tribe of Levi, Moses' tribe. In fact, he was Moses' maternal cousin.[245] God had given him so much treasure that its keys alone proved heavy for a group of strong men.[246] Despite being an Israelite, he betrayed his people and Moses[247] and joined ranks with the Pharaoh.

Korah arrogantly asserted, "I have been given all this wealth because of my own knowledge and skill." He had forgotten that

---

242. Qur᾿ān 10:83

243. He is known in the Qur᾿ān as *Qārūn*. His story is mentioned in detail in Qur᾿ān 28:76–81. He is also mentioned in several verses alongside Pharaoh and Hāmān. While the major commentaries do not claim this, I believe that Korah, though an Israelite, had joined Pharaoh's court. He had amassed tremendous wealth, and, apparently, he felt the status quo would better preserve his wealth than Moses' reforms. My main evidence for this claim is verse 43:23–4. God says, "We sent Moses with our signs and our clear proof to the Pharaoh, Hāmān, and Korah at which they said, 'He is a sorcerer and a mendicant.'" These verses make it clear that Korah was also part of the Pharaoh's court for the statement, "He is a sorcerer and a mendicant," is attributed to all three together. Accordingly, the Biblical story must be misplaced, for the Bible tells his story in Numbers 16 along with the stories of Dathan and Abiram. It narrates almost the same story as Qur᾿ān 28:76–81 but places these events after the exodus from Egypt while they are wandering in the desert. Since Korah had shown allegiance to the Pharaoh during the Egyptian period, it is not possible for him to have been spared until the time of the exodus. God would have purged him from the ranks of the Israelites during the exodus. Furthermore, the Qur᾿ān explicitly says that he and his home (*dār*) were swallowed up. The word *dār* does not refer to a tent. Finally, even if he had been allowed to live that long, and his tent were called a *dār*, it seems unlikely that he could have hauled all his wealth into the desert for forty years.

244. Qur᾿ān 28:76

245. *al-Burhān fī tafsīr al-qur᾿ān* vol. 4 p. 289

246. Qur᾿ān 28:76

247. Qur᾿ān 28:76

God had destroyed people before him who were more powerful than he and more numerous for such empty claims.[248]

Moses and his fellow Israelites admonished him, "Do not exult. God does not like the exultant.[249] Use what God has given you to attain the abode of the hereafter. Do not forget the formidable share that has been given to you in this world, and be benevolent as God has been benevolent to you. And do not cause corruption in this land, for God does not like agents of corruption."[250]

Nonetheless, he flaunted his wealth and finery before his people.[251] Those among them who were infatuated with the life of this world would say, "We wish we could have the likes of what Korah has been given. He is very fortunate."[252]

But others who had been blessed with sound knowledge told them, "Woe to you. God's reward is better in the eyes of one who has faith and acts righteously, but no one attains it except the perseverant."[253]

Because of his pomp and arrogance,[254] God caused the earth to swallow Korah along with his mansion. He had no army to protect him from God nor could he rescue himself. The next day at dawn, when Korah's fate became known, those who had longed to be in his place the day before were saying, "Amazing! It seems we were wrong—God increases and withholds the provision from whomever he wishes from his servants. If God had not shown us favor, he might have made the earth swallow us too. It appears that the faithless are actually *not* felicitous."[255]

---

248. Qurʾān 28:78

249. Qurʾān 28:76

250. Qurʾān 28:77

251. *Man lā yaḥḍuruhu al-faqīh* vol. 4 p. 13

252. Qurʾān 28:79

253. Qurʾān 28:80

254. Qurʾān 28:81

255. Qurʾān 28:82

Building a Community

God told Moses and his brother, "Settle your people in the city, and let your houses face each other, and maintain the prayer, and give good news to the faithful."[256] This command gave Moses the inspiration to take practical steps toward organizing his people as a free and functioning society. They moved close together and built their houses so that their doors faced one another, thereby facilitating easy communication and commerce among themselves. They built a place of worship and gathered regularly for prayer there.

Moses urged his small group of followers to trust in God saying, "My people, if you have faith in God and are among those who submit themselves wholly to him, then put your trust in him."[257]

In response, they prayed, "In God do we place our trust. O Lord! Do not make us a test for these wrongdoers, and deliver us by your mercy from these faithless people."[258]

Thus, Moses and Aaron were able to lay the foundations of a Godly society.

The Golden Heifer

In this community there lived a righteous young man with his father and mother. The father owned a prized heifer with an unblemished golden coat. He felt this heifer was so perfect, and he enjoyed gazing at her so much, that he never made her do any work. He simply let her graze and come and go as she pleased.

His son was an ardent follower of Moses. He once heard Moses extol Muḥammad and ʿAlī and their family, and he too began praying for them and praising them over all God's creatures. He worked as a merchant. He stored his merchandise in a room in his house which he kept under lock and key. When he was out, he left the key with his father so that his father could open the room and let customers view the merchandise.

---

256. Qurʾān 10:87

257. Qurʾān 10:84

258. Qurʾān 10:85–6

One day, he brought home some customers who wished to see his merchandise. When the young man went to retrieve the key from his father, he saw that his father was sleeping, and he knew that, as usual, the key would be tucked beneath his pillow. The young man, out of consideration for his father, decided not to disturb his father's rest even if it meant losing his customers. When his father awoke, he realized what had happened and that his son had sacrificed a profitable sale for his comfort. He gave him his prize heifer to compensate him for the lost sale and to reward him for his selfless devotion.[259]

Unsolved Murder

Around the same time, there was a murder in the Israelite community.[260] A man's body was found, and people began to blame

---

259. *Biḥār al-anwār* vol. 13 p. 259 tr. 1 and p. 262 tr. 2

260. Two comments are significant here.

- First, there is no clear indication in the sources when the incident of the heifer took place. Moses was obviously present, so it must have occurred after he returned from Midian. The traditions mention that it took place in a city, thus it must have occurred before the exodus. It seems that the Israelites exercised a level of autonomy in dealing with the murder, thus it must have taken place during the brief window after the Festival and before the Pharaoh's renewed crackdown. Based on all these facts, I have placed the incident here in the story as a best guess.
- Second, the traditions mention various motives for the murder. I will summarize them here. As it is not possible to determine which motive is correct, and the motive has little bearing on the story, I have chosen one that fits better with the overall narrative.
    - Two cousins proposed to a young woman. She accepted the righteous one and rejected the wicked one. The latter became jealous, killed the former, and then took the body to Moses and pretended not to know who killed his cousin (*Biḥār al-anwār* vol. 13 p. 259 tr. 1 and p. 265 tr. 3).
    - A man killed his relative and then framed one of the best tribes of the Israelites and demanded blood money from them (*Biḥār al-anwār* vol. 13 p. 262 tr. 2).
    - Three cousins proposed to their female cousin. She chose one and the other two killed him and then acted as though they mourned

one another for his murder.[261] Without any clear evidence or known witnesses,[262] Moses ruled that all who were potentially involved must swear to their innocence with the following words, "By God, the Almighty and Severe, Lord of the Israelites, who has favored Muḥammad and his family over all of his creation, we solemnly swear that we did not kill this man, and we do not know who killed him." If they all swore thus to their innocence, he would distribute the burden of paying the blood money to the victim's heirs upon all of their shoulders. They were given the choice to swear their innocence, admit their guilt, identify the real murderer, or face imprisonment.[263]

All who were involved felt that this resolution was too harsh. They exclaimed, "O Prophet of God! You penalize us so heavily when we have committed no crime. And you make us swear such intense oaths, yet our oaths vindicate us of nothing."[264]

God heard their complaints and decided to offer them a way to uncover the identity of the true murderer and, with the same stroke of a brush, to further reward the young man who had been such a devotee of Moses and Muḥammad and so good to his father.

Slaughter a Cow

Moses told his people, "God commands you to slaughter a cow."

They asked, "Do you take us for fools?" They could not comprehend how slaughtering a cow had anything to do with solving the murder.

---

him (*Biḥār al-anwār* vol. 13 p. 267 tr. 7).

- A rich man had only one nephew as an heir. The heir was poor and could not wait for his uncle to die, so he killed him to hasten his inheritance (*Biḥār al-anwār* vol. 13 p. 274).

261. Qur'ān 2:72

262. Certainly Moses would have had access to knowledge of the murderer. However, the prophets were meant to be role models in, among other things, the dispensation of justice. For this reason, he acted based on normally accessible information, not on divinely bestowed information.

263. *Biḥār al-anwār* vol. 13 p. 266 tr. 6

264. *Biḥār al-anwār* vol. 13 p. 267 tr. 6

Moses responded, "I seek refuge in God lest I should be one of the senseless who jests with the commands of God."[265]

They saw that he was serious, so they said, "Ask your Lord on our behalf that he clarify for us what kind of cow it is that we must slaughter."[266] They could have slaughtered any sort of cow, and it would have sufficed, but they were presumptuous in their questioning and sought a way to undermine God's wisdom, so he tightened the reigns and made their task more difficult.[267]

Moses asked God and told them, "He says, 'It is a cow, neither too old nor too young—rather, middle-aged, between the two.' Do what you have been commanded."[268]

They said again, "Ask your Lord on our behalf that he clarify for us its color."[269]

He asked God and told them, "He says, 'It is golden—brilliant gold—pleasing to those who gaze on it.'"[270]

They said again, "Ask your Lord on our behalf that he clarify for us precisely what kind of cow it is that we must slaughter, for all cows appear the same to us. We shall, if God wills, be guided to the right cow."[271]

Once again, Moses asked God and told them, "He says it is a cow neither broken to till the earth nor to water the crops; healthy and without blemish."[272]

Finally, as though struck by an epiphany, they said, "*Now* you have come forth with the truth."[273]

---

265. Qur'ān 2:67

266. Qur'ān 2:68

267. *Biḥār al-anwār* vol. 13 p. 266 tr. 4

268. Qur'ān 2:68

269. Qur'ān 2:69

270. Qur'ān 2:69

271. Qur'ān 2:70

272. Qur'ān 2:71

273. Qur'ān 2:71

A Hefty Price

In the interim, the young man whose father had given him his golden heifer saw a dream. In the dream, he met Prophet Muḥammad and Imam ʿAlī along with their progeny. They told him, "You have been our devotee, and we would like to present you in this life with some of your reward for this devotion. When your people come to you to buy your cow, do not sell it without first consulting your mother, for God will tell her a price that will ensure your well-being and that of your progeny."[274]

It happened just as they had predicted. The next day, a delegation of Israelites came asking after the young man's heifer. He asked his mother, and she set the price at as much gold as the heifer's hide would hold.[275] They complained to Moses that such an exorbitant price was beyond what they were prepared to pay. He explained to them that it was their own fault for being presumptuous with God rather than submitting to his first command. He advised that they seek the help of some wealthy individuals to raise the funds.[276] In the end, they bought the heifer, promised to pay the agreed amount, and slaughtered it, but only with great reluctance.[277]

When they had slaughtered the heifer, Moses told them to sever its tail and strike the dead man's body with it.[278] They did as they were told, but nothing happened. They asked Moses, "Where is the verdict that your Lord promised us?"

Moses replied, "My Lord's promise is true. There must be some other problem."

He asked God who told him, "I never fail in my promise, but these people must first pay the young man the agreed price. Only then will I allow this murdered man to be revived." They gathered their

---

274. *Biḥār al-anwār* vol. 13 p. 269 tr. 7

275. *Biḥār al-anwār* vol. 13 p. 266 tr. 5

276. There is not evidence for this. However, I can imagine no other way for slaves of Egypt to pay such a hefty price.

277. Qurʾān 2:71

278. Qurʾān 2:73 and *Biḥār al-anwār* vol. 13 p. 260 tr. 1

money and filled the heifer's hide with gold and begrudgingly gave it to the young man.

When they struck the dead man again, he sprung to life. He identified his two cousins as his murderers and explained that their motive had been jealousy over his marriage to their mutual cousin. Moses ordered these two men to be executed, and the entire affair was resolved.[279]

Reward For Devotion

One man confided in Moses, "I do not know which is more unusual—that God raised this man and made him speak or that he enriched this young man with such immense wealth."

God told Moses to tell the Israelites, "If any of you wishes for me to give him a good life in this world and a high station in my proximity, then he should act as this young man has acted. He but heard Moses mention Muḥammad and ʿAlī and their family, and he began praying for them and praising them over all of my creatures. For this reason, and for the concern he shows his father, I diverted this immense amount of money to him so that he may benefit from my blessings, be honored among men by bestowing gifts, gain others' love by showing kindness to them, and eschew the guiles of his enemies by earning their friendship."[280]

The young man asked Moses, "How shall I guard such immense wealth from my enemies and those who are jealous of me?"

Moses told him, "Send prayers on Muḥammad and his family just as you used to before you were given this wealth. He who provided you with this wealth for the sake of such prayers will certainly protect it for you for the sake of such prayers as long as you remain steadfast in your beliefs." The young man did as he was instructed, and God protected his wealth for him as long as he lived.

A Life Redeemed

When the newly-revived dead man heard God's promise, he prayed, "O God! I beg you with the same prayer that this young man has

279. *Biḥār al-anwār* vol. 13 p. 270 tr. 7

280. *ibid.*

offered for Muḥammad and his family that you allow me to remain alive so that I may live happily with my wife; that you protect me against my enemies and those who are jealous of me; and that you bless me through my life with her."

God told Moses to tell him, "You were meant to live sixty years. Because of these heartfelt prayers of yours, I shall extend your life an additional seventy for a total of 130 years.[281] As long as you live, your senses shall be intact, your mind shall be sound, and your desires shall be virile so that you may avail yourself of the lawful pleasures of this world. You shall not die before your wife; and she shall not die before you. When she dies, so shall you die, and you shall enter paradise together."

Then God told Moses:

> If those two murderers had asked me, with the same conviction and through the same prayers as these young men, to protect them against jealousy and to make them content with what I had provided them, I would have done so. If, after committing the murder, they had repented and asked me, in this way, to keep their sin concealed, I would have done so. I would have diverted these people from their insistence on knowing the murderer, and I would have found some other way to bestow all this wealth on this righteous young man. If, after having their sin revealed to all, they had repented and asked me, in this way, to make people forget what they had done, I would have satisfied the victim's heirs and made them forgo retribution and made everyone forget what crime they had committed. This is grace that I dispense to whom I wish, for I am the Dispenser of vast Grace. But I deprive of my grace whom I wish, for I am the Almighty and Wise.[282]

---

281. This is a clear example of *badā'* through which God changes his apportionment because of the choices we make.

282. *Biḥār al-anwār* vol. 13 p. 271–2 tr. 7

Controlling the Rain

During this period, the Israelites were able to farm for themselves. Seeing that God listened to Moses' prayers, the Israelites decided to ask God if he would give them control over the rain so that they could make it rain and make it stop at will. In this way, they hoped to maximize their yield. God conceded, and commanded the angels of rain to answer to Moses, and for Moses to base his command on the will of his people.

They planted all kinds of crops and told Moses to make rain in abundance. In a short time, their plants were many times their normal size. At the end of the season, they were excited at the prospect of an enormous harvest. Their hopes were dashed when they saw that their enormous plants had produced nothing of worth.

They became angry and complained to Moses. But he explained to them that God is the All-Wise. He makes the rain fall in due measure to ensure that they are provided for. He gave them control only to teach them that they lack the knowledge to manage such affairs on their own. Rather, they must trust in God as their provider.[283]

Return to Persecution

During these years, as their followers increased and their movement gained traction, there was renewed talk among the upper echelons of Egyptian society about Moses' troublesome activities. They came to the Pharaoh and said, "Will you leave Moses and his people to cause corruption in the land and to abandon you with your gods?"

The Pharaoh was elated to see that he once again had his people's support to root out the Israelites. He replied, "We shall once again slaughter their sons and spare their women. We can do this with utter impunity, for we are dominant over them."[284]

Hamān counseled that killing their newborn sons would not be enough to stop them. He advised that they round up all of Moses'

283. *Biḥār al-anwār* vol. 13 p. 340 tr. 17

284. Qur'ān 7:127

followers and imprison them.[285] This would strip Moses of his support. Those who believed in him would be in prison, and those who did not would be too scared to join.

News of the Pharaoh's abrupt change in policy hit Moses' followers hard. All but the most steadfast were confirmed in their fear, for now they would be singled out for persecution for having joined with Moses. Moses urged them saying, "Turn to God for help and persevere. And remember that this land belongs to God. He bestows it on whom he wishes from among his servants, and the final outcome will be in favor of the God-fearing."[286]

The most jaded of the Israelites smugly rebuffed his prophecy and words of encouragement saying, "We were tormented before you came to us, and we are now to be tormented after you have come to us," as if to say that his promises to free them from the Pharaoh's clutches were false.

Moses replied, "I am still hopeful that your Lord will destroy your enemy and let you inherit their land." He knew that God would fulfill his promise and that any delay was only a test. But he warned them that the fulfillment of this promise would not be the end but the continuation of a life-long test. For this reason, he said, "Then, after giving you their land, he will see how you act."[287]

Besieged by Calamities

God saw their frailty and had mercy on them. He besieged Pharaoh and his fellow Egyptians with a series of calamities.[288] He wished

285. *Biḥār al-anwār* vol. 13 p. 111 tr. 1

286. Qur'ān 7:128

287. Qur'ān 7:129

288. The Qur'ān tells us that Moses was given nine signs (17:101). While it is true that he performed many more than nine miracles, those performed for the benefit of the Pharaoh numbered only nine. Of the nine, two, his staff and his white hand, were miracles but not calamities, and each is referred to in the Qur'ān as an *āyah* or "sign" (43:48) and *burhān* or "proof" (28:32). The other seven were both miracles and calamities, and each is referred to in the Qur'ān as an *āyah* or "sign" (17:101) and *ʿadhāb* or "punishment" (43:48). Verse 7:130 mentions one—years of drought and loss of produce (there is some discussion over whether these are two punishments or just one, but I will shortly argue that they constitute one). Verse 7:133 mentions another five—a catastrophic storm, locusts, beetles, frogs, and blood. Verse 7:134 mentions the seventh and final one—a plague on their livestock. It is true that two traditions (*Biḥār al-anwār* vol. 13 p. 136 tr. 45–6) name the parting of the Red Sea and the stone from which twelve springs flowed instead of the first and seventh calamities I have enumerated here. However, considering the wording of the Qur'ān, I believe that these two should not be considered part of the seven.

The Bible (Exodus 7:14 to 12:30) also mentions a series of calamities which it calls "plagues," some of which match the seven calamities mentioned in the Qur'ān. In the following table, I have listed all the plagues from the Bible next to the seven calamities from the Qur'ān.

	The Seven Calamities in the Qur'ān	**The Plagues in the Bible**
1	Years of drought and loss of produce	Hail
2	Hailstorm	Locusts
3	Locusts	Gnats
4	Beetles	Frogs
5	Frogs	Blood
6	Blood	Boils
7	Plague on livestock	Flies
8		Plague on livestock
9		Darkness
10		Death of the firstborn

Five of the seven of the calamities mentioned in the Qur'ān (drought and loss of produce, locusts, frogs, blood, and plague) are clear in that we know what each one entailed. The other two, *al-ṭūfān* and *al-qummal,* are not as clear since the lexicographers and Qur'ānic commentators have various opinions as to their meaning.

A *ṭūfān* is literally something that "encompasses." It usually refers to a flood. For instance, the Qur'ān refers to Noah's flood as a *ṭūfān* (29:14). Most commentators have construed *ṭūfān* in Moses' story also to be a flood of the Nile. This interpretation is problematic for the following reasons:

- The Nile was naturally prone to flooding. In fact, the annual flooding between July and October was crucial for the success of agriculture in Egypt from ancient times until 1970 when the Aswan Dam was built. Egyptologists believe that the ancient Egyptians constructed their houses in places and in ways that mitigate the harmful effects of these annual floods. It follows that a flood would not be an unusual occurrence for the Egyptians that would cause much distress, unless, of course, we assume that this particular flood was more catastrophic than usual.

- The nature of a flood is that it encompasses an affected area indiscriminately. Unless it was by another miracle, the flood would naturally have devastated Egyptian and Israelite homes alike. However, it is clear that these calamities were sent only against the Egyptians and that the Israelites were spared. Perhaps it is to account for this that al-Zamakhsharī explains that the flood only affected the Egyptians and was miraculously held back from the Israelites homes (see *al-Kashshāf*). While this is possible, there does not appear to be any evidence for this.
- There is no flood mentioned in the Bible. While this by itself does not constitute evidence against this interpretation, it does further confirm that construing *ṭūfān* as a flood is problematic.
- Many commentators have offered other interpretations for *ṭūfān*. For instance, al-Bayḍāwī, after favoring "flood," mentions that it could mean a leprosy epidemic, death, or the plague.

In conclusion, I have chosen to translate *ṭūfān* as a "hailstorm" borrowing from the Old Testament. While there is no more evidence for this than the other interpretations of *ṭūfān*, it is easier to imagine how a hailstorm could selectively strike one part of Egypt and not another without need for an additional miracle.

There are numerous opinions on *qummal*. Commentators have construed them to be small monkeys, locust nymphs, beetles, and gnats, among other things. According to the recension that reads *qaml*, they are construed as lice or ticks. A tradition from *Tafsīr al-Qummī* asserts that, as a result of the *qummal* infestation, the Egyptians' crops were destroyed indicating that it was an infestation of their crops, not of their bodies. *Tafsīr Nimūneh* also draws the same conclusion. Accordingly, I have construed *qummal* to be beetles while wholeheartedly admitting that this could be incorrect.

It was challenging determining what the seventh calamity was. Most commentators have construed "years of drought and loss of produce" (7:130) as two different calamities. However, when they try to explain the difference, they are not able to separate them to my satisfaction. Loss of fruits and other produce are natural results of drought, so it is not meaningful to call them two different calamities. To find the seventh calamity, I looked to 7:134 which mentions a *rijz* or "punishment" from the sky. Admittedly the word *rijz* is used in the Qur'ān to refer to various kinds of punishment. For this reason, most commentators have construed verse 7:134–5 to be a reference to the repeated pattern of sin, calamity, repentance, relief, and a return to sin in which the Egyptians were engaged, not as a reference to a seventh and independent calamity. However, a

at once to give strength to the believers and to break the Egyptians' will in hopes that they too may come to believe.[289]

Droughts and Loss of Produce

The first calamity was a series of droughts.[290] God withheld rain, and without rain, the Nile receded and failed to flood. Without the annual flood, the land could not be replenished with silt. Their crops withered. With a depressed water table, fruit trees failed to produce their normal harvest. The Israelites were accustomed to eking out an existence on next to nothing, so they were immune to the effects of drought and famine.[291] But the drought hit the Egyptians hard. They recalled the Pharaoh's oration on the Day of Adornment when he had said, "O my people! Do the kingdom of Egypt and these rivers that run at my feet not belong to me? Do

---

few commentators (namely *al-Taḥrīr wa al-tanwīr* and *Majma῾ al-bayān*) mention the possibility that *rijz* was the seventh punishment and that it entailed either a plague or a hailstorm. I have construed it as a plague—not a plague of humans but of livestock. I believe it cannot be a plague of humans because the apparent spirit behind these seven calamities was to warn the Egyptians and leave them no excuse for refusing to listen to Moses, not to kill them. Accordingly, none of the other calamities caused death, and so I believe this one also did not cause death, at least not human death.

It is also worth noting that there is no apparent crescendo in the severity of these calamities. It is tempting to think that verse 43:48 which says, "Not a sign did we show them but that it was greater than the other," is speaking of these calamities. However, this is incorrect. This portion of verse 43:48 is speaking of the staff and the white hand, not the calamities. Then, when it mentions, "We gripped them with punishment in hopes that they would return to us," "punishment" is a reference to the calamities.

289. Qur᾿ān 43:48

290. Qur᾿ān 7:130

291. The underlying assumption is that all of these calamities affected the Egyptians, not the Israelites. The only way I can imagine for a drought not to affect a segment of the population is if that segment of the population is immune to the effects of the drought because they have always lived on drought-like rations.

you not perceive?"[292] So they now begged, "O King! Make the Nile flow freely once again."

He lied to them, "I am not pleased with my subjects. That is why I have made it stop flowing."

They argued, "O King! If you do not make the river flow, we will have no choice but to seek out another god besides you."

Seeing little choice, the Pharaoh ordered his subjects to accompany him to the river bank. He made them stand in one place while he went off on his own where they could no longer see him or hear him. He knelt on the ground and lay his cheek upon the earth and raised his index finger toward the sky and said, "Lord! I have come here to you as a lowly servant comes before his master. I know that nobody can make the Nile flow but you, so please make it flow."

When he returned to his people, they were cheering and celebrating for torrents of rain were falling, and the Nile was flowing as it had not flowed in a while. He told them that it was he who had done this for them, and they all fell prostrate before him.

The Pharaoh Condemns Himself

Later, Gabriel appeared before the Pharaoh in the form of a nobleman from Egypt. He said, "O King! Counsel me on what I should do with a servant of mine."

The Pharaoh asked, "What is your difficulty with him?"

Gabriel said, "I gave this servant authority over my other servants. I entrusted him with my keys, but he has rebelled against me—he has allied with my enemies, and he is an enemy to my allies."

Pharaoh shook his head and said, "What a terrible servant you have! If I were in your place, I would drown him in the Red Sea."

Gabriel looked pleased with the counsel. He asked, "O King! Please write this advice for me."

The Pharaoh called for paper, pen, and ink, and he wrote, "The punishment for a servant who rebels against his master and aligns

292. Qur'ān 43:51

with his enemies and is an enemy to his allies is that he be drowned in the Red Sea."

Gabriel pressed, "O King! Please place your royal seal upon this letter of yours." He complied and then handed the letter to him which Gabriel stowed for safe-keeping.[293]

Recurring Droughts

Again the rain stopped. The Pharaoh called on Moses and asked him to call off the drought. Moses let him know that he would do so only if the Pharaoh promised to release the Israelite prisoners and cease all aggression against his people. The Pharaoh promised, and the rain fell. But again Pharaoh told his people that it was he who had made it rain.[294]

Again the rain stopped. The Pharaoh told his people the drought was an ill omen brought on by Moses and his followers, though the true cause of what they termed "ill omens" was actually God's retribution for their ill actions, but most of his people did not realize this.[295] He made more empty promises, God let the rain fall, he reneged on his promises, the rain stopped, and so the cycle continued for years. Finally, the Pharaoh declared to Moses, "Whatever so-called 'miracle' you may bring us to bewitch us, we are not going to believe in you."[296]

Hailstorm

Next, God sent a catastrophic hailstorm upon them.[297] The hailstones rained only upon the Egyptians' neighborhoods, causing damage where they fell but stayed clear of the area occupied by Moses and his followers. After a few such storms, Moses came to the Pharaoh and demanded the release of all Israelite prisoners and cessation of all aggression against Moses' followers. The Pharaoh managed to

---

293. *Biḥār al-anwār* vol. 13 p. 132–3 tr. 37

294. Qur'ān 7:131

295. *ibid.*

296. Qur'ān 7:132

297. Qur'ān 7:132

condescend, "O magician! Invoke your Lord for us by the covenant he has made with you. We will then heed your guidance."

But when the storm stopped, Hāmān advised him against conceding anything to Moses. He said, "If you do, Moses will conquer you and seize Egypt for himself."[298] The Pharaoh accepted this advice and refused to honor his promise.[299]

Locusts

The next year, when their grains were ripe to harvest, God told Moses to point his staff toward the eastern and western horizons. Grey clouds of locusts swarmed like rain clouds from both directions and descended upon their crops. Within minutes they had decimated the food supply of Egypt.[300] Again, there were empty promises, gracious relief, and betrayal at the egging of Hāmān.

Beetles

The next year, God told Moses to strike the earth with his staff. Millions of beetles crawled out of the ground and began devouring their crops.[301] Again, there were empty promises, gracious relief, and betrayal at the egging of Hāmān.

Frogs

The next year, God told Moses to stand on the bank of the Nile and call every frog that lived among the reeds to come to shore. Hordes of these creatures entered the city and overwhelmed the Egyptians, filling their houses and getting into their food and water supplies.[302] Again, there were empty promises, gracious relief, and betrayal at the egging of Hāmān.

---

298. *Biḥār al-anwār* vol. 13 p. 111–112 tr. 15

299. Qur'ān 43:49–50

300. *Biḥār al-anwār* vol. 13 p. 115 tr. 16

301. *Biḥār al-anwār* vol. 13 p. 115 tr. 16. This tradition seems to describe *qummal* as lice while another tradition describes them as a plant pest.

302. *Biḥār al-anwār* vol. 13 p. 114 tr. 16

Blood

The next year, God told Moses to strike the water of the Nile with his staff. In an instant, the water turned to blood. When the Israelites drew water from it, the water was pure, but when the Egyptians tried to drink it, it would remain blood. One Egyptian woman, in her vain effort to thwart God's plan, ordered her Israelite slave to draw water for her and serve it to her. But as soon as it touched her own lips, it turned to blood.[303] Again, there were empty promises, gracious relief, and betrayal at the egging of Hāmān. They acted arrogantly, for they were an evil people.[304]

Plague on Livestock

Their last chance came in the form of a plague on their livestock.[305] Once again, only the livestock of the Egyptians was affected. When it struck, they begged Moses saying, "If you remove this plague, we will certainly believe in you and we will let the Israelites leave with you."[306] But when God lifted the plague from their midst, they reneged on their promise yet again.[307]

Neither God nor Moses nor Aaron was naïve in believing the Pharaoh's empty promises. The purpose of these calamities was to awaken his and his people's conscience or to seal their fates if they chose to ignore the clear miracles that Moses performed before their very eyes. When the calamities had run their courses, all who remained with Pharaoh had proven to the world that their hearts, like his, were blind to truth.

---

303. *Biḥār al-anwār* vol. 13 p. 114 tr. 16

304. Qur'ān 7:133

305. Qur'ān 7:134. I explained in an earlier footnote why I have construed *rijz* as a plague and as a seventh calamity. I also explained why I believe it was not a human plague but perhaps a plague on their livestock.

306. Qur'ān 7:134

307. Qur'ān 7:135

Shift in Strategy

From here on, the focus of Moses' and Aaron's mission in Egypt changed. They had fulfilled their duty to call Pharaoh and his people, largely to no avail. Now, their entire focus centered around the Israelites. In prayer, Moses said, "O Lord! You have given the Pharaoh and his courtiers glamour and wealth in this temporal world, and, as a result, they have led people away from your path. O Lord! Blot out their wealth, and harden their hearts so that they do not believe until they see the painful punishment."[308]

As Moses prayed, Aaron and all the angels said, "Amen," in chorus.[309]

God replied, "Your supplication has been answered, so be steadfast, but do not follow the way of those who are ignorant among the Israelites."[310] At once, God promised them relief from the clutches of Pharaoh and foreshadowed the perils that lay ahead in their dealings with their own people. While God's answer came instantly, in his wisdom, he decided, unbeknownst to them, to delay fulfilling his promise for another forty years.[311]

Campaign to Kill Moses

In the aftermath of the seven calamities, Egypt was in ruins, and Pharaoh was all the more desperate to be rid of Moses completely. His advisors had sanctioned the persecution of Israelite slaves, but with the power Moses wielded, they were loath to harm him directly. Pharaoh now felt he had reason enough to convince them otherwise.

He summoned Moses to his court. He recounted all the upheaval Moses had caused and pleaded with his advisors saying, "Let me slay Moses, and let him go on invoking his lord while I do it. I do not care, for his lord will not be able to save him. I fear that Moses will change your religion or bring forth more corruption in the

308. Qur'ān 10:88

309. *Biḥār al-anwār* vol. 13 p. 135 tr. 42

310. Qur'ān 10:89

311. *Biḥār al-anwār* vol. 13 p. 128 tr. 29

land than he already has."[312] A hall full of nodding heads evinced a near consensus among the members of the court. The Pharaoh, eager to be rid of his nemesis and too impatient to risk waiting on an executioner, unsheathed his dagger and advanced toward Moses.

Moses prayed, "I seek the protection of my Lord and your Lord from every arrogant person who does not believe in the Day of Reckoning."[313]

As the Pharaoh raised his hand to strike, his hand trembled. He was of legitimate birth, and no one of legitimate birth has the depravity to kill a prophet.[314]

The Believer From the House of the Pharaoh

Suddenly, and to the Pharaoh's relief, in an uncharacteristically bold voice, Ezekiel intoned, "Will you kill a man for saying, 'My Lord is God,' when he brings you manifest proofs from your Lord?" It was Ezekiel, who had never worshiped an idol a day in his life,[315] who had helped Moses escape from Egypt so many years before. Ever since, he had been a silent witness to all that had passed between Moses and his own cousin, the Pharaoh. He believed wholeheartedly in every word Moses preached, but, with the utmost tact, he had completely concealed his faith. The Pharaoh stopped in his tracks and lowered his blade. He glared at Ezekiel as he continued, "Should he be lying, his lie will be to his own detriment. But if he is truthful, that means you are profligate liars, and at least some of what he promises will afflict you, for God does not guide one who is a profligate liar.[316] My people, granted

---

312. Qur'ān 40:26

313. Qur'ān 40:27

314. *Kāmil al-ziyārāt* p.78

315. *Biḥār al-anwār* vol. 13 p. 161 tr. 2

316. Qur'ān 40:28. While all the statements of Ezekiel are quoted in one section of *Ghāfir*, I do not believe they were all spoken in one gathering for the following reasons:

- The content of each section is different. In the first section, his tone is impartial and removed. However, in the following sections, he makes

that today sovereignty belongs to you as you dominate over the land. However, who will help us against God's punishment should it overtake us?"

The Pharaoh tried desperately to sound as even-keeled as Ezekiel as he told his court, "I just show you things the way I see them, and I only guide you to the path of rectitude."[317] But the damage was done. Ezekiel's words had struck a chord with their intellects, and they could see no sense in killing Moses.

In the coming months, Ezekiel began speaking in small gatherings of Egyptians wherever he thought his words might have an effect. In one such gathering, he said:

> My people, I fear for you a day like the day that met the heathen factions of old[318]—like the divine punishment that repeatedly overtook the people of Noah, ʿĀd, Thamūd, and those who came after them. And what was meted out to them was undoubtedly just, for God does not desire any injustice for his servants.[319] My people, I fear for you the day of shouts and calls[320]—a day when you will turn to flee though you will have none to protect you from God, for whomever God leads astray has no guide.[321] Centuries ago, Joseph had

---

it clear that he is a believer. Had he said these things in the initial exchange with the Pharaoh, he would not have succeeded in stopping him from killing Moses.

- The usage of the particle *wāw* in 40:30 and 40:38 shows a disconnect between what comes after and what went before.
- The interjection of Pharaoh's request to Hāmān to build him a tower. This request is a non-sequitur with respect to Ezekiel's previous soliloquy, therefore, it must be an independent incident, and, therefore, the subsequent statements from Ezekiel must have been spoken at different gatherings from the first.

317. Qur'ān 40:29

318. Qur'ān 40:30

319. Qur'ān 40:31

320. Qur'ān 40:32

321. Qur'ān 40:33

> brought you manifest proofs, but you remained in doubt concerning what he brought you. When he died, you thought, 'God will never send another messenger after him.' That is how God leads astray those who are profligate and skeptical,[322] those who dispute the signs of God without having any proof come to them. Such disputation is outrageous to God and to those who have faith. This is how God seals the heart of every arrogant tyrant.[323]

In another gathering, he said:

> My people, follow me. I will guide you to the path of rectitude.[324] My people, the life of this world is only fleeting enjoyment while the hereafter is a lasting abode.[325] Whoever commits a sin shall be requited with its like, but whoever acts righteously, whether male of female—if he or she is faithful—shall enter paradise with unlimited provisions.[326] My people, why is it that I invite you to salvation while you invite me to the fire?[327] You invite me to defy God and to ascribe to him partners of which I have no knowledge while I call you to the Almighty, the Forgiving.[328] Undoubtedly, that to which you invite me has no call in this world nor in the hereafter, and our return is to God, and the profligates will be inmates of the fire.[329] Soon, you will remember

322. Qurʾān 40:34

323. Qurʾān 40:35

324. Qurʾān 40:38

325. Qurʾān 40:39

326. Qurʾān 40:40

327. Qurʾān 40:41

328. Qurʾān 40:42

329. Qurʾān 40:43

> what I am telling you. I entrust my affairs to God.
> God is watchful of His servants.[330]

Ezekiel's Accusers

There were some who heard Ezekiel speak these words of heresy. They took the news to the Pharaoh and accused Ezekiel of having joined ranks with Moses. The Pharaoh was enraged at the accusation. He said, "Ezekiel is my cousin and my deputy. However, if what you say is true, then he deserves the worst punishment for having betrayed my trust in him. If, on the other hand, you have falsely accused him, then it will be you who face my wrath."

The Pharaoh summoned Ezekiel to his court. The informants repeated their accusations in his presence. They alleged, "You reject the Pharaoh as your lord, and you show ingratitude for his great blessings upon you!"

In his calm tone, Ezekiel said, "My King! Have you ever known me to tell a lie?" The Pharaoh conceded that he had not. He continued, "I ask my accusers, 'Who is your lord?'"

They replied in unison, "The Pharaoh, of course!"

"Who is your creator, your provider, the one responsible for your livelihood and for thwarting harm from your path?" He asked.

They replied in unison, "The Pharaoh, of course!"

Ezekiel nodded in approval and turned to the Pharaoh and said, "My King! I hereby testify before you and all who are present that their lord is my lord; their creator is my creator; their provider is my provider; the one who manages their life is the one who manages my life. Furthermore, I have no lord, no creator, and no provider other than their lord, their creator, and their provider. I hereby testify before you and all who are present that I disavow any lord, creator, or provider other than their lord, their creator, and their provider, and I deny that he is my lord or my god?"

The Pharaoh grinned in approval of his cousin's wise and convincing reply, oblivious to the double entendre in his words.

330. Qur'ān 40:44

He ordered those who had falsely accused him to a summary execution.[331] In this way, God saved Ezekiel from their evil schemes.[332]

The Royal Hairdresser

Ezekiel was neither the first nor the last person from the Pharaoh's inner circles to accept Moses' religion. The hairdresser who served the Pharaoh's daughters was also a believer.[333] The Pharaoh's daughter[334] once heard her mention God's name as she began her work. She questioned the hairdresser about this. With complete peace of mind, she explained to the Pharaoh's daughter that God was her Lord and the Lord of all creation. The daughter reported this development to her father who summoned the hairdresser along with her children. When she refused to recant, Pharaoh ordered that she and all of her children be burned alive in the palace furnace. Her only request was that their bones be collected and buried after they were dead. When her last child was being thrown into the fire, he told his mother, "Be patient, for you are in the right."[335]

---

331. *Biḥār al anwār* vol. 13 p. 160 tr. 1

332. Qur'ān 40:45. Some traditions claim that his life was saved as I have indicated here (*Biḥār al-anwār* vol. 13 p. 161 tr. 1). Others claim he was killed, but his faith was saved (*Biḥār al-anwār* vol. 13 p. 163 tr. 7). I believe there is a stronger case for the former since this verse is praising God for saving him. If, on the other hand, God had not saved him, but he was nonetheless able to safeguard his faith in the face of torture and death, God would have praised him instead of praising himself.

333. In the traditions, she is called a *māshiṭāh* or hairdresser. One or two traditions from Sunnī sources allege that she was Ezekiel's wife (*Biḥār al-anwār* vol. 13 p. 163 tr. 7). While this is within the realm of possibility, I have not mentioned this detail in my story for several reasons:

- I could not find evidence of this in Shi'ī traditions.
- If Ezekiel was a noble in the court of the Pharaoh, it seems unlikely that his wife would be a lowly servant to his daughters.
- It seems unlikely that the Pharaoh would have spared the husband but punished the wife so harshly.

334. According to this report, the Pharaoh had a daughter, perhaps through another wife, since, as I mentioned earlier, it seems Āsiyah was barren.

335. *Biḥār al-anwār* vol. 13 p. 163 tr. 7. Admittedly, since this tradition is taken

Āsiyah's Martyrdom

The Pharaoh's wife, Āsiyah, had always been devoted to Moses and to the one God he served and had despised her husband. She too had managed to conceal her beliefs from her husband all these years. But as she saw her husband's brutality spiral out of control, she grew more eager to disavow him, no matter what the cost. When she witnessed the fate to which he subjected the poor hairdresser, she could take no more. She said defiantly, "Damn you, Pharaoh! What has made you so audacious in the face of God!"

Surprised, he said, "Perhaps you have been overcome by the same insanity that afflicted your servant."

She retorted, "I am not insane. I believe in God who is my Lord, your Lord, and the Lord of all realms."

He grew furious and pledged to spare no effort to see that she paid dearly for her treachery. He forced her to lie on her back in the hot sand and had her wrists and ankles bound with rope and staked to the ground. He proceeded to torture her to force her to recant.[336] She looked to the heavens and prayed, "My Lord, build me a home near you in paradise, and deliver me from the Pharaoh and his evil deeds, and deliver me from these wrongdoers."[337] Her prayers were immediately answered. God showed her the gardens of paradise, and while her body was still being tormented, a smile crept across her face. Pharaoh took this as evidence that she was indeed mad, but it was the pleasure of God's acceptance that made her smile.[338] She would be known until the end of time as one of the four best women who ever lived[339] and as a role model for all who believe.[340]

---

from Sunnī sources, I have modified it slightly.

336. *Biḥār al-anwār* vol. 13 p. 164 tr. 7

337. Qur'ān 66:11

338. *Biḥār al-anwār* vol. 13 p. 164 tr. 7

339. *Biḥār al-anwār* vol. 13 p. 162 tr. 3

340. Qur'ān 66:11

Build Me a Tower

The Pharaoh's entire edifice of power was now under attack, not only from the Israelites without, but from within his inner circles as well. He had always been adept at manipulating his people, so in a desperate fit, he decided to launch one more campaign to regain their support. He told his courtiers, "My nobles, I know of no god for you besides me."[341] He told them, if Moses' god were real, he must exist in the skies, because there was no sign of him on earth. He told them he would prove once and for all that no such god existed, not even in the heavens. To this end, he commanded his vizier saying, "Hamān, give orders to the brick makers to light their kilns and churn out bricks.[342] I want you to build me a tower so that I can reach these portals that lead into the skies to find out about this god of Moses—though I suspect he is a liar."[343]

His scheme was ingenious. He knew very well that Moses' god could not be found in the sky and that the existence of such a god could not be disproven by such a ploy. However, he accomplished two important goals through his scheme. First, he bought himself timc. No one could pass final judgment upon him without giving him a chance to carry out his new plan; and this plan promised to take months to complete, if not years.[344] Second, the massive project demanded a huge number of laborers and tremendous resources. The completion of this project became the sole goal and occupation of most of Egypt. With a tower of this magnitude on their mind and the sizable pay they received for their labor, the Egyptians could think of little else.[345]

---

341. Qurʾān 28:38

342. Qurʾān 28:38

343. Qurʾān 40:36–7

344. There is no evidence linking this tower to the famed pyramids of ancient Egypt. However, as the true purpose of the pyramids, aside from being tombs, remains a mystery, it is tempting to wonder whether the first pyramid may have been built as part of this pharaoh's schemes against Moses.

345. The aforementioned verses mention Pharaoh's order to have this tower built. However, the Qurʾān does not say whether it was actually built. The

Prepare to Leave Egypt

Moses and Aaron took advantage of this opportunity. The Pharaoh's scheme gave them ample time and relative freedom to organize themselves and plan their next move. God told Moses, "Leave with my servants by night, and move quickly, for you will be pursued.[346] Strike a dry path for them in the sea. You need not fear being caught.[347] And leave the path in the sea as it lies behind you. Theirs is an army doomed to drown."[348] God wanted a mass exodus of the Israelites from Egypt toward the east. They were to pack lightly and leave quietly so as not to alert Pharaoh's distracted forces before they were out of harms way.

Joseph's Remains

Within a few days, all preparations were made. But one task remained. God ordered Moses to exhume the remains of Joseph and carry them with him to the Levant to be reunited with his ancestors' remains. Moses asked God how he should know where Joseph's remains lay. God guided him to an old woman, blind and decrepit. He asked her, "Do you know where Joseph's remains are interred?"

---

traditions are also surprisingly silent about the tower. I found only two traditions from Shīʿī sources about it. One seems implausible because it speaks of the Pharaoh using four kites or eagles to lift himself into the air (*Biḥār al-anwār* vol. 13 p. 125 tr. 22). Another places this event much earlier in the story before the seven calamities (*Biḥār al-anwār* vol. 13 p. 114 tr. 16). This is improbable because the ploy of building a tower is the desperate act of one at his wits end, not a powerful tyrant who still believes he is god. One Sunnī tradition also speaks of the event (*Biḥār al-anwār* vol. 13 p. 151). However, at the end of this version, Gabriel destroys the tower and everyone involved in its construction. Again, this seems a stretch. If the tower that defied God had been destroyed in such a dramatic way and every last worker had been sought and killed, it seems hard to imagine how anyone would join the Pharaoh's army as he chased Moses to the sea. Due to the dearth of details about the fate of this tower, I have left the rest of its story unmentioned.

346. Qurʾān 20:77 and 26:52

347. Qurʾān 20:77

348. Qurʾān 44:24

She replied that she did. But when he requested that she show him, she said, "No, not until you do four things for me. First, you must restore my legs so I can walk. Second, you must restore my youth to me. Third, you must restore my sight. And fourth, you must promise me that I will be at the exact station of paradise that you will occupy."

Moses sought to clarify and asked "You mean that you want to be in paradise, correct?"

She corrected him emphatically, "No, by God! I want to be *with you* in paradise!"

Moses felt her demands were too grand. He complained to God who replied, "Promise her what she has asked, for it is I who will give her, not you."

Moses promised her, God gave her what she asked, and she guided him to Joseph's grave which lay nested along the shore of the Nile. They exhumed the sarcophagus of white marble and prepared it for the long journey ahead.[349]

Exodus

When all was ready, with minimal detection and at Moses' command, more than 700,000 Israelites[350] slipped out of Egypt. It took several hours for news to reach the Pharaoh. When he was alerted of these developments, he was infuriated. He immediately sent criers by night to the surrounding cities to announce that the Israelites had rebelled and risen against him. He called on every able-bodied Egyptian to join him on an early morning campaign to wipe them out once and for all. The heralds announced, "These Israelites are but a small band of people.[351] But they have aroused our wrath. We are a cautious society."[352]

---

349. *Biḥār al-anwār* vol. 13 p. 127 tr. 25 and p. 128 tr. 30 and p. 130 tr. 32 and p. 130 tr. 33

350. *Biḥār al-anwār* vol. 13 p. 218 tr. 11

351. Assuming that the number of Israelites was indeed at 700,000, this propaganda of Pharaoh's was a lie meant to belittle the threat and rally more people.

352. Qur'ān 36:54–56

Pharaoh set off at sunrise at the head of an enormous army consisting of his regular soldiers and all the reserves his criers had been able to recruit. They followed the Israelites' trail due east.[353] The Israelites had been moving without rest since the previous night. But their pursuers were traveling much faster and were closing in on them.

Defectors

There was a small band of Israelites who defected and joined with the Pharaoh. They were opportunists and wanted to ensure their future. They knew if they were with Moses when the Pharaoh caught him, they too would be killed along with the rest of the Israelites. But if Moses succeeded in escaping, they could always defect from the Pharaoh's army and join with him later.[354]

Balaam, Son of Beor

Balaam, son of Beor,[355] also wished to ride with the Pharaoh's forces. Balaam had been a righteous follower of Moses and a devoted servant of God. Because of his sincerity, God had given him special signs,[356] always answered his prayers, and showered him with

353. Qur'ān 26:60

354. *Biḥār al-anwār* vol. 13 p. 127 tr. 26

355. In Arabic he is known as *Bal'am ibn Bā'ūrā* or *Bā'ūr*. His story is mentioned in great detail in Numbers 22–24. While the general plot of the Biblical story is similar to that reported in a tradition attributed to Imam al-Riḍā, the Bible sets the story after the death of Moses and after Joshua has led the Israelites across the Jordan. Imam al-Riḍā's tradition, on the other hand, explicitly states that it was the Pharaoh who sought Balaam's aid in defeating Moses (*Biḥār al-anwār* vol. 13 p. 377 tr. 1). Interestingly, the Biblical version of the story has also found its way into Islamic traditions. The one recorded by al-Jazā'irī (*Biḥār al-anwār* vol. 13 p. 377 tr. 2) does not mention an imam as its source and is presumably taken from Jewish scriptures. One major point of deviation is that the Bible considers Balaam to be a prophet while the Qur'ān clearly states that he was a fallible man who had been blessed with divine gifts that were later revoked when he turned evil.

356. Qur'ān 7:175

worldly blessings.[357] But Pharaoh was able to win his loyalty. He goaded him to use his power and pray for Moses' destruction.[358] Balaam could have risen to great heights of spirituality by means of God's gifts, but he clung to the earth and followed his base desires and thus lost his gifts. He became so twisted that even Satan became his disciple.[359]

Balaam mounted his donkey to ride with Pharaoh, but the animal would not budge. He began beating the poor animal, frantic that he was being left behind. God gave the donkey power to speak. It asked, "Why do you beat me? Do you want me to assist you by carrying you to God's prophet so that you can pray for his destruction?"[360]

Balaam, blinded by his ambition, ignored this sign and continued to beat the donkey to death. In his indifference to these warnings from God, he became like a stray dog which pants if you attack it and pants if you leave it alone.[361]

Cross the Sea

The Israelites reached the shore of the Red Sea.[362] Moses had promised them that God would save them, but many had their doubts, especially because they saw the sea as a dead end in their escape route. Moses reassured them that God would open a way where they saw none.

357. *al-Kāfī* 35.1.2 p. 29–30

358. *Biḥār al-anwār* vol. 13 p. 377 tr. 1

359. Qur'ān 7:175–6

360. *Biḥār al-anwār* vol. 13 p. 377 tr. 1

361. There is no mention of Balaam's worldly fate. I do not know whether he was destroyed along with the Pharaoh or whether he lived a life of misery like Sāmirī.

362. I believe they crossed at what is now known as the Gulf of Suez. This offshoot of the Red Sea is about 15 to 20 miles across at various locations. This width concurs with the four *farsakh* (13.6 miles) mentioned in one tradition (*Biḥār al-anwār* vol. 13 p. 138–9 tr. 54) as the length of the path through the sea. Naturally, they must have crossed far enough south of the mouth of the current Suez Canal to prevent Pharaoh from simply taking his troops around from the north.

God told Moses:

> Tell the Israelites to renew their commitment to me as their one God; to call to mind Muḥammad, the foremost of all my slaves; and to call to mind the station of ʿAlī, the brother of Muḥammad, and his pure progeny. Tell them to say, "O God! Through their intercession let us cross over the surface of this vast water before us." If they do this, the water will become like solid earth beneath their feet.

When Moses told the Israelites this, they were horrified. They said, "Will you now make us do what we fear most? We fled from the Pharaoh for fear of just such a death. Now will you force us across these murky waters with only these words to protect us? What do we know about what is in store for us on the other side?"

Caleb, son of Jephunneh,[363] asked Moses, "Did our Lord tell us to say this and walk upon the water?"

Moses replied, "Yes, he did."

Caleb asked, "And do you order me to do this?"

Moses replied, "Yes, I do."

Caleb mounted his horse, advanced toward the water's edge, renewed his commitment to God, called to mind Muḥammad and the station of ʿAlī and his pure progeny just as he had been ordered. Then he said, "O God! Through their intercession let me cross over the surface of this vast water before me." With a spur to the side of his horse, he charged out over the surface of the water. His steed's hooves clapped across the water no differently from if it had been dry land. He rode out some distance and then turned to face the Israelites. He said emphatically, "My brothers and sisters! You must follow Moses, for these are words that open the gates of paradise, lock the gates of hell, bring down provision, and secure for God's servants his everlasting pleasure."

---

363. In Arabic his name is *Kālib ibn Yuḥannā*. In another tradition, it was Joshua, son of Nūn, who did this (*Biḥār al-anwār* vol. 13 p. 122 tr. 21).

His impassioned and charismatic appeal to the Israelites evoked nothing from them. They were wholly unconvinced. They demanded, "We will only walk on land."[364]

At that instant, God commanded Moses, "Strike the sea with your staff."[365]

Parting of the Sea

He invoked God's name, saying, "O God! For the sake of Muḥammad and his pure progeny, make it part."[366] He raised his staff and brought it down with a splash on the surface of the sea. Suddenly, it parted. The sea water was driven back to their right and to their left leaving a long, cavernous road descending into the depths of what, moments before, had been an endless sea. The escarpment of water on each side of the road seemed like the sides of a canyon, dark and still.[367]

The Israelites were in utter awe at what they were witnessing. Moses urged them, "Now go!"

But they refused. They complained, "The sea floor is wet. We fear our feet will get stuck in the quagmire."

Moses prayed, "O God! For the sake of Muḥammad and his pure progeny, make it dry."

God made a powerful gale blow along the seaway, drying the earth as it blew. The ground before them became dry, as though no water had touched it in days. Again, Moses urged them, "Now go!"

But they refused. They complained, "We are twelve tribes, the progeny of twelve brothers. If we all set upon this roadway, each tribe will vie to advance ahead of the others. We fear the bad feelings that we will feel toward our brethren. If only there were twelve different paths, each tribe could take one and we would feel safe from what we now fear."

God ordered Moses to strike the sea eleven times more to the right and left of the first road to make twelve roads total, the

---

364. *Biḥār al-anwār* vol. 13 p. 138–9 tr. 54

365. Qur'ān 26:63

366. *Biḥār al-anwār* vol. 13 p. 138–9 tr. 54

367. Qur'ān 26:63

number of the tribes of Israel. He prayed, "O God! For the sake of Muḥammad and his pure progeny, expose the sea bed for us, and clear out the water before us." In an instant, the eleven additional roadways formed and the wind blew to dry each of them.

But they refused. They complained, "When each tribe enters its own roadway, they will not know what has happened to their fellow tribes."

God ordered Moses to strike with a horizontal blow the escarpment of water on either side of each roadway and say, "O God! For the sake of Muḥammad and his pure progeny, make these escarpments of water part so that they can see each other."[368]

When they were finally content to begin their trek across the sea, they heard the thunder of hoof beats behind them in the distance. Over the western horizon, they could see the specter of the Pharaoh's army advancing on them, and many cried out, "We have been caught."[369]

But Moses reassured them saying, "No we have not. My Lord is with me. He will guide me."[370] Moses sent Aaron forward to lead the way while he remained back to ensure that the last of his people had safely crossed.

I Must Save My Father

As Moses helped the last stragglers begin the trek across the seaway, there was one young man who kept looking to the west with interest. Moses reassured him that the Pharaoh's forces would not overtake them and urged him to move along with the rest. The young man said he knew that they would be safe, but he wondered what the fate of the Egyptian army would be. Moses told him that God would destroy them. The young man wept and confessed, "My father joined the Pharaoh's army and now marches with them. I must go to him and persuade him to come back to you."

Moses applauded his devotion to his father but warned that he would not be spared God's punishment if he was caught in the

368. *Biḥār al-anwār* vol. 13 p. 138–9 tr. 54

369. Qur'ān 26:61

370. Qur'ān 26:62

ranks of the Pharaoh's army. He accepted the warning but raced back toward the advancing troops anyway.[371]

The Pharaoh's Folly

By the time the Egyptian forces reached the shore of the Red Sea, Moses was nearly halfway across the seaway, and Aaron and the first members of each tribe had reached the far side safely. The Pharaoh masterfully concealed his shock at seeing the twelve gaping passageways carved through the sea. He turned to address his officers and said, "You know that I am your highest lord? This is why the sea has parted for me. We must pursue these slaves upon these pathways through the sea."

Not a soldier budged. The Pharaoh, distraught by their insolence, spun his horse around to lead the charge into the seaway. His astrologer urged him not to go. But the Pharaoh, blinded by hubris, refused to listen. He kicked his stallion's sides, but it refused to advance. It was as terrified as the soldiers were. At that moment, Gabriel appeared along one of the paths through the sea riding a mare in heat. The Pharaoh's stallion saw the mare and raced after it, forgetting its fear. With the Pharaoh in the lead, his legions of troops followed suit.[372]

The small band of Israelites who had defected and joined with the Pharaoh now realized what power Moses wielded, and they saw that the Pharaoh was leading his army into a calamitous trap. Terrified, they broke ranks and tried to scramble to the front hoping to make it to the other side before it was too late. But God sent an angel to spook the horses upon which they rode to keep them from advancing ahead of the Pharaoh himself. They were doomed to the fate of the rest for their hypocrisy.[373]

The Destruction of the Pharaoh

By the time the last of the Pharaoh's troops entered the seaway, Moses and the last of the Israelites had reached the far shore

---

371. *Biḥār al-anwār* vol. 13 p. 128 tr. 27

372. *Biḥār al-anwār* vol. 13 p. 123 tr. 21 and p. 134 tr. 41

373. *Biḥār al-anwār* vol. 13 p. 127 tr. 26

safely. Moses waited until the Pharaoh was in clear sight of the Israelites so that they could witness what would happen next.[374] As the Pharaoh and his legions charged into view, Moses struck the dry sea bed. Like the sides of a canyon crumble in a quake, so the sides of the twelve passageways began to crumble. The first to be crushed by the crumbling walls of water were the troops in the rear. Their cries of terror reached the Pharaoh's ears like a thunderous shockwave. He stopped dead in his tracks and spun around to see what was happening. Then he spun again and saw the Israelites standing triumphantly on the far shore, terror no longer in their eyes, and it struck him that Moses had trapped him. He glared at Moses[375] and frantically screamed at him, "I hereby believe that there is no god except him in whom the Israelites believe, and I am one of those who submit!"[376]

Moses shook his head in disbelief, and Gabriel's voice[377] boomed louder than the Egyptian soldiers' screams, "What? Now? When you have disobeyed us until now and were among the agents of corruption?"[378] Such penitence in the face of death is too little, done too late. To boot, the Pharaoh looked to Moses as his savior and did not even address God.[379] Gabriel appeared before him and solemnly announced, "Today we shall deliver your body so that

---

374. Qur'ān 2:50. This verse states that he was drowned as the Israelites looked on. It also makes sense that God would allow them to witness his destruction so they would feel assured that he was truly dead and could no longer persecute them.

375. The verse does not specify whom he is addressing. However, one tradition indicates that he was speaking to Moses (*Biḥār al-anwār* vol. 13 p. 131 tr. 34).

376. Qur'ān 10:90

377. *Biḥār al-anwār* vol. 13 p. 123 tr. 21

378. Qur'ān 10:91

379. *Biḥār al-anwār* vol. 13 p. 131 tr. 34

you may be a sign for those who come after you.[380] Though many people are oblivious to our signs, just as you were.[381]

Moses and the Israelites gazed on as the water engulfed the Pharaoh's army and even the Pharaoh himself. In minutes, the chaos of death and destruction subsided into gentle waves lapping at the sandy beach. Neither did the sky weep for them, nor the earth, nor the sea, and they were not granted any respite.[382]

Moses addressed the Israelites saying, "Give thanks to God, for he has fulfilled his promise and delivered you from the Pharaoh and destroyed him." Forty years had passed since God had promised Moses and Aaron the arrival of such a day.[383]

But the Israelites were not ready to celebrate and give thanks. The Pharaoh had ruled over them with god-like impunity for so long that they could sooner believe that he had somehow saved

---

380. The Pharaoh has come to represent the inevitable defeat that God metes out to even the most powerful forces of evil. It was imperative, for this purpose, that his body be preserved so that the Israelites and the surviving Egyptians could see with their own eyes that he was indeed dead. Otherwise, the Israelites, who had been terrorized for so long by this larger-than-life personality, would not have been able to break free of his grip. Also, it would have been easy for others to manipulate the facts and claim that he had used his godly powers to somehow save himself (*Biḥār al-anwār* vol. 13 p. 110 tr. 14). We may find parallels in modern tyrants whose executions have often been veiled in secrecy, leaving their former victims with a continued sense of fear of their imminent return. In summary, the verse says that God saved Pharaoh's body so that the Israelites and the remaining Egyptians could know that he was dead so that the story of his ultimate defeat at the hands of God would go down in history as a lesson for all who are tempted by power.

It should be noted that there is nothing in this verse that suggests that the Pharaoh's body would be preserved indefinitely for posterity. The verse simply says that the Pharaoh would be a sign for others, not that his body would be a sign. Some contemporary commentators and many lay people have tried to link this verse with the discovery of certain mummies from ancient Egypt as though the truth of this verse depends on the presence of a particular mummy in a museum somewhere. As I wrote earlier, there is no scientific evidence to link any of the existing mummies to the Pharaoh of Moses' time.

381. Qur'ān 10:92

382. Qur'ān 44:29

383. *Biḥār al-anwār* vol. 13 p. 128 tr. 29

himself than they could that he was dead. To reassure them, God ordered the sea to cast the Pharaoh's body upon the shore so that they could see for themselves that he was indeed dead.[384] Despite his immense weight from being clad from head to toe in polished iron armor, at God's behest, the sea easily washed his body ashore.[385] Moses invited each Israelite to examine the corpse and to be a witness to the demise of the Pharaoh who thought he was a god.

Moses told them:[386]

> The Pharaoh's punishment is not limited to the quick death you have just witnessed. Rather, beyond the veil of death, a terrible punishment has already besieged him and all who aided him.[387] Morning and evening until the Day of Judgment they will be subjected to the fire of hell in purgatory.[388] Believers far and wide will call down God's damnation upon them,[389] and with every call, the intensity of their punishment will increase. Then on the Day of Judgment, they will be among the hideous,[390] and God will damn them[391] and decree, "Cast Pharaoh and his family into the severest punishment!"[392] All this because in this life, they were leaders who invited others to the fire. On the Day of Resurrection, too, they will lead their people and usher them into the

---

384. *Biḥār al-anwār* vol. 13 p. 118 tr. 18

385. *Biḥār al-anwār* vol. 13 p. 131 tr. 34

386. Note that the following lines, which I have attributed to Moses, are not actually attributable to him. However, I took the liberty of putting these Qurʾānic words in his mouth as a way to incorporate things beyond death into the story.

387. Qurʾān 40:45

388. Qurʾān 40:46

389. Qurʾān 28:42

390. Qurʾān 28:42

391. Qurʾān 28:42

392. Qurʾān 40:46

> fire. And what an evil destination it will be for the incoming![393] And though they received much aid in this life, on the Day of Resurrection they will receive none.[394]
>
> When they and their followers argue with one another in the fire, the meek followers will say to their domineering leaders, "We used to follow you, so will you now protect us even a little from the fire?"
>
> To this, those who were domineering will say, "We are all in this together. God has already judged between us."
>
> Those in the fire will say to the keepers of hell, "Ask your Lord to relieve us from at least a day's punishment."
>
> The keepers will ask, "Didn't your apostles bring you clear proofs?"
>
> They will reply, "Yes."
>
> The keepers will say, "Then ask him yourselves; although you should know that the requests of the faithless are to no avail."[395]

Some who had witnessed the young Israelite man return for his father asked Moses what had become of him. He told them that he was in the mercy of God, but he had not escaped the punishment, for when such a punishment strikes, it strikes the sinner and all who are in his midst.[396]

---

393. Qur'ān 11:98

394. Qur'ān 28:41

395. Qur'ān 40:47–50

396. *Biḥār al-anwār* vol. 13 p. 128 tr. 27

A Delegation to Occupy Egypt

God instructed Moses to move with his people to the northeast toward the Levant,[397] for he had granted them the eastern and western portions of that blessed land and all that lay between, and he would fulfill his promise to them because of their patience.[398] However, he also told him to send a smaller delegation of about 100,000[399] capable individuals back to Egypt by the land route to the north.[400] With the Pharaoh, his courtiers, advisors, and his entire army destroyed, Egypt was on the brink of a complete power vacuum. Moses announced that the Israelites were the inheritors of the land of Egypt and all that it contained.[401] He described to them the gardens, springs, fields, and splendid places—the bounties in which the Egyptians had once rejoiced. All of that would now belong to them.[402] He assembled a delegation of men, established a chain of command, and gave them detailed instructions that they were to follow to a tee upon entering Egypt.[403] Among these instructions, he ordered them to seize much of the gold jewelry of the Egyptians. He told them to transport this vast wealth to his custody, for they would need this treasure to establish their government in the Holy Land.[404]

---

397. *Biḥār al-anwār* vol. 13 p. 110 tr. 14

398. Qur'ān 7:137

399. This number is not mentioned explicitly. However, one tradition says that 700,000 Israelites escaped from Egypt. Another says that there were 600,000 at the time of the revelation of the tablets. Thus, I have inferred that 100,000 must have been sent back to Egypt.

400. *Biḥār al-anwār* vol. 13 p. 110 tr. 14 and *Majmaʿ al-bayān* under 26:59

401. Qur'ān 26:59

402. Qur'ān 44:25–28

403. No mention is made of the nature of this delegation, and no names are given. However, I presume the leader of the delegation would have been Aaron, Joshua, Caleb, or someone else near to their caliber.

404. There is no explicit evidence for this specific instruction. However, I believe something like this must have happened. I will present my arguments for this inference when I discuss Sāmirī's construction of the golden calf.

Countless Blessings

As the small delegation moved west to Egypt, Moses set out with the majority of the Israelites northeast in the direction of the Levant.[405] Some of the Israelites asked him, "Moses, by which power and through which strength and upon which mounts do you foresee us reaching the Holy Land, for we have in our midst children and women and the elderly and disabled?"

Moses replied, "I know of no people whom God has made to inherit a land as vast as the land he has made you inherit. I know of no people whom God has given of the world's blessings as much as he has given you. You have been given more blessings than can be counted by any other than God. God will find a way for us, so remember him and turn your affairs over to him. For he is more merciful to you than you are to yourselves."

They requested, "Pray to him that he may give us food and drink, clothing, mounts, and shade from the heat."

God spoke to Moses in secret saying, "I have commanded the sky to shower them with manna and quail; I have commanded the wind to fan the flames of their hearths and roast their quail; I have commanded a stone to burst forth with water; I have commanded the clouds to shade them from the sun; and I have commanded their clothing to grow with them as they grow."[406]

Make us an Idol

On the way, they encountered a pagan people who were devoted to their idols, one of which was a masterfully wrought golden calf.[407] They said, "O Moses, make for us a god as they have gods." The Israelites had been persecuted so ruthlessly by the Pharaoh that they had lost all sense of identity and self-worth. They were easily

---

405. *Biḥār al-anwār* vol. 13 p. 110 tr. 14

406. *Biḥār al-anwār* vol. 13 p. 178 tr. 7

407. That one of their idols was a golden calf or a golden bull is only an educated guess, but such a hypothesis is helpful in understanding why Sāmirī is later successful in promoting a golden calf as the idol of choice. It could also be that the Egyptian pantheon contained a calf or a bull.

impressed by the idols and temples and rituals they saw, and they longed to be like them.

Moses told them, "You are a foolish lot.[408] What these idol-worshipers are engaged in is doomed to perish, and what they do shall come to naught."[409] He pressed further, "Shall I seek for you a deity other than God when he has graced you more than he has all other nations?[410] Just bear in mind that God delivered you from the Pharaoh's clan who had inflicted on you a terrible torment—slaughtering your sons and sparing your women. In that was a great test from your Lord, and he now wishes to test your gratitude and loyalty."[411] He then threatened, "The punishment for idol worship is death, so put these thoughts out of your mind."[412] He promised them that God would soon reveal a book to them as he had revealed books to the prophets of old.[413] This would give them the identity they needed so badly.

Manna and Quail

They had left Egypt with little more than the clothes they wore. In his infinite benevolence, as he had promised Moses, God provided for all of their needs. He provided manna and quail in abundance[414]

---

408. Qur'ān 7:138

409. Qur'ān 7:139

410. Qur'ān 7:140

411. Qur'ān 7:141

412. There is no evidence of this statement in the sources; however, at some point Moses must have warned his people of the consequences of idol worship, otherwise it would have been unjust for him to punish with death those who later worshiped the golden calf.

413. *Biḥār al-anwār* vol. 13 p. 230 tr. 42 and Qur'ān 20:80

414. Qur'ān 2:57, 7:160, and 20:80. We do not know exactly what was meant by *mann* and *salwā*. What is clear is that they were two kinds of food, for everywhere they are mentioned in the Qur'ān, God says immediately afterward, "Eat from the good things we have provided to you." According to some explanations, manna were mushrooms; according to others, they were coriander seeds from which they used to make flour and bread; and according to another, they were beans from the camelthorn bush (*taranjabīn*) which is a legume (*Biḥār al-anwār* vol. 13 p. 183 tr. 19). It seems there is an agreement that *salwā* was some species

which they could collect without the exertion of hunting or gathering or cultivating. Manna and quail would rain down upon them from first light until sunrise each morning. Moses instructed them to rise early and collect what they needed for the day, lest they be forced to ask their brethren for favors.[415] He conveyed to them, on God's behalf, the message, "Eat from the good things we have provided for you, but do not overstep the bounds by being ungrateful lest my wrath should descend upon you. He upon whom my wrath descends will definitely perish.[416] But if you do overstep, then also know that I am All-Forgiving to him who turns to me, becomes faithful, acts righteously, and above all, remains true to guidance."[417]

Clouds and Water

Moses divided the Israelites along tribal lines to facilitate governance.[418] He appointed leaders within each of the twelve tribes whom he charged with various duties. All were in turn answerable to him.

The desert sun provided the first test of this new system of governance. It hung high in the sky, its searing heat bore down upon them and made them thirsty beyond their limits. Moses prayed to God to help them, so he sent clouds to fill the sky and shade them from the sun's unbearable heat.[419] To quench their thirst, Moses placed a small cuboid stone in the middle of their camp. He then told the leaders of each tribe to have their people dig shallow ditches from the stone leading back to the heart of their tribe's encampment. When the work was done, he prayed to God

---

of bird. Since we do not know precisely what kind of food this was, I have simply translated it as "manna and quail" in keeping with the Biblical translations (see Exodus 16).

415. *Man lā yaḥḍuruhu al-faqīh* vol. 1 p. 503 tr. 1449

416. Qur'ān 20:81

417. Qur'ān 20:82

418. Qur'ān 7:160

419. Qur'ān 7:160 and 2:57

for water[420] saying, "O God! I beg you by the right of Muḥammad, the Foremost of the Prophets; by the right of ʿAlī, the Foremost of the Successors; by the right of Fāṭimah, the Foremost of Women; by the right of al-Ḥasan, the Foremost of your Friends; and by the right of al-Ḥusayn, the Foremost of the Martyrs, to quench the thirst of these servants of yours."[421]

God answered his prayer and told him, "Strike the rock with your staff." He did, and twelve springs gushed forth from it like twelve spokes of a wheel. The fresh water streamed into the twelve ditches, and every tribe knew its drinking place.[422]

Return to Sinai

From the time they left Egypt, Moses had promised his people that God would give them a book of guidance.[423] As the sacred month of Dhū al-Qaʿdah approached,[424] Moses guided the Israelites toward the mountain from which God first spoke to him.[425]

---

420. Qurʾān 2:60

421. *Biḥār al-anwār* vol. 13 p. 184 tr. 19

422. Qurʾān 7:160 and 2:60

423. Qurʾān 20:80

424. The Torah was given to Moses at the end of a forty-day period that started with the first of Dhū al-Qaʿdah and ended on the tenth of Dhū al-Ḥijjah (*Biḥār al-anwār* vol. 13 p. 213 tr. 7). It does not matter that their months and even their calendar may have been different. According to this tradition, those forty days corresponded to what we now call by these two names in the Islamic calendar. Another tradition claims that the Torah was "sent down" on the sixth of Ramaḍān (*al-Kāfī* 7.13.6). It could be that one report is untrue. It is also possible that each describes a separate part of the process of revelation. Just as it is mentioned that the Qurʾān was revealed in stages, it is also possible that the Torah was revealed in stages.

425. I am not certain that it was the same mountain from earlier in the story. Nonetheless, there are clues that suggest that it was.

- First, the Qurʾān uses the same phrase to describe the mountain in both stories: "the right flank of the mountain" (*jānib al-ṭūr al-ayman*; see Qurʾān 19:52 and 20:80). While this is not conclusive evidence, it is coincidence enough to warrant investigation. Most commentators do not seem to have considered this possibility, but a few have (see *al-Baḥr al-madīd*, *Rūḥ al-bayān*, *al-Tafsīr li kitāb allāh al-munīr*).

They encamped around the same place Moses had left Ṣafrāʾ along with their children and belongings on that epic night when he had been appointed God's prophet. He reminded the Israelites that God would continue to provide them with food, water, and shade and that they must remain steadfast and patient. He told them that God had promised to reveal their long-awaited book at the culmination of thirty nights.[426]

His people insisted that they wanted to hear God too, just as he had heard God on the mountain. Some even said they would not believe in any book he brought them unless they could hear God's voice. He warned them about making such demands but agreed to let them hear God. He announced he would not go to receive this book alone. He would choose a delegation from among them to accompany him up the mountain so that they could bear witness to the revelation and testify before the rest.[427]

From more than 700,000 Israelites,[428] he narrowed the pool to 70,000. From 70,000 he narrowed the pool to 7,000. Finally, he chose, according to his best judgment,[429] the 70 best men from their midst.[430]

- Second, after crossing the Gulf of Suez (Red Sea), the Israelites would have found themselves in the Sinai Peninsula which also fell on the route Moses had taken on his way back from Midian.

For these two reasons, in my story I have assumed that it was the same mountain in both instances.

426. Qurʾān 7:142

427. *Biḥār al-anwār* vol. 13 p. 218 tr. 11

428. I believe this number refers to the 600,000 who were with him at the camp and the 100,000 who he had sent back to Egypt.

429. There is an interesting tradition related to this story, which tells us that Moses believed that these 70 men were the best men of his community but that he was mistaken. In the tradition, a man asks Imam al-Mahdī why people cannot choose their own imam. The Imam explains that even Moses, despite his infallibility and great knowledge, was not able to choose righteous men who would remain steadfast. Rather, he chose men with seeds of hypocrisy latent in their hearts. If he could not choose the right companions, then how could fallible and limited people choose the right imam? (*Kamāl al-dīn* 2.43 p. 461).

430. Qurʾān 7:155

As was his wont, he appointed his brother Aaron as his deputy for the duration of his absence. Moses told him, "Be my deputy over my people and set things right and do not follow the way of the agents of corruption."[431] By the same token, he admonished the Israelites to obey Aaron just as they would obey him.

On the first of Dhū al-Qaʿdah, Moses set out with his seventy companions. He retraced the steps he had taken all those years before when he had been searching for the source of a flickering flame so that he could warm his family. This time there was no flame, but he knew the way. As they proceeded into the valley and then turned to climb the mountain, they were transported as he had been before, hundreds of miles to the northeast, across the vast Arabian desert. He told his companions that they were entering the Sacred Valley of Ṭuwā and instructed them to remove their shoes as a sign of deference to the Almighty. He showed them the tree that had been ablaze on that blessed night. Now, there was no flame and no light. He told them that they must camp in this place for thirty days, fasting by day, worshiping by night, to purify themselves and prepare themselves spiritually to witness the revelation of the divine book.

Shares of Gold

Back at base camp, there was much excitement among the Israelites. Members of the delegation Moses had sent to Egypt to seize the Egyptian jewelry had arrived and delivered their massive cache of gold. They dutifully turned the chests of gold over to Aaron. Aaron in turn, as Moses' vicegerent, doled out a portion of this cache to each person, according to Moses' instructions to him, since this wealth now belonged to them.[432]

---

431. Qurʾān 7:142

432. As I mentioned earlier, there is no explicit evidence for the seizure or delivery of Egyptian gold. However, I believe something like this must have happened. I will present my arguments for this inference shortly when I discuss Sāmirī's construction of the golden calf.

Thirty Days Extended

On the mountain, when thirty days had passed, Moses' companions eagerly awaited the promised event. But Moses informed them that God had extended the preparatory period for ten more days to make forty days total.[433] This caused great consternation among his companions as their confidence in Moses' promise waned.

At base camp, the close of the thirtieth day left a palpable feeling of disappointment as a shadow of doubt engulfed the camp. Rumors sprang up that Moses was dead or that he had run away and abandoned them. Rapidly, doubts grew into outright rage.[434]

Aaron demonstrated the utmost forbearance and wisdom in silencing these rumors and admonishing the people to be patient but to little avail.

---

433. Qur'ān 7:142. One verse mentions that the promised period was to last forty nights (Qur'ān 2:51). Another mentions thirty days that were then completed with ten additional nights to make forty in all (Qur'ān 7:142). From these two verses, it is not clear whether Moses knew from the beginning that it would be forty nights or whether he was told it would be thirty and the ten were added later. There is one tradition that indicates that he knew it would be forty nights but was instructed by God to say thirty (*Biḥār al-anwār* vol. 13 p. 213 tr. 7). The upshot of this view is that Moses lied at God's command, thus, I have dismissed this version. Another tradition says that the initial promise was only for thirty days and that the additional ten were added based on *badā'* where God's determination for things apparently changes because of certain choices that people make (*Biḥār al-anwār* vol. 13 p. 227 tr. 27). This latter view is strong for two reasons:

- It explains why Qur'ān 7:142 splits up the forty nights into thirty and ten.
- It corresponds with other instances of *badā'* where God tests people's patience by making them wait longer than they expected. We saw a similar situation in Noah's story.

434. *Biḥār al-anwār* vol. 13 p. 213 tr. 7

Sāmirī's Idol

Sāmirī was a prominent member of one of the Israelite tribes and a generous man.[435] He was a smith by profession.[436] He had been one of the first to cross the Red Sea.[437] When he had crossed, he had stood upon the shore looking back as the remaining Israelites poured frantically out of the seaway to safety. When the last of them were ashore, he had watched intently as Gabriel brought up the rear, riding his mare with which he had led the Pharaoh's army to their doom. As Gabriel rode past them, it had occurred to Sāmirī to collect the sand from one of this mare's hoofmarks as a keepsake, for he fancied it might hold some special power.[438] He grabbed a fistful of sand and furtively tucked it away in a pocket.

Now, as the Israelites' discontent festered in the base camp, Sāmirī devised a plan.[439] He had been among those who had asked Moses to make them an idol like the wondrous idols other people worshiped.[440] With the rising wave of discontent, Moses' possible

---

435. *Biḥār al-anwār* vol. 13 p. 230 tr. 40

436. This is an educated guess based on the skill he demonstrates in making the golden calf.

437. *Biḥār al-anwār* vol. 13 p. 209 tr. 4

438. Qur'ān 20:96. The common explanation given for this verse is that there was, in fact, some supernatural quality to the earth upon which the angel's horse trod. Sāmirī alone noticed this and collected the earth from one hoofmark and later used it to magically make the golden calf low. Perhaps a better explanation is the one put forward in *Tafsīr al-kāshif*. Shaykh al-Mughniyyah suggests that there was no actual power in the hoofmark. Sāmirī imagined that there was and conjured a tale to explain to Moses how he made the golden calf. This is a much more satisfying explanation, especially considering that no supernatural powers are required to cast a golden calf. All that one needs is a hot fire and the skills of a goldsmith. The sound effects were also easy enough to come by. Perhaps Sāmirī created some hollow mechanism within his calf that produced a low when blown upon. Alternatively, as one tradition suggests, perhaps God himself made the calf low as an additional test (*Biḥār al-anwār* vol. 13 p. 209 tr. 4), though this last explanation is problematic as far as it relates to divine justice.

439. Sadly, the Old Testament blames Aaron for making the golden calf and calling people to worship it (Exodus 32). The Qur'ān sets the record straight.

440. Qur'ān 7:138

desertion, and Aaron's inability to maintain full control, Sāmirī saw a golden opportunity to provide for his people what Moses had been unable, or unwilling, to do.

He bypassed Aaron and spoke secretly with those who had been party to having an idol. He convinced them that Moses was not returning and that he could make the idol they had been dreaming about. It would be a single idol to worship the one God but in a form that rivaled the Egyptians and the other peoples they had seen after the exodus. His idea struck a chord with many of his brethren.

When Aaron caught wind of this plot, he was enraged by the Israelites' contempt for Moses' and his authority. They had shown them more miracles and more blessings than had ever been shown to any people.[441] Nonetheless, they were seemingly eager to contravene even the most basic precepts of their religion. Aaron set out to find Sāmirī and put an end to his machinations.

Meanwhile, Sāmirī set to work on a clay mold using the skills he had honed through years of practice as a smith. When the mold was complete, he sent word to all his supporters to bring their shares of gold from the Egyptian cache. He lit a blazing fire, stoked with desert hardwoods that burnt exceptionally hot.[442] When the temperature was hot enough, he told everyone to cast his gold into the large crucible. He also cast his share of gold.[443] Then he reached into his pocket, grabbed a handful of sand from Gabriel's mare's hoof print, and with great fanfare, cast it in with the gold. He swung the crucible into the heart of the blaze, and they waited for the heat to do its work. After some time, he adroitly tipped the molten contents of the crucible into the clay mold.

---

441. Qur'ān 5:20

442. The melting point of pure gold is 1,948 degrees F. Some gold alloys melt as low 1,580 degrees F. A normal wood fire burns between 1,100 to 1,500 degrees F. Based on these numbers, it would have taken some great skill to generate enough heat from a wood fire to melt gold. Nonetheless, it seems that it is possible—if we suppose that Sāmirī possessed extraordinary skill in this regard and that the gold he melted was gold alloy.

443. Qur'ān 20:87

The gold cooled, and Sāmirī cracked open the mold. Word had spread like wildfire throughout the camp, and people gathered around eagerly to see the fruits of Sāmirī's labor. He carefully chiseled away the mold, and, within minutes, they were staring at the scintillating statue of a golden calf. Sāmirī placed his mouth on a hole in the calf and took a deep breath and blew. He had designed it to make a sound like the lowing of a real cow.

There were gasps of childlike excitement. Sāmirī had built them an idol, a calf, a lifeless body with a low. The crowd said to one another with general approbation, "This is your God and the God of Moses!"[444]

Aaron Tries to Stop Them

Aaron approached with a few of his steadfast followers in tow. He chided Sāmirī and admonished and argued with his people, hoping to dissuade them. He told them, "My people, you are being tested through this golden calf. Your Lord is the All-Merciful, so follow me and obey my command."[445] He asked them, "Do you not see that this idol neither speaks to you, nor guides you in any way?[446] It causes you no benefit or harm?"[447]

But they ignored his admonishment, and they took it for a god anyway, for they were wrongdoers.[448] Besides Sāmirī, there were five others who advocated for worshiping the calf. Their names were Adhīnūh, his brother Mīdhawayh along with Mīdhawayh's son, daughter, and wife.[449] They insisted, "We will continue to worship this idol until Moses returns to us."[450] When Aaron stepped forward to take Sāmirī into custody, the mob attacked him. They

---

444. Qur'ān 20:88

445. Qur'ān 20:90

446. Qur'ān 7:148

447. Qur'ān 20:89

448. Qur'ān 7:148

449. *Biḥār al-anwār* vol. 13 p. 216 tr. 8. I am not sure about the pronunciation of their names, but I included them because they are mentioned in a tradition.

450. Qur'ān 20:91

restrained Aaron and threatened to kill him if he laid a finger on Sāmirī or the golden calf.[451]

There was nothing left for Aaron to do. He lacked the support to fight against Sāmirī. All he could do was bide his time, let his disapproval be known for the record, and wait for Moses to return to set things aright. Anything more would have caused irreparable rifts in this volatile and nascent community.

The Seventy Hear God

Back on the mountain, the ten days had come to an end. Moses gathered the seventy men around the olive tree where God had first spoken to Moses. Then he turned to climb further up the mountain and told them to follow behind him. Moses, so eager to meet the Lord, rushed ahead leaving his people to struggle to catch up.

When he reached the appointed place, God asked, "What has hurried you on before your people, O Moses?"[452]

He replied, "They are close upon my heels. I hurried on to you, my Lord, that you may be pleased."[453]

Shortly, all seventy men gathered behind him. God addressed Moses[454] in a sonorous tone that they felt emanated from below them and above, from their right and left, and from before them and behind. He said, "Moses, I have singled you out from among your people to be the recipient of my messages and the addressee

---

451. Qur'ān 7:150. It is important to note that Aaron's portrayal in Islamic sources is very different from his portrayal in the Old Testament (Exodus 32). The Old Testament, in typical form, maligns this great prophet and accuses him of having created the golden calf and of calling on the Israelites to worship it. Furthermore, it claims that he led them in revelry. By contrast, the Qur'ān exonerates Aaron and lays full blame on Sāmirī and the foolish among the Israelites who followed him.

452. Qur'ān 20:83

453. Qur'ān 20:84

454. Qur'ān 7:143

of my speech. Take these tablets that I now give you, and be among the grateful."[455]

The Tablets

Gabriel appeared before him and ceremoniously placed several wooden tablets in his hand.[456] These tablets were inscribed with

---

455. Qur'ān 7:144

456. There are several questions regarding these tablets:

- Were the tablets different from the Torah?
    - The Bible indicates that they were two things. It speaks of two sets of two tablets each. The first pair were "the work of God; the writing was the writing of God" (Exodus 32:16). When Moses allegedly broke these (Exodus 32:19), God had him carve another set so that he could "write on them the words that were on the first tablets" (Exodus 34:1). In Jewish and Christian tradition, the tablets contained the Decalogue or Ten Commandments, meant for all people. The Torah on the other hand, comprises the Pentateuch, the first five books of the Old Testament. There seems to be great uncertainty among Jews and Christians as to whether these were also given to Moses along with the tablets or whether Moses wrote these later.
    - The majority view among Muslim scholars is that the tablets (*alwāḥ*) were the medium upon which the Torah (*tawrāh*) was inscribed, and thus, they are the same thing. The Qur'ān's description of each suggests that they were the same thing. It describes the tablets saying, "We inscribed for him in the tablets various things: admonishment and an elaboration of all things" (7:145). In another place it says, "He took up the tablets in whose inscriptions there was guidance and mercy" (7:154). It describes the Torah saying, "We sent down the Torah in which there was guidance and light" (5:44). A few commentators, such as al-Balāghī and Ibn ʿĀshūr, have asserted that the tablets were different from the Torah. In their defense, it does seem far-fetched to imagine that the entire Pentateuch was inscribed in tablets. There would have been very many tablets, indeed, and it would have been difficult for Moses to hold and carry them. One possible explanation is that the Torah was different and much shorter than the current Pentateuch, in which case it could have fit more easily on the tablets.
- How many were the tablets?
    - As I indicated above, the Bible claims there were two tablets, each double-sided.

things—with admonishment and an elaboration of all things. God continued:

> Hold fast to them, and bid your people, and they too will hold fast to the best of its teachings. Those who do not hold fast are corrupt, and I shall show you the state of those who are corrupt.[457] I shall withhold my signs from them, for they are arrogant without cause. As a result, even if they were to see every sign, they would not believe in them; and if they were to see the path of rectitude they would not follow it; but if they were to see the way of error, they would follow it. That is because they denied our signs and were oblivious to them.[458] Those who deny our signs and deny that they will meet me in the hereafter, their works shall be effaced. Is this anything but justice for what they did?[459]

Moses received the tablets and fell to the ground in prostration to thank God for his guidance. Then he turned to the seventy men who stood around him and showed them the tablets, expecting

---

- The Qur'ān uses the plural *alwāḥ* to describe them. In Arabic, the plural is only used for three or more indicating that there were at least three tablets.

- Of what were the tablets made?
    - The Bible claims they were stone and that the original pair of tablets shattered when Moses cast them down (Exodus 32:19).
    - The Qur'ān refutes the assertion that they shattered. It does say that he cast them down (7:150) but a few verses later says he picked them up again (7:154). The Qur'ān does not address the material out of which they were made. There are some traditions, from Sunnī sources, that claim they were wooden tablets. This would make it more plausible that Moses easily carried them and that he cast them down without breaking them, but more than this, we have no evidence.

457. Qur'ān 7:145

458. Qur'ān 7:146

459. Qur'ān 7:147

them to be overwhelmed with joy or at least awestruck at having witnessed the act of revelation. Instead, in their eyes, he saw only skepticism.

Let Us See Him

They had expected to see God, as they believed Moses had seen God in the form of a burning olive tree. They were not content to only hear his voice.[460] They said, "Moses, we shall not believe in this scripture of yours until we see God with our own eyes."[461]

Moses explained to them that it is impossible to see God in this world or the next; that God is not confined to a particular space or located in a particular direction; and that our eyes are far too weak to gaze at the Almighty. He explained that what he had seen all those years before had only been a fire, not God. And what they had just heard altogether had been a voice created by God, not God himself.

The seventy men refused to accept his excuses. They insisted that they would see God, or they would refuse to testify that the scripture was from God.[462]

Moses dejectedly turned in the direction from which he had heard the voice of God. He silently apologized to God for the foolish request he was about to make. Then he said, "My Lord, show yourself to me, that I may gaze at you."

God replied, "You shall not see me. But look at that mountain there in the distance. I shall disclose something of myself to it. If it abides in its place, then perhaps you shall be able to see me." God disclosed something of himself to the mountain. In an instant, the mountain, in its enormity, exploded.[463] Moses and his companions simply gazed on in utter disbelief until,[464] a moment later, the

---

460. *Biḥār al-anwār* vol. 13 p. 218 tr. 11

461. Qurʾān 2:55

462. *Biḥār al-anwār* vol. 13 p. 226 tr. 22

463. Qurʾān 7:143

464. Qurʾān 2:55

shock wave hit them. The thunderous blast instantaneously killed all seventy men.[465] Moses himself was knocked unconscious.[466]

Eventually Moses regained consciousness. When he recalled what had happened, he fell prostrate and said, "You are immaculate! I turn to you penitently, and I am the first of the faithful."[467] He lifted his head and gazed around at the seventy companions. He checked a few to see if they would wake, but he realized that they were dead. He prayed, "My Lord, had you wished, you might have destroyed them earlier along with me." He dreaded the thought of returning to his people to report that the seventy people who were supposed to witness the revelation of their scripture had all been killed. Without their testimony, and under such suspicious circumstances, he knew he would never be able to convince them of the authenticity of these scriptures.[468] He continued, "Lord, will you destroy us because of the actions of fools among us? This was simply a test by which you misguide whom you wish and guide whom you wish. You are our master, so forgive us and have mercy on us, for you are the best of those who forgive.[469] Apportion a share of goodness for us in this world and in the hereafter, for we have returned to you."

God replied, "I inflict my punishment on whom I will, but my mercy embraces all things. I shall apportion my special mercy for those among your people who fear me and give charity and those who believe in our signs;[470] those who follow the last messenger, the unlettered prophet, whose mention they will find written in this Torah; who will bid them to do what is right and forbid them from what is wrong; who will make lawful for them all good things and forbid them from all filth and will relieve them of their burdens and the shackles that were upon them—those who believe

---

465. Qurʾān 2:55

466. Qurʾān 7:143

467. Qurʾān 7:143

468. *Biḥār al-anwār* vol. 13 p. 226 tr. 22

469. Qurʾān 7:155

470. Qurʾān 7:156

in him, honor him, and help him and follow the light that will be sent down with him, they alone shall be felicitous."[471]

In response to Moses' prayer, God revived his seventy companions in hopes that they would be grateful.[472] They came to life as if they were waking from a slumber. Moses explained what had happened, and they realized that they had been foolish to demand that they see God.

Moses gathered the tablets in his arms, and together they prepared to return to their camp.

God told Moses, "We tried your people in your absence, and Sāmirī has led them astray."[473] Moses had witnessed Sāmirī's prior eagerness to have an idol for them to worship God. He now intuited that that seed of eagerness had germinated into something more. He became angry and distraught at the thought, and he quickened his pace on the descent.[474]

Moses Returns

When they entered camp, Moses saw an immense crowd of more than 500,000[475] gathered. Without a moment's hesitation, he made a beeline for the gathering. When he approached, he stopped in his tracks as his gaze fell upon the golden calf to which all were facing. He broke the silence when he bellowed, "How awful have you all been in my absence!"[476] Everyone turned, aghast. He continued, "My people, didn't your Lord make you an irrevocable promise? Was my absence too long for you? Did you desire that your Lord's wrath should descend on you, and for that, you reneged on your covenant with me?"[477]

---

471. Qur'ān 7:157

472. Qur'ān 2:56 and *Biḥār al-anwār* vol. 13 p. 218 tr. 10

473. Qur'ān 20:85

474. Qur'ān 20:86

475. *Biḥār al-anwār* vol. 13 p. 235 tr. 43

476. Qur'ān 7:150

477. Qur'ān 20:86

They replied, "We did not renege on our covenant of our own accord. Rather, we were laden with the weight of the Egyptians' jewels, so we cast them into the fire, and likewise, did Sāmirī cast."[478]

Moses scanned the ashen faces to see if Aaron was among them. He was not. He spotted him in the distance, sitting apart from the crowd with a smaller crowd of about 12,000[479] around him. Moses rushed in his direction. In one sweeping motion, he cast aside the tablets which were still nestled in his arms and unceremoniously seized his brother's head, pulling him near.[480] He asked, "Aaron, what kept you from coming for me when you saw them going astray? Did you disobey my command?"[481]

Aaron uttered, "O my mother's son![482] Do not grab my beard or my forelock to chide me.[483] These people overpowered me and nearly killed me.[484] I feared lest you should say, 'You have caused a rift among the Israelites, and you did not heed my words.'[485] Do not give our enemies opportunity to gloat over me, and do not count me among these wrongdoers."[486]

Moses exhaled deeply in relief. He had known that his brother had not let him down. But he had to be sure. His grip on Aaron's head loosened into a hug. He uttered, "My Lord, forgive me and

---

478. Qurʾān 20:87

479. *Biḥār al-anwār* vol. 13 p. 235 tr. 43

480. Qurʾān 7:150

481. Qurʾān 20:92–3

482. In one tradition, Imam al-Ṣādiq mentions that Aaron called Moses "my mother's son" instead of "my father's son" to remind him of the closeness between them. Half-brothers who share a father are more likely to have rivalries than half-brothers who share a mother. Moses and Aaron were full brothers, yet Aaron chose to mention their mother to remind Moses that they are not supposed to be enemies (*Biḥār al-anwār* vol. 13 p. 219 tr. 14).

483. Qurʾān 20:94

484. Qurʾān 7:150

485. Qurʾān 20:94 and *Biḥār al-anwār* vol. 13 p. 220 tr. 14

486. Qurʾān 7:150

my brother, and admit us into your mercy, for you are the most merciful of all."[487]

Confrontation With Sāmirī

With Aaron at his side and their faithful supporters in tow, Moses turned to face the massive crowd who encircled the golden calf. Moses approached Sāmirī, stared him in the face and inquired, "What do you have to say, Sāmirī?"[488]

He replied tentatively, "I noticed something that the others did not. So I took a handful of dust from the messenger's hoofmarks and cast it into the molten gold. That is what my soul prompted me to do."[489]

Sāmirī and his cohorts had perpetrated a cardinal sin, idol worship, for which they knew the punishment was death. Sāmirī's culpability in this matter was greater than the others because he had pioneered the way. Nonetheless, God told Moses to show him clemency because of his enduring generosity.[490] God is loath to ignore the manifestations of his own attributes, even if he finds them in the worst of his creatures. Instead of executing him, Moses banished him saying, "Get away from here! Henceforth, it shall be your lot in life to say, 'Do not touch me!'[491] This is your worldly punishment. Soon, you shall meet your maker at a predetermined time from which you shall not be absent. Now look at this idol to whom you were so devoted. We shall grind it into shards and then scatter its shards into the sea.[492] Your god is solely the one God

---

487. Qur'ān 7:151

488. Qur'ān 20:95

489. Qur'ān 20:96

490. *Biḥār al-anwār* vol. 13 p. 230 tr. 40

491. The commentators have offered various possible meanings for this sentence. Some have suggested that it is wholly figurative to communicate his banishment from Israelite society. Others have suggested that he was compelled to repeat this phrase whenever anyone tried to come close to him. Yet others have suggested that he was afflicted with some mental or physical sickness because of which he felt pain whenever he was near people.

492. Qur'ān 20:97. The word *nuḥarriqannahu* is usually construed to mean

other than whom there is no god. His knowledge encompasses all things."[493]

The Punishment For Idol Worship

When the calf was destroyed and it was filed into shards and Sāmirī was banished, Moses turned his attention to those who had followed Sāmirī and had reneged on their covenant to worship the one God. He scolded them for their foolishness and impatience. He told them, "Those of you who worshiped the calf shall be seized by their Lord's wrath and shall be denigrated in this life. Thus, do we requite the fabricators of lies against God. However, toward those of you who commit misdeeds but repent after committing them and reaffirm their faith, I tell you your Lord is, after such repentance, all-forgiving, all-merciful."[494] He continued addressing both groups together, "My people, you have wronged yourselves by making the calf an idol. Therefore, repent to your creator. Then execute the idol worshipers among you! This is the best thing to repair your relationship with your creator."[495]

"we shall burn it." However, this raises the problem of whether a golden statue can be burned. Many commentators have concluded, based on this meaning of the verb, that Sāmirī had miraculously turned the golden calf to a living calf with flesh and bones which Moses then burned. However, this is incorrect for at least two reasons. First, the Qur'ān refers to the statue as a *jasad* which is a lifeless body, not a living one. Second, it would be unjust for God to allow a person who is leading others away from him to perform a miracle. For this reason, other commentators have concluded that the verb *nuḥarriqannahu* should be construed to mean "we shall file or grind it into shards." A variant of this verb is used to denote the filing of metal with a file or rasp. This meaning is mentioned in one tradition (*Biḥār al-anwār* vol. 13 p. 234 tr. 43). It is also far more appropriate in Moses' circumstance. If he had melted down the calf or broken it using an axe, it would have been possible for some deviant people to procure pieces of the broken statue and preserve them as sacred relics, and the spirit of idolatry would have endured. By filing it into tiny shards and dispersing the shards into the sea, they could wholly consign the calf to history.

493. Qur'ān 20:98

494. Qur'ān 7:152–3

495. Qur'ān 2:54

Such a severe sentence took everyone by surprise—those who were guilty of idol worship because they feared death and those who were not because they were reluctant to kill their brethren. The idol worshipers were too fearful to admit their guilt. When they were asked, they would simply say, "I am not guilty. It was others who worshiped the calf." God told Moses to mix some of the golden shards with water and have everyone drink from the water. The lips and nose of all who were guilty turned black thereby indelibly revealing their guilt.[496]

Those who were innocent complained to Moses, "Our punishment is worse than that of our brethren. With our own hands, you want us to kill our fathers, mothers, sons, and brothers though we did nothing wrong to deserve this. In this way, we are being punished as they are."

God sent the message through Moses, "You are being made to do this because you did not disavow them or fight with Aaron against them."

Moses added, "If you pray to God through Muḥammad and the family of Muḥammad, he has promised to make it easy for you to carry out these executions against those who deserve it."[497]

They all felt remorseful and realized that they had gone terribly astray. They said, "Should our Lord have no mercy on us or forgive us, we shall indeed be among the losers."[498]

Moses ordered the 588,000 who had worshiped the calf to stand and face their punishment. Then he ordered the 12,000 who had not followed Sāmirī to unsheathe their swords. He announced to the executioners, "I pray that God damn any among you who hesitates to execute a person to consider whether he is an acquaintance or a relative and thus spares him."[499] With that, the mass execution began.

---

496. *Biḥār al-anwār* vol. 13 p. 239 tr. 48

497. *Biḥār al-anwār* vol. 13 p. 234 tr. 43

498. Qurʾān 7:149

499. *Biḥār al-anwār* vol. 13 p. 234 tr. 43

A Stay of Execution

When thousands had been killed, a group of the survivors said to one another, "Has God not made the intercession of Muḥammad and his family such that no favor that is coupled with their names is rejected? Is it not through their names that the prophets of old sought intercession with God? Then why do we not seek their intercession?" Together they prayed, "Lord! Through Muḥammad the noble; through ʿAlī the virtuous and magnificent; through Fāṭimah the virtuous and immaculate; through al-Ḥasan and al-Ḥusayn the grandsons of the foremost of all messengers and the foremost of all people in paradise; and through their pure and good progeny, we beg you to forgive us our transgressions and grant us a stay of execution!"

At that moment, Moses received word from God, "Cease the killing! For I swore to myself that if any of them begs me, as they have begged me, to protect them from perpetrating such a sin again that I would forgive them and protect them. Even if Iblīs had prayed to me thus, I would have guided him. And if Nimrod and the Pharaoh had prayed to me thus, I would have saved them."[500]

Moses ordered that the executions be curtailed. He told those who were left, "God has accepted your penance. Indeed, he alone is the one who always accepts the sinners' repentance, for he is the All-Merciful."[501]

They buried the dead, and with heavy hearts, regrouped for what lay ahead.

The First Covenant

Moses' anger had now abated, so he gathered up the tablets whose inscriptions contained guidance and mercy for those who are in awe of their Lord.[502] He gathered all his people. He stood before them with Aaron on his right and the seventy men who had accompanied him up the mountain behind him. He showed his

500. *Biḥār al-anwār* vol. 13 p. 235 tr. 43

501. Qurʾān 2:54

502. Qurʾān 7:154

people the tablets God had given him. Then he ordered the seventy men to step forward, one by one, and bear witness that the tablets he now held in his hand had indeed been given to him by God. Then he read what was written upon them. He exhorted his people to abide by every word inscribed on the tablets and then bound them by a covenant to live and die by its teachings. They accepted.

The tablets contained some of the following teachings:

> He has succeeded who has given charity and remembered his Lord's name and prayed. Instead, you give priority to this temporal life when the hereafter is better and longer lasting.[503]
>
> O Moses! I have created you, chosen you, strengthened you, commanded you to obey me, and forbidden you to sin against me. If you obey me, I shall help you to obey. But if you sin, I shall not help you to sin. Moses, if you obey me, then it is because of my favor to you; and if you sin against me, then it is I who have all-conclusive and incriminating evidence against you.[504]
>
> O Moses! Fear me in even your secret affairs, and I shall guard your weaknesses. Remember me in private and during the joy of pleasure, and I shall remember you when your guard is down. Restrain yourself from being angry at those over whom I have given you power, and I shall refrain from being angry at you.[505]
>
> Do not transgress the sanctity of the Sabbath.[506] Hereafter, if anyone observes the Sabbath and does not allow himself to break it out of the fear of God, God will admit him to paradise. But if

503. Qur'ān 87:14–7

504. *Biḥār al-anwār* vol. 13 p. 328 tr. 5

505. *Biḥār al-anwār* vol. 13 p. 328 tr. 6

506. Qur'ān 4:154

anyone takes it lightly and deems it lawful to do work, though God has prohibited it on that day, God will cast him in hellfire.[507]

The Second Covenant

Then God said to Moses, "Moses, they have now accepted the scripture, the Torah inscribed upon these tablets. You must now present them with the standard[508] by which I will distinguish between the true believers and the weak of faith. Therefore, make another covenant with them, for I have sworn to myself not to accept anyone's faith or deeds unless they also accept this standard."

Moses asked, "Lord, what is this standard?"

God said, "They must swear that Muḥammad is the best of humankind and the foremost of the prophets; that his brother and successor ʿAlī is the best of the successors; that his friends and allies whom he guides are the foremost of creation; and that his followers who submit to him and bow before his directives and prohibitions and before the directives and prohibitions of his successors are the stars of the highest station of paradise and the kings and queens of the everlasting gardens."

Moses conveyed God's message and made the second covenant with his people. Some believed firmly in the covenant, but others made it only with their tongues.[509]

God knew the weakness of many of their resolve and wanted to leave them no excuse to renege on this covenant. He ordered Gabriel to uproot a nearby mountain with his wings and to suspend the mountain over their heads. It hung their like an enormous cloud, and they were convinced it was going to fall upon their

---

507. *al-Kāfī* 5.17.1

508. This tradition makes reference to the *kitāb* and *furqān* mentioned in Qurʾān 2:53. I have translated *kitāb* as "scripture" and *furqān* as "standard."

509. *Biḥār al-anwār* vol. 13 p. 233 tr. 43

heads.[510] God's voice rang out, "Hold firmly to what we have given you and remember what is in it!"[511]

They replied in unison, "We hear, and we obey!" But some uttered quietly, "We hear, and we *disobey*," for they were captivated by the golden calf and could not relinquish it.[512]

Ingratitude

With the promised scripture revealed and the covenant made, it was time for Moses to move the Israelites north toward the Holy Land. Throughout their journey, they continued to receive God's blessings of shade and manna and quail and water. But they lost sight of the blessings and grew ungrateful, able only to see the monotony of their diet and not its lifesaving grace. They complained, "Moses, we can no longer tolerate only one kind of food. So ask your Lord on our behalf if he would bring forth for us from that which the earth produces—of its greens and cucumbers and garlic and lentils and onions."

Moses answered, "Will you exchange what is better with what is inferior?"[513] When his question failed to elicit the desired compunction, he admonished them to be grateful saying, "My people, remember God's blessings upon you. Remember when he

---

510. Qur'ān 7:171, 2:63, and 2:93 and *Biḥār al-anwār* vol. 13 p. 213 tr. 6 and p. 241 tr. 48.

511. Qur'ān 2:63. Most commentaries and all of the traditions indicate that the Israelites initially refused to accept the covenant and that the mountain was raised over their heads to coerce them into accepting. Clearly, such a forced covenant would be of no value, for the nature of a covenant is that it is a consensual agreement between two parties. The two verses from *al-Baqarah* that mention this part of the story say, "Remember when we made with you a covenant and we lifted the mountain over you. We said, in hopes that you would be God-fearing, 'Hold firmly to what we have given you and remember what is in it'" (Qur'ān 2:63 and 2:93). The apparent meaning of the verse is that the covenant was made before the mountain was lifted over them. I have given precedence to this apparent meaning of the verse and the rational argument over the version transmitted in the traditions.

512. Qur'ān 2:93

513. Qur'ān 2:61

appointed prophets among you[514] and made you kings[515] and gave you what he gave no other nation."[516]

Enter Jerusalem

Then he exhorted them, "Go into this city, and you will have what you have requested.[517] Enter the city of Jerusalem, the Holy Land that God has ordained for you,[518] and eat thereof freely wherever you wish. Enter its gates with humility and say, 'We beg for *ḥiṭṭah* (forgiveness).' God shall forgive you your sins and increase the reward of the righteous.[519] But do not turn on your heels or you will be among the losers."[520]

There were some among them who uttered a prayer other than what they were told.[521] For them, Moses' exhortation was but a joke and so they mockingly said, "We beg for *ḥinṭah* (wheat)," instead of saying, "We beg for *ḥiṭṭah* (forgiveness)."[522] God sent down a plague from the sky to punish those individuals for their transgressions which they were wont to commit.[523]

The others complained, "Moses, a tyrannical people lives here. We shall not enter it until they leave. Once they leave, then we shall proceed."[524]

---

514. This is an allusion to Joseph and Jacob in addition to any other prophets from the Israelite line.

515. This is an allusion to Joseph and his successors who ruled over Egypt prior to the Pharaoh's coup.

516. Qur'ān 5:20

517. Qur'ān 2:61

518. Qur'ān 5:21

519. Qur'ān 2:58 and 7:161

520. Qur'ān 5:21

521. Qur'ān 2:59 and 7:162

522. *Biḥār al-anwār* vol. 13 p. 174 tr. 2

523. Qur'ān 2:59 and 7:162

524. Qur'ān 5:22

Moses and Aaron's two closest disciples, Joshua[525] and Caleb, were God-fearing and had been blessed by God with sound faith and courage. They urged the Israelites, "Go at them through the gate as Moses has commanded you. Once you have entered it, you shall be victorious. And put your trust in God, if you are faithful."[526]

They ignored Joshua and Caleb and said, "Moses, we shall never enter it so long as those people remain in it. You go along with your Lord and fight! We shall sit right here and await the outcome."[527]

Exasperated, Moses turned to God and said, "I have power over no one but myself and my brother, so distinguish between us and these transgressors."[528]

Forty Years Exile

God replied, "Because of their ingratitude and stubborn disobedience, the Holy Land shall hereby be forbidden for them for forty years."[529] Because of their choices, God revoked his decision to grace them with the Holy Land, and he transferred this grace to their children.[530] He continued, "They shall wander the earth. Moses, though you are concerned for their well-being, do not grieve for these transgressors."[531]

For the next forty years, the Israelites wandered the deserts outside the borders of the Holy Land. Each day, they would

---

525. In Arabic his name is *Yūshaʿ ibn Nūn.*

526. Qurʾān 5:23

527. Qurʾān 5:24

528. Qurʾān 5:25

529. Qurʾān 5:26

530. *Biḥār al-anwār* vol. 13 p. 180 tr. 11 and p. 181 tr. 13 and 14. This is another example of *badāʾ* by which God's decree changes based on the choices made by people. There is a tradition that I quoted in Abraham's story which said Moses was one of four prophets who were destined to fight with the sword (*Biḥār al-anwār* vol. 14 p. 2 tr. 2). It is clear from this part of the story that he was prepared to fight the people who occupied Jerusalem, but because of his people's desertion, God changed his plan for him.

531. Qurʾān 5:26

trudge more than 12 miles.[532] When they slept at night, God would transport them back to their starting point from the previous day, adding to their frustration and the futility of their situation.[533]

At some point during these forty years, God withheld revelation from Moses for thirty or forty days. Moses grew concerned that his people had once again displeased God. He climbed up Mount Arīḥā and prayed, "Lord, if it is because of the sins of the Israelites that you have withheld your revelation from me, then I beg you by your age-old precedent of forgiveness to forgive them."[534]

Hajj

One year,[535] Moses and Aaron, along with Aaron's two sons, Shabbar and Shabīr, excused themselves from the tedious fate of their people to perform the Hajj. Along the way, they met seventy other prophets of God[536] and altogether they proceeded toward Bakkah. The invitation of Abraham still hung in the air and Moses answered, "*Labbayk*! At your service, my Lord!"[537] and all the prophets who were with him repeated, "*Labbayk*! *Labbayk*!"[538] During their time there, Shabbar and Shabīr made it a point to pray in their great uncle Ishmael's house, directly beneath the place where the golden water spout now pours down.[539]

---

532. The tradition mentions four *farsakh*. Each *farsakh* is approximately 3.4 miles. So the distance they traveled was 13.6 miles per day.

533. *Biḥār al-anwār* vol. 13 p. 177 tr. 6

534. *Biḥār al-anwār* vol. 13 p. 8 tr. 9

535. There is no indication when they performed this Hajj. I have only placed it here in the story because it seems to fit best.

536. *Biḥār al-anwār* vol. 13 p. 11 tr. 16

537. *Biḥār al-anwār* vol. 13 p. 10 tr. 11

538. *Biḥār al-anwār* vol. 13 p. 10 tr. 13–14

539. *Biḥār al-anwār* vol. 13 p. 11 tr. 17

Quest For Khiḍr

Also during the forty years in the desert,[540] Moses journeyed to visit Prophet Khiḍr.[541]

Moses was with his people one day when someone commented, "I do not believe there is anyone on earth more knowledgeable than you, O Moses!"

Moses immediately felt indignant at this person's praise of him, for such praise threatens to sow the seed of arrogance in even the best of people. He asked God, "Is there any man more knowledgeable than I?" He wanted desperately to reaffirm his humility by meeting someone who could remind him how limited his own knowledge was.[542]

God told him to go and meet Khiḍr. Khiḍr's name was Tāliā, son of Milkān, son of ʿĀbir, son of Arfakhshad, son of Shem, son of Noah. He was a prophet and a messenger sent by God to his people to call them to the belief in the one God, his prophets, his messengers, and his scriptures. He was one of God's servants whom God had granted special mercy and whom he had taught special knowledge.[543] His miracle, with which he was able to prove

---

540. There is no clear indication when this story took place with respect to the rest of Moses' story. One tradition indicates that it took place after Moses had performed all of his miracles and fulfilled much of his mandate as a prophet (*Biḥār al-anwār* vol. 13 p. 278 tr. 1). Thus, it seems appropriate to place it late in his story.

541. There is a difference of opinion over whether he was a prophet or not. At least one tradition explicitly says that he was (*Biḥār al-anwār* vol. 13 p. 286 tr. 4). *Al-Mīzān* also concludes with confidence that the Qur'ān describes him in terms appropriate for a prophet (see his discussion of Qur'ān 18:60–82). Many traditions mention that Khiḍr has been allowed by God to live indefinitely. There are mentions of him meeting with Prophet Muḥammad and some of the imams.

542. Several traditions quote Moses' question, "Is there any man more knowledgeable than I?" and spin it in a way that reeks of arrogance, as though he were boasting about being unrivaled in his knowledge. No righteous person, and certainly not a prophet of God, would be boastful. I have therefore kept his words but spun it a way that is in keeping with what we know of a prophet's character.

543. Qur'ān 18:65

his credentials as God's prophet, was that the ground around any place he sat would burst into verdure and flowers. This is why he came to be known as Khiḍr, the Green One.[544] God told Moses he would find Khiḍr at the Confluence of the Two Seas where a dead fish would miraculously come to life.[545]

Moses placed Aaron in charge of the Israelites and took Joshua with him on his journey.[546] He told him, "I intend to travel until I reach a place called the Confluence of the Two Seas or spend my life searching."[547] They packed meager provisions including a whole dried fish which Moses entrusted to Joshua's care. They traveled until they reached a place where two seas met. They sat for a time upon a rock to rest. Joshua laid the fish and his pack down at the water's edge so he could drink and wash himself. He must have inadvertently splashed a little water on the fish because it suddenly jerked and flicked its tail, and before he could react, it found its way into the sea and vanished into the depths.[548] Joshua was so amazed he wished to alert Moses, but he saw that Moses was napping, and he did not want to disturb him. By the time Moses awoke, Joshua had forgotten what had happened to the fish and they continued on their way.[549]

They walked on for a while until midday. Moses said to Joshua, "Bring us our meal. We have met with much fatigue due to this journey of ours."[550] Suddenly, Joshua remembered what had happened to the fish. He said, "You know, when we took a rest at that rock, I forgot to tell you about the fish—none but Satan made

---

544. *Biḥār al-anwār* vol. 13 p. 287 tr. 4

545. Qur'ān 18:60–64. The commentators of this verse have offered various guesses as to the location referred to by the Confluence of the Two Seas. Moses' statement, "or spend my life searching," indicates that he too did not know where this place was but was on a quest to find it.

546. *Biḥār al-anwār* vol. 13 p. 286 tr. 3

547. Qur'ān 18:60

548. An alternative explanation is that the dead fish simply slipped into the sea and sank out of reach without miraculously coming to life.

549. Qur'ān 18:61

550. Qur'ān 18:62

me forget. Anyway, amazingly, the dried fish made its way into the sea."[551]

Moses exclaimed, "That is what we were after!" So they returned, retracing their footsteps to the spot where they had been.[552]

Encounter With Khiḍr

They found Khiḍr who was praying, sitting in a bed of flowers that had blossomed around him. They approached him and sat nearby until he was done. He greeted them and asked, "Who are you?"

Moses replied, "I am Moses, son of Amram, and this is Joshua, son of Nūn."

Khiḍr asked with a hint of recognition, "You are Moses with whom the Almighty spoke?" When he admitted that he was, he asked, "What can I do for you?"[553]

Moses said, "I have come to learn from you. May I follow you? And will you teach me of the guidance you have been taught?"[554]

He replied, "You will never have the patience to be with me.[555] I have been assigned a task that you cannot bear, just as you have been assigned a task I cannot bear.[556] You have not been given awareness of the secrets that I bear, so how can you possibly have patience in the face of events of whose underlying wisdom you are unaware."[557]

Moses said eagerly, "You will, God willing, find me to be patient, and I will not disobey you in any matter."[558]

Khiḍr said sternly, "If you follow me, do not question me concerning anything until I myself make a mention of it to you."[559]

---

551. Qur'ān 18:63

552. Qur'ān 18:64

553. *Biḥār al-anwār* vol. 13 p. 279 tr. 1

554. Qur'ān 18:66

555. Qur'ān 18:67

556. *Biḥār al-anwār* vol. 13 p. 279 tr. 1

557. Qur'ān 18:68

558. Qur'ān 18:69

559. Qur'ān 18:70

Moses agreed to the terms. He dismissed Joshua and told him to return to join the Israelites.[560]

He Knocks a Hole in the Boat

Khiḍr set off with Moses in tow. They boarded a small boat at a nearby dock. It was a simple vessel owned in partnership by several poor sailors who eked out a meager living by catching fish and shuttling passengers here and there.

As they waited for the sailors to settle in, Moses caught a glimpse of a tiny swift that was darting across the water's surface, chirping and snatching up tiny sips of water. A broad smile appeared on Khiḍr's otherwise straight face. He asked, "Do you know what she is telling us?"

Moses replied, "No. Tell me."

Khiḍr said, "She says, 'By the Lord of the sky and earth and by the Lord of the sea, your combined knowledge in relation to God's knowledge is like this sip of water I draw with my beak in relation to this sea, rather less still!'"[561]

Just as the sailors were about to set sail, Khiḍr stood up, raised his staff, and without notice, knocked a hole through the boat's bottom. The sailors pounced on him and kicked them both off their boat before resigning to the task of repairing their beloved vessel. Moses was shocked. He chastised Khiḍr saying, "Did you make a hole in it to drown those poor sailors? You have done a monstrous thing!"[562]

Khiḍr knowingly smiled and shook his head, saying, "Did I not say, 'You will never have the patience to be with me?'"[563]

---

560. There is no evidence of this except that there is no mention, even in a pronoun, of Joshua accompanying them on the following three adventures. In fact, all the pronouns refer to "two people," Moses and Khiḍr, indicating that Joshua was no longer present.

561. *Biḥār al-anwār* vol. 13 p. 302 tr. 22

562. Qur'ān 18:71

563. Qur'ān 18:72

Moses realized he had breached the terms to which he had agreed. He said, "Please, do not take me to task for having forgotten, and do not be hard on me."[564]

He Slays a Boy

They set off from the docks until they encountered a young boy. Without a moment's hesitation, Khiḍr drew a blade and slew the child.

Again Moses stood aghast. He exclaimed, "Have you just slain an innocent soul without his having slain anyone else? You have done a despicable thing."[565]

Again Khiḍr knowingly smiled and shook his head, saying, "Did I not tell you, 'You will never have the patience to be with me?'"[566]

Moses conceded, "If I question you about anything after this, do not keep me in your company. You will be released from our agreement as far as I am concerned."[567]

He Takes No Wages

So they set off once more. They were extremely hungry as they had taken no provisions with themselves. They came upon the people of a town. They asked the people for food, but they refused to extend any hospitality to them. In that town, they found a wall which was about to collapse. Khiḍr set out to erect it and prevent it from toppling. Moses expected him to ask the owners of the property to compensate him for his efforts with some food, but he did not. As they walked away, Moses blurted, "Had you wished, you could have taken wages for that work."[568]

---

564. Qurʾān 18:73

565. Qurʾān 18:74

566. Qurʾān 18:75

567. Qurʾān 18:76

568. Qurʾān 18:77

Khiḍr Explains

Khiḍr said with finality, "This, I am afraid, is where you and I shall part. But I shall first inform you of the reality of these things for which you did not have sufficient patience.[569] As for the boat, it belongs to those poor people who work at sea. I wanted to make it defective, for on their tail was a king who was wrongfully confiscating every vessel he found."[570] By knocking a hole in it, he was able to convince the king's men that this boat was of no use to the king's fleet and so they left it to its rightful owners.

Khiḍr continued, "As for the boy, his parents are believers, and we feared he would overwhelm them with rebellion and disbelief."[571] He knew that this boy, though innocent now, would eventually turn against God and sway his parents from belief because of their love for him.[572] He continued, "We hope their Lord will give them, in exchange, a child who is purer than he and more compassionate."[573] It was not long before God provided them with a righteous daughter who would later be married to a prophet,[574] and from their line would arise seventy prophets.[575]

Khiḍr continued, "As for the wall, it belongs to two orphans in the city. Under it lies a treasure belonging to them.[576] Their treasure comprises not only gold and silver but a tablet upon which the following words are inscribed:

> In the name of God, the All-Beneficent, the Ever-Merciful.

---

569. Qurʾān 18:78

570. Qurʾān 18:79

571. Qurʾān 18:80

572. *Biḥār al-anwār* vol. 13 p. 310 tr. 42

573. Qurʾān 18:81

574. *Biḥār al-anwār* vol. 13 p. 285 tr. 1

575. *Biḥār al-anwār* vol. 13 p. 280 tr. 1

576. Qurʾān 18:82

> I am God; there is no god but me. Muḥammad shall be my messenger.[577]
>
> I wonder how a person can be exultant when he is certain of death.
>
> I wonder how a person can laugh without restraint when he is certain of the reckoning.
>
> I wonder how a person can fret over a loss or be impatient with what he is provided when he is certain of God's decree.
>
> I wonder how a person can place his hopes in the temporal world when he sees how fickle it is with its denizens.
>
> I wonder how a person can deny the life to come when he sees the life that is here.[578]

Their father was a righteous man.[579] So your Lord, out of his mercy, desired that his sons should recover their treasure when they come of age. I did not do any of these things according to my own judgment." Khiḍr was executing the decree of God in the same way God's angels usually do. He concluded, "This is the reality of these things for which you did not have sufficient patience."[580] Thus, Moses reaffirmed that his knowledge, as vast as it may be, paled in the face of God's knowledge.

As Moses prepared to leave, he asked Khiḍr for some parting advice. Khiḍr said, "Never denigrate a person because of a sin he has committed. There are three things that are most beloved to God: moderation in times of plenty; forgiveness despite having the

---

577. *Biḥār al-anwār* vol. 13 p. 295 tr. 10

578. *Biḥār al-anwār* vol. 13 p. 295 tr. 9 and tr. 10

579. Several traditions mention that it was not their immediate father but a forebear who lived some seven hundred years before (*Biḥār al-anwār* vol. 13 p. 310 tr. 44). The lesson is that a person's goodness brings benefit for generations to come.

580. Qur'ān 18:82

power to take revenge; gentleness with God's other servants. If a person is gentle with others in this world, God will be gentle with him on the Day of Resurrection. Finally, the key to wisdom is the fear of God Almighty."[581]

Death in the Wilderness

In the course of the forty years in the wilderness, one entire generation of Israelites died[582] including Aaron and Moses.[583] Only Joshua, Caleb, and their families survived from that generation because they had been willing to obey Moses' every command.[584] Aaron died before Moses, leaving behind his two sons, Shabbar and Shabīr.[585] Moses bathed his body and performed his funeral rites.[586]

Soon afterward, as Moses lay on his deathbed, he placed the wooden tablets upon which the Torah was inscribed,[587] his armor, his staff,[588] some of his garments, some manna, his sandals, Aaron's turban,[589] and other relics in the wooden box Gabriel had given Moses' mother, Jochebed, so she could stow her infant away in case the authorities came for him. This box, thereafter known as the Ark of the Covenant, he entrusted to his successor, Joshua.[590] The Ark became a sign of the rightful Jewish prophet.

581. *Biḥār al-anwār* vol. 13 p. 294 tr. 8

582. *Biḥār al-anwār* vol. 13 p. 177 tr. 6

583. *Biḥār al-anwār* vol. 13 p. 27 tr. 2

584. *Biḥār al-anwār* vol. 13 p. 177 tr. 6

585. *Biḥār al-anwār* vol. 13 p. 11 tr. 15. This tradition further explains that these two names translate into Arabic as al-Ḥasan and al-Ḥusayn. According to another famous tradition, when Imam al-Ḥasan was born, God ordered Prophet Muḥammad to name him Shabbar, further extending the Tradition of Rank which stated that ʿAlī was to the Prophet what Aaron was to Moses. According to this later commandment, al-Ḥasan and al-Ḥusayn were to the Prophet what Shabbar and Shabīr were to Moses (*Amālī al-Ṭūsī* 1.13.32).

586. *Biḥār al-anwār* vol. 13 p. 364 tr. 4

587. *Biḥār al-anwār* vol. 13 p. 438 tr. 2

588. *Biḥār al-anwār* vol. 13 p. 443 tr. 8

589. *Biḥār al-anwār* vol. 13 p. 444 tr. 9

590. *Biḥār al-anwār* vol. 13 p.439–40 tr. 4

Then, at the age of 240,[591] on the eve of the 21st of Ramaḍān,[592] Moses died leaving no children to survive him.[593] After his death, a herald announced in the heavens, "Moses has died! But then what creature does not?"[594]

Eventually Joshua would lead the next generation of Israelites out of the desert and into the Holy Land just as God had promised.[595]

---

591. *Biḥār al-anwār* vol. 13 p. 6 tr. 2

592. *Biḥār al-anwār* vol. 13 p. 365 tr. 6

593. *Biḥār al-anwār* vol. 13 p. 27 tr. 2

594. *Biḥār al-anwār* vol. 14 p. 2 tr. 1

595. There is mention in several traditions that Ṣāfrā', Moses' wife, led a rebellion against Joshua in a story that parallels 'Ā'ishah's rebellion against Prophet Muḥammad's successor, Imam 'Ali (*Biḥār al-anwār* vol. 13 p. 366 tr. 8 and p. 367 tr. 10). I have not incorporated these into my story because the incident falls outside the current timeline. However, two questions come to mind regarding that story:

- There are no indications in the traditions that Ṣafrā' was rebellious toward Moses or Aaron or Joshua during Moses' lifetime the way 'Ā'ishah was clearly rebellious toward Prophet Muḥammad and his family, especially toward Fāṭimah and 'Alī. This is not to say that it is impossible for her to change, but the lack of earlier symptoms should make us pause before attributing such a heinous act to her.
- Her age would have been a factor. She would have been more than 200 years old according to the ages given in the traditions.

Ezekiel

Moses' Third Successor

After Moses died in the wilderness, according to Moses' express appointment, Joshua, son of Nūn,[1] assumed leadership of the Israelites and led them on their conquest of Jerusalem. Likewise, after Joshua, Caleb, son of Jephunneh[2] assumed this leadership role. Caleb's successor was the prophet Ezekiel[3] who was known in his time as *Ibn al-ʿAjūz*, or Son of the Old Woman. His mother had been old and barren. But when she prayed to God for a child, she was granted Ezekiel.[4]

City Destroyed by a Plague

During Ezekiel's time, there was a city in the Levant comprising some 70,000 households. Periodically, this city would be struck by a plague. During these outbreaks, the rich and powerful of the city would escape into the surrounding lands and wait out the disease. But the poor and disenfranchised would have no choice but to remain in the city and weather the storm of death brought by the plague.

In the aftermath of one such outbreak, the rich of the city commented, "If we stay in this city of ours, many of us will die."

---

1. In Arabic his name is *Yūshaʿ ibn Nūn*.

2. In Arabic his name is *Kālib ibn Yuḥannā*.

3. In Arabic his name is *Ḥizqīl*. Though his name is not mentioned in the Qurʾān, there is one verse that, according to the traditions of the Prophet's family, refers to an incident in which he took part (*Biḥār al-anwār* vol. 13 p. 385 tr. 6). For this reason, I have mentioned his story in this book.

4. *Majmaʿ al-bayān* quoted in *Biḥār al-anwār* vol. 13 p. 383 after tr. 5

Likewise, the poor commented, "If only we could escape from this city, we would no longer be decimated by this incessant plague."[5]

The rich and powerful decided that they would aid the poor, and together they would escape from their city and, thereby, the clutches of looming death.[6] They traveled a short distance to a neighboring city that had itself been wiped out by the plague not too long before. They took up residence there and began making their life anew when suddenly, at God's command, they all contracted the plague and died a quick death.[7]

Their plan had been laudable in every way except that they had begun to believe that the power to escape death was in their own hands, and they forgot that life and death were solely in the jurisdiction of God Almighty. God snatched away their lives to teach the world that, when people strive to stave off death, which they should do, they must simultaneously remember that their ability to do so and their success or failure is wholly dependent on God's will.[8]

Resurrected by Ezekiel

Some years later, Ezekiel was traveling in the vicinity of this city of the dead. He found their remains strewn all around in various stages of decomposition. He asked God to tell him their story.

Ezekiel pondered a while about the finality and inevitability of death and then prayed, "Lord, if you wish, please revive them just as you killed them so they can rebuild your land, populate it with believing offspring, and worship you."

God asked, "Ezekiel, if this is what you want, then I shall revive them all."

---

5. Admittedly, I have altered their comments slightly to make sense of the story.

6. Qurʾān 2:243

7. Qurʾān 2:243 and *al-Kafi* quoted in *Biḥār al-anwār* vol. 13 p. 385 tr. 6

8. This explanation is my own. I was not able to find any better justification of God's actions in the commentaries on this verse.

Ezekiel uttered some words that God taught him, and, immediately, bones and body parts that had been strewn all around, lurched to life and moved with a frenzy as they were reunited with their counterparts. Within moments, the entire population of the city stood before Ezekiel, bewildered, but very much alive.[9] He told them what had happened, and they praised God for having been merciful with them by reviving them and giving them a second lease on life.

Ezekiel, feeling a renewed sense of conviction at seeing the act of resurrection, proclaimed, "God is indeed all-powerful!"[10]

---

9. In the Old Testament, we find a similar account, although it seems to be told as a parable, not a real event (Ezekiel 37:1–14).

10. Qur'ān 2:243 and *al-Kafi* quoted in *Biḥār al-anwār* vol. 13 p. 385 tr. 6

Ishmael, Son of Ezekiel

Moses' Fourth Successor

God appointed Ezekiel's son Ishmael[1] as a prophet and messenger after him.[2] He was charged with the guidance of a people, but they refused to hear him and persecuted him relentlessly. Nonetheless he persevered in calling them to faith. He diligently exhorted his family to pray and give charity, undeterred by their incorrigible recalcitrance.[3]

True to His Word

He became known as *Ṣādiq al-Waʿd* because he was "true to his word."[4] Once, he promised to wait for someone at a particular place. The person forgot about their rendezvous and failed to show up. Ishmael, true to his word, waited for the person for an inordinate length of time until the person happened to pass by the agreed upon place, thereby releasing Ishmael from his promise.[5]

---

1. His name in Arabic is *Ismāʿīl*.

2. Qurʾān 19:54 mentions the name Ishmael among other prophets. There is a difference of opinion among Muslim scholars over the identity of this Ishmael. The predominant opinion among Sunnī scholars is that he is Ishmael, son of Abraham. The predominant view among Shīʿī scholars is that he was Ishmael, son of Ezekiel. Two facts corroborate the latter opinion:
    - One fact is that the imams explicitly refute that this verse refers to Abraham's son and name Ezekiel's son instead (*Biḥār al-anwār* vol. 13 p. 388 tr. 2 and p. 390 tr. 6).
    - A second fact is that that verse 19:54 mentions Ishmael after Moses (19:51) when it would have been more appropriate, had this been Abraham's son, to mention him after Abraham (19:41). *Al-Mīzān* also uses this point to argue for the latter view.

3. Qurʾān 19:55

4. Qurʾān 19:54

5. Some of the traditions mention that the person told him to wait (*Biḥār al-*

Last Request

Toward the end of his life, Ishmael's people became so rebellious that they began attacking him and were intent on killing him. God sent an angel named Saṭāṭāʾīl,[6] invested with the power to destroy his people and deliver him from their hands.

Saṭāṭāʾīl manifested before him as his people beat him to the brink of death and said, "Ishmael, I am Saṭāṭāʾīl, the Angel of

---

anwār vol. 13 p. 389 tr. 4). If this had been the case, he would not have been bound to wait since he would not have been bound by a promise. Others mention that he waited for an entire year until the person finally returned (*Biḥār al-anwār* vol. 13 p. 388 tr. 1). This seems to be extreme, and it raises the following questions:

- Did he have no duty more pressing than to wait idly?
- Why did he not send someone to remind the delinquent person?

Considering these points, I have concluded the following:

- He was not simply *told* to wait but rather *promised* the other person that he would wait. This fits better with his honorific, "True to his Word." If he had been told to wait and he did, it would have been more fitting to call him "the Obedient" than "True to his Word."
- He clearly waited a long time to have become a symbol of this virtue. However, the traditions that mention that he waited a *ḥawl* or "year" may have been exaggerating for emphasis. In English vernacular we sometimes use such extreme timeframes as in the phrases "He's taking forever" and "Sometime this century would be nice!" I should note that *al-Mīzān* rationalizes the possibility that he waited for a year by saying that people's level of diligence in fulfilling their promises varies. Some would wait until some other duty called. Some would wait until nightfall. Others are so diligent that they would wait forever and sacrifice everything to forestall breaking their promise. He asserts that Ishmael was at this level.
- The underlying message is important here, not the specific timeframe. Being true to one's word is not only a virtue but a duty. Accordingly, when asked to enumerate the cardinal sins in Islam, Sayyid Sīstānī enumerates "breaking a promise" as number 23 (www.sistani.org. Arabic Questions and Answers under the topic "*al-muḥarramāt*"). Accordingly, Ishmael clearly made a promise to wait for this person without qualifying the length of time he was willing to wait. For this reason, he was bound to wait indefinitely or risk failing to keep his word.

6. alternatively, Isṭāṭāʾīl

Destruction. God Almighty has sent me to you to punish your people if you so wish. What would you like me to do?"

Ishmael replied, "I do not need such help at this time, Saṭāṭā'īl."

God intervened and asked him, "Then what do you need?"

Ishmael replied, "Lord, you made a covenant with mankind, and, thus, they must accept you as their Lord, they must accept Muḥammad as their prophet, and they must accept his successors as his vicegerents. You have prophesied for us what Muḥammad's nation will do to his grandson Ḥusayn after him. You have promised that you will bring Ḥusayn back to life in this world so that he can take revenge upon those who will murder him and mutilate his body.[7] Lord, my request of you is that you bring me back to life along with Ḥusayn so that I too may take revenge upon these who now murder me."

God granted him his request just before he was killed. He will raise him again during the *Raj'ah* along with Imam al-Ḥusayn.[8]

---

7. This is a reference to the *raj'ah* or "second coming" when certain individuals who embodied pure good will be brought back to life along with those who embodied pure evil for a final battle of good against evil. Belief in the *raj'ah* is one of the core tenets of Islam and has been affirmed by the imams in countless traditions.

8. *Biḥār al-anwār* vol. 13 p. 390 tr. 6 and p. 388 tr. 2 and 3

Elijah

Ahab, King of Baalbek

While Joshua ruled over the Israelites, he divided the Holy Land into twelve regions and assigned each to one of the twelve tribes. The Levites, including the descendants of Aaron, occupied one of these regions, located in what later came to be known as Baalbek.[1]

This region was ruled by the Levite king, Ahab.[2] Ahab fell in love with a woman called Jezebel[3] from a distant land where the people worshiped idols. He proposed to her, but she insisted that she would marry him only if he allowed her to bring one of her idols whom her people called Baal.[4] At first he adamantly refused, but with time, his conscience succumbed to his desire, and he capitulated to her demand. Jezebel arrived at his city with a massive retinue of servants and priests whose purpose was to serve Baal.[5] With time, Jezebel's fervent devotion to her idols influenced Ahab and, eventually, the people of that region to follow her religion. Ahab even renamed his region Baalbek in honor of their newfound god.

---

1. *Biḥār al-anwār* vol. 13 p. 393 tr. 2. In Arabic, this city is known as *Baʿlabakka*, but the Lebanese have corrupted it to Baʿalbek or simply Baalbek.

2. He is referred to in the traditions only as "king." He is called Ahab in the Bible (1 Kings 17–22).

3. She is referred to in the traditions only as the wife of the aforementioned king. The Bible calls her Jezebel of the Sidonites (1 Kings 21).

4. The name Baal or Baʿl is not mentioned in this tradition. She simply refers to an idol without mentioning the name. However, I have inserted this name to bring out the connection between this tradition, other traditions, and the Qurʾānic reference to Baʿl (37:125). The Bible also mentions her devotion to Baal and how she influenced Ahab (1 Kings 16:29–34).

5. *Biḥār al-anwār* vol. 13 p. 400 tr. 6

Jezebel's Crimes

Idolatry was not Jezebel's only vice. She proved to be a vicious and bloodthirsty ruler. When Ahab was away on military campaigns, she would rule in his stead with an iron fist, persecuting those who still held firm to Moses' teachings. There was one man in particular with whom she dealt with unconscionable ill will. His name was Naboth.[6] He had lived in the vicinity of the palace, his property adjacent to Ahab's. The king had always liked Naboth for his strength of faith and kindness. Once, when the king was away, Jezebel seized the opportunity to usurp Naboth's land and property and execute him and his entire family. When Ahab returned, he was outraged, but as always, he let his love for his wife drown out the screams of his conscience.[7]

Elijah Sent to Baalbek

God sent one of his prophets from that region, from the line of Aaron,[8] named Elijah,[9] as a messenger to Baalbek.[10] Elijah had been working in the region to guide the Israelites. His new mission was to rebuke Ahab and guide him back to the right path. He lambasted Ahab saying, "God gave you your kingdom and a long life, and you

---

6. He is named in the Bible (1 Kings 21).

7. *Biḥār al-anwār* vol. 13 p. 393 tr. 2

8. *al-Mīzān* under 37:123–132

9. In Arabic his name is *Ilyās*. Some traditions refer to someone named *Ilyā*. ʿAllāmah al-Majlisī is of the opinion that they refer to the same person because the stories and the names are similar (*Biḥār al-anwār* vol. 13 p. 400 after tr. 7). I have accordingly assumed that Ilyā is a mistaken or alternate form of Ilyās and combined the stories. Interestingly, it seems some Christians are of the opinion that Elijah is pronounced "el-ī-YAW" which makes it very similar to Ilyā and Ilyās.

There are several traditions that mention that he, like Khiḍr, has been given perpetual life. In particular, one narrates an encounter between him and Prophet Muḥammad (*Biḥār al-anwār* vol. 13 p. 401 tr. 9). Another mentions his encounter with Imam al-Bāqir (*Biḥār al-anwār* vol. 13 p. 398 tr. 4).

10. Qurʾān 6:85

thank him by rebelling against him![11] Will you not fear God? Do you now pray to Baal and disavow God who is the Best of Creators and is your Lord and the Lord of your forebears?"[12]

Elijah's admonishment fell on deaf ears. Ahab refused to accept it. Even when Elijah conveyed God's threat to destroy him unless he repented, Ahab ridiculed him and banished him from Baalbek.[13]

Elijah took refuge in the surrounding mountains. Elijah remained in the mountains eating what fruits and greens he could gather, concealed through God's grace.[14] He asked God to withhold rain from Baalbek to bring the region to its knees, which he did, creating a drought that led to an intense famine that decimated their wealth and livestock.[15]

Ahab's son fell deathly ill as a result of the famine. Ahab called on his priests to make sacrifices to Baal to restore his health but to no avail. Seeing their god's inability to remedy their plight, Ahab thought of Elijah who, all those years before, had called him to renounce Baal and return to God Almighty.[16]

God told Elijah, "Return to Ahab for he is now ready to repent."[17]

In the meantime, Ahab sent delegations into the surrounding mountains where Elijah had last been seen to invite him back. Elijah heard their calls, and, according to God's instructions, he agreed to come back if they agreed to certain stipulations. He said, "My Lord has sent me to you and to your king. You must listen to his message to you. God orders you to return to your king and tell him, 'I, Elijah's god, am God, other than whom there is no god. I am the God of the Israelites and their creator. I provide for them, give them life, mete out death, cause them harm, and bring benefit

---

11. *Biḥār al-anwār* vol. 13 p. 400 tr. 6

12. Qur'ān 37:124–126

13. *Biḥār al-anwār* vol. 13 p. 393 tr. 2

14. *Biḥār al-anwār* vol. 13 p. 393 tr. 2

15. *Biḥār al-anwār* vol. 13 p. 400 tr. 6

16. *Biḥār al-anwār* vol. 13 p. 394 tr. 2

17. *Biḥār al-anwār* vol. 13 p. 400 tr. 6

to them, yet you dare to seek cure for your son from other than me?'"[18]

They bore Elijah's message to Ahab who realized the error of his ways.[19] He summoned Elijah to his court and guaranteed him amnesty and safe passage. Elijah asked him, "Do you promise to do whatever I say?" Ahab agreed and swore a solemn oath to that effect.

Elijah then ordered all of Ahab's courtiers out of his presence. He ordered Ahab to renew his covenant with God by sacrificing two bulls to him. Then he ordered him to execute his wife, Queen Jezebel, and to destroy the idol of Baal. Ahab did all that he was told and freed himself of the shackles of vice. He repented and reformed himself. God let the rain fall once again and restored Ahab's son to health.[20]

Elijah's Prayers

Elijah was a devoted servant of God who spent long hours in devotion. He used to prostrate and utter the following prayer:

> Is it fitting for you to punish me, Lord, when I have parched my throat for your sake?
>
> Is it fitting for you to punish me when I have rubbed my face in the dirt for your sake?
>
> Is it fitting for you to punish me when I have abstained from sin for your sake?
>
> Is it fitting for you to punish me when I have kept the night vigil for your sake?[21]

---

18. *Biḥār al-anwār* vol. 13 p. 394 tr. 2

19. There are two conflicting accounts. According to one, Ahab rebels and his son is killed (*Biḥār al-anwār* vol. 13 p. 394 tr. 2). According to another, he repents and Elijah triumphs (*Biḥār al-anwār* vol. 13 p. 400 tr. 6).

20. *Biḥār al-anwār* vol. 13 p. 400 tr. 6

21. *Biḥār al-anwār* vol. 13 p. 393 tr. 1

> Is it fitting for you to punish me despite the long nights I have spent standing in worship?
>
> Is it fitting for you to punish me despite my lengthy prayers to you?[22]

God responded, "Lift your head for I shall never punish you."

Elijah insisted, "What is to stop you from punishing me after you have promised not to punish me? Are you not my Lord, and am I not your slave? Am I not completely at your mercy?"

God repeated, "Lift your head for I shall never punish you. When I make a promise, I unfailingly fulfill it."[23]

He also used to offer the following prayer, morning and evening, to seek protection from death by drowning, burning, and choking:

> In the name of God. God's will be done. None thwarts harm but God.
>
> In the name of God. God's will be done. None brings goodness but God.
>
> In the name of God. God's will be done. There is no blessing but from God.
>
> In the name of God. God's will be done. We have no power or strength except through God, the High, the Great.
>
> In the name of God. God's will be done. May God shower his blessings on Muḥammad and his pure family.[24]

---

22. *Biḥār al-anwār* vol. 13 p. 400 tr. 7

23. *Biḥār al-anwār* vol. 13 p. 393 tr. 1

24. *Biḥār al-anwār* vol. 13 p. 399 tr. 5

Elisha

We know very little about Elisha.[1] We are told that he did many of the miracles that Jesus later did. He walked on water, raised the dead, and cured the leprous and the congenitally blind.[2]

He is mentioned twice in the Qurʾān in the ranks of prophets[3] indicating that he, too, was a prophet.

In the Old Testament, he is portrayed as the successor to Elijah[4].

---

1. In Arabic he is known as *al-Yasaʿ*. Elisha is pronounced "el-EE-shaw."

2. *Biḥār al-anwār* vol. 13 p. 401 tr. 8

3. He is mentioned in Qurʾān 6:86 among those favored above all people and in Qurʾān 38:48 among the good.

4. 2 Kings 2–9 and 13:14–21

Dhū al-Kifl

We know very little about Dhū al-Kifl. He is mentioned twice in the Qurʾān in the ranks of prophets.[1]

In one tradition, when Imam al-Jawād is asked about Dhū al-Kifl, he says he was one of the 313 messengers from among God's 124,000 prophets.[2]

Elisha's Successor

One tradition portrays him as the successor of Elisha. According to this tradition, when Elisha grew old, he wished to see his successor assume his duties during his lifetime so he could be assured that he would perform them well. He gathered his people and announced, "Whoever accepts three challenges from me shall be my successor. He must fast every day, spend the night in prayer, and control his anger."

A man named ʿUwaydiyā ibn Adrīm, who was slight in stature, rose and volunteered. Elisha paid him no heed. The next day, Elisha made the announcement again. Again ʿUwaydiyā rose. This time, after having given everyone ample chance to speak up, he chose him. ʿUwaydiyā became known as Dhū al-Kifl.[3]

The Devil Tests His Self-Control

Witnessing all this, Satan challenged his underlings to make Dhū al-Kifl angry. A devil named al-Abyaḍ volunteered.

When Dhū al-Kifl had just lain down for his siesta, al-Abyaḍ came in the form of a frail man crying, "I have been wronged!" Dhū al-Kifl listened patiently to his complaint and told him to summon the person who had wronged him. Al-Abyaḍ reluctantly agreed.

1. He is mentioned in 21:85 as one of the patient and in 38:48 as one of the good.

2. *Biḥār al-anwār* vol. 13 p. 405 tr. 2

3. No satisfying explanation is given for the meaning of his epithet.

The next day, he returned at the same time, claiming that his assailant refused to come. This time Dhū al-Kifl wrote a summons ordering the person to appear. On the following day, again, al-Abyaḍ came and cried his heart out. Dhū al-Kifl took him by the hand and agreed to follow him home and settle the matter there. Seeing his unending patience, al-Abyaḍ lost hope of ever angering him and disappeared.[4]

Another tradition places Dhū al-Kifl chronologically after Solomon.[5]

---

4. *Biḥār al-anwār* vol. 13 p. 404 tr. 1

5. *Biḥār al-anwār* vol. 13 p. 405 tr. 2

Samuel

Destruction at the Hands of the Copts

After Moses, the Israelites became steeped in sin and corruption. They rebelled against God's law and adulterated his religion despite the presence of prophets among them who strove to admonish them and lead them. In response, God allowed the Copts,[1] under the command of Goliath,[2] to decimate them. They massacred their men and boys, enslaved their women, looted their wealth, and drove them from house and home.[3] They destroyed their houses of worship and stole the Ark of the Covenant.[4]

This unassuming wooden box measured only two by three cubits.[5] It was the very box Gabriel had given Moses' mother,

---

1. In the Bible, they are referred to as Philistines. I found no mention of any equivalent term in our traditions, but in one they are referred to as Copts, Egyptians, so I have used the same.

2. In Arabic his name is *Jālūt*.

3. *Biḥār al-anwār* vol. 13 p. 439 tr. 4

4. *Biḥār al-anwār* vol. 13 p. 451 tr. 15. I was first tempted to think that this attack was one of the two promised destructions of the Temple mentioned in Qur'ān 17:4–7. However, this is definitely not the case. First, there is no mention of the Temple of Jerusalem in the story of Samuel. In fact, it was David or Solomon who first built the temple. Second, the aforementioned attacks on the temple probably refer to the Babylonian Captivity during Nebuchadnezzar's reign which began in 586 B.C.E. and the second destruction of the temple at the hands of the Roman, Titus, in 70 C.E. These events happened much later than the story of Samuel, Saul, David, and Goliath. Mention of this story can be found in 1 Samuel although much that is there must be taken with a grain of salt.

5. *Biḥār al-anwār* vol. 13 p. 443 tr. 8. A cubit was on the order of half a meter, so the ark's dimensions were 1m by 1.5m according to this tradition. This seems to be an odd dimension for a box made to hold a newborn. Either the dimension mentioned here is not accurate or the ark was not the same as the box made for Moses.

Jochebed, so she could stow the infant Moses away in case the authorities came for him.[6] Many years later, as Moses lay on his deathbed, he placed the wooden tablets upon which the Torah was inscribed,[7] his armor, his staff,[8] some of his garments, some manna, his sandals, Aaron's turban,[9] and other relics in it and entrusted it to his successor, Joshua.[10] From that time forward, the Ark became a sign of the rightful Jewish prophet. God only allowed those whom he had chosen to possess it.[11] It became a source of blessing and tranquillity for the Israelites.[12] They would carry it into battle and derive strength from it.

Appoint a King

Now, it was gone, and the ensuing chaos in the ranks of the Jews was crippling. Prophet Samuel[13] had grown very old and could no longer provide the leadership they needed to combat the Copts and free themselves of their hold.[14] It was time for God to make Samuel's successor known.

6. Qur'ān 20:39 and *Biḥār al-anwār* vol. 13 p. 439–40 tr. 4

7. *Biḥār al-anwār* vol. 13 p. 438 tr. 2

8. *Biḥār al-anwār* vol. 13 p. 443 tr. 8

9. *Biḥār al-anwār* vol. 13 p. 444 tr. 9

10. *Biḥār al-anwār* vol. 13 p.439–40 tr. 4

11. *Biḥār al-anwār* vol. 13 p. 456 tr. 18 and 19

12. Qur'ān 2:248

13. In Arabic his name is *Ushmū'īl.*

14. In studying this story, it is noteworthy that the Israelite elders did not ask Samuel to lead them but to appoint a king for them. If Samuel had been capable of leading, it would have made sense for them to have asked him or for him to have asserted himself to fill the role. It also contradicts what we know about God's divine guides (prophets and imams) to say that he was not possessed of sufficient leadership ability since these guides were meant to be guides and leaders in the most global sense. I could not find a tradition or commentary to satisfactorily answer this question. One tradition does suggest that there was a division of responsibility between prophets and kings—"kings led the troops, and prophets kept the king's affairs in order and gave him good omens" (*Biḥār al-anwār* vol. 13 p. 450 tr. 11). This "separation of temple and state" hardly accords with the Islamic model of prophethood. I believe the Bible provides a plausible

The Israelite leaders came to him and said, "Appoint for us a king that we may fight in the way of God."[15]

Besides the fact that appointing a successor was not in his hands, Samuel did not believe they had the wherewithal to actually fight. He said, "You have no sense of loyalty to God's cause or a desire to fight in his way.[16] Perhaps you will not fight if fighting is prescribed for you?"[17]

They asked incredulously, "Why would we not fight in the way of God when we have been expelled from our homes and separated from our children?[18] If God prescribes fighting for us, we will obey our Lord and fight our enemies."[19]

How Can Saul Be Our King?

Samuel then received his orders from God and conveyed to them, "God has appointed Saul[20] as your king."[21]

The very leaders who, a moment before, had claimed total subservience to the will of God now objected to his choice saying, "How shall *he* rule over *us* when *we* are more worthy of ruling than *he*, and he has not even been given ample wealth as we have?" The precedent until that time had been that all prophets were from the tribe of Levi, and all kings were from the tribe of Joseph.[22] God had favored these two tribes for these honors, and according to the Jews'

---

answer. There we are told that "Samuel grew old" (1 Samuel 8:1), and this is why his people came and requested that he appoint a king. If this is correct, then we can assume that Samuel was capable of leading them except that he was too old and weak. Accordingly, their request for a king was tantamount to saying, "When you appoint your successor, let him be one who will rule as a king."

15. Qur'ān 2:246

16. *Biḥār al-anwār* vol. 13 p. 450 tr. 11

17. Qur'ān 2:246

18. Qur'ān 2:246

19. *Biḥār al-anwār* vol. 13 p. 450 tr. 11

20. In Arabic his name is *Ṭālūt*.

21. Qur'ān 2:247

22. Some mention that the tribe of Judah was the tribe of kings (see *Majma' al-bayān* in his discussion on these verses).

misguided beliefs, once God gives such favor, he cannot retract it for his hands are tied.[23] Saul was from the tribe of Benjamin and so, in their eyes, was undeserving of such an appointment since God could not possibly transfer favor from them and their tribe to him and his.[24]

Samuel replied, "God himself has chosen him over you and enhanced him vastly in his physique and knowledge."[25] By this, he wished to refute their claims to superiority, for God, the Omnipotent, does as he wills. If he had deemed their tribes worthy of favor in the past, he was not compelled to continue his favor in the present when there was someone more worthy of it than they. And Saul was, indeed, worthy of God's favor for he possessed the two critical virtues of a successful military leader: knowledge and physical might. Physically, Saul was the heftiest of the Israelites and brave and strong. That he was also poor or from a less prominent tribe had no bearing on his irrefutable merits.[26] Samuel continued, "God gives dominion, which is his to give, to whomever he wishes. God is vastly generous and omniscient."[27]

The Israelite leaders were not convinced. So Samuel told them, "Proof of his dominion is that the Ark of the Covenant shall come to you. In its arrival, you will find comfort bestowed upon you by your Lord, and in it are what remains of the artifacts left by the family of Moses and the family of Aaron. Angels shall bear it. In all this there is proof for you, if you are going to believe."[28] With the miraculous return of their their long lost Ark, no grounds remained for them to deny that Saul was indeed their rightful king.

---

23. Qurʾān 5:64

24. *Biḥār al-anwār* vol. 13 p. 439 tr. 4, p. 438 tr. 1, and p. 450 tr. 11

25. Qurʾān 2:247

26. *Biḥār al-anwār* vol. 13 p. 439 tr. 4

27. Qurʾān 2:247

28. Qurʾān 2:248

Saul Tests His Troops

Saul set off with his troops and soon thereafter told them, "God shall test you by means of a river—whoever drinks freely from it shall no longer be part of my army, and whoever tastes but a handful of it shall remain part of my army."[29] He needed faithful troops, not just vast numbers, to stand up to Goliath's forces. Nonetheless, when they reached the river, his troops drank from it freely save some of them. He dismissed those who drank and sent them home.

He and, with him, those of strong faith who remained crossed the river and soon reached the field where Goliath's forces were entrenched. Those who had tasted but a handful, upon seeing the host before them, lost their resolve. They said, "We do not have the strength on this day to fight Goliath and his troops." These too, Saul dismissed.

Few Against Many

Only those who had exercised enough self-control to refrain completely from even a handful of water—who knew they would meet God—said, "How many a company of few has vanquished a company of many by God's leave! For God is with the perseverant."[30] The next day, when they faced Goliath and his troops at the commencement of battle, they prayed, "Lord, bestow on us the capacity to persevere, make firm our feet, and aid us against these unbelieving people."[31]

---

29. Qur᾿ān 2:249

30. Qur᾿ān 2:249. One tradition mentions that the final count of soldiers left to fight was 313 (*Biḥār al-anwār* vol. 13 p. 438 tr. 1). Another mentions 60,000 (*Biḥār al-anwār* vol. 13 p. 443 tr. 6).

31. Qur᾿ān 2:250

They fought strongly and remained firm. David killed Goliath,[32] and, without a leader, his troops could not muster a fight. In the end, by God's leave, Saul and his troops vanquished their enemy.[33]

---

32. There is a record of some details surrounding the circumstances by which David killed Goliath including the popular story that he killed him with a single pebble launched by his sling (*Biḥār al-anwār* vol. 13 p. 452 tr. 17). This account follows the Biblical account verbatim and contains several questionable points that portray Saul and David in questionable light, thus I have decided to disregard it and stick to the terse, unembellished Qur'ānic account.

33. Qur'ān 2:251

David

When David[1] was born, he had already been circumcised, indicating that he had been chosen for God's special service.[2] When he was a young man, he fought in King Saul's army along with his brothers and father. Despite his youth, he was mighty and fierce.[3] It was he who dealt Goliath the death blow that had ended the Coptic occupation of Jerusalem.[4] He eventually became king of the Israelites and was chosen by God as his prophet.

God revealed a book to David known as the Psalms,[5] on the twenty-eighth of Ramaḍān,[6] altogether as a complete book.[7] The Psalms contained epic stories, praise of God, and supplications[8] but not law since David and his followers were still bound to follow the law of Moses. David used to recite the Psalms in a voice so

---

1. His name in Arabic is *Dāwūd*. One tradition indicates that the meaning of his name was derived from the phrase meaning "He cured his own wounds with love...presumably his love for God (دَاوَى بِوُدٍّ) (*Biḥār al-anwār* vol. 14 p. 2 tr. 4).

2. *Biḥār al-anwār* vol. 14 p. 2 tr. 3

3. Qur'ān 38:17

4. Qur'ān 2:250

5. It is referred to in the Qur'ān as the *Zabūr* (4:163) which seems to be a generic name for a "book."

6. *Biḥār al-anwār* vol. 14 p. 33 tr. 1

7. *Biḥār al-anwār* vol. 14 p. 33 tr. 2

8. *Biḥār al-anwār* vol. 14 p. 37 tr. 12

enchanting that the mountains and birds exalted God alongside him[9] morning and evening.[10]

In the Psalms was written, "The righteous shall inherit the earth."[11]

For this gift of revelation and divine knowledge, David thanked God saying, "Praise is for God who favored me more than he did many of his other believing servants."[12]

God favored David because he spent much time in prayer,[13] and he used to fast one day out of every two.[14]

A Frog Teaches Him

Once, when David had finished reciting the Psalms, God sent a small frog to remind him to remain humble despite his beautiful voice and his accompaniment by the chorus of birds and mountains. The frog asked, "David, are you pleased with your worship today?" He replied that he was. The frog continued, "Do not be too pleased for each night I and my kind exalt God one thousand times, and each exaltation is followed by three praises. We do this from our watery abode. Then, when we hear the screech of a bird flying overhead, and we perceive the hunger in his voice, we jump and

---

9. Qur'ān 21:79, 34:10, 38:19 and *Biḥār al-anwār* vol. 14 p. 3 tr. 7. Some commentators suggest that the exaltations of the mountains and birds that are mentioned here are the same ones that are mentioned in Qur'ān 17:44. I, however, do not believe such silent, indiscernible exaltations would warrant mention as one of David's miracles since everything is constantly exalting him in this way anyway. Thus, what happened during David's time must have been something more than this. For instance, their exaltations must have been audible to all—not that God made a sound be heard from them but that their natural exaltations were made audible to all.

10. Qur'ān 38:18

11. Qur'ān 21:105. This phrase also appears in the current Psalms in the Old Testament. There we read, "The righteous will inherit the land and dwell in it forever" (Psalm 37:29). One tradition construes this statement as a prophecy for Imam al-Mahdī and his companions (*Biḥār al-anwār* vol. 14 p. 37 tr. 12).

12. Qur'an 27:15

13. Qur'ān 38:17

14. *Biḥār al-anwār* vol. 14 p. 15 tr. 26

splay ourselves in full view of the bird so that it may eat us up."[15] He hoped to show David how his exaltations of God were fewer in number than theirs and required no great sacrifice the way theirs did.

A Caterpillar Teaches Him

Another time, David was reciting especially loudly. When he was done, he noticed a tiny red caterpillar inching along next to him. He watched it until it stopped in front of him. He thought to himself, "I wonder why God has created such a creature."

God gave the caterpillar power to speak to David. It asked, "O Prophet! Have you ever heard my movements or seen any sign of my having passed your way?" David said that he had not. The caterpillar continued, "God Almighty hears my footsteps and my breaths and sees where I have passed. So lower your voice."[16]

The Rock

During the eleventh year of his rule, a plague descended on the people of Jerusalem. He instructed them all to gather with him at the great rock where they used to worship. David had witnessed a constant stream of angels rising and descending from that spot, and so he knew it would be the best place for him to plead with God. He stood upon the great rock and begged God to relieve his people of the plague. His prayer was answered and the plague was lifted.

David decided to make that rock a formal place of worship, and so he began construction of a sanctuary on that spot. This sanctuary came to be known as the Holy of Holies. Millennia later, it would come to be known as the Dome of the Rock.[17]

---

15. *Biḥār al-anwār* vol. 14 p. 16 tr. 28

16. *Biḥār al-anwār* vol. 14 p. 17 tr. 29

17. *Biḥār al-anwār* vol. 14 p. 14 tr. 23 from *al-Kāmil fī al-taʾrīkh*

Two Disputing Parties

God consolidated David's power, fortified his kingdom, and gave him wisdom and decisive judgment[18] but only after testing him. To this end, God sent a group of angels in the guise of two disputing parties. David was holed up in his sanctuary, deeply engaged in worship, when these parties scaled the sanctuary's wall. Their sudden appearance by way of such an odd entrance frightened David.

They told him, "Do not be afraid. We are two disputing parties. One of us has transgressed against the other, so judge truly between us, and do not be unjust, and guide us to the straight path." Still bewildered, David agreed to hear their dispute.

One of them said, pointing to another, "This is my brother. He has ninety-nine sheep, and I have only one. Yet he demanded, 'Hand her over to me,' and when he said this, he was overbearing in his address."

David, who was a sworn advocate of the downtrodden and oppressed, was wholly convinced by this man's complaint. He hastily said, "Your brother has wronged you by demanding that your sheep be added to his. Many among the masses[19] wrong one another thus. Only those who believe and do good deeds are exempt. Alas, how few they are!"

No sooner had David said this than he realized that we had just tested him and that he had failed to hear both sides of the dispute. He had been so eager to rescue this man from his brother's oppression, and so convinced that this brother had acted unscrupulously, as most people do, that he had failed to be impartial and fair. With deep regret, David sought forgiveness from his Lord and bowed low and repented.

---

18. Qur'ān 38:20

19. All the commentaries to which I referred construed the word *khulaṭā'* (sing. *khalīṭ*) to mean "partners," meaning that most business partners wrong one another. This is indeed one of the meanings of the word, but it has nothing to do with the story at hand. There is no indication that the two brothers are partners who own the hundred sheep together. Instead, I think the word is used in the same meaning as *akhlāṭ* meaning "the masses."

Because he realized his mistake and sought forgiveness, God forgave him his oversight and raised him to a high station.[20] God told him, "O David! We hereby make you our vicegerent on earth, so judge between people justly, and do not follow your whims, or they will lead you away from God's path. And those who lose God's path shall suffer a severe punishment because they have forgotten the Day of Reckoning."[21]

Judgment Through Unseen Evidence

With his newly gotten authority, David set about judging cases and delivering justice. But he soon realized the limitations of his court. Every once in a while, it happened that he was sure of a person's guilt, but he could not prosecute him because of a lack of incriminating evidence. He asked God to allow him to judge, not based on evidence and the testimony of witnesses, but based on God's divine knowledge. God told him, "You have asked me for information of which I have never apprised anyone, and upon which it is not fitting for anyone but me to judge."

David insisted. God sent Gabriel to warn him once more. But when David continued to insist, he told him, "God has answered your request. The first case that will be presented to you tomorrow will be such a case.

The next morning, two men appeared before him, one old and the other young. The young man held a bunch of grapes in his hand. The old man said, "O Prophet of God! This young man came into my garden and destroyed my grape vines and ate from my grapes without my permission."

David asked the young man, "What is your side of the story?" He admitted that he had done whatever he was accused of.

---

20. There is a connection between David's mistake, his repentance, and God making him a vicegerent and, hence, judge. David's response to his own mistake shows his own humility and willingness to submit to truth. This is the raw material needed for God to choose someone and fortify him with infallibility. There is clearly a strong parallel between this story and the story of Adam. In both cases, God created a scenario to teach a crucial lesson under safe circumstances where the person could cause no real harm and break no real laws.

21. Qur'ān 38:21–26

God warned David once again, "If I reveal the true verdict in this case and you pass judgment accordingly between these two, your heart will not like it, and your people will not accept it. David, the old man broke into the young man's father's garden and killed him. He stole his garden and stole forty thousand silver pieces from him and buried them in a corner of the garden. Give the young man a sword and order him to execute the old man. Then turn the garden back over to him, and tell him to dig is such-and-such a place to recover his father's money."[22]

David passed judgment as God instructed him. There was an uproar among the Israelites. They exclaimed, "He has ordered a thief to execute his victim!"

David beseeched God to save him from the impending backlash of his people. God informed him where the young man's father was buried. He told him to go there with the Israelites and resuscitate and invoke him so that he could himself describe the circumstances of his death. He did this, and the Israelites were satisfied.[23]

God told David, "In the future, judge based on evidence and the testimony of witnesses, and do not ask to pass judgment based on my knowledge until the Day of Judgment."[24]

Judgment Through Interrogation

In another case, David did not dare ask for God's secret knowledge of the truth, but he employed ingenious interrogation methods to uncover the truth. A woman complained that her husband had taken all his money and journeyed to do business along with a company of men from their village. When the company returned, her husband was not among them. When she asked after him, they

---

22. *Biḥār al-anwār* vol. 14 p. 7 tr. 13

23. *Biḥār al-anwār* vol. 14 p. 6 tr. 12

24. *Biḥār al-anwār* vol. 14 p. 8 tr. 14. Admittedly, I have combined several stories into one. In one of the stories, the stolen item is grapes (*Biḥār al-anwār* vol. 14 p. 7 tr. 13), in one it is a cow (*Biḥār al-anwār* vol. 14 p. 8 tr. 14), and in a third, no specifics are mentioned (*Biḥār al-anwār* vol. 14 p. 6 tr. 12). Clearly, such a story could only have taken place once. For one thing, each story says that David asks for unprecedented knowledge. And each one ends with God telling David never to ask such a thing again. For this reason, I have combined them into one.

simply said that he had died. She asked about his money, but they said they knew nothing about any money.

David asked her, "Do you know these men who journeyed with your husband?" She said she did. "Are they alive or dead?" he asked. She said they were alive. He ordered all of the men to be rounded up and detained for interrogation. He lined them up and asked them, "Do you think I don't know what you did to this woman's husband?"

He then assigned one guard to each man and ordered hoods to be cast over each one's head. He sent each detainee with his guard to a separate corner of his court. With the detainees out of earshot, he whispered to the crowd that had gathered to watch the trial, "When I call out, 'God is great!,' you also call out 'God is great!'"

With the stage set, he called the first detainee forward. He uncovered his head, and began interrogating him in a subdued voice. "On what day did you set out on your journey with this woman's husband? What month was it? Where had you reached when he died? Of what sickness did he die? How many days was he ill? Who nursed him? On which day did he die? Who bathed him? Who shrouded him? Who prayed for him? Where did you bury him?"

One by one, the man answered his questions, hesitating here and there. When he was done, David shouted in a loud voice, "God is great!" And all who were present shouted, right on cue, "God is great!"

On hearing the chorus of shouts, the rest of the men grew worried. They were convinced that the first man had caved to David's interrogation and revealed their crime. David had the first man taken away and brought a second in the same way. This time, he stared the frightened man in the face and asked, "Do you think I don't know what you did to this woman's husband?"

Without another thought, this man exclaimed, "O Prophet of God! It is true that I was party to his murder, but I did not want to kill him."

One by one, David had all the men brought forth, and one by one, they each admitted to their role in the man's murder.[25] He punished them and restored the victim's wealth to his widow and her family.

Laboring For a Living

Although he was king, David lived a humble life. He did, however, depend on the public treasury for his personal upkeep. Once, God told him, "David, you would be a perfect servant to me if only you did not depend on the public treasury instead of earning your own keep by working with your own hands."[26] David wept profusely for having fallen short of the Lord's expectations. He decided to devote some time each day to weaving strips of palm leaves into mats with his own hands. He would then sell these and make a loaf of barley bread from the money he earned from the sale.[27]

On seeing David make such a noble effort, God told him that he would teach him the art of blacksmithing which would be more profitable and more useful. He taught him how to melt iron to the consistency of warmed wax[28] and shape the softened metal and how to manufacture armor to protect himself from armed attacks.[29] He told him, "Manufacture chain mail, and be precise in linking the rings. And do good things with these gifts, for I see what you do."[30]

He eventually developed his skills so that he could make a set of mail each day. These he sold for 1000 silver pieces each. He thereby became independent of the support of the public treasury.[31]

---

25. *Biḥār al-anwār* vol. 14 p. 13 tr. 20

26. *Biḥār al-anwār* vol. 14 p. 13 tr. 21

27. *Nahj al-balāghah* sermon 160

28. *Biḥār al-anwār* vol. 14 p. 3 tr. 7

29. Qur'ān 21:80

30. Qur'ān 11:34. Some traditions mention that David could melt iron without fire (*Biḥār al-anwār* vol. 14 p. 3 tr. 6) indicating that this was a miracle of his. This is plausible, however, if this was meant to be a way for him to earn a living and, perhaps, usher in a new industry of metal working, it seems more likely that he would have done this in the conventional way.

31. *Biḥār al-anwār* vol. 14 p. 13 tr. 21

Letting Widows Remarry

David was one of four prophets chosen to battle with the sword.[32] During one of his battles, his general and close friend, Uriah, fell. Uriah had been a faithful supporter to David, and David wished to honor him in death. He personally delivered news of his death to his wife, Bathsheba.[33] He saw that she took it badly. It was the custom among the Israelites that a widow would not ever remarry.

After several months, when Bathsheba's mourning period was over, God commanded David to go and seek her hand in marriage precisely to break, through his own deeds, this last vestige of celibacy in his people's culture.[34] As he expected, the Israelites saw his proposal to Bathsheba as an affront to their customs. They began spreading rumors that David had purposely had Uriah killed so that he could marry his wife.[35] Nonetheless, David did as God commanded him to do thereby establishing the right of a widow to remarry.

---

32. *Biḥār al-anwār* vol. 14 p. 2 tr. 2. The others mentioned are Abraham, Moses, and Muḥammad.

33. This is the name mentioned for her in the Bible (2 Samuel 11:3).

34. *Biḥār al-anwār* vol. 14 p. 24 tr. 2. There is a clear parallel in this story to Prophet Muḥammad's effort to overcome the cultural prohibition against marrying one's adopted son's ex-wife which he did by marrying Zaynab bint Wahb who had previously been married to Zayd ibn al-Ḥārithah, his adopted son.

35. These false rumors have survived to this day. The Bible recounts a tale that accuses David of voyerism, fornication, and conspiracy to murder among other things (2 Samuel 11:1–27). These defamatory tales existed in the time of Prophet Muḥammad and the imams. Jewish storytellers (*qaṣṣāṣūn*) would recount them for Muslims, many of whom unthinkingly accepted them as fact. According to one tradition, Imam ʿAlī and Imam al-Ṣādiq threatened to lash anyone who recounted such a story about David or any other prophet. In their words, they threatened to "strike the *ḥadd* twice." Presumably, *ḥadd* in this context refers to the eighty lashes due to someone who falsely alleges sexual misconduct (*qadhf*). Despite the imams' best efforts to eradicate this story, Sunnīs have stubbornly preserved it (*Biḥār al-anwār* vol. 14 p. 26 tr. 5).

David Performs Hajj

One year, David took the Israelites south to Bakkah to perform Hajj. At ʿArafāt, David felt the congestion of so many people was hindering his ability to concentrate, so he climbed to the top of the Mountain of Mercy to continue his prayers. People began to whisper among themselves saying, "Perhaps God can hear our prayers better if we climb to a higher place as David has done."[36]

Gabriel came to David and said, "God asks you, "Why did you climb atop this mountain? Did you think I could not hear you amidst the throngs of people below?" Gabriel then showed David a vision in which they traveled to the bottom of the sea. There, beneath a tremendous rock, lived a tiny worm-like creature. Gabriel told David, "God wants me to tell you, 'I hear the prayers of this tiny creature, beneath this tremendous rock, at the bottom of the sea. So do not ever think that I cannot hear your prayers.'" David took this message back to his people to ensure that they did not misconstrue his actions as an indication that God is not omniscient.[37]

David Meets Ezekiel

Once, David was trekking through the countryside, praising God in the company of the mountains and the birds. He heard a human voice from one of the surrounding mountains. He tracked the source of the voice to a cave. As he approached, he called out. The voice said in disdain, "I hear the voice of one who is soft and whose belly is full. Who are you?"

David replied, "I am David."

The voice said, "The David who has many wives and many servants?"

David replied, "Yes, I am he. And you?

"I am Ezekiel,"[38] replied the voice.

---

36. I have inferred this question to justify God's following rebuke to David.

37. *Biḥār al-anwār* vol. 14 p. 16 tr. 27

38. This Ezekiel should not be confused with the Ezekiel who was the Believer from the House of the Pharaoh or Prophet Ezekiel who was the third successor

David asked, "Ezekiel, would you allow me to enter your cave with you?"

Ezekiel replied, "No." Ezekiel clearly did not realize David was a prophet. He had only heard some rumors and assumed that David was like every other king.

God communicated to Ezekiel, "Do not insult my prophet." Ezekiel realized his mistake and apologized and welcomed David into his cave.

On entering the cave, David commented on its stark poverty. Ezekiel replied, "Neither am I in true hardship as long as I am not in hellfire, nor are you in true ease as long as you are not in paradise,"[39] meaning that the ease and hardship of this world is insignificant compared to the ease and hardship of the hereafter.

David asked him, "Have you ever felt tempted by worldly pleasures?" Ezekiel replied that he had. David asked, "What do you do to overcome your desire?"

Ezekiel replied, "I go into this gorge you see below and contemplate on what is to be found there." David took his advice and wandered into the gorge. There he found an ancient iron dais, rusted and deteriorating. Upon the dais lay a skull and a full skeleton. Affixed to the dais was a sign that read, "I am Arwāsalam. I ruled for many years, I built many cities, and I married many women. Yet, in the end, the bare earth has become my bed, a stone, my pillow, and worms and snakes my neighbors. He who sees me should never allow himself to be beguiled by the temporal world."[40]

Marry Before Death

Once David was sitting with a young man who used to frequent his company and sit quietly awaiting David's pearls of wisdom. The Angel of Death appeared before David and greeted him. Then he turned toward the young man. David asked him, "Why do you look at him?"

---

to Moses.

39. *Biḥār al-anwār* vol. 14 p. 26 tr. 4

40. *Biḥār al-anwār* vol. 14 p. 25 tr. 3

Azrael said, "I have been ordered to take his soul after seven days in this very place."

David felt compassion for his young companion. He asked him, "Are you married?" The young man replied that he was not. So David said, "Go to the house of so-and-so. He is a man of high standing among the Israelites. Tell him that King David orders him to marry his daughter to you. Marry her and consummate the marriage on this very night. Stay with your wife for the next seven days. On the seventh day, come back and meet me here."

At the end of the week, the young man returned. David asked him, "How have you enjoyed what you have experienced?"

He replied, "I have never experienced such a blessing and such happiness."

David praised God and told his companion to be seated. Seven days were over, and he expected the Angel of Death to appear any moment. Some time passed, and there was no sign of Azrael, so David dismissed the young man and told him to return to his wife. When he was gone, David summoned Azrael and asked, "Did you not tell me that you would take this man's life at the end of the week?"

Azrael said, "I did, but God decided to show compassion on him because you did. He has extended the young man's life for thirty years."[41]

David's Companion in Heaven

God once told David, "Go to Khalādah, daughter of Aws, and give her tidings of paradise, and tell her that she is to be one of your companions in the hereafter."

David went to her house and knocked at her door. She opened the door and, seeing his expression, asked, "Has some revelation come that concerns me?" When he delivered God's message to her, she ask incredulously, "Is it possible that it is someone else he means whose name happens to be the same as mine?"

David replied reassuringly, "It is you."

---

41. *Biḥār al-anwār* vol. 14 p. 38 tr. 17

She said, "Prophet of God, I do not doubt what you say. But I do not know any quality within me that qualifies me for what you have promised me."

David said, "Tell me about yourself."

She said, "No pain has ever afflicted me, nor harm, nor need, nor hunger of any kind but that I have endured it without asking God to deliver me from it. I always wait until he himself chooses to give me relief.[42] I thank him for everything and praise him."

David said, "It is because of this quality that you have reached such a station."[43]

Ostentation Forgiven

Once, David came to know a pious man. He was very impressed with him, but God told him, "Do not be impressed with him for he is ostentatious in his piety."

When this man died, David refused to attend his funeral. However, fifty men attended who each testified that they witnessed nothing but goodness from the deceased. Following his burial, God asked David, "Why did you not attend that man's funeral?"

David answered, "Because of what you told me about him."

God said, "Notwithstanding his ostentation, when fifty people testified to his righteousness, I accepted their testimony and forgave him for what I knew of him." In this way, God wished to teach David the importance of keeping one's flaws hidden from others. Though the deceased's deeds were not good, his ability to keep his flaws hidden was, and for this, God was willing to forgive him those flaws.[44]

---

42. One level of trust in God dictates that we ask only him for all of our needs. Another higher level of trust dictates that we not even ask God for our needs but simply trust that he, in his infinite wisdom, will fulfill them when and how he deems best. Khalādah possessed this ultimate level of trust which is reminiscent of Abraham's trust in God as he was about to be hurled into Nimrod's blaze.

43. *Biḥār al-anwār* vol. 14 p. 39 tr. 18

44. *Biḥār al-anwār* vol. 14 p. 42 tr. 31

The Sabbath-Breakers

The city of Aylah[45] was a fishing community on the Red Sea coast. It was named after a descendant of Abraham.[46] They were blessed with great prosperity. Each day the tides would bring fish-laden water into their harbor and inland waterways and allow them to easily catch what fish they desired.[47] With time, their economy grew and, with it, their need for more and more fish.

Jewish law forbade them to, among other things, fish on the Sabbath. The Torah said:

> Do not transgress the sanctity of the Sabbath.[48] Hereafter if anyone observes the Sabbath and does not allow himself to break it out of the fear of God, God will admit him to paradise. But if anyone takes this prohibition lightly and deems it lawful to do work on the Sabbath, though God has prohibited it on that day, God will cast him in hellfire.[49]

Aylah's denizens, being devout followers of Moses' law, observed the Sabbath and ceased fishing from dusk on Friday until early Sunday. But the temptation to increase their yield weighed heavy on many. They felt they could gain an economic advantage if they fished seven days a week instead of only six. A small group of righteous and devout individuals admonished them to continue to observe the Sabbath as they had been commanded and reminded them of God's threat to cast them in hellfire if they transgressed. They advised them that no economic advantage could justify defying God's law.

Seeing the weakness and latent corruption in many of Aylah's denizens, God decided to test their observance of the Sabbath. He

45. *Majmaʿ al-bayān*

46. *Biḥār al-anwār* vol. 14 p. 52 tr. 5 footnote 4

47. *Biḥār al-anwār* vol. 14 p. 52 tr. 5

48. Qurʾān 4:154

49. *al-Kāfī* 5.17.1

made the fish come to them in clear sight only on the Sabbath. On the other days of the week when they did not observe the Sabbath, no fish came with the tide.[50]

For a few weeks they endured and maintained the Sabbath. But eventually, they could not resist. During the week, before the Sabbath was upon them, they dug trenches leading from the high tide mark into large spill-over holding ponds. On Friday afternoon, they opened the gates to their trenches and then went about their Sabbath rituals. The next day, as the tide rose and the fish teemed, the fish-laden waters poured into the trenches and spilled over into the holding ponds. When the tide receded, the fish were trapped, unable to exit. Sunday morning, the fisherman proceeded to their holding ponds to collect the fish.[51] They felt they had effectively outsmarted God. They were not, after all, technically violating the Sabbath in this way since they were not actively fishing on the Sabbath.

The small group of righteous and devout individuals admonished them against employing such ruses. They warned them that this was a test from God and that if they endured, God would bring relief and reward them. But if they tried to deceive God, they would be deceiving only themselves. Their admonishment fell on deaf ears, yet they persisted.

There were some in the city of Aylah who were not party to the fishermen's deceit but saw no benefit in admonishing them since they believed they were clearly unwilling to listen. They told the admonishers, "Why do you bother admonishing a people whom God is going to destroy or punish severely anyway?"

The admonishers replied, "We do so to exonerate ourselves before God and in hopes that they may come to fear God and cease their transgression."[52]

Despite the admonishers' good intentions, the fishermen grew numb to the admonishment. God grew angry with them though they neither associated partners with God nor doubted in Moses'

---

50. Qur'ān 7:163

51. *Biḥār al-anwār* vol. 14 p. 52 tr. 5 and p. 56–8 tr. 13

52. Qur'ān 7:164

commandments in any way.[53] God seized the wrongdoers with a terrible punishment because they were corrupt and had rebelled and done what they had been forbidden to do and broke their covenant with God.[54] He damned them[55] and told them, "Be outcast apes!"[56] All of the fishermen who had violated the Sabbath, along with their families who supported them, turned instantly to apes. For three days, they neither ate nor drank. On the third day, they were dead.[57]

The admonishers were saved from any hardship because they had fulfilled their duty to God.[58] However, those who had discouraged and even ridiculed the admonishers were also destroyed.[59]

When God told David about the deceptions the people of Aylah had tried to employ, he damned them.[60] The Sabbath-breakers of Aylah would thereafter be an example for their contemporaries and for those who came after them and a source of admonishment for the God-fearing.[61]

David's Retreat to His Sanctuary

David often secluded himself in his sanctuary so that he could focus fully on worship. On one such occasion, God asked him, "Why are you alone?"

David replied, "My desire to be with you was too great, but people were preventing me from being with you."

---

53. *al-Kāfī* 5.17.1

54. Qur'ān 5:13

55. Qur'an 4:47

56. Qur'ān 7:165–6 and 2:65

57. *Biḥār al-anwār* vol. 14 p. 59 tr. 13

58. Qur'ān 7:166

59. *Biḥār al-anwār* vol. 14 p. 54 tr. 6

60. Qur'ān 5:78. There is nothing explicit in the Qur'ān to link this verse to the aforementioned story. However, the traditions link the two.

61. Qur'ān 2:66

God said, "Go back to them for if you bring even one of these fugitive slaves of mine back to me, I shall write your name in the tablet among those who are praised."[62]

God asked him, "Why are you silent?"

David replied, "My awe of you has silenced me."

God asked him, "Why are you so tired?"

David replied, "My love for you and my worship of you has exhausted me."

God asked him, "Why are you so poor when I have provided for you?"[63]

David replied, "My fulfillment of the obligations you have written for me has left me destitute."

God asked him, "Why are you so meek?"

David replied, "Your indescribable might has made me meek. You are deserving of all this, my Master!"

God said, "For all this, I give you tidings of my grace. You shall have whatever you want on the day when you meet me. Now go, and live in harmony with people. Treat them well, and if they do not return the favor, do not take it to heart. If you do this, you shall have whatever you want on the Day of Resurrection."[64]

God also told David, "Rejoice in me. Take pleasure in remembering me. Enjoy whispering your prayers to me. For I shall soon purge the world of the corrupt and damn the wrongdoers."[65]

God also told David, "David, just as the sun does not fail to shine on him who basks in it, so too my mercy does not fail to encompass him who seeks it. And just as certainly as ill omens fail to harm those who ignore them, so those who fear them fail to save themselves from them. And just as the closest of people to me

---

62. *Biḥār al-anwār* vol. 14 p. 40 tr. 26

63. Once he began earning his own keep, his personal wealth was presumably separate from his kingdom's wealth. So it is possible for him to have been a wealthy and powerful king but a destitute person, similar to Imam ʿAlī during his own caliphate.

64. *Biḥār al-anwār* vol. 14 p. 34 tr. 3

65. *Biḥār al-anwār* vol. 14 p. 34 tr. 3

on the Day of Judgment are the humble, so too the farthest people from me on the Day of Judgment are the arrogant."[66]

God's Wise Words For David

God also told David, "If a servant of mine brings me a particular good deed, I shall open the gates of paradise to him."

David asked, "And what is this good deed?"

God replied, "If he relieves another believer of a hardship, if only by feeding one who is hungry a date or part of a date."

David commented, "He who knows this ought never to lose hope in your mercy."[67]

God also told David, "Tell your people, 'If any of you endeavors to obey God's commands, he will help you to obey him. If you ask him, he will give you. If you supplicate him, he will answer you. If you seek his protection, he will protect you. If you ask him to suffice you, he will suffice you. If you trust in him, he will guard you, and if all God's creatures were to turn on you, God would fend them off of you.'"[68]

God also said to David, "Remember me in your times of happiness, and I shall remember you in your times of grief."[69]

God also said to David, "Love me and endear me to my creatures."

David said, "Lord, I love you, but how should I endear you to your creatures?"

God replied, "Mention my favors to them, for if you mention my favors to them, they will love me."[70]

God also said to David, "Beware the hearts of those attached to this world for their minds are veiled from knowing me."[71]

God also said to David, "David, give tidings to the sinners and warn the righteous."

---

66. *Biḥār al-anwār* vol. 14 p. 34 tr. 4 and p. 39 tr. 21

67. *Biḥār al-anwār* vol. 14 p. 35 tr. 5–7

68. *Biḥār al-anwār* vol. 14 p. 37 tr. 13

69. *Biḥār al-anwār* vol. 14 p. 37 tr. 15

70. *Biḥār al-anwār* vol. 14 p. 38 tr. 16

71. *Biḥār al-anwār* vol. 14 p. 39 tr. 19

David asked in surprise, "Why should I give tidings to the sinners and warn the righteous?"

God replied, "Give the sinners tidings that I accept repentance and forgive sins. And warn the righteous not to exult over their deeds, for if I were to judge them based on their deeds they would perish."[72]

God gave the following message to David concerning a tyrannical king, "David, tell this tyrant, 'God did not install you as a king so that you could add wealth to your wealth but to answer, on his behalf, the call of the oppressed with aid. God has sworn a solemn oath to aid the oppressed and take revenge for them on any in whose presence they were oppressed and who failed to aid them.'"[73]

God also exhorted him, "David, thank me as I deserve to be thanked."

David said hopelessly, "Lord, how can I thank you as you deserve to be thanked when every thanks I offer is itself a blessing from you requiring yet another thanks?"

God said, "David, by recognizing this very fact, you have thanked me as I deserve to be thanked."[74]

God also told David, "If any of my servants sincerely asks me for protection from another, and then the heavens and the earth and all they hold conspire against him, I shall make a way out for him. But if any of my servants asks another for protection, I shall cut off all heavenly paths of assistance to him and make the earth swallow him up, and I shall not care in what valley he perishes."[75]

God also told David, "Tell the tyrants of the world never to remember me, for whenever someone remembers me, I remember him, and when these tyrants remember me, I remember them and damn them."[76]

God also said, "David, tell the oppressed, 'I have only delayed my answer to your prayers for relief from your oppression, though

---

72. *Biḥār al-anwār* vol. 14 p. 40 tr. 22

73. *Biḥār al-anwār* vol. 14 p. 40 tr. 24

74. *Biḥār al-anwār* vol. 14 p. 40 tr. 25. A similar exchange took place with Moses.

75. *Biḥār al-anwār* vol. 14 p. 41 tr. 29

76. *Biḥār al-anwār* vol. 14 p. 42 tr. 30

I have indeed answered them, for one of many reasons that are hidden from you. Perhaps you in turn wronged another who called down my help against you, in which case I consider this repayment for that. Perhaps there is a station in paradise to which you cannot attain except by struggling against this person's oppression, for I test my servants through their money and their lives..."[77]

David's Proverbs

What follows are some of David's many wise statements:

> Son of Adam, how is it that you mention guidance when you cannot even raise yourself out of the vices that lead to perdition? Son of Adam, your heart has grown hard and forgetful of God's greatness. If you knew God and knew of his greatness, you would be ever in fear of him and in wait of the promised meeting with him. Poor soul! How is it that you forget so easily your grave and the loneliness you will feel therein?[78]

> One with intellect ought to be aware of his times, attentive to his personal development, and vigilant of his tongue.[79]

> One with intellect ought not forget about four times during the day: one to pray to his Lord; one to take account of himself; one to mingle with his brethren in faith who truthfully reveal his faults; and one in which he lets himself enjoy lawful and respectable pleasures, for this fourth one will help him with the others.[80]

77. *Biḥār al-anwār* vol. 14 p. 43 tr. 34

78. *Biḥār al-anwār* vol. 14 p. 36 tr. 10

79. *Biḥār al-anwār* vol. 14 p. 39 tr. 20

80. *Biḥār al-anwār* vol. 14 p. 41 tr. 27

David's Son

God gave David a son named Solomon.[81] He gave Solomon knowledge just as he had given it to David, and for this, Solomon too was immensely grateful.[82] Once David said to Solomon, "My son, beware of too much laughter for too much laughter leaves you empty-handed on the Day of Judgment. I advise you to maintain lengthy silence unless there is something good that must be said, for to regret once over a lengthy silence is better than to regret always for having said too much. My son, if speech is of silver, then silence must be of gold."[83]

David's wife once told their son, "Beware of sleeping too much at night, for doing so will render you poor on the Day of Judgment."[84]

David's Successor

God ordered David to appoint Solomon as his successor. Solomon was only thirteen years old, so David tested his intellect to ensure that he was prepared to serve.[85] Nonetheless, this appointment caused a great stir among the Israelite elders. They complained to one another, "He installs such a young man to rule over us when there are those among us who are older than he."

David gathered them together and said, "News of your objections has reached me. I call on you all to present your staffs to me. He whose staff comes to life and sprouts and blossoms shall be ruler over my kingdom after me." The elders agreed to this arrangement. Each one wrote his name on his staff. Solomon also wrote his name on his staff. These staffs were then locked in a room that was guarded by the elders overnight. The next morning, when they

---

81. In Arabic his name is *Sulaymān.*

82. Qur'ān 27:15

83. *Biḥār al-anwār* vol. 14 p. 35 tr. 8

84. *Biḥār al-anwār* vol. 14 p. 134 tr. 8

85. *Biḥār al-anwār* vol. 14 p. 72 tr. 13

unlocked the room, only Solomon's had miraculously sprouted and blossomed. Reluctantly, the elders accepted David's appointment.[86]

David announced, "O people! We have been taught the language of birds, and my son shall be given dominion over *jinn* and humanity and over the wind."[87]

David's Death

When David reached the age of 100, the Angel of Death came for him.[88] God had decreed only fifty years for him, but since Adam had gifted him fifty years from his life, he lived to 100.[89] When he saw Azrael, David asked why he had not given him due warning so he could prepare for death. Azrael replied, "I sent you so many warnings."

David asked, "Who were your messengers?"

Azrael replied, "Where are your father, your brother, your neighbor, and your other acquaintances?"

David said, "They have all died."

Azrael said, "They were my messengers to you to tell you that you too shall die as they died."[90]

86. *Biḥār al-anwār* vol. 14 p. 68 tr. 2 and p. 81 tr. 25

87. *Biḥār al-anwār* vol. 14 p. 71 tr. 10

88. *Biḥār al-anwār* vol. 14 p. 8 tr. 16

89. *Biḥār al-anwār* vol. 14 p. 9 tr. 17

90. *Biḥār al-anwār* vol. 14 p. 14 tr. 23

Solomon

Solomon[1] was born circumcised[2]—one early sign that he was destined to succeed his father, David, to the station of prophethood. He was God's gift to David. He became a great servant for he turned to God often in prayer.[3] The name Solomon was chosen for him because he had a *good* heart, and he was, therefore, content with whatever God gave him.[4]

Demonstration of Wisdom

God endowed Solomon with knowledge as he had endowed David, and he too responded by saying, "Praise is for God who favored us more than he did many of his other believing servants."[5] Nonetheless, because of his young age, the Israelite elders questioned his appointment as David's successor. Through miracles and public demonstrations of his wisdom, God sought to allay their worries.

In one such case, a grape farmer came before David complaining that flocks of sheep belonging to a group of local shepherds had wandered into his vineyard by night[6] and severely damaged his vines. The law demanded that the responsibility for protecting crops be shared between the farmers and shepherds. Farmers were responsible during the day for keeping watch over their crops and warding off any unwanted grazers. In turn, shepherds were responsible during the night for keeping track of their flocks

---

1. In Arabic his name is *Sulaymān*.
2. *Biḥār al-anwār* vol. 14 p. 80
3. Qur'ān 38:30
4. *Biḥār al-anwār* vol. 14 p. 93 from al-Tha'labī. This tradition indicates that there is a connection between the name *Solomon* and the word *salīm* meaning "sound" or "good."
5. Qur'ān 27:15
6. Qur'ān 21:78

and preventing them from trespassing into others' crops.[7] This law, according to which all past Israelite prophets had judged, demanded that the offending shepherds surrender enough heads of sheep to the farmer to compensate him for the damage to his crops.[8]

David summoned Solomon to court.[9] Before his son's arrival, David told his courtiers that he would defer to his son and allow him to pass judgment to further convince them of his God-given wisdom. Solomon arrived and listened attentively to the plaintiff and to the shepherds' admission of guilt. God made Solomon understand the

---

7. *Biḥār al-anwār* vol. 14 p. 132 tr. 5

8. *Biḥār al-anwār* vol. 14 p. 132 tr. 6

9. The traditions differ widely over the details of this judgment.

- Some claim that both David and Solomon issued contradictory verdicts independently (*Biḥār al-anwār* vol. 14 p. 131 tr. 4 and p. 132 tr. 6).
- Others claim that only one verdict was issued and that was Solomon's. Everything else was just a discussion between the two (*Biḥār al-anwār* vol. 14 p. 131 tr. 3).
- Yet others claim that David wholly refrained from passing judgment and immediately referred the case to Solomon to demonstrate his wisdom and prowess in judgment (*Biḥār al-anwār* vol. 14 p. 131 tr. 2).

I believe that the third tradition fits best in the context of the story. For them to issue independent and contrary verdicts is highly improbable. Such a move would undermine David's authority, create questions about each one's infallibility, and make for very bad government. On the other hand, it is clear that David's intention was to demonstrate Solomon's wisdom. Furthermore, if they discussed the affair in private, skeptics could easily have claimed that it was all staged and that David taught Solomon what to say to one-up the old prophets. Thus, it is most probable that David refrained from passing any verdict and invited Solomon to hear the case without coaching him in any way. In this way, Solomon's verdict would have had the greatest impact on a court of skeptics.

ʿAllāmah al-Majlisī suggests that Solomon's ruling was an abrogation (*naskh*) of the prophets' rulings (*Biḥār al-anwār* vol. 14 p. 133–4). However, considering the tradition that quotes Solomon differentiating between instances where the plants were destroyed from the root and those where the only the fruits are eaten (*Biḥār al-anwār* vol. 14 p. 131 tr. 2), it is more likely that Solomon understood that the details of this case were unprecedented, and that is why his ruling differed.

correct ruling in this case.[10] Based on God's inspiration, Solomon decided that this case was slightly different from all preceding cases. In the past, the animals had completely destroyed the plants such that they could not recover in the subsequent growing season. For this reason, the prophets had always ruled as they had. In this case, on the other hand, the sheep had only destroyed this year's crop leaving the vines intact. Accordingly, he ruled that the shepherd should retain ownership of all his sheep, but he must surrender all lambs born in the coming year[11] along with all milk and wool produced during that same period to the farmer.[12]

The Language of Birds

When Solomon reached the age of thirteen,[13] David died, and Solomon successfully succeeded him to the throne.[14]

Like his father, Solomon was taught the language of birds. He told his people, "We have been taught the language of birds, and we have been given every kind of blessing. This is certainly a clear advantage."[15]

---

10. Qur'ān 21:79

11. *Biḥār al-anwār* vol. 14 p. 131 tr. 2

12. *Biḥār al-anwār* vol. 14 p. 131 tr. 4

13. The timeline for Solomon's life is not clear since there are contradictory reports in the traditions. One tradition says that he succeeded his father at the age of 13 (*Biḥār al-anwār* vol. 14 p. 73 tr. 13). Another says that he died at the age of 712 (*Biḥār al-anwār* vol. 14 p. 140 tr. 8). And a third says he ruled for 40 years (*Biḥār al-anwār* vol. 14 p. 73 tr. 13). I have arbitrarily chosen to disregard the claim that he ruled for 40 years to make the other two numbers fit.

14. Qur'ān 27:16

15. Qur'ān 27:16. Clearly, Solomon's ability to converse with the birds was miraculous. It follows that it was an ability beyond the scope of what behavioral ecologists and observers of nature are able to decipher from the sounds and movements of birds; otherwise, his ability would not have qualified as a miracle. We can further corroborate this assertion by observing the kinds of conversations Solomon has with the hoopoe (Qur'ān 27:22–24) and the ant (Qur'ān 27:18). Their thoughts are far more sophisticated than the simple warning cries and mating calls that biologists are able to decipher. They demonstrate keenly human intelligence. For this reason, I believe, not only was Solomon's ability to

A Lesson on Love

He once observed a male sparrow complaining to its mate, "Why do you rebuff my advances." Then with bravado, he added, "If I wished, I could seize the dome from atop King Solomon's palace in my beak and hurl it into the sea."

Witnessing the sparrow's bluster, Solomon smiled amusedly and asked, "Can you truly do this?"

The sparrow replied, "No, Messenger of God! But a male must sometimes puff his chest and aggrandize himself before his mate. Besides, one in love must not be blamed for what he says."

Solomon turned to the female sparrow and asked, "Why do you rebuff his advances when he loves you so?"

She replied, "O Prophet of God! He is not truly in love with me. He only claims to be so, for he loves another besides me." Her words affected Solomon deeply. Without tarrying a moment longer, he retreated into the temple for forty days, weeping intensely and begging God to purify his heart of all love but the love of God, for the sparrow had reminded him that a heart has room for only one love.[16]

A Child to Praise God

On another occasion, Solomon overheard a male sparrow tell his mate, "Let us mate. Perhaps God will provide us with a child who will praise him, for we are old, and we may not live to see another mating season."

Solomon was amazed by the sparrow's sense of purpose. He said, "His intention alone is worth more than my entire kingdom."[17]

Tribute For the King

Another pair of birds built their nest near a road. As Solomon's entourage approached, they feared that he may destroy their nest

---

converse with birds and beasts miraculous, but their ability to reason and speak to him as humans was also miraculous.

16. *Biḥār al-anwār* vol. 14 p. 95 tr. 3

17. *Biḥār al-anwār* vol. 14 p. 95 tr. 3

and their clutch of eggs unawares. The male bird retrieved a date he had been saving for his chicks, and the female retrieved a locust she had been saving. Together they approached Solomon and offered him their presents with their request to spare their nest. He accepted their gifts, gifted them back to the birds, and steered his entourage clear of their nest.[18]

A Legion of Birds

Not only could Solomon speak to and understand the language of birds, many birds were also in his army. Whenever he sat upon his throne and summoned his court, a myriad of birds would swarm and hover over his throne in perfect formation awaiting his command.[19]

The Kingdom of Solomon

Solomon was married young,[20] and despite his youth, began thinking of an heir. He assumed that his firstborn would be a son and that this son would naturally succeed him.[21] His wife became pregnant, and he grew hopeful as her term came to and end. But then one day, to his horror, Solomon entered his court and found the corpse of his stillborn son cast upon his throne. When he recovered from his initial shock, he realized that God was disciplining him for his presumptuousness, and he repented with all his heart.[22] He said,

18. *Biḥār al-anwār* vol. 14 p. 82 tr. 26

19. *Biḥār al-anwār* vol. 14 p. 110 tr. 3

20. There are traditions that claim that he had 1000 women in his palace: 300 wives and 700 concubines (*Biḥār al-anwār* vol. 14 p. 70 tr. 5). While it is conceivable that the law of the Israelites allowed for this or that this was a special exception made for him, these numbers make him sound more like the decadent Abbasid, Ottoman, and Mogul sultans—may God damn them all—than the righteous prophet of God he was. Certainly, another tradition, which claims he used to have conjugal relations with them all every 24 hours (*Biḥār al-anwār* vol. 14 p. 74 tr. 17), is a fabrication since he would have had exactly 1.4 minutes with each with no time left for any other activity in his life!

21. It is not completely clear that this was his assumption, however, as you will see, it is the most plausible explanation that ties all the verses together.

22. Qur'ān 38:34. There is much speculation among the commentators as to

"Lord, forgive me, and grant me a kingdom unbefitting anyone after me.[23] You alone are the Bountiful."[24] Far from stemming from greed or jealousy, his prayer was the ultimate act of asceticism and renunciation of worldly gains. He realized his mistake in trying to extend his ownership of his worldly possessions by appointing his own heir. He wanted to purify himself of any trace of presumptuousness before God by attaining a kingdom too great for him to ever bequeath to his heirs. He was, in reality, asking to be subjected to one of life's hardest tests: to have supreme power and wealth along with utter impotence to control the ultimate fate of any of it. In this way, he hoped to break himself and teach himself to trust totally in God.

God accepted his repentance and granted him his request. He subjugated the wind, in all its tempestuousness, to blow toward the Holy Land on his command.[25] It would then blow gently wherever he wished.[26] It conveyed him in a morning the distance traveled in a month by any other conveyance and conveyed him in an afternoon the distance traveled in a month by any other conveyance.[27] Thus, he could travel with the wind billowing in his ship's sails the same distance in a day that it would have otherwise taken him two months to traverse.

God also set a river of molten copper in motion for him[28] by teaching him advanced techniques of metallurgy.

---

the identity of the "body" that was "cast upon his throne." I believe that it was the body of his son because this ties the story together best.

23. This prayer of his is almost always misconstrued as a prayer for "a kingdom unmatched by anyone after me." After misconstruing the verse in this way, many commentators go to great lengths to explain why his prayer was not spoken out of greed and jealousy. Interestingly, neither the words of his prayer, nor the context in which he speaks them, allow for such an interpretation.

24. Qur'ān 38:35

25. Qur'ān 21:81

26. Qur'ān 38:36

27. Qur'ān 34:12

28. Qur'ān 34:12

God subjugated the devils to his command after making their spirit-like bodies material and solid.[29] From their ranks, he made some dive to uncover the hidden treasures of the sea, and he made others build for him. They constructed temples for him and sculptures of trees;[30] bowls the size of small pools and cauldrons fixed in the earth.[31] Those devils who were prone to flee from his service were bound in chains and guarded to ensure they did not escape.[32] If any of them were to veer from God's command, God gave him a taste of the torment of the blaze.[33]

God told him, "This is our gift to you, so give it or keep it without any oversight from us."[34] God saw how hard Solomon was on himself, so he rewarded him with the kingdom he asked for and the freedom to bequeath it how and to whom he wished. Then God said, "Give thanks, family of David, and do not be like most, for the grateful among my servants are few."[35]

Solomon was given a ring inscribed with the following words: "Glory be to the one by whose words the *jinn* were muzzled."[36]

The Kingdom's Godly Purpose

Solomon decided to devote his mighty kingdom and miraculous powers to overpower infidel kings, not to live in luxury.[37] In the

29. *Biḥār al-anwār* vol. 14 p. 70 tr. 4

30. The Qur'ān mentions the word *tamāthīl* (sing. *timthāl*) which is most commonly understood to mean statues. However, as the production of statues representing animate beings is forbidden in both Islamic and Jewish law, this is problematic. In one tradition, Imam al-Ṣādiq explains that they were sculptures of trees (*Biḥār al-anwār* vol. 14 p. 74 tr. 15). Perhaps it is a reference to columns sculpted of stone.

31. Qur'ān 34:13. I have seen cauldrons of this size when I visited the shrine of the Sufi saint Moinuddin Chishti in Ajmer, India.

32. Qur'ān 38:37–8 and 21:82

33. Qur'ān 34:12

34. Qur'ān 38:39

35. Qur'ān 34:13

36. *Biḥār al-anwār* vol. 14 p. 80

37. *Biḥār al-anwār* vol. 14 p. 82 tr. 29

capacity of a king, he carried himself with dignity and composure. However, beneath his regal garments, he wore coarse clothing made of goat hair and a fiber made of palm fronds which he wove together himself.[38] He would serve his guests meat with fine white bread. But he would provide his own family lower grade whole wheat bread. He himself would eat coarse barley bread.[39] And whenever possible, he would have his meals with the poor and avoid the company of the wealthy saying, "I am a poor man among many poor people."[40] While other kings, and even his own subjects slept soundly, he would spend the night in worship, weeping until dawn.[41]

Most people mistakenly saw his kingdom and wealth as a luxury to be envied. One farmer gazed upon Solomon's entourage as it passed in the distance. He muttered to himself some words of amazement and envy. The wind conveyed his words to Solomon who stopped the caravan. He walked over to the farmer and said, "I have walked over to you to warn you not to wish for what you do not have the strength to bear. A single word of praise to God, uttered with sincerity, is better than all the wealth and power that lies in the hands of the House of David because the reward for that praise will last an eternity while the kingdom of Solomon will inevitably perish."[42] He continued, "We have been given whatever people have been given in addition to things they have not been given. We know what people know in addition to what they do not know. Considering this, we have found nothing to be better than the following: to fear God though he is unseen just as though he

38. *Biḥār al-anwār* vol. 14 p. 82 tr. 29

39. *Biḥār al-anwār* vol. 14 p. 71 tr. 8

40. *Biḥār al-anwār* vol. 14 p. 82 tr. 28. There is a tradition that says Solomon will be the last prophet to be admitted to paradise because he will have to account for his worldly wealth (*Biḥār al-anwār* vol. 14 p. 74 tr. 16). However, this tradition is highly suspect considering, first, that God said, "This is our gift to you, so give it or keep it without any oversight from us" (Qur'ān 38:39) and, second, that Solomon lived humbly in private. Thus, I have disregarded that tradition and its implications.

41. *Biḥār al-anwār* vol. 14 p. 82 tr. 29

42. *Biḥār al-anwār* vol. 14 p. 81

were seen; to be frugal in times of wealth and poverty; to speak the truth whether you be happy or angry; and to be meek before God in every circumstance."[43]

Bring Back the Sun

Among his duties as king was to raise and maintain an army to defend his kingdom and wage war on other states that refused to submit to God's law. His army consisted not only of men but of birds and beasts and *jinn* as well.[44] He took charge of these duties personally and oversaw the selection and training of his soldiers and the horses upon which they rode. Once, on the eve of battle, he was engaged in such an inspection. The swift steeds that had been selected were being shown to him one after another. The work was so much and so pressing that he could not break for prayer.[45] The sun set and darkness descended, and he confessed to God, "I became so engrossed with these horses and was distracted from the remembrance of my Lord that the sun has now disappeared beyond the horizon's veil."[46] He begged the angels, "Angels of God, bring it back for me!"[47] Within moments, the sun reappeared, and he and his companions prepared for prayer by wiping their calves and necks for the ablution.[48]

---

43. *Biḥār al-anwār* vol. 14 p. 131 tr. 1

44. Qur'ān 27:17

45. *Biḥār al-anwār* vol. 14 p. 103

46. If Jewish law prescribed a prayer such as ʿAṣr, then he failed to pray that obligatory prayer on time. Al-Mīzān justifies this action arguing that his inspection was also obligatory and when two obligatory acts conflict, one must choose the more important and more pressing. However, it is also possible that the prayer he missed was not an obligatory one but one he was wont to offer of his own accord.

47. Many traditions claim that Solomon killed his horses because they distracted him from prayer. Shaykh al-Ṣadūq dismisses such traditions as *taqiyyah* because the horses were not at fault (*Biḥār al-anwār* vol. 14 p. 101 from *al-Faqīh*).

48. Qur'ān 38:31–33

Seeking Rain

Once, the Levant was struck by a severe drought. He and his subjects gathered in the desert outside of their city to pray for rain. They passed an ant who was also praying for rain saying, "God, we are your creatures. We are dependent on you for our sustenance. Thus, do not punish us for the sins of Adam's children, and bring us rain."

Solomon overheard her prayer and was so moved that he told his people, "Let us return home for our work has been done by another."[49]

Valley of the Ants

When renovations to the temple were complete, Solomon set off with a tremendous army on a pilgrimage to Bakkah. They marched until they came upon a valley inhabited by a colony of ants. A guard ant from the colony sensed the army's approach and cried out, "O ants! Take cover in your mounds. Let Solomon and his army not trample you unawares!"[50] The wind carried her faint but strident cry to Solomon's ears.[51] He was at once grateful for God's gift of comprehension and troubled by her warnings. He approached her and asked, "Dear ant, do you not know that I am God's prophet and that I wrong no one?"

She replied with the utmost humility, "I know this, but I feared that my sisters might gaze upon your mighty army and be distracted from their duty to God."[52]

He smiled joyously at her reply and prayed, "Lord, inspire me to be grateful for the blessings you have bestowed on me and my parents, and inspire me with the ability to do good deeds with which you are pleased, and include me, through your mercy, in the ranks of your righteous servants."[53] He maneuvered his troops to avoid the ant mounds.

---

49. *Biḥār al-anwār* vol. 14 p. 72 tr. 12 and vol. 14 p. 94 tr. 3

50. Qur'ān 27:18

51. *Biḥār al-anwār* vol. 14 p. 92 tr. 2

52. *Biḥār al-anwār* vol. 14 p. 92 tr. 2

53. Qur'ān 27:19

Hajj

As they approached Bakkah, he told his troops:

> This is a land in which God will raise an Arab prophet. He will be given victory over all his enemies. His enemies will be instilled with awe of him up to a distance of one month's travel in every direction. He will be just with his family and others alike. And he will not be perturbed by naysayers. He will follow the path of Abraham. Glad tidings to all who live to meet him, believe in him, and stand by him! Let those of you who are present tell those who are absent, for he will be the Foremost of all the Prophets, the Seal of the Messengers, and his name is recorded in all the scriptures of old.[54]

To prepare for the rites of Hajj, he told his troops to remove their body hair with a depilatory agent called *nūrah*,[55] to bathe, and to don clean garments.

Solomon and his troops performed the rites of the Hajj according to the ancient custom of Abraham and Adam.[56] He then had the entire Kaʿbah draped in fine fabric from Egypt.[57] He thus became the first to ever drape the Kaʿbah in a *kiswah*.[58]

Where Is the Hoopoe?

Pilgrimage complete, Solomon led his troops home to the Holy Land.[59] En route, they needed to stop for water to drink and wash

54. *Biḥār al-anwār* vol. 14 p. 128

55. *Biḥār al-anwār* vol. 14 p. 115 tr. 10

56. *Biḥār al-anwār* vol. 14 p. 128

57. *Biḥār al-anwār* vol. 14 p. 75 tr. 1

58. *Biḥār al-anwār* vol. 14 p. 75 tr. 20

59. The tradition transmitted by al-Thaʿlabī (*Biḥār al-anwār* vol. 14 p. 128) asserts that they moved from Bakkah to Yemen. However, since it is clear from the Qurʾānic story that Solomon was home when he corresponded with Bilqīs, I

for prayer. Solomon called his troops to attention so he could assign the hoopoe the task of seeking out water.[60] His army of birds hovered in perfect formation overhead as always. Solomon gazed up into the sky to inspect the legions of birds.[61] But to his surprise, a single ray of light shone through the otherwise impervious avian cloud above, revealing a gap where the hoopoe was supposed to be.[62] He sternly asked, "Why do I not see the hoopoe? Is he absent?"[63] When he heard no response, he barked, "I shall punish him severely or even execute him if he does not bring me a good reason for his absence."[64]

Two Hoopoes Meet

Earlier that day, the hoopoe bird, whose name was Yaʿfūr, had decided to explore and had happened into the land of Sheba. There he met another hoopoe named ʿAnqīr.

ʿAnqīr asked him, "From where have you come, and where do you want to go?"

Yaʿfūr replied, "I have come from the Holy Land with my master Solomon, son of David."

ʿAnqīr asked, "Who is Solomon, son of David?"

Yaʿfūr replied, "He is king of men, *jinn*, birds, animals, and devils. Where are you from?"

---

have disregarded this detail from al-Thaʿlabī's report.

60. The hoopoe is known in Arabic as the *hudhud.* According to some traditions, this bird had the ability to sense water hidden beneath the earth (*Biḥār al-anwār* vol. 14 p. 112 tr. 4). It is not clear whether this was a special ability of that individual hoopoe from Solomon's court or a general property of the species of bird. I was not able to find any scientific literature confirming such an ability for the species. Either this question has not yet been explored by the scientific community, or I was simply not able to locate the research, or this was a gift of that specific individual.

61. Qur'ān 27:20

62. *Biḥār al-anwār* vol. 14 p. 110 tr. 3

63. Qur'ān 27:20

64. Qur'ān 27:21

ʿAnqīr replied, "I am from this land. It is ruled by a woman named Bilqīs. It seems your master has a great kingdom. Bilqīs' kingdom is not much less than that. She is the ruler of all of Yemen. Will you come with me to see her kingdom?"

Yaʿfūr said, "I am worried that Solomon may look for me at the time for prayer when he will need water."

ʿAnqīr said, "I am sure he will be pleased if you bring him information about this kingdom."

News From Sheba

Back in Solomon's camp, his patience was growing thin. He called on the falcon who was commander of the birds and asked if he knew where the hoopoe was. He replied, "I do not know. I did not send him on any mission."

The falcon summoned the eagle and ordered him to rise into the sky and seek out the hoopoe. As he soared ever higher, he spotted the hoopoe flying swiftly in their direction. He swooped to intercept him. Yaʿfūr, the hoopoe, exclaimed, "For the sake of God almighty who gave you power over me, have mercy on me."

The eagle ceased his attack but scolded him saying, "The Prophet of God has sworn to punish you severely or even execute you."

Yaʿfūr asked hopefully, "Did he mention any chance of clemency?"

The eagle said, "Yes. He said, 'If he does not bring me a good reason for his absence.'"

With renewed hope, Yaʿfūr approached Solomon with the ultimate posture of submission. Even so, Solomon laid hold of him roughly. Yaʿfūr managed to utter, "O Prophet of God! Call to mind the day when you will stand before your Lord as I now stand before you."

The anger from Solomon's face vanished as he heard these words.[65] He asked, "Where have you been?"

Yaʿfūr said, "I have become aware of information of which you are unaware. I have brought you certain news from the land of Sheba.[66] I found there a woman who rules over them. She has been

---

65. *Biḥār al-anwār* vol. 14 p. 82 tr. 29

66. Qurʾān 27:22

given every sort of blessing. In particular, she has an immense throne.[67] I found her and her people prostrating before the sun instead of God. Satan has made their deeds seem decorous to them and thereby swayed them from the path, so they are not guided."[68]

Letter to Bilqīs

Solomon considered this news and said, "We shall see whether you have told the truth or whether you are a liar."[69] He dictated a letter for the queen of Sheba to his scribe,[70] Āṣif ibn Barkhiyā.[71] He stamped it with his royal seal and told Yaʿfūr, "Take this letter of mine, and deliver it to them. Then, withdraw from them, and see what reply they give."[72]

Like a passenger pigeon, Yaʿfūr, the hoopoe, carried Solomon's letter to Sheba. He swooped into Bilqīs' court and, evading notice, dropped the letter upon her throne. He then retreated out of sight and waited to see her reaction.

Upon reading the letter, Bilqīs grew worried. She turned to her courtiers and said, "O advisors! A gracious letter has been delivered to me.[73] It is from King Solomon. It begins, 'In the name of God, the All-Beneficent, the Ever-Merciful,'[74] and continues, 'Do not be impertinent with me, and come to me in surrender.'"[75] After a pause, she glanced up from the letter and said, "Advisors! Give me your opinions regarding this matter. I am not wont to decide a matter until I hear your testimony."[76]

---

67. Qur'ān 27:23

68. Qur'ān 27:24

69. Qur'ān 27:27

70. *Biḥār al-anwār* vol. 14 p. 114 tr. 8

71. *Biḥār al-anwār* vol. 14 p. 127 tr. 13

72. Qur'ān 27:28

73. Qur'ān 27:29

74. Qur'ān 27:30

75. Qur'ān 27:31

76. Qur'ān 27:32

Her advisors discussed the matter among themselves for some time. Then her vizier told her, "We have might and unyielding resolve, but the decision is yours whether to fight or surrender. So tell us what you would command us to do."[77]

She contemplated her options aloud saying, "When kings invade cities, they ruin them and make its nobles into paupers. This is what they are wont to do.[78] Let us neither fight them and risk our security nor surrender and lose our civilization. Rather, I shall send them some gifts as appeasement. Then I shall see with what response my messengers return."[79]

Yaʿfūr hurried to Solomon's court and arrived long before Bilqīs' messengers, where he reported all that he had witnessed.

Bilqīs' Tribute

When Bilqīs' messenger came to Solomon,[80] Solomon asked him, "Do you dare pay monetary tribute to me as appeasement for rejecting my demand for surrender? I have no need for your tribute, for what wisdom and guidance God has given me is better than what material wealth he has given you. Nonetheless, you undoubtedly exult over these gifts of yours.[81] Return to them with your gifts, and tell them to prepare themselves for destruction for we shall meet them with an army against which they will have no strength to fight, and with it we shall expel them from Sheba in utter disgrace."[82]

He was hopeful that his threat and his rejection of her gifts would convince the queen of Sheba that he was no ordinary king and compel her to come to him in submission.

---

77. Qurʾān 27:33

78. Qurʾān 27:34

79. Qurʾān 27:35

80. Apparently she sent a group of people bearing gifts and made one of them the group's head. For this reason, some verses refer to them in the singular and some in the plural.

81. Qurʾān 27:36

82. Qurʾān 27:37

Bilqīs' Throne

Some weeks later, when he was sure the messengers would have returned to Sheba with his message, he said to his courtiers, "O advisors! Who among you will bring me her throne before they come to me in surrender?"[83] If she was not already convinced, he wanted to prepare a miracle that would leave no room for her to doubt.

A demon from among the *jinn* said, "I can bring it to you before you rise from where you are seated. I have the strength to do so and am trustworthy in this charge."[84] Solomon asked if anyone else could do better.

Āṣif ibn Barkhiyā[85] spoke. To him, Solomon had given knowledge of the book. If all knowledge were divided in seventy-three parts, Solomon had taught one part of seventy-three to Āṣif.[86] Āṣif said, "I can bring it to you before you blink an eye." He was destined to be Solomon's successor, and while Solomon could have performed the miracle himself, he wished his people to know Āṣif's virtue and power, in this way, just as David had shown the Israelites Solomon's virtue by letting him judge that fateful case.[87] In the blink of an eye, Āṣif folded the earth, stepped into Bilqīs' court, and transported her throne to Solomon's court.[88]

When Solomon saw it displayed before him, he said, "This is by my Lord's grace. He has allowed this to be done to test me to see whether I am grateful or not. If one is grateful, his gratitude only benefits himself, and if one is ungrateful, he harms only himself for God is free of need for our gratitude and generous in spite of our ingratitude."[89]

---

83. Qur'ān 27:38

84. Qur'ān 27:39

85. *Biḥār al-anwār* vol. 14 p. 127 tr. 13 and p. 113 tr. 5

86. *Biḥār al-anwār* vol. 14 p. 113 tr. 5–12. The tradition goes on to say that 72/73 were given to Prophet Muḥammad and his successors.

87. *Biḥār al-anwār* vol. 14 p. 127 tr. 13

88. *Biḥār al-anwār* vol. 14 p. 110 tr. 2

89. Qur'ān 27:40

Soon, news reached Solomon that Bilqīs was approaching with her entourage, ready to submit. He commanded his courtiers, "Disguise her throne before she arrives, so we may see whether she is guided by her intellect or whether she is one who is not guided."[90] Part of his goal was to convince her that he was God's prophet, but he also wanted to test her intellect and her discernment. By making some minor alterations to her throne, he wished to test her ability to observe and draw sound conclusions from her observations.

When Bilqīs arrived, she was welcomed into Solomon's court. As she walked by her throne, it was asked of her, "Is your throne like this one?"

She replied, "This seems to be it." She observed the alterations and thus refrained from assuming that it was in fact her throne. She understood that this miracle was an attempt to convince her that Solomon was no ordinary king. She said, "We were given knowledge of the truth of your message even before seeing this miracle, and we had submitted right then."[91] The fact that his letter demanded her submission to God and that he refused her tribute had convinced her that he was God's prophet. It had been the idols she worshiped instead of God that had prevented her from accepting Solomon's message at first for she was of an unbelieving people.[92]

Bilqīs Surrenders

Solomon invited her saying, "Enter my palace." When she entered and saw its courtyard, she thought it was a pond, and she lifted her skirt slightly, exposing her calves.

Solomon told her, "It is a courtyard whose floor is made of polished crystal."

Amazed by such a feat of architectural genius, atop all the virtue and miracles she had witnessed, she said, "Lord, I had wronged

---

90. Qur'ān 27:41

91. Qur'ān 27:42

92. Qur'ān 27:43

myself by not believing before now. I hereby surrender alongside Solomon to the Lord of all realms."[93]

Justice for the Wind

Once an old woman came to Solomon's court. She lodged a complaint against the wind. She had been working atop her roof when a gust of wind blew with such force that she was thrown from her roof and had sustained a broken wrist as a result. Solomon summoned the angel who controlled the wind so that he could hear the woman's complaint against him. Solomon asked the angel, "What made you do what you did to her?"

The angel replied, "God Almighty ordered me to save a ship that was stranded at sea. As is my wont, I rushed to fulfill my Lord's command. As I blew upon the ship, I also blew on this woman, and as a result, she must have broken her wrist."

Solomon asked God, "How should I judge between your wind and this lady?"

God told him, "You must recover the cost of restitution for this woman's broken wrist from the owner of the ship which I saved with my wind. I am God, and no one is wronged in my kingdom."[94]

Solomon's Advice to His Son

Solomon once told his son, "Beware of being argumentative for there is no benefit in it. It only serves to foment enmity among brethren."[95]

---

93. Qur'ān 27:44

94. *Biḥār al-anwār* vol. 14 p. 74 tr. 14. While this story is told in a way that seems more akin to legend or fable, it actually communicates an important principle. God's justice dictates that hardships that afflict us for no fault of our own must be made up to us. It seems that Solomon, as God's special agent, was in charge of dispensing this form of justice usually reserved for God himself.

95. *Biḥār al-anwār* vol. 14 p. 134 tr. 9

Solomon's Death

Solomon used to seclude himself, especially in his old age, in the temple. During his absence, Āṣif would handle his affairs.[96] During his 712th year, while he was in his seclusion, God decided to take his life.[97] He sent the Angel of Death to retrieve his soul as he stood in worship leaning upon his staff. His lifeless body remained rigidly supported for days, giving his servants the impression that he was still alive. Eventually, God sent a termite to weaken his staff so that his body would collapse. Only when it fell did his people realize that he had died and had been dead for some time. God arranged his death in such an unusual manner to prevent the *jinn* from making false claims to having knowledge of the unseen. Clearly, if they had known the unseen, they would not have endured their degrading punishment a moment longer than they had to.[98]

Generations later, it would be said about the inevitability of death, "If anyone had been able to find a path to everlasting life or to ward off death, it would have been Solomon, son of David who was given dominion over jinn and humanity in addition to prophecy and a station of proximity to the Divine. Nonetheless, when he consumed his allotted provisions and completed his appointed term, the crossbows of mortality launched at him arrows laced with death. As a result, his palaces lay empty, unused, and inherited by another people."[99]

---

96. *Biḥār al-anwār* vol. 14 p. 141

97. *Biḥār al-anwār* vol. 14 p. 140 tr. 8

98. Qur'ān 34:14

99. *Nahj al-balāghah* sermon 182

Jonah

Amittai's Two Guests

Amittai[1] was out in the forest one day securing a bundle of timber atop his head. When he returned to his usual spot in the market of Nineveh, his crowd of regulars were already lined up to bid for his wood, for he was known to have the choicest selection and to be scrupulously honest in all his dealings. Unbeknownst to the rest, there were two new faces in the crowd concealed under heavy hoods. King David and his son Solomon had been sent here by divine decree so that David could secretly meet one of his companions with whom, God had told him, he would reside in paradise.[2]

Amittai's arrival caused a great stir. He called out as always, "Who will buy my pure wood with pure money?" There were several bids for the entire bundle, each decidedly outdoing the other, until the bidding stopped and the exchange was made.

The two strangers approached and greeted Amittai. He invited them to follow him home and enjoy a meal with him. They complied. On their way, Amittai spent his newly gained earnings on a sack of wheat. When they arrived at his humble home, he offered them a seat and quickly began grinding the wheat in his stone mill. He mixed the stone-ground flour with water to make dough. He lit a fire and threw the formed dough against the wall of the oven to cook. This gave him a few minutes to sit with his guests and talk.

When the bread was done, they washed their hands. He placed the steaming loaf before them, sat upon his knees, broke the loaf

---

1. In Arabic his name is *Mattā*. He is the father of Jonah.

2. Previously, there was mention of Khalādah who was also given this rank. There is nothing far-fetched about David having more than one companion in paradise.

in a few pieces, and sprinkled some salt over it. As he brought the first morsel near his lips he uttered, "In the name of God," and then ate it with relish. When he had swallowed he uttered, "Praise is for God." Morsel after morsel, he did the same. Then he gulped down some water after saying, "In the name of God." And when his thirst was quenched, he said, "Praise is for God."

He lifted his hands and, with tears in his eyes, said:

> Lord, whom have you blessed as much as you have blessed me? You have given me keen vision and hearing and a sound body. You gave me the strength to go to a tree, which I did not even have to plant or care for, and you made it a source of sustenance for me. Then you brought someone to me to buy my wood, and with the earnings from that sale, I bought wheat, which, again, I did not grow. You subjugated fire for my use to cook that wheat, and you let me eat it with relish so that I may gain strength to serve you. For all this and more, to you belongs all praise!

Seeing that Amittai was lost in prayer, David whispered to Solomon, "Let us go now. I have never seen anyone so thankful as this man."[3]

Jonah Is Chosen

Nineveh was a massive city of more than one hundred thousand people.[4] It was located at the site of modern day Karbalā,' distant from the seat of David's and Solomon's power in Jerusalem, and thus its people had strayed far from the path of divine guidance

---

3. *Biḥār al-anwār* vol. 14 p. 403 tr. 16

4. Qur'ān 37:147

with little consequence.[5] God appointed Amittai's son, Jonah,[6] as a prophet and messenger to these profligate and misguided people.[7]

Jonah was thirty years old when he was made a messenger.[8] For the next thirty-three years, he called his people to believe in God and to follow the law of Moses, to almost no avail. Only two people accepted his call.

Jonah's Patience Wears Thin

Jonah saw that his tireless efforts were yielding no fruits on the people of Nineveh. He thought back to Noah, Abraham, and Moses and their unswerving fortitude in calling their stubborn people and felt ashamed before God for his own weakness in this regard. He prayed to God for patience and said:

> Lord, you sent me to my people when I was thirty years old. I have remained among them thirty-three years, calling them to believe in you and in my message and warning them of your wrath. Yet they have rejected me, and hardly any have believed in me. They have denied that I am your

---

5. One tradition mentions that Amittai was a contemporary of David, thus I have inferred that Jonah was a contemporary of Solomon. That said, there is nothing else in the Qurʾān or traditions that pins down his exact time frame.

6. In Arabic his name is *Yūnus*. One tradition traces the etymology of his name to the triliteral root, *anasa*, meaning "to be friendly with" or "to take comfort in." We have encountered such unconventional linguistic derivations before with the names of other prophets. Linguistic problems aside, this tradition claims that his name signifies that he "found comfort in God and was averse to his people. Later, when they reformed themselves, he found comfort in his people also" (*Biḥār al-anwār* vol. 14 p. 391 tr. 9).

7. Qurʾān 37:139. There is no mention in the Qurʾān or traditions of the exact crimes and moral vices of which the people of Nineveh were guilty. The emphasis of the story of Jonah is on Jonah's personal struggle. Nonetheless, that a prophet of God would call down God's wrath upon his people is clear indication that their crimes and vices were on par with the ʿĀd and Thamūd people, the Sodomites, and the people of Noah.

8. Most of the rest of the story is based on a single lengthy tradition (*Biḥār al-anwār* vol. 14 p. 392–9 tr. 12).

> messenger and mocked me. Now they threaten me, and I fear they will kill me. I lack the patience to continue calling them for I see no hope for them. So I beg you to send down your worst punishment upon them, for they are a hopeless people.

God reminded Jonah:

> Among them are unborn babies, children, elderly people, and frail women. I am just and wise, and my mercy trumps my anger. I do not punish the young for the crimes of the old. Jonah, these are my creatures and my dependents. I wish to give them more time to repent and reform. Jonah, I sent you to be merciful with them; to treat them with the gentleness characteristic of the prophets; to be for them like a doctor who cures their sickness. Yet, you have been harsh with them and unkind. You have not dealt with them as my past messengers dealt with their peoples. You ask me to punish them because you lack the patience to persevere. Noah was more patient with his people than you have been. For this reason, I angered when he angered and answered him when he called on me.

Jonah felt ashamed at his own weakness and lack of patience. He said:

> Lord, I am only angry with them for your sake, and I only call down your punishment upon them because they have sinned against you. For this reason, I can never feel compassion toward them. I can never feel goodwill for them because they have defied me and rejected me as their prophet. So I beg you again to send down you punishment upon them for I do not believe they will ever believe.

God told him:

> Jonah, they number more than one hundred thousand. They bring prosperity to this city, and they give birth to children who may become my servants. My preferred course of action is to defer their punishment because of what I know about them and about you. My plans and arrangements are different from yours. Remember that you are only a messenger, and I am the wise Lord. My knowledge of them is hidden; you do not know how deep it goes. Whereas your knowledge about them is superficial, with no depth. Nonetheless, I shall comply with your request. Their punishment shall descend upon them on the middle Wednesday of the month of Shawwāl, just after sunrise. Go, and announce it to them.[9]

---

9. Clearly, there are some problematic elements in this story as transmitted by this tradition. Parts of the story seem to contradict Jonah's infallibility, and parts seem to contradict the requisite subservience we have come to expect from the prophets, and parts seem to contradict the supremacy of God.

As with all such discussions, we must maintain a firm hold on those conclusions that are the product of pure reason (*ʿaql*) for such conclusions are necessarily true and trump all other statements when there is a contradiction. The following three principles are such products of the intellect:

- Rationally, we know that the prophets must be infallible exemplars of the highest ethical traits. The simplest argument for this claim is that their fallibility would undermine the very purpose for which they were sent since we would always have room to doubt whether they were mistaken in conveying God's message and, hence, God could not hold us accountable for disobeying them and rejecting their teachings.
- Prophets must be at the forefront of subservience before God, for if they were not, how could they be role models of subservience to the rest of mankind?
- We know without question that God is supreme. He does as he wishes, and no one, not even one of his prophets, can stop him once he decides to do something.

With these three principles in hand, whenever we see something that contradicts the prophets' infallibility, their subservience to God, or God's supremacy, we must see if it could reasonably be construed in a way that fits with these

Jonah was immensely pleased with this outcome.

Prophecy for Nineveh

Jonah had two close friends, Rūbīl and Tanūkhā. Rūbīl was Jonah's lifelong friend and was a shepherd by trade. He was from a family of scholars and wise men, and he too was a wise and knowledgable follower of Jonah. Tanūkhā was neither wise nor knowledgeable but devoted nonetheless. He made a living by collecting and selling firewood.

Jonah rushed to Tanūkhā and informed him of the news. Tanūkhā's opinion was to keep the punishment a secret so that the people of Nineveh would continue in their evil ways right up until the punishment destroyed them.

Jonah remembered that God had instructed him to announce the punishment to the people, so he did not take Tanūkhā's advice. He said, "Let us go find Rūbīl and ask his opinion since he is a wise and knowledgeable man from a family of scholars."

They found Rūbīl and gave him the news. Rūbīl said, "I advise that you speak with God again and ask him to withhold this

---

principles and if not, it must be rejected outright.

With this methodology, let us examine Jonah's story. It is clear from the sources that Jonah lacked a level of patience. Using our principles, we must put this in context, for Jonah is a prophet, and prophets are chosen precisely because they possess all the prerequisite virtues needed for guiding people. Accordingly, we must conclude that his deficit in patience was in comparison with the great prophets of old, not in comparison with the rest of humankind.

It follows that this exchange I have quoted between God and Jonah is really God's way of actively nurturing a heightened level of patience in Jonah. If God had wished, he certainly could have vetoed Jonah's request. But he chose to argue with him, and he attempts to convince him to be more patient, clearly to no avail. Jonah, in turn, understood that he was being given the opportunity to speak his mind and "argue" with God. Thus, this exchange does not contradict God's supremacy or Jonah's subservience. Think of it more like the exchange between a teacher and a disciple where the teacher brings himself to the disciple's level and gives him freedom to make his own mistakes, and thereby learn. As we shall see later in the story, God's concession to send down punishment kills two important birds with one stone. The people of Nineveh are frightened into reform, and Jonah rushes off and gets swallowed by the whale, and through that ordeal, learns patience.

punishment for he has no need for it. He loves to be compassionate with his creatures. Who knows? Maybe these same people, after having rejected you and disobeyed you, may come to believe one day."[10]

They debated back and forth until, finally, Jonah decided to announce the impending punishment without asking God for a reprieve.

The people of Nineveh responded with more disrespect than they had ever previously dared. They rebuked Jonah and mocked him and threatened to banish him from their city. Jonah, utterly disgusted with them, decided, without waiting for God's express instructions, to abandon Nineveh. He left feeling angry at his people, assuming that God would not take him to task and straiten his circumstances for leaving the city without receiving express permission to do so.[11]

Rūbīl's Admonishment

When the fateful day arrived, the black clouds approached. Within the city, Rūbīl began frantically warning his people. He said, "I am Rūbīl, your well-wisher. It is the middle of Shawwāl, and Jonah warned you that God has promised to send down punishment upon you on this day. God does not fail in his promise. Now, you must decide what you wish to do."

For the first time in the history of man, a people condemned by God, on the verge of utter destruction, grew penitent and reflective.[12] They asked Rūbīl, "What do you advise us to do?"

---

10. It seems that Tanūkhā and Rūbīl are reflections of Jonah's two conflicting sides. Tanūkhā feels the same hot anger in the face of sin as Jonah and cannot bring himself to have mercy on the sinner. Rūbīl feels so much compassion that he cannot see the wisdom in threats and punishments. They reflect the two extremes between which Jonah is struggling to find the balance. I do not mean that they are imaginary alter egos but only that each friend is similar to Jonah in a different way.

11. Qur'ān 21:87. God had promised to send down a punishment, so Jonah felt justified in leaving his people. He should have been patient and awaited God's command. This was all part of God's ploy to teach him greater patience.

12. Qur'ān 10:98

He told them, "You must beg God with tears and cries. Humble yourselves before him. Repent for your past transgressions and pledge to reform yourselves. Raise your hands to the skies and pray, 'Lord, we have done wrong! We rejected your prophet, but we now repent to you for all of our sins. If you do not have mercy on us and forgive us, we shall be among the losers. So accept our repentance and have mercy on us, O Most Merciful!' Do not stop praying in this way with all your heart until God repeals his punishment from you."

They agreed unanimously to follow his advice. Rūbīl hastily fled the city so that he would not be caught by God's punishment. He watched from a distant mountain as the clouds of God's punishment pressed upon his city.

The people of Nineveh did exactly as Rūbīl advised them. Rūbīl too, from his vantage point, prayed to God to spare his people. And God did. His plan had worked. For the first time, the sight of his punishment had instilled enough fear in a people to bring them to their senses before it was too late. He told Seraphiel, "Go down to the people of Nineveh, for they have called out to me with tears and cries and repented and sought forgiveness. I wish to show them mercy and accept their repentance for I am God, the Clement, the Ever-Merciful. I rush to accept the repentance of my servants whenever they repent for their sins. Jonah asked me to send my punishment upon these people, and I promised I would, and I always fulfill my promise. I have now fulfilled my promise by sending my punishment upon them. Happily, there is no need to destroy them. Go down and command my army of angels to cease the advance of the punishment."

Jonah Escapes by Boat

While all this was taking place in Nineveh, Jonah continued his trek. Because he had left Nineveh without God's express permission to do so, God had left him to his own devices without any new revelation or guidance or moral support.[13] He had no idea that a revolution had swept over his people and assumed they had

13. *Biḥār al-anwār* vol. 14 p. 387 tr. 6 and p. 384 tr. 2

been utterly destroyed. He walked on with no goal but to distance himself from Nineveh, like a fugitive on the run,[14] until he finally reached a port city. He decided to board a small boat that was laden and ready to sail.[15]

At sea, the boat was caught in the middle of choppy waters. With the boat so full, the sailors felt sure they would sink if they could not lighten their load. They agreed that they would draw lots. Whoever's lot was drawn would tether himself by a rope to the boat and swim alongside until the rough seas had subsided.[16] Jonah drew the short lot.[17] He tethered himself and jumped overboard. As a result, the boat floated a little higher in the water, and they felt the danger had passed.

Swallowed by a Whale

Suddenly, out of the depths arose an enormous whale, mouth gaping. In an instant, it swallowed Jonah whole. The rope that secured him snapped, and the whale slunk back into the depths. The sailors simply gazed on dumbfounded as their poor companion disappeared.[18]

God had ordered this whale to swallow Jonah. He ordered it to guard him in its mouth without crushing him or hurting him. For three days,[19] Jonah remained trapped in the whale's mouth, unable to see for the darkness and unable to move for the lack of space.

---

14. Qur'ān 37:140

15. Qur'ān 37:140

16. It is not clear from the sources what necessitated such drastic measures. It is clear that they drew lots, and Jonah lost (37:141). Whether it was a storm or the appearance of the whale or something else, is not clear. All versions of the story in the traditions and the Book of Jonah seem very far-fetched. It is hard to justify why the sailors would be so callous as to throw a person overboard to die rather than struggle together against the elements. It is harder to justify why Jonah would willingly jump. I have tried to create a scenario that seems more plausible than what is contained in the sources.

17. Qur'ān 37:141

18. Qur'ān 37:142

19. *Biḥār al-anwār* vol. 14 p. 383 tr. 2

Jonah understood that this hardship was a direct result of the impatience he had shown to his people and the haste with which he had abandoned them. He cried out through those layers of darkness, swallowing his anger for his people,[20] "There is no god but you! You are exalted! I was one of the wrongdoers!"

God had been prepared to keep Jonah in the whale's belly indefinitely, until the Day of Resurrection, if necessary. But he had realized his shortcomings and exalted God, so God accepted his prayer[21] and ordered the whale to release him upon a desolate shore. Sick and weak, Jonah collapsed upon the shore, unconscious.[22]

Lying on that beach, he would have died in the sun,[23] but God made a gourd vine to grow over him as shade.[24] When he awoke, he praised God for the shade he had provided him. When he felt thirsty, he sucked at the vines and imbibed the juices to be found therein.[25]

A Lesson in Compassion

He regained his strength and was ready to leave the shade of the vine when he noticed an infestation of insects at the base of the vine. Before he could react, they gnawed at the base of the vine and severed its connection with the soil. Within an hour, the leaves were wilted and the plant died. Jonah felt sad for the fate of this vine.

God asked him, "Jonah, do you feel such compassion for this vine which you did not plant or water or nurture, yet you cannot find compassion in your heart for more than one hundred thousand people in Nineveh who are your people and whom you have spent so many years nurturing? You asked me to send my punishment upon them, and I did. But seeing it, they repented and reformed

---

20. Qur'ān 68:48

21. Qur'ān 21:88

22. Qur'ān 37:143–145

23. Qur'ān 68:49

24. Qur'ān 37:146

25. *Biḥār al-anwār* vol. 14 p. 383 tr. 2

themselves and have become believers. They now await your return so that you can guide them."[26]

Jonah returned to his people with a renewed sense of fortitude and patience. God gave the people of Nineveh a new lease on life because they believed in Jonah and accepted his teachings.[27]

---

26. *Biḥār al-anwār* vol. 14 p. 383 tr. 2

27. Qur'ān 37:148 and 10:98

Zecharíah, John the Baptist, & Jesus

Two Blessed Families

Jesus' story begins two generations before him. His grandmother Anna[1] was married to Joachim[2] who was one of God's chosen prophets and a messenger sent to the Israelites.[3] Anna's sister, Elizabeth,[4] was married to Prophet Zechariah.[5] The stories of these

---

1. Anna is referred to in traditions alternatively as *Ḥannah* (see *Biḥār al-anwār* vol. 14 p. 202 tr. 14) and *Martā* (see *Biḥār al-anwār* vol. 14 p. 213 tr. 11).

2. Joachim is pronounced jo-uh-KEEM and is said to mean "God makes firm." Perhaps this was an honorific given to him since the Qur'ān refers to him by the name *'Imrān*.

3. *Biḥār al-anwār* vol. 14 p. 202 tr. 14

4. Elizabeth is referred to in the traditions as *Ḥanānah* (see *Biḥār al-anwār* vol. 14 p. 202 tr. 14).

5. It is important to note that the Prophet Zechariah mentioned in the Qur'ān as the father of John the Baptist is not the same as the Prophet Zechariah to whom is attributed the Book of Zechariah in the Old Testament. The former is not even considered a prophet in the Bible. In Luke 1 he is called a priest, and his conversation with an angel is recounted, though he is shown to have doubted in God's promise and to have been punished because of this. The latter is believed to have been a prophet during the reign of Darius the Great, after the destruction of the temple around 520 B.C.E. There is no mention of this prophet in Islamic sources. Rather, whenever the Prophet Zechariah is mentioned in Islamic sources, it is the father of John the Baptist who is meant.

two pious families and their children are intricately intertwined.[6]

Joachim's Prophecy

God communicated to Joachim, "I shall bestow upon you a blessed male child who will heal the blind and the leprous and revive the dead by God's leave. I shall make him a messenger to the Israelites."[7]

He rushed to convey these tidings to Anna who had yearned so long for a child to no avail.[8] They were immensely grateful to God for this gift, and they prepared for the child's arrival. As her pregnancy progressed, Joachim reassured Anna saying, "God has promised to grant me in this very month a child who will be a prophet."[9]

Sadly, Joachim died shortly thereafter, less than a month before his child's birth. In an act of utter selflessness and in accordance with her late husband's wishes, Anna committed her unborn child to the service of the temple in Jerusalem. In earnest prayer she said, "My Lord, I dedicate to you what is in my womb as one free to serve you, so accept him from me. You are the All-Hearing, the All-Knowing."[10] It was from her forefather Abraham that she had

6. Jesus' Family Tree:

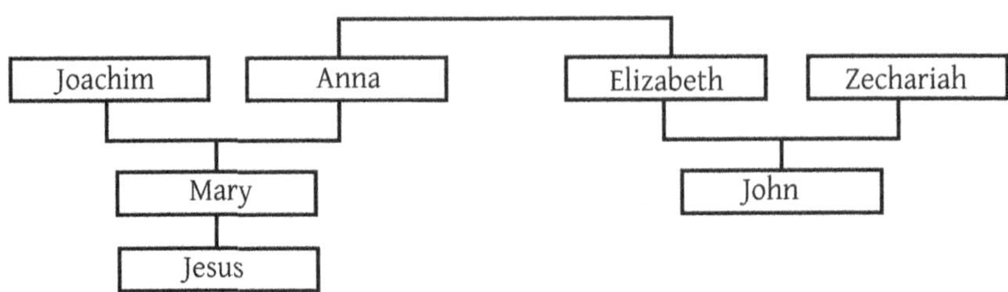

7. *al-Kāfī* 1.4.127.1

8. *Majma' al-bayān* under verse 3:35

9. *Biḥār al-anwār* vol. 14 p. 203 tr. 16

10. Qur'ān 3:35 It was the practice of the most devout Jewish families in that time to dedicate their children in this way to God's service. They would renounce their rights as parents, foremost of which were their rights to care for their children and to be obeyed by them. They would sacrifice their rights and dedicate the child to the service of God in the temple where he or she would be raised by the priests, serve the temple and the worshipers, and learn his or her

learned that the key to pleasing God is to sacrifice for his sake what you hold most dear.[11]

Prophecy Deferred

When she bore a girl, she was perplexed. In utter incredulousness she told God, "My Lord, I have borne a female child!"[12] It was not that she was misogynistic, as is common in many primitive societies. On the contrary, Anna was perplexed by the birth of a girl in light of Joachim's prophecy. She had submitted so wholly to her husband's prophecy that she was certain her child would be its fulfillment. Indeed, he had explicitly promised her this. But now she had borne a girl, and, for a moment, she was both disappointed that she had somehow failed to play her part and bewildered that the prophecy was left unfulfilled.[13] Little did she know that the boy she had expected was nothing like this girl she had been given.[14]

---

religious obligations. The child would not necessarily be bound to this service for life; rather, the parents could only renounce their rights for the time in which they had rights, presumably until the child reached puberty. At that age, he or she could choose for himself whether to continue or leave the service of the temple (*Majmaʿ al-bayān* under verse 3:35).

11. See Qur'ān 37:102–111 and 3:92

12. Qur'ān 3:36

13. The authors of *al-Mīzān* and *Majmaʿ al-bayān* have hypothesized that the cause of Anna's bewilderment was that she had borne a girl while, according to Jewish custom, girls could not be dedicated to the service of the temple. However, it seems these dedications were not limited to boys. Rather, there were other "virgin" girls who had been dedicated in the same capacity as Mary (see *Gospel of the Nativity of Mary* in Roberts, Rev. Alexander and James Donaldson, eds. *Ante-Nicene Fathers.* Vol. 8. Grand Rapids, MI: WM. B. Eerdmans Publishing Co., 1995. p. 385b). Accordingly, I have construed the cause of her bewilderment differently in my narrative.

14. Qur'ān 3:36. The vast majority of commentators believe the phrase "*wa laysa al-dhakaru ka al-unthā*" to be a continuation of what Anna said to God. ʿAllāmah al-Ṭabāṭabāʾī and al-Marāghī believe it is God who says this as an aside to us, and that if Anna had said it, she would have said it the other way around, "This female I have borne is not like the male I had hoped for."

God's statement, "The boy she had expected was nothing like this girl she had been given," is not meant to debase Jesus in any way or to say that Jesus' status

Then, she understood everything. Of course, her late husband had spoken the truth. He was an infallible prophet of God and could have neither misunderstood God's revelation to him nor misspoken. Rather, like so many of God's decrees, this one had been contingent on factors beyond even his prophet's knowledge. As those factors had changed, so too had the fate of their child.[15]

When Anna had understood this, she said with a renewed sense of devotion, "I hereby name her Mary."[16] The name "Mary" means "servant,"[17] and this was Anna's way of showing her resolve to follow through on her oath and turn her child's affair over to God to do as he willed. Then she begged, "And I seek refuge for her and her progeny from the evil of the outcast Satan."[18] With this prayer, she demonstrated to God not only her willingness to sacrifice for his sake but her undying faith in the promise God had made to Joachim—that he would have a blessed male child who would heal the blind and the leprous and revive the dead by God's leave and be a messenger to the Israelites. It no longer mattered to her whether that child was born directly to her or many generations later, it was God's promise, and he would undoubtedly fulfill it.

As is God's wont with his sincere servants, he accepted Anna's dedication and her prayer. He accepted the girl graciously as his servant, and he ensured that, though she was separated from the nurturing care of her mother, she would be reared excellently and want for nothing.[19]

---

was less than his mother's. Anna had expected her child to be a messenger and a worker of miracles as per Joachim's prophecy. However, she had not expected him to be one of the Messengers of Great Resolve and one of God's greatest messengers. Thus, the comparison is between *the prophet she expected* and Mary, not Jesus and Mary.

15. *al-Kāfī* 1.4.127.1-2 and *Biḥār al-anwār* vol. 14 p. 203 tr. 16 and p. 205 tr. 21

16. Qurʾān 3:36

17. *Majmaʿ al-bayān* under verse 3:36

18. Qurʾān 3:36

19. Qurʾān 3:37. Some traditions imply that Anna immediately placed her newborn infant in the temple (*Biḥār al-anwār* vol. 14 p. 202 tr. 12–13). There is no indication that she or any other woman nursed her. However, it is reasonable to speculate that someone nursed her and cared for her until she was old enough

Mary's Guardian

Without her father, Mary was an orphan with no male guardian. Zechariah, as her maternal aunt's husband, and more importantly, as God's prophet, was naturally the only candidate. However, there were others in the temple, five in particular, who thought themselves more deserving of this privilege.[20] So they concurred that they would cast lots to decide the affair.[21] Despite their machinations, God's will was done, and Zechariah's lot was drawn. Thus, God answered Anna's prayer and charged Zechariah with Mary's care.[22]

Childhood in God's Service

For the entire duration of her childhood, as per her mother's dedication, Mary remained in the temple and never set foot out of it.[23] Her work was to serve the worshipers and priests alongside the other girls and boys who had been dedicated.[24] It was hard work, but the rewards justified her toil. In the presence of priests, especially her guardian, Zechariah, she gained a deep knowledge of God and learned the intricacies of the law. Even at her tender

---

not to need constant care, perhaps at the age of three or four. We can speculate that her mother or a hired wet nurse might have had the responsibility of doing this. Alternatively, the *Gospel of the Nativity of Mary* relates that the angel promised Anna that Mary "shall remain three years in her father's house until she be weaned" (Roberts, Rev. Alexander and James Donaldson, eds. *Ante-Nicene Fathers*. Vol. 8. Grand Rapids, MI: WM. B. Eerdmans Publishing Co., 1995. p. 385a).

20. *Biḥār al-anwār* vol. 14 p. 198 tr. 5. Several traditions (*Biḥār al-anwār* vol. 14 p. 202 tr. 13 and p. 204 tr. 18) mention that the other parties to the quarrel were prophets; however, it is inconceivable that prophets of God would "quarrel" as the Qur'ān expressly mentions that these parties did. Thus, we cannot accept these traditions.

21. Qur'ān 3:44

22. Qur'ān 3:37

23. *Biḥār al-anwār* vol. 14 p. 202 tr. 12–13

24. *Biḥār al-anwār* vol. 14 p. 205 tr. 20

age, she discovered the secret delights of intimately worshiping God.[25]

This state of affairs continued as long as Mary was a child. It was when she came of age that her continued service to the male worshipers became problematic. The presence of women, even an exemplar of chastity[26] like Mary, was a distraction to the exclusively male priests. Mary in particular was as beautiful as she was chaste.[27] Even Mary herself would have found it unbearable to have continued serving them as she had. More urgently though, she was about to begin menstruation,[28] and it was against the law for a woman in that state to remain in the temple. Thus, for the first time, since the day she was born, she left the temple.[29]

As her mother, Anna, had passed away some time before,[30] the most fitting place for her to bide her time outside the temple was with Zechariah and Elizabeth for they had filled for her the role of loving parents after the loss of her own. In their house, she spent

---

25. These last few sentences are speculation.

26. Qur'ān 21:91

27. *Biḥār al-anwār* vol. 14 p. 192 tr. 1. One tradition tells us that God will use her on the Day of Judgment to argue against those women who believe their inordinate beauty justifies their acts of sexual indecency. He will present Mary to them and ask, "Are you more beautiful or she? We made her beautiful, yet she was not tempted" (*Biḥār al-anwār* vol. 12 p. 341 tr. 2).

28. *Biḥār al-anwār* vol. 14 p. 193 tr. 2 and p. 202 tr. 12. It is commonly believed in some cultures that Mary did not menstruate and that menstruation somehow contradicts her immaculate nature. Menstruation is a normal bodily function like eating, drinking, and defecating. There is no shame in it. In the Islamic worldview, menstruation is not a scourge meant to punish women for some original sin. It is simply the biological outcome of a woman's fertility. Thus, menstruation does not contradict her immaculate nature. More importantly, the two traditions I have cited here explicitly state that she menstruated. Many other traditions imply the same. In conclusion, since there is no rational reason why she could not have menstruated, and there are numerous traditions that explicitly and implicitly mention that she did, we can safely and confidently say that she did.

29. *Biḥār al-anwār* vol. 14 p. 202 tr. 12–13

30. *Biḥār al-anwār* vol. 14 p. 193 tr. 2. One recension of this tradition says that "she was orphaned of both her parents."

a week or ten days until she was clean.[31] Then she withdrew from her new foster family to return to the temple.[32]

Mary's Cloister

When she returned to the temple, it was under circumstances very different from what they had been when she had left ten days prior. With her coming of age, she was no longer bound by her mother's dedication.[33] Nevertheless, she longed to be no place more than in the temple. It was holy ground, blessed by God.[34] It was upon the Temple Mount that her forefathers,[35] David and Solomon, had built the original temple centuries before.[36] Despite the corruption that had crept into it, the extirpation of which was the main occupation of her father and Zechariah,[37] this place was where she felt closest to God and could immerse herself in his worship.

It fell upon Zechariah, as her guardian, to find a suitable place for her residence that allowed her to worship while remaining cloistered from the presence of men.[38] He chose for her the

---

31. I have made this inference from the verse 19:16 which says, "*She withdrew from her family to an easterly place.*" This "easterly place" was within the temple. It only makes sense to say that she "withdrew from her family" if she was with her family before she withdrew. If, on the other hand, she were simply continuing to live in the temple, only in a new place within the temple, she could not be said to have "withdrawn from her family."

32. Qur'ān 19:16

33. *Majmaʿ al-bayān* under verse 3:35

34. Qur'ān 17:1, 21:71, and 21:81

35. *Biḥār al-anwār* vol. 14 p. 194 tr. 2

36. 1 Chronicles 22:1–19 and 2 Chronicles 3:1–16

37. We can infer the presence of great corruption and their struggle against it from verse 19:5 since Zechariah had reason to fear for the integrity of God's religion if he died without an heir. We can also infer it from 3:44 since the leadership of the temple staked a claim against that of their prophet and quarreled with him over it. Greatest of all, the imminent birth of Jesus, who was sent as a last attempt to reform a nation with a long and dark history of corruption and treachery, leads us to be certain that corruption in the temple was at an all-time high.

38. *Biḥār al-anwār* vol. 14 p. 205 tr. 20

sanctuary where the altar of incense was kept.[39] It was located just

---

39. The Qur'ān gives us two clues as to the whereabouts of Mary's cloister. It says it was within the *miḥrāb* (3:37) and it describes its location as being in "an easterly place" (19:16). I have used these two clues, along with the help of other verses, the Bible, and scholarly reconstructions of the Temple of Herod to try to identify the place where Mary's cloister was located.

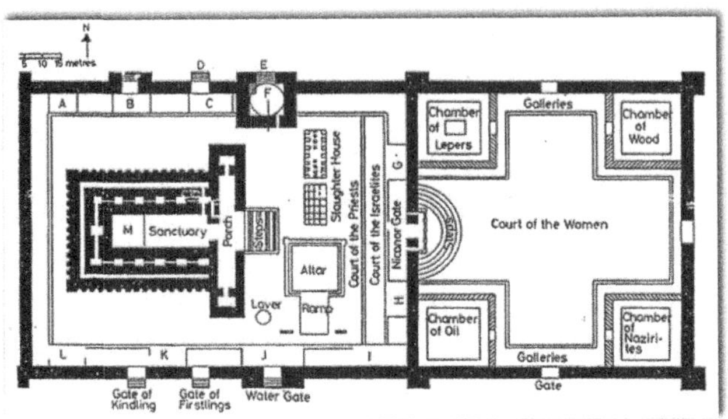

When verse 19:16 mentions that her cloister was in "an easterly place," it is tempting to assume it was in the Court of Women since this was the easternmost part of the Temple Mount. However, several verses tell us that this "easterly place" was also in the "*miḥrāb*." It is improbable that the Court of Women would have been referred to as the *miḥrāb*.

The term *miḥrāb*, which in the Islamic context has come to refer to a prayer niche at the front of a mosque indicating the direction of the Kaʿbah, refers more generally in the Qur'ān to a place of worship. Various etymologies have been suggested for the word, but most commentators are in agreement that it is roughly the equivalent of *masjid* or "mosque" or in this case, "temple."

One verse indicates clearly that Mary's cloister was in the *miḥrāb*. It says, "Whenever Zechariah visited her in the *miḥrāb*, he would find provisions near her" (3:37). 3:38 continues to tell us that Zechariah prayed on the spot for God to grant him a son, a prayer mentioned in greater detail in 19:1–6. And 3:39 tells us that his prayer was answered immediately "while he stood in the *miḥrāb*." Thus, the place in which Mary's cloister was located, the place of Zechariah's prayer, and the place where he was given the news of the birth of his son, John, all took place in the *miḥrāb*.

In the Gospel of Luke, no mention is made of Mary's presence in the temple, but Zechariah's story is told like this:

> One day Zechariah was doing his work as a priest in the temple, taking his turn in the daily service. According to the custom followed by the priests, he was chosen by lot

east of the Holy of Holies, into which tradition allowed only the high priest to enter, and that, only on the Day of Atonement.[40] There he built for her a small, simple, room where she could devote herself

---

> to burn incense on the altar. So he went into the temple of the Lord while the crowd of people outside prayed during the hour when the incense was burned. An angel of the Lord appeared to him, standing at the right side of the altar where the incense was burned. When Zechariah saw him, he was alarmed and felt afraid. But the angel said to him, "Don't be afraid, Zechariah! God has heard your prayer, and your wife Elizabeth will bear you a son. You are to name him John. (Luke 1:8–13)

Luke's narration until here does not contradict the narration of the Qurʾān. And it does confirm that Zechariah was addressed by the angel at the altar of incense which is located in the sanctuary. While this place is not at the easternmost part of the Temple Mount, it is at the easternmost part of the most sacred parts of the temple located at the uppermost level of the temple. It is fitting that this uppermost level, which was the most sacred part of the temple, be referred to as the *miḥrāb*.

Qurʾān 19:11 further strengthens this claim for it tells us that when he exited the *miḥrāb*, after this incident, he exited to a place overlooking his people where he was the center of attention. If you look at archeological models that recreate the Temple of Herod, so called because it was Herod who commissioned its renovation around the time period in question, you see that the porch, the sanctuary (where the altar of incense would have been housed), and the Holy of Holies were all at the same level, higher than the rest of the temple structures. Qurʾān 19:11, which tells us that he exited to a place overlooking his people, bolstered by the passages from Luke, indicates that the *miḥrāb* was the sanctuary and that when Zechariah exited, it was from the steps leading down from the porch.

There is one final verse that confirms these claims. In Qurʾān 38:21 we are told that "the two parties scaled the sanctuary's wall to enter the *miḥrāb*" to present their case to David. Since it is David who originally built this temple, we can assume that its structure in that time was similar to its structure in the time of Zechariah and Mary, even though it was destroyed and rebuilt several times in the interim. In any case, my point is to emphasize that the Qurʾān uses the word *miḥrāb* to identify the place where David was sitting when these people came to him and that they had "to scale the wall" to get to him. It seems all these verses in both books are talking about the same place and, accordingly, I have translated the word *miḥrāb* as "sanctuary."

40. *Oxford Companion to the Bible*. p. 734a

to worship far from the gazes of men while remaining within the confines of the holy temple. Only Zechariah was permitted to enter her quarters.

It might seem unusual for Mary to receive so much attention from the community elders. However, Zechariah, for one, was well aware of the prophecies given to Joachim, and he knew that Mary was destined for greatness. She epitomized the ideal of human perfection through complete servitude to God. She was akin in virtue to the great queen of Egypt, Āsiyah, who had been martyred millennia before for her heroic stand against the Pharaoh in support of Moses.[41]

The Voices of Angels

In her new quarters in this holy place, Mary was granted the special privilege by God of being able to hear and converse with angels.[42] On one occasion, they told her, "O Mary! God has chosen you and purified you."[43] With these words, they bore a reminder from God that he held true to the promise he had made to her mother, Anna. He had accepted her into his service and chosen her as his *mary*, his special "servant." And he had agreed to purify her by protecting not only her but her progeny from the evil hand of Satan. They continued, "And he has favored you over all the women of the world."[44] With these words, they foreshadowed a favor God wished to do for Mary that was unprecedented in the history of humankind and would remain unmatched until the end of time. They concluded, "O Mary! Thus obey your Lord and prostrate and bow with those who bow to show your gratitude."[45]

One year on the first of Muḥarram,[46] Zechariah, being a priest, was chosen by lot to conduct the ceremonial burning of incense at the altar of incense within the sanctuary. He entered and shut the

41. *Biḥār al-anwār* vol. 14 p. 201 tr. 9–11 and Qur'ān 66:11–12

42. In Arabic such a person is called a *muḥaddath* or *muḥaddathah*, "one who is spoken to."

43. Qur'ān 3:42

44. Qur'ān 3:42

45. Qur'ān 3:43

46. *Biḥār al-anwār* vol. 14 p. 1674 tr. 2

colossal doors behind him while the other priests and Israelites waited below for the rite to be fulfilled.[47] Before performing the rite, as was his wont, he visited Mary. It was Zechariah's habit to visit her regularly in her quarters to check on her. He would knock and announce himself. As close as he was to her, even he had to observe certain limits. When she had covered herself appropriately, she would bid him to enter. A thing that never ceased to amaze Zechariah was the provisions he would find laid out for her.[48] She would have winter fruits even in the summer and summer fruits even in the winter.[49]

Zechariah's Prayer

On this occasion, he asked her, "Mary, from where do you get this?"

She replied, "It is from God. God provides for whomever he wishes without any reckoning."[50]

Zechariah was thus reminded by Mary of God's limitless bounty. He felt a spiritual upwelling within himself, and without a moment's delay, he rose to pray right where he was in the sanctuary. As he burnt the incense, he prayed for what he and Elizabeth most wanted and what seemed the most far-fetched. He was an old man, and she had been barren throughout their marriage.[51] But he knew God's power was limitless. He knew his forefather Abraham had been granted Ishmael and Isaac in old age. Most of all, he was certain that God would do whatever was best. So he prayed from the bottom of his heart saying, "My Lord! My bones have grown feeble, my head has turned gray with age, yet never, my Lord, have I been disappointed when praying to you. I fear what my kinsmen will do after me." He had seen the lust for power in his relatives who longed to employ the priesthood for self-interest, and he thought a son could keep them in check after his death. He continued, "And my wife is barren, so grant me an heir out of your

47. Luke 1:8–10

48. Qur'ān 3:37

49. *Biḥār al-anwār* vol. 14 p. 204 tr. 17

50. Qur'ān 3:37

51. Qur'ān 3:40 and 19:4–5

grace who will inherit from me and thereby inherit from part of the family of Jacob, and make him, my Lord, pleasing to you."[52] He continued, "Lord, grant me righteous progeny out of your grace. You are the hearer of prayers."[53]

God answers sincere prayers without delay. While Zechariah yet stood there in the sanctuary with his hands raised to the sky, Angel Gabriel appeared before him with an entourage of angels and declared, "O Zechariah! We bring you tidings of a boy whose name shall be John.[54] Never before have we made anyone with this name."[55] Then they conveyed a message directly from God saying, "God conveys to you tidings of John who shall confirm the Word of God, be a leader, a celibate,[56] and a prophet from among the righteous."[57]

Zechariah was elated to hear God's tidings and immensely grateful. Yet, he was in awe of God's power and a bit surprised to have been graced like this, for while others view the prophets as men close to God, they view themselves to have fallen short of the mark, and they do not dare to presume that God will answer their prayers.[58] He feebly asked, "Lord! How will I possibly have a son

---

52. Qur'ān 19:4–6

53. Qur'ān 3:38

54. His name is *Yaḥyā* in Arabic and John the Baptist in the New Testament.

55. Qur'ān 19:7

56. While celibacy is not a virtue in Islam, John the Baptist was singularly praised for this trait because it resulted from his total renunciation of temporal pleasure for the sake of God's pleasure. In nearly all people, denying oneself carnal pleasure altogether yields some form of deviant behavior. John the Baptist was uniquely blinded to the satisfaction of his own desires by his eagerness to satisfy God's. One commentator has appropriately said, "The legality, commendation, and praise of celibacy is specific to him (i.e., John the Baptist) since its legality and commendation in any general sense are unprecedented in any divine legal system. As for Islamic law, it is transmitted without dispute that the Messenger of God said, 'Marriage is part of my example. He who renounces my example is not of me'" (*Ālā' al-raḥmān* vol. 1 p. 281).

57. Qur'ān 3:39

58. Abraham's statement in Qur'ān 19:48 provides another example of the humility of the prophets.

when old age has overtaken me and my wife is barren?"[59] He did not doubt that God could do it.[60] But after a lifetime of prayers, and nearly losing hope—not in God's unlimited grace, but in his own worthiness to receive that grace—he was still in awe. He longed to know how God would do it. Would he make him and his wife young again? Would he have him marry a younger wife?

The answer came, "The matter is as I have said. God does whatever he wishes.[61] Your Lord says, 'Such a thing is easy for me considering I created you before this when you were nothing.'"[62]

A Sign for Zechariah

Still in awe, but having gained some composure, he begged, "Lord! Make me a sign." He wanted a tangible sign to increase his certainty and to remind himself that God would undoubtedly fulfill his promise. The answer came, "Your sign is that you shall not be able to speak to the people for three days except through gestures. And remember your Lord much and exalt him night and day."[63]

Zechariah was euphoric. He opened the grand doors of the sanctuary and exited. As he stepped out onto the porch, he glanced down to his people who were waiting for him below. They could see from his expression and manner that something had happened. They asked him about it, but he only gestured to them that he could not speak and would not be able to for another three days.

---

59. Qurʾān 3:40 and 19:8

60. The author of the Gospel of Luke writes, "Zechariah said to the angel, 'How shall I know if this is so? I am an old man, and my wife is old also.'

'I am Gabriel,' the angel answered. 'I stand in the presence of God who sent me to speak to you and tell you this good news. But you have not believed my message which will come true at the right time. Because you have not believed, you will be unable to speak—you will remain silent until the day my promise to you comes true'" (Luke 1:18–20).

Sadly, this author did not understand the station of God's prophets and imagined that Zechariah's question stemmed from his doubt in the truth of God's promise.

61. Qurʾān 3:40

62. Qurʾān 19:9

63. Qurʾān 3:41 and 19:10

As God had ordered him, he now gestured to them to "exalt God day and night!"[64]

Zechariah and Ḥusayn

Zechariah spent the next few days praising God for answering his prayer. During this time, Gabriel taught him the names of the final prophet and his family, Muḥammad, ʿAlī, Fāṭimah, al-Ḥasan, and al-Ḥusayn. Zechariah noticed that mention of the first four names evoked a great feeling of elation within him. But when al-Ḥusayn's name was mentioned, he choked up with tears and felt that he was drowning in sorrow. He asked God about this to which he replied by recounting what would happen to al-Ḥusayn at Karbalāʾ in all its gruesome detail.

Zechariah was so affected by this story that he spent the next three days in solitude, weeping. He said, "Lord, will you torment the best of your creatures through his son? Lord, will you let such a calamity descend upon his doorstep? Lord, will you afflict Fāṭimah and ʿAlī with such a tribulation? Lord, grant me a son, as you have promised me, despite my old age, and let him be the apple of my eye. When you have granted him to me, make me smitten with love for him. And then torment me through him as you have decided to torment your beloved Muḥammad through his son." Within six months, Elizabeth gave birth to a boy whom Zechariah named John.[65] God's peace was with him the day he was born, the day he

---

64. Qurʾān 19:11

65. *Biḥār al-anwār* vol. 14 p. 178 tr. 14. Several traditions, including this one, assert that John was born after six months of gestation, like Imam al-Ḥusayn. Some traditions claim that no one other than John and al-Ḥusayn were born after only six months and survived. Others claim that only Jesus and al-Ḥusayn had this honor. It is possible, based on pure speculation, that the names Yaḥyā (John) and ʿĪsā (Jesus) were confused in some of the traditions since, in Arabic, these two names look very similar. It seems more likely, based on the other similarities between John and Ḥusayn, that he is the one who was born after six months, not Jesus. Nonetheless, because we have traditions claiming both, and because this is not a significant issue, I have attributed this miracle to both John and Jesus.

would die, and the day he would be raised to life.[66]

Gabriel Visits Mary

It was sometime afterward, on a Friday, as the sun reached its zenith,[67] that Mary was engaged in worship in her cloister. She had become accustomed to her solitude. Aside from Zechariah, she saw no one. The rest of the priests knew that her quarters were expressly off limits. This was all the more reason why Mary was stunned when she saw inside her cloister, unannounced, a handsome man.[68] She exclaimed, "I seek protection with the All-Beneficent from you, so stay away from me if you truly fear God!"[69] Not knowing who this was or what intentions he had, she hoped her appeal to his fear of God would make him desist from any harm he wished to inflict upon her.

In an instant, he allayed her fears intimating, "I am but a messenger from your Lord whom he has sent so that I may give you a pure son."[70] It was Archangel Gabriel whom God had sent in the form of a handsome man.[71] His was not an unfamiliar name to her. He had been a friend and servant to all the prophets of God, many of whom had been her forefathers. Now he would serve her.

She asked, "How will I have a son since no man has touched me in wedlock, and I have never been unchaste?"[72] Like Zechariah, she had no doubt in God's omnipotence and his infinite wisdom. Yet she could not help but to be surprised at this news. Her mother

---

66. Qur'ān 19:15

67. *Biḥār al-anwār* vol. 14 p. 213 tr. 11

68. Qur'ān 19:17

69. Qur'ān 19:18

70. Qur'ān 19:19

71. Qur'ān 19:17

72. Qur'ān 19:20 and 3:47. There is no evidence for Joseph, the carpenter, or Mary's betrothal to him in Islamic literature. On the contrary, when ʿAlqamah complained to Imam al-Ṣādiq about the false allegations people were making at the Shīʿah as perpetrators of sin, he cited this betrothal as an example of the false allegations those same sorts of people had made at even God's prophets and saints (*Amālī al-Ṣadūq* p. 102).

had told her of the prophecy God had given to her father Joachim. She knew the prophecy would be fulfilled in her progeny. However, Mary thought being a virgin had disqualified her from bearing that child. Ironically, God had chosen her to bear this child precisely because she was a virgin and chaste.[73]

Gabriel replied, "The matter is as I have said. Your Lord says, 'Such a thing is easy for me.' We shall do this, among other reasons, so that we may make it a sign for humankind to know our power[74] and a source of mercy from us that they may know their prophet and be guided by him. It is a matter already decided.[75] When God decides a thing, he need only say to it 'Be!' and it is."[76] With this final statement, she knew that this promise from God was not subject to any contingencies as his promise to her father had been. Rather, it was decided, and would happen without fail. With that, and by the power invested in him by God, Gabriel breathed into her womb the spirit of life—the same spirit that had given Adam life[77]—and the embryo of Jesus, son of Mary, was conceived.

Tidings From the Angels

Thereafter, Mary was hailed and congratulated by delegations of angels. They told her, "O Mary! God gives you the good news of a *word* from him whose name is the 'Messiah, Jesus, son of Mary,' distinguished in this world and the hereafter, and one of those near to God."[78] They called Jesus God's *word* because he was created, not through the natural systems God has ordained for the conception of all other living creatures but merely by the will of God, symbolized by a single word, the imperative "Be!"[79] And they

---

73. Qur'ān 66:12 and 21:91

74. *Biḥār al-anwār* vol. 14 p.218 tr.23

75. Qur'ān 19:21

76. Qur'ān 3:47

77. *Biḥār al-anwār* vol. 14 p. 219 tr. 25

78. Qur'ān 3:45

79. Qur'ān 4:171

called him the "Messiah" because he was blessed, a source of much good.[80]

The angels continued saying, "And he will speak to the people while in the cradle and as an adult just the same,[81] and he will be among the righteous. And God will teach him the law and wisdom and in particular the Torah[82] and the Evangel.[83] And he will be a messenger to the Israelites."[84]

A Distant Place

Mary felt immense gratitude to God for honoring her with this gift. She devoted herself ever more diligently to worship as her child grew in her womb. When she had borne him for nearly six months, she felt the time was nearing for her to give birth.[85] At the behest of

---

80. The Hebrew term *māshiāḥ* means "anointed." It was used as a synonym for "king" because kings would be anointed with blessed oil. Jews have not traditionally accepted him as the Messiah since he was not a king. Christians believe he is a king whose kingdom is in heaven. ʿAllāmah al-Ṭabāṭabāʾī believes he may have been called the "messiah," not because he was, or will be, a king anointed with blessed oil, but simply because he was *blessed*. He himself declares, "He has made me *blessed* wherever I may be" (Qurʾān 19:31). Thus, he understands "messiah" to be a synonym for the Arabic *mubārak*.

81. For him to speak as an adult is nothing special. It is mentioned here to emphasize that his speech as an infant will be the same as his speech as an adult.

82. The Torah refers to the writing on the tablets given to Moses upon the mountain. The tablets themselves were destroyed during the destruction of Jerusalem under Nebuchadnezzar in 586 B.C.E. In 457 B.C.E., Cyrus defeated the Babylonians, freed the Jews and set up Ezra as the ruler of Jerusalem. Ezra is responsible for reconstructing much of the extant Old Testament.

83. The Evangel refers to one single book revealed to Jesus, not the various gospels now included in the New Testament that were authored by several people.

84. Qurʾān 3:46–49

85. *Biḥār al-anwār* vol. 14 p. 207 tr. 2 and 3. These traditions tell us that Jesus and Imam al-Ḥusayn were the only two people to be born at six months (24 weeks) and survive. Imam al-Ṣādiq's intent was apparently that they were the only two people ever to have survived these circumstances *until that time*. Incidentally, 24 weeks is still a critical cut-off age for survival in babies. At 24 weeks, even with modern medical advancements, survival and prospects for a

angels, she slipped out of the temple unbeknownst to anyone and withdrew to a distant place.[86] God carried her miraculously, more than 530 miles due east to the outskirts of Kūfah, to a place that later came to be known as Karbalāʾ.[87]

---

healthy life are very slim. It is safe to say that in pre-modern times, death was certain, so Jesus' and Imam al-Ḥusayn's survival was truly miraculous.

Earlier, when I narrated the birth of John the Baptist, I discussed the presence of conflicting traditions, some of which mention that John was born after six months and others of which mention that it was Jesus.

86. Qurʾān 19:22

87. The Qurʾān tells us only that she withdrew to "a distant place." One tradition tells us that the place was Bethlehem. While this tradition concurs with the New Testament (Luke 2:4), at six miles it is not a very "distant place." More importantly, it is contradicted by many traditions that tell us that she gave birth around Kūfah. A close examination of these traditions shows that they are all in agreement.

- One says explicitly that she traveled from Syria (which includes Jerusalem) to Karbalāʾ where she gave birth at the place where Imam Husayn is now buried (*Biḥār al-anwār* vol. 14 p. 212 tr. 8). This tradition not only is the most explicit in specifying the exact location of Jesus' birth, but it also clearly states that her journey was miraculous. She was able, through God's power, to travel there and back in less than a day for each leg, and she returned to Syria the very night she gave birth.
- A second tradition says vaguely that she gave birth next to the Euphrates (*Biḥār al-anwār* vol. 14 p. 214 tr. 11). While the Euphrates does pass through parts of Syria, it does not pass near Bethlehem, but it does pass through Karbalāʾ.
- A third tradition tells of Imam al-Ṣādiq seeking out a date palm among the orchards of Kūfah and then praying next to one in particular. He then explains to his companion that it is "by God, the very tree about which God has said, 'Shake the trunk of the date palm toward yourself and it will drop freshly picked dates upon you'" (*Biḥār al-anwār* vol. 14 p. 208 tr. 5). We can safely guess either that the transmitter referred to Karbalāʾ as Kūfah because it is on the outskirts of Kūfah or that the palm the Imam prayed near was a descendant or graft from the original palm in Karbalāʾ.
- A fourth tradition speaks of Imam ʿAlī's visit to Barāthā, which is today part of Baghdad (*Biḥār al-anwār* vol. 14 p. 211 tr. 7). While this tradition speaks of a spring that bubbled forth for Mary, it does not explicitly refer to Jesus' birth but rather refers to Barāthā as "Mary's home." I

Jesus Is Born

Her labor pains gripped her. In the barren wasteland, she saw no shelter. There was only the emaciated trunk of a date palm, still standing, but barely, evincing no signs of life. As she approached it, a shot of pain forced her to the ground at its base. She exclaimed, "I wish I had died before this and become a thing forgotten beyond recall."[88] It was not the pain that made her speak so. It was the thought of what would happen after she had delivered. She was a chaste woman from a chaste family. She was about to bear a child out of wedlock, and all she had to defend herself against her people's wicked tongues was her word, and she knew it would stand for little under the circumstances. Of course, she knew God was her protector, but she did not yet know what plan he had in store.

There, in the barren plain of Karbalāʾ, with no one to help her, or even to hear her screams, without even the shade of a tree, on Tuesday,[89] the 25th of Dhū al-Qaʿdah,[90] Mary gave birth.

Eat, Drink, and Be Comforted

From the ground where he lay, Jesus, son of Mary, called out to his mother with strength and comfort saying, "Do not fret! Your Lord has made a spring to flow at your feet. Shake the trunk of the date

---

believe this tradition has nothing to do with Jesus' birth and is rather speaking of another place that Imam ʿAlī had excavated which was Mary's home, perhaps at some later time in life.

- A fifth and sixth tradition explain that the verse "We made the son of Mary and his mother a sign, and we sheltered them on a plateau with a place to stay and fresh water" (23:50) refers to Najaf and the Euphrates (*Biḥār al-anwār* vol. 14 p. 217 tr. 19–20). It is possible that this verse is referring to the time of Jesus' birth; however, considering that it says that they were sheltered there, it seems it is referring to a longer stay than the few hours they would have spent following his birth.

88. Qurʾān 19:23

89. *Biḥār al-anwār* vol. 14 p. 213 tr. 11

90. *Biḥār al-anwār* vol. 14 p. 214 tr. 13

palm toward yourself and it will drop fresh dates upon you. Eat, drink, and be comforted."[91]

She recognized her son's words as a sign of God. No sooner had he spoken than she heard the gurgling of water and felt the cool freshness bubbling between her toes. She reached out and cupped the water in her hands and quenched her parched tongue. She washed away the dust and felt as though she were imbibing life itself. She cleansed and bathed herself.[92] She bathed her child and swaddled him in what she could spare of her own clothing.

Then she reached out to the lifeless palm trunk and shook it feebly. In an instant, it sprang to life. It sprouted long, verdant fronds that cast a cool shade over her, and tremendous clusters of ripened dates hung low and glistened as their sticky syrup seeped out in golden halos around each plump fruit. Some of these landed with a thump beside her, and she ate and regained her strength. She now felt at ease, with renewed physical strength, and most importantly, a renewed surety in God's promise and grace. The God who provided all this, would never forsake her.

Satan's Vow

In the meantime, Satan was informed by his spies that a child had been born because of whom every idol would fall prostrate. He searched the east and the west and finally found him and his mother surrounded by angels. They kept him at bay. Satan asked who his father was. When the angels told him he was created like Adam had been, he swore that he would misguide four fifths of all humanity through him.[93] He knew that such a miraculous birth could easily be twisted to make people think him divine.

---

91. Qur'ān 19:24–25

92. *Biḥār al-anwār* vol. 14 p. 240. Al-Majlisī explains that the spring in which she bathed herself and Jesus was the same spring used centuries later to bathe the head of Imam al-Ḥusayn.

93. *Biḥār al-anwār* vol. 14 p. 215 tr. 14

Vow of Silence

Mary rose, with baby in hand, ready to return home. Jesus spoke to her again and told her, "If you see any person, say, 'I hereby make a vow to the All-Beneficent to maintain silence,[94] so I shall not speak to any person today.'"[95] With this, he set her mind at ease. She would not have to speak. She was relieved of the duty of defending herself. He would somehow defend her.

Allegations

As easily as God had carried her to Karbalā', he returned her along with baby Jesus. On the very evening of her delivery,[96] she found herself on the outskirts of Jerusalem walking somberly toward the temple with Jesus in her hands.[97] At first people looked at her amicably with their usual greetings. As their gazes fell upon the child in her arms, they glanced quizzically at one another as if to ask whose child Mary was carrying. In her wake, people's wonder turned to malice as they began to speculate that it might be hers. By the time they collectively realized the scandal of it all, Mary had reached the temple and an eager mob had gathered. With self-righteousness and feigned indignation, they berated her saying, "O Mary! You have done something novel! O sister of Aaron![98]

---

94. Such a vow of silence was clearly allowed for Mary or perhaps more generally in Jewish law. It is, however, not permitted in Islamic law.

95. Qur'ān 19:26

96. *Biḥār al-anwār* vol. 14 p. 212 tr. 8

97. Qur'ān 19:27

98. Several reasons have been offered for why she was called "sister of Aaron."

- It was most likely a reference to Aaron since she was from his progeny. There is a precedent for referring to the members of a tribe as brothers and sisters of the patriarch of that tribe. For instance, we are told, "And we sent to 'Ād, their brother Hūd" (11:50). Hūd was a "brother of 'Ād" because he belonged to a city or tribe that was founded by 'Ād. Similarly, Ṣāliḥ and Shu'ayb are referred to as a "brother of Thamūd" and "brother of Midian," respectively.
- She could alternatively have had a brother named Aaron about whom

Your father was not a lascivious man nor was your mother an adulteress."[99] With cutting sarcasm, they told her she was a pioneer of sin in a family renowned for chastity. In reality, they cherished the opportunity to denigrate Joachim's family and Zechariah's ward.

The people became increasingly impatient with what they viewed as Mary's impudence. She refused to talk. They were accusing her of fornication, yet she did not speak a word in her own defense. When all had gathered around and the indictments had reached a crescendo, Mary simply pointed at the child in her arms as if to refer everyone's addresses to him.[100] They demanded incredulously, "How can we speak to one who is yet an infant in his cradle?"[101]

Jesus Speaks

Then he spoke. Mary's son, Jesus, an infant swaddled in his mother's arms, spoke to them as a grown man would speak. With poise and a resonant voice he announced so that all could hear him, "I am a servant of God! He has given me the book and made me a prophet. He has made me blessed wherever I may be, and he has exhorted me to pray and give charity as long as I live and to be good to my mother, and he has not made me a miserable tyrant to her. May God's peace be with me the day I was born, the day I die, and the day I am raised again to life."[102]

---

we have no other information.

- Aaron may have been an exemplar of chastity. By referring to her as Aaron's sister, they were trying to drive the dagger of their sarcasm deeper.
- Aaron may have been an exemplar of lasciviousness in which case they were not being sarcastic but simply vicious (see *Majmaʿ al-bayān*).

99. Qurʾān 19:27–28

100. Qurʾān 19:29

101. Qurʾān 19:29. Since he was still in her arms and not in a cradle, the phrase "an infant in his cradle" seems to be a figurative way to refer to an infant whether or not it is actually in a cradle.

102. Qurʾān 19:30–33. It is transmitted that these three moments are the most frightening moments in a person's existence: when he is born and lays his eyes

When he finished, there was absolute silence. People were overwhelmed, filled with awe and wonder and a renewed faith in God's omnipotence.[103] Zechariah and his infant John rejoiced to have witnessed the fulfillment of Joachim's prophecy. Others were sorely disappointed. Those who despised God's prophets and had leveled false allegations at Mary and were prepared moments before to have her stoned for fornication,[104] now found themselves tongue-tied. Not an inkling of doubt remained. Mary had been exonerated fully in the eyes of all.[105]

Gifts From the East

Some time afterward, when things had settled down in Jerusalem, a delegation of Zoroastrians arrived and sought out Mary's house and requested an audience with her. They addressed her as follows:

> We are a people who gaze at the stars. When your son was born, one of the stars of dominion appeared in the sky. We examined it closely and found that his dominion is to be the dominion of prophethood and that it will never part from him until he is raised into the heavens where he will be in the proximity of God as long as the world remains as it is. Then he will enter a dominion that is longer and more lasting than that in which he previously lived.
>
> We have traveled from a place in the east until we reached this place where we found the star to be shining directly overhead. This is how we knew where he is. We have brought presents for him as a means to become close to him. No one has ever

---

for the first time on the temporal world; when he dies and sees the reality of life after death; when he is raised and witnesses a world he could not have imagined (*Biḥār al-anwār* vol. 14 p. 246 tr. 26).

103. *Biḥār al-anwār* vol. 14 p. 218 tr. 23

104. *Biḥār al-anwār* vol. 14 p. 216 tr. 16

105. *Biḥār al-anwār* vol. 14 p. 216 tr. 16

> been given such gifts as these. We chose these gifts because each resembles him in some way. They are gold, myrrh, and frankincense. We bring gold because it is the leader of all commodities, and, similarly, your son will be the leader of all people as long as he lives. We bring myrrh because it is a panacea for wounds, and, similarly, through your son, God will cure wounds, diseases, insanity, and all ailments. And we bring frankincense because its smoke rises into the sky like nothing else, and, similarly, God shall raise your son into the heavens like no other contemporary.[106]

John's Precociousness

After his first divinely-inspired words, Jesus, the infant, spoke no more. On the seventh day, his umbilicus and foreskin were shed.[107] For the next two years, Zechariah continued his lifelong mission to guide the Israelites and root out corruption. His son, John, from a very young age, demonstrated an intense devotion to God. He watched his father and the other priests at the temple, wearing their simple cassocks and burnooses, worshiping with selfless devotion. He returned home and asked his mother, "Please sew me a cassock and burnoose so that I may go to the temple and worship with the priests."

Elizabeth replied, "Let's wait until the prophet of God returns so that I may consult with him on this." When Zechariah returned, she told him of their son's request.

Zechariah asked John, "Why do you wish to join us in the temple when you are but a small boy?"

John replied, "Father, have you not seen boys who are younger than I who have tasted death?" John had deeply understood the urgency of life and the imminence of death and wished not to waste a moment for fear that he might die without having worshiped

106. *Faraj al-mahmūm* p. 28

107. *Biḥār al-anwār* vol. 12 p. 3 tr. 4

God as much as he could. Without further discussion, Zechariah turned to Elizabeth and asked her to do as the child had requested.

John devoted all his waking moments to worship. He wept endlessly and grew emaciated until his cheek bones protruded painfully through his skin. The priests expressed their concern for John's health to Zechariah. Zechariah asked him why he wept so much and said, "I asked God to grant me a son to make me *happy*."

John replied softly, "Father, you are the one who told me to weep so much."

Zechariah, surprised by this assertion, asked, "When did I say such a thing?"

John replied, "Did you not say, 'Between heaven and hell there is a bridge which no one may cross except those who weep out of fear of God?'"

Zechariah admitted that he had and that it was true. From then on, Zechariah made sure that when he mentioned hell, John was not within earshot for he was more sensitive to the fear of God than anyone else.

Elizabeth begged John to return home with them. After much cajoling, he conceded. She nursed him to health and fed him. Then one day, as he slept, God spoke to him in a dream and said, "Have you found a home that is better than mine?"

John started from sleep. He asked his mother to give him his cassock and burnoose and told her that he must return to the temple. Despite Elizabeth's protestations, he insisted that he had no choice. Zechariah saw in his eyes that he had seen a vision, so he convinced his wife to let their son go. He told her, "He has been shown something in his heart that will prevent him from ever partaking in the pleasures of this worldly life."

John Succeeds His Father

When Zechariah passed away, his son John, though still a child, and only slightly older than Jesus, donned the mantle of prophethood and continued his father's mission.[108] God made him wise despite

---

108. *Biḥār al-anwār* vol. 14 p. 255 tr. 51

his youth.[109] He was compassionate, pure, God-fearing, and good to his parents.[110] God appointed him saying, "John, hold fast to the Book of Moses."[111]

He would address the Israelites, praising God and warning them about the Day of Judgment and reminding them that the plight of the Israelites was due to their many sins. He promised that they would be delivered at the hands of the Messiah who would rise up in some twenty years.[112]

Jesus' Childhood

During Jesus' first seven years, Mary and Jesus returned to the land of Iraq where he had been born. They lived in peace and in the unending grace of God for a time in Barāthā[113] and for a time in Kūfah on the banks of the Euphrates.[114] Here God "sheltered them on a plateau with a place to stay and fresh water."[115] They also spent some part of these years in Egypt.[116]

Jesus' Mission

It was when Jesus reached the age of seven that God conferred upon him his mission as a messenger, a role in which he superseded even John as God's proof over humanity.[117] He was to be the seal of 600 prophets sent specifically to the Israelites.[118] As with all his

109. Qur'ān 19:12

110. Qur'ān 19:13

111. Qur'ān 19:12

112. *Biḥār al-anwār* vol. 14 p. 179 tr. 16

113. *Biḥār al-anwār* vol. 14 p. 211 tr. 7

114. *Biḥār al-anwār* vol. 14 p. 217 tr. 19–20. There are some indications in the traditions and in the New Testament that they spent some time in Egypt. As there is nothing absurd about this possibility, I have included it too.

115. Qur'ān 23:50

116. *Biḥār al-anwār* vol. 14 p. 273 tr. 2

117. *Biḥār al-anwār* vol. 14 p. 255 tr. 51

118. *Biḥār al-anwār* vol. 14 p. 251 tr. 41 and p. 250 tr. 40. Like Moses and the other Hebrew prophets, Jesus' mission was, in one sense, specifically to his

predecessors, God made a covenant with him to believe in and worship him, to support the other prophets, and to work sincerely for the guidance of all people.[119] He was given the light of guidance, knowledge, and wisdom along with the canon of knowledge of all the prophets before him.[120] Additionally, he was chosen to join the ranks of the Messengers of Great Resolve. He was the fourth and penultimate of five bearers of law. It was to be his mandate to amend the law of Moses. He returned to Jerusalem to begin his mission and, with it, the final chapter in the history of his people.

---

people, the Jews, and in another sense, to all of humanity. Insofar as Jesus was an infallible prophet bearing divinely-inspired guidance, his mission was to guide all people to whom he could convey his message directly or indirectly. In particular, he guided them to correct beliefs and to the general and universal laws of morality and worship to which God holds all people accountable. On the other hand, insofar as Jesus bore a law that both upheld and amended Moses' law, he was specifically a messenger to the Israelites, and only they were bound to obey his law (see *Maʿārif-e Qurʾān* by Shaykh Miṣbāḥ Yazdī vol. 5 p. 31–42).

Based on this difference, we can conclude that all Jews were obligated to accept him as their Messiah and prophet and to obey his law with all its amendments to Moses' law. All other people were only obligated to believe in him if word reached them of his prophethood. If they did not learn of his prophethood, they were not responsible for believing in him. And none of these non-Jews were obligated to follow the specific law that he had brought for the Jews.

By way of example, we see that the group of *jinn* referred to in Qurʾān 46:29–32 were followers of Moses' book up until they heard that the Qurʾān had been revealed, at which point they converted directly from Judaism to Islam. They were apparently not Jews and so were obligated only to follow the tenets and general laws of Moses' law. They apparently were not informed of Jesus' book and so they make no mention of it.

Another example may be ʿAbd al-Muṭṭalib and Abū Ṭālib, Prophet Muḥammad's grandfather and uncle, respectively. They are reported to have been *ḥanafī*, followers of the religion and law of Abraham. They were justified in adhering to Abraham's law since neither Moses' nor Jesus' law would have abrogated the patriarch's law for the Arabs.

Finally, we shall see shortly Jesus' unusual interaction with the Canaanite woman who was a Gentile and, hence, not obligated to follow Jesus' law.

119. Qurʾān 3:81 and *Biḥār al-anwār* vol. 14 p. 234 tr. 4

120. *Biḥār al-anwār* vol. 14 p. 250 tr. 39

On the twelfth or thirteenth of Ramaḍān of that year, God revealed to Jesus the Evangel.[121] Like all revealed books before it, it was given to Jesus intact as a complete book, not in separate parcels over the course of his mission.[122]

To establish his credibility among people, God bolstered him with miracles. He stood before his people and declared, "I have brought you signs from your Lord: I shall create for you out of clay the form of a bird, then I shall breathe into it, and it will become a bird by God's leave.[123] And I shall heal the blind and the leprous and revive the dead by God's leave.[124] And I shall tell you what you eat and what you store in your houses. There are signs in that for you, should you truly be believers."[125]

Healer of the Sick, Raiser of the Dead

In his infinite wisdom, God equipped Jesus with miracles that spoke to his time. He lived in an era when diseases were epidemic and people needed medical treatment. He brought for them, on God's behalf, a panacea the likes of which they did not have and by which he raised for them the dead, cured the congenitally blind and the leprous, and sealed his case against them.[126]

Some days, thousands of people with a variety of maladies would gather to receive treatment from Jesus. He would treat them and at the same time, call them to faith, hoping that being touched by the infinite power of God would soften their hearts to truth.[127]

---

121. *Biḥār al-anwār* vol. 14 p. 283 tr. 2–3

122. *Biḥār al-anwār* vol. 14 p. 284 tr. 4

123. A similar story is narrated in the *Infancy Gospel of Thomas.*

124. While all of his miracles are done by God's leave, he makes doubly sure to mention this condition for the creation of birds and the revival of the dead because these are truly godly acts, and there is more chance that people will fall into error and believe he is God when they see him doing what they believe only God can do.

125. Qur'ān 3:49

126. *al-Kāfī* 1.1.20

127. *Biḥār al-anwār* vol. 14 p. 259

Bringing Shem to Life

Jesus practiced these miracles on numerous occasions. On one such occasion, his disciples asked him to raise a dead person for them to see and thereby strengthen their faith. He took them to the grave of Shem, the son and successor of Noah. Jesus stood at the head of the grave and cried out, "Stand, by God's leave, Shem, son of Noah!" With that the grave cracked open. He repeated the cry and there was movement from within. At the third cry, Shem emerged from the grave, and he and Jesus exchanged greetings. Jesus asked him, "Which would you prefer, to remain alive or to return to your grave?"

Shem replied that he would prefer to return. He said, "Until this very moment, I still feel the sting of death in my belly." He did not want to face the pangs of death for a second time.[128]

Jesus' Friend

Jesus had a friend whom he had been accustomed to visiting regularly. He was unable to visit him for a while, and when he went to visit him again, the friend's mother said he had died. Jesus asked her if she would like to see her son again and she eagerly replied that she would. He came the next day, and they went together to his grave. He prayed to God and, by his leave, his friend rose from his grave. When Jesus saw him and his mother weeping with joy, his heart went out to them. He asked his friend if he would like to remain alive for another twenty years and marry and have children. He said he would, and he lived for another twenty years just as Jesus had promised.[129]

The Canaanite Woman

On another occasion, a Canaanite woman who was not a Jew brought a son of hers to Jesus. She said, "O Prophet of God! This son of mine is paralyzed. Please pray for him before God."

---

128. *Biḥār al-anwār* vol. 14 p. 233 tr. 2

129. *Biḥār al-anwār* vol. 14 p. 233 tr. 3

Jesus replied, "I have only been authorized to heal the paralyzed from among the Israelites."

She beseeched humbly, "O Spirit of God! Even dogs receive scraps from the tables of their masters when they are done. So bestow upon us some of your wisdom so that we also may benefit." Jesus sought permission from God, and it was granted, so he healed the boy.[130]

Jesus' Wisdom

Once, Jesus reflected on the miracles he had been able to perform. He said to his disciples, "I have treated the sick and cured them by God's leave. I have healed the congenitally blind and the leprous by God's leave. With a mere touch, I have revived the dead by God's leave. However, I have tried to cure the fool, but I have not been able to heal him."

His disciples asked, "Whom do you intend by this "fool"?

He replied, "I mean him who admires himself and his own opinion; who considers all obliged to him and himself obliged to no one; who considers all rights to be due to him while no rights are due to anyone else. Such is a fool for whom even I do not have a cure."[131]

An Elixir For Jesus

Ironically, though God had endowed Jesus with miraculous powers to heal others, God required him to resort to mere mortal remedies for himself. When he fell ill once in his childhood, he asked his mother, Mary, to prepare an elixir of oil, honey, and bitter herbs.

---

130. *Biḥār al-anwār* vol. 14 p. 253 tr. 45. As I explained earlier, this Gentile woman was not responsible for obeying Jesus' law, and, hence, he was not obligated or even authorized to perform his miracles for her. However, she was responsible for believing in him as a prophet which she obviously did. As an exception, because of her sincere display of devotion to him as a prophet of God, he heals her son.

It is noteworthy that a similar story is narrated in the Gospel of Matthew 15:21–28. However, the story narrated there contains elements that are much more difficult to justify and accept.

131. *Biḥār al-anwār* vol. 14 p. 323 tr. 35

When she offered it to him, he tasted it and cringed in disgust. She asked him why he cringed when he himself had asked for it. He replied, "I prescribed this concoction for myself based on my prophetic knowledge, but I now cringe in disgust because I am but a child." With that, he took one more waft and then drank it.[132]

Walking on Water

Jesus' miracles were not limited to healing the sick and raising the dead. He was once traveling with a close companion of his. They arrived at a body of water and Jesus said, "In the name of God," with solid conviction, and he was able to walk on the surface of the water. His companion saw him and also said with solid conviction, "In the name of God," and he too was able to walk on the surface of the water. This was a gift God gave him for his devotion to Jesus and his solid belief.

However, the man was overcome with a sense of conceit. He thought to himself, "The Spirit of God walks on water, and I walk on water. What merit does he have over me?" No sooner had he thought this then he splashed beneath the surface and scrambled to grab hold of Jesus to save himself.

Jesus caught hold of him and brought him safely to shore. He told the man, "You forgot your place and thought yourself better than you are. This is why God became angry with you and stripped you of your gift. Repent to God." He did, and God returned his gift to him.[133]

Jesus' Teachings

The purpose of these miracles was to establish his credentials beyond a shadow of a doubt. When he felt this purpose was served and people were ready to listen to him, he announced, "I have

---

132. *Biḥār al-anwār* vol. 14 p. 253 tr. 46 and 47

133. *Biḥār al-anwār* vol. 14 p. 254 tr. 49. This story is similar to the one recorded in Matthew 14:22–33. The Bible identifies the person "of little faith" as Peter, Jesus' successor. As Muslims, we know that Peter, as Jesus' infallible successor, would never have had "little faith" or thought himself Jesus' equivalent. Thus, we can accept the story but reject the identification of the man with Peter.

brought you wisdom, and I have come to clarify for you some of the things about which you differ. So fear God and obey me. God is my Lord and your Lord, so worship him. This is the straight path."[134] And he announced, "I come to confirm the Torah which came before me and to make lawful for you some of the things that you were forbidden. And since I have brought you these signs from your Lord, fear God and obey me. God is my Lord and your Lord, so worship Him. This is the straight path."[135]

Jewish law, as it had stood since the time of Moses, had been onerous and not without cause. It was because of the wrongdoings of the Jews and, in particular, because they had blocked so many from the path of God, dealt in usury after being forbidden to do so, and devoured the wealth of others wrongfully, that God had forbidden them things they had previously been permitted.[136]

Not only had they blatantly contradicted God's injunctions, they had continually demonstrated their unbending recalcitrance to obeying God's command. When he had commanded them to slaughter the heifer, they had asked for all its specifications hoping to find an excuse not to comply, so God had imposed increasingly stringent conditions until he left them no choice but to purchase and slaughter the only heifer that fit the specifications for an exorbitant price.[137]

Jesus came, not to abrogate the law of Moses altogether, but to amend it and make it easier for them to follow.[138] In this vein, he once said, "Do not imagine that I have come to abolish the law or the prophets. I have come not to abolish but to complete them."[139] In particular, he abrogated the Sabbath and amended

---

134. Qur'ān 43:63–64

135. Qur'ān 3:50–51

136. Qur'ān 4:160–161

137. Qur'ān 2:67–71 and *Tafsīr nūr al-thaqalayn* vol. 1 p. 87

138. *Biḥār al-anwār* vol. 14 p. 234 tr. 4

139. Matthew 5:17. Matthew's narration goes on to quote Jesus saying that he will not change a thing of the law but fulfill and implement it. This part of the passage contradicts the Qur'ānic quotation of Jesus saying, "And I come to confirm the Torah which came before me and to make lawful for you some of the

the laws for consuming animal fat and birds.[140] On the other hand, the law he preached still contained the obligation to offer regular prayers, to enjoin good and forbid evil, and it designated things as permissible or prohibited. God commanded Jesus to pray facing the east following the example of Noah, an example which had, in the interim, been abrogated once by Abraham who prayed to the Kaʿbah and again by Moses who prayed to the west.[141] Other than this, the Evangel contained mainly admonishment and parables.[142] It contained no new amendments to the laws of retribution, capital punishment, or inheritance.[143]

God's Teachings to Jesus

God spoke to Jesus throughout his life, sometimes through direct inspiration, sometimes from behind a veil, and sometimes through the mediation of an angel.[144]

Once God told him, "O Jesus! I do not forget those who forget me, so how could I possibly forget those who remember me? And I am not stingy with those who disobey me, so how could I possibly be stingy with those who obey me?"[145]

God also told him, "Do not be deceived by him who rebels against me through disobedience. He eats what I provide for him but worships other than me. Then he calls on me in his hardship, and I answer him. Then he goes back to his ways. Does he dare disobey me and tempt my anger? I swear by my own name! I shall seize him such that he shall have no deliverance, and, in other than me,

---

things that you were forbidden" (3:50).

140. *Biḥār al-anwār* vol. 14 p. 246 tr. 25

141. *Jesus Through Shi'ite Narrations* p. 288

142. Qur'ān 5:46

143. *Biḥār al-anwār* vol. 14 p. 234 tr. 4

144. Qur'ān 42:51

145. *Jesus Through Shi'ite Narrations* p. 286

he shall find no refuge. After all, how can he possibly flee from my skies and my earth?"[146]

God also told him, "Let him who considers me slow in providence beware of my wrath lest I open a gate of worldly pleasure for him."[147] Some of God's most terrifying punishments are disguised as blessings. When this person becomes so insolent that he criticizes God's providence, despite the fact that it is precisely calibrated for each of his creatures' needs, God increases his provision, not as a blessing but as a means of drawing him deeper and deeper into sin.[148]

God also told him, "It is ironic that my believing servant is saddened when I withhold worldly pleasure from him even though that is potentially when he is most beloved and nearest to me. And he exults when I lay forth worldly pleasure for him even though that is potentially when he is most despicable to me and furthest from me."[149]

God also told him, "Be forbearing toward people like the earth beneath them, generous like free-flowing water, and merciful like the sun and the moon which shine upon the righteous man and the sinner alike."[150]

God also told him, "O Jesus! Make me a gift of tears on behalf of your eyes and of humility on behalf of your heart; and adorn your eyes with contemplative sadness when those who are frivolous laugh in gaiety; and stand beside the tombs of the dead and call to them in a loud voice; perhaps you will receive admonishment from them. And say to yourself, 'I shall be joining them soon.'"[151]

---

146. *Jesus Through Shi'ite Narrations* p. 286

147. *Jesus Through Shi'ite Narrations* p. 288

148. This is an example of the divine policy of *istidrāj* mentioned in Qur'ān 7:182

149. *Jesus Through Shi'ite Narrations* p. 288

150. *Jesus Through Shi'ite Narrations* p. 292

151. *Jesus Through Shi'ite Narrations* p. 292

God also told him, "O Jesus! I entrusted you with the destitute, and you have shown them mercy. You love them, and they love you. They are pleased with you as their leader and guide, and you are pleased with them as your companions and followers. These characteristics—being pleased with a divinely-appointed leader and for him to be pleased with you—are two characteristics such that whoever meets me on Judgment Day with them has thereby met me with the most pure and most beloved of deeds."[152]

God also told him, "O Jesus! I urge you to follow the path of your predecessors so that you join their ranks. Say, O brother of the warners, to your people, 'Do not enter any of my houses of worship but with pure hearts, blameless hands, and lowered gazes, for I shall not hear the prayer of one who supplicates me if even one of my servants has a claim against him, and I shall not answer his prayer if I have a right upon him that he has left unfulfilled.'"[153]

God also told him, "O Jesus! Let your tongue be the same in private and in public and likewise your heart...It is not proper to have two tongues in a single mouth, nor two swords in a single scabbard, nor two hearts in a single breast, and likewise two minds."[154]

God also told him, "When I give you a blessing, receive it with humility, and I shall perfect it for you."[155]

Once Jesus passed by a grave and witnessed angels of chastisement punishing the person in it. When he passed by the same grave again, he witnessed angels of mercy and streams of light around the grave. He was surprised to see this, and he asked God about it. God told him, "O Jesus! This person was a sinner. He left his wife pregnant. She bore and raised his child until he grew up. She turned him over to the charge of the scribes to be educated. His teacher instructed him to say, 'In the Name of God, the All-

---

152. *Jesus Through Shi'ite Narrations* p. 292

153. *Jesus Through Shi'ite Narrations* p. 294

154. *Jesus Through Shi'ite Narrations* p. 296

155. *Jesus Through Shi'ite Narrations* p. 296

Beneficent, the Ever-Merciful.' Because of this, I felt embarrassed[156] that I was chastising this man with fire in the bowels of the earth while his child was remembering my name on the surface of the earth."[157]

Prophecy of Aḥmad

Jesus fulfilled God's commandment and prophesied the coming of the unlettered prophet. He said, "O Israelites! I am God's messenger to you who confirms the Torah which came before me and brings the good news of a messenger who will come after me whose name is Aḥmad."[158] In reality, he was only restating what God had revealed to him in the Evangel. There he told him of a prophet to come who would "enjoin them to do good and forbid them to do evil; who would make all good things lawful for them and make all filthy things unlawful; who would relieve them of their burdens and the chains that bound them." And he promised them that those who "believed in him, honored him, aided him, and believed in the light that was revealed with him" would be successful in the hereafter.[159] God also portrayed that prophet and his truest companions saying they would be like a plant that first sprouts and then grows thick and strong until it can finally stand on its own such that it pleases the farmer who planted it.[160] And he described that prophet's successor, the "bald man of the Quraysh,"[161] along with his physical and personality traits, and he prophesied that he would one day pass through Barāthā, the childhood home of Jesus, and that he would excavate the stream from which they used to draw water

---

156. Of course, God does not "feel embarrassed" the way we do. He does nothing to be embarrassed and he is perfect and unchanging. Nonetheless, he often uses anthropomorphic imagery to help us understand better.

157. *Jesus Through Shi'ite Narrations* p. 300

158. Qur'ān 61:6. Aḥmad is another name for Prophet Muḥammad.

159. Qur'ān 7:157

160. Qur'ān 48:29

161. Imam ʿAlī was known as *Aṣlaʿ Quraysh* because of his distinctive receding hairline.

and the flat rock upon which Mary used to keep Jesus and say her prayers.[162]

From the Evangel

One passage in the Evangel reads as follows:

> O Jesus! Strive for my sake and never flag. Listen and obey. O son of the immaculately pure woman, the virgin, Mary. I created you without a father as a sign to all people. So worship me alone. Trust in me alone. Hold fast to the book, and explain it to the people in their language. Convey to all that I am the eternal God who will never perish. Confirm for them the coming of my unlettered prophet who will ride a camel and wear a woolen mantle, a turban, and sandals...When he will speak to a person, he will turn to him fully. When he will walk, he will walk with the weighty dignity of a rock...He shall marry many women but have few progeny. His progeny shall issue from a blessed woman, (Fāṭimah), who shall be with your mother in paradise. She will have two children who will be martyred. His book will be the Qur'ān and his religion will be Islam...For those who meet him, listen obediently to him, and fight alongside him, there is Ṭūbā."

When Jesus read this he asked, "My Lord, what is Ṭūbā?"

God replied, "It is a tree in paradise...beside which flows a stream. Anyone who drinks from it shall never thirst again."

Jesus begged, "O Lord, give me a sip of it."

He replied, "No, Jesus! That stream is prohibited for all the prophets until that prophet drinks. And that garden is prohibited for all nations until that prophet's nation enters it. I shall raise you up before long and then send you back to earth at the end of time so that you can see the wonders of that nation and aid them

---

162. *Biḥār al-anwār* vol. 14 p. 210 tr. 7

against the damned Dajjāl (Antichrist). I shall send you down at the time of prayer so that you can pray with them. They are a nation to whom I shall show mercy."[163]

The Disciples

As with all his predecessors, Jesus faced staunch opposition from many of the Israelites to whom he was sent.[164] The faithless among them said, "This is nothing but plain magic."[165]

He needed to distinguish between his supporters and enemies, so he asked them, "Who will be my helpers in this path to God?" A group of the Israelites believed in him, and a group did not believe.[166]

There were twelve men in particular who supported him with deep conviction.[167] They told him, "We shall be your helpers in this path to God. We believe in God and ask you to testify that we have submitted."[168] They knew that Jesus, as a prophet, was a witness over his people and that he would be called by God to testify for and against people depending on whether or not they accepted his call. After asking him to testify in their favor, they turned to address God and said, "O Lord! We believe in all that you have sent down, and we follow your messenger, so record us among those who testify that he fulfilled his duty." It was as though they sought to repay the favor to Jesus, for even the prophets are not exempt from interrogation on the Day of Judgment.[169] They volunteered themselves as witnesses to testify that Jesus had done everything humanly possible to convey God's message and guide his people. These twelve came to be known as the *ḥawāriyyūn*, or "disciples," a tribute to their own purity and their mission to purify others of

---

163. *Biḥār al-anwār* vol. 14 p. 285 tr. 6 and p. 323 tr. 33

164. *Biḥār al-anwār* vol. 14 p. 249 tr. 39

165. Qur'ān 5:110

166. Qur'ān 61:14

167. *Biḥār al-anwār* vol. 14 p. 250 tr. 40

168. Qur'ān 3:52

169. Qur'ān 7:6

the filth of sin by admonishing and reminding them.[170]

Lessons for the Disciples

Jesus expended great effort to train and nurture these disciples so that they could continue his mission after him. He would take them with him wherever he went and draw lessons from the world around. Once, they walked along the coast of a nearby sea. Each person had his own rations of food with him. Jesus took a small loaf of bread which was part of his ration for the journey and flung it into the water. When his disciples questioned him about this, he replied, "I did this so the creatures of the sea could eat it. The reward for such an act before God is great."[171] He hoped to teach them the lessons of self-sacrifice and of kindness to all of God's creatures.

On another occasion, he gathered his disciples together and told them, "O disciples! I have a favor to ask of you. Please do it for me."[172]

They replied in unison, "Consider it done, O Spirit of God!"[173] At

---

170. The word *ḥawāriyy* conveys the general meaning of a disciple or close companion. However, it is used in the Qurʾān exclusively for the disciples of Jesus. Imām al-Riḍā was asked, "Why were the disciples of Jesus called *ḥawāriyyūn?*" Imam al-Riḍa replied, "According to people, they were called *ḥawāriyyūn* because they were washermen—they used to purify clothes of dirt by washing them. It is a word derived from *al-khubz al-ḥuwwārā* (white bread baked with flour that has been sieved multiple times). According to us, they were called *ḥawāriyyūn* because they themselves were pure and they purified others of the filth of sin by admonishing and reminding them" (*ʿUyūn akhbār al-Riḍā* 2.32.10 and see ITI's commentary on *al-Kāfī* 2.5.6).

171. *Biḥār al-anwār* vol. 14 p. 257 tr. 55

172. Clearly, for him to wash their feet is not a favor to him but to them. However, he calls what he wants to do for them a favor to himself so that they will concede without hesitation. If he had told them, "I want to serve you," they presumably would not have conceded so easily.

173. Jesus is called the "Spirit of God" because of his miraculous birth without a father. God created his spirit, not through a natural process as he creates all other people's spirits, but directly by his will and infinite power. Thus, he is the "spirit created by the will of God," or simply, the "Spirit of God." The Qurʾān

this, he stood and washed their feet.[174] They told him, "It was more fitting that we do this, O Spirit of God!"

At this he said, "The person most fit to serve is a scholar.[175] I have only humbled myself like this so that you will humble yourselves after me before people just as I have humbled myself before you."[176]

---

describes him as such in the following verse: "The Messiah, Jesus, son of Mary, is but a messenger of God, and God's word, which he cast into Mary, and a spirit from him" (4:171).

174. In some recensions, the word *qabbala*, meaning, "he kissed their feet," is mentioned instead of *ghasala*. According to those recensions, we must construe his mention of "service" in the following line broadly as a reference to the "honor" he showed them by kissing their feet.

175. It is important to note the following about Jesus' statement, "The person most fit to serve is a scholar."

- Perhaps the reason a scholar is the one most fit to serve is that one of his main purposes is to impart his knowledge, and service provides a way for him to soften people's hearts so they more readily accept what he has to impart.
- By "scholar," he means a scholar of religion since any other kind of scholar is not obligated to impart wisdom and thus would not be enjoined to serve in this way.
- His statement is general, but his intent is to apply it to his own situation with regard to his disciples—he is a "scholar" and they are students to whom he wants to impart wisdom.
- By saying the scholar is "most fit to serve," he implies that the rest of people are "fit to serve." Thus, this statement in no way lifts the burden of service from non-scholars.

176. There is hyperbole in this statement. He says he has shown them humility *only* so that they show others humility. Certainly, he does not mean that this is his *only reason*. Otherwise his humility would be lacking in sincerity, and he would be enjoining them to something without having acted on it himself. Rather, it is so important to him that they follow his lead that he treats it as though it were his only reason for being humble.

Then Jesus said, "Wisdom is imparted through humility, not through pride,[177] just as[178] plants grow in soft soil, not in rock."[179]

---

177. The Arabic phrase "*tuʿmaru al-hikmah*" is a figurative expression meaning "wisdom is constructed" or "erected." "Wisdom" is likened to an abandoned house or a house that needs to be built. Because this figurative expression is not helpful in English, we have left it and translated the intent.

This sentence could be construed in two ways. It could be construed, as we have translated it, to mean that through humility a person can soften other people's hearts and prepare them to learn wisdom. Alternatively, it could be translated as "Wisdom is imparted *because* of humility, not *because* of pride." This translation implies that there is an existential relationship between humility and wisdom such that a person's humility is rewarded with an effusion of wisdom within that same person. This is a relationship that we would not necessarily have understood were it not for this tradition. The first interpretation is stronger because it ties the end of the tradition together with the beginning. In effect, Jesus' statement, "Wisdom is imparted through humility," is the reason why he has shown humility to his disciples and why he wants them to show humility to others—so that they become ready to accept the wisdom he wants to impart to them.

178. The word *kadhālik* normally translates as "likewise," and we would expect the sentence order to be reversed as follows: "Plants grow in soft soil, not in rock. Likewise, wisdom is imparted through humility, not through pride." Reversed sentence structure like this is not uncommon in Arabic. We find the following examples in the Qurʾān: "Is he who creates like him who does not create?" (16:17) when the intended meaning is "Is he who does not create like him who creates?" Similarly, "Shall we treat the God-fearing like the sinful?" (38:28) when the intended meaning is "Shall we treat the sinful like the God-fearing?" Rather than switch the word order in the translation, we have translated *kadhālik* to mean "just as" instead of "likewise" so that the English corresponds with the intended meaning of the Arabic.

Jesus' statement, "plants grow in soft soil, not in rock," is a metaphor for a student's heart. A teacher's humility through service is like a plow that tills the soil to prepare it for seed.

179. *al-Kāfī* 2.5.6. Translation and commentary taken from ITI's work on *al-Kāfī*.

Once, his disciples asked him, "O Spirit of God! Whose company should we keep?"

He replied, "He whose outward aspect reminds you of God, whose speech increases your knowledge, and whose actions make you desirous of the hereafter."[180]

They asked him, "What is the severest of all things?"

He replied, "The severest of all things is God's anger."

They asked, "How can we guard ourselves against God's anger?"

He replied, "By not getting angry."

They asked, "And what is the root cause of anger?"

He replied, "That you think yourself better than others, you feel the need to dominate them, and you look upon them with derision."[181]

He told them, "Do not do to anyone what you would not like others to do to you. If anyone strikes you on your right cheek, then offer him your left also."[182]

He taught them the following:

> O Children of Adam! Flee from this temporal world toward God, and wrench your hearts free from it, for neither are you fit for it, nor is it fit for you. You shall not remain for it, and it shall not remain for you. It will deceive you and cause you much pain. He is truly deceived who is fooled by it. He is a loser who trusts in it. He is doomed for destruction who loves it and seeks it. So turn to your creator. Fear your Lord. And instill in yourselves the terror of a day when no father can avail his son, nor can any son avail his father.
>
> Where are your fathers, mothers, brothers, sisters, and children? They were called by death,

180. *al-Kāfī* 2.8.3. Translation taken from ITI's work on *al-Kāfī*.

181. *Biḥār al-anwār* vol. 14 p. 287 tr. 9

182. *Biḥār al-anwār* vol. 14 p. 287 tr. 10

so they answered. And now they have been consigned to the earth to become neighbors of the dead...They are in dire need of the good deeds they sent forth for themselves, and they have no need of the things they left behind. How many of you will heed the admonishment?

You all are like animals in this world—your greatest concern is your appetite for food and sex. Have you no shame before him who created you for he has threatened all who disobey him with hellfire? And you will not be able to withstand the fire. And he has promised those who obey him that they will be in his proximity in the loftiest paradise. So race toward it, and make yourself deserving of it.

Be fair to people by giving them their due even if it means taking from yourself. Show compassion to the weak and needy among you. Turn toward God sincerely. Be righteous servants. Be not tyrannical kings, nor rebellious despots who rule their subjects with the constant threat of death. The one who dominates those who dominate others is the Lord of the sky and earth, the Lord of the first and the last, the Master on the Day of Judgment, whose retribution is severe, whose punishment is agonizing, from whom no oppressor is safe, whom nothing escapes, from whom nothing is hidden, whose knowledge encompasses all things, and who places everything in its proper place in heaven or in hell.

O weak son of Adam! Where do you flee from him who seeks you out in the black of night and the glare of day in any state in which you find yourself?

> I have herein conveyed my admonishment; he who heeds it shall succeed."[183]

In one gathering, he taught, "O Israelites! Do not share wisdom with the foolish, lest you wrong it; and do not withhold it from those who seek it, lest you wrong them."[184]

Feast From Heaven

Once, he exhorted the disciples to fast for thirty days and promised them that they could ask anything of God, and he would grant it. When they had completed the fast, they came to Jesus and said, "When we work for people and we fulfill our task for them, they feed us. We have now fasted and felt the pangs of hunger for God's sake.[185] So we ask you, O Jesus, son of Mary! Can your Lord send down to us a tray laden with food from heaven?"[186]

He warned them, "Fear God, if you are truly believers."[187] Of course he knew they were believers. These were the elite among his followers, his devotees. They were tried and tested. However, they had misspoken by asking if God "could" send down a tray. For the disciples of a prophet, such a question belied doubt in the very omnipotence of God, and he felt he must teach them a lesson.

They clarified their intent and said, "We want to eat from it, and we want our hearts to find peace, and we want to know that you have told us the truth, and we want to be among those who testify."[188]

This was a positive amendment to their first request, but it was clumsy and unworthy of God, so Jesus restated their prayer in perfect form as a perfect servant begging a perfect master. He donned a coarse woolen cassock and turned his attention to God,

---

183. *Biḥār al-anwār* vol. 14 p. 288 tr. 12

184. *al-Kāfī* 2.10.4. Translation taken from ITI's work on *al-Kāfī*.

185. *Majma' al-bayān* vol. 3 p. 372 under verse 5:115

186. Qur'ān 5:112

187. Qur'ān 5:112

188. Qur'ān 5:113

weeping,[189] and said, "O God! O Lord! Send down to us a tray laden with food from heaven which will be the starting point of a festival for us and for the coming generations of our people and a sign from you; and through it provide for us, for you are the best of providers."

God replied, "I shall send it down to you. But should any of you refuse to believe after this, I shall punish him in a way that I shall not punish anyone else in all of creation."[190]

With that, a red-colored table spread descended from the sky, suspended between two clouds until it came to rest on the ground before them. Jesus wept and prayed, "O God! Make me among the grateful. Let this food be a source of mercy for us and not a means of exemplary punishment."

All around them the Israelites stood dumbfounded, seeing something the likes of which they had never before seen and smelling something the likes of which they had never before smelled. Jesus performed the ablutions and prayed at length. Then he lifted the wispy veil that covered the food as he recited, "In God's name, the Best of Providers." It was a single roasted fish. It had been scaled and its oils seeped out of it in streams. Near its head there was salt for seasoning, and near its tail there was vinegar, and it was garnished all around with different varieties of herbs and greens. Along with the fish, there were five loaves of bread. One was topped with olive oil, another with honey, another with butter, another with cheese, and the last with bits of dried, salted meat.

Jesus told his disciples not to eat any of it until he had given the word. One of them thought he saw another steal a bite, and he told Jesus. Jesus confronted the accused man and asked him if he was guilty of eating before being given permission. He said he was not. When his accuser insisted that he had seen him with his own eyes, Jesus told him, "Believe your brother over your eyes."[191]

---

189. *Majmaʿ al-bayān* vol. 3 p. 373 under verse 5:115

190. Qurʾān 5:114–115

191. *Biḥār al-anwār* vol. 14 p. 235 tr. 7

Simon Peter asked, "O Spirit of God! Is this food of this world or of the next?"

Jesus replied, "What you see is neither of this world nor the next; rather it is something God has conjured through his infinite power. Eat, now, of what you have requested, and God will give you strength and bounty out of his grace."

Some of the disciples asked, "Would you show us another miracle within this miracle?"

Jesus addressed the fish and said, "Fish, come to life, by God's leave." The fish gave a jerk and its scales and fins were returned to it. The disciples were appalled to see their food flipping like this. Jesus asked them, "Why then did you ask for something that appalls you when it is granted? I honestly fear for your salvation." He addressed the fish again and said, "Fish, return to your former state, by God's leave." And it did.

The disciples said, "O Spirit of God! You should be the first to eat of this. We will only eat after you."

Jesus replied, "God forbid that I eat from it. Those who asked for it should eat from it." At hearing this, some of the disciples hesitated. So Jesus called on all who were poor, crippled, sick, or otherwise afflicted. He told them, "Eat, all of you together. May it bring you well-being and may it bring those who refuse it hardship. When all was done, 1,300 men and women had eaten from the fish and bread, each to his fill.[192] When Jesus looked at the fish, it was just as it had appeared when it had descended from the sky. The table spread rose until it disappeared as mysteriously as it had appeared. On that day, every cripple who ate of the fish was cured, every sick person was restored, and every poor person was relieved of his poverty and they remained so until they died.

Those among the disciples who had hesitated felt deeply remorseful, and they repented for it.

For forty days, on alternate days, the spread would descend at noon. The rich and poor, old and young would crowd around it to eat from it. Jesus saw the chaos and so he organized them and

192. Another tradition mentions 4,700 (*Biḥār al-anwār* vol. 14 p. 249 tr. 37). It could be that this greater number takes into account the total number of beneficiaries over the forty-day period.

let them eat by turns. By evening, as the shadows became long, it would rise up and disappear.

After some time, God commanded Jesus to restrict the spread to the poor. The rich did not take this well. They began to doubt and to spread doubt among others. God reminded them, through Jesus, of the ultimatum he had issued when he first sent down the spread, "but should any of you disbelieve after this, I shall punish him in a way that I shall not punish anyone else in all of creation."[193] Despite having seen, even eaten from, God's miraculous provisions, 330 people persisted in their doubts. Jesus prayed for the damnation of these people.[194] For the first and last time in the history of humankind, God punished a people by transforming them into swine. They wallowed in the streets for three days eating waste, and then they died.[195]

Death Deferred

Once he and his disciples were passing through a community where the people were singing in celebration. When he asked what was happening, Jesus was told that they were celebrating a wedding. Jesus said forebodingly, "Today they sing, but tomorrow they will cry."

His disciples asked him to explain. He said, "Their matriarch is going to die this very night."

The next day, they asked about the matriarch and found that she was still very much alive. They confronted Jesus over this, so he simply said, "God does as he wishes. Let us go to her." They went to her house and knocked on the door. When her husband came to the door, Jesus asked permission to speak with his wife. The husband entered the house and informed her that God's messenger wished to see her, so she covered herself and bid them enter. He asked her, "What did you do last night?"

She replied, "I did not do anything out of the ordinary. Every Thursday evening a particular beggar has been coming to our

193. Qur'ān 5:115

194. *Biḥār al-anwār* vol. 14 p. 64 tr. 15

195. *Majma' al-bayān* vol. 3 p. 373–4 under verse 5:115

house. We give him enough to hold him over until the following week. Last night, when he came, I was busy and so was my family. He came and cried out, but none of us could answer him. When I was finally free, he had already left, so I covered myself and went searching for him and gave him provisions as we always have."

When Jesus heard her story, he urgently asked her to rise from where she sat. When she rose, he pointed out a snake that had been hiding near her but had not struck her. He told her, "Because of your act of charity, God averted this death from you."[196]

Emissaries to Antioch

Jesus sent his disciples as emissaries to various centers of civilization so that they could spread his teachings among the Israelites and others who would listen. Once he sent two emissaries to the city of Antioch.[197] With great zeal, they proceeded to proclaim their mission and call people to believe in the one God and his messenger, Jesus. The people of Antioch were pagans, so they peremptorily captured and imprisoned the emissaries. When news of their capture reached Jesus, he sent his closest disciple, Simon Peter, to free them and assist them in fulfilling their mission.

Simon acted with exemplary forbearance. He began to associate discreetly with the close associates of the king without making his beliefs or his mission known. They took a liking to him and

---

196. *Biḥār al-anwār* vol. 14 p. 244 tr. 22. This is an example of *badā'*, the contingency of God's decrees.

197. This story is narrated with various details in *Biḥār al-anwār* vol. 14 p. 240 tr. 20 and in *Majma' al-bayān* vol. 8 p. 202 under verse 36:20. It is presented in both places as though it corresponds to the story of the three messengers mention in Qur'ān 36:13–30. However, there are several key discrepancies between the two stories. Chief among these is that the Qur'ānic story ends with the destruction of the city because its people refuse to believe in the messengers and kill the local man who speaks out in their support. In the traditions, on the other hand, the people of the city and even their king come to believe (see *al-Mīzān* and *Tafsīr-e nimūneh* under Qur'ān 36:13–30). I have included the basic story from the traditions in this narrative with the assumption that it is true but was mistakenly associated with the story from the Qur'ān because of some similarities between them. I have not included the story from the Qur'ān only because there is nothing in that story to indicated that it has to do with Jesus.

mentioned him to their king. The king called on him in court and also was impressed by his noble manner and wisdom. When he had established a relationship with the king, Simon addressed him saying, "My king! I am informed that you have imprisoned two men who called your people to a strange religion. I am wondering if you listened to what they had to say."

The king replied, "My anger prevented me from that."

Simon said, "If it please my king, allow me to debate with them. If they speak the truth, let us follow them, and if we speak the truth, they will join us in our religion."

When the two emissaries were brought forth, they were both shocked and relieved to see Simon, but they concealed their emotions well. Simon asked them, "Who sent you to this place?"

They replied, "We were sent by Jesus, the messenger of the one God, the creator, other than whom there is no god."

Simon asked them, "What proof do you have to confirm your claim? Can this god of yours restore the sight of a blind man?"

They replied, "If we ask him to do so, he can if he wills it."

Simon turned to the king and said, "My king, bring forth two blind men who have never seen in their life."

His guards brought two men whose eyes were sealed shut with the growth of skin such that their eyes were indistinguishable from their foreheads. The two emissaries prayed and asked God to restore the sight of the first. In an instant, he opened his eyes, and saw the light of day for the first time in his life.

Simon also prayed and restored the sight of the second. He turned to the king triumphantly and said, "My king, we have matched their miracle with our own. Bring forth two men who are paralyzed and unable to walk." His guards did so.

Again, the two emissaries prayed and Simon prayed, and both were able to restore the men's ability to walk. Simon said, "My king! I have matched them in their miracles. However, there is one more test. If they are able to pass it, I shall join them in their religion. I have heard that my king had a son who died. If their god is able to revive your son, I shall admit defeat and believe in their god."

The two emissaries prayed and fell prostrate begging God to revive the boy. When they lifted their heads, they told the king,

"Proceed to your son's grave, and you shall find him alive, if God wills."

All who were present in the court proceeded excitedly to the grave of the king's son. When they reached it, they found the boy standing next to his grave with dirt still falling from his head. The king was overwhelmed with emotion. He hugged his son and asked him what he had experienced. The boy said, "I was dead. I saw two men prostrating before God begging him to raise me, so he did."

The king asked him, "If you saw these two men, would you recognize them?" He said he would. So the king ordered all the men present to stand in a line and had his son look at each one. When he came to the two emissaries, he identified them.

Simon, declared, "I, for one, hereby declare my belief in their one God and in the truth of what they claim." The king also believed and the people of Antioch with him.[198]

Jesus' Character

Jesus' behavior was impeccable. He never did anything the least bit reprehensible, he never turned away an orphan, he never laughed boisterously, he never even shooed a fly from his face, and he never held his nose in aversion to a rotten smell for fear of offending the one who was responsible for it.[199] He was an optimist and encouraged his companions to see the best in things. Once they passed by the rotting corpse of a dog, and his disciples exclaimed in disgust, "How rotten is its smell!"

Jesus calmly noted, "How brilliantly white are its teeth!"[200]

Jesus the Ascetic

Jesus chose an ascetic life for himself. He used to have no pillow except a bare rock, he wore coarse clothes, he ate plain bread flavored only by the intensity of his hunger. At night, his lantern was the light of the moon. In the winter, his shelter from the cold

198. *Biḥār al-anwār* vol. 14 p. 240 tr. 20 and *Majma' al-bayān* vol. 8 p. 202 under verse 36:20

199. *Majma' al-bayān* vol. 3 p. 373 under verse 5:115

200. *Biḥār al-anwār* vol. 14 p. 327 tr. 46

was the open lands of the east and west. His fruits and vegetables were what the earth produced for beasts. He did not have a wife to infatuate him, nor a child to cause him regret, nor wealth to distract him, nor greed to abase him. His mount was his legs. And his servant was his own two hands.[201]

When he was asked, "Why do you not marry?" he replied, "What shall I do with marriage?"

The man replied, "It may provide you with children."

Jesus said, "What shall I do with children? As long as they live, they are a temptation, and when they die, they cause grief."[202]

Jesus did wear a ring. The inscription in its stone was taken from two lines of the Evangel. It read, "Good for him because of whom God is remembered. Woe to him because of whom God is forgotten."[203]

Jesus was of medium build with intensely curly hair.[204]

He was not quite as ascetic as his mother's cousin, John the Baptist. John cried constantly but never laughed. Jesus both cried and laughed, and through this, gained greater favor with God.[205]

Jesus was successful in instilling in his disciples this same spirit of indifference to worldly pleasures. They too lived poorly in their

---

201. *Nahj al-balāghah* sermon 160. As with John the Baptist and Mary, Jesus' stark lifestyle was not meant as a model for all people. He did exemplify the ideal of indifference to the temporal world (*al-zuhd*). However, most people cannot, and should not, deny themselves the legal pleasures of the world to such an extreme. Perhaps he chose his lifestyle because of the dire circumstances of the people he was serving. We should look to him as a model of the virtue of indifference to the temporal world, not of the extent to which to impose this ideal on ourselves.

202. *Biḥār al-anwār* vol. 14 p. 238 tr. 15. Again, I must reiterate that these statements, if they are correctly attributed to Jesus, do not reflect the Islamic ideal in which marriage and having children are highly encouraged.

203. *Biḥār al-anwār* vol. 14 p. 247 tr. 31

204. *Biḥār al-anwār* vol. 14 p. 248 tr. 35

205. *Biḥār al-anwār* vol. 14 p. 249 tr. 38

attempt to escape temptations. It was precisely because of this that God granted some of them abilities similar to Jesus'. They could walk on water and cure the sick as Jesus could.[206]

When God saw that Jesus' disciples had been nurtured to a lofty state, he addressed them directly through divine inspiration and said, "Believe in me and my messenger." For a non-believer, this would have been a command to enter the faith. For the disciples, it was a call to rise to the apex of faith.

They responded, "We believe, and we beg you to bear witness that we have submitted."[207]

His disciples were not the only ones to affirm their faith so strongly. There was one family in particular. One member of this family would not make any extraordinary effort to worship other than what was obligatory upon him. Yet, whenever he prayed to God, his prayer was answered. Another man from the same family would spend forty days at a time worshiping and fasting to prepare himself for supplicating God, yet in the final measure, his prayers remained unanswered. He came to Jesus and asked him what was wrong with him. Jesus offered a prayer and then asked God to tell him what was wrong with the man. God inspired him saying, "O Jesus! This servant of mine has tried to approach me without coming through the proper channels. He supplicated me while he harbored an iota of doubt in you. If he were to supplicate me forever, I would never answer him." When Jesus told the man what God had said, the man admitted to having some doubts. He asked Jesus to intercede on his behalf and supplicate God to remove this doubt from his heart, and he did. Thereafter this man became among the closest of Jesus' companions.[208]

In Pursuit of a Treasure

Once, Jesus was traveling with his disciples when they passed by a town. Jesus asked his companions to set up camp on the outskirts

206. *Biḥār al-anwār* vol. 14 p. 278 tr. 9

207. Qur'ān 5:111

208. *Biḥār al-anwār* vol. 14 p. 278 tr. 10

so that he could enter the city and retrieve a treasure he was seeking. When he entered, he wandered through its streets and alleys until he came upon a decrepit house. He knocked and was greeted reticently by an old woman. He asked if she lived with anyone. She told him that her orphaned son,[209] now a young man, lived with her and that he spent his days gathering kindling in the desert so that he could sell it at market and support himself and his mother. He asked her if he could be their guest and she welcomed him. She prepared a place for him to sleep and left him to settle in.

When her son returned home she told him, "God has blessed us with a righteous guest. The light of indifference to the temporal world and goodness virtually emanates from his face. Rise to the occasion and serve him and keep him company." The young man served Jesus and showed him what hospitality his poverty would afford him. They began talking, and Jesus asked him about his life and his work and about other things. He found him to have a strong intellect and saw in him great potential for spiritual development. He also perceived that his heart was occupied with some deep sadness. He asked him about it and cajoled him to reveal its cause so that he could help to find a cure.

The young man told him, "I was gathering kindling one day when I passed by the palace of the king. From a distance, I caught a glimpse of the king's daughter but quickly looked away to preserve my chastity. However, from that moment, I have not been able to stop thinking about her, and my desire for her increases each day. I do not see any escape except death."

Jesus said with a smile, "If you would like, I shall devise a plan so that you can marry her."

The young man consulted with his mother before taking Jesus up on his offer. She advised him, "I do not think this man would promise you something if he could not fulfill it. Listen to him and do whatever he says."

The next morning, Jesus told the boy to go to the king's palace and announce to his guards that he has come to ask for his

---

209. An orphan is a child who has lost his father. Thus, we must not think it a contradiction that he is an orphan while his mother still lives.

daughter's hand in marriage and to then return and tell him what passed between him and the king.

The young man did as Jesus told him. The guards took one look at his simple, even shabby, appearance and scoffed at him. They conveyed the message to their king who was both enraged and curious to see what impudence had compelled such a suitor to come for his daughter, so he admitted him into his presence. Once again, the young man repeated his intent, and so the king mockingly told him, "I will not give you her hand in marriage unless you bring me a chest full of rubies, corals, and diamonds," and he proceeded to enumerate a treasure he knew to be greater than any one king possessed. The young man politely replied that he would bring the king an answer the next day.

When he told Jesus what had passed between them, Jesus walked with the boy into a nearby hut made of mud brick which was in a state of disrepair. He prayed to God, and God made the hut into rubies, corals, diamonds, and whatever else the king had demanded, and better. He told the man, "Take what you need and go back to the king."

Needless to say, the king and his courtiers were astounded, but they greedily demanded more before they would consent. The man returned, gathered more jewels and brought them to the king. This time, the king realized that there was something special about this young man. He spoke to him in private and the boy told him all about Jesus and his own love for the king's daughter. The king consented and told the young man to bring Jesus to the court so that he could conduct the marriage.

They were married that very night. The next day, the king spoke with his new son-in-law and perceived the intellect and intelligence that had impressed Jesus. As this daughter of his was his only child, he decided to make the young man his crown prince and heir to his kingdom.

The next day, the king died suddenly, and the crown prince became the king.

The following day, Jesus came to his court to bid farewell. The young man, who was now a king, said to him, "O wise man! You have many rights over me, and I cannot thank you sufficiently for even one of them if I were to live eternally. However, something occurred to me yesterday, and if you do not explain it to me, I shall never be able to enjoy all that you have helped me attain."

Jesus asked him, "What is it?"

He asked, "When you were able to raise me from that lowly state to this lofty state in two days, why have you not done the same for yourself?"

At great length, Jesus replied, "If a person knows God, his magnanimity, and his reward and perceives the fleeting nature of this world and its baseness, he will not desire fleeting power and fleeting things. In God's proximity, and in our knowledge and love of God, we take spiritual pleasure in the face of which those fleeting pleasures count for nothing."

The king thought for a while and then said to Jesus, "When this is the case, why have you chosen for yourself what is better and placed me in this great affliction?"

Jesus calmly replied, "I did this to test your intellect and intelligence and so that you could procure a greater reward for having chosen to abandon all this which is now at your fingertips and so that you could be an example for others."

This king who ruled for less than a day abdicated his throne, donned a cassock, and returned with Jesus. When they reached the camp where the disciples had been waiting all these days, Jesus told them, "This is the treasure I had been seeking in this city. I have now found it. To God belongs praise."[210]

John the Baptist's Martyrdom

Jesus sent twelve of his disciples with John to preach to the people and order them to cease the marriages of uncles and nieces. The king in the land where they were preaching was in love with his niece, and, according to custom, he wished to marry her. When the king's sister, the girl's mother, heard rumors that John was threatening to destroy her daughter's future as a queen, she decided to act fast before the king learned of the new prohibition. She dressed her daughter in her most provocative clothes and told

210. *Biḥār al-anwār* vol. 14 p. 280

her to seduce her uncle and coerce him to promise her anything she wished. The king was so taken with his niece that he promised her whatever her heart desired. As her mother had coached her, the girl demanded the head of John the Baptist on a platter. He protested, but she insisted, and being a bastard himself, he conceded.[211] When John arrived in the city, the king summoned him to his court. He slaughtered him with his own hands and placed his severed head on a golden platter for his new bride.[212]

John's companions retrieved his body and head and buried him.[213] The sky and earth mourned his death for forty days.[214] Jesus missed his cousin, John, dearly. He often visited his grave. Once, he asked God to revive him. When John rose from his grave, they exchanged greetings and hugs. Jesus was so elated to see him once again. John asked him why he had had him revived. When Jesus told him that he simply longed to visit with him and to be comforted by his presence, John became a little upset. He said, "Jesus, I have not yet forgotten the pangs of death, and now you bring me back to life so that I must taste death again!" With this terrifying warning of the reality of death, John said farewell and reentered his grave.[215]

Satan Tries to Tempt Jesus

For his devotion to God, Jesus made many enemies. But none was as persistent and deceptive as Satan. When Jesus was thirty, Satan came to him outside of Jerusalem and asked him, "Jesus, are you the one who is so great that you came to exist without a father?"

Jesus retorted, "Rather, greatness is his who created me in such a way and created Adam and Eve before me."

---

211. *Biḥār al-anwār* vol. 14 p. 175 tr. 13

212. *Biḥār al-anwār* vol. 14 p. 182 tr. 24. There are several contradictory versions of this story narrated in various traditions. I have simply chosen one that seemed more coherent than the others and agreed in large part with the story narrated in Matthew 14.

213. Matthew 14:12

214. *Biḥār al-anwār* vol. 14 p. 175 tr. 13

215. *Biḥār al-anwār* vol. 6 p. 170 tr. 47

Satan asked, "Are you the one who is so great that you spoke as an infant in his cradle?"

Jesus retorted, "Rather, greatness is his who made me speak and who could have, if he had so wished, made me mute."

Satan asked, "Are you the one who is so great that you create out of clay the form of a bird and then breathe into it and it becomes a bird?"

Jesus retorted, "Rather, greatness is his who created me and created all that he has subjugated for me."

Satan asked, "Are you the one who is so great that you cure the sick?"

Jesus retorted, "Rather, greatness is his by whose leave I cure them and who can, whenever he so wishes, make me ill."

Satan asked, "Are you the one who is so great that you revive the dead?"

Jesus retorted, "Rather, greatness is his by whose leave I revive them and who will unfailingly take their life again and take mine."

Satan asked, "Are you the one who is so great that you walk across the sea without wetting your feet or sinking into the water?"

Jesus retorted, "Rather, greatness is his who subjugated the sea to me and who could, if he so wished, drown me."

Satan asked, "Are you the one who is so great that a day will come when the skies and the earth and all who are therein will be below you and you shall be above all of them managing their affairs?"

Jesus was appalled by these remarks and finally retorted, "Exalted is God above me and all his creatures commensurate with the volume of his skies and earth, with the ink needed to write all his words, with the weight of his throne, and with what is sufficient to please him!"[216]

In another instance, Satan appeared to Jesus on a mountain. He said, "O Spirit of God! You have revived the dead and healed the congenitally blind and leprous. Surpass all this by throwing yourself off this mountain and then reviving yourself." He appealed

---

216. *Biḥār al-anwār* vol. 14 p. 270 tr. 1

to Jesus' sense of pride to push him to surpass his own feats and in the process Satan hoped to rid himself of his greatest foe.

Jesus simply replied, "I had been given leave to do all those things, but I have not been given leave to revive myself."[217]

In another challenge, Satan asked Jesus, "Can your Lord insert the whole world into an egg while the egg remains as it is?"

Jesus answered, "Impotence is not an attribute of God. However, what you speak of cannot be."[218] In other words, God can do anything that is possible, but what cannot possibly exist will not exist, because it is impossible, not because God is in any way impotent.

When his tricks failed, Satan sent an army of devils to attack Jesus in Jerusalem. God ordered Gabriel to defend his prophet. He simply and easily wiped out the entire army with one flap of his right wing and consigned them all to the fire of hell.[219]

Satan Misguides Jesus' Followers

Eventually, Satan realized he would not be able to shake Jesus. All those years before, when he had heard Anna utter, "I seek refuge for her (Mary) and her progeny from the evil of the outcast Satan,"[220] he had not thought God would answer her prayer.[221] He had thought he could still find a way to misguide this grandson of hers who performed such godly acts. He had thought he would be able to find even an iota of pride in him which he could cultivate and use to destroy him. When he realized that his efforts were in vain, he turned his efforts from Jesus himself to his followers. He was determined to fulfill the oath he had made when Jesus was born—to misguide four fifths of all humanity through him.[222]

---

217. *Biḥār al-anwār* vol. 14 p. 271 tr. 2

218. *Biḥār al-anwār* vol. 14 p. 271 tr. 3

219. *Biḥār al-anwār* vol. 14 p. 245 tr. 24

220. Qur'ān 3:36

221. *Biḥār al-anwār* vol. 14 p. 271 tr. 4

222. *Biḥār al-anwār* vol. 14 p. 215 tr. 14

Plot Against Jesus

Though so many had witnessed, even personally been touched by, Jesus' miracles, or perhaps because so many had been touched, the leadership of the Jewish community could no longer tolerate his existence. For 33 years,[223] he had worked his miracles, amended the law of the Torah with the law of the Evangel, taught and demonstrated wisdom, and challenged the leadership of the temple. The leaders of the temple and the powerful and wealthy knew as well as the destitute and disenfranchised that Jesus was the Messiah. He had proven this beyond a doubt, yet they easily wrote him off as a sorcerer.[224] Thus, these leaders of the Jewish community followed precisely in the footsteps of their predecessors back to the time of Moses—they connived to undermine the greatest blessing God could have given them, a prophet. By this act, they evinced the extent of their ingratitude for God's countless blessings to them.

Just as they plotted, so too did God. Sadly for them, God is the best of plotters.[225]

As the Jews and their Roman allies closed in on Jesus, God told him, "O Jesus! I shall take you from them, and I shall raise you into my proximity, and I shall free you of the filth of those who have not believed, and I shall make those who follow you dominate those who do not believe in you until the Day of Resurrection. Then to me will be your return whereupon I shall judge among you concerning that about which you used to differ. As for those who did not believe in you, I shall have punished them severely in the temporal world by subjugating them to those who did, and I shall punish them in the hereafter at which point they will have no helpers. And as for those among your followers who believe in the truth and do righteous deeds, I shall pay them their rewards in full. I do not like the wrongdoers."[226]

---

223. *Biḥār al-anwār* vol. 14 p. 336 tr. 3

224. Qur'ān 5:110

225. Qur'ān 3:54

226. Qur'ān 3:55–57

The Last Supper

With the calm of one who acts solely for God, Jesus called on his twelve disciples to assemble in a house. It was the eve of the twenty-first of Ramaḍān.[227] When they had convened, they wondered where their teacher was. Then he appeared before them from a corner of the room. He informed them of God's promise to him—that he would be raised up within the hour and that he would be saved from the hands of the Jews.

According to God's express command, he conveyed the light of divine guidance, his wisdom, and the knowledge of God's book to Simon Peter, his rightly appointed successor and his vicegerent over the believers.[228] He announced Simon's successorship to his disciples and made a covenant with them to support him and follow him.

Then he looked each of them in the eye and asked, "Which of you is willing to be disguised like me and to be killed, crucified in my place? Whoever accepts this burden shall be with me at my station in paradise."

Without a moment's hesitation, one of the younger disciples spoke with placid determination, "I shall do it, O Spirit of God!"

Jesus turned to the rest and said, "There is one among you who shall go against me twelve times before morning."

One of them asked in agitation, "Is it I?"

Jesus told him, "If you feel it within yourself, then it shall be you." He looked back at the group and spoke gravely, "After I am raised up, you shall become divided into three factions. Two will fabricate lies against God and for it, enter the fire. Only one group will faithfully follow Simon Peter and for it, enter paradise." As his disciples gazed upon him, contemplating these somber words, he moved back to the corner from which he had appeared and just as swiftly disappeared and was raised up.

Shortly thereafter, the Jewish leaders came in pursuit of Jesus. They apprehended the young disciple whom they perceived to be

227. *Biḥār al-anwār* vol. 13 p. 365 tr. 6

228. *Biḥār al-anwār* vol. 14 p. 250 tr. 39. See also Matthew 16:16–18.

Jesus along with the disciple whose betrayal Jesus had prophesied a few moments earlier.[229]

They crucified this young man in a most gruesome manner. He bravely faced death with surety in his heart that he would be reunited with his teacher and God's prophet. To those who looked on, it seemed that Jesus was being executed. Some were pleased, many were indifferent. The Jews claimed, "We killed the Messiah, Jesus, son of Mary, the messenger of God." But they did not kill him nor did they crucify him, but so it was made to appear so to them. Those who differ over him are steeped in doubt about him. They do not have any knowledge about him and only chase conjectures. But they definitely did not kill him. Rather, God raised him into his proximity.[230]

When God lifted Jesus into the sky, 9,313 angels accompanied him.[231] Jesus had draped around himself a garment of coarse wool. Mary had spun the yarn, woven the fabric, and then stitched this garment for him. Yet, when he reached his destination, he was commanded to "cast off the adornment of the temporal world!"[232] Even a garment so pure and simple had no place in God's realm.

In that realm, which is neither part of this world nor the hereafter, Jesus took up residence, and he shall remain there until God sees fit for him to return to earth. When he entered that abode, God addressed him saying, "O Jesus, son of Mary! Remember my blessing upon you and upon your mother, when I supported you through the Holy Spirit so that you could speak to the people in the cradle and in adulthood just the same, and when I taught you law, wisdom, the Torah, and the Evangel, and when you created from clay the form of a bird by my leave, and you breathed into it and it became a bird by my leave; and you healed the blind and the leprous by my leave, and you raised the dead by my leave; and when I held off the evil of the Israelites from you when you brought

---

229. *Biḥār al-anwār* vol. 14 p. 337 tr. 6

230. Qur'ān 4:157–158

231. *Biḥār al-anwār* vol. 14 p. 339 tr. 15

232. *Biḥār al-anwār* vol. 14 p. 338 tr. 9

them clear proofs, whereat the faithless among them said, 'This is nothing but plain magic.'"[233]

Then God asked him, "O Jesus, son of Mary! Was it you who said to the people, 'Take me and my mother for deities alongside God'?"[234]

Jesus replied, "Immaculate are you! It does not behoove me to say what I have no right to say. Had I said it, you would have known it. You know what is in my mind, but I do not know what is in your mind. You know well all that is unseen. I only said to them what you had commanded me to say: 'Worship God who is my Lord and your Lord.' And I was a witness over them as long as I was among them. But when you took me from them, only you were watchful over them, and you are witness over all things. If you punish them, it is your right for they are your creatures. And if you forgive them, no one can or should stop you for you are the Invincible, the Wise."[235]

---

233. Qur'ān 5:110

234. It is possible that this conversation has not yet taken place and that it will take place on the Day of Judgment as is indicated by two traditions (*Biḥār al-anwār* vol. 14 p. 236 tr. 12 and 13). However, it is also possible that it took place in the past at this particular point in the story as indicated by the apparent meaning of the word "*idh*" which is used in the sense of "Remember when..." to introduce stories of the past.

235. Qur'ān 5:116–118

Index

B

C

D

E

F

G

H

I

J

K

R

S

T